THEORY TESTING
IN ORGANIZATIONAL
BEHAVIOR:
The *Varient* Approach

FRED DANSEREAU

State University of New York at Buffalo

JOSEPH A. ALUTTO

State University of New York at Buffalo

FRANCIS J. YAMMARINO

University of Kentucky

With the collaboration of
MacDonald Dumas
University of West Indies, Trinidad

PRENTICE-HALL, INC., Englewood Cliffs, N.J. 07632

Library of Congress Cataloging in Publication Data

DANSEREAU, FRED
    Theory testing in organizational behavior.

    Bibliography; p.
    Includes index.
        1. Organization.   2. Paradigms (Social sciences)
    3. Organizational behavior.   4. Multivariate analysis.
    I. Alutto, Joseph A.   II. Yammarino,
    Francis J.   III. Title.
    HM131.D34   1984   302.3′5   83-19057
    ISBN 0-13-914408-0

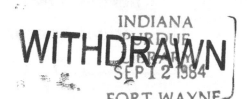

Editorial/production supervision and
    interior design: Sonia Meyer
Cover design: Lundgren Graphics, Ltd.
Manufacturing buyer: Ed O'Dougherty

©1984 by Prentice-Hall, Inc.
Englewood Cliffs, New Jersey 07632

Printed in the United States of America

10   9   8   7   6   5   4   3   2   1

ISBN 0-13-914408-0

Prentice-Hall International, Inc., *London*
Prentice-Hall of Australia Pty. Limited, *Sydney*
Editora Prentice-Hall do Brasil, Ltda., *Rio de Janeiro*
Prentice-Hall Canada Inc., *Toronto*
Prentice-Hall of India Private Limited, *New Delhi*
Prentice-Hall of Japan, Inc., *Tokyo*
Prentice-Hall of Southeast Asia Pte. Ltd., *Singapore*
Whitehall Books Limited, *Wellington, New Zealand*

*To those willing to experience the challenge
of exploring new solutions
to traditional problems of science*

CONTENTS

PREFACE   ix

INTRODUCTION   1

PART I
BASIC CONCEPTS

1 TRADITIONAL APPROACHES AND THE VARIENT PARADIGM   3

A Varient Approach to Statistics *4*   **A Varient Approach to Entities** *9*
A Varient Approach to Variables *16*   **The Varient Paradigm** *24*
Overview of the Book *26*   **Perspectives on the Varient Paradigm** *29*
        Summary *31*   *Review Questions* *32*

2 THE VARIENT MATRIX: CONCEPTUALIZATIONS   33

Introduction *33*   **The Entity Axis** *37*   **The Variable Axis** *53*
        Summary *63*   *Review Questions* *64*

PART II
HOW THEORIES ARE FORMULATED

3 THEORY: FORMULATIONS   65

Introduction *65*   **Selecting Entities** *67*   **Selecting Variables** *82*
        Summary *86*   *Review Questions* *86*

v

4 THEORY: AN ILLUSTRATIVE FORMULATION   87

Theory A: Role Theory *88*   Theory B: Exchange Theory *95*
Comparison of Theory A and Theory B *104*
          Summary *108*   *Review Questions* *108*

PART III
HOW DATA ARE ANALYZED

5 DATA ANALYTIC TECHNIQUES   110

The General Linear Tensor *111*   Total Correlation Analysis *116*
Within and Between Analysis (WABA) *120*   Varient Applications of
WABA *135*   Traditional Applications of WABA *141*
          Summary *144*   *Review Questions* *144*

6 DEDUCTIVE ALIGNMENT   145

Single-Level Analysis *145*   Multiple-Level Analysis *153*
Multiple-Variable Analysis *157*   Multiple-Relationship Analysis *161*
          Summary *164*   *Review Questions* *165*

7 INDUCTIVE ALIGNMENT   166

Tests of Significance *166*   Single-Level Analysis *168*
Multiple-Level Analysis *185*   Multiple-Variable Analysis *186*
Multiple-Relationship Analysis *187*
          Summary *188*   *Review Questions* *188*

PART IV
HOW CONCLUSIONS ARE DRAWN ABOUT THEORY
AND DATA

8 INFERENCES   190

Theory and Deduction *191*   Data Analysis and Induction *192*
Inferences *198*
          Summary *199*   *Review Questions* *200*

9 TESTING THEORIES: A GROUP-COLLECTIVITY
ILLUSTRATION   201

Theory and Deduction *201*   Data Analysis and Induction *206*

Inferences and Summary *220*   *Review Questions* *221*

10 TESTING THEORIES: A PERSON – DYAD – GROUP
ILLUSTRATION   222

Theory and Deduction *222*   Data and Induction *227*

Inferences and Summary *239*   *Review Questions* *241*

11 TESTING THEORIES: COMPLETING THE ANALYSIS   242

Theory and Deduction *242*   Data Analysis and Induction *243*

Inferences and Summary *258*   *Review Questions* *261*

PART V
ADDITIONAL WAYS CONCLUSIONS ARE DRAWN
ABOUT THEORY AND DATA

12 SUMMARY AND EXTENSIONS OF THE VARIENT PARADIGM   262

WABA in More General Terms *263*   Time in the Varient Paradigm *264*
The Extended Varient Paradigm *275*   Theoretical Issues *276*
Empirical Issues *277*

Summary *278*   *Review Questions* *279*

13 IMPLICATIONS   280

Bivariate Correlations *280*   Partial Correlations *283*   Multiple
Correlation and Regression *288*   One-Way Analysis of Variance
(ANOVA) *295*   Analysis of Covariance (ANCOVA) *299*   The *n*-Way
Analysis of Variance *300*

Summary *307*   *Review Questions* *308*

14 COMPARISON TO OTHER APPROACHES   309

Measurement *309*   Methodological Approaches *316*
Inferences *318*

Summary *320*   *Review Questions* *320*

15 **THE VARIENT PARADIGM AND THEORY TESTING IN THE FUTURE   321**

Varient Conceptualizations *321*   **Theory** *324*   **Data Analysis** *324*
Inferences *324*   **Applied Issues** *325*

Conclusion   328   *Review Questions   328*

APPENDICES

Appendix A   Tables *330*   **Appendix B   Key Geometric
Properties** *336*   **Appendix C   Key Algebraic Properties** *339*
Appendix D   Mathematical Proofs *343*   **Appendix E   Degrees
of Freedom** *350*   **Appendix F   Traditional Applications
of WABA** *354*   **Appendix G   Measures Used at MCO** *362*
Appendix H   Computerized WABA *372*   **Appendix I
Answers to Review Questions** *382*

REFERENCES   397

NAME INDEX   407

SUBJECT INDEX   410

PREFACE

In this book we present and illustrate a framework or paradigm for use in attempting to investigate why and how human beings function in organizations. The paradigm provides a way to (1) formulate theories, (2) analyze data, and (3) align theory and data so as to (4) encourage theory testing by a comparison of competing alternative hypotheses. Standard approaches to testing theories (such as tests of statistical significance) are integrated and used in the paradigm. Additional tests are developed that permit empirical assessments of theoretical assertions about (1) networks of variables (performance, satisfaction, and climate) and (2) multiple entities and levels of analysis such as persons, dyads, groups, and collectivities. Because *variables* and *entities* are integral components of the framework, a new term—*varient*—is used to characterize the paradigm.

The varient paradigm can be employed with variables and levels of analysis that are typically of interest in organizational behavior and the social sciences. Specifically, the levels of analysis discussed in this book are often of interest in psychological, social psychological, and sociological approaches to organizational analysis. When the paradigm is used, the theoretical and empirical significance of all or some of these levels of analysis can be evaluated. In addition, theoretical and empirical distinctions can be made between the different types of contingent and noncontingent formulations of variables that are often of interest in disciplinary and interdisciplinary work.

Individuals who are interested in theoretical work will find a framework for organizing, comparing, contrasting, and generating theories that specify variables and entities. The illustrations of how to formulate theories have implications for theories of personality, leadership, dyads, informal work groups, and professional and organizational subsystems, as well as for the theoretical constructs of roles and exchanges. When theories are formulated with the use of the paradigm, they are automatically testable with data.

The book addresses empirical work through within and between analysis (WABA). This analytical procedure is based on mathematical theory and provides a way to reduce data to a set of key empirical indicators compatible with widely used contemporary approaches to data analysis, such as univariate and multivariate analyses of variance and correlational analysis. An advantage of the varient paradigm is that it permits inferences to be drawn about the entities and levels of analysis which may underlie obtained empirical relationships between variables. Moreover, when within and between analysis is used as specified in the paradigm, data are automatically aligned with theory-based hypotheses.

Individuals who carry out both theoretical and empirical work are offered a method for choosing among multiple hypotheses about one set of variables and entities; thus, a complete inferential system for drawing conclusions about theory and data is presented.

Essentially, this book provides an explication of how theories are formulated (Part II), how data are analyzed (Part III), and how conclusions are drawn about theory and data (Parts IV and V), based on the basic "varient" concepts presented in the first part of the book. For readers with limited exposure to this type of work, a detailed theoretical and data analytic inferential system is presented and illustrated. For more experienced readers, the varient paradigm, building on traditional approaches, provides an alternative means for the consideration of multiple variables and levels of analysis in theory formulation and data examination. The book is not, however, intended to be all things to all people. Rather, by extending the usefulness of specific and widely used contemporary approaches, it presents the integrated varient method for engaging in the research process.

Individuals who wish to draw conclusions about theory and data in this way will be interested in the FORTRAN and SPSS computer programs described in the appendix to the book. In addition, the computer program and user's manual we employ in this work can be obtained by writing to Fred Dansereau, SUNY at Buffalo, 212 Crosby Hall, Buffalo, New York 14214. Individuals who teach others about theory testing can obtain an instructor's manual from Prentice-Hall.

Throughout this book, various applications of the paradigm are illustrated with data collected from employees of a metal extraction company. We wish to express our appreciation to these individuals for their willingness to respond to in-depth interviews and lengthy questionnaires and hope they found our feedback sessions about multiple levels of analysis in their setting useful in building a better organization.

A number of colleagues have made intellectual contributions to the development of the varient paradigm since we began this work in 1976. Specifically, Steven Markham at Virginia Polytechnic Institute and State University, Thomas Naughton at Wayne State University, and Sidney Nachman at New York University provided insights at various stages in the development of the paradigm. G. Chandrasekaran at the State University of New York at Buffalo was particularly important in the development of a FORTRAN program for within and between analysis, as well as for assisting in the development of a proof for linking the analysis of variance with bivariate correlations.

In addition, portions of the paradigm have been presented at professional meetings and in books, journals, and doctoral dissertations. The responses of the participants in these meetings and of reviewers, as well as those of our colleagues at Buffalo, served to focus our thoughts and reinforce the view that our approach is very compatible with contemporary and traditional work. We are grateful to those colleagues at the State University of New York at Buffalo School of Management who have helped create a climate in which the free exchange and challenge of ideas is commonplace. We would also like to thank various individuals who read versions of the manuscript at different points in its development for their insights and criticisms, as well as the reviewers of our manuscript. These include Professors Nealia Bruning (Kent State University), G. Chandrasekaran (SUNY at Buffalo), Peter Dubno (New York University), Janet Dukerich (University of Minnesota), Robert House (University of Toronto), Jerry Hunt (Texas Tech), Frank Krzystofiak (SUNY at Buffalo), Steven Markham (Virginia Polytechnic Institute and State University), George Milkovich (Cornell University), Ian Miners (University of Toledo), Michael Moore (Michigan State University), Thomas Naughton (Wayne State University), Eric Nielsen (Case Western University), Jerry Newman (SUNY at Buffalo), Saroj Parasuraman (Drexel University), Denise Rosseau (Northwestern University), John Slocum (Southern Methodist University), William Snavely (Miami University), Barry Staw (University of California, Berkeley), Donald Vredenburgh (Baruch College, City University of New York).

We owe a special debt to Sabina Schneider, who was able to quickly transform numerous handwritten (scribbled) versions of text and tables into clear, typewritten manuscript. After all these years, Sabina could probably retype this book from memory. Irene Forster's and Debra Kiel's expert typing and supervisory skills and the outstanding editing ability of Nola Healy Lynch greatly facilitated the completion of this project. In the final stages of the project James Bergantz, Daniel Coleman, Sanford Ehrlich, and Mark Lawton helped with various tasks. In addition, a number of typists worked diligently to help us complete the manuscript in a timely fashion. These include Elaine Csont, Linda Lucas, Mary Guadagna and Joan Mahoney.

We must also acknowledge the perceptive and constructive criticism received from Jayne Maerker and her reviewers, as well as the helpful encouragement and support provided by Jayne and her associates Linda Albelli and Ken Knickerbocker at Prentice-Hall during the development of the book. As the book moved into print, the excellent design and editing ability of Sonia Meyer and the copyediting of Jeannine Ciliotta greatly enhanced the clarity of the presentation of our work. Finally, the efforts of Paul Misselwitz at Prentice-Hall increased the visibility of our work in the market place. Obviously, we remain responsible for the content of the book.

Fred Dansereau
Joseph A. Alutto
Francis J. Yammarino

INTRODUCTION

This book can be used in formulating and testing theoretical assertions about variables (performance, satisfaction, and climate) and entities at any level of analysis (persons, dyads, groups, collectivities). For example, a theorist may have a hunch and therefore hypothesize that a particular variable (such as leadership) refers to entities at one level of analysis (such as persons). The *varient* approach to variables and entities presented in this book allows an individual to test such an assertion with data. Empirical results may be in line with a theorist's hunch, or the variable may be associated with a different level of analysis (such as leader-follower dyads) than originally hypothesized. The idea that one should allow for the disproof of hypotheses is compatible with approaches in the physical sciences and is, of course, the key to theory testing —unless a theory can fail by being replaced by another theory, it is untestable. To incorporate into our field the excitement and fun of not knowing before data analysis which of several theories (if any) will be supported, we created a paradigm.

As suggested by Masterman (1970) the term paradigm has been defined in a number of ways. We define a **paradigm** as a cognitive framework that can serve to initiate and guide scientific investigation (Barrett, 1972; Behling, 1978; Roberts, Hulin, and Rosseau, 1978) through multiple-hypothesis generation and testing (McGuire, 1973). To call an approach a paradigm, we require that a cognitive framework must be specified; it must be possible to use the framework to formulate theories and analyze data in such a way that theoretical formulations and data analytic techniques are aligned and an inferential system for drawing conclusions about theory and data must be specified. In addition, we require the inferential system specified in a paradigm to be compatible with the approach used in the physical sciences to test hypotheses. Specifically, a hypothesis of interest should be viewed as passing a critical test when it is not replaced by an alternative hypothesis, and as failing when it can justifiably be replaced by a competing hypothesis. A classic example of this

1

testing process can be found in physics, where Newton's theories were replaced by Einstein's.

We believe the varient approach satisfies the requirements of a paradigm because: A basic cognitive (varient) framework is presented in Chapters 1 and 2; the way in which theories are formulated when the paradigm is used is presented in Chapters 3 and 4; data analytic techniques and theoretical formulations are aligned as presented in Chapters 5 to 7; and an inferential system is summarized and illustrated in Chapters 8 to 15. The varient approach also incorporates the physical science approach to theory or hypothesis testing. As an illustration, consider two substantive hypotheses about three variables and two levels of analysis. One hypothesis may include an assertion that two of the variables are related, independent of a third variable, and applicable to groups but not collectivities. An alternative hypothesis may include an assertion that these three variables are all related and that they are applicable only to collectivities. The first, or group, hypothesis suggests that multiple interpersonal processes underlie the three variables and their relationship. The second, or collectivity, hypothesis suggests that collectivized or large-scale social movements, rather than small-group processes, may underlie variables and relationships. The varient paradigm can be used to formulate these two theories in such a way that an empirical analysis can be performed to test the probable validity of each competing hypothesis.

The following four analytical procedures comprise the varient paradigm:

1. Single-level analysis
2. Multiple-level analysis
3. Multiple-variable analysis
4. Multiple-relationship analysis

Single- and multiple-level analyses are used to specify and test assertions about entities. Multiple-variable and multiple-relationship analyses are used to identify and test assertions about variables. These four analytical perspectives on variables and levels of analysis are considered in every chapter of this book. Thus the entire book has been used as a vehicle for presenting and illustrating the varient paradigm. Our point of departure in Chapter 1 is, of course, traditional and contemporary approaches to theory testing, since these approaches are the basis of the varient paradigm.

1

TRADITIONAL APPROACHES
AND THE
VARIENT PARADIGM

Most contemporary theories in organizational behavior and the social sciences either implicitly or explicitly include an assertion of (1) the relationships among variables and (2) the entities, and therefore levels of analysis, to which the variables apply. Whether about personal feelings, group level phenomena such as leadership, or organizational attributes such as climate or technology, **theories** and **hypotheses** include assertions about both variables and types of entities. This characteristic of theories is usually mentioned in writings that attempt to define theory-building processes (Blalock, 1969; Dubin, 1976; Miller, 1978). However, problems do remain in contemporary approaches designed to test theoretical assertions about variables, their relationships, and entities, and this chapter will demonstrate how the varient paradigm addresses many of these problems.

It has been suggested that current investigatory work might be viewed as using a complex set of assumptions and beliefs which are adopted during the research process (Bass, 1974; Bronfenbrenner, 1971; Cartwright, 1973; Myrdal, 1973). The ad hoc character of much research hardly ensures that assertions have been adequately tested in relation to alternative explanations. Indeed, some writers have gone as far as to suggest that there are no articulated paradigms in organizational behavior or in the social sciences in general (Barrett, 1972; Bass, 1974; Behling, 1978; Eckberg and Hill, 1979; Lindzey, 1978; McGuire, 1973; Meehl, 1967; Roberts et al., 1978; Van den Berghe, 1978; Watson, 1982; Ziman, 1978). For example, Watson (1982, p. 448) states: "Work done in the social and behavioral sciences is piecemeal, unsystematic, and lacking in consensuality.... The result is that social behavioral scientists work in small, disjointed areas employing idiosyncratic concepts and methods."

We believe, however, that at least one approach to theory testing is widely used. It is based on the multiple hypothesis testing approach used in the physical sciences (see Behling, 1980; Braithwaite, 1973; Chamberlin, 1890; Cohen and Nagel, 1934; Diesing, 1971; Dunnette, 1966; Fisher, 1973; Graen, 1976; Kaplan, 1964; Kuhn, 1970; Lerner, 1959; MacKenzie and House, 1978;

Meehl, 1967; Nagel, 1961; Platt, 1964, 1966; Popper, 1959; Staw, 1974; Staw and Ross, 1978). In **multiple hypothesis testing** at least two hypotheses are compared, and the hypothesis that is viewed as the more likely explanation for an outcome is adopted. The version of multiple hypothesis testing currently used in the social sciences and studies of organizational behavior involves tests of statistical significance. In these tests, a **substantive hypothesis** based on a theory of interest is evaluated by comparison against a statistically based **null hypothesis**. If a substantive hypothesis seems more likely than a null hypothesis, the substantive hypothesis passes the test and the results are viewed as **statistically significant**. When results of a study do not pass the test, and thus do not allow for the rejection of a statistical or null hypothesis, the inference is that the study has produced random results. The failure could be due to poor (for example, random) data, a poor theory, or both. In essence, these statistical procedures place a theory in only limited jeopardy. Consequently, for example, the American Psychological Association suggests in its guide to authors that results which allow for the rejection of statistical hypotheses are appropriate for publication, although substantive theories cannot be publicly rejected when only standard statistical procedures are used.

Because the statistical approach is widely used and seems to be based on multiple hypothesis testing, it is a starting point for evaluating theoretical assertions about variables and entities. A complementary approach is necessary, however, if there is interest in testing theories in such a way that a hypothesis can visibly fail through replacement by another substantive, rather than simply statistical, hypothesis. From this perspective, our objective is to develop an approach that permits preferred substantive hypotheses to be compared to competing substantive hypotheses — that is, the varient paradigm. Before we illustrate how this conceptualization can be first derived from traditional and contemporary work involving variables and entities and then integrated into a paradigm, the following review of the statistical approach to multiple hypothesis testing will demonstrate the need for an additional investigative paradigm.

A VARIENT APPROACH TO STATISTICS

Statement of the Problem

Tests of statistical significance are known to have limited usefulness. For example, Bolles (1962), Meehl (1967), and Rozeboom (1960) have attempted to draw attention to a distinction made by Fisher, a biologist and one of the pioneers in developing statistical theory, between the process of statistical hypothesis testing based on numbers and the testing of scientific hypotheses about variables and relationships. According to Fisher (1973), the statistical testing procedures were not designed to provide a basis for acceptance of theoretical or scientific hypotheses about variables and relationships; rather, they were designed to be used as a basis for rejection of statistical hypotheses about numbers. In a similar vein, as pointed out by Hays (1973, p. 415), "Any study can be made to show significant ($p \leq 0.05$) results if one uses enough subjects, regardless of how nonsensical the content may be."[1]

A Varient Approach to the Problem

Our approach to these problems was to develop a set of tests of **practical significance** (see Part III) that parallel the traditional statistical tests but are not sensitive to increases in the number of subjects in a study. Although we use tests of statistical significance, we view these tests as inherently limited. To illustrate these limitations, it is helpful to view the statistical approach as a paradigm. If the approach is a paradigm, we should be able to identify the cognitive framework that underlies the approach and to show how it is used to formulate theories and analyze data in such a way that theoretical formulations and data analytic techniques are aligned into an inferential system.

Basis of the Cognitive Framework

The statistical paradigm can be found in virtually any basic statistics book. Although the paradigm was first used in biology (Fisher, 1925), its underlying cognitive framework is statistical in nature and is based on a general conceptualization of randomness commonly called a **normal distribution**. This conceptualization permits a large number of distributions to be generated from a general equation for a normal curve.

F, Z, t Distributions Specifically, various theoretical distributions, such as the $\hat{F}$, $\hat{Z}$, and $\hat{t}$, are deduced from the general normal conceptualization and a probability is associated with each value of the distributions, in this case $\hat{F}$, $\hat{Z}$, or $\hat{t}$. (The use of hats [^] indicates that these distributions are purely theoretical in nature and involve predicted values.) It is well known that the $\hat{F}$, $\hat{Z}$, and $\hat{t}$ distributions are similar. Although these indicators will be described in more detail in later chapters, a brief statement of their relationship may be helpful. $\hat{F} = \hat{t}^2$, and $\hat{Z}$ has been shown by Fisher to underlie the $\hat{F}$ distribution — indeed, Fisher labeled values for $\hat{F}$ as $\hat{Z}$ values. From a theoretical perspective, the paradigm aligns a variety of well-known mathematical indicators (such as correlations) with $\hat{F}$, $\hat{Z}$, and $\hat{t}$ values. By means of this alignment, a probability is then associated with all values that can be taken on by mathematical indicators.

In the paradigm, theoretical formulations (the $\hat{F}$, $\hat{Z}$, and $\hat{t}$ distributions) and data analytic indicators (expressed as F, Z, and t scores) are aligned so that any value for a particular mathematical indicator can be assigned a probability. For making inferences, these probabilities can be viewed as indicating the degree to which a statistical hypothesis is a likely explanation for an obtained value. If the probability is low in value (such as $p \leq 0.05$), a statistical explanation is rejected. An illustration of a correlational problem the statistical paradigm attempts to solve may be helpful at this point.

---

[1] From *Statistics for the Social Sciences*, 2d ed., by William L. Hays. Copyright © 1973 by Holt, Rinehart and Winston, Inc. Reprinted by permission of Holt, Rinehart and Winston, CBS College Publishing.

Correlation It is quite common for a theory to specify that two variables are related. A **correlation** serves as a mathematical indicator of the degree of relationship between two sets of scores on two variables (X and Y) paired in the following fashion:

	X	Y
Pair one	1	1
Pair two	2	2

In this case, the scores on X are identical to the scores on Y for each pair, and the correlation takes on a value of 1. However, it is known that the value of a correlation is determined in part by the number of pairs of scores that are considered. Therefore, it is not appropriate simply to interpret a correlational value. In fact, every time a correlation is calculated based on two pairs of scores ($n = 2$), it has a magnitude of 1 and the probability of a statistical explanation is 1. But if an infinite number of pairs ($n = \infty$) of scores are examined, then by definition the number of pairs would not influence the value taken on by a correlation, and the probability of statistical explanation is 0. Between these two extremes, the number of pairs on which a correlation is based should have some influence on the values taken on by this indicator. Simply stated, the statistical paradigm offers a way of testing whether an obtained correlational value is due to what we call "statistical artifacts" (in this case, the number of pairs of scores on which it is based).

The notion of an ideal true or **population correlation** — which is a theoretical correlational value — is introduced in order to perform such tests. Assume that a correlation "really" or "truly" equals 0 (or some other value); then it can be asked what the probability is that the correlation will take on a value greater than 0 due solely to the number of pairs of scores. Given only two pairs of scores, the probability is 1 that a correlation will take on a magnitude of 1. Suppose, however, that three pairs of scores are considered, as in the following example:

	X	Y
Pair one	1	1
Pair two	2	2
Pair three	3	3

In this illustrative case, the correlation again equals 1. If it is assumed that the true correlation between these scores equals 0, what is the probability of obtaining this or any other value simply as a result of using three pairs of scores in calculating the correlation? This question is addressed in the statistical paradigm by generating a theoretical distribution of scores, in this case of $\hat{t}$ scores, based on the number of pairs of scores. Since every correlational value can be converted to an obtained t score (see Chapter 5), the probability of any correlational value given three pairs of scores is determined. This procedure is applied for any number of pairs of scores or, more generally, for any number of degrees of freedom.

The resulting probabilities can be interpreted as indicating the likelihood that various correlational values are due to the number of pairs of scores in the data. By convention, probabilities less than or equal to 0.05 are taken to indicate that a correlational value is not very likely to be explained by the number of pairs of scores on which the correlation is based. The result of applying these conventions and procedures can be illustrated from the following values presented by Guilford (1965, pp. 580–81):[2]

Pairs of Scores	Correlational Values Required at the 0.05 Level
3	0.997
5	0.878
12	0.576
202	0.138
502	0.088

How would one evaluate the case of three pairs of scores resulting in a correlation of 1? A correlational value of 1 is greater than 0.997 and is therefore viewed as unlikely ($p \leq 0.05$) to be simply a result of the number of pairs of scores used to calculate the correlation.

This example and the illustrative values from Guilford (1965) serve to indicate the cognitive structure that underlies the statistical paradigm. Essentially, as the number of pairs of scores or degrees of freedom increases, the magnitudes of the correlations required to be statistically significant decrease. As shown above, in a case with 502 pairs of scores, a correlational value of 0.088 would be statistically significant. Of course, given an infinite number of pairs of scores, any correlation that is not exactly 0 would be viewed as statistically significant. Consequently, as pointed out by Hays (1973), any set of results can be made statistically significant by increasing the number of scores included in a study. This is a logical and appropriate limitation inherent in the paradigm and one that affects any research relying on the statistical approach. Nevertheless, the statistical paradigm, as is apparent from its widespread use, provides a number of ways to formulate theory and analyze data such that theory and data analytic indicators are aligned into an inferential system.

Theory

In order for a researcher to use the statistical paradigm, a theory only need specify or provide a way to generate scores, which in turn can be reduced to values for an empirical indicator; a wide variety of variables is thus permitted when the paradigm is used. For example, variables with space-time metrics (height, width, depth, and time) are permitted in addition to variables with non-space-time metrics that reflect purely intellectual constructs (such as organizational climate). There are differing views about variables in the social sciences; for example, Ghiselli (1974) has indicated that many variables of interest in organizational behavior are intellectual constructs, whereas Miller (1978) has suggested that only variables with space-time metrics should be

---

[2] From *Fundamental Statistics in Psychology and Education*, by J. Guilford. Copyright © 1965 by McGraw-Hill. Used with the permission of the McGraw-Hill Book Company.

employed in the social sciences. One clear advantage of the traditional statistical paradigm is that it can accommodate and even encourage the examination of variables with differing metrics. This paradigm also allows for point predictions about the amount of a variable (as suggested by Meehl [1967]), as well as for the specification of relationships between variables in a general (for example, correlation) or specific (for example, beta weights) sense. In summary, an advantage of the traditional statistical paradigm is that a variety of theories that specify relationships among variables with different metrics can be formulated and then tested against a statistical hypothesis.

Data Analytic Techniques

For testing purposes, the data analytic techniques used in the statistical paradigm must permit a clear determination of the influence of degrees of freedom (based on the number of pairs of objects under consideration) on the value of an empirical indicator. Geometrically based data analytic indicators, which have been developed over centuries, readily meet this requirement and are used in the paradigm. For example, a number of indicators of relationships among variables are based on what we call the "general linear tensor" (see Chapter 5 and Misner et al., 1973). These indicators express the degree to which scores (expressed as vectors) are related to one another. Variations on this linear tensor approach include bivariate and multiple correlations, regressions, and analyses of variance (see Chapters 5 and 13). Moreover, being geometrically based, these indicators are also coordinate-free and therefore can be used with variables claiming a variety of metrics.

Theory-Data Alignment

In the statistical paradigm, theoretical formulations and data analytic techniques are aligned by the use of theoretical distributions (such as $\hat{F}, \hat{Z}, \hat{t}$) based on statistical theory and by the use of data analytic indicators that can be converted to these distributions (F, Z, t). When the paradigm is used a theoretical $\hat{F}, \hat{Z}$, or $\hat{t}$ distribution is deduced, an ideal null condition is defined, and the probability that any value approximates a null condition is determined. An obtained value is temporarily assumed to be random or aligned with a statistically random distribution, thus allowing the obtained result to be viewed as potentially due to the degrees of freedom in the data. The obtained indicator is then converted to an F, Z, or t score, and the probability that the obtained value approximates a chosen null hypothesis is known. This probability is viewed as indicating the degree to which data approximate an ideal random condition.

Inferences

Essentially, in the statistical paradigm, a hypothesis based on a substantive theory of interest is compared to a statistically based null hypothesis. In many fields, a probability less than or equal to 0.05 is viewed as indicating that an ideal random or null condition is not a likely explanation for data. The 0.05

level of statistical significance is due to convention; as Fisher (1973, p. 45) states: "In fact no scientific worker has a fixed level of significance at which from year to year and in all circumstances he rejects hypotheses." If the statistically based hypothesis can be rejected in that it seems very unlikely ($p \leq 0.05$ or $p \leq 0.01$), then at least one competing alternative explanation for a set of results has been evaluated and denied support. If a statistical hypothesis cannot be rejected, such a finding does not actually disprove the theoretical substance of a hypothesis. Rather, the failure to reject simply suggests that the results are in line with a theory of random dispersal and that they could be predicted using statistical methods alone.

Paradigm Characteristics

The traditional statistical paradigm thus is not designed to allow for the replacement of one substantive hypothesis by another; but this inability should not be viewed as eliminating the value of the approach. The traditional paradigm provides an important test of one statistical explanation for any set of results. Therefore we will retain use of this approach in the development of our paradigm. The need to develop another paradigm, however, stems from problems that arise from using only the statistical paradigm. Specifically, an exclusive use of the statistical paradigm can result in hypotheses that at best fade away, since scholars will tend to focus on correcting sampling deficiencies rather than on finding data analytic support for selecting one substantive hypothesis over another. Bass (1974), Myrdal (1973), and Starbuck (1972), among others, have suggested that it would be preferable if hypotheses were rejected through being replaced by other substantive hypotheses which were found to be more likely explanations of data.

Of course, it could be argued that if a study which had originally produced statistically significant results were replicated exactly and the results failed to reject the theory of random dispersal, such results might be informative. However, an exact replication of any study, particularly in the social sciences, is virtually impossible, if only because two studies must differ at least in where or when they are conducted. On the other hand, instead of pursuing a replication approach, we prefer to test multiple substantive hypotheses in a single study with identical characteristics for each hypothesis. We have developed this approach as a response to contemporary problems in dealing with entities and variables.

A VARIENT APPROACH TO ENTITIES

Statement of the Problem

Recall that the requirement that a theory must specify types of entities or levels of analysis is not novel. We use the term **entity** to refer to specific objects of interest to a researcher (persons such as Sam, Harry, or Jane; collectivities such as General Motors, Chrysler, or Ford). **Levels of analysis** refer to categories or classifications of entities arranged in a hierarchical order such that higher levels (such as collectivities) encompass or include lower levels of analysis (such as persons).

Even if a theory is to be tested with the statistical paradigm, a specification of levels of analysis is necessary. For example, as suggested by Stone (1978, pp. 36–37), the measurement of variables or scaling depends on the theoretical specification of entities, since a "scale may be looked upon as a set of 'items' so constructed that entities... being measured (i.e., scaled) can be systematically assigned scores on the scale, the assignment of such scores being related to the amount of the measured attribute the entity possesses." Despite this obvious requirement for any theory, in our view entities and levels of analysis are often not explicitly specified in social science theories. In part, this problem may be due to the lack of a conceptual basis for making assertions about appropriate levels of analysis. As a temporary solution to the problem, the issue of entity groupings is often divorced from mainstream substantive research employing the statistical paradigm. This separation is accomplished by referring to a statistical problem of levels of analysis that is viewed as somehow distinct from basic requirements for formulating theories. Our view of the problem with entities is consistent with Roberts et al.'s (1978) suggestion that a clear conceptualization of levels of analysis and entities is lacking as a basis for most theoretical formulations, with a subsequent weakening of the logical basis for theory testing. A number of other theorists and critics also refer to the lack of such a conceptualization (Boulding, 1980; Cummings, 1981; Hannan, 1971; Homans, 1958; Katz and Kahn, 1978; Kuhn, 1980; Miller, 1978; Parsons, 1980; Rapoport, 1980; Staw, 1980; Staw and Oldham, 1978; Staw, Sandelands, and Dutton, 1981; Van de Ven and Astley, 1981).

From an empirical rather than a theoretical perspective, Blalock (1979) has identified at least three schools of thought on the subject, all disagreeing to some extent on the method proposed to accomplish the resolution of level of analysis problems. Numerous others have offered differing views on the reasons entities are often not specified and have proposed statistical techniques designed to compensate for such uncertainty or lack of specificity (Blalock, 1964; Epstein, 1980; Firebaugh, 1978; Hage and Aiken, 1969; Hannan, 1971; James, 1982; Katerberg and Hom, 1981; Lazarsfeld and Menzel, 1961; Lincoln and Zeitz, 1980; Roberts et al., 1978; Robinson, 1950; Vecchio, 1982). Again, one explanation for these problems is that researchers lack a conceptualization of entities.

A Varient Approach to the Problem

Because mainstream research uses the traditional statistical paradigm and because levels of analysis are specified, even if only implicitly, in order to collect data, we believe some conceptualization of entity categories must underlie these traditional studies. Therefore, one purpose for developing the varient paradigm is to specify a conceptualization of levels of analysis that is compatible with the methods employed in the traditional statistical paradigm. A general conceptualization is presented in Chapter 2; here we will consider how contemporary problems stimulated the varient conceptualization of entities.

Single Levels of Analysis

Human beings in organizational settings are often viewed in different ways, and therefore there are many definitions of entity groupings or levels of analysis. For example, some theorists and researchers view human beings or individuals in organizational settings as independent of one another, or as **persons** (see Campbell et al., 1970). Human beings or individuals can also be viewed as interdependent on a one-to-one basis, or as **dyads** (see Weick, 1978). Likert (1961, 1967), for example, tends to view human beings in organizational settings as interdependent with a number of other individuals who interact face to face, or as **groups**. Katz and Kahn's (1978) approach suggests that individuals can also be viewed as interdependent due to the hierarchical structuring of multiple individuals, or as **collectivities**. Van de Ven and Astley (1981) have suggested that psychologists often focus on persons, social psychologists on groups, and sociologists on collectivities. In a similar fashion, based on an extensive review of work in a variety of sciences, Miller (1978) defined and distinguished several levels of analysis, three of which (organisms, groups, and organizations) are of particular interest for the purposes of this presentation.

Miller (1978, p. 515) distinguishes between persons ("organisms" in his language) and groups in this way: "An experiment deals with groups rather than organisms if the outputs studied result from interaction among group members and are not simply outputs of individual organisms that are near one another in space-time."[3] This distinction implies an interdependence between human beings at the group level that is not present at the person level of analysis. In this formulation a dyad, composed of two human beings, is viewed as distinguishable from groups, which are composed of more than two individuals. Miller (1978, p. 515) goes on to distinguish between groups and collectivities ("organizations" in his language): "Groups differ from organizations, the next higher level of living systems in three ways: (a) the members though ordinarily mobile are usually near enough together to see and hear one another; (b) each one potentially can communicate directly with every other one over two way channels although some of these may not be open at all times; (c) there are no echelons, since by definition an organization is a system with echelons composed chiefly of groups."[4] This distinction between groups and collectivities highlights the notion that collectivities do not involve a direct interaction between individuals, but rather are held together by echelons or hierarchies.

Each of these four levels of analysis or entity groupings (persons, dyads, groups, and collectivities) may be viewed in two different ways or as two different **units of analysis**. For example, some psychologists focus on individual differences — in other words, on characteristics that distinguish between persons (such as inherited abilities). Other psychologists focus on processes and characteristics that occur within persons (such as learning). Some social

---

[3] From *Living Systems*, by J. G. Miller. Copyright © 1978 by McGraw-Hill. Used with the permission of the McGraw-Hill Book Company.
[4] From *Living Systems*, by J. G. Miller. Copyright © 1978 by McGraw-Hill. Used with the permission of the McGraw-Hill Book Company.

psychologists see dyads as being composed of different interdependent human beings and focus on differences within dyads (Hollander, 1958, 1974, 1978). Still others view dyads as being composed of similar human beings (Byrne and Nelson, 1965). Social psychologists who have a more sociological orientation consider groups with three or more people as homogenized entities and focus on differences between groups, whereas others concentrate on the parts within groups; or as indicated by Blau (1964, p. 284) the work of Simmel suggests that "the elements of differentiated social circles are undifferentiated, those of undifferentiated ones are differentiated." One way to interpret this statement is that differentiation between and not within groups is a different conceptualization of groups than that of differentiation within and not between groups. Finally, from a sociological perspective, characteristics that distinguish between whole collectivities or a large number of human beings who are linked not face to face but indirectly (for example, by a hierarchy) may be of interest (Durkheim, 1933). Alternatively, the focus of interest may be within these collectivities.

This notion of viewing a single entity at one level of analysis in two very different ways is not unusual in science. For example, in chemistry a molecule is viewed as being composed of atoms that contain electrons. Nonetheless, at least two theories of molecules are widely known (Sienko and Plane, 1974). In one theory, the entire molecule is viewed "as a unit with all the electrons moving under the influence of all the nuclei and all the other electrons.... This approach recognizes that the electron belongs to the molecule as a *whole* and may move throughout the entire molecule" (Sienko and Plane, 1974, p. 80; emphasis added). A second theory focuses on the parts of the molecule: "It assumes that the atoms in a molecule are very much like isolated atoms except that one or more electrons are accommodated in the outer shell of another atom"[5] (Sienko and Plane, 1974, p. 80). In this theory the focus is on the interdependent *parts* (atoms) that make up a molecule. Indeed, various individuals have suggested the importance of considering parts and wholes in general in the behavioral and social sciences as well as in organizational behavior (Blau, 1964; Kaplan, 1964; Lerner, 1963; Miller, 1978; Nagel, 1963; Simmel, 1908; Van de Ven and Astley, 1981).

As noted previously, despite interest in various levels of analysis (see Bobbitt et al., 1978; Hellriegel and Slocum, 1979; Korman, 1977; Schein, 1980), a conceptualization that includes all these views of levels and units of analysis does not seem to be available. Although theoretical assertions have been made about entities, it is often unclear whether parts or wholes are asserted at a particular level of analysis. (A review of various approaches to the level of analysis problem is presented in Chapter 13.) Furthermore, as far as we can determine, only some of the empirical testing procedures that are compatible with and derivable from the statistical paradigm have been identified. Contemporary empirical techniques, however, do not seem to allow for an assessment of assertions about entities.

---

[5] From *Chemistry: Principles and Properties*, by M. Sienko and R. Plane. Copyright © 1974 by McGraw-Hill. Used with the permission of the McGraw-Hill Book Company.

In order to deal with these omissions, we have attempted to organize basic approaches to entity groupings in the following way: Human beings or individuals can be viewed (1) as independent of one another as persons, (2) as interacting directly on a one-to-one basis in dyads, (3) as interacting face to face in multiperson patterns in groups, or (4) as members of hierarchically structured collectivities. The degree and nature (direct or indirect) of interdependence between individuals distinguishes among these four levels of analysis. In addition, each of the levels of analysis can be viewed in terms of two units of analysis — either as a whole unit or in terms of the parts which make up that unit. Finally, one must allow for the possibility that any particular level of analysis may prove to be irrelevant in order to test theoretical assertions about entities. Therefore, a single level of analysis can be viewed in two ways, always allowing for rejection of a level effect. This approach can be illustrated for one level of analysis (dyads) in the following fashion:

Level of Analysis	Alternative Views
Dyads	Whole dyads
	Dyad parts
	Reject level

Wholes and parts are seen to be very different characterizations of a single entity; a theorist must therefore consciously select one of these alternatives. For a set of empirical results, the question is whether, for a given level of analysis, parts, wholes, or neither seems the most likely explanation. We use the term **single-level analysis** to refer to a consideration of one level of analysis independently of other levels of analysis.

Multiple Levels of Analysis

Single-level analysis, however, does not include a consideration of the possibility that a finding at one level of analysis may have implications for other levels of analysis. We call a consideration of more than one level of analysis **multiple-level analysis**. Indeed, the work on the level of analysis problem suggests that multiple levels of analysis must be taken into consideration. For example, Hannan (1971) indicates that the two major metatheoretical positions on levels of analysis are the polar theses of homology and discontinuity.

The **homology thesis** posits a basic consistency across all levels of analysis. For example, a relationship among variables could be hypothesized to hold for whole collectivities, groups, dyads, and persons, and such results should be empirically demonstrable. Although traditionally various authors have suggested that variables and relationships of interest should hold across all levels, we define a **cross-level approach** as one which asserts that an effect holds across at least two levels. From the more traditional perspective, Parsons (1956, pp. 190, 194) states: "The contrast between small scale partial social systems and the large scale is not on the same order as the shift from personality or psychological to social system or from organism to psychologi-

cal.... There are continuities all the way from two person interaction to the
United States as a social system.... If this theoretical continuity is genuine
then you can generalize from levels where things are demonstrated most
freely."[6] Following Parsons' approach, Katz and Kahn (1978) assert that
effects at one level of analysis (person level) are representative of other levels of
analysis.

In contrast to the homology thesis, two types of **discontinuities** have been
discussed by various theoreticians and researchers. According to one approach,
which we labeled **level-specific**, relationships among variables at lower levels of
analysis do not hold at higher levels of analysis. For example, a relationship
may be hypothesized to hold for whole dyads (lower level of analysis) but not
for groups (higher level of analysis). Various authors suggest that their theories
are level-specific. For example, Homans (1961) writes:

> In their private speculations, some sociologists were once inclined to think of the
> small informal group as a microcosm of society at large: they felt that the same
> phenomena appeared in the former as in the latter but on a vastly reduced scale
> — a scale that incidentally made detailed observation possible. And no doubt
> there are striking resemblances between the two.... But to say that the two
> phenomena have points in common is not to say that one is a microcosm of the
> other, that the one is simply the other writ small.... The reason lies... in
> the fact that, in the institutions of society at large, the relations between the
> fundamental processes are more complex. [pp. 379–80]

A second type of discontinuity is viable. In this approach, which we call
emergent, a relationship at a higher level of analysis does not hold at lower
levels of analysis. For example, a relationship may be hypothesized to be based
on whole collectivities (higher level of analysis), but to not hold for groups,
dyads, or persons (lower level of analysis). In this sense, a relationship emerges
at the collectivity level of analysis. Various authors have suggested that such
emergent effects may occur. For example, Miller (1980) states:

> These reviewers [Boulding, 1980; Kuhn, 1980] are right in saying my theory does
> not directly generate special theories. But... a special theory can be generated
> from studying relationships among variables dealt with in the general theory.
> Special theories concerning phenomena that occur at one level but may be absent
> from other levels, moreover, are not inconsistent with general living systems
> theory. Each level has emergent properties not found at levels below and also
> characteristics dropped out in the course of evolution of levels above. Systems
> theory asserts, however, that it is important to determine whether findings made
> at one level are relevant to other levels. [p. 70]

Although these three types of theoretical formulation have been asserted,
without a general conceptualization, no method for organizing these different
assertions — and certainly no method for assessing whether data correspond to
such assertions — is currently available. Our approach to this problem is to

---

[6] From *Toward a Unified Theory of Behavior*, by T. Parsons. Copyright © 1956 by Basic
Books. Used with the permission of Basic Books.

TABLE 1.1.   Illustrative entity axis

Entity Axis	Illustrative Cross-Level Formulation	Illustrative Emergent and Level-Specific Group Parts Formulation
Collectivities		
Wholes	#	
Parts		
Reject level		——
Groups		
Wholes	#	
Parts		——
Reject level		
Dyads		
Wholes	#	
Parts		
Reject level		——
Persons		
Wholes	#	
Parts		
Reject level		——

create an axis along which two units of analysis (wholes and parts) and a "reject" alternative for each level of analysis are arrayed. To simplify this illustration, assume that one set of individuals can be viewed potentially as persons and as forming dyads, groups, and collectivities. When this set of individuals is viewed as collectivities, there are fewer distinct entities, although the entities are larger. Therefore, collectivities can be viewed as the **highest**, most encompassing, and persons as the **lowest**, most delimited, **level of analysis**. Therefore **lower** and **higher levels of analysis** are defined based on this conceptualization. The axis in Table 1.1 is used to represent this hierarchical ordering of levels of analysis.

On this axis, theoretically based assertions about entities are identified by the location of double lines along the entity axis. The locations of data are indicated by the number signs. Perhaps the most useful feature of this approach is that the degree to which results are compatible with the assertions of one theory or another can be assessed. For example, a hypothesis that a relationship between variables applies at the collectivity level of analysis and across all levels of analysis is shown in Table 1.1 by the location of double lines in the second column at each level of analysis. Likewise, a second hypothesis that a relationship between variables emerges at the group parts level of analysis, and is level-specific to groups (does not hold at higher levels of analysis), is indicated by the location of the double lines in the third column of the table. In this example, the locations of the number signs indicate that the data are more compatible with the cross-level formulation.

Furthermore, with this approach it is not necessary to assume that wholes are either greater than or equal to the sum of their parts. The paradigm treats one set of individuals in multiple ways; but no requirement is imposed that persons fit into dyads and dyads into groups like Chinese boxes, although the paradigm does permit such a view. Moreover, because the paradigm allows for emergent and cross-level effects, the approach is compatible with both re-ductionist and nonreductionist views of entities. Essentially, the entity axis can be viewed as a set of alternative hypotheses that can be chosen on a theoretical and empirical basis when the varient paradigm is employed. In order to make these decisions, however, variables must also be considered.

A VARIENT APPROACH TO VARIABLES

Statement of the Problem

Unlike the situation found in our consideration of entities, problems with analyzing variables are more widely known, since they tend to be viewed as related to mainstream research. Even so, contemporary approaches to variable specifications have been criticized for their failure to consider the generation and interrelatedness of nomological networks of variables (Bass, 1974; Bould-ing, 1980a, 1980b; Campbell and Fiske, 1959; Cook and Campbell, 1976; Cronbach and Meehl, 1955; Cummings, 1981; Kaplan, 1964; McGuire, 1973; Meehl, 1967; Nunnally, 1967; Roberts et al., 1978; Schwab, 1980). From an empirical perspective, some critics suggest that contemporary approaches have a tendency to focus narrowly on isolated relationships, on small segments of entire networks, and on nonreplicative and nonextensive studies (Barrett, 1972; Bass, 1974; Ghiselli, 1974; McGuire, 1973).

One traditional response to these criticisms has focused on using various methods for simultaneously considering multiple variables (such as multiple regression). Another set of responses has focused on so-called moderator variables. In the latter case, interest is usually in the degree to which a relationship between two variables differs under dissimilar conditions (that is, defined by values of the moderator variable). In a brief review of approaches to moderator variables, Arnold (1982) suggests:

> Interest in these topics has spawned a number of attempts to outline the appropriate statistical techniques which should be employed to test the validity of hypotheses regarding the existence of moderator variables and moderated relationships. (Saunders, 1956; Zedeck, 1971; Guion, 1976; Peters and Champoux, 1979). However, these attempts by their own admission have not been successful in clarifying all of the issues surrounding exactly which statistical and analytic techniques are appropriate for testing various moderator variable hypotheses. [p. 144]

A Varient Approach to the Problem

Problems arising from not focusing on multiple variables or nomological networks may very well be related to problems with contemporary approaches to moderator variables or multiple relationships. Therefore, a second purpose for developing the varient paradigm was to derive a general reconceptualization of variable specifications that is compatible with existing techniques for examining nomological networks of variables and multiple relationships. Our approach is to use two perspectives on one network of variables. Although any number of variables can be considered in a network, for purposes of providing a more readily understood overview, only the case of three variables is considered in this chapter. Our two perspectives on networks of variables result in two analytical conceptualizations (multiple-variable analysis and multiple-relationship analysis), which are used to specify relationships among variables and to test empirically the accuracy of such specifications. Although a general conceptualization is presented in Chapter 2, here we will provide an overview to illustrate how contemporary problems stimulated the varient conceptualization of multiple variables and multiple relationships.

Multiple-Variable Analysis

To focus on multiple variables as one network requires a consideration of each variable separately and of the relationships between variables in the network. We call such a consideration **multiple-variable analysis**. From this perspective, each variable is viewed as a node in a network of variables. In addition, the assertion of a set of relationships among variables in a network has implications for each variable. For ease of presentation, the focus here will be on simple relationships, in which one variable can affect another variable, and vice versa. (The temporal ordering of variables is considered in Chapter 12.)

When two variables are viewed as components of a potentially infinite network of variables, it is useful to indicate the linkage between the two variables by a dotted line, as follows:

$$X \dots Y$$

Logically, two variables may be viewed as related or unrelated. For notational purposes, to indicate that two variables are related we use a double-headed arrow ($\leftrightarrow$), and to indicate that two variables are unrelated we use the perpendicularity symbol ($\perp$). The double-headed arrow is not meant to imply anything about the temporal or causal ordering of variables. The linkage between two variables can then be characterized in either of two mutually exclusive ways, as illustrated below:

Related Variables Case	Unrelated Variables Case
$X \leftrightarrow Y$	$X \perp Y$
$\dots$	$\dots$

From a testing perspective, the related and unrelated cases can be defined as the two ends of a degree-of-relatedness continuum. At one extreme is a relationship of 1 between variables, and at the other extreme is a relationship of 0 between variables. Therefore, when two variables are viewed as related on an empirical or a theoretical basis, the alternative hypothesis that two variables are unrelated is being rejected.

This approach to characterizing linkages between variables and corresponding notation is particularly useful when a three-variable network is being considered. The three-variable network is represented schematically as follows:

Using a formulation that will be more fully presented in Chapter 2, this three-variable network can be characterized in eight different ways by viewing each of the three linkages (XY, YZ, XZ) in two ways and in combination:

Related variables:	$X \leftrightarrow Y$	$Y \leftrightarrow Z$	$X \leftrightarrow Z$
Generally related variables:	$X \leftrightarrow Y$	$Y \leftrightarrow Z$	$X \perp Z$
	$X \leftrightarrow Y$	$Y \perp Z$	$X \leftrightarrow Z$
	$X \perp Y$	$Y \leftrightarrow Z$	$X \leftrightarrow Z$
Generally unrelated variables:	$X \leftrightarrow Y$	$Y \perp Z$	$X \perp Z$
	$X \perp Y$	$Y \perp Z$	$X \leftrightarrow Z$
	$X \perp Y$	$Y \leftrightarrow Z$	$X \perp Z$
Unrelated variables:	$X \perp Y$	$Y \perp Z$	$X \perp Z$

Each of these eight characterizations can be seen as forming a different assertion about the relationship among the three variables.

First, the three variables may be viewed as related to each other. This **related variables case** can be expressed by the following notation, assuming that variables X and Z are also related:

$$X \leftrightarrow Y \leftrightarrow Z \tag{1.1}$$

At the other extreme, all three variables may be viewed as unrelated; this **unrelated variables case** can be expressed in the following way, assuming that variables X and Z are also unrelated:

$$X \perp Y \perp Z \tag{1.2}$$

Six cases can occur between these two extremes. In one set of three cases only one pair of variables is related, and these variables are independent of a third variable. We refer to these cases as **generally unrelated variables**, and we use the following notation:

$$(X \leftrightarrow Y) \perp Z \tag{1.3}$$

Here parens are used to indicate that variables X and Y are related, but that both are unrelated to variable Z. In a final set of three cases, one variable shares a relationship with two others, but two variables are also unrelated. We refer to these as cases of **generally related variables** and use the following notation:

$$(X \perp Z) \leftrightarrow Y \qquad\qquad \textbf{(1.4)}$$

The understanding in this notation is that variables X and Z are unrelated, although each is related to variable Y. The four basic cases can be illustrated schematically and summarized in the following way:

Case	Related variables	Generally related variables	Generally unrelated variables	Unrelated variables
Schematic				
Notation	$X \leftrightarrow Y \leftrightarrow Z$	$(X \perp Z) \leftrightarrow Y$	$(X \leftrightarrow Y) \perp Z$	$X \perp Y \perp Z$
Assertion	1.1	1.4	1.3	1.2

These four cases are frequently asserted and then tested in contemporary social science research. Although contemporary approaches will be discussed and explained in more detail in Chapter 13, an overview of some key problems may be helpful for the reader familiar with traditional approaches.

From a traditional theoretical perspective, there are few difficulties. For example, a theorist may be interested in the related variables case, in which two variables are hypothesized to be related owing to a third (often called situational) variable. If interested in the generally unrelated case, however, a theorist may wish to assert that a relationship between two variables is not due to some third factor. In other formulations, a theorist may assert that two unrelated variables (usually called "independent") can be predictors of a third variable (usually called "dependent"); this is the generally related case. And, of course, in the unrelated variables case a theorist may assert that there is no relationship among any of the variables. Any one of these four types of assertions may be quite reasonable on a theoretical basis.

Empirically, testing such assertions with contemporary methods can be problematic. For example, the use of partial correlations will have no impact in the case of unrelated variables, and in the related case it will be unclear which variable should be partialed out from the others. One response to this problem is to choose a third variable to be partialed out, based on theory alone. Such a solution places a theory beyond empirical testing, since the theory is used to determine the data. Instead, it would seem more appropriate to identify a related case empirically. After such an identification, there might be some interest in examining the consequences of holding constant a third variable when exploring the relationship between two other variables. There is, however, currently no empirical test to determine whether a relationship between two variables of interest is significantly reduced by partialing out a third variable; such a test will be presented in Chapter 13.

Another contemporary empirical approach that may seem useful in examining networks is multiple regression. When variables are generally related $[(X \perp Z) \leftrightarrow Y]$, a multiple regression formulation of $X + Z = Y$ would be useful. However, an attempt to apply this equation in a related variables case is a violation of critical assumptions, for as Lin (1976, p. 327) states: "When independent variables are highly correlated... regression models should not be used."[7] Furthermore, Heise (1975, p. 187) indicates that calculating a multiple regression is problematic "when the correlations between two or more determinants of a dependent variable are much higher than the correlations between the dependent variable and the determinants."

As an illustration of the difficulties with the multiple regression approach, assume that the following generally related case holds:

$$(X \perp Y) \leftrightarrow Z$$

which can also be written

$$X \perp Y \leftrightarrow Z \leftrightarrow X$$

In this case, a multiple regression of the form $X + Y = Z$ would be appropriate. Assume, however, that data can be characterized as follows:

$$(X \leftrightarrow Y) \perp Z$$

Applying the equation $X + Y = Z$ to this generally unrelated network would result in a case in which the relationship between the independent variables would be higher than the zero relationship between each independent variable and the dependent variable. In this case, the application of a multiple regression methodology would be questionable due to the problem of multicollinearity, as identified by Heise (1975), Kerlinger (1973), and numerous others. Therefore, multiple regression has clear limitations as a general way to examine networks of relationships.

In light of these contemporary problems in testing theories empirically, our approach is to view any one of the eight assertions as plausible when three variables are considered. In a somewhat more general sense, any one of the four conditions (unrelated, generally unrelated, generally related, and related)

---

[7] From *Foundations of Social Research*, by N. Lin. Copyright © 1976 by McGraw-Hill. Used with the permission of the McGraw-Hill Book Company.

should be theoretically assertable. Once asserted, however, each of the relationships between the variables must be considered empirically in order to identify which of the eight assertions or four general cases seems more likely. Of course, once a network is characterized, any number of methodological tools (such as partial correlation or multiple regression) can be employed. Until Chapter 13, however, the focus in this book will be on distinguishing between networks of variables theoretically and empirically rather than on methodological tools.

To summarize, for the three-variable case, four different conditions are identified and viewed as forming a variable axis arrayed as follows:

Related Variables	Generally Related Variables	Generally Unrelated Variables	Unrelated Variables

These four general cases can be specified for any number of variables. In this way, a nomological network can be expanded to include an infinite number of variables, and the plausible networks can be identified and considered in formulating theories and analyzing data.

The three-variable case in multiple-variable analysis does not fully explain relationships since, for example, variables are known to be able to moderate or mediate the relationship between other variables (Arnold, 1982). The conceptualization of such effects is called **multiple-relationship analysis** because the relationship between at least two variables (X and Y) is examined under different conditions defined by at least one other variable (Z). As in studies of moderator effects, the same relationship is examined in each of several conditions in multiple-relationship analysis.

Multiple-Relationship Analysis

The study of moderator effects is sometimes influenced by the use of ambiguous jargon. For example, the term **contingency** in the statistical paradigm usually refers to an assertion that two variables are in some way directly related. We call this type of contingency a **direct contingency**, in that one variable directly affects another variable.

In addition, in organizational behavior and the other social sciences, the notion of contingency implies that a relationship between at least two variables is dependent or contingent on the values of a third variable (see Fiedler, 1967; Hellriegel and Slocum, 1979; House, 1971; Neilsen, 1974). We label this case an **indirect contingency** condition, a term meant to convey the same notion as moderated effect (Arnold, 1982). We use these two terms interchangeably but favor the use of the former term because, as pointed out by Rosenzweig (1980), the term "moderator" is confusing even in a grammatical sense.

A consideration of the three-variable case helps to illustrate a distinction between indirect and direct contingencies. In order completely to examine a network of variables in the three-variable case, the effect of each variable on the relationships between the other two variables should be considered. Specifically, in a network of three variables, three cases are plausible: First, a relationship between variables X and Y may be contingent on the values taken on by variable Z; second, a relationship between variables Z and Y may be contingent on the values taken on by variable X; and third, a relationship between variables X and Z may be contingent on the values taken on by variable Y. The directed lines in the following diagram illustrate these three indirect contingencies:

Using this conceptualization, it is possible to illustrate how moderator effects and the identification of relationships in multiple-variable analysis are integrated by considering the four cases definable in multiple-variable analysis (related, generally related, generally unrelated, and unrelated).

In the unrelated variables case, knowledge about one variable provides no information about the others; therefore the variables are not directly contingent. The unrelated variables, however, may or may not be indirectly contingent. If they are indirectly contingent, the outcome of an examination of unrelated variables should reveal that under one value for a variable, a relationship between the two other variables holds, and under another set of values for the same variable, a relationship between the two other variables does not hold. In such a case, then, the relationship between two variables may depend on the values taken on by another variable. This is an indirect contingency, because the variables are not directly related across values of a third variable; their relationship depends on values of a third variable. For notational purposes, brackets can be placed around the unrelated variables to illustrate that these variables are indirectly contingent and form a set:

$$[X \perp Y \perp Z]$$

A key alternative to this contingent case is a formulation that the relationships among the variables are not indirectly contingent on the value of other variables. In this case (labeled **multiplexed**), not only the variables but also the relationships among variables are uninfluenced by other variables in the network. This case can be written without brackets in order to indicate the lack of a set of variables:

$$X \perp Y \perp Z$$

In the unrelated variables case, any relationship may be multiplexed with or be indirectly contingent on a third variable. Because the variables are not directly contingent, an examination of the relationship between any two variables within values of a third variable involves a full distribution of scores on the correlated variables. As a result, in the unrelated case it is appropriate to examine relationships within values of a distinct third unrelated variable.

In contrast, in the related case all the relationships are by definition directly contingent on values taken on by other variables. For example, if values for X are known, then values for Y and Z are known. In this case, if Y and Z are related, then their relationship is directly contingent on X because Y and Z are directly contingent on X. The same logic holds for any of the relationships. In effect, to examine the relationship between any two variables within a third variable amounts to examining the relationship between the variables within the variables. Theories may, for example, specify that low values on a particular variable may be related to low values on another variable and that high values on the two variables are not related. The use of a third variable that is related to X and Y can amount to a test of this high-low specification rather than a test of whether a third variable affects a relationship between two other variables. Therefore, in the related case it is inappropriate to examine relationships within values of a nondistinct third variable. For notational purposes, brackets can be placed around the entire set of variables to indicate that the three variables are directly contingent on one another and form a set of variables:

$$[X \leftrightarrow Y \leftrightarrow Z]$$

Between these two extremes are the generally related and generally unrelated cases. Since all the variables are related in some way in the generally related case, a specification that the values of a third variable influence the nature of a relationship between two other variables amounts to an examination of the two variables within themselves, and multiple-relationship analysis is inappropriate. In this generally related case, then, the variables are viewed as directly contingent on one another and the following notation is used:

$$[(X \perp Y) \leftrightarrow Z]$$

In the generally unrelated case, one of the variables is very different from the other two and is unrelated to them. As a result, for example, the relationship between X and Y can be examined within values of a distinct third variable. In the indirect contingency case, the relationship between X and Y may be contingent on the values of this different third variable, or

$$[(X \leftrightarrow Y) \perp Z]$$

Alternatively, in the multiplexed case the third variable may have no impact on the relationship, or

$$(X \leftrightarrow Y) \perp Z$$

Our approach to clarifying the nature of direct and indirect contingencies can be simplified in the following fashion. Multiple-variable analysis can identify four general networks based on the relationships between variables; these relationships can then be viewed through multiple-relationship analysis as directly or indirectly contingent on the variables. The resulting general

TABLE 1.2.   Derivation of a variable axis[a]

| KEY CONDITIONS | | OUTCOMES | |
Multiple-Variable Analysis	Multiple-Relationship Analysis	Multiple-Variable Analysis	Multiple-Relationship Analysis
Related variables	Direct contingency	$X \leftrightarrow Y \leftrightarrow Z$	$[X \leftrightarrow Y \leftrightarrow Z]$
Generally related variables	Direct contingency	$(X \perp Y) \leftrightarrow Z$	$[(X \perp Y) \leftrightarrow Z]$
Generally unrelated variables	Indirect contingency	$(X \leftrightarrow Y) \perp Z$	$[(X \leftrightarrow Y) \perp Z]$
	Multiplexed	$(X \leftrightarrow Y) \perp Z$	$(X \leftrightarrow Y) \perp Z$
Unrelated variables	Indirect contingency	$X \perp Y \perp Z$	$[X \perp Y \perp Z]$
	Multiplexed	$X \perp Y \perp Z$	$X \perp Y \perp Z$

[a]The second and last columns of the table contain the six conditions along a variable axis.

conditions are presented in Table 1.2. As shown by the notation in the table, the issue of whether the relationship among variables is indirectly contingent on other variables becomes important only when variables are generally unrelated or unrelated; only in these cases is a third variable independent of the other variables.

From a theoretical perspective, the specification of indirect contingencies requires the identification of a third variable that differs from the variables whose relationship is expected to vary depending on values of the third variable. Once this third variable is identified, it is possible to argue that relationships are indirectly contingent (vary in magnitude depending on the values taken on by the third variable), or that a relationship is multiplexed (does not vary within conditions defined by the third variable). From an empirical perspective, the relationships between variables must be examined first; when an unrelated or generally unrelated case is identified, the degree to which relationships are indirectly contingent on an independent third variable should be examined. In a general sense, multiple-relationship analysis permits assertions to be made about indirect contingencies and provides the basis for an empirical method to test such assertions that will be illustrated in later chapters. By using multiple-variable and multiple-relationship analyses in this way, a variable axis along which conditions are arrayed is defined.

THE VARIENT PARADIGM

The six alternative formulations of variables that arise from a consideration of the three-variable case (see Table 1.2) are listed in the top row of Table 1.3 and form a variable axis. These conditions are mutually exclusive alternative

TABLE 1.3. Illustrative varient matrix (three-variable and four-entity case)

	VARIABLE AXIS					
	Related Variables	**Generally Related Variables**	**Generally Unrelated Variables**		**Unrelated Variables**[a]	
ENTITY AXIS	Direct Contingency $[X \leftrightarrow Y \leftrightarrow Z]$	Direct Contingency $[(X \perp Z) \leftrightarrow Y]$	Contingent $[(X \leftrightarrow Y) \perp Z]$	Multiplexed $(X \leftrightarrow Y) \perp Z$	Contingent $[X \perp Y \perp Z]$	Multiplexed $X \perp Y \perp Z$
Collectivities						
Wholes	||					
Parts						
Reject		#|				
Groups						
Wholes	||			|||		
Parts		#|		|||		
Reject			||			
Dyads						
Wholes	||		||			
Parts						
Reject		#|		||		
Persons						
Wholes	||		||			
Parts						
Reject		#|	||	||		
Analyses						
Single level / Multiple level	Whole collectivities / Across levels	Group parts / Level-specific and emergent	Whole dyads / Level-specific and emergent	Whole groups / Level-specific and emergent		
Multiple variable	$X \leftrightarrow Y \leftrightarrow Z$	$(X \perp Z) \leftrightarrow Y$	$X \leftrightarrow Y$	$X \leftrightarrow Y$		
Multiple relationship	Direct contingency	Direct contingency	$X \leftrightarrow Y$ indirectly contingent on Z	$X \leftrightarrow Y$ multiplexed with Z		
Theory	A	B	C	D		

[a] Unrelated contingent and multiplexed formulations are also plausible and will be considered in subsequent chapters.

assertions about the relationships among variables. An entity axis (see Table 1.1) is listed in the first column of Table 1.3. The axis contains eight alternative units of analysis (and four reject conditions) that may underlie variables. What we call a **varient matrix** results from combining the variable and entity axes.

The varient matrix is a summarizing device for locating both theoretical assertions and the results of empirical analysis, and for assessing the degree of isomorphism between theory and data. Using the varient matrix, a theorist can choose from any number of formulations of the relationships among variables (in this case six) and any number of levels of analysis (in this case four). The matrix, however, serves to emphasize that the choice of one theory also means that another is not chosen. In Table 1.3, four alternative theories (A through D) are shown by the double lines along the variable and entity axes to occupy different spaces in the matrix. A theorist can choose one of these formulations. If theory A is chosen, a set of variables is expected to be related based on differences among whole collectivities, groups, dyads, and persons. In contrast, if theory B is preferred, the variables are expected to be generally related based on differences among group parts; and so on for theories C and D.

It is important to notice that these formulations are different ways to specify the relationships among a single set of variables and a single set of types of entities. In other words, the cells contained in the matrix form alternative hypotheses about one set of variables and types of entities; obtained data should be locatable in the matrix independently of a theorist's preferences. For example, a theorist may specify theory A, and data may be obtained for a set of variables and entities that are more supportive of theory B. Data are listed in the matrix by the location of number signs. In Table 1.3, data are illustrated to be more compatible with theory B than with theory A, C, or D.

The varient matrix can be expanded infinitely to include any number of variables and entity sets. As a result, any theoretical assertion can be shown to be more likely only relative to the set of theoretical assertions against which it is tested. It is this multiple-hypothesis testing format that we refer to as the varient approach, and the entire conceptualization of variables and entities that underlies theory, data, and inferential processes is referred to as the varient paradigm.

OVERVIEW OF THE BOOK

Basis of the Cognitive Framework (Chapter 2)

The four basic variable and entity components of the paradigm (single- and multiple-level analyses and multiple-variable and multiple-relationship analyses) that have been linked to traditional and contemporary approaches can also be viewed in relation to the varient conceptualization presented in Chapter 2. The focus in Chapter 2 is on developing a conceptualization of variables and entities in which theory and data are aligned in a way compatible with the traditional statistical paradigm but that also permits the comparison of substantive hypotheses on a theoretical and empirical basis.

Theory (Chapters 3 and 4)

Procedures for generating hypotheses that include an explicit consideration of single and multiple levels of analysis and multiple variables and
relationships are presented in Chapter 3. An illustration of the use of these
procedures in formulating role and exchange theories is presented in
Chapter 4.

Data Analytic Techniques (Chapter 5)

After a consideration of theoretical issues, the focus of the book shifts to
standard data analytic techniques. A general linear tensor approach that
permits examination of data without the trappings of the statistical paradigm is
presented in Chapter 5. Most standard techniques (such as the analysis of
variance and correlational analysis) are shown to be derivable from the linear
tensor, which is used in a variety of scientific fields of study. Moreover, an
extension of the tensor called within and between analysis, or WABA
(Dansereau et al., 1982a, 1982b; Dansereau and Dumas, 1977; Markham,
Dansereau, and Alutto, 1983) is presented in this chapter. WABA provides an
exact rather than approximate link between correlations and the analysis of
variance that is somewhat different from other formulations (Bechtoldt, 1959;
Cohen, 1977; Cronbach, 1971; Cronbach and Meehl, 1955; Kerlinger, 1973;
Loevinger, 1965; McNemar, 1955). However, this link is compatible with the
exact mathematical formulation stated by Robinson (1950). Although the
traditional F, Z, t indicators are used in WABA, another set of three indicators
(E, A, R) is used to test for practical significance before using the statistical
indicators. An overview of the way WABA is employed in single- and
multiple-level analyses and in multiple-variable and multiple-relationship
analyses is presented at the end of Chapter 5.

Theory-Data Alignment (Chapters 6 and 7)

A set of ideal values for all indicators (F, Z, t and E, A, R) deduced
from the varient conceptualization is presented in Chapter 6. A method for
assessing the degree to which any value of an indicator approximates these
ideal conditions is presented in Chapter 7. The E, A, R indicators are
constructed so that inferences can be based on the magnitude of relationships
regardless of degrees of freedom. In this way the paradigm can be viewed as a
response to suggestions that greater attention should be paid to the practical
significance of the magnitude of indicators, independent of sample size effects
(Bakan, 1966; Bass, 1974; Bolles, 1962; Boulding, 1980; Dunnette, 1966;
Fisher, 1973; Ghiselli, 1974; Meehl, 1967; Rozeboom, 1960; Signorelli, 1974).

Inferences (Chapters 8 to 11)

The alignment of theory with data results in an inferential system based
on tests of both practical and statistical significance. Inferential procedures are
summarized in Chapter 8 and are illustrated in Chapters 9 to 11 with data

collected from managers employed in a manufacturing firm and with a theoretical formulation described in Chapter 4. In Chapters 9 and 10, the focus is on testing separately two nomological networks consistent with role and exchange theories. A key point of these separate illustrations is that even if only one theory is of interest, multiple hypotheses about variables and entities can still be tested. A means to examine multiple networks is illustrated in Chapter 11.

Paradigm Characteristics (Chapters 12 to 15)

The varient paradigm is presented and illustrated in the first eleven chapters of the book. The remaining chapters provide additional ways to draw inferences about theory and data. The focus in this part of the book is on illustrating the implications of various characteristics of the paradigm for contemporary and traditional approaches and problems.

Specifically, the way in which the paradigm can be extended to include time is presented in Chapter 12. This extension provides a number of responses to traditional problems in dealing with change (see Harris, 1963). For example, sometimes changes are interpreted as indicating a lack of reliability, and at other times as indicating temporal effects (Campbell, 1976; Kimberly, 1976; Nunnally, 1967; Stanley, 1971). The varient paradigm permits a choice between an inference of change and one of no change. As a result of this extension, multiple-variable and multiple-relationship analyses as well as single- and multiple-level analyses can be performed based on differences that occur over time (process differences), in addition to those between or within entities (structural differences).

Chapter 13 shows how the paradigm encompasses and extends traditional univariate, bivariate, and multivariate analyses of variance and correlational analyses. A procedure is derived for inferring whether partialing out one variable from a relationship between two variables has a significant effect. In addition, a procedure for testing theoretical formulations specified in a multiple regression format is developed. The general formulation is also employed to clarify and extend a number of approaches to aggregation or levels of analysis (Epstein, 1980; Firebaugh, 1978; Hage and Aiken, 1969; Hannan, 1971; Katerburg and Hom, 1981; Lincoln and Zeitz, 1980).

The focus of Chapter 14 is on the implications of the paradigm for contemporary approaches to measurement, methodology, and drawing inferences from data. Concerning measurement issues, the paradigm provides a response to difficulties with contemporary approaches to content, predictor criterion, and construct validity (Bechtoldt, 1959; Campbell, 1976; Campbell and Fiske, 1959; Cronbach, 1971; Dunnette, 1966; Kalleberg and Kluegel, 1975; Kerlinger, 1973; Loevinger, 1965; Nunnally, 1967; Schwab, 1980). In addition, various approaches to assessing the characteristics of measures (such as factor analysis and Cronbach's alpha) are expanded so that multiple indicators of measurement reliability are readily available. For example, procedures are identified for generating two alpha coefficients in the analysis of any one attitude scale. Concerning methodology, the varient paradigm is compatible with experimental and nonexperimental studies. Finally, other perspectives on generalizing from data are shown to be compatible with the varient approach.

The varient paradigm provides a way to define the domain of theories and concepts in terms of both variables and levels of analysis, and thus it can be viewed as a response to the problem of "fuzzy concepts" (Zadeh, 1968). Some of the future implications of using the paradigm to clarify concepts and research are presented in Chapter 15.

PERSPECTIVES ON THE VARIENT PARADIGM

Figure 1.1 illustrates how the varient matrix conceptualization (Chapter 2) underlies the way theories are formulated (Chapters 3 and 4), the choice of data analytic techniques (Chapter 5), and the deductive (Chapter 6) and inductive (Chapter 7) alignment of theoretical formulations and data analytic techniques into an inferential system, which is summarized in Chapter 8. As a result, the actual testing of theories (Chapters 9 to 15) is based on all the concepts of the paradigm. This last point is illustrated in Figure 1.1 under the heading Testing Theories. For testing purposes, theories are viewed as specifying a space in the varient matrix; data are then mapped into a varient matrix, and the degree of isomorphism between the spaces occupied by theory and by data is examined. In the figure, data indicated by number signs are shown as aligned with theory A because the data occupy the same space in the matrix as the predictions based on that theory. In contrast, theory B is viewed as disproved, since an alternative theory is necessary to explain the location of the data aligned with theory B. An overlay of the theory and the data matrices shown in Figure 1.1, which results from deductive and inductive alignments, is always used for drawing inferences. Specifically, when double lines are used to indicate the predictions or space occupied by theories A and B and number signs are used to locate data, the result is the following overlay:

In this overlay (varient matrix), theory A (represented by the double lines in the left side of the figure) is aligned with data (as indicated by the number signs). In contrast, theory B is not aligned with data. Traditional null results, although identified, are viewed as outside the varient matrix and are not used to disprove theories. Finally, as shown in the figure, the varient matrix can be expanded to include the time dimension.

The term "paradigm" seems an appropriate characterization of the varient approach because the varient matrix as a basic conceptualization explicitly provides a means to (1) formulate theories, (2) analyze data, and (3) align theoretical formulations and analyze data in a way that (4) encourages

Chapters	2	3,4	5	6	7	8	9 to 11	12 to 15
Substance	Varient matrix	Theory: Formulations	Data: Analytic techniques	Deductive alignment	Inductive alignment	Inferences	Testing theories	Other features

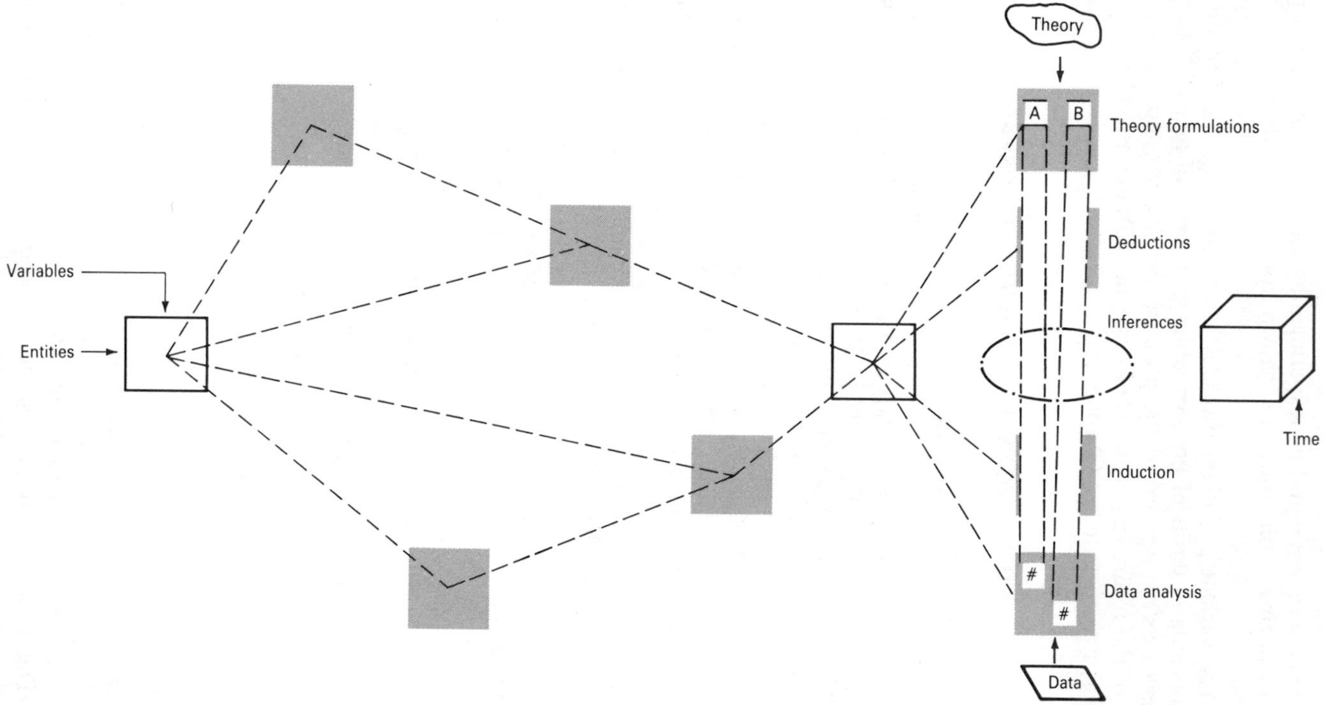

Theory formulations

Deductions

Inferences

Induction

Data analysis

Time

Theory

A   B

#   #

Data

Variables

Entities

FIGURE 1.1. The varient paradigm

multiple-hypothesis testing. The book is therefore divided into the following parts:

Part I   **Basic Concepts**

         Chapters 1 and 2

Part II   **How Theories Are Formulated**

         Chapters 3 and 4

Part III **How Data Are Analyzed**

         Chapters 5 to 7

Part IV   **How Conclusions Are Drawn about Theory and Data**

         Chapters 8 to 11

Part V   **Additional Ways Conclusions Are Drawn about Theory and Data**

         Chapters 12 to 15

If the term "paradigm" is problematic, this book might simply be viewed as presenting an integrated approach to a series of widely known problems. Alternatively, readers might choose to characterize it as merely a logical extension of contemporary approaches of this type. Indeed, we have attempted to avoid an idiosyncratic approach by retaining the widely used traditional statistical approach. Regardless of which characterization seems preferable, the conceptualization of variables and entity sets underlying the varient matrix — and, by definition, single- and multiple-level analyses and multiple-variable and multiple-relationship analyses — forms the basis of this varient approach and is presented in the next chapter.

SUMMARY

The traditional statistical paradigm places hypotheses in limited jeopardy. Therefore, in order to test substantive hypotheses against each other and to respond to contemporary problems with variables and levels of analysis, the varient paradigm is proposed. The paradigm is designed to be compatible with traditional approaches and contains four key components, two of which deal with entity issues (single- and multiple-level analyses) and two of which deal with variable issues (multiple-variable and multiple-relationship analyses). These four components, which underlie the varient approach to formulating theory, analyzing data, aligning theory and data, and drawing inferences, are discussed in each succeeding chapter of the book.

REVIEW QUESTIONS

1. What is the state of the art in contemporary approaches to theory testing?
2. What type of multiple-hypothesis testing is common in social science research?
3. What effect does sample size have on the adequacy of theory testing under the traditional statistical paradigm?
4. Why is multiple substantive hypothesis testing in a single setting preferable to simple tests against a statistical standard?
5. How are the concepts of unit of analysis and level of analysis related?
6. (a) Can variables be valid across levels, or are only level-specific effects valid? (b) Can emergent effects be asserted if the focus is on only a single level of analysis?
7. Why is it important to specify on theoretical grounds whether variables should be related or unrelated?
8. Is the concept of a contingent condition similar to that of a moderated effect? If so, in what way?
9. Why does the varient paradigm include a number of definitions of terms?
10. To what extent can the varient paradigm be used with previous and contemporary approaches to theory testing?

2

THE VARIENT MATRIX:
Conceptualizations

INTRODUCTION

The varient conceptualization of variables and entities presented in this chapter is based on the premise that the assertion of one hypothesis implies the rejection of a specific set of equally likely alternative hypotheses. This premise can be stated more formally as follows:

> In any theoretical model, hypothesis, or statement of research focus, a set of mutually exclusive and competing formulations is defined by the number of variables and the number of different types of entities specified.

For example, if three variables and one level of analysis (for example, dyads) are asserted, a specific set of alternative formulations of these three variables and one level of analysis can be generated. In initiating any investigation, a theorist should recognize that he or she chooses only one formulation from a more complete set of plausible alternative formulations. Likewise, empirical analyses involve choosing which one of a set of alternative formulations appears to be more plausible. Theorists and researchers make choices explicitly or implicitly among a set of alternative formulations about variables and entity sets. In order to explicate and to provide an overview of these choices, Table 2.1 presents the four key decisions that are made on a theoretical and an empirical basis through using the varient paradigm. These decisions are the focus of attention in this chapter. The principles underlying these analyses are also given in the table.

Entities

One level of analysis (for example, dyads) can be viewed as being composed of whole entities, as being composed of the parts of each entity, or as irrelevant. As shown in item I of Table 2.1, the derivation of these

TABLE 2.1.   Key theoretical and empirical decisions in the varient paradigm

---

I. Single-Level Analysis

Principle:	Parts and wholes are different views of one entity.
Choices:	Choose *one* of the following alternatives:
	1. Whole entities
	2. Entity parts
	3. Equivocal (reject entity)
	4. Inexplicable (reject entity)

II. Multiple-Level Analysis

Principles:	**W** Wholes at a lower level of analysis can be followed by wholes, parts, and equivocal conditions at higher levels of analysis.
	P Parts can be followed by an inexplicable condition.
	EI Equivocal and inexplicable conditions can be followed by wholes or parts.
Choices:	For a two-level analysis, choose *one* of the following alternatives:
	1. Cross-level wholes (principle *W*).
	2. Cross-level parts (principle *W*).
	3. Level-specific wholes (principle *W*).
	4. Level-specific parts (principle *P*).
	5. Emergent wholes (principle *EI*).
	6. Emergent parts (principle *EI*).
	7. Reject level (eight conditions).

III. Multiple-Variable Analysis

Principle:	Generate a set of alternative ways to formulate relationships among variables, assuming variables may be related or unrelated.
Choices:	For a three-variable formulation, choose *one* of the following alternatives:
	1. Related (do not go to IV).
	2. Generally related (do not go to IV).
	3. Generally unrelated (go to IV).
	4. Unrelated (go to IV).

IV. Multiple-Relationship Analysis

Principle:	Variables whose relationship is indirectly contingent on a third variable should be different from or independent of a third variable.
Choices:	Given the identification of at least a third variable, choose *one* of the following alternatives:
	1. Indirectly contingent.
	2. Multiplexed (noncontingent).

---

alternative formulations for a single level of analysis is based on the principle that four conditions (parts, wholes, and two rejection conditions, equivocal and inexplicable) are mutually exclusive. From this conceptualization of a single level of analysis follows a model for multiple levels of analysis. The principles of this multiple-level conceptualization are summarized in item II of Table 2.1. The available choices for two levels of analysis where one level of analysis is viewed as a lower level and a second as a higher level are also given in the table. For example, when two levels are considered, a choice that a relationship holds at both levels of analysis (a cross-level formulation) by definition rejects the alternative formulation that the relationship holds at only one level of analysis (as in emergent and level-specific formulations).

Single- and multiple-level analyses may also be illustrated in a decision format for two levels of analysis. From this perspective, the entity axis of the varient matrix is used to specify a set of alternatives and may be summarized as shown in the upper portion of Figure 2.1. For each level of analysis, only one of the four alternatives may be hypothesized, and data analysis should lead to an inference that one alternative is the most likely plausible explanation for the variable-entity relationship. Given four alternatives at each level of analy-

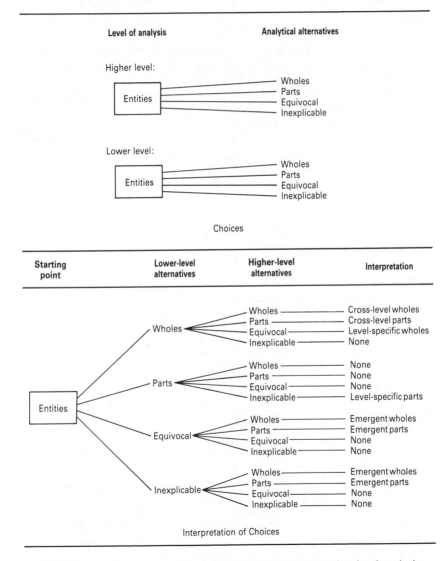

FIGURE 2.1.   Choices and interpretation of choices at two levels of analysis

sis, 16 alternatives and associated interpretations are plausible when two levels of analysis are considered. Although these 16 alternatives will be discussed in detail in this chapter, the decision tree shown in the lower portion of Figure 2.1 illustrates the choices that are made when one alternative is chosen at each of two levels of analysis. One of these 16 alternatives is chosen on a theoretical and empirical basis when a choice of one alternative is made at each level of analysis. The alternatives become more complex as more levels of analysis are considered; thus, the varient matrix is used to identify alternatives.

Variables

Assuming that a particular number of variables is specified and that two variables can be either related or unrelated, a series of competing alternatives is constructed. Item III of Table 2.1 lists conditions that arise when three variables are considered. Item IV shows that for multiple-relationship analysis, a relationship between two variables may be viewed as contingent on or multiplexed with values of a third variable. These assertions about variables can also be summarized in a decision tree format by viewing components of the variable axis as alternatives to be chosen on a theoretical or empirical basis. For example, in a three-variable case, one of 6 alternatives shown in Figure 2.2 is chosen when both multiple-variable and multiple-relationship analyses are performed.

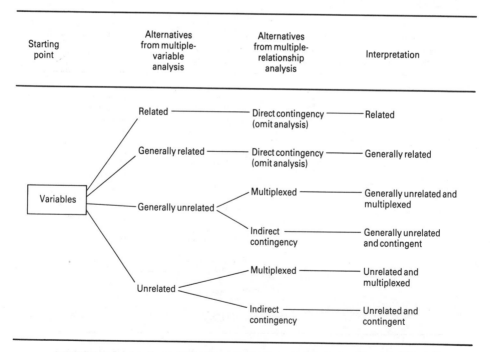

FIGURE 2.2. Choices and interpretation of choices between formulations of three variables

The Varient Matrix

The overview presented in Table 2.1 illustrates the choices that must be made between competing formulations of the same set of variables and entities in order to formulate and test hypotheses. The decision trees illustrate that varient matrices provide a means of locating each of several formulations relative to one another. With the use of a varient matrix, a theory and a data set are located in one position in the matrix by ruling out alternative placements. Moreover, a theoretically based placement is free to vary from an empirically based placement. The focus of the remainder of this chapter is on explaining the derivation of these choices from a set of basic principles. For the broadest possible application, this conceptualization was developed to be compatible with indicators from the traditional statistical paradigm.

THE ENTITY AXIS

Not surprisingly, the statistical paradigm, which was developed by physical scientists, requires a specification of **physical entities**, which are defined as objects that exist in space and time. Nonphysical entities are beyond the scope of this and other scientific paradigms. As Miller (1978, p. 10) notes: "Physical space is shared by all scientific observers and all scientific data must be collected in it. This is equally true for natural science and behavioral science."[1] Some care must be taken, however, that theories in the social sciences and organizational behavior are not dismissed as nonphysical in nature. As long as variables that may seem to be nonphysical (such as satisfaction, leadership, and so on) are linked to some set of objects which exist in physical space and time (such as persons, groups, collectivities), theories that include these variables are not intended to address nonphysical issues. Indeed, as will be discussed in subsequent chapters, even concepts that may seem nonphysical in nature can and must be translated into theories of physical objects.

Although levels of analysis must exist in physical space-time, this requirement does not mean that all such entity sets are readily observable. On the contrary, a lower level of analysis may be hypothesized and then data employed to assess whether a hypothesized level seems likely. This approach is common in physics, where attempts are made to identify the smallest entity set and to assess whether effects are due to activity at one (such as neutron) or another (such as molecule) level. When the varient paradigm is used, a particular level and unit of analysis is hypothesized and then data are examined to determine the likelihood that data support the hypothesized unit and level of analysis. In this way, a number of different types of entities can be hypothesized (other than, for example, persons, dyads, groups, and collectivities), and data can then be employed to evaluate such hypotheses.

Correspondingly, in terms of effects, a lower level of analysis (such as persons) may or may not be embedded in a higher level of analysis (such as collectivities). With the use of the varient paradigm, an embedding of entities

---

[1] From *Living Systems*, by J. G. Miller. Copyright © 1978 by McGraw-Hill. Used with the permission of the McGraw-Hill Book Company.

can be hypothesized and then tested empirically. For example, individual human beings may be embedded in work groups (a lower level of analysis), which are in turn embedded in departments or collectivities (a higher level of analysis). A key question becomes how to assert theoretically and ascertain empirically whether certain variables are associated with both departments and work groups (a cross-level formulation), or with work groups but not collectivities (a level-specific formulation), or with collectivities but not work groups (an emergent formulation). In order to consider such questions of multiple levels of analysis, a focus on single levels of analysis will serve as a useful starting point.

Single-Level Analysis

Although entities will later be considered in a conceptual sense, we begin with the variables associated with them. For our purposes, a **variable** is defined when different values or points, identifiable along a continuum, are assigned to entities. Moreover, one entity can be characterized along a number of variables. For example, a person might be characterized in terms of two variables (for example, degree of his or her satisfaction and performance). In this case two values are assigned to each entity and the relationship among the two variables across entities can be assessed.

Four Key Conditions   In many, if not most, traditional applications of the statistical paradigm, one score for each variable is assigned to each entity. Each score is then a characterization of the entity as a **whole**, or an undivided unit of analysis. In other words, the focus is on whole entities. This notion can be illustrated schematically by representing one entity as a circle:

The entire circle then is characterized by a score. The shading of the circle can represent the score on some variable, as follows:

In this case, assume that a whole entity is characterized as having a value of 2 on a variable. In testing theories, however, generally more than one score along a dimension is of interest in defining a variable. Therefore, in order to obtain a range of scores, additional entities must be considered. For example, consider the case in which two entities are examined. Say that one entity has a score of 2 and the other a score of 1 on some dimension. This case can be illustrated schematically as follows:

Score = 2   Score = 1

Notice that differences occur between these two entities.

For our purposes, a **whole condition** is defined as a focus between entities and a lack of focus within entities. In this case, differences between these entities on a single dimension are viewed as valid; differences within these entities are viewed as error and irrelevant. This conceptualization of entities is quite compatible with contemporary work in organizational behavior, and with individual difference approaches in psychology and other fields. As stated by Bakan (1966, p. 433): "The basic datum for an individual difference approach is not anything that characterizes *each* of two subjects but the difference *between them*" (emphasis in original).

As an alternative to the whole condition, a theorist or researcher may be interested in the same level of analysis (such as persons), but each entity may be viewed as containing interdependent parts. In this case the focus is on the interdependent components within each entity, or **parts**. If triangles represent these parts and circles represent an entity of interest, this condition can be illustrated as follows:

Here two parts are contained inside an entity. One part might have a score of 1 and the other part a score of 2, which can be illustrated as follows:

Score = 1 Score = 2

It is not necessary to introduce an additional set of similar entities with parts in order to obtain variability, because the dimension varies within an entity. But if other entities are added, each entity should contain a similar set of parts and a similar distribution of scores should be obtained.

As should be apparent, the entity **parts condition** is defined as a lack of focus between entities and a focus within entities. In this case, valid differences are expected within entities, and error occurs when differences between entities are the focus of interest. This conceptualization of parts is compatible with an alternative nonindividual difference approach in which each entity is viewed as a particular context within which a general proposition is manifested (Bakan, 1966). In this sense, the focus is not on differences between entities, but rather on differences within each of several entities.

Wholes and parts are thus seen as mutually exclusive alternative conditions—that is to say, only one of these two different views can be maintained about one entity-based dimension. In a whole condition, a focus within entities is erroneous; in contrast, in a parts condition, the same focus within entities is valid. Likewise, in a whole condition, a focus between entities is valid; in a parts condition, the same focus between entities is error. Therefore, the notion that parts and wholes are mutually exclusive conditions is based on the premise that one set of differences (such as between entities) on one dimension cannot be both valid and erroneous at the same time. This conceptualization of parts and wholes, which allows a focus either between or within entities to be error, is quite compatible with various applications of the traditional statistical paradigm. For example, Bakan (1966) indicates that "error" is a kind of umbrella term for variation among scores from different individuals (between-entity variation), and variation among measurements for the same individual (within-entity variation).

It should be apparent as a result of this conceptualization that one variable may reflect mainly differences between rather than within entities and be compatible with a whole condition, and that a second variable may reflect differences mainly within rather than between entities and be compatible with a parts condition. In other words, wholes and parts may be hypothesized or inferred; however, different variables must be associated with wholes than with parts. Stated somewhat differently, when one variable is of interest, wholes and parts are mutually exclusive. When two variables are of interest, one variable may reflect wholes and the other parts. Therefore, both a whole and a parts view may be maintained, provided different variables are associated with each view.

Returning to the case where one variable is of interest, logic dictates that two other conditions in addition to wholes and parts must be plausible. These two conditions permit the rejection of a particular level of analysis when neither wholes nor parts can be asserted at that level. One of these conditions is similar to a whole condition in that a focus between entities is valid, and it is similar to a parts condition in that a focus within entities is valid. Clearly, it differs from the whole and parts conditions for the same reasons. The label "equivocal" is therefore appropriate for this condition. Stated more formally, the **equivocal condition** is defined as a focus both between and within entities. In the final condition, too, a particular entity is viewed as irrelevant; therefore, a focus within or between entities is erroneous. This condition is called the **inexplicable condition**, which is defined as a lack of focus within and between entities.

The mutually exclusive nature of these four conditions should be apparent, since, as mentioned above, a particular focus cannot be viewed as erroneous and valid at the same time. The four conditions can be summarized as follows:

	Focus Between	*Focus Within*
Wholes	Valid	Error
Parts	Error	Valid
Equivocal	Valid	Valid
Inexplicable	Error	Error

This summary also demonstrates that each of the four conditions involves two statements—one about a focus within and one about a focus between entities.

The antithetical nature of the two statements contained in the conceptualization of parts and wholes permits multiple-hypothesis testing. For example, the choice of an inference toward wholes involves a rejection of the remaining three conditions. On the other hand, the lack of decision inherent in the equivocal and inexplicable conditions involves a rejection of a particular level of analysis. In this way, two interpretable conditions (parts and wholes) and two conditions which indicate that a particular level of analysis may be inappropriate (equivocal and inexplicable) have been generated. The degree to which this conceptualization is compatible with empirical procedures used in the statistical paradigm can now be considered.

Assessing the Four Conditions Empirically In the traditional statistical paradigm, a major concern is the relative difference between scores. These differences are traditionally measured by **signed deviation scores**, which provide an indication of the degree to which each score (X) varies from all other scores. **Total signed deviation scores** are calculated by determining the average of a set of scores ($\bar{X}$) and subtracting this average from all other scores ($X - \bar{X}$). Total signed deviation scores can be partitioned into within- and between-cell scores. Specifically, a **within-cell signed deviation score** is defined by determining the average of the scores in a cell ($\bar{X}_J$) and then subtracting this cell mean from each score in that cell ($X - \bar{X}_J$). **Between-cell signed deviation scores** are calculated by subtracting the average of all scores ($\bar{X}$) from the average for each cell ($\bar{X}_J - \bar{X}$). The calculation of these scores can be illustrated by considering five scores which are contained in two cells representing distinct entities and which take on the values 1, 2, 3, 4, and 5, yielding an overall average of 3. The calculations are as follows:

	Cell I		Cell II		
Scores (X)	1	2	3	4	5
Grand average ($\bar{X}$)	3	3	3	3	3
Cell averages ($\bar{X}_J$)	1.5	1.5	4	4	4
Total deviations ($X - \bar{X}$)	−2	−1	0	1	2
Within-cell deviations ($X - \bar{X}_J$)	−0.5	0.5	−1	0	1
Between-cell deviations ($\bar{X}_J - \bar{X}$)	−1.5	−1.5	1	1	1

In the varient paradigm, cells are aligned with entities (see Chapters 6 and 7), and within- and between-entity scores are calculated and examined. However, whether the resulting within and between deviations should be viewed as valid or error depends on which of the four conditions (wholes, parts, equivocal, or inexplicable) is under consideration.

For hypothesis testing, a definition of error and lack of error is necessary. Although definitions for error will be presented in Chapters 5, 6, and 7, an overview may be helpful at this point for readers familiar with statistics. In the one-variable case, error is defined as a lack of variability in scores, and validity is defined as the presence of variability in scores. Therefore, between- and within-cell scores can be compared in order to assess which focus (within, between, or neither) results in more variability. An F ratio can be employed in this regard; however, an F ratio is a creature from the statistical paradigm and is sensitive to degrees of freedom in a data set. For this reason, an additional direct comparison between the within- and between-cell deviations was developed, which we call an E ratio. This ratio also involves a comparison of within and between deviation scores, and its calculation is equal to the F ratio without a degree of freedom component. As such, the E ratio equals the ratio of two empirical indicators (within- and between-eta correlations).

In the two-variable case, given the fact that the correlation between two independent random variables is known to be zero, error is defined as a zero correlation. Since within- and between-cell scores can be used to calculate the correlations between two variables (Robinson, 1950), the difference between a within-entity correlation and a between-entity correlation for the same variables can be calculated by using a Z test because these two correlations are independent (see Appendix C). In addition, in order to assess the practical significance of the difference between the magnitudes of these correlations (independent of degrees of freedom), we have developed an indicator, which we call the A test, designed to assess angular differences.

This approach to single levels of analysis is summarized in Table 2.2 from theoretical, empirical, and inferential perspectives. In the one-variable case, the ratio of between- and within-cell scores (E and F ratios) is considered. In the two-variable case, correlations based on within and between signed deviation scores are considered separately (R and t tests) and in combination (A and Z tests). Therefore, one of four conditions can be hypothesized on a theoretical basis and data can be analyzed to ascertain which condition seems more likely based on tests of practical and statistical significance. Inferences are drawn mainly by comparing indicators based on within-entity deviations with indicators based on between-entity deviations. Statistical tests involving a comparison of an obtained value with a theoretical population value are also used. Essentially, tests for statistical (F, Z, t) and practical (E, A, R) significance are an integral part of the varient paradigm. The general framework for choosing among the four conditions on both a theoretical and an empirical basis will be developed and illustrated in subsequent chapters, as indicated in the lower portion of Table 2.2.

TABLE 2.2. Plausible theoretical, empirical, and inferential conditions at a single level of analysis

	GENERAL CASE		ONE-VARIABLE CASE			TWO-VARIABLE CASE		
	Theoretical		*Empirical*		*Inferential*	*Empirical*		*Inferential*
	Focus	Specification	Specification	Indicator	E, F	Specification	Indicator	A, Z, R, t
Wholes								
Between	Yes	Valid	Variable	$B \neq 0$	∞	Systematic	$\lvert B > 0\rvert$	∞
Within	No	Error	Constant	$W = 0$		Nonsystematic	$-\lvert W = 0\rvert$	$+$ 0
Parts								
Between	No	Error	Constant	$B = 0$	0	Nonsystematic	$\lvert B = 0\rvert$	0
Within	Yes	Valid	Variable	$W \neq 0$		Systematic	$-\lvert W > 0\rvert$	$-$ ∞
Equivocal								
Between	Yes	Valid	Variable	$B \neq 0$	1	Systematic	$\lvert B > 0\rvert$	∞
Within	Yes	Valid	Variable	$W \neq 0$		Systematic	$-\lvert W > 0\rvert$	0 ∞
Inexplicable								
Between	No	Error	Constant	$B = 0$	l	Nonsystematic	$\lvert B = 0\rvert$	0
Within	No	Error	Constant	$W = 0$		Nonsystematic	$-\lvert W = 0\rvert$	0 0
Chapter	3	4		5	6 and 7		5	6 and 7
	←			8 to 15				

Transition to Multiple-Level Analysis

This conceptualization of four conditions at one level of analysis can be used at each of several levels of analysis. The transition from single- to multiple-level analysis will be eased by a consideration of these four conditions from a reductionist and a nonreductionist perspective. Moreover, it helps demonstrate the compatibility of our single-level conceptualization with reductionist and nonreductionist approaches found in the social sciences and studies of organizational behavior.

The Reductionist Approach From a **reductionist viewpoint**, any entity should be reducible to its fundamental components. For our purposes, components are defined as wholes at a lower level of analysis. Theoretically, a whole entity at one level of analysis can be viewed as being composed of homogeneous components from a lower level of analysis. An entity parts condition at one level of analysis can be viewed as involving a configuration of heterogeneous components from a lower level of analysis. The equivocal condition at one level of analysis can be seen as indicating independent components from a lower level of analysis that are not organized into an identifiable heterogeneous or homogeneous entity. Finally, an inexplicable condition at one level of analysis can be viewed as indicating some type of error. From this viewpoint, each of the four conditions is viewed as consisting of the same components from a lower level of analysis, and the distributions of scores reflect different configurations of these more fundamental or lower-level components. In other words, the values given to components from a lower level of analysis are taken to indicate whether a whole, parts, equivocal, or inexplicable condition seems most likely.

We will illustrate this reductionist approach by making circles represent components (such as persons) and ovals represent the higher level of analysis of interest (such as dyads) that can be reduced. As in previous examples, assume that the shading of the circles represents the degree of a particular variable assigned to a component. A reductionist formulation can thus be illustrated as shown in Figure 2.3.

From an empirical perspective, it is important to note from this illustration that between-cell scores based on the averages of scores in the same cell (or entity) are valid representations of scores only when the values for the components are the same within each entity. Therefore, in the whole condition, regardless of whether one component score or the average of a set of component scores is employed, the same value will be obtained. From a reductionist perspective, however, components need not always be organized in this way; rather, they may be combined in a way that makes the average an inappropriate representation of a set of scores. Specifically, in a parts condition there are differences between scores within each entity, and they may be accurately represented by scores within each entity. Alternatively, a set of components from a lower level of analysis may not actually form an entity at a higher level of analysis. In this latter case, each component may be unique, as in the equivocal condition, which prohibits viewing a higher level of analysis type of entity as a viable way to summarize the formation of components. As a

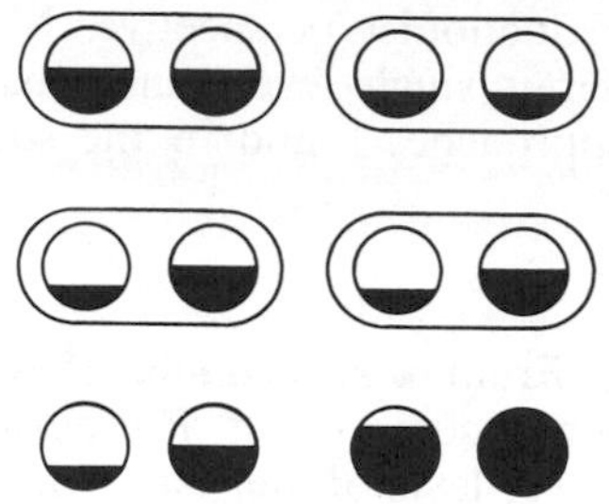

Condition	SCHEMATIC ILLUSTRATION		NUMERICAL ILLUSTRATION	
	Entity A	Entity B	Entity A	Entity B
Wholes			2 2	1 1
Parts			1 2	1 2
Equivocal (reject level)			1 2	3 4
Inexplicable (reject level)	—	—		

FIGURE 2.3. A single (dyad) level of analysis from a reductionist perspective

result, both within- and between-cell scores at a higher level of analysis are necessary to represent the independent components.

An extreme reductionist view implies that wholes are always equal to the sum of their components. Such an extreme view precludes the possibility that an entity may emerge that is not explicable solely in terms of its components. The use of within- and between-cell (entity) scores permits a reductionist view —for example, that a set of scores for a component may be homogeneous at a higher level of analysis and indicate a whole entity. An advantage of the use of these scores, however, is that there is no requirement that components must always sum to other, larger wholes at a higher level of analysis. In other words, the use of averages or between-cell or entity scores, rather than the summation of scores, permits tests of nonreductionist formulations in addition to re- ductionist formulations.

The Nonreductionist Approach As pointed out by Hunt, Sekaran, and Schriesheim (1982), researchers in organizational behavior sometimes prefer **nonreductionist positions**, which assert that entities at higher levels of analysis are not reducible to more fundamental components. In such formulations, for example, group phenomena are not viewed as simply person-level phenomena expressed at a higher level of analysis (Brown and Turner, in press). Even in the physical sciences, in a nonreductionist approach the components of an entity are sometimes conceptualized from an aggregation perspective. Consider this example from physics: A gas is composed of molecules; however, the basic characteristics of a gas are determined not by the complex behavior of each molecule, but by the action of all the molecules taken together. According to Gnedenko (1966) and others, molecules within a gas seem to vary in a way depending on chance. As a result, an average (between-gas) score is employed to characterize the aggregate gas. In this case, the unique deviations of each molecule are averaged out in order to obtain a measure of the entity gas.

An important feature of this nonreductionist approach is that the variation of the components is shown empirically to be compatible with error (randomness). In our example from physics, the within-entity (cell) variation of molecules is shown to be error before it is asserted that an average is a valid indicator. In other words, an average is not assumed to represent the sum of the individual components. Instead, the averaging procedure is viewed as removing the error due to individual components. According to our definition of the whole condition, an assertion of wholes means that differences or values contained within entities (cells) should be error. A key point of this discussion is that the deviation of scores within an entity should be demonstrated to be compatible with some notion of error if between-cell scores are to be interpreted as valid.

Of course, an extreme nonreductionist position implies that averages of scores are always and everywhere appropriate because any deviations from averages are always and everywhere error. Such extreme approaches have been criticized by a number of individuals. For example, Kimberly (1980, p. 367) asks: "How valid is it to define leadership style in terms of averaged subordinate ratings?" In a more general critique of social science research Gould (1982, p. 8), suggests: "There is also a growing tendency to perform all sorts of undefined and totally inappropriate, mathematical operations on data (such as... taking averages), operations that a mathematician can only stare at in horror and disbelief."[2] In line with these criticisms, consider an example in which two component scores of 1 and 999,999 are given and an average of 500,000 results. In this case, unlike cases in which scores are equal or approximately so, the average and individual scores are not similar, and each provides a different characterization of an entity. In order to deal with this type of problem, the varient paradigm requires a demonstration that within-cell deviations are error before employing averages (between-cell scores) and asserting a whole condition. In addition, the parts and equivocal conditions are viewed as plausible and are not rejected on an a priori basis.

Another widespread nonreductionist viewpoint asserts that only a single score should be employed for each entity, since the average of the components of an entity may not represent that entity's true score. At the extreme, this position is untenable. The use of one score for each entity involves an assumption that differences on that variable within that entity are error, without providing a means for assessing such an assumption. Moreover, and perhaps more important, the use of a single score for each entity does not allow for a distinction to be made between the whole and equivocal conditions. Such a distinction becomes quite important when multiple levels of analysis are considered. Despite these problems with the use of one score for each entity, such scores can be clarified by considering their relationship with between-entity scores.

Therefore, the conceptualization of the four conditions (wholes, parts, equivocal, and inexplicable) presented in this chapter is compatible with less

---

[2] From *The Sciences*, May–June 1982. © 1982 by The New York Academy of Sciences.

extreme nonreductionist and reductionist positions. Essentially, a single level of analysis can be viewed in any one of these four competing and alternative ways. This four-condition conceptualization serves as the basis for examining multiple levels of analysis.

Multiple-Level Analysis

In the framework of a single level of analysis, the four conditions identified concern the same entity set, or the same level of analysis. Multiple-level analysis involves a focus on at least two entity sets or levels of analysis (such as persons and dyads). Of particular interest to us is the way in which one level of analysis can be linked with one other level of analysis. Once plausible linkages are defined, any number of levels of analysis can be considered by sequentially considering two levels of analysis at a time. Therefore, in this section of the chapter we will define the plausible linkages between two levels of analysis before extending the conceptualization to any number of levels of analysis.

When the four plausible conditions at one level of analysis are crossed with the four conditions at a second level of analysis, the 16 distinct conditions listed at the beginning of this chapter, and summarized later in variant matrix form in Table 2.3, are generated. Eight of these conditions have substantive meaning, whereas the other eight result in the rejection of two levels of analysis or are logically inconsistent. One way to illustrate the meaning of these 16 conditions is to view one level of analysis, labeled a lower level of analysis, as potentially embedded in a higher level of analysis. For example, a set of persons may be viewed as a lower level of analysis contained in a higher level of analysis (such as dyads). Such a reductionist starting point does not preclude the possibility of asserting or finding empirically that a nonreductionist formulation is more likely (that a higher or lower level of analysis is irrelevant). However, beginning with a reductionist perspective simplifies the following presentation of the way in which the four conditions at a lower level of analysis take on a slightly different meaning, depending on which condition is asserted or obtained empirically at a higher level.

The Whole Condition at a Lower Level   First, wholes at a lower level of analysis are defined as a focus between rather than within entities. The differences between entities at a lower level of analysis may be due to differences at a higher level of analysis. The condition where wholes are asserted both at a lower and at a higher level of analysis is called **cross-level wholes** and is illustrated in the upper portion of Figure 2.4. In addition, wholes at a lower level of analysis may form parts at a higher level of analysis. This condition is called **cross-level parts** and is illustrated in the middle portion of Figure 2.4. In some cases, however, between-entity differences at a lower level of analysis may not form wholes or parts at a higher level of analysis, but may be scattered both within and between entities. This condition is called **level-specific wholes** and is illustrated in the lower portion of Figure 2.4. Wholes, however, imply valid differences between entities at a lower level of analysis; these differences should manifest themselves at higher levels of

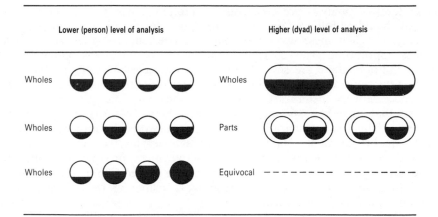

FIGURE 2.4. Three types of whole entities at a lower (person) level of analysis, and wholes, parts, and an equivocal condition at a higher (dyad) level of analysis

analysis and should therefore not become error at the next higher level of analysis. As a result, when whole conditions are asserted or identified empirically at a lower level of analysis, an inexplicable condition at the next higher level of analysis is interpreted as inconsistent.

The principle that underlies these interpretations is called the **principle of wholes** and can be stated as follows: Wholes at lower levels of analysis can be followed by a whole, a parts, or an equivocal condition, but not by an inexplicable condition at the next higher level of analysis. In other words, the four combinations of conditions at two levels of analysis are conceptualized and interpreted as follows:

Lower Level	Higher Level	Interpretation
Wholes	Wholes	Cross-level wholes
Wholes	Parts	Cross-level parts
Wholes	Equivocal	Level-specific wholes
Wholes	Inexplicable	Inconsistent

As should be apparent, wholes at a lower level of analysis take on a different meaning depending on the way a higher level of analysis is viewed as influencing scores. Specifically, a whole condition at a lower level of analysis may reflect a whole or parts conditions at the next higher level of analysis. Cross-level wholes and parts are defined in this way. Alternatively, whole conditions at a lower level of analysis may be level-specific and not a reflection of a higher level of analysis.

The Part Condition at a Lower Level Second, the case when parts are asserted at a lower level of analysis implies that any differences between entities are erroneous. As a result, within- or between-entity differences at a higher level of analysis are erroneous. Therefore, parts at a lower level of analysis should be followed only by an inexplicable condition at a higher level of analysis. When these two conditions are asserted, the label **level-specific parts** is appropriate. This conceptualization seems quite reasonable. In the parts condition, there are several entities at one level of analysis, but each entity is the same as other entities—that is, several entities exist without valid differences between them. As a result, any of the conditions at higher levels of analysis that include a specification of valid between-entity differences are erroneous. This conceptualization can be expressed as the **principle of parts**, which can be stated as follows: Parts at a lower level of analysis can be followed by an inexplicable, but not by a whole, parts, or equivocal condition at the next higher level of analysis. This principle and conceptualization can be stated in a somewhat different fashion by considering the interpretations consistent with each possibility:

Lower Level	Higher Level	Interpretation
Parts	Wholes	Inconsistent
Parts	Parts	Inconsistent
Parts	Equivocal	Inconsistent
Parts	Inexplicable	Level-specific parts

Wholes and Parts at a Lower Level   Four key interpretable conditions that result when multiple levels of analysis are considered can now be summarized as follows:

Lower Level	Higher Level	Interpretation
Wholes	Wholes	Cross-level wholes
Wholes	Parts	Cross-level parts
Wholes	Equivocal	Level-specific wholes
Parts	Inexplicable	Level-specific parts

As should be apparent from this tabular summary, not only do the parts and wholes condition take on different meaning when multiple levels of analysis are considered, but the equivocal and inexplicable conditions at a higher level of analysis take on important meaning when parts or wholes are obtained at a lower level of analysis. Furthermore, because the four conditions at each level of analysis are mutually exclusive, the principles of parts and wholes result in definitions of cross-level and level-specific wholes and parts that are mutually exclusive (when one variable is considered).

The Equivocal and Inexplicable Conditions at a Lower Level   What are the consequences of multiple-level analysis for the equivocal and inexplicable condition when each is asserted at a lower level of analysis? If an equivocal condition is asserted at a lower level of analysis and parts are asserted at a higher level of analysis, the label **emergent parts** is appropriate. Moreover, given an equivocal condition at a lower level of analysis, when wholes are asserted at a higher level of analysis, the label **emergent wholes** is appropriate. An equivocal condition may also be followed at the next higher level of analysis by another equivocal condition, which indicates that both levels of analysis should be rejected. Furthermore, an equivocal condition asserted or inferred at a lower level of analysis may become inexplicable at the next higher level of analysis. *In general, however, in a single setting an equivocal condition at a lower level of analysis implies valid differences both between and within entities, and these differences should not become error at the next higher level of analysis.* This set of emergent and rejection alternatives can be summarized as follows:

Lower Level	Higher Level	Interpretation
Equivocal	Wholes	Emergent wholes
Equivocal	Parts	Emergent parts
Equivocal	Equivocal	Reject both levels
Equivocal	Inexplicable	Reject both levels

A final conceptualization and interpretation of conditions applies when an inexplicable condition is asserted at a lower level of analysis. This formulation may be represented as follows:

Lower Level	Higher Level	Interpretation
Inexplicable	Wholes	Emergent wholes
Inexplicable	Parts	Emergent parts
Inexplicable	Equivocal	Reject both levels
Inexplicable	Inexplicable	Reject both levels

As should be apparent, emergent wholes and parts are defined as occurring when the lower level of analysis is rejected (with the equivocal or inexplicable condition) and when wholes or parts are asserted at the upper level of analysis. Therefore, eight conditions are viewed as having substantive meaning.

Performing Multiple-Level Analysis   Essentially, for two levels of analysis interpretations have been derived for 16 plausible alternative conditions. This conceptualization is summarized in Table 2.3 with the use of the entity axis of the varient matrix. Specifically, at each of the two levels of analysis shown in the table for each of the 16 cases, one of the four conditions is chosen on a theoretical and an empirical basis; the double lines indicate the space selected on a theoretical basis, and number signs indicate an empirically based choice of a cross-level wholes formulation. The interpretation of each of the 16 mutually exclusive alternatives is shown in the column headings of the table.

An essential point underlying this conceptualization of multiple levels of analysis is that if a particular level of analysis is of interest, the starting point is wholes (or between-cell scores) at a lower level of analysis. *From this perspective, any set of scores is viewed as averages of scores from the lower level of*

TABLE 2.3. Plausible conditions for multiple levels of analysis

TYPE OF THEORY

ENTITY AXIS	Cross-Level Wholes	Cross-Level Parts	Level-Specific Wholes	Level-Specific Parts	Emergents Wholes	Emergents Parts	Reject Level A	Reject Level B	Reject Level C	Reject Level D	Inconsistent Wholes	Inconsistent Parts	Inconsistent Parts
Higher Level													
Wholes	#		—		—		—	—	—	—	—	—	
Parts		—	—		—	—	—	—	—	—		—	—
Equivocal		—	—	—			—	—	—	—			—
Inexplicable				—			—	—	—	—	—		
Lower Level													
Wholes	#		—		—		—	—	—	—	—	—	
Parts		—	—		—	—	—	—	—	—		—	—
Equivocal		—	—	—			—	—	—	—			—
Inexplicable				—			—	—	—	—	—		

analysis, which means that the entire formulation and analytical procedure can be seen as being based on averaged scores. At first glance this may appear to be very problematic; using unaveraged scores might appear to be safer. However, as indicated previously, such scores, if purported to reflect differences between entities, also by definition require an assertion that any deviations within entities are error. In the varient paradigm, an attempt is made to test the accuracy of this assertion. Therefore, the use of one score for each entity is less rigorous than the use of an average. Nevertheless, a question that can be asked empirically is whether the use of averages (once identified as appropriate) yields results similar to those obtained with the use of single scores. Nothing in this formulation of single and multiple levels of analysis precludes the use of an average, as well as of one score for each entity. Simply stated, analyses can be performed by focusing on the relationship between scores based on averages and on nonaveraged scores for each entity.

A method for formulating theories at each level of analysis is provided by this conceptualization of entities. Empirically, the likelihood of one of the four conditions can be assessed at one level of analysis. Once a decision has been reached at one level of analysis, the same type of analysis can be performed at a higher level and a condition can be inferred. Thus, theoretical predictions and data can be located in one of four conditions at each of two levels of analysis.

Although we are considering two levels of analysis at a time, the multiple-level conceptualization can be extended to any number of levels of analysis. For example, a higher level of analysis could be viewed as contained in a still higher level of analysis, and so on. In this extension, the relationships among the four conditions remain as outlined in Table 2.3 for two levels of analysis. For example, suppose one were interested in a variable that was believed to reflect only group and dyadic face-to-face interaction and not person or collectivity level phenomena. Moreover, assume that these variables are asserted to apply to both whole groups and dyads. This assertion means an equivocal condition at the person level, a whole condition at the dyad level, a whole condition at the group level, and an equivocal condition at the collectivity level. The entire formulation can then be characterized as follows: The variable emerges at the dyad level and holds across whole dyads and groups and is level-specific (does not apply to collectivities). This is an **emergent, cross-level, level-specific formulation**. This formulation is illustrated in the varient matrix presented in Table 2.4. As shown in the table, the characterization of this formulation is accomplished by considering two levels at a time. Given this illustration of the ability of the entity axis to expand infinitely, the length of the axis and the number of alternative explanations specified by an assertion of a particular number of entities can now be stated.

Since at each level of analysis four conditions are possible, the length of any entity axis and number of theoretical and empirical conditions equals four multiplied by the number of levels of analysis of interest. Stated more formally, if L represents the number of levels of analysis of interest, then the length of the entity axis can be written as follows:

$$\text{Length of the entity axis} = 4L$$

TABLE 2.4.   A level-specific and emergent cross-level
whole dyad and group formulation in a varient matrix

ENTITY AXIS	LOCATION OF THEORY AND DATA
Collectivities	
Wholes	
Parts	
Equivocal #	
Inexplicable	Level-specific
Groups	
Wholes #	
Parts	
Equivocal	Cross-level wholes
Inexplicable	
Dyads	
Wholes #	
Parts	
Equivocal	
Inexplicable	Emergent
Persons	
Wholes	
Parts	
Equivocal #	
Inexplicable	

For example, for four levels of analysis, there are 16 conditions on the entity axis.

In addition, since various combinations of conditions can be chosen, the number of multiple-level alternative formulations for a given number of levels of analysis is equal to 4^L, where L equals the number of levels of analysis of interest. For example, recall in the two-level illustration presented in Table 2.3 that 16 alternative multiple-level formulations were possible. This is compatible with the rule for determining the number of alternative explanations ($4^2 = 16$). In the case of four levels of analysis 4^4 or 256 different formulations are possible, in which one condition is chosen at each level of analysis. These alternative competing formulations apply for each variable of interest and are all plausible when four levels of analysis are of interest. Moreover, these 256 formulations compete because the four conditions within each level of analysis are mutually exclusive. In addition, any number of entities can be considered at each of the levels of analysis.

The simplest way to illustrate the nature of the entity axis is with one variable. A variable can be hypothesized to represent differences among whole entities, among the parts inside each of several entities, or as not applicable to a particular level of analysis (the equivocal or inexplicable conditions). However, such an illustration requires a consideration of the variable axis of the varient matrix in addition to the entity axis.

THE VARIABLE AXIS

Obviously, the number of alternatives along the variable axis varies depending on the number of variables under consideration. In the one-variable case there is, of course, only one alternative along the variable axis (such as X). However, there can be several different ways to formulate hypotheses about that variable. As an example, for one variable, wholes across two levels of analysis ($L = 2$) may be hypothesized. The length of the entity axis is $4L$ or 8, and the number of competing alternative explanations is 4^L or 16. Suppose one of these 16 explanations is chosen on a theoretical basis (such as cross-level wholes). An empirical analysis may result in the inference that a whole effect seems more likely. Using number signs to indicate a choice based on data and double lines to indicate the hypothesized formulation, the following varient matrix of one variable can be constructed:

		VARIABLE AXIS
	ENTITY AXIS	X
Level II	Wholes	#
(higher)	Parts	
	Equivocal	
	Inexplicable	
Level I	Wholes	‖
(lower)	Parts	
	Equivocal	#
	Inexplicable	

As indicated in this varient matrix for one variable and two levels of analysis, at the higher level of analysis the hypothesized condition (wholes) corresponds to the condition chosen from data. In contrast, at level I the lack of correspondence between the double lines and number sign indicates a lack of agreement between hypothesis and data. The data indicate that an emergent formulation is more appropriate than a cross-level condition.

Multiple-Variable Analysis

The Two-Variable Case   When only one variable is of interest, multiple hypotheses that involve different levels of analysis can be considered. When two variables are specified, the relationship between the two generates the formation of two alternatives along the variable axis. Specifically, two variables may be related or unrelated. Using a perpendicularity sign ($\perp$) to indicate unrelated variables and a double-headed arrow to indicate related variables, a varient matrix for the two-variable case at one level of analysis is displayed as follows:

| | VARIABLE AXIS | |
ENTITY AXIS	*Related Variables* *X ↔ Y*	*Unrelated Variables* *X ⊥ Y*
Wholes	‾‾ ‾‾	
Parts	# #	
Equivocal		
Inexplicable		

In this illustrative case, two variables X and Y are hypothesized to be related based on differences between whole entities, as indicated by the location of double lines in the table. Empirically, as indicated by the location of number signs for each variable in the table, the variables seem to be related as predicted, but are more compatible with an assertion of parts than of wholes. In the two-variable case, first each variable is considered separately and then their relationship is examined. In this way, multiple hypotheses about variables and entities as well as their relationship can be generated. Since variables should not be viewed as both related and unrelated at the same time, two mutually exclusive competing alternatives always occur when two variables are of interest. Because any network of variables can be characterized by the relationship between all variables, taken two at a time, the two-variable case forms a basis for constructing a general procedure for specifying the variable axis of the varient matrix.

The General Formulation   In general, the variable axis of a varient matrix is formed by considering all plausible relationships that can be examined, given a particular number of variables. The general equation for the number q of possible relationships given V variables is written in the following way:

$$q = \frac{V^2 - V}{2} \tag{2.1}$$

The logic that underlies this equation is rather straightforward and is as follows. Given V variables, the number of possible relationships that can be specified or examined can be determined by beginning with a (nonvarient) matrix formed by V variables crossed by V variables. This matrix is illustrated in Figure 2.5. The total number of entries in the $V \times V$ matrix is V^2. The diagonal in this matrix contains V comparisons of each variable with itself. Therefore V, the number of variables, is subtracted from the total number of entries, V^2, to remove these identities. The two triangular submatrices illustrated in the diagram are mirror reflections of each other. Therefore the total number of unique relationships that involve a comparison of one variable with another is one-half the total number of remaining comparisons, $(V^2 - V)/2$.

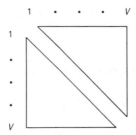

FIGURE 2.5. Matrix resulting from a correlation of V variables

Since each of the total number of possible relationships (q) among variables taken two at a time may indicate that two variables are related or unrelated, the total number of alternative conditions that can be generated given V variables is written as:

$$\text{Total number of alternative formulations of variables} = 2^q \qquad \textbf{(2.2)}$$

For example, in the case of three variables, from Equation 2.1 the total number of comparisons or relationships that should be considered is $q = (3^2 - 3)/2 = 3$, and the total number of alternative formulations of variables is $2^q = 2^3 = 8$. The eight conditions for the three variables were illustrated in Chapter 1. In the case of four variables, q equals $(4^2 - 4)/2$ or 6, and the total number of alternative formulations of variables is 2^6 or 64.

One particularly useful feature of this general conceptualization is that smaller varient matrices are subsumed by larger matrices. An illustration of this feature is presented in Table 2.5. The table shows a variable axis based on two variables X and Y, where two alternative conditions (related and unrelated) are listed. The unrelated and related conditions in a two-variable case are also included in a three-variable axis and take on additional meaning. This point is illustrated in the middle columns of Table 2.5. Specifically, an assertion or finding that two variables X and Y are related is compatible with any of the conditions which can arise when a third variable Z is considered *and* in which the same two variables X and Y are related. Data about a relationship between two variables X and Y provide no information about the relationship of these variables to a third variable.

The crucial point is not that the relationship between two variables is unimportant, but rather that a three-variable axis includes a two-variable axis in an extended form. The same principle applies to four, five, and V variable cases; for that reason, an illustration of the specification of alternatives in a three-variable case will be sufficient for our purposes. In a sense, a four-variable case with a variable axis containing 64 conditions can be reduced to a three-variable case by focusing on key alternative conditions. The key alternatives of interest to us are listed in the last column of Table 2.5. This approach to reducing a four-variable case to a three-variable case is employed solely for the purpose of simplifying the presentation of procedures for generating a variable axis. In fact, any one of the 64 alternative formulations that are

TABLE 2.5. Linkages between two-, three-, and four-variable cases

TWO-VARIABLE CASE

Related $X \leftrightarrow Y$	Unrelated $X \perp Y$	THREE-VARIABLE CASE	FOUR-VARIABLE CASE
		Related (direct contingency)	
$X \leftrightarrow Y$		$[X \leftrightarrow Y \leftrightarrow Z]$	$[X \leftrightarrow Y \leftrightarrow Z \leftrightarrow W]$
		Generally related (direct contingency)	
	$X \perp Y$	$[(X \perp Y) \leftrightarrow Z]$	$[(X \perp Y) \leftrightarrow (W \leftrightarrow Z)]$
$X \leftrightarrow Y$		$[(X \perp Z) \leftrightarrow Y]$	
$X \leftrightarrow Y$		$[(Y \perp Z) \leftrightarrow X]$	
		Generally unrelated (indirect contingency)	
$X \leftrightarrow Y$		$[(X \leftrightarrow Y) \perp Z]$	$[(X \leftrightarrow Y) \perp (W \leftrightarrow Z)]$
	$X \perp Y$	$[(X \leftrightarrow Z) \perp Y]$	
	$X \perp Y$	$[(Y \leftrightarrow Z) \perp X]$	
		Generally unrelated (multiplexed)	
$X \leftrightarrow Y$		$(X \leftrightarrow Y) \perp Z$	$(X \leftrightarrow Y) \perp (W \leftrightarrow Z)$
	$X \perp Y$	$(X \leftrightarrow Z) \perp Y$	
	$X \perp Y$	$(Y \leftrightarrow Z) \perp X$	
		Unrelated (indirect contingency)	
	$X \perp Y$	$[X \perp Y \perp Z]$	$[X \perp Y \perp Z \perp W]$
		Unrelated (multiplexed)	
	$X \perp Y$	$X \perp Y \perp Z$	$X \perp Y \perp Z \perp W$

plausible when four variables are considered can be specified and identified empirically. For illustrative purposes, our preference is to focus on the structure of the eight alternative conditions that can occur when only three variables are considered.

The Three-Variable Case These eight competing formulations for the three-variable case are presented in the upper portion of Table 2.6. From a theoretical perspective, any one of the eight cases might be preferred. For example, on a theoretical basis one might hypothesize that organizations are designed such that all variables are related as one set. This assertion of a related variables case involves a rejection of seven other formulations. Alternatively, one might assert that two variables (X and Y) are independent but combine to form a third variable (Z) based on some theoretical rationale. In this case, a generally related case is asserted. Moreover, the formulation might be written as $X + Y = Z$. This assertion, of course, involves a rejection of six other formulations as well as the assertion that $X + Z = Y$. Despite any theoretical assertion and rejection of alternative assertions, the data may or may not correspond to the selected assertion.

In order to test the adequacy of any assertion empirically, it is necessary to distinguish empirically, in this case, among the eight conditions. The related

TABLE 2.6. Plausible theoretical, empirical, and inferential conditions in multiple variable analysis (the three-variable case)

	Related	Generally Related			Generally Unrelated			Unrelated
CHOSEN FOCUS (VARIABLE AXIS)	X↔Y↔Z	(X⊥Y)↔Z	(X⊥Z)↔Y	(Y⊥Z)↔X	(X↔Y)⊥Z	(X↔Z)⊥Y	(Y↔Z)⊥X	X⊥Y⊥Z
Theoretical								
XY relationship	↔	⊥	↔	↔	↔	⊥	⊥	⊥
XZ relationship	↔	↔	⊥	↔	⊥	↔	⊥	⊥
YZ relationship	↔	↔	↔	⊥	⊥	⊥	↔	⊥
Empirical								
Magnitude (R and t)								
XY relationship		0				0	0	0
XZ relationship			0		0		0	0
YZ relationship				0	0	0		0
Differences (A and t')								
$\|XY\| - \|XZ\|$	0	−	+	(0)	+	−	0	0
$\|XY\| - \|YZ\|$	0	−	(0)	+	+	0	−	0
$\|XZ\| - \|YZ\|$	0	(0)	−	+	0	+	−	0

and unrelated conditions are distinguishable by the different magnitudes of the relationships contained in each case. Specifically, zero correlations between all pairs of variables are shown for the unrelated case; in the related case, all correlations are presented as nonzero (see the middle section of Table 2.6). A consideration of the number of zero relationships implied by each of the eight alternatives also permits a distinction to be made between the generally related and generally unrelated conditions, although not between the subcases within the generally related and generally unrelated conditions.

As a result, a consideration of the differences between the correlations among the variables is necessary in order to distinguish among the last six conditions (three in each of the generally related and generally unrelated cases). The differences that result from subtracting each relationship from all other relationships are presented in the lower portion of Table 2.6. The signs of these differences distinguish between the three generally related and the three generally unrelated cases. Essentially, the magnitude of and the differences between these relationships can be used to choose among the eight conditions.

From an inferential perspective, the magnitude of a relationship (whether it is or is not close to zero) can be assessed by employing a traditional t test. Since the test is statistical, however, the result depends on the number of degrees of freedom in the data. Therefore, an R test was developed to assess the degree that the magnitude of a relationship varies from zero in a practical sense. Evaluating the difference between relationships involves an additional assessment of whether one relationship is larger in magnitude than another relationship. These relationships, however, are not by definition independent of each other. For example, if two variables are related, then a third variable is likely to be related with both or neither of these variables. In the traditional statistical paradigm, Hotelling's t' test is used to test the difference between two nonindependent correlations; but since this test is also influenced by degrees of freedom, an A test is used to assess the practical significance of such a difference.

Therefore, from an empirical perspective, the eight conditions are distinguishable in terms of both the magnitudes of the relationships among the variables and the differences between the relationships among the variables. In addition to specifying a relationship among variables, a theory must specify the entity or entities to which it applies. For the purpose of simplifying the illustration, assume that a theory specifies either wholes or parts at one level of analysis and a relationship among variables.

In order to assess empirically the accuracy of such theoretical assertions, two additional terms, **chosen focus** and **other focus**, are helpful. Specifically, in the case of wholes, the focus is on differences between entities and a focus within entities is viewed as error. In contrast, in the case of parts, the focus is on differences within rather than between entities. In both cases, one focus is chosen and the other focus is viewed as error. Solely for the purpose of simplification, wholes and parts can be viewed as specifying that a chosen focus is viewed as valid, or not error, and that the other focus is viewed as error. Therefore, any specification about multiple variables involves both a chosen and an other focus. In general, the other focus involves the specification of relationships that would occur when a focus is viewed as error (the unrelated case). The chosen focus usually involves a specification that variables are related.

Finally, the widespread contemporary use of multiple regression calls for the following comments about the three generally related cases. In these three cases, the differences specified may seem to imply that each variable must contribute equally to a third variable. This does not necessarily follow, and in order to illustrate this point, the zero values for the differences for these cases were placed in parens in Table 2.6. Although this issue will be considered in more detail in subsequent chapters, it is useful to point out that multiple regression can be applied to any one of the eight conditions summarized in Table 2.6 and is not necessarily limited to the generally related case. The interpretation of the application of a multiple regression methodology will, however, vary depending on which of these cases seems more likely (see Chapter 13).

In summary, from a theoretical perspective, given a set of variables, a number of alternative explanations are derived from which one formulation is selected. From an empirical perspective, a choice of one condition is based on the demonstration that the other, theoretically equally likely, conditions are less plausible. The condition selected based on a theoretical basis, of course, may or may not correspond to the condition selected on an empirical basis. For example, one may assert that $X + Y = Z$ and find that the formulation $X + Z = Y$ is supported by the data.

Multiple-Relationship Analysis

If one or several variables are conceptualized as being different from another set of variables (as in the generally unrelated or unrelated cases), the multiplexed and indirectly contingent formulations are plausible. From a theoretical and an empirical perspective, a choice must be made between these two alternatives.

The requirement that at least two different sets of variables be asserted theoretically and identified empirically before choosing between the multiplexed and contingency formulations is rather important. First, it assures theoretical clarity in that the variable or variables that may serve as moderator or contingency factors are specified, as distinct from those variables whose relationship is contingent. Second, an empirical identification of variables that are unrelated ensures that the ranges of the variables which are examined within a condition formed by the values of a (moderator) variable are not truncated in each condition.

From a theoretical perspective, it is necessary to specify a "third" variable (Z) which (1) is different from other variables and (2) can be used to form categories. For illustrative purposes, assume that two categories or conditions (Z_1 and Z_2) are formed, based on different values of variable Z. Within each condition two variables of interest (X and Y) may be related or unrelated. This results in the four plausible theoretical alternatives shown in the upper portion of Table 2.7. In each case, the same two variables are of interest. However, when a contingent formulation is asserted, the variables are hypothesized to be related in one category and unrelated in the second category; when a multiplexed formulation is asserted, the variables are hypothesized to show the same relationship under each condition defined by values of a third variable.

From an empirical perspective, the contingent and multiplexed alternatives can be distinguished by the magnitude of the relationship in each condition and the differences between the magnitudes of these relationships. In the multiplexed cases, the difference between the relationships in each condition equals zero. In the contingent cases, a difference other than zero is obtained when the correlations are subtracted from each other. In order to distinguish between the two multiplexed formulations, there must also be a consideration of the magnitude of the relationships in each condition. Both the magnitude of the relationships in each category and the differences between them should be considered. The upper portion of Table 2.7 shows the calculations involved in distinguishing between these alternatives empirically for the case where two categories are formed by values of a third variable.

From an inferential perspective, the magnitude of the relationship in each condition can be tested with a t test from the traditional statistical paradigm and with the R test, which examines the magnitude of the relationship independent of degrees of freedom. To test the differences between the correlations in the two conditions, a Z test is typically employed, given that the two correlations are independent. This statistical test can be supplemented with an A test of the practical significance of the difference between the correlations from each condition.

In this way, the choice of a multiplexed or contingent formulation is based on theoretical and empirical considerations. The theoretical and empirical choices may differ or be similar; for example, a multiplexed formulation may be hypothesized and a contingent formulation may be selected on an empirical basis. In addition to focusing on the relationship among variables, one should also consider characteristics of entities in multiple-relationship analysis.

TABLE 2.7. Plausible theoretical and empirical conditions for the multiplexed and indirect contingency formulations with a focus on variables and entities (two categories)

VARIABLE FOCUS

	Multiplexed		Contingent	
Theoretical	**Case A**	**Case B**	**Case C**	**Case D**
Condition Z_1	$X \perp Y$	$X \leftrightarrow Y$	$X \leftrightarrow Y$	$X \perp Y$
Condition Z_2	$X \perp Y$	$X \leftrightarrow Y$	$X \perp Y$	$X \leftrightarrow Y$
Empirical				
Magnitudes (R and t)				
Condition Z_1	0			0
Condition Z_2	0		0	
Difference (A and Z)				
Cond. Z_1 − Cond. Z_2	0	0	+	−

ENTITY FOCUS

	Multiplexed		Contingent				Error
Theoretical	**Case 1**	**Case 2**	**Case 3**	**Case 4**	**Case 5**	**Case 6**	**Case 7**
Condition Z_1:	Parts	Wholes	E or I	E or I	Parts	Wholes	E or I
Condition Z_2:	Parts	Wholes	Parts	Wholes	E or I	E or I	E or I
Empirical							
Differences inside Conditions							
Condition Z_1							
Between	0	+	0	0	0	+	0
Within	+	0	0	0	+	0	0
Differences ($B - W$)	−	+	0	0	−	+	0
Condition Z_2							
Between	0	+	0	+	0	0	0
Within	+	0	+	0	0	0	0
Differences ($B - W$)	−	+	−	+	0	0	0
Differences among Conditions							
Condition Z_1 (between) minus Condition Z_2 (within)	−	+	−	0	0	+	0
Condition Z_2 (between) minus Condition Z_1 (within)	−	+	0	+	−	0	0

Note: E indicates equivocal, I indicates inexplicable.

From an entity perspective, each condition based on different values of a third variable can be viewed as a separate study containing potentially different entities. A level of analysis may be hypothesized to be relevant under only some conditions (contingent), or the same entity set may be hypothesized to be relevant under all conditions (multiplexed). For example, certain collectivities that contain groups may or may not be compatible with the operation of certain group processes. The varient approach permits formulations which include either a specification that under certain conditions a lack of wholes or parts will be obtained, or a specification that wholes and parts apply across all conditions. Although this entity perspective on multiple relationships will be discussed and illustrated in subsequent chapters (see Chapter 11), an example and overview of the ability of the paradigm to deal empirically with these formulations about entities may be helpful at this point.

In a case where two conditions are defined by values of a third variable, seven different formulations involving entities are plausible. These different formulations are summarized in the lower portion of Table 2.7. For example, consider the case where parts are asserted in both conditions, Z_1 and Z_2. This means that for each condition, within-entity deviations are viewed as valid or systematic. This is indicated in the table by the use of plus signs. In addition, in the case of parts, a focus between entities is viewed as erroneous; this is indicated in the table by the use of zeros. When the within-entity score of plus is subtracted from a between-entity score of zero, the difference is negative. Essentially, as shown in the lower portion of Table 2.7, this procedure is employed for each condition. In addition, a determination of whether error in one condition differs from the supposedly valid variation in the other condition can be made. The results, shown in the last two rows of Table 2.7, illustrate that these seven cases are distinguishable based on the difference between the values in each condition. Therefore, an entity may be hypothesized to be relevant across all conditions (a multiplexed formulation), but empirically it may be found that the entity is relevant only under certain conditions defined by values of a third variable (a contingent formulation), or vice versa.

This general procedure, illustrated for the case of two conditions defined by values of a third variable, can be extended to include any number of conditions defined in this way. Table 2.8 demonstrates the application of this general procedure to the case in which four conditions are defined by the values of a third variable. In this illustration, 16 different formulations of

TABLE 2.8. Plausible theoretical and empirical conditions for the multiplexed and indirect contingency formulations with a focus on variables (four categories)

	MULTIPLEXED	CONTINGENT													
		1	2	3	4	5	6	7	8	9	10	11	12	13	14
Theoretical															
Condition Z_1	↔	⊥	↔	↔	↔	⊥	↔	⊥	⊥	↔	↔	⊥	⊥	⊥	↔
Condition Z_2	↔	⊥	↔	↔	⊥	↔	↔	↔	⊥	⊥	⊥	↔	⊥	↔	⊥
Condition Z_3	↔	⊥	↔	⊥	↔	↔	⊥	↔	↔	↔	⊥	⊥	⊥	↔	⊥
Condition Z_4	↔	⊥	⊥	↔	↔	↔	⊥	⊥	↔	⊥	↔	↔	⊥	⊥	⊥
Empirical															
Magnitudes (R, t)															
Condition Z_1	0				0		0	0			0	0	0	0	
Condition Z_2	0			0			0	0	0		0	0			0
Condition Z_3	0		0		0			0	0	0				0	0
Condition Z_4	0	0				0	0			0			0	0	0
Differences (A, Z)															
Condition Z_1 minus															
Condition Z_2	0	0	0	0	+	−	0	−	0	+	+	−	0	0	−
Condition Z_3	0	0	0	+	0	−	+	−	−	0	+	0	0	−	0
Condition Z_4	0	0	+	0	0	−	+	0	−	+	0	−	−	0	0
Condition Z_2 minus															
Condition Z_3	0	0	0	+	−	0	+	0	−	−	0	+	0	−	+
Condition Z_4	0	0	+	0	−	0	+	+	−	0	−	0	−	0	+
Condition Z_3 minus															
Condition Z_4	0	0	+	−	0	0	0	+	0	+	−	−	−	+	0

variables are viewed as equally plausible. For example, two variables may be hypothesized to be related in none, one, two, three, or all four conditions. The magnitude of the correlations and the differences between conditions distinguish among these 16 cases. From an empirical perspective, differences are examined using A and Z tests, and magnitudes are assessed with R and t tests. In Table 2.8, two cases are compatible with the view that the relationship among the variables of interest is multiplexed. The 14 remaining cases all involve contingent formulations.

A simplified extension of this approach for focusing on entities in the four different conditions is summarized in Table 2.9. In multiplexed cases, differences occur between the within- and between-entity deviations in each condition formed by values of a third variable. This formulation is illustrated in the first and second columns of Table 2.9. For purposes of simplicity, only one of a number of contingency formulations plausible for this set of variables and entities is presented in the third and fourth columns of the table. In this illustrative contingency case, wholes or parts are viewed as viable only in condition Z_1.

Assertions that the emergence of a level or a relationship between variables is contingent on the values of some third variable involves a large

TABLE 2.9. Plausible theoretical and empirical conditions for the multiplexed and indirect contingency formulations with a focus on entities (four categories)

	ILLUSTRATIVE MULTIPLEXED		ILLUSTRATIVE CONTINGENT	
	A, Z Differences Between – Within	Interpretation	A, Z Differences Between – Within	Interpretation
Inside Conditions				
Condition Z_1 $(B - W)$	+ or −	W or P	+ or −	W or P
Condition Z_2 $(B - W)$	+ or −	W or P	0	E or I
Condition Z_3 $(B - W)$	+ or −	W or P	0	E or I
Condition Z_4 $(B - W)$	+ or −	W or P	0	E or I
Among Conditions				
Condition Z_1 (B) minus				
Condition Z_2 (W)	+ or −	W or P	+ or −	W or P
Condition Z_3 (W)	+ or −	W or P	+ or −	W or P
Condition Z_4 (W)	+ or −	W or P	+ or −	W or P
Condition Z_2 (B) minus				
Condition Z_1 (W)	+ or −	W or P	+ or −	W or P
Condition Z_3 (W)	+ or −	W or P	0	E or I
Condition Z_4 (W)	+ or −	W or P	0	E or I
Condition Z_3 (B) minus				
Condition Z_1 (W)	+ or −	W or P	+ or −	W or P
Condition Z_2 (W)	+ or −	W or P	0	I or E
Condition Z_4 (W)	+ or −	W or P	0	E or I
Condition Z_4 (B) minus				
Condition Z_1 (W)	+ or −	W or P	+ or −	W or P
Condition Z_2 (W)	+ or −	W or P	0	I or E
Condition Z_3 (W)	+ or −	W or P	0	I or E

Note: W, P, E, and I indicate wholes, parts, equivocal, and inexplicable, respectively.

number of alternative explanations and is based on the demonstration that variables, their relationships, and entities are not multiplexed across these conditions. The varient paradigm allows for the possibility that variables associated with entities at a higher level of analysis may form contingencies for entities at lower levels of analysis. In addition, contingency formulations may be derived at a single level of analysis. (Such assertions will be further discussed in the next chapter.) Finally, this conceptualization of contingent and multiplexed cases does not preclude a specification that the direction of relationships between variables is contingent on values taken on by a third variable. The details of this type of formulation follow logically from the general conceptualization and will not be considered in this book.

Essentially, in multiple-relationship analysis one multiplexed or contingent formulation involves a choice of one alternative from an entire set of plausible alternatives. Nevertheless, at a more abstract level, the decision-making process can be simplified by focusing on a choice between only two alternatives (multiplexed and contingent). In general, multiplexed formulations include a specification of no differences between conditions created by values of a third variable, and contingency formulations specify differences.

Similarly, the choice of one set of relationships among variables at one or several levels of analysis involves a selection from several alternatives. These choices can be justified on theoretical grounds (see Part II), and on empirical bases (see Part III), and they can be used as a means for drawing inferences from data (see Parts IV and V).

SUMMARY

Once a certain number of variables and levels of analysis have been chosen, a varient matrix provides a way to summarize and identify a set of plausible alternative explanations. For a single level of analysis, entities can be viewed in four mutually exclusive ways (wholes, parts, equivocal, and inexplicable). For multiple levels of analysis, the general formula for determining the number of alternative explanations is 4^L where L equals the number of levels of analysis. In terms of multiple-variable analysis, the number of alternative formulations that can be derived for a certain number of variables is given by Equation 2.2. For purposes of multiple-relationship analysis, a decision must be made between a multiplexed and a contingent formulation. The theoretical and empirical implications of this conceptualization for single- and multiple-level analyses and for the formulation and analysis of multiple variables and relationships are presented in the remainder of the book.

REVIEW QUESTIONS

1. Why is it important to specify the number of variables and types of entities asserted in a theory?

2. (a) What is the varient matrix? (b) How does filling in a varient matrix assist in theory building?

3. How does one deal with purely ideational entities—that is, entities with no physical representation in the space-time dimensions?

4. When one expects to find differences at one level between entities but not within each entity, is one focusing on wholes or on parts?

5. How can one conclude that both wholes and parts are appropriate for one variable associated with one entity?

6. (a) How is an inexplicable condition interpreted? (b) Why can reliance on average scores cause interpretation difficulties?

7. How does one interpret findings that the effect of a hypothesized level or unit is of little or no relative significance?

8. Why are findings at lower levels of analysis important in interpreting findings at higher levels of analysis?

9. On what basis does one distinguish between the following two formulations of one set of variables: $X + Y = Z$; $X = Y = Z$?

10. If one asserts that a relationship between two variables will hold under one condition and not under another condition, is this a multiplexed or a contingent formulation?

3

THEORY:
Formulations

The varient approach to theory building—that is, the way in which theory serves as a basis for deciding between equally likely alternative formulations (see Table 2.1), is presented in this chapter and illustrated in Chapter 4. First, however, it is necessary to consider general approaches to theory construction. Traditionally, theories are thought to be built either inductively by observation or deductively by concept formation, followed by some form of empirical verification. In reality, both processes serve to guide theory development in the social sciences. Although the varient paradigm may help in theory formulation, it is particularly useful in ensuring that theories can be converted into a set of testable assertions. For our purposes, theories are considered to differ primarily in size and level of abstraction.

Theory Size

The number of variables and levels included in a theory determines its size. At one extreme, large or **grand theories** attempt to explain or include all variables or levels. Theories of this type attempt to unify a large number of more delimited theories. For example, a theory in physics that applies to all of physical space is a grand theory, even though only a few variables may be specified. At the other extreme are **simple theories** that specify only two variables, their relationship, and one unit of analysis (such as why satisfaction and age might be related at the whole-person unit). Between the extremes are **middle-range theories**, which include formulations about a limited number of variables and entities.

Of course, theories of different size, scale, or scope may overlap. A grand theory includes a number of middle-range and simple theories; likewise, middle-range theories include a number of simple theories. Any attempt to make distinctions among these three types of theories is arbitrary because the differences are of degree rather than kind. It can be helpful to represent schematically the relationships among these three types by using concentric circles. Grand theories are represented by large circles that contain smaller circles representing middle-range and simple theories, as in the following example:

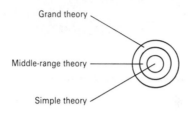

Level of Abstraction

In addition to varying in size, theories differ in level of abstraction. More abstract **general theories** are typically viewed as attempts at specifying general (Braithwaite, 1973), universal (Behling, 1980), or scientific (Merton, 1949) laws or lawlike propositions (Blalock, 1969). Less abstract **specific theories** or empirical generalizations (Behling, 1980) are derived from general formulations. For example, as pointed out by Blalock (1969), a highly abstract theory may be viewed as applicable to all living systems, and a less abstract formulation of the theory may make predictions about a particular subset of living systems (such as human beings). Likewise, as pointed out by Homans (1961), a universalistic or more abstract principle may be specified and predictions that are specific or less abstract may be derived from it. In a similar way, as suggested by Dubin (1969), when a general abstract proposition is asserted, specific-level variables must be identified.

According to Behling (1980), research in organizational behavior (and probably in most of the social sciences) tends to focus on specific-level or less abstract theories. One advantage of this orientation is that less abstract specifications can be more readily tested empirically. Usually, in order to test general theories, a less abstract specific set of predictions must be derived from the more general formulation. Once these specific predictions are derived, testing is possible with the use of the varient matrix described in this book. It is important to note that the varient approach is compatible with inductive, deductive, and mixed modes of theory generation.

The Varient Matrix

Regardless of whether one begins with grand theories or systematically develops some simple theoretical notions based on observations, using the varient matrix is appropriate—in fact, we believe it is essential. For our purpose, any theory must refer to two or more concepts, specify a network of relationships among critical concepts, and explicitly or implicitly assert appropriate levels of analysis. Regardless of the logical process accounting for the specific structure of a theory, and independent of a theory's level of abstraction, these three components will be present and can be summarized as follows:

VARIENT REQUIREMENTS FOR ALL LEVELS AND TYPES OF THEORIES

I. Theory Formulation Elements
- A. Variables
- B. Networks of relationships
- C. Entities

II. Theory Testing Elements
- A. Measurement of variables
- B. Indicators of relationships
- C. Assessments of entities or levels represented by measures and indicators

---

Use of the varient matrix (1) forces recognition of this structure in assessing theoretical validity and (2) provides a means of determining whether data gathered to test any theoretical model meet the basic structural requirements in reference to variables, relationships, and entities. We believe these two characteristics of the varient approach are its most attractive features, for these attributes begin to provide researchers with a means of dealing with a number of roadblocks to theory building.

Specifically, Blalock (1969), Conant (1947), Miller (1978), and Pascal (1670) have noted the difficulties in attempting to engage in systematic theory building in the physical and social sciences when there is little consistency in concept definition, specification of relationships, clarification of appropriate levels for theoretical effects, and investigation into whether measures of concepts represent those constructs effectively. If one approaches theory formulation and empirical research from a varient perspective, those shortcomings are quickly identified and provide a focus for corrective action. In essence, the varient approach forces a resolution or clarification of basic issues rather than providing a means to gloss over basic theoretical inadequacies. Even if a reader fails fully to understand the bases for all varient-related data analytic techniques, we believe that an appreciation of the extent to which this perspective imposes a discipline for theory development and validation should result in an orientation of benefit to the individual theorist or investigator and to the cumulative development of understanding in the social sciences.

SELECTING ENTITIES

Formulations and Entities

For theorists interested in social events, dealing with human beings as entities can indeed be quite complex. Human beings can be viewed as persons independent of others, or as forming dyads, groups, or collectivities. Although these entities can be defined in a variety of ways, in order to formulate and then test theories, it is necessary to agree on some definition as a starting point. Our choice in developing the varient approach is to begin by focusing on relatively concrete rather than abstract categorizations of entities. In our experience, most social science research of significance attempts to explain the dynamics of easily perceived social realities, such as individuals, groups, organizations, governments, and social movements. Although permitting abstract qualities (such as norms and motivations) to be investigated, those concrete entities have an everyday reality that makes them attractive for study.

Of course, we are not alone in suggesting the desirability of beginning with apparently real or easily observed entities. Miller (1978, p. 22) argues for the use of concrete rather than abstract systems in the following way: "Behavioral scientists, if they deal with abstracted systems and establish their own conceptual boundaries which cut across concrete systems, easily forget the intrasystem relationships in concrete systems which influence processes *within* and *among* these (abstracted) systems. Consequently, their understanding of the phenomenon they study is often incomplete and inaccurate" (emphasis added).[1]

The definitions of entities and levels used in this book should be viewed only as a means to initiate an investigation or as a working hypothesis because, in fact, data may eventually require the rejection of any chosen specification of entities. One must remember that multiple definitions of entities and a comparison among definitions can be made empirically with the use of the varient paradigm. The eight units representing four levels of analysis for our purposes are listed in the first column of Figure 3.1. We prefer to view these units as equally plausible and different ways to describe characteristics of human beings located within finite space and time boundaries. Persons, dyads, groups, and collectivities are represented in Figure 3.1 by circles, ovals, rectangles, and pentagons, respectively. In this formulation, persons serve as the parts for dyads and groups; whole groups serve as the parts for collectivities.

This formulation of units and levels of analysis has several advantages. Specifically, the total number of human beings represented is constant across all levels of analysis; eight human beings are represented in Figure 3.1. In addition, as higher levels of analysis are considered, the number of entities and independent observations decreases as the size of each entity increases.

Perspectives on Entities The perspective taken, thus far, is that of an outside observer looking at a number of objects (human beings in this case) in a variety of ways. This **outsider perspective** is compatible with a natural science approach to research and can be defined in this way. As pointed out by Miller (1978, p. 6): "Natural scientists attempt to view all phenomena dispassionately, somewhat as the supernatural observers looked down upon the Napoleonic era in Hardy's epic *The Dynastas*. These celestial beings watch the movements of human armies and the vacillation of men's fortunes just as

---

[1] From *Living Systems*, by J. G. Miller. Copyright © 1978 by McGraw-Hill. Used with the permission of the McGraw-Hill Book Company.

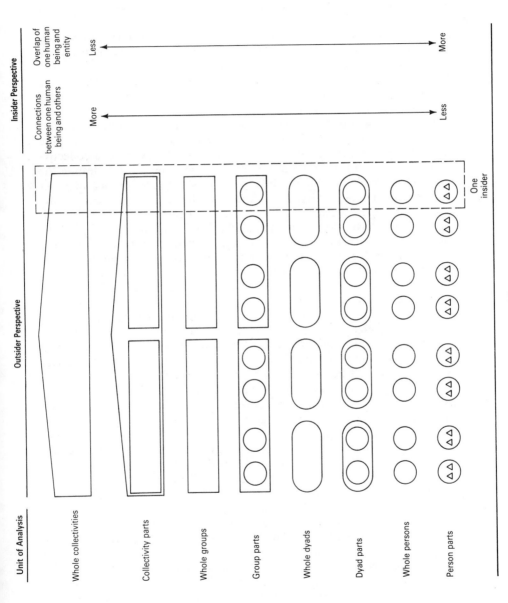

FIGURE 3.1. Insider and outsider perspectives on entities

the natural scientist views the stars."[2] From this outsider perspective, one human being is viewed as potentially influenced by the processes that can occur at any one or all of these units of analysis because he or she is viewed as being embedded in a variety of entities whose relative influence must be assessed.

From the view of any one individual, or from an **insider perspective**, membership in any entity may be seen as influencing his or her perceptions and sensations. For example, a whole collectivity unit of analysis implies more connections between human beings than the whole person unit of analysis. As is shown in Figure 3.1, the number of connections between individuals increases as one moves from lower to higher levels of analysis. These connections may enhance or constrain a human being's ability to function independently of others. Nevertheless, an insider is viewed as dependent on these connections for either freedom or lack of freedom. At the extreme, a collectivity may even appear to function independently of any one insider, despite the fact that it is composed of human beings, just as any one insider may act independently of the collectivity. In addition, as shown in Figure 3.1 by the dashed lines, the space occupied by one human being overlaps more with entities at a person level of analysis than at a collectivity level of analysis. For example, at the dyad level of analysis, one human being composes 50 percent of the entity and each individual in a dyad can destroy it. At higher levels of analysis, an individual composes even less of an entity, and when he or she leaves a collectivity or a group it may continue to exist and exert influence over members and nonmembers.

Although we are stressing that the ability of an outside observer to identify levels will affect research and theory formulation, we do not in any way deny the validity of insider perceptions. Indeed, the experiences of insiders or participants can provide the basic data for the testing of theoretical structures and may well be the basis for initial theory formulation. Calls for more insider insights (see Mintzberg, 1982) are useful, as they can form the contextually rich basis for generating theories that can then be tested from an outsider perspective.

As is widely known, there are severe problems with employing either perspective as the sole basis of a research strategy. An insider's perspective can produce data that are so rich and so detailed they cannot be effectively analyzed and from which appropriate inferences will not be extracted. On the other hand, an outsider's perspective can produce data that are far removed from any insider's perspective; their meaning for what occurs in a setting can be obfuscated to such an extent that a research project appears to be simply an exercise in manipulating numbers. The varient model encourages theory generation and testing based on both approaches.

Clearly, the general approach to entities summarized in Figure 3.1 can be made specific to work settings. In order to illustrate the application of this general approach, we will present a simple case followed by a more complex example.

---

[2] From *Living Systems*, by J. G. Miller. Copyright © 1978 by McGraw-Hill. Used with the permission of the McGraw-Hill Book Company.

Persons, Groups, and Collectivities in Work Settings In a single work setting human beings may be viewed as persons, as embedded in **supervisory work groups** in which each subordinate reports to the same superior, and as embedded in departments (collectivities). A schematic illustration of this typical work setting is presented in Figure 3.2.[3] In the figure a hierarchical configuration is viewed in six different ways. Similar hierarchical structures in various forms occur in many organizations. In developing such applications, it is helpful to recognize that individuals reporting to a supervisor beyond the first level of supervision in an organization often can be characterized in several ways. For example, such individuals can be viewed as independent heads of different departments (collectivities); or as subordinates they can be viewed as forming a group of subordinates reporting to one superior. One way to deal with this issue of multiple perspectives is to view a setting as work groups composed of individuals. Another alternative would be to view individuals rather than groups as the potential components of a collectivity. One disadvantage of the latter approach is that it ignores the possibility of group-level effects. Although hierarchical structuring of persons, work groups, and departments is not necessarily universal, our experience suggests it is a quite common by-product of attempts to organize work around technological constraints. For this reason, we will tend to refer to departments as collectivities and treat each set of individuals who report to the same supervisor as a work group in an aggregation of work groups, which in turn determines how departments are defined.

In the example shown in Figure 3.2, one set of human beings in a setting is conceptualized as potentially embedded in six different units of analysis. This is a simple application, and for this setting a varient matrix containing three levels of analysis (persons, groups, and collectivities) can readily be generated. Such a matrix is then used to formulate hypotheses about each level of analysis; that is, a choice can be made between the wholes, parts, equivocal, and inexplicable conditions at each level of analysis. These hypotheses are indicated in a varient matrix by the placement of double lines. Table 2.3 is then used to ensure that the hypothesis made at one level is consistent with the hypothesis at the next level. For example, a theorist may be interested in a cross-level, whole-collectivity formulation (variables of interest apply to whole collectivities as well as to the work groups and persons embedded in such collectivities). In this case, double lines would be placed in the varient matrix after the whole condition for each level of analysis; this placement is consistent with the principle of wholes and the placements specified in Table 2.3. The location of hypotheses with double lines along the varient axes guides the use of the empirical testing procedures presented in this book.

Superiors and Subordinates in Work Settings Although the way hypotheses are framed in a varient matrix will be illustrated in the next chapter, a

[3] In Figure 3.2 the individual at the top of the organization shown at the person level is not included at the group and collectivity level because he or she by definition has no superior. As illustrated in later chapters, this individual may be considered in this way or as a group or be included in other groupings of individuals at levels of analysis above the person level. In addition, to simplify the example, the dyad level of analysis has been omitted.

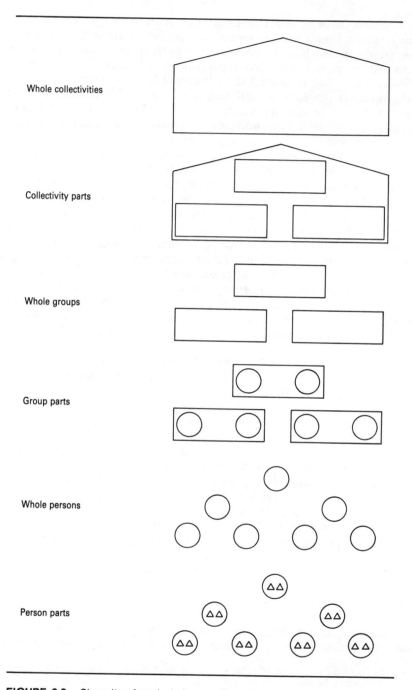

Whole collectivities

Collectivity parts

Whole groups

Group parts

Whole persons

Person parts

FIGURE 3.2. Six units of analysis in a work setting

more complex application of the general conceptualization to work settings may be helpful at this point. The second application is a result of recognizing that in most work settings, each individual tends to report to one superior. This leads to the interesting issue of how to think about the entities formed by superiors and subordinates. A review of the way vertical relationships can be established also serves to introduce the interpretation of several approaches to superior-subordinate relationships. With this in mind, we will turn to leadership research for substantive illustrations (see, for example, Jacobs, 1970; Yukl, 1981).

The literature exploring leadership issues in organizations indicates that a given superior has the option of forming interpersonal linkages with the individuals who report to him or her. When a superior is viewed as a whole person, established relationships with all reporting subordinates should be the same. Under such conditions, each subordinate is seen as being treated similarly or identically. This view of a superior has been called the **average leadership style (ALS) approach** (Dansereau, Cashman, and Graen, 1973; Dansereau, Graen, and Haga, 1975).

An alternative to the ALS approach is the view that the actions of each superior toward his or her subordinates may be based on the position of one subordinate relative to that of other subordinates. In this **vertical dyad linkage (VDL) approach** (Graen, 1976), the parts of a superior can be viewed as reflecting each subordinate's relationship to that superior. In other words, within a superior, comparisons may occur between subordinates, and the relative position of subordinates "inside" the superior may be dependent on this comparison process. A superior may maintain distinctions in the assignment of latitude or in other supportive behavior based on personal perceptions of comparative differences in ability, personality, or other characteristics of the subordinate. In the VDL case, a superior is viewed in terms of parts.

A very different, dyadic—not person- or leadership-centered—view of superior-subordinate relationships is also plausible. In such a **dyadic formulation**, the entity of interest is the dyad, defined as composed of one superior and one subordinate. Superiors are viewed as forming multiple relationships with individuals. These relationships, however, are based not on a superior alone (such as leadership), but rather on both superiors and subordinates. In other words, from a reductionist perspective, the "components" of a superior are viewed as independent pieces of different interpersonal or dyadic relationships formed with subordinates. Instead of a superior behaving in a similar way toward all subordinates (wholes) or differentiating among subordinates relative to each other (parts), he or she may form multiple independent relationships with a number of individuals. In this condition a superior may grant latitude or flexibility to a given subordinate independent of any behaviors exhibited toward other subordinates. A set of schematic diagrams may help clarify distinctions among ALS, VDL, and dyadic formulations before locating these formulations in a varient matrix.

At the person level, one person may form a relationship with two other individuals, each of whom is a potential component in a perceptual field. In the case of behavior based on whole person assumptions (no differentiation), these two components are homogenized. We represent this case by a circle indicating a whole person, as follows:

Alternatively, the superior's relationship to individuals reporting to him or her may be dependent on comparisons between individuals. This case can be illustrated by the two triangles representing components and a circle indicating that these components are contained within a person (the superior):

These whole and part conditions at the person level of analysis specify a dependency between components within a person. In contrast, in the equivocal condition the components need not be anchored in a person. Instead, the components associated with a person can be viewed as not dependent on that person. This notion can be illustrated by using triangles without a circle as a representation of the components independent of the superior:

△ △

In this case, the basis of the component is *not* the person level of analysis, and this level of analysis is rejected.

Of course, these independent components can be viewed as belonging to dyads. At the dyad level of analysis, these components may constitute parts of two dyads. The drawing in the lower portion of Figure 3.3a represents this condition. Alternatively, these components for one superior and two subordinates may be homogenized and viewed as forming whole dyads. This

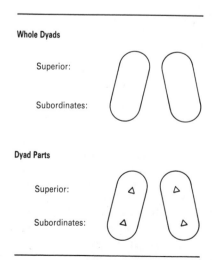

FIGURE 3.3a. Two dyad-level formulations for one superior and two subordinates

whole dyad condition is illustrated in the upper portion of Figure 3.3a. Essentially, in this dyadic formulation dyads are hypothesized to emerge and the person level of analysis is asserted to be irrelevant. In other words, a lack of person parts or whole persons is hypothesized at the person level of analysis. Therefore, the person level of analysis is rejected.

In contrast to this dyadic formulation, superior-subordinate relationships can be viewed as reducible to whole person–work group relationships, as in the ALS approach. For example, in a work setting in which whole superiors are of interest, whole work groups and superiors can be viewed as linked in the ways shown in the upper portion of Figure 3.3b. In this cross-level formulation each of the superior-subordinate dyads (relationships) is homogenized, making the dyads all the same for the superior and the members of the work group. Therefore, this type of formulation can be viewed as a hypothesis about whole persons and work groups. When superior parts are the focus of interest, work group and superior parts may be viewed as linked. This condition is illustrated in the lower portion of Figure 3.3b. In this VDL type of formulation, superior-subordinate dyads differ within each of the superiors and their respective work groups; however, the position of one subordinate is relative to the position of other subordinates within the same work group. As a result, this case can be viewed as a person–work group parts formulation.

Essentially, four different formulations of a work setting have been derived: person–work group wholes and parts (Figure 3.3b) and dyad wholes and parts (Figure 3.3a). Figure 3.3c illustrates these different formulations for a work setting with three superiors and six subordinates. In the case of dyad wholes and parts, notice that a superior's relationship with each subordinate is viewed as independent of his or her relationship with other subordinates. In

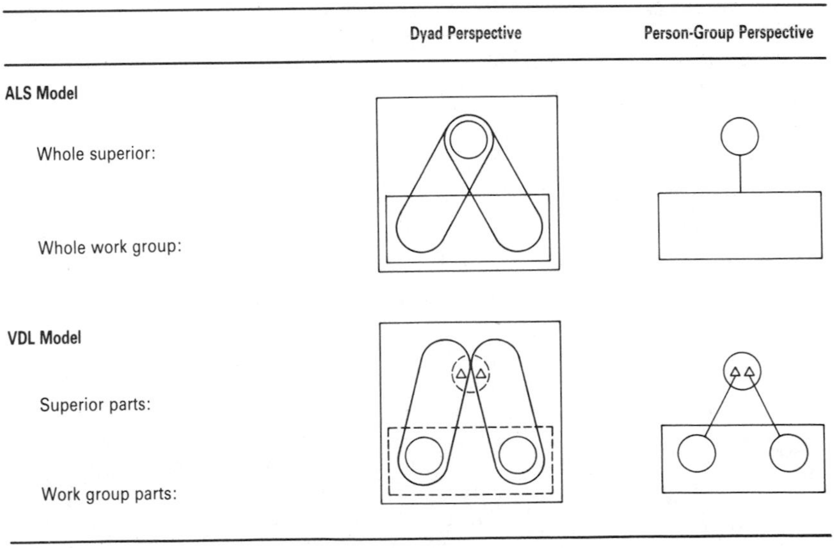

FIGURE 3.3b. ALS and VDL formulations for one superior and two subordinates from dyad and person-group perspectives

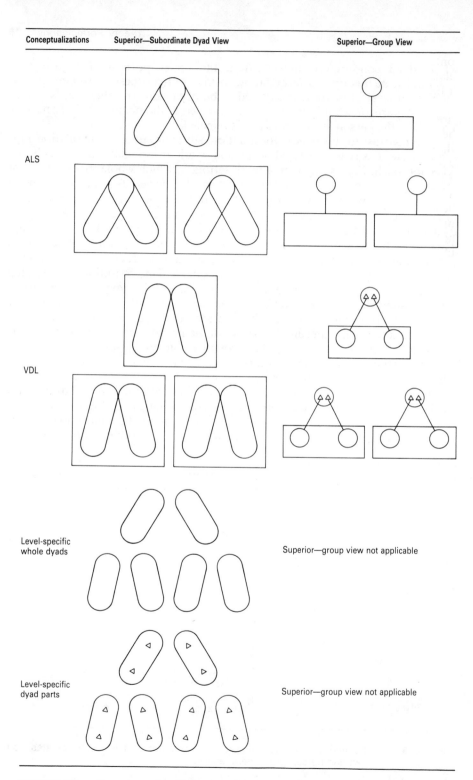

Conceptualizations	Superior—Subordinate Dyad View	Superior—Group View
ALS		
VDL		
Level-specific whole dyads		Superior—group view not applicable
Level-specific dyad parts		Superior—group view not applicable

FIGURE 3.3c. Superior-subordinate dyads and work groups in a work setting

contrast, in the superior–work group parts and whole formulations, a superior's relationship with one subordinate is viewed as related to and dependent on his or her relationship with another subordinate.

This illustration of four different formulations for work settings based on superiors and subordinates can be summarized, and we believe simplified, by the use of a varient matrix. From Figure 3.3c, four perspectives (ALS, VDL, whole dyads, and dyad parts) can be viewed as constituting hypotheses about two levels of analysis: (1) superior-subordinate dyads and (2) superior-subordinate work groups. The predictions about each level of analysis are summarized in the varient matrix presented in the upper portion of Table 3.1. In the ALS model, whole superior-subordinate dyads are homogenized into whole superior-subordinate work groups (a cross-level, whole group formulation). In the VDL model, whole superior-subordinate dyads form parts within superior-subordinate work groups (a cross-level, group parts formulation). The two dyadic models are level-specific formulations.

This type of analysis is linked to the simple conceptualization presented in Figure 3.2. Specifically, in the simple illustration work groups were considered without regard to superiors. Instead, all the individuals in the setting were viewed in terms of work group membership. The predictions for such a work

TABLE 3.1. Four alternative theoretical positions located in a varient matrix and predictions for two levels of analysis

	ALS	VDL	WHOLE DYADS	DYAD PARTS
Varient Matrix Predictions				
Superior – Subordinate Work Groups				
Wholes	—			
Parts		—		
Equivocal			—	
Inexplicable				—
Superior – Subordinate Dyads				
Wholes	—	—	—	
Parts				—
Equivocal				
Inexplicable				
Type of hypothesis	Cross-level Whole groups	Cross-level Group parts	Level-specific Whole dyads	Level-specific Dyad parts
Other Predictions				
Subordinate – Work Group Analysis				
Wholes	—			
Parts		—		
Equivocal			—	
Inexplicable				—
Superior Analysis				
Wholes	—			
Parts		—		
Equivocal			—	
Inexplicable				—

group analysis, focusing on only subordinates, are shown in the lower portion of the table. In other words, the more complex conceptualization provides additional information about the degree to which work group analyses based on the simple conceptualization may be extended by considering superiors. In addition, as shown in Table 3.1, a varient matrix can be used to specify the predictions made by each model about superiors.

Of course, this more complex conceptualization can be extended to consider other theoretical issues. For example, a superior may form a relationship not only with subordinates but also with an immediate superior or boss. Interpersonal relationships of a superior with subordinates may or may not be similar to a superior's interpersonal relationship with the boss. In work group–superior formulations this issue is particularly important, because in these cases a superior serves as a linking pin between his or her subordinates and boss (Likert, 1967).

In order to examine such a possibility, a superior's interpersonal relationship with his or her boss can be viewed as yet another component of a superior. From the perspective of wholes, a superior may treat his or her subordinates and boss in the same manner. For example, a superior may allow equal participation to the boss and subordinates and in this way serve as a link between them that assumes consistency in behavior and outlook. From the perspective of parts, a superior may differentiate among a boss and subordinates. In this case a superior serves as a link between the boss and subordinates, but in a differentiated rather than homogeneous fashion. In the dyadic formulation, a superior may not link the boss and subordinates; rather, each relationship may be unique, different from other interpersonal relationships. Because our interest is in using and illustrating the simple (Figure 3.2) and more complex (Figure 3.3c) conceptualizations with data in Chapters 9 and 10, the focus in the remainder of this book is not on superior-boss relationships. Nevertheless, the simple and more complex models should serve to illustrate that the general conceptualization of levels of analysis summarized in Figure 3.1 can be employed in a variety of ways in work settings. At this point, we will return to more general concerns.

Single-Level Analysis

In formulating a theory, one out of several levels of analysis is usually of particular interest. On an a priori basis this level is not rejected, and therefore an equivocal or inexplicable condition is not asserted. A decision must then be made whether the entity of interest should be viewed as an intact whole or in terms of its parts. From a theoretical perspective, wholes are chosen when interest is in differences between similar entities and when processes within entities are viewed as irrelevant. In contrast, when interest is in processes or differences within entities, or in the interdependent parts that compose an entity, parts are asserted.

A diagram such as the one presented in Figure 3.4 is sometimes helpful in making a choice between parts and wholes. In this illustration, the shadings of the geometric figures represent distributions of scores on some variable or dimension of interest. Person parts (such as interpersonal relationships with

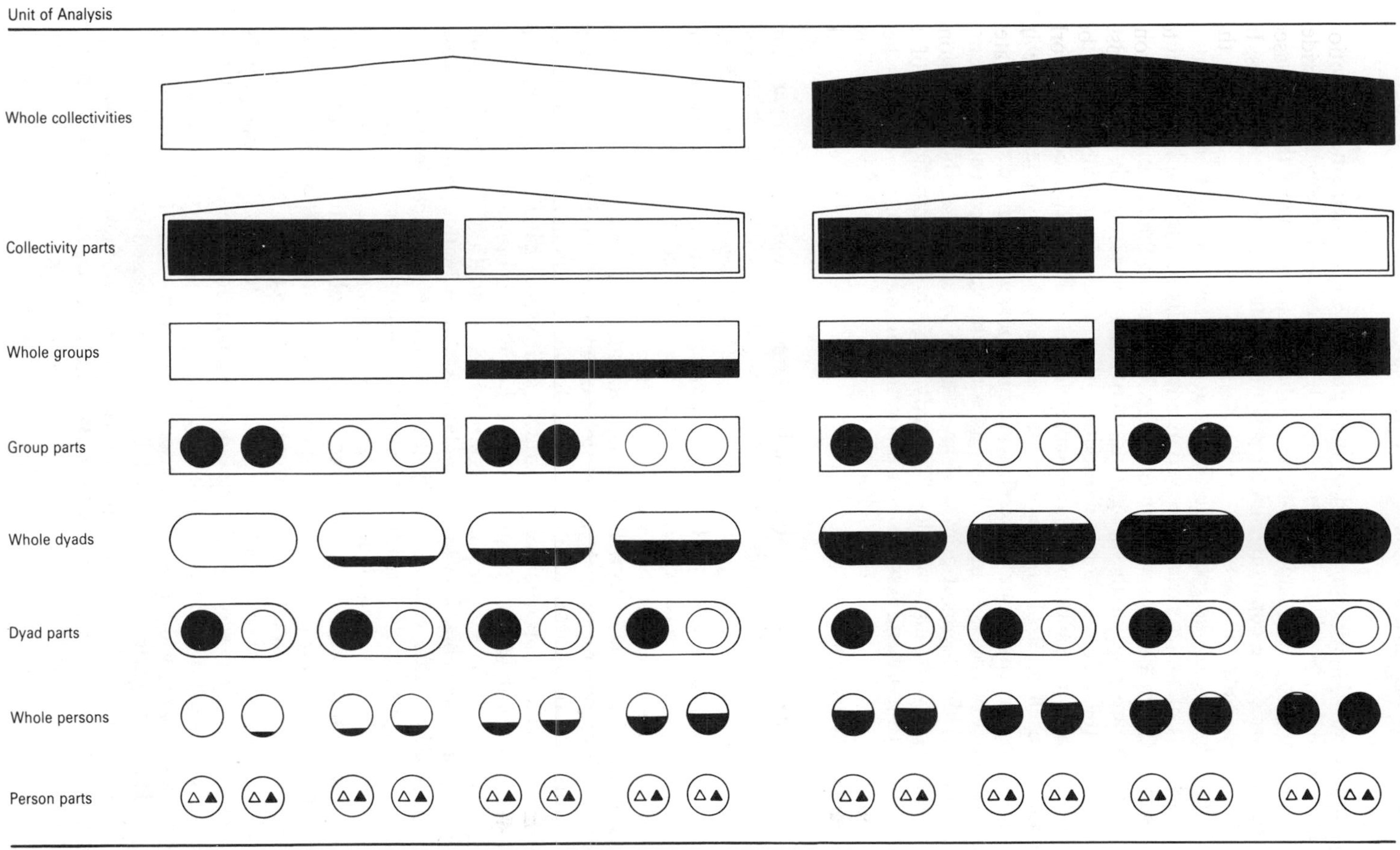

FIGURE 3.4. Uniqueness of the eight units of analysis

Unit of Analysis

Whole collectivities

Collectivity parts

Whole groups

Group parts

Whole dyads

Dyad parts

Whole persons

Person parts

several individuals) are represented in the figure by the shaded small triangles within the circles, which are the same at each level of analysis. Whole persons are represented by the shading differences between the circles; the shadings within the circles are constant. Similar schematic illustrations for other levels of analysis are shown in the figure.

The shading of the geometric shapes at each level of analysis illustrates that each unit of analysis can be viewed as entirely distinct from all other units of analysis. Given a set of scores (in this case 32 scores at the person parts level of analysis), any one of these eight units of analysis is equally likely. For example, in the case of whole collectivities, the 16 scores contained in each collectivity are the same, but those scores differ for the two collectivities. Essentially, each level of analysis can be viewed as unique in terms of one variable at a particular time. Different variables, however, can be specified for different units of analysis. In all cases, as was summarized in Table 2.1, one must decide either to reject a level of analysis or to choose a whole or parts view of an entity at a particular level of analysis. Such determinations must be made for both more and less abstract theoretical formulations.

Multiple-Level Analysis

Although each unit of analysis can be viewed as unique in that a variable may emerge and remain level-specific, theories need not be restricted to one unit of analysis. Using the principle that wholes at a lower level of analysis may be followed by wholes, parts, or an equivocal condition at the next higher level of analysis, effects across levels may be specified by a theory. For example, effects or relationships may be hypothesized as cross-level whole; that is, applicable to whole collectivities, groups, dyads, and persons. This illustrative cross-level specification is represented schematically in Figure 3.5, using the entity axis of the varient matrix. In addition, a formulation of emergent and level-specific group wholes is illustrated, as it was in Figure 3.4. However, in this figure multiple levels of analysis are taken into account.

Since the entity axis shown in Figure 3.5 has a length of 16, 256 different assertions are plausible. The two formulations shown in the figure, however, can be used to illustrate the contradictory nature of such formulations. Specifically, consider the situation in which one theorist asserts a cross-level formulation. In this formulation, observed differences between groups are viewed as manifestations of differences between collectivities. In contrast, another theorist who prefers a level-specific group formulation would view differences between groups not as attributable to collectivities, but as reflecting only group-level processes. These two theorists, then, look at the same groups in two very different ways. In the varient paradigm both views are plausible, and the analytical procedures described in later parts of the book are used to resolve such theoretically based differences of opinion.

Clearly, a number of additional formulations based on four levels of analysis can be created. For example, effects can be hypothesized to emerge at one level (not to be applicable at lower levels), continue across a few levels, and then become level-specific. The rules for developing formulations of this type were summarized in Table 2.1. Provided the link between each level of

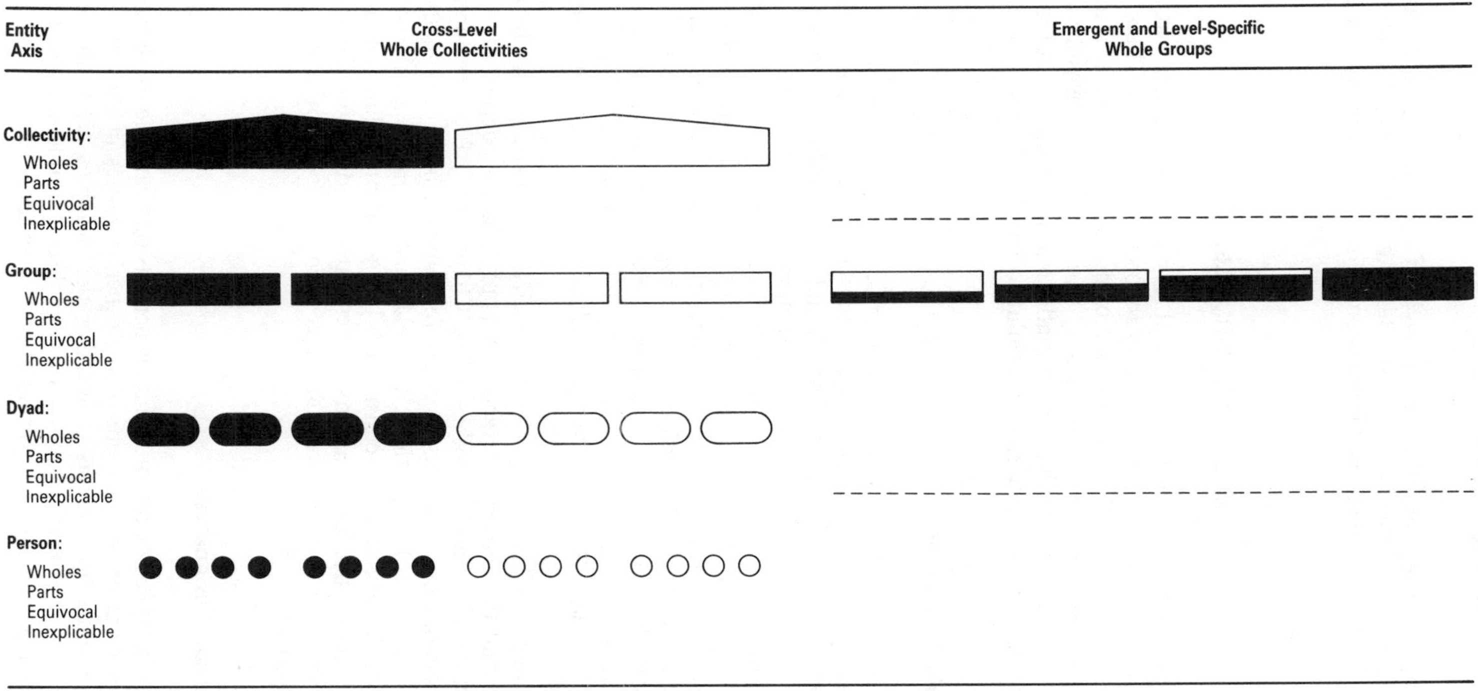

Entity Axis

Cross-Level Whole Collectivities

Emergent and Level-Specific Whole Groups

Collectivity:
Wholes
Parts
Equivocal
Inexplicable

Group:
Wholes
Parts
Equivocal
Inexplicable

Dyad:
Wholes
Parts
Equivocal
Inexplicable

Person:
Wholes
Parts
Equivocal
Inexplicable

FIGURE 3.5. Cross-level whole collectivities and emergent-level specific whole groups

analysis is not inconsistent with these principles (see Table 2.3), a variety of mutually exclusive specifications can be derived for the case of four levels of analysis. Such multiple-level formulations can be created by general- or specific-level theories.

SELECTING VARIABLES

For research purposes, the selection of variables and their interrelationships, as well as of entities, can be based on purely theoretical concerns. The variables chosen, however, must be aligned with one or more level and unit of analysis. In addition, a general theory should specify various ways to measure abstract variables. Once these choices have been made, multiple-variable and multiple-relationship analyses can be used to formulate a testable theory.

Multiple-Variable Analysis

Whenever possible, a complete nomological network of variables should be considered. Therefore, relationships or the lack of relationship among all variables taken at least two at a time should be identified in general- and specific-level theories. Although somewhat more complex procedures can be employed, a focus on two variables at a time and a specification that each pair of variables is related or unrelated is sufficient to generate a network. Once all the linkages among the variables of interest are hypothesized, alternative formulations—which are by definition not hypothesized to hold—can be generated with the use of a varient matrix. For example, in the three-variable case the choice of a generally unrelated formulation of variables is an assertion that the three remaining alternatives (related, generally related, and unrelated) are less likely.

In building theories we prefer to specify two abstract variables, their relationship, and the entities to which they apply; then we derive a number of specific-level variables and hypotheses (see Chapter 4). After developing this integrated network of constructs, another formulation is created in the same way. Given these two formulations, the relationship among all the variables specified by each formulation is considered. Using this procedure, an entire set of plausible alternative explanations is generated and summarized with a varient matrix. The chosen formulation is then located in the matrix and assessed empirically.

Multiple-Relationship Analysis

If a chosen specification of variables permits one variable to be viewed as very different from or independent of the other variables in the formulation, then a choice must be made as to whether the variables are multiplexed or contingent—as, for example, in the case of a three-variable specification, if a generally unrelated or unrelated formulation is asserted.

In making this choice, an entire set of variables may be hypothesized to reflect differences based on one unit of analysis; or one variable may be asserted to be at a higher level of analysis than other variables. In the latter case, the relationships between variables at a lower level of analysis are examined within values taken on by a variable at a higher level of analysis. The general principle underlying this specification is that lower-level entities occupy the same space but are contained in higher-level entities. For example, a number of dyads may be contained in one collectivity, but one dyad cannot contain a number of collectivities.

Such an approach to defining an environment for any object is similar to the position taken by Miller (1978). In general, an **environment** is defined as something within which other objects are contained, not simply as everything outside a particular entity of interest (see Aldrich, 1979; Weick, 1978). Instead, an environment is an entity that encompasses other entities of interest—which is not to suggest that industry or geographic location, for example, cannot serve as the environment for a set of organizations. From this perspective, an organization is contained within a larger level of analysis (industry or environment).

Essentially, any definition of an environment is viewed as an arbitrary slicing of the total environment. At the highest level of analysis the universe can be viewed as the environment for all entities. A particular type of environment may or may not affect an entity of interest. This approach to defining an environment is not intended to dismiss the importance of so-called environmental factors, but rather is an attempt to conceptualize environments from an outsider's perspective. An insider may very well experience different phenomena depending on the society or industry within which he or she is embedded, when effects are contingent. Alternatively, different types of environments may have little effect on what is experienced by an insider, when effects are multiplexed.

The outsider view of environments can be illustrated by considering a work setting. For example, a whole-collectivity variable may be viewed as distinguishing between various departments or collectivities. In a contingent formulation, one type of collectivity may be hypothesized to be conducive to finding relationships between variables based on differences between groups in that collectivity. In a second type of collectivity, the work groups may emerge but a relationship may not hold. This is an indirect contingency formulation. When the same group-level effects are specified for each type of collectivity, a multiplexed formulation is asserted.

From an entity rather than a variable perspective, in one type of collectivity whole dyads may be hypothesized to underlie a relationship between two variables. In a different type of collectivity, dyads may not serve as the basis for a relationship. This indirect contingency formulation is illustrated in the upper portion of Figure 3.6. In an alternative, multiplexed hypothesis, dyads are hypothesized to underlie results in both collectivities. For example, it might be hypothesized that levels of behavioral latitude in supervisory relationships are formed on a dyadic basis in all functional or subsystem units (such as production or adaptive) in an organization. This case is represented in the lower portion of Figure 3.6.

Indirect Contingency Formulation

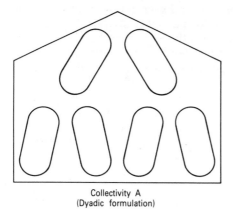
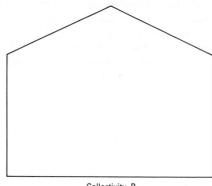

Collectivity A
(Dyadic formulation)   Collectivity B
                                        (Nondyadic formulation)

Multiplexed Formulation

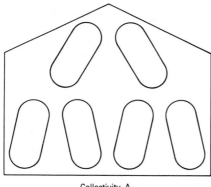
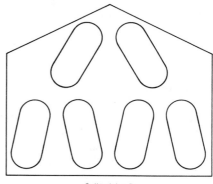

Collectivity A
(Dyadic formulation)   Collectivity B
                                        (Dyadic formulation)

FIGURE 3.6.   Indirect contingency and multiplexed formulations

Considering eight units of analysis, the plausible ways in which higher levels of analysis can serve as an environment for lower-level entities can be summarized on a case-by-case basis:

- Whole collectivities may serve as the environment for:
    Whole work groups, dyads, and persons
    Collectivity, work group, dyad, and person parts

- Collectivity parts may serve as the environment for:
    Whole work groups, dyads, and persons
    Work group, dyad, and person parts
- Whole work groups may serve as the environment for:
    Whole dyads and persons
    Work group, dyad, and person parts
- Work group parts may serve as the environment for:
    Whole dyads and persons
    Dyad and person parts
- Whole dyads may serve as the environment for:
    Dyad and person parts
    Whole persons
- Dyad parts may serve as the environment for:
    Whole persons
    Person parts
- Whole persons may serve as the environment for:
    Person parts

The specification of a contingency formulation imposes the additional requirement that at least one variable be different from other variables. The logical framework that results from this approach when three variables are of interest can be presented as follows:

MULTIPLE-VARIABLE ANALYSIS	CONTINGENCY	MULTIPLE-RELATIONSHIP ANALYSIS
Unrelated case	Indirect	Contingent
	Possible	Multiplexed
Generally unrelated case	Indirect	Contingent
	Possible	Multiplexed
Generally related case	Direct	Not applicable
Related case	Direct	Not applicable

This framework can be used in two ways. First, when an assertion of an indirect contingency is preferred, one begins with multiple-relationship analysis and the choices listed in the last column. Specifically, the assertion of an indirect contingency involves the rejection of multiplexed assertions and the rejection of assertions that the variables of interest are generally related or related. Second, one can begin with the multiple-variable analysis, or one of the four conditions listed in the first column of the table. If the generally unrelated or unrelated cases are chosen in multiple-variable analysis, a choice of an indirect contingency or a multiplexed formulation is necessary. If a direct contingency formulation is selected, multiple-relationship analysis is inappropriate. An illustration of the use of multiple-variable and multiple-relationship analyses and single- and multiple-level analyses in formulating theories is presented in the next chapter.

SUMMARY

The formulation of theories requires a consideration of variables and entities, regardless of whether simple, middle-range, or grand theories at a general or specific level of abstraction are of interest. Four levels of analysis, each with two units of analysis, are important for both general- and specific-level formulations about variables. The perspective taken on formulations about entities is that of an outsider watching a number of individuals or human beings. This outsider perspective has implications for what an insider (one individual) may experience due to the number of connections between that individual and others and the overlap of one human being with entities which can contain many individuals. From this outsider perspective, single- and multiple-entity formulations that include multiple variables and relationships can be asserted.

REVIEW QUESTIONS

1. What are the minimal requirements for a theory?
2. (a) What are the elements necessary for theory formulation?
   (b) What elements must be addressed if theory testing is to be successful?
3. How can insider and outsider perspectives be viewed in relation to theory development and theory testing?
4. What is the purpose of generating simple and complex applications of a general conceptualization of levels of analysis?
5. Give an example of how only one level of analysis can be considered on a theoretical and an empirical basis.
6. What are the basic levels of analysis, and why are they particularly appropriate for research in the social sciences?
7. How does one validate theoretical assertions about relationships between variables and the importance of levels of analysis?
8. How are environments conceptualized?
9. How can the following assertion be translated into a testable hypothesis: Multidimensionality and multicollinearity in the description of organizational events is inherent in the construction of any system to be studied, particularly in attitude research.
10. Why is the process of formulating theories not limited to social psychological theories?

4

THEORY:
An Illustrative Formulation

The purpose of this chapter is to illustrate the development of two sets of testable hypotheses based on a varient approach. The presentation strategy will be to (1) evolve the critical theoretical basis for each set of hypotheses, (2) identify variables and relationships believed to be consistent with each theory, and (3) specify appropriate types of entities or levels of analysis to be included in data analyses presented later in the book. In this chapter we will work through two examples of how the varient approach can be used to test in single- and multiple-level analyses and multiple-variable and multiple-relationship analyses the validity of two abstract theoretical notions: role theory and exchange theory. A major part of the remainder of the book entails a presentation of the data analytic and inferential consequences of the research strategy flowing from ideas and concepts illustrated in this chapter.

Because we are interested both in specific and in general (lawlike) formulations, a consideration of two basic theories that have endured over time seems appropriate. Various theories about roles and exchanges have been asserted not only by scientists, but also by philosophers. For example, as pointed out by Blau (1974, p. 207), Aristotle viewed exchange as a "gift or service given as to a friend, although the giver expects to receive an equivalent or greater return as though it had not been a free gift but a loan." Aristotle distinguished exchange from a second type of interaction, which involved stated terms; these stated terms may be considered similar to contemporary notions of roles. Essentially, our purpose is to develop two testable middle-range formulations of roles and exchanges (theory A and theory B) at both specific and general levels of abstraction. In the process, an outsider perspective is used to develop the entity component of the formulation. Although the testable formulation presented in this chapter can be viewed as a contribution to the richness of these long-lived theories, we prefer to view the formulation as a first step in developing general-level theories. No matter how the formulation is viewed, the starting point for analytical work should be contemporary approaches to role and exchange theory.

THEORY A: ROLE THEORY

Reviewers of various approaches to role theory are often quite critical. For example, consider the following sample of reviewer comments from over a 25-year period:

> The concept of role is at present still rather vague, nebulous and non-definitive. [Nieman and Hughes, 1951, p. 149]

> The plethora of conflicting definitions causes some confusion especially when different writers use different words for the same theory. [Banton, 1965, p. 2]

> Of definitions of role as the following chapters amply reveal there seems to be no end. [Newcomb, from Biddle and Thomas, 1966, p. v]

> In summary then role and role related concepts suffer from a high degree of redundancy which is often compounded by imprecision and implicitly assumed distinctions. [Alutto, 1968, p. 8]

> By now readers may have concluded that role theory is as broad as the ocean and as shallow as a mud puddle. [Biddle, 1979, p. 8]

Critics have also raised questions about research guided by role theory. For example, in 1951 Nieman and Hughes indicated that the literature on roles is more distinguished for its conceptual promise than for its research fulfillment. In 1968 Alutto, in a review of several hundred studies, suggested: "By and large most empirical investigations of role related phenomenon have had only a vague and indirect impact upon the development of role related concepts" (p. 11). Similarly, Katz and Kahn stated: "The research evidence for the model of role taking in organizations is irregular in quality and relevance" (1978, p. 199).

Moreover, a substantial body of empirical work has focused on outcomes from roles rather than on formulating a basic testable theory of roles. Concepts such as role conflict and ambiguity (Gross, Mason, and McEachern, 1958; Kahn et al., 1964; Rizzo, House, and Lirtzman, 1970), role demands, role location, role skills, and role learning (Sarbin and Allen, 1968) tend to suggest that roles preexist in some way and that their outcomes can be studied without a test of the basic notions underlying the concept of roles. In this vein, Biddle (1979), in an extensive review of role theory and empirical studies of roles, states:

> The empirical picture is not entirely rosy.... Above all, few investigators have yet taken up basic research in the role field. [p. 336]

> I shall argue that basic research concerns the central concepts upon which role theory is created: roles, identities (or positions), and expectations. These are the core concerns of the field, and until we have useful information about the forms, conditions of occurrence, causes, and effects of these events it is unlikely that role theory can grow as an integrated science. [pp. 339–41]

The key implication of these comments for us is that a focus on a general-level theory has been suggested as a viable approach. In formulating such a theory, the consistencies in various approaches should be identified and incorporated.

Although roles have been defined in a number of ways, a common theme runs through the definitions. Consider, for example, the following:

> When he puts the rights and duties which constitute the status into effect he is performing a role. [Linton, 1936, pp. 113–114][1]

> A set of expectations applied to an incumbent of a particular position. [Gross, Mason, and McEachern, 1958, p. 60]

> A set of norms and expectations applied to the incumbent of a particular position. [Banton, 1965, p. 29]

> Both a position and its associated expectations. [Secord and Backman, 1974, p. 405][2]

> Those behaviors characteristic of one or more persons in a context. [Biddle, 1979, p. 393]

Essentially, each definition seems to imply two notions: position and expectations. In general, only expectations that are shared by a number of individuals are considered to be relevant to role theory. Likewise, the notion of position implies an individual's rank or status, which is presumably shared by individuals in similar positions.

These aspects of role theory have been described as applicable to multiple levels of analysis. For example, the concept of role has been characterized as an interdisciplinary concept of interest in psychology, social psychology, sociology, and anthropology (see Alutto, 1968; Biddle, 1979; Biddle and Thomas, 1966; Katz and Kahn, 1978; Secord and Backman, 1974), with individuals in each discipline focusing on different levels and units of analysis. Following this tradition, Katz and Kahn have suggested that sociological concepts can be translated to lower levels of analysis, since "the two levels of analysis by and large do not have different types of facts to worry about" (1978, p. 15). It is this interdisciplinary focus and associated assumptions of multilevel effects which lead one to conclude that any formulation of role theory should hold across levels rather than be level-specific in nature.

At the person level of analysis, individuals are frequently viewed as actors playing a role, which suggests that individual personalities do not determine the nature of a role. Instead, factors external to an individual (at higher levels of analysis) specify how an individual is to play a role. For example, Blau (1974, p. 78) apparently implies a distinction between what we have called cross-level and level-specific formulations in the following way: "There is a fundamental difference between these two interpretations: the former implies that social processes external to individual personalities are responsible for the differences in discrimination, the latter that internal psychological processes are responsible." In a similar vein, at the dyad and group levels of analysis, Katz and Kahn (1978) have proposed a role-taking model. This model implies that the relationship between two individuals is rather

---

[1] From *The Study of Man*, by R. Linton. Prentice-Hall, Englewood Cliffs, New Jersey © 1936, renewed 1964. Used with the permission of Prentice-Hall.
[2] From *Social Psychology*, by P. Secord and C. Backman. Copyright © 1974 by McGraw-Hill. Used with the permission of the McGraw-Hill Book Company.

impersonal in that each actor behaves or is socialized to behave in a way compatible with a role rather than with the personal preferences of the individuals taken either separately or together.

The tendency to view roles as rather impersonal creates controversies at times about the nature of roles. For example, as pointed out by Miller (1978), Ruesch (1967) has asserted that roles and social systems are composed of human beings and should not be viewed as independent of human beings. In contrast, Parsons (1967) is often portrayed (for example by Ruesch) as arguing that roles exist independent of human beings.

General-Level Formulation

One approach to this apparent controversy is to reject the metaphysical argument and assert that roles do not exist independent of all humanity. If human beings did not exist, roles as we know them could not exist. In other words, roles can be viewed as human contrivances. However, this assertion in no way suggests that one individual or human being will find it very easy to change roles. Indeed, from an insider perspective roles may appear to be nonmalleable, a perception that may arise from the entities that underlie roles. Nevertheless, this focus on roles as embedded in the social fabric of human existence provides the basis for a general-level formulation of role theory.

Single-Level Analysis   As discussed in the previous chapter, at the collectivity level of analysis individuals are expected to view themselves as relatively small compared to the collectivity and as dependent on a large number of indirect connections with other actors. In this regard, recall that collectivities are based on hierarchical or other types of impersonal and indirect linkages rather than on personal, face-to-face interactions; in a collectivity, an individual should in a sense be able to view himself or herself as simply a cog in a large gear. Moreover, the greater number of connections with other individuals at the collectivity level of analysis, as opposed to the group, dyad, and person levels of analysis, may enhance the feeling that roles are not easily changed. At the collectivity level, groups serve as parts of the collectivity. Therefore, with the choice of a whole collectivity unit of analysis rather than collectivity parts, the connections between individuals can be viewed as impersonal and not based on group processes inside a collectivity.

This choice means that variables associated with whole collectivities should be homogeneous within collectivities and different between collectivities. If this formulation of role theory is correct, in terms of variables and their relationship we hypothesize that titles will be related to expectations at the collectivity level of analysis.

The variable **title** represents a labeling process residing within human beings who occupy physical space. In contrast, the term **position** can be taken to mean a location in some type of social (and perhaps nonphysical) space. We define titles as categories or labels that are properties of collectivities and that reside in human beings. This definition of title is compatible with Secord and Backman's (1974) notion of role category and with Biddle's (1979) notion of identities.

Expectations have typically been defined as having an anticipatory and normative quality (Hollander, 1958; Secord and Backman, 1974) and as referring to activities or behaviors (Katz and Kahn, 1978). We define **expectations** as beliefs about what should or will be done by oneself or others.

Our key assertion—that titles are related to expectations—can be examined and tested in a number of ways. For example, a change in title may be followed in time by a change in expectations. Alternatively, a change in expectations may result in a change in title over time. (The issue of temporal ordering of relationships is deferred until Chapter 12.) Another part of this assertion is that titles and expectations are properties of collectivities. Therefore, collectivities are predicted to differ in terms of their titles and expectations, and these differences are hypothesized to be related. At this point, the general proposition may be stated as follows:

> Titles and expectations will be related based on differences between whole collectivities.

This proposition must be clarified by considering multiple levels of analysis.

Multiple-Level Analysis   Suppose human beings could associate titles and expectations not at a collectivity level of analysis, but only at a person level. In such a case, each individual would construct titles and expectations independent of other human beings. A similar level-specific formulation would result if groups or dyads based on face-to-face interactions were viewed as forming titles and expectations. Therefore we chose a cross-level formulation, which suggests that titles and expectations are based on large-scale social movements; persons, dyads, and groups remain important but are viewed differently.

Specifically, in this formulation face-to-face interactions in groups or dyads are viewed as a reflection of the titles and expectations associated with the collectivities within which these other entities are embedded. Likewise, differences between persons are viewed as simply a reflection of the different collectivities within which different persons are embedded; when an individual takes a new job and title, for example, his or her expectations are hypothesized to be drawn in line with the titles and expectations associated with a new collectivity. This cross-level view of persons, dyads, and groups is compatible with previous work (see Alutto, 1968; Biddle, 1979; Katz and Kahn, 1978).

From a reductionist perspective, our cross-level formulation means that collectivities are dependent on an alignment of persons, dyads, and groups within each collectivity. From an outsider perspective, titles and expectations are viewed as somewhat fragile because their maintenance depends on a large number of individuals sharing a similar set of titles and expectations. In contrast, titles and expectations can seem to be quite powerful when viewed from the perspective of one insider, because a large number of persons, dyads, and groups share similar titles and expectations for themselves and for others in similar roles.

A key question that arises in attempting to formulate a general theory is this: What would be the consequences for human beings if the theory did not hold or if human beings were unable to associate titles and expectations at a collectivity level of analysis? If this association were not possible, the use of titles (professor, nurse, doctor, production superintendent) would not trigger any expectations about what an individual with such a title would or should do. Expectations (standing in front of a classroom for so many hours a week) would not be organized into a particular category (teacher). Moreover, a collectivity-level formulation implies that a number of individuals recognize such titles and that the titles are not the result of each person's idiosyncratic ideas or face-to-face interactions with others. Therefore, the following general proposition is asserted:

> Titles and expectations will be related based on differences between whole collectivities, groups, dyads, and persons.

Multiple-Variable and Multiple-Relationship Analyses   This general proposition contains two variables. Therefore, the variable axis of the varient matrix contains two alternatives—that is, titles and expectations are related or unrelated. In schematic form, the variable axis can be represented as follows, where T and E are abbreviations for titles and expectations, respectively:

Related   Unrelated

$T \leftrightarrow E$ $T \perp E$

Based on our stated proposition, titles and expectations should be related at multiple levels of analysis, that is, at the person, dyad, group, and collectivity levels.

Since only two variables are specified, their relationship cannot be viewed as being contingent on a third variable. Thus multiple-relationship analysis is unnecessary. We will consider a set of additional variables, but first the general formulation of theory A can be clarified by a less abstract formulation.

Specific-Level Formulation

Although an extensive consideration of specific large-scale (collectivity level) social movements that may bring about changes in titles and expectations is beyond the scope of this book (see, for example, Merton, 1949; Weber, 1947), such phenomena and their outcomes can be useful in understanding processes within a work setting. For example, according to one interpretation of the work of Weber (1947), the Industrial Revolution was due in part to a change in the basis of titles and expectations. Specifically, rather than basing roles on birthright and allegiance to royalty, a shift appears to have occurred in which roles were based on function to society or to a large number of individuals. It should be clear that one way to define titles in a more specific fashion is in terms of their function to society (Katz and Kahn, 1978; Parsons, 1960; Weber, 1947).

From this perspective, considering shared (collectivized) individual preferences (values) for producing outputs, the earliest titles may well have been **production titles**, which focused on the production of goods and services. As people attempted to produce goods and services, the law of entropy (which in oversimplified form means that things tend to fall apart) probably influenced organizing processes. This tendency of organizing efforts to fall apart may then have been overcome by activities that involved the maintenance of the production function (**maintenance titles**). Another method of keeping an organization from decomposing is to control inputs and outputs; as a result, a new set of titles called **support titles** may have evolved. Finally, an additional way to overcome entropy is by making changes inside an organization based on **adaptive titles**.

These four functional general categories have been suggested by various theorists (see Katz and Kahn, 1978) and provide one method for systematically categorizing titles. For example, titles such as production superintendent, foreman, general foreman, and the like are viewed as production titles. Titles such as maintenance engineer, mechanical engineer, and personnel supervisor are viewed as maintenance titles because their function is to service production titles. Production control, quality control, and purchasing can be viewed as support titles because their focus is on controlling inputs and outputs. Titles such as research engineer and chemist can be viewed as adaptive titles because of their focus on change or research and development.

Quite frequently in a work setting titles are linked within a hierarchy in which **upper-level titles** involve integrating various functions, and **lower-level titles** focus mainly on the performance of a function. Therefore, the following specific eight types of **functional titles** can be asserted as having theoretical meaning: upper- and lower-level production, maintenance, support, and adaptive titles.

Titles can also be categorized in terms of degree of professionalism. The concept of professionalism has been tied to a general (collectivity level) shift in individuals' preferences (values) for providing goods and services to society at large. For example, Kornhauser (1962) saw a mutual dependence between organizations and professionals. From this perspective, organizations are viewed as having evolved from small, family-centered economic units, and the criterion for filling jobs has become functional knowledge rather than inherited status. In this way professional associations can be thought of as providing certification or a title which indicates that an individual has a certain degree of functional knowledge. Because **professionalism** involves an association or organization of individuals, the collectivity level again seems appropriate for understanding titles.

Some researchers have argued that conflicts arise for individuals who are members of both a profession and a work organization. As pointed out by Hall (1977), this type of conflict is not inevitable. In fact, in a work setting professional titles may complement functional titles. For example, adaptive or research and development titles in a work setting may require greater professionalism on the part of individuals who hold such titles. In contrast, production titles may rely on the specifics of the particular situation, rather than on professional titles and expectations. Essentially, collectivities in work settings are hypothesized to have different titles and degrees of professionalism.

Different titles may trigger different expectations about how much **freedom from constraints** should be given to an individual. For example, some titles (such as production) may trigger an expectation of greater attention to rules and regulations, greater interaction with a superior, and greater use of machines. Other titles (such as adaptive) may trigger less attention to rules and regulations, less interaction with superiors, and less reliance on machines. Given our theory, expectations of greater freedom from various constraints might be expected in upper-level adaptive collectivities than in lower-level production collectivities.

These specific-level definitions of expectations are of particular interest, at least to us, because expectations which are shared across levels imply that within work settings the behavioral latitude expected of or given to a human being may vary with his or her title. One individual may have greater control over job-related behavior, whereas others may possess less freedom. Perhaps due to a variety of social and personal values, titles that imply a lack of freedom from constraints are often viewed as objectionable. As a solution to this problem, it is occasionally suggested that collectivities should be enriched to incorporate greater freedom from various constraints, thereby granting increased latitude to all members regardless of title. From the perspective of our formulation of titles and expectations, an individual who holds a title implying a great deal of latitude can experience at least as many problems as one who holds a title signifying little freedom from constraints. The titles and expectations are viewed as determined by collectivity-level processes and not just by individual preferences.

For our purposes then, at a less abstract level titles can be defined in terms of different functions and professionalism. Expectations can be viewed as involving the following types of variables: freedom from machines and superiors, as well as expectations about how much freedom superiors should offer subordinates. A formal hypothesis concerning these variables can be stated as follows:

> Titles (functional and professional) will be related to expectations about freedom from constraints (such as from machines or superiors), at the whole collectivity, group, dyad, and person levels of analysis.

Single- and Multiple-Level Analyses   Clearly, this hypothesis implies that different collectivities with different titles (functional and professional) and with different expectations (about freedom from various constraints) can be identified in a work setting and that these titles and expectations will covary. Moreover, differences between whole persons, whole dyads, and whole groups are expected to be manifestations of membership in different collectivities.

Multiple-Variable and Multiple-Relationship Analyses   At least four specific-level variables have been asserted (functional and professional titles, freedom from machines and from superiors). However, these variables are viewed as one network through their interrelationships. In particular, certain functional titles are considered more professional than others. Likewise, freedom from various constraints forms one multifaceted definition of expectations. In this sense, titles and expectations are represented by multiple interrelated variables.

TABLE 4.1.   Location of theory A predictions in a varient matrix

	VARIABLE AXIS[a]			
ENTITY AXIS	**Related** $T \leftrightarrow E$	**Generally** **Related** **(T, E)**	**Generally** **Unrelated** **(T, E)**	**Unrelated** $T \perp E$
Collectivities				
Wholes	____			
Parts	____			
Equivocal				
Inexplicable				
Groups				
Wholes	____			
Parts	____			
Equivocal				
Inexplicable				
Dyads				
Wholes	____			
Parts	____			
Equivocal				
Inexplicable				
Persons				
Wholes	____			
Parts	____			
Equivocal				
Inexplicable				

Prediction: Whole collectivities across levels.

[a]T indicates titles; E indicates expectations.

In terms of a varient matrix, a four-variable case can be simplified to the three-variable case (see Chapter 2) and a choice must then be made between the related, generally related, generally unrelated, and unrelated conditions. The related case was chosen in this specific-level formulation because all variables representing titles and expectations are hypothesized to be related.

Since a related case is asserted, the variables are hypothesized to be directly contingent, and a multiple-relationship analysis is unnecessary. The entire formulation can be summarized in terms of a varient matrix, as shown in Table 4.1.

THEORY B: EXCHANGE THEORY

The assertion of one theory can be enhanced by generating a second theory and comparing it to the first. In order to generate our theory B, we started with previous work on exchange theory (see, for example, Gergen, Greenberg, and Willis, 1980). Reviewers have tended to be somewhat less critical about exchange theory than role theory. Nevertheless, Chadwick-Jones (1976), in an extensive consideration of exchange theory, suggests that lack of an overall scheme from which hypotheses are derived may account for a number of theoretical and empirical problems associated with exchange theory. Since there are few other specific criticisms, it is appropriate to review traditional exchange approaches before we formulate a general theory. Essentially, two key notions seem to underlie exchange theory.

First, the **law of effect** is typically included in various formulations of exchange theory; that is, individuals tend to engage in behaviors leading to or providing pleasure (see Thorndike, 1911). For example, Secord and Backman (1974) indicate that exchange relies on a principle of profit maximization; that is, an individual attempts to maximize outcomes and avoid inputs in an exchange. Ekeh (1974) states that profitable exchange is an attempt to obtain outcomes based on the principle of maximization, which is the cornerstone of the first four principles of social exchange (Homans, 1958, 1961, 1974). According to Chadwick-Jones (1976), an attempt to maximize or optimize outcomes by an individual is common in a variety of work (see Blau, 1964, 1974; Homans, 1961; Thibaut and Kelley, 1959).

Second, reviewers also indicate that notions of equity are typically included in formulations of exchange theory. For example, Chadwick-Jones (1976) states that the principles of reciprocity, equity, and distributive justice are "almost identical" ideas. Alexander and Simpson (1964) and Pepitone (1981) point out that works on balance (Heider, 1958), congruity (Newcomb, 1953), dissonance (Festinger, 1957), and equity (Adams, 1963, 1965, 1968) are based on the same general principle. Ekeh (1974) discusses the similarities among the ideas of fair exchange, distributive justice, and numerous types of reciprocity. Secord and Backman (1974) point out that the principle of equity (Adams, 1963, 1965, 1968) is closely related to the principle of distributive justice (the fifth principle of social exchange for Homans [1958, 1961, 1974]).

The notion of equity requires further elaboration. Basically, **equity theory** postulates that a person engages in an internal comparison process in which he or she assesses his or her own position relative to that of some created referent other. For example, consider a focal individual, Joe, and some created referent, Harriet. According to equity theory, first Joe assesses his own inputs (I_J) and outcomes (O_J) from an exchange. Second, Joe defines a referent (Harriet) and the inputs (I_H) and outcomes (O_H) of that referent. Third, Joe compares the ratio of his inputs and outcomes to that of his referent Harriet.

In mathematical terms, **equity** is defined as the theoretical case in which Joe's ratio of inputs to outcomes is equal to Harriet's. In other words, equity is defined as:

$$\frac{I_H}{O_H} = \frac{I_J}{O_J} \tag{4.1}$$

Inequity is defined as a theoretical case in which Joe's ratio is not equal to Harriet's ratio of inputs and outcomes. In other words:

$$\frac{I_H}{O_H} \neq \frac{I_J}{O_J}$$

Since the same variables cannot be viewed as both equal and unequal, these equations are definitional in nature and are not testable hypotheses stated in terms of related (or unrelated) variables.

Most formulations of exchange contain the notions of equity and hedonism or optimizing. The marriage of these two notions, however, is quite problematic. For example, Ekeh (1974) indicates that equity notions can be viewed as providing some type of justification for the exploitation implied by the hedonistic or optimizing notions in exchange theories. When these two notions are linked in this way, an individual takes everything from the source of an exchange and then justifies his or her actions by choosing another referent who also exploits others. In general, exploitation can be avoided only when each party to an exchange incurs no costs.

As an alternative to this approach, Blau's work (1974) suggests that an individual may react to exploitation by another and attempt to strike down an oppressor or exploiter. Indeed, when both parties to an exchange are taken into account, a different linkage between the notions of hedonism and equity may be possible. For example, Emmerson (1969) attempted to develop exchange theory by incorporating concepts from reinforcement theory (Skinner, 1953). In this formulation, presumably a person exhibits a behavior and then receives a reinforcement. Therefore, from the point of view of either party to an exchange, the individual acts and receives something in return. In a similar vein, Blau (1974) implies that if rewards or returns are given to one individual, then that party becomes obligated or indebted to another individual. As a result, notions of reinforcement can be viewed as providing a hedonistic component to exchange.

From this perspective, the notions of giving and getting can be viewed as implied in exchange theory. For example, Secord and Backman (1974, p. 225) state: "In part, however, attempts to elicit rewards from the other person take the form of *giving* progressively greater rewards that prompt the other to *return* in kind" (emphasis added).[3] To our knowledge, although the ideas of giving and getting seem to be implied by various exchange theories, the specific manner in which equity notions are accounted for with these ideas has not been articulated. Before we attempt to make this linkage, it is necessary to consider how levels of analysis are included in exchange theory formulations.

Although different levels of analysis are associated with exchange theory, the dyad level of analysis is typically asserted, perhaps because exchange implies a transaction between two actors. Homans' work (1961) indicates that exchanges at the dyad level of analysis can be reduced to person-level characteristics. Blau (1974, p. 212) takes issue with this perspective and states: "To be sure, the concept of exchange itself refers to emergent properties of social relations that cannot be reduced to the psychological processes that motivate individual behavior." Another approach to exchange theory focuses on groups and kinship (Lévi-Strauss, 1969), and still another assertion (across levels) is that groups can be explained in terms of dyads. Taking the latter perspective, Ekeh (1974, pp. 125, 127) states: "Here, immediately, we arrive at another contradiction in Homans' theory. Although it is stated in dyadic terms, the

---

[3] From *Social Psychology*, by P. Secord and C. Backman. Copyright © 1974 by McGraw-Hill. Used with the permission of the McGraw-Hill Book Company.

evidence offered to validate the theory is in connection with multi-person interactions.... I argue that *Homans forced these data to fit his theory by reducing multi-person interactions to multiple dyadic interactions*" (emphasis in original). From still another perspective, Bredemeir (1977) concludes that people exchange with other people, not with collectivities.

General-Level Formulation

Clearly, different levels of analysis have been implicitly associated with exchange theory. But before dealing explicitly with the levels of analysis issue, we prefer to begin by linking equity and hedonistic notions with an assertion about variables—specifically that investments and returns are related. **Investments** are what one party gives to another party. **Returns** are what one party gets back from another. These definitions are intended to convey that investments trigger returns and returns trigger investments, thus incorporating the principle of reciprocal reinforcement. The concept of returns is also compatible with the idea of hedonism—that an individual always receives something in an exchange. Although the law of effect is included in this formulation, the notion of optimizing is removed because of widely known problems with this concept (see March and Simon, 1958).

One way in which this formulation includes equity notions can be illustrated with Figure 4.1a and 4.1b. In Figure 4.1a, investments and returns are hypothesized to be positively correlated, as represented by the diagonal line. In this case, as investments increase, returns increase, and vice versa. In Figure 4.1b two points (*C* and *D*) are located off the diagonal. These two points represent inequitable situations in that investments are not equal to returns. Equity can be maintained by reducing investments or increasing returns for an individual located at point *C*. For an individual at point *D*, equity can be maintained by increasing investments or reducing returns. In either case, the exchange point is pushed back onto the diagonal, as illustrated by the directed lines in Figure 4.1b. From this perspective, inequity is viewed as occurring when investments and returns are not perfectly related. A more detailed explanation of this general theory is beyond the range of our illustra-

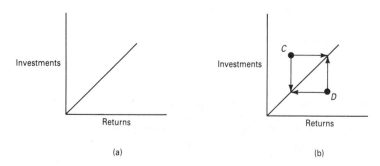

(a)   (b)

FIGURE 4.1. Investments and returns relationship and projection of points onto the investment-return diagonal

tion. However, the concepts of hedonism, equity, and reciprocal reinforcement have been incorporated into this formulation; the point can be explicated a little further by considering levels of analysis.

Single-Level Analysis   An assertion that the dyad level of analysis is appropriate for exchange theory is compatible with many contemporary approaches (Blau, 1964; Ekeh, 1974; Homans, 1958). Moreover, by focusing on dyads, the notions of reciprocal reinforcement can be clarified. For example, consider two human beings (Harriet and Joe) who compose a dyad. Assume that Joe is attempting to socialize Harriet (to use reinforcement theory). In this case, Joe waits for Harriet to behave or make an investment. When the investment is a return for Joe, he makes an investment in Harriet; as a result, Harriet receives a return from Joe. This sequence of events can be illustrated schematically, as shown in Figure 4.2.

In this case, Joe reinforces some behavior (investment) of Harriet by making an investment in Harriet. She can also reinforce Joe by giving additional investments to Joe after he makes an investment. As a result, Joe essentially learns to reinforce Harriet and she learns which behaviors will trigger investments from Joe. Moreover, Joe can make investments in Harriet in order to place her in his debt. The process can be reversed (Harriet may invest in a way that places Joe in her debt). In the case where a debt is incurred, one of the actors will have more returns than the other, and the two actors will be distinguishable. This notion is compatible with a dyad parts unit of analysis. In contrast, if whole dyads are chosen, then both parties, Harriet and Joe in this case, will be expected to have equal investments and returns.

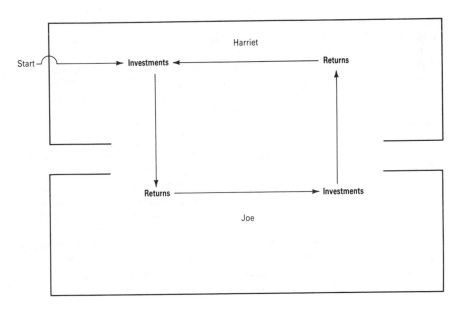

FIGURE 4.2.   General formulation of investment-return cycle

The choice of whether to assert whole dyads or dyad parts depends on the theorists' preferences. In Hollander's (1958) idiosyncrasy credit theory, an imbalance between members of a dyad is viewed as being offset by the party in debt allowing the other party (or creditor) freedom in behaving, in a sense as an investment to offset the debt to a creditor. Based on a preponderance of additional work (see Byrne and Nelson, 1965), however, we prefer to choose whole dyads as more appropriate than dyad parts in an exchange formulation. This general formulation, which includes notions from the law of effect, equity theory, reciprocal reinforcement, and Hollander's idiosyncrasy theory, can be summarized by the following general proposition:

Investments and returns are related based on differences between whole dyads.

In other words, some dyads can be viewed as "richer" in the sense that substantial investments and returns occur, and other dyads can be viewed as less rich.

As noted previously, in formulating a general theory, this key question must be considered: How different would human existence be without some notion of exchange at a dyad level of analysis? In order to consider this question, picture a world in which the human beings with whom we come in contact are unable to make a link between investments and returns. Without such a connection, it would perhaps be impossible to negotiate or bargain with any other human being; if we were to make an investment, the other party would simply take the return and we would not receive anything for our investment. If such an inequitable event were to occur, our theoretical formulation predicts that an attempt would be made to gain a return from the other person or that the dyad would dissolve. In a more general sense, the survival of human beings is somewhat difficult to imagine without some type of investment and return mechanism. Consider, for example, a newborn infant, whose dependence on other individuals for survival is almost complete. A child requires an investment on the part of some other human being for survival. The newborn has few immediate returns to offer another human being, except perhaps affection. Therefore, unless a child can somehow provide a set of long- or short-term returns, he or she will not become a member of a dyad and will probably die or be abandoned.

The choice of whole dyads as an appropriate unit of analysis suggests that from an insider's perspective, a human being is connected with one other individual and that each can destroy the dyad. The notion that one human being can destroy a dyad is compatible with the general idea from exchange theory that individuals may feel they have some control over, or some ability to optimize, their returns. In addition, the choice of a dyad as a unit of analysis is compatible with equity notions in the sense that the referent for each individual is the other member of a dyad. Since whole dyads have been chosen as a unit of analysis, a relationship between investments and returns may be hypothesized to hold across levels or to emerge at or be specific to the dyad level of analysis. Therefore, a consideration of multiple levels of analysis is necessary.

Multiple-Level Analysis Starting at the person level of analysis, an assertion of wholes means that each individual treats other individuals in the same way. Although persons may have different interpersonal styles, as is implied by the whole-person unit of analysis, in the investments and returns formulation two individuals are viewed as being involved in an exchange in which the style of each actor is not critical. Therefore, the whole-person unit of analysis is hypothesized not to be relevant to investments and returns.

At the person-parts unit of analysis, dyadic relationships are viewed as being based on the comparative positions of the other individuals with whom one individual interacts. In other words, each dyadic relationship is dependent on the other dyadic relationships formed by a person. Again, in this case one person influences the formation of a dyad. Our investments and returns formulation is interpreted to mean that two actors interact and form dyads.

To summarize, each human being is capable of forming multiple dyads, and these dyads are influenced not by one individual's style (wholes) or by his or her relationship with other persons (parts), but rather solely by the other actor in each independent dyad. As a result, an equivocal condition is hypothesized for the person level of analysis. Therefore, a relationship between investments and returns is hypothesized to emerge at the dyad level of analysis.

In terms of the group level of analysis, as illustrated in the previous chapter, the whole-persons unit of analysis can be considered to be compatible with the whole-group unit of analysis (for example, in the average leadership style approach). Likewise, person parts can be viewed as being compatible with the group-parts unit of analysis (for example, in the vertical dyad linkage approach). At the group level of analysis, individuals are seen as being influenced by a group of other individuals, so that linkages occur between persons and groups. Since our investments and returns formulation implies that two actors are influenced by each other rather than by individuals outside the dyad, the group level of analysis is hypothesized to be not applicable. As a result, an equivocal condition is chosen at the group level of analysis. In terms of multiple levels of analysis, this means that the relationship between investments and returns is hypothesized to be *specific* to the dyad level of analysis and not applicable to groups.

From the perspective of multiple-level analysis, the following proposition can be stated:

> Investments and returns will be related based on differences between whole dyads and will emerge at the dyad level of analysis and be specific to that level.

Multiple-Variable and Multiple-Relationship Analyses Only two variables, investments (I) and returns (R), have been specified. Therefore, the following two alternatives are plausible along the variable axis of a varient matrix:

Related   Unrelated

$I \leftrightarrow R$ $I \perp R$

In light of our proposition, the unrelated condition is rejected, and since only two variables are specified, an analysis of multiple relationships is not required.

Specific-Level Formulation

A specific-level formulation is helpful in clarifying the general investments and returns formulation. Less abstract variables representing investments and returns can be specified by considering a work setting in which superior-subordinate dyads are of interest. Possible investment variables include those of superior investments in subordinates and subordinate investments in superiors. A superior may provide interpersonal support to the subordinate; allow the subordinate to participate in decisions that are of importance to him or her; give him or her inside information; and show confidence in and consideration for the subordinate's unique abilities and preferences. This set of investments can be viewed as a superior's providing **attention** to a subordinate. In addition, a superior may allow a subordinate to make changes or to modify his or her job or tasks in a manner consistent with the subordinate's preferences. This set of investments can be viewed as a superior's providing **latitude** to a subordinate.

If attention and latitude are a superior's investments, they should also serve as a return to a subordinate. This seems plausible because the two constructs imply support of a subordinate as a unique human being and the allowing of an individual to perform in a way compatible with his or her own preferences and abilities. In exchange for the returns of attention and latitude, a subordinate may invest in his or her superior in a number of ways. For example, a subordinate may act in a way that satisfies his or her superior, an

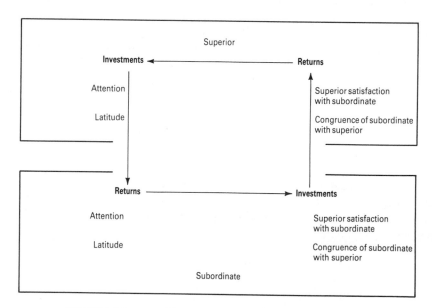

FIGURE 4.3. Specific formulation of investment-return cycle

investment known as **superior satisfaction with subordinate**. In addition to satisfying the superior, a subordinate may bring his or her actions in line with a superior's preferences, an investment called **congruence of subordinate with superior**. These two investments by subordinates may in turn serve as returns to a superior.

The specific-level formulation presented thus far is meant to imply that an investment-return cycle can be initiated from either a superior's or a subordinate's perspective. The diagram presented in Figure 4.3 may be helpful in illustrating the investment-return cycle. An investments-returns cycle can be initiated anywhere in the flow of investments and returns indicated by the lines in the diagram. For example, a subordinate's actions may align with a superior's preferences, which then serves as an investment on the part of the subordinate and as a return for the superior. This return may then spark an investment, such as attention, on the part of the superior. The cycle may continue or end depending on the maintenance of a relationship between investments and returns. This specific-level formulation also includes the notion that investments and returns between superiors and subordinates are highly personalized and depend on both superiors and subordinates rather than on each separately as a person or in a group. The specific-level formulation can be summarized with the following hypothesis:

> Investments (attention and latitude) will be related to returns (satisfaction of superior with subordinate and subordinate congruence with superior) based on differences between whole (supervisor-subordinate) dyads rather than differences between superiors or subordinate work groups.

Single- and Multiple-Level Analyses   The focus of this specific-level formulation is on whole dyads composed of one superior and one subordinate. In addition, this formulation specifies that effects at the whole dyad unit of analysis are specific to that level. Given this level-specific formulation, differences between whole dyads are expected to vary both between and within groups; therefore, an equivocal condition is predicted based upon a group or collectivity level analysis. In addition, the notion of emergence means that at the person level of analysis, each individual's interpersonal connection with others is based not on that person as a whole or on some comparison process within that individual, but rather on both persons in a dyad. As a result, an equivocal condition is asserted at the person level of analysis. These assertions are summarized in Table 4.2 by the location of the double lines along the entity axis.

Multiple-Variable and Multiple-Relationship Analyses   On the variable axis, two variables were specified for investments and two for returns. Since a four-variable case can be reduced to a three-variable case (see Chapter 2), and since all these variables are viewed as one network, this assertion can be mapped in the column labeled "Related" in the varient matrix, as shown in Table 4.2. Since all these variables (latitude, attention, superior satisfaction with subordinate, and subordinate congruence with superior) are viewed as one network of investment and return variables, multiple-relationship analysis is not necessary.

TABLE 4.2.   Location of theory B predictions in a varient matrix

	VARIABLE AXIS[a]			
ENTITY AXIS	*Related* *I ↔ R*	*Generally* *Related* *(I, R)*	*Generally* *Unrelated* *(I, R)*	*Unrelated* *I ⊥ R*
Collectivities				
Wholes				
Parts				
Equivocal	—			
Inexplicable	—			
Groups				
Wholes				
Parts				
Equivocal	—			
Inexplicable	—			
Dyads				
Wholes	—			
Parts	—			
Equivocal				
Inexplicable				
Persons				
Wholes				
Parts				
Equivocal	—			
Inexplicable	—			

Prediction: Level-specific and emergent whole dyads.

[a]*I* indicates investments; *R* indicates returns.

COMPARISON OF THEORY A AND THEORY B

Single- and Multiple-Level Analyses

At a single level of analysis, theory A includes an assertion of whole collectivities and theory B includes an assertion of whole dyads. But in terms of multiple levels, theory A is a cross-level formulation and theory B is a level-specific and emergent whole-dyad formulation. The locations of the theories along the entity axis have been presented in Tables 4.1 and 4.2.

Multiple-Variable Analysis

For the purpose of simplifying the presentation, this four-variable formulation (titles, expectations, investments, and returns) is reduced to a three-variable formulation. As a result, a choice among four cases is necessary.

First, the unrelated case is rejected because theories A and B both include a specification of relationships among the variables. In other words, the following configuration of the variables is rejected:

$$T \perp E \perp I \perp R$$

A second plausible assertion is that theory A and theory B contain essentially the same variables. From a theoretical insider perspective, recall that titles and expectations as properties of collectivities are viewed as impersonal or as independent of face-to-face interactions. In contrast, the emergent and level-specific dyadic formulation of investments and returns involved variables that are hypothesized to be personal in nature. Therefore, based solely on theory, titles and expectations are hypothesized to be different from investments and returns. Therefore, the related case is not selected. In other words, the following configuration of variables is rejected.

$$T \leftrightarrow E \leftrightarrow I \leftrightarrow R$$

Instead, the variables specified by theory A and those of theory B are hypothesized to be independent of each other. Specifically, a generally unrelated formulation of these variables is chosen. In other words, the following configuration of these variables is hypothesized to be more likely:

$$(T \leftrightarrow E) \perp (I \leftrightarrow R)$$

This assertion is the generally unrelated case because the following four pairs of variables are viewed as unrelated:

$$T \perp I \qquad T \perp R \qquad E \perp I \qquad E \perp R$$

As we have seen, two of the possible pairs of variables, those of theory A and those of theory B, are hypothesized to be related.

Finally, this assertion of a generally unrelated case means a rejection of the hypothesis that the four variables are generally related; thus we reject as unlikely the following configuration of variables:

$$(T \perp E) \leftrightarrow (I \perp R)$$

Our choice of a generally unrelated case based on theoretical considerations can be summarized in terms of the variable axis of the varient matrix in the following way.

Case:	Related	Generally related	Generally unrelated	Unrelated
Decision:	Rejected	Rejected	Chosen	Rejected

Therefore, the following proposition is asserted:

> Titles and expectations at the collectivity level of analysis and across levels of analysis are unrelated to investments and returns, which emerge and are level-specific at the whole-dyad level of analysis.

A less abstract proposition can be derived by inserting specific variables and entities associated with theories A and B into this general proposition.

Multiple-Relationship Analysis

Since we have rejected the two conditions that include specifications of direct contingencies (the related and generally related cases), indirect contingencies are possible, and multiple-relationship analysis must be performed. Because collectivities are physically larger and occur at a higher level of analysis than dyads, collectivity-level variables can serve as an environment or contingency for dyads. The opposite assertion (that dyads contain collectivities) is not viewed as plausible.

This suggests that the collectivity-level variables specified in theory A may create conditions under which the dyad-level variables specified in theory B should be examined. Specifically, when a multiplexed formulation is chosen, investments and returns based on dyad differences are hypothesized to occur regardless of the titles and expectations that characterize a collectivity. When a contingency formulation is chosen, depending on the titles and expectations associated with a collectivity, a relationship between investments and returns based on dyad differences would be expected in some collectivities and not in others.

In the absence of extensive previous research on levels of analysis, or T, E, I, and R, a multiplexed formulation seems appropriately conservative. In order to test this assertion, investments and returns must be examined within collectivities with different titles and expectations (provided a generally unrelated case has been demonstrated empirically). Nevertheless, the following proposition serves as one way to summarize the multiplexed formulation:

> Titles and expectations of whole collectivities and across levels of analysis will be unrelated to investments and returns, which will emerge and remain at the whole-dyad level of analysis. In addition, investments and returns will be related only at the dyad level of analysis, regardless of the titles and expectations associated with the collectivities within which the dyads are embedded.

In contrast, a contingency formulation would require a specification of the particular titles and expectations that would be more or less conducive to a relationship between investments and returns based on dyads. Our choice is to reject a contingent formulation—that is, $[(T \leftrightarrow E) \perp (I \leftrightarrow R)]$—in favor of a multiplexed formulation—that is, $(T \leftrightarrow E) \perp (I \leftrightarrow R)$.

Theory A and Theory B on the Varient Matrix

Theories A and B can now be mapped onto the larger varient matrix shown in Table 4.3. Through multiple-variable analysis, the generally unrelated

TABLE 4.3. Location of theory A and B predictions in a varient matrix

VARIABLE AXIS[a]

ENTITY AXIS	Generally Related — Related $[(T \leftrightarrow E) \leftrightarrow (I \leftrightarrow R)]$	Generally Related $[(T \perp E) \leftrightarrow (I \leftrightarrow R)]$	Generally Unrelated — Contingent $[(T \leftrightarrow E) \perp (I \leftrightarrow R)]$	Generally Unrelated — Multiplexed $(T \leftrightarrow E) \perp (I \leftrightarrow R)$	Unrelated — Contingent $[T \perp E \perp / \perp R]$	Unrelated — Multiplexed $T \perp E \perp / \perp R$
Collectivities						
Wholes						
Parts				||	||	
Equivocal						
Inexplicable						
Groups						
Wholes						
Parts				||	||	
Equivocal						
Inexplicable						
Dyads						
Wholes				||	||	
Parts						
Equivocal						
Inexplicable						
Persons						
Wholes						
Parts				||	||	
Equivocal						
Inexplicable						

Prediction: Whole collectivities across levels and level-specific and emergent whole dyads.

[a] T, E, I, and R indicate titles, expectations, investments, and returns, respectively.

case has been chosen. Through multiple-relationship analysis, a multiplexed formulation has been chosen. These choices are represented in Table 4.3 by the two sets of lines at each level of analysis for wholes. The same procedure is employed to locate investments and returns at the dyad level of analysis. The summaries in Tables 4.1 and 4.2 are consistent with the summary in Table 4.3. Networks of related variables are asserted in theory A and in theory B. Therefore, when each theory is considered separately, a related case should be chosen. However, when the variables associated with each theory are hypothesized to be independent of each other, the combined prediction for both theory A and theory B becomes a generally unrelated case. Table 4.3 presents the prediction for theories A *and* B.

From a testing perspective, the key question is whether these conditions seem more likely when data are analyzed. In actuality, any one of the conditions in the varient matrix could occur, so an empirical procedure for locating data in one position versus another is necessary. The focus of the next three chapters is on developing such a procedure. In Chapter 8, the overall procedure is summarized. A way to test theory A predictions (see Table 4.1) with data will be presented in Chapter 9; similarly, tests of theory B predictions (see Table 4.2) will be illustrated in Chapter 10. In Chapter 11, one way in which the predictions for theories A and B (see Table 4.3) were tested with data is presented.

SUMMARY

Theory A includes a specification of a relationship between variables (titles and expectations) and a specification of single (whole-collectivity) and multiple levels of analysis (it is a cross-level formulation). Theory B includes a specification of a relationship among variables (investments and returns), a specification of a single level of analysis (dyads), and a rejection of other levels of analysis (it is an emergent and level-specific formulation). At a higher level of abstraction, these theories are simple in that they consider only two variables each, and middle range in terms of the number of types of entities included in each. At a lower level of abstraction the theories are also middle-range in terms of the number of variables specified. A consideration of both theories simultaneously illustrates the use of single- and multiple-level analyses and multiple-variable and multiple-relationship analyses. In general, the two theories are viewed as very different (generally unrelated and multiplexed). In Chapters 5 through 8, the details of an empirical testing procedure are presented; one way to test theories A and B is illustrated in Chapters 9 through 11.

REVIEW QUESTIONS

1. How does one test a theory when relationships between variables are specified, but appropriate units or levels are not?

2. How can the validity of role and exchange theory be assessed?
3. Which units, as opposed to levels, of analysis were selected as critical for theory A and B?
4. Why was a cross-level formulation adopted for theory A?
5. Why was a level-specific formulation adopted for theory B?
6. Why was a generally unrelated condition specified for variables contained in theories A and B?
7. What implications does the assertion that the variables in theory A are independent of the variables in theory B have for multicollinearity?
8. Is the following a multiplexed or contingent formulation of variables: Investments and returns based on differences between whole dyads are related only in support collectivities.
9. If theory A, titles and expectations, had been used to predict the same outcomes as theory B, how would the varient matrix appear?
10. Why are the specific, less abstract, formulations of variables presented in this chapter not operationalizations of variables?

5

DATA
ANALYTIC TECHNIQUES

At least three key questions about data analysis arise in the course of locating data in a varient matrix. First, how can data be reduced based on mathematical principles or theories into a set of key indicators? In this chapter we will illustrate how geometry, one of the most basic of mathematical systems, underlies data reduction techniques. The identification of key mathematical indicators, however, would be of little interest without a consideration of substantive theoretical issues. The second question which therefore arises is this: What are the ideal numerical values of mathematical indicators that correspond to the theoretical conditions of interest (wholes, parts, and so on)? We will focus on this issue in Chapter 6. The third question is how to assess the degree to which different values of mathematical indicators approximate ideal values. In Chapter 7, we will deal with this issue and illustrate how data are located on a varient matrix. In Chapter 8, a full description of the process of theory testing involving theoretical formulations and data analysis is presented and illustrated. To introduce the varient approach to data analysis, this chapter presents the way in which data are reduced.

Our position on data reduction is that it must be based not only on theories of interest to investigators, but also on mathematical principles. In contrast, some investigators seem to believe that tradeoffs can be made between mathematics and their own substantive interests. As a result, indicators are sometimes used that do reduce data but for which the mathematical characteristics are unclear. We reject this approach and focus in this chapter on identifying a set of key and widely used empirical indicators derived from mathematical theory.

The specific mathematical theory underlying these key indicators is geometry. Since geometry transcends all coordinate systems (see Misner, Thorne, and Wheeler, 1973), the key indicators presented in this chapter permit a variety of metrics (such as space-time and non-space-time scales) to be examined. In our view, the geometric basis of the key indicators in the statistical paradigm permits traditional methods to be widely used. The mathematical basis of indicators, however, should be distinguished from the inferential procedures used in the statistical paradigm (tests of statistical significance), which are based on assumed ideal normal distributions rather than on geometry alone.

A critical set of geometrically based indicators can be derived from what we call the general linear tensor. Although the general linear tensor permits a determination of the degree of association between variables, it is indifferent to the entities characterized by variables. Within and between analysis (WABA) was developed to extend the tensor to include entities.

Therefore, this chapter contains (1) a presentation of the general linear tensor in geometric terms, (2) an illustration of how it is used to examine total correlations in most traditional work, (3) a demonstration of how the key empirical indicators in within and between analysis are calculated and derived from geometry, and (4) an overview of the way in which these key indicators in WABA are used in the varient paradigm and in traditional approaches (for example, one-way analysis of variance and correlational analysis). We recognize that a number of other indicators and methods (such as multiple regression and multivariate analysis of variance) are based on the principles presented in this chapter, but discussion of these techniques is deferred until Chapters 12 and 13 in favor of focusing on and extending with WABA the use of the general linear tensor.

THE GENERAL LINEAR TENSOR

The general linear tensor is called by different names in different scientific disciplines—"metric tensor" by physicists (see Misner et al., 1973) and "scalar product" by mathematicians (see Olmstead, 1966).

Essentially, the **general linear tensor** can be viewed as the geometric principles (from Euclidean geometry) that specify how to calculate the length of a vector and the scalar product between two vectors in space. The notion that the scalar product equals the cosine of the angle between two vectors (or the degree of association between two variables expressed as unit length vectors) is widely known (see Harman, 1970; Fisher, 1925). Descriptions of the general linear tensor, explanations of its underlying geometry, and associated mathematical proofs are readily available. Our purpose is not to provide redundant information, but rather to use the general linear tensor as a basis for analyzing data.

Degree of Association (cos θ)

From a geometric perspective, a variable takes on meaning depending on the degree to which it is associated with another variable; the degree of association can be expressed in terms of angles, where variables are viewed as vectors. Variables as vectors are illustrated in the upper portion of Figure 5.1. A variable is a vector because it has direction (usually from lower to higher values).

At one extreme, when variables are perfectly related the two vectors should overlap so that a change or movement in one vector from low to high results in the same degree of movement in a second vector. In this case, the angle between the two vectors equals 0°, and the two vectors X and Y overlap to such an extent that they are indistinguishable, as is illustrated in the middle portion of Figure 5.1. At the other extreme, two vectors can be independent, with a change in one vector having no effect on a second vector. In this case, two vectors are at a right angle (90°) to each other, as illustrated in the lower portion of Figure 5.1.

Any number of angles can occur between these two extremes. A subset of such intermediate angles is illustrated in the upper portion of Figure 5.2. As shown in the figure, the degree to which each angle is closer to a 0° or to a 90° angle can be determined except in the case of 45°, which represents the exact midpoint between the extremes. The sines, cosines, and cotangents associated with each angle are also shown in the upper portion of Figure 5.2.

Although the degree of association between vectors can be expressed in angles, the cosines of angles are typically used to express empirically the relationship between two lines in space (Smail, 1953), two vectors in space-time (Misner et al., 1973), or two variables in a space formed by objects (Harman, 1970). The angles that can occur between two vectors vary from 180° to 0°.

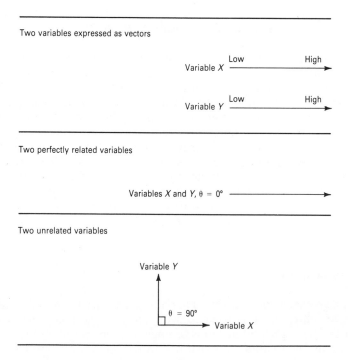

FIGURE 5.1.   Vectors and related and unrelated variables

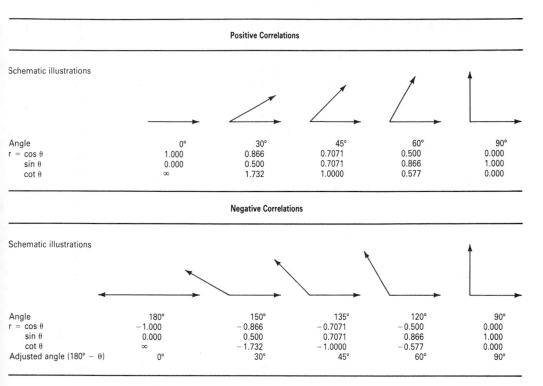

Positive Correlations

Schematic illustrations					
Angle	0°	30°	45°	60°	90°
r = cos θ	1.000	0.866	0.7071	0.500	0.000
sin θ	0.000	0.500	0.7071	0.866	1.000
cot θ	∞	1.732	1.0000	0.577	0.000

Negative Correlations

Schematic illustrations					
Angle	180°	150°	135°	120°	90°
r = cos θ	−1.000	−0.866	−0.7071	−0.500	0.000
sin θ	0.000	0.500	0.7071	0.866	1.000
cot θ	∞	−1.732	−1.0000	−0.577	0.000
Adjusted angle (180° − θ)	0°	30°	45°	60°	90°

FIGURE 5.2.   Geometric examples of degree of correlation

The cosines of these angles vary from -1 to $+1$, and they are symmetric in magnitude. This point is illustrated in Figure 5.2. For example, an angle of 150° results in a cosine of -0.866, which is identical in magnitude to the cosine of a 30° angle. The symmetry is illustrated in more detail in section 1 of Appendix B. Essentially, any angle between 90° and 180° can be subtracted from 180°; the result will be 90° or less. Such adjusted angles are shown at the bottom of Figure 5.2. Thus, because of the symmetry of cosines, the magnitude of association between variables expressed as cosines can be viewed as always ranging from 0° to 90°.

This leads to a consideration of the **general correlation** (r_{XY}), which is equal to the cosine of the angle between two vectors (Fisher, 1915; Harman, 1970) and is an indicator of the degree of association between two vectors. The general correlation must vary from $+1$ to -1, and it must be symmetric; that is, a correlation of $+0.7071$ indicates the same degree of association as a correlation of -0.7071. The minus sign simply indicates that the two variables operate in opposite directions. These points can be summarized with the equation

$$\cos \theta_{XY} = r_{XY} \qquad (5.1)$$

Degree of Association and Lack of Association (cot θ)

Although in empirical work interest is often focused on the relationship expressed as a cosine between variables or vectors, the value of such a relationship also implies a degree of nonrelationship. To understand this point, it is helpful to view a relationship between two vectors solely in terms of its magnitude and therefore in terms of an angle between 0° and 90°. As a result, any correlation (cos θ) between two variables can be viewed as contained in the first quadrant of 90°. Given a relationship between two vectors of interest X and Y, a third vector called V which is perpendicular to one of the vectors of interest can always be drawn. The three angles ($\theta_{XY}, \theta_{VY}, \theta_{VX}$) that result in this case can be diagramed as follows:

The angle between vectors V and X always equals 90° and has a cosine of 0, a sine of 1, and a cotangent of 0 (see Table A.1). The two remaining angles (θ_{VY}, θ_{XY}) are useful in drawing inferences about the strength of the relationship (cos θ_{XY}) between two variables (X and Y).

Specifically, the angle between X and Y indicates the degree to which the two vectors are associated. The angle between vectors V and Y (θ_{VY}) indicates the degree to which X and Y are not associated. When, for example, θ_{VY} equals 90°, X and Y are perfectly associated because the third vector is independent of variables X and Y. However, if the angle between vectors V and Y equals 0°, variables X and Y form a 90° angle and are not associated. Because the two angles θ_{VY} and θ_{XY} must sum to 90°, given a value for one cosine (or correlation), the two angles (one indicating association between two variables and one indicating lack of association) are known.

From a derivation presented in the third section of Appendix B, the cotangent can be used in two ways to express the degree of association (θ_{XY}) and lack of association (θ_{VY}). First, it can be viewed as the ratio of the cosines of two different angles. These cosines, given Equation 5.1, can be expressed in terms of two general correlations. The ratio of these cosines is called a **general E ratio**, which can be defined as

$$\cot \theta_{XY} = \frac{\cos \theta_{XY}}{\cos \theta_{VY}} = \frac{r_{XY}}{r_{VY}} = E \tag{5.2}$$

A second derivation of the cotangent occurs when it is expressed in terms of the cosine of one angle or one correlation. This definition of the cotangent can be summarized as follows:

$$\cot \theta_{XY} = \frac{\cos \theta_{XY}}{\sqrt{1 - \cos^2\theta_{XY}}} = \frac{r_{XY}}{\sqrt{1 - r_{XY}^2}} = R \qquad (5.3)$$

This ratio defined by one correlation is called the **general *R* ratio**.

Equation 5.3 should be familiar from the traditional statistical paradigm. When this equation is squared, r_{XY}^2 equals the percentage of variance accounted for in one variable by another and $1 - r_{XY}^2$ equals the percentage of variance unaccounted for in one variable by another variable. At one extreme, if a correlation (r_{XY}) equals 0, then the *R* ratio (cotangent) equals 0. At the other extreme, if a correlation (r_{XY}) equals 1, then the *R* ratio or cotangent is undefined and approaches infinity. The cotangent has a value of 1 at 45°, and this value occurs when an obtained correlation equals 0.7071. This midpoint is quite compatible with the view that squared correlations indicate the percentage of variance accounted for in one variable by another variable. (Specifically, the square root of 0.50 equals cos 45° or approximately 0.7071.) Therefore, an obtained correlational value of 0.7071 results in an *R* value of 1, in that 50 percent of variance in the variables of interest is common and 50 percent is unique. Although the *E* ratio is based on two different correlations as a cotangent, it has the same range of values and midpoint as the *R* ratio. We prefer to view both ratios (expressions of one cotangent) as indicating the degree to which two variables are associated relative to the degree to which two variables are not associated.

The Key Indicator (θ)

The key indicator in the general linear tensor is the angle between two vectors. Such angles are typically obtained by the use of the cosine and with Equation 5.1 by the use of general correlations (r). Once the value for the general correlation is known, a value for the cotangent can be obtained in either of the two ways described previously. Thus, the general linear tensor can be summarized as in Table 5.1. As indicated in the table, the cosine and cotangent underlie many of the equations and associated data reduction techniques to be discussed in the remainder of this chapter. The key indicator from a data analytic perspective, however, is the calculation of the cosine of an angle (r_{XY}), since the *R* and *E* ratios can be calculated based on values for the cosine (r_{XY}).

The calculation of the angle between two vectors based on the data is known to be based on geometric principles (see Harman, 1970; Misner et al., 1973; Olmstead, 1966; Smail, 1953), and is referred to in this book as the general linear tensor. In physics, this tensor is viewed as a machine (Misner et al., 1973) with two slots into which vectors are inserted and one number

TABLE 5.1.   Illustration of the general linear tensor

	GEOMETRIC MEANING	RANGES	THEORY-DATA LINK	
			Mathematical Indicator	*Equations*
Degree of association of two variables (X and Y)	$\cos \theta_{XY}$		r_{XY}	5.4, 5.8, 5.9, 5.12, 5.13
Sign and magnitude		−1 to 1		
Magnitude only		0 to 1		
Degree of association relative to lack of association	$\cot \theta_{XY}$	0 to ∞[a]		
One correlation			R	5.5, 5.16, 5.18
Two correlations			E	5.10

[a]The range of the cotangent is actually $-\infty$ to $+\infty$. However, given the symmetry of correlations around 0, the range from 0 to ∞ is sufficient to capture the range of the *magnitudes* of correlations. This approach is used throughout the varient paradigm and is also used in the statistical paradigm.

comes out:

Slot 1	**Slot 2**
↓	↓

$$(\qquad \cdot \qquad)$$

When the same vector (X) is inserted into both slots, the square of the vector (X^2) is output. When two different vectors are inserted, a **scalar product** of X on Y, or the cosine, is output. From geometry, we know that the cosine of the angle between two vectors of unit length (one) is equal to the scalar product of the two vectors (Harman, 1970).

To calculate the angle between two vectors, the following requirements must be met. First, each vector should be of unit length; and second, the scalar product should be used to obtain the $\cos \theta$ between the two vectors. Signed deviation scores are typically used for this purpose because they meet these two requirements. But herein lies a problem. Since we have shown that there are at least three types of signed deviation scores (total, within, and between), the correlation between any or all such deviation scores may be considered using the general linear tensor. In traditional work, only total signed deviation scores are considered. Although we will use the total deviation scores to illustrate how such total correlations can be calculated, it is important to keep in mind that this is only one application of the general linear tensor and that other applications will be presented here.

TOTAL CORRELATION ANALYSIS

In traditional work, total signed deviation scores ($X - \overline{X}$) or total deviation scores are calculated by taking the average of a set of scores ($\overline{X}$) and then subtracting that average ($\overline{X}$) from each score (X). These total deviation scores

$(X - \bar{X})$ are then distributed back to the source of the score (X). A vector of unit length is formed by dividing each total signed deviation score by the square root of the sum of the squared deviations. For example, two points on vector X are written as follows:

$$\frac{X_1 - \bar{X}}{\sqrt{\Sigma(X - \bar{X})^2}} \qquad \frac{X_2 - \bar{X}}{\sqrt{\Sigma(X - \bar{X})^2}}$$

The length of this vector is obtained by squaring each point and then adding the terms. The length of a vector, formed in this way regardless of the number of points, always equals 1.

Given two unit-length vectors, one for variable X and one for variable Y, the scalar product given two points on each vector is written as follows:

$$\frac{X_1 - \bar{X}}{\sqrt{\Sigma(X - \bar{X})^2}} \cdot \frac{Y_1 - \bar{Y}}{\sqrt{\Sigma(Y - \bar{Y})^2}} = \frac{(X_1 - \bar{X})(Y_1 - \bar{Y})}{\sqrt{\Sigma(X - \bar{X})^2 \Sigma(Y - \bar{Y})^2}}$$

$$\frac{X_2 - \bar{X}}{\sqrt{\Sigma(X - \bar{X})^2}} \cdot \frac{Y_2 - \bar{Y}}{\sqrt{\Sigma(Y - \bar{Y})^2}} = \frac{(X_2 - \bar{X})(Y_2 - \bar{Y})}{\sqrt{\Sigma(X - \bar{X})^2 \Sigma(Y - \bar{Y})^2}}$$

$$\text{Total} \qquad \frac{\Sigma(X - \bar{X})(Y - \bar{Y})}{\sqrt{\Sigma(X - \bar{X})^2 \Sigma(Y - \bar{Y})^2}}$$

The total in this case is written in a general form.

The scalar product for any number of points on each vector results in the following general formula for the **total correlation**, is based on total deviation scores, and is equal to the cosine of the angle between two variables X and Y (Harman, 1970). The formula is

$$\cos \theta_{XY} = r_{TXY} = \frac{\Sigma(X - \bar{X})(Y - \bar{Y})}{\sqrt{\Sigma(X - \bar{X})^2 \Sigma(Y - \bar{Y})^2}} \qquad (5.4)$$

Any formula for correlations in any statistics book can be derived from Equation 5.4. Once the total correlation has been calculated, the associated cotangent or **total R ratio (R_T)** can be obtained from Equation 5.3 as follows:

$$\cot \theta_{XY} = R_T = \frac{r_{TXY}}{\sqrt{1 - r_{TXY}^2}} \qquad (5.5)$$

A t test, which is typically employed to test the statistical significance of total correlations, can be derived from the R_T ratio. If N is the number of pairs of scores that comprise a correlation, the traditional t test (t_T) **for a total**

correlation is written

$$t_T = R_T\sqrt{N-2} = \frac{r_{TXY}}{\sqrt{1 - r_{TXY}^2}}\sqrt{N-2} \qquad (5.6)$$

Equation 5.6 is identical to the equation for a t test found in standard statistics books. Nevertheless, a demonstration that the appropriate degrees of freedom for any correlation are exactly $N-2$ is presented in Appendix E. Equation 5.6 is also in line with statistical methods in that the traditional test, which includes the cotangent (the inverse of a tangent), is referred to as a t test, which apparently stands for the term "tangent" (Student, 1908). The following illustration of the procedures for calculating r_{TXY}, R, and t should clarify the nature of these indicators.

Illustrative Data Reduction

For the purpose of illustration, assume that seven scores on variable X and seven scores on variable Y have been obtained and that they are paired as shown in Table 5.2. For example, pair A involves a score of 9 on one variable and a score of 12 on a second variable. As shown in the table, the scores on variable X and then on variable Y are added together; this addition of rows is indicated by a summation sign (Σ). Likewise, the average of all scores is obtained and then distributed back to their source, as shown in the table. The sum of these averages ($\Sigma \bar{X}$) is always equal to the sum of the scores. (A proof of this statement is presented in Appendix C.) Total deviation scores are calculated by subtracting the mean from each score. As shown in the table, the summation of these scores equals 0. Finally, in order to obtain the denominator for Equation 5.4, each deviation score is squared, and these squared scores are added to form $\Sigma(X - \bar{X})^2$ and $\Sigma(Y - \bar{Y})^2$. The above calculations are shown for variables X and Y in Table 5.2 and provide two terms required by the formula for the total correlation (Equation 5.4). In order to obtain the numerator for Equation 5.4, the deviation scores for X and Y are multiplied. These calculations can be summarized as follows:

1. Calculate the averages for variables X and Y.
2. Calculate the signed deviation scores for X and Y by subtracting the average for the variable from each score.
3. Square the signed deviation scores $(X - \bar{X})^2$ and $(Y - \bar{Y})^2$ and then sum them. Multiply these summations and take the square root. The value that results is the denominator in Equation 5.4.
4. Multiply each signed deviation score on variable X by the corresponding signed deviation score on Y. The sum of these cross products forms the numerator in Equation 5.4.

From these calculations, the following value for the total correlation results by substitution into Equation 5.4:

$$\cos \theta_{XY} = r_{TXY} = 0.679$$

TABLE 5.2. Calculation of a total correlation from signed deviation scores

			SOURCE OF SCORES					SUMMATION (Σ)	
	A	B	C	D	E	F	G	Numerical	Symbolic
Variable X									
Scores (X)	9	2	4	1	7	8	4	35	ΣX
Average ($\bar{X}$)	5	5	5	5	5	5	5	35	$\Sigma \bar{X}$
Total deviations ($X - \bar{X}$)	4	−3	−1	−4	2	3	−1	0	$\Sigma(X - \bar{X})$
Squared total deviations ($X - \bar{X})^2$	16	9	1	16	4	9	1	56	$\Sigma(X - \bar{X})^2$
Variable Y									
Scores (Y)	12	5	7	3	9	5	1	42	ΣY
Average ($\bar{Y}$)	6	6	6	6	6	6	6	42	$\Sigma \bar{Y}$
Total deviations ($Y - \bar{Y}$)	6	−1	1	−3	3	−1	−5	0	$\Sigma(Y - \bar{Y})$
Squared total deviations ($Y - \bar{Y})^2$	36	1	1	9	9	1	25	82	$\Sigma(Y - \bar{Y})^2$
Variables X and Y									
Cross products ($X - \bar{X})(Y - \bar{Y}$)	24	3	−1	12	6	−3	5	46	$\Sigma(X - \bar{X})(Y - \bar{Y})$
Calculations									
Total correlation									

$$\frac{\Sigma(X - \bar{X})(Y - \bar{Y})}{\sqrt{\Sigma(X - \bar{X})^2 \Sigma(Y - \bar{Y})^2}} = \frac{46}{\sqrt{(56)(82)}} = 0.679$$

The value for the total R is obtained by substitution into Equation 5.5, as follows:

$$\cot\theta_{XY} = R_{TXY} = \frac{r_{TXY}}{\sqrt{1 - r_{TXY}^2}} = \frac{0.679}{\sqrt{1 - 0.679^2}} = 0.925$$

The value for the t test of the total correlation is obtained by substitution into Equation 5.6, as follows:

$$t_{TXY} = R_{TXY}\sqrt{N - 2} = 0.925\sqrt{7 - 2} = 2.068$$

These three values (r_{TXY}, R_{TXY}, and t_{TXY}) provide a simple way to reduce a set of data into a smaller set of indicators, which are themselves interrelated: Values for R are essentially determined by the value of the correlation (r), and values for t are determined by R and the number of pairs of scores.

The Need for WABA

This approach to reducing data is summarized in Table 5.3. The value of 0.679 for the total correlation has little meaning, however, until some type of theory (for example, statistical) is considered, although even with the consideration of statistical theory, difficulties remain. For one thing, the widespread use and analysis of total correlations and other indicators based on total deviations fails explicitly to take into account the entities or levels of analysis that may be specified on a theoretical basis. In fact, the example presented in Table 5.2 is based on a set of numbers that are not specified to be characterizations of any entities. Therefore, it is necessary to extend this traditional approach by using

TABLE 5.3. Illustration of total correlation analysis

	EQUATION	MATHEMATICAL INDICATOR	RANGE	ILLUSTRATIVE RESULTS (TABLE 5.2)
Degree of association of total deviations on variable X and total deviations on variable Y	5.4	r_{TXY}	-1 to 1	0.679
Degree of association relative to lack of association (one correlation)	5.5	R_T	0 to ∞	0.925
Adjustment for degrees of freedom	5.6	t_T	0 to ∞	2.068

the general linear tensor explicitly to include entities and levels of analysis. We call this extension within and between analysis (WABA).

WITHIN AND BETWEEN ANALYSIS (WABA)

The WABA extension of the traditional approach is based on the general linear tensor and on the work of Robinson (1950) and Duncan, Cuzzort, and Duncan (1961). Most work on levels of analysis has also been based on Robinson's (1950) seminal paper. At this point we will illustrate that WABA includes the total correlation and that it provides additional information.

In the numerical example of the general linear tensor presented in Table 5.2, only one correlation between two variables, X and Y, was calculated. This correlation was based on the total deviations on variable X and variable Y. The correlation of interest in this approach (r_{TXY}) can be illustrated in matrix form as follows:

	VARIABLE X TOTAL	VARIABLE Y TOTAL
VARIABLE X TOTAL	1.00	
VARIABLE Y TOTAL	r_{TXY}	1.00

In this matrix, one correlation r_{TXY} was calculated based simply on the total deviation scores.

When WABA is employed, cells are created so that any variable (X or Y) can be expressed in terms of total, between-cell, and within-cell deviation scores. Therefore, if two variables are of interest, six scores are calculated and distributed. Mathematically, of course, two of the signed deviation scores (within and between) sum to a total deviation; for variable X

$$X - \bar{X} = \left(X - \bar{X}_J \right) + \left(\bar{X}_J - \bar{X} \right)$$

and for variable Y

$$Y - \bar{Y} = \left(Y - \bar{Y}_J \right) + \left(\bar{Y}_J - \bar{Y} \right)$$

The calculation of these scores was illustrated in Chapter 2 and is illustrated again in Tables 5.5a and 5.5b. Since all these scores are signed deviation scores,

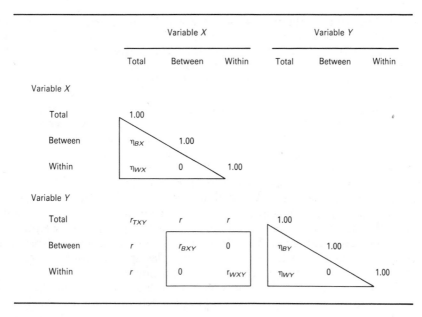

FIGURE 5.3. Key correlations in WABA

the general linear tensor can be used to calculate the relationship among them. The result is the correlation matrix shown in Figure 5.3. This matrix demonstrates that given two variables, 15 correlations (ignoring the values of 1) can be calculated using the general formula from the linear tensor. A consideration of all 15 correlations is not necessary, as some redundancy occurs between the correlations. We will now define and discuss the six correlations that determine all other correlations in this matrix (η_{BX}, η_{BY}, r_{BXY}, η_{WX}, η_{WY}, and r_{WXY}).

A **within-cell eta correlation** (η_W) is the correlation of total deviation scores with within-cell deviation scores on a single variable. A **between-cell eta correlation** (η_B) is the correlation of total deviation scores with the between-cell deviation scores on a single variable. Eta correlations for variables X (η_{BX}, η_{WX}) and Y (η_{BY}, η_{WY}) are contained in the triangles shown in the matrix of 15 correlations. The choice of these correlations as one set of key indicators is based on the fact that between- and within-cell deviation scores are always independent (see section 1 of Appendix D for a proof). This fact is indicated by the zero values contained in the triangles shown in the matrix of 15 correlations.

The independence is important from a practical perspective, because scores for one variable are written in two different ways, and the eta correlations indicate the degree to which scores are represented in one way or the other. From a statistical perspective, the independence of the within- and between-cell scores permits the total degrees of freedom in signed deviation scores to be partitioned into two components. A focus on eta correlations we call **WABA I**, because one variable (X or Y) is considered. Although values for these correlations are obtained by using the general linear tensor, the term eta (η) correlation is used because it is identical to the square root of eta squared, an indicator used in many traditional approaches. Essentially, four of the correlations ($\eta_{BX}, \eta_{BY}, \eta_{WX}, \eta_{WY}$) in the matrix of 15 correlations have been discussed, and since two zero correlations have been identified, nine correlations remain to be considered.

A **within-cell correlation** (r_{WXY}) is the correlation of one variable (X) with another variable (Y) based on within-cell deviation scores. A **between-cell correlation** (r_{BXY}) is the correlation of one variable (X) with another variable (Y) based on between-cell deviation scores. These correlations are contained in the rectangle shown in the matrix of 15 correlations. The choice of these correlations as key indicators is based on the mathematical fact that the two correlations are independent. (See section 7 of Appendix D for a demonstration of this fact.) This independence is indicated by the zeros in the rectangle shown in the matrix of 15 correlations. Again, the independence is helpful in a practical and statistical sense. We refer to a focus on the within- and between-cell correlations as **WABA II**, because two variables are correlated. Therefore 5 correlations in the matrix of 15 remain to be considered.

The total correlation is simply equal to the following mathematical combination of the eta and within- and between-cell correlations:

$$\eta_{BX}\eta_{BY}r_{BXY} + \eta_{WX}\eta_{WY}r_{WXY} = r_{TXY} \tag{5.7}$$

where

η_{BX} = between-eta correlation for variable X

η_{BY} = between-eta correlation for variable Y

r_{BXY} = between-cell correlation for two variables (X and Y)

η_{WX} = within-eta correlation for variable X

η_{WY} = within-eta correlation for variable Y

r_{WXY} = within-cell correlation between two variables (X and Y)

r_{TXY} = total correlation between two variables (X and Y) based on total deviations

Equation 5.7 is the **WABA equation**, and its proof is found in section 5 of Appendix D.

A simple proof of the WABA equation can be derived. From section 5 of Appendix D, within-eta correlations can be written as

$$\eta_{WX} = \sqrt{1 - \eta_{BX}^2}$$

$$\eta_{WY} = \sqrt{1 - \eta_{BY}^2}$$

By substitution, Equation 5.7 can be written in the following form, expressed by Robinson (1950):

$$r_{TXY} = r_{BXY}\eta_{BX}\eta_{BY} + r_{WXY}\sqrt{1 - \eta_{BX}^2}\sqrt{1 - \eta_{BY}^2}$$

Essentially, any total correlation has two mathematically based components: the **between-cell component** ($\eta_{BX}\eta_{BY}r_{BXY}$) and **within-cell component** ($\eta_{WX}\eta_{WY}r_{WXY}$). Therefore, 4 correlations in the matrix of 15 remain, but these are composites of the within and between eta and cell correlations (see Chapter 12 for the equations that demonstrate this fact).

As should now be apparent, the WABA equation (Equation 5.7) defines the 6 key correlations in the matrix of 15. In the case of WABA I, the independence of the within- and between-cell vectors means that knowledge of a between-cell score provides no information about a within-cell score. Likewise, in the case of WABA II, knowledge about a between-cell correlation provides no information about a within-cell correlation. Unique information is therefore possessed by the indicators. The WABA equation specifies the way these within- and between-cell indicators combine to form a total correlation. In other words, the total correlation whose calculation was illustrated in Table 5.2 is actually an aggregate of within- and between-cell components. A discussion of these components is now appropriate.

WABA I (Eta Correlations)

In WABA I, each variable is considered separately. The procedures for calculating an eta correlation are derived from the geometric theory on which WABA I is based. Given that within- and between-cell deviation scores are independent, two vectors (B and W) form a 90° angle (see section 1 of Appendix D). The total deviation scores are represented as one vector (T) that varies between the within and between vectors. This notion can be represented in the following standard geometric form, with the addition of arrows to represent the variability of vector T:

Degree of Association The angle between the total (T) and between-cell scores (B) indicates the degree to which a total set of scores is represented by between-cell scores (or averages). The formula for calculating the correlation ($\cos\theta$) between the total ($X - \bar{X}$) and between-cell ($\bar{X}_J - \bar{X}$) vector or the between-eta correlation is obtained by using the general linear tensor or by substitution in the formula for the total correlation (Equation 5.4), and is

$$\cos \theta_{TB} = \eta_{BX} = \frac{\Sigma(X - \bar{X})(\bar{X}_J - \bar{X})}{\sqrt{\Sigma(X - \bar{X})^2 \Sigma(\bar{X}_J - \bar{X})^2}} = +\sqrt{\frac{\Sigma(\bar{X}_J - \bar{X})^2}{\Sigma(X - \bar{X})^2}} \quad (5.8)$$

A proof that a between-eta correlation equals the positive square root of the sum of squared between-cell deviations divided by the sum of the squared total deviations is presented in section 2 of Appendix D. This formula is the traditional definition of the square root of eta squared (see Hays, 1973). Given this proof, the between-cell eta correlation must vary from 0 to +1.

Similarly, the degree to which total scores on a single variable are described by within-cell scores is indicated by the angle between the total and within-cell vectors. The formula for calculating the correlation ($\cos \theta$) between the total ($X - \bar{X}$) and within-cell ($X - \bar{X}_J$) vector, or the within-eta correlation, is obtained by using the general linear tensor or by substitution in the formula for the total correlation (Equation 5.4):

$$\cos \theta_{TW} = \eta_{WX} = \frac{\Sigma(X - \bar{X})(X - \bar{X}_J)}{\sqrt{\Sigma(X - \bar{X})^2 \Sigma(X - \bar{X}_J)^2}} = +\sqrt{\frac{\Sigma(X - \bar{X}_J)^2}{\Sigma(X - \bar{X})^2}} \quad (5.9)$$

A proof that within-eta correlations equal the positive square root of the sum of the squared within-cell deviations divided by the sum of the squared total deviations is presented in section 3 of Appendix D. The fact that a squared within-cell eta correlation equals the sum of the within-cell deviations squared divided by the total sum of squares means that the within-cell eta correlation varies from 0 to +1 (from 90° to 0° in angular terms). In reference to the traditional statistical paradigm, it might be helpful to point out that given Equations 5.8 and 5.9, the within-cell eta squared correlation can be written as $\eta_{WX}^2 = 1 - \eta_{BX}^2$.

Degree of Association and Lack of Association   Using Equation 5.2, the cotangent of the angle between the total vector and the between vector can be written as the between-eta correlation divided by the within-eta correlation:

$$\cot \theta_{TB} = \frac{\cos \theta_{TB}}{\cos \theta_{TW}} = \frac{\eta_{BX}}{\eta_{WX}} = E \quad (5.10)$$

We refer to this cotangent as an *E* **ratio**. At one extreme, a total vector (T) on one variable may be entirely represented by its own between-cell deviation scores ($\theta_{TB} = 0°$). In this case, the between-eta correlation equals 1, and in order to satisfy the equation $\eta_{BX}^2 + \eta_{WX}^2 = 1$ (see section 4 of Appendix D), the within-eta correlation must equal 0. In this extreme case, the *E* ratio is undefined and approaches infinity. At the other extreme, a total vector (T) on one variable is perfectly represented by its own within-cell deviation scores

$(\theta_{TW} = 0°)$. In this case, the within-eta correlation equals 1, the between-eta correlation equals 0, and the E ratio equals 0.

As is the case for any cotangent, given the symmetry of cosines, the E ratio can be viewed as having a range from 0 to ∞. Within this range, an E ratio equals 1 when the total deviations are represented equally well by the between- and within-cell vectors ($\theta_{TB} = 45°$ and $\theta_{TW} = 45°$). As the total deviation vector approaches the between-cell vector, the cotangent becomes larger (greater than 1). In contrast, when the total deviation vector approaches the within-cell vector, the cotangent becomes smaller (less than 1). Unlike the R ratio, the E ratio is based on two correlations rather than one.

Adjustments for Degrees of Freedom　Finally, from a statistical perspective, the eta correlations can be influenced by degrees of freedom. An **F ratio** can be written in terms of the E ratio as follows:

$$F = E^2 \frac{N - J}{J - 1} \tag{5.11}$$

where N equals the number of scores and J equals the number of cells. A derivation of Equation 5.11 may be helpful at this point. Specifically,

$$E^2 = \frac{\eta_{BX}^2}{\eta_{WX}^2}$$

which can be expressed in traditional terms as the sum of squares between (SS_B) divided by the sum of squares within (SS_W). In other words, given that

$$\eta_{BX}^2 = \frac{\Sigma(\bar{X}_J - \bar{X})^2}{\Sigma(X - \bar{X})^2} = \frac{SS_B}{SS_T} \quad \text{and} \quad \eta_{WX}^2 = \frac{\Sigma(X - \bar{X}_J)^2}{\Sigma(X - \bar{X})^2} = \frac{SS_W}{SS_T}$$

then

$$E^2 = \frac{\eta_B^2}{\eta_W^2} = \frac{SS_B}{SS_W}$$

By multiplying E^2 by the ratio of the degrees of freedom for the between- and within-eta correlations (see Appendix E), the traditional F ratio is obtained:

$$F = \frac{SS_B}{SS_W} \frac{N - J}{J - 1} = E^2 \frac{N - J}{J - 1}$$

Summary of WABA I　This geometric formulation is summarized in Table 5.4. As is shown in the table, the degree to which a single set of scores is represented by between- or within-cell scores is indicated by the between- and within-eta correlations. The ratio of these two correlations forms a cotangent

TABLE 5.4. Illustration of WABA I

	EQUATION	MATHEMATICAL INDICATOR	RANGE	ILLUSTRATIVE RESULTS Variable X	Variable Y
Degree of association of total deviations and					
Between-cell deviations	5.8	η_B	0 to 1	$\eta_{BX} = 0.267$	$\eta_{BY} = 0.605$
Within-cell deviations	5.9	η_W	0 to 1	$\eta_{WX} = 0.964$	$\eta_{WY} = 0.796$
Degree of between association relative to lack of association					
Two correlations	5.10	E	0 to ∞	$E_X = 0.277$	$E_Y = 0.760$
Adjustment for degrees of freedom	5.11	F	0 to ∞	$F_X = 0.153$	$F_Y = 1.155$

of an angle, called an E ratio, and the F ratio is a function of this ratio. When the eta correlations and degrees of freedom are known, all the key indicators for WABA I are known. From this formulation, the procedures for calculating these cosines and cotangents can be illustrated.

Illustrative Data Reduction The same set of scores used in Table 5.2 for variables X and Y is used in Tables 5.5a, 5.5b, and 5.5c to illustrate how WABA extends the total correlation. At this point, however, the focus is on the eta correlations for variables X and Y separately (WABA I). Using this

TABLE 5.5a. Calculations for a within and between analysis (variable X)

	CELL I A	B	C	CELL II D	E	CELL III F	G	SUMMATION (Σ) Numerical	Symbolic
Variable X									
Scores (X)	9	2	4	1	7	8	4	35	$\Sigma(X)$
Average ($\bar{X}$)	5	5	5	5	5	5	5	35	$\Sigma(\bar{X})$
Cell averages ($\bar{X}_J$)	5	5	5	4	4	6	6	35	$\Sigma(\bar{X}_J)$
Total deviations ($X - \bar{X}$)	4	-3	-1	-4	2	3	-1	0	$\Sigma(X - \bar{X}) = 0$
Within-cell deviations ($X - \bar{X}_J$)	4	-3	-1	-3	3	2	-2	0	$\Sigma(X - \bar{X}_J) = 0$
Between-cell deviations ($\bar{X}_J - \bar{X}$)	0	0	0	-1	-1	1	1	0	$\Sigma(\bar{X}_J - \bar{X}) = 0$
Squared total deviations ($X - \bar{X}$)^2	16	9	1	16	4	9	1	56	$\Sigma(X - \bar{X})^2$
Squared within deviations ($X - \bar{X}_J$)^2	16	9	1	9	9	4	4	52	$\Sigma(X - \bar{X}_J)^2$
Squared between deviations ($\bar{X}_J - \bar{X}$)^2	0	0	0	1	1	1	1	4	$\Sigma(\bar{X}_J - \bar{X})^2$
Cross Products for Variable X									
Total by between ($X - \bar{X}$)($\bar{X}_J - \bar{X}$)	0	0	0	4	-2	3	-1	4	$\Sigma(X - \bar{X})(\bar{X}_J - \bar{X})$
Total by within ($X - \bar{X}$)($X - \bar{X}_J$)	16	9	1	12	6	6	2	52	$\Sigma(X - \bar{X})(X - \bar{X}_J)$
Between by within ($\bar{X}_J - \bar{X}$)($X - \bar{X}_J$)	0	0	0	3	-3	2	-2	0	$\Sigma(\bar{X}_J - \bar{X})(X - \bar{X}_J)$

Calculations for Variable X

Between-eta correlation $\eta_{BX} = [\Sigma(X - \bar{X})(\bar{X}_J - \bar{X})]/\sqrt{\Sigma(X - \bar{X})^2 \Sigma(\bar{X}_J - \bar{X})^2}$

$$= \sqrt{\Sigma(\bar{X}_J - \bar{X})^2/\Sigma(X - \bar{X})^2} = 4/\sqrt{(56)(4)} = 0.267$$

Within-eta correlation $\eta_{WX} = [\Sigma(X - \bar{X})(X - \bar{X}_J)]/\sqrt{\Sigma(X - \bar{X})^2 \Sigma(X - \bar{X}_J)^2}$

$$= \sqrt{\Sigma(X - \bar{X}_J)^2/\Sigma(X - \bar{X})^2} = 52/\sqrt{(56)(52)} = 0.964$$

Between with within correlation $\eta_{BWX} = [\Sigma(\bar{X}_J - \bar{X})(X - \bar{X}_J)]/\sqrt{\Sigma(\bar{X}_J - \bar{X})^2 \Sigma(X - \bar{X}_J)^2} = 0;$

$$0/\sqrt{(4)(52)} = 0$$

TABLE 5.5b. Calculations for a within and between analysis (variable Y)

| | CELL I | | | CELL II | | CELL III | | SUMMATION (Σ) | |
	A	B	C	D	E	F	G	Numerical	Symbolic
Variable Y									
Scores (Y)	12	5	7	3	9	5	1	42	$\Sigma(Y)$
Average ($\bar{Y}$)	6	6	6	6	6	6	6	42	$\Sigma(\bar{Y})$
Cell averages ($\bar{Y}_J$)	8	8	8	6	6	3	3	42	$\Sigma(\bar{Y}_J)$
Total deviations ($Y - \bar{Y}$)	6	−1	1	−3	3	−1	−5	0	$\Sigma(Y - \bar{Y}) = 0$
Within-cell deviations ($Y - \bar{Y}_J$)	4	−3	−1	−3	3	2	−2	0	$\Sigma(Y - \bar{Y}_J) = 0$
Between-cell deviations ($\bar{Y}_J - \bar{Y}$)	2	2	2	0	0	−3	−3	0	$\Sigma(\bar{Y}_J - \bar{Y}) = 0$
Squared total deviations ($Y - \bar{Y}$)²	36	1	1	9	9	1	25	82	$\Sigma(Y - \bar{Y})^2$
Squared within deviations ($Y - \bar{Y}_J$)²	16	9	1	9	9	4	4	52	$\Sigma(Y - \bar{Y}_J)^2$
Squared between deviations ($\bar{Y}_J - \bar{Y}$)²	4	4	4	0	0	9	9	30	$\Sigma(\bar{Y}_J - \bar{Y})^2$
Cross Products for Variable Y									
Total by between ($Y - \bar{Y}$)($\bar{Y}_J - \bar{Y}$)	12	−2	2	0	0	3	15	30	$\Sigma(Y - \bar{Y})(\bar{Y}_J - \bar{Y})$
Total by within ($Y - \bar{Y}$)($Y - \bar{Y}_J$)	24	3	−1	9	9	−2	10	52	$\Sigma(Y - \bar{Y})(Y - \bar{Y}_J)$
Between by within ($\bar{Y}_J - \bar{Y}$)($Y - \bar{Y}_J$)	8	−6	−2	0	0	−6	6	0	$\Sigma(\bar{Y}_J - \bar{Y})(Y - \bar{Y}_J)$

Calculations for Variable Y

Between-eta correlation $\eta_{BY} = [\Sigma(Y - \bar{Y})(\bar{Y}_J - \bar{Y})]/\sqrt{\Sigma(Y - \bar{Y})^2\Sigma(\bar{Y}_J - \bar{Y})^2}$

$= \sqrt{\Sigma(\bar{Y}_J - \bar{Y})^2/\Sigma(Y - \bar{Y})^2} = 30/\sqrt{(82)(30)} = 0.605$

Within-eta correlation $\eta_{WY} = [\Sigma(Y - \bar{Y})(Y - \bar{Y}_J)]/\sqrt{\Sigma(Y - \bar{Y})^2\Sigma(Y - \bar{Y}_J)^2}$

$= \sqrt{\Sigma(Y - \bar{Y}_J)^2/\Sigma(Y - \bar{Y})^2} = 52/\sqrt{(82)(52)} = 0.796$

Between with within correlation $\eta_{BWY} = [\Sigma(\bar{Y}_J - \bar{Y})(Y - \bar{Y}_J)]/\sqrt{\Sigma(\bar{Y}_J - \bar{Y})^2\Sigma(Y - \bar{Y}_J)^2} = 0;$

$0/\sqrt{(30)(52)} = 0$

TABLE 5.5c. Calculations for a within and between analysis (variables X and Y)

| | CELL I | | | CELL II | | CELL III | | SUMMATION (Σ) | |
	A	B	C	D	E	F	G	Numerical	Symbolic
Variables X and Y									
Cross products									
Total ($X - \bar{X}$)($Y - \bar{Y}$)	24	3	−1	12	6	−3	5	46	$\Sigma(X - \bar{X})(Y - \bar{Y})$
Between ($\bar{X}_J - \bar{X}$)($\bar{Y}_J - \bar{Y}$)	0	0	0	0	0	−3	−3	−6	$\Sigma(\bar{X}_J - \bar{X})(\bar{Y}_J - \bar{Y})$
Within ($X - \bar{X}_J$)($Y - \bar{Y}_J$)	16	9	1	9	9	4	4	52	$\Sigma(X - \bar{X}_J)(Y - \bar{Y}_J)$

Calculations for Variables X and Y

Total correlation $\quad r_{TXY} = [\Sigma(X - \bar{X})(Y - \bar{Y})]/\sqrt{\Sigma(X - \bar{X})^2\Sigma(Y - \bar{Y})^2} = 46/\sqrt{(56)(82)} = 0.679$

Between-cell correlation $\quad r_{BXY} = [\Sigma(\bar{X}_J - \bar{X})(\bar{Y}_J - \bar{Y})]/\sqrt{\Sigma(\bar{X}_J - \bar{X})^2\Sigma(\bar{Y}_J - \bar{Y})^2} = -6/\sqrt{(4)(30)} = -0.548$

Within-cell correlation $\quad r_{WXY} = [\Sigma(X - \bar{X}_J)(Y - \bar{Y}_J)]/\sqrt{\Sigma(X - \bar{X}_J)^2\Sigma(Y - \bar{Y}_J)^2} = 52/\sqrt{(52)(52)} = 1.00$

Between component $\quad \eta_{BX}\eta_{BY}r_{BXY} = (0.267)(0.605)(-0.548) = -0.0885$

Within component $\quad \eta_{WX}\eta_{WY}r_{WXY} = (0.964)(0.796)(1.00) = 0.7673$

Total of components $\quad \eta_{BX}\eta_{BY}r_{BXY} + \eta_{WX}\eta_{WY}r_{WXY} = -0.0885 + 0.7673 = 0.679 = r_{XY}$

illustrative data for variable X, the average ($\overline{X}$) of all seven scores and the cell averages ($\overline{X}_J$) are calculated. These averages are distributed back to the source of each score. The total, within-cell, and between-cell deviations are calculated. Each of these signed deviation scores is squared, and these squared scores are then summed. The square root of these terms forms the denominator for correlations. In addition, cross products for one variable must be calculated. In WABA I, the cross products are calculated based on different representations of one variable. Specifically, the total by between, total by within, and between by within cross products are calculated. When combined with the values for the denominator, the cross products form the values for the eta correlations. These calculations are illustrated in Table 5.5a for variable X and in Table 5.5b for variable Y.

The values shown in the tables are obtained by using the four general steps for calculating any correlation, which were presented for the total correlation (Equation 5.4) in the previous section. The following shorthand method for calculating eta correlations can also be used:

$$\eta_{BX} = \sqrt{\frac{SS_B}{SS_T}} \quad \text{and} \quad \eta_{WX} = \sqrt{\frac{SS_W}{SS_T}}$$

(See sections 2 and 3 of Appendix D for a proof that this is an appropriate procedure.)

As is shown in Table 5.5a for variable X, the between- and within-eta correlations equal

$$\cos \theta_{TB} = \eta_{BX} = 0.267$$
$$\cos \theta_{TW} = \eta_{WX} = 0.964$$

The E ratio equals

$$\cot \theta_{TB} = E = \frac{\eta_{BX}}{\eta_{WX}} = \frac{0.267}{0.964} = 0.277$$

The F ratio equals

$$F = E^2 \frac{N - J}{J - 1} = (0.277)^2 \frac{4}{2} = 0.153$$

For variable Y, as is shown in Table 5.5b, the between- and within-eta correlations equal 0.605 and 0.796, the E ratio equals 0.760, and the F ratio equals 1.155.

As indicated by the eta correlations, variables X and Y both vary mainly within cells. This is confirmed by the E ratios, which are less than 1. To summarize: In WABA I, each variable is considered separately; then the eta components of the WABA equation (η_{BX}, η_{WX}, η_{BY}, and η_{WY}) are examined and compared using E and F ratios.

WABA II (Within- and Between-Cell Correlations)

The within- and between-cell correlations of WABA II differ from the eta correlations in WABA I in that the relationship between two variables is considered in WABA II. From a geometric perspective, the relationship between two variables X and Y can be expressed based on between- and within-cell vectors. Two angles between X and Y are formed in this case, one based on two between-cell vectors (BX and BY) and a second based on two within-cell vectors (WX and WY). This can be illustrated schematically as follows:

Because between- and within-cell vectors are independent, the angles between X and Y based on between- or within-cell vectors are totally free to vary. (In section 7 of Appendix D an example is provided in which a between-cell correlation equals -1 and a within-cell correlation equals $+1$.)

Degree of Association In terms of between-cell vectors, the cosine of the angle θ_{BXY} can be obtained. The range of the cosine is from -1 to $+1$ (or from 0 to 1 if only the magnitude of the cosine is considered). The equation for a between-cell correlation can be written using the general linear tensor or by substitution into the equation for the total correlation (Equation 5.4) as

$$\cos \theta_{BXY} = r_{BXY} = \frac{\Sigma(\bar{X}_J - \bar{X})(\bar{Y}_J - \bar{Y})}{\sqrt{\Sigma(\bar{X}_J - \bar{X})^2 \Sigma(\bar{Y}_J - \bar{Y})^2}} \qquad (5.12)$$

In terms of the within-cell correlation, the cosine of the angle θ_{WXY} can be written using the general linear tensor or by substitution into the equation for the total correlation (Equation 5.4) as

$$\cos \theta_{WXY} = r_{WXY} = \frac{\Sigma(X - \bar{X}_J)(Y - \bar{Y}_J)}{\sqrt{\Sigma(X - \bar{X}_J)^2 \Sigma(Y - \bar{Y}_J)^2}} \qquad (5.13)$$

Because the two angles are free to vary, the ratio of their cosines does not form a cotangent. Therefore, different procedures must be used in comparing between- and within-cell cosines from the cotangent used for eta correlations. After a consideration of a way to assess the differences between these within- and between-cell correlations, the cotangents associated with each will be defined.

Differences The differences between the within (θ_{WXY}) and between (θ_{BXY}) angles provide a basis for assessing which of the two angles is larger.

Given the symmetry of correlations around a 90° angle, the magnitude of cosines (correlations) can be expressed in the range from 0 to 1 (or in angular terms from 90° to 0°). When the between (θ_{BXY}) and within (θ_{WXY}) angles are subtracted,

$$A_{BWXY} = \theta_{WXY} - \theta_{BXY} \tag{5.14}$$

where

$$0° \le \theta \le 90°$$

what we refer to as an **angular difference of the within- and between-cell correlations** or an A_{BW} value results. In this case, the larger the resulting angular difference value, the larger the between-cell correlation. We prefer to have a positive value indicate that a between-cell correlation is larger and a negative value indicate that a within-cell correlation is larger. Since we are interested in the magnitude of correlations regardless of sign, the within and between angles will be restricted such that they vary from 0° to 90° and thus the range of the angular difference A is from $-90°$ to $+90°$. (Throughout the book radians and degrees are used interchangeably in characterizing an angle. The conversion between angles and radians is quite common and is presented in Table A.1 in Appendix A.)

The value for this angular difference can be calculated from the two correlations or cosines. Specifically, since the magnitudes of the within- and between-cell correlations are of interest, the absolute value of these cosines (or correlations) is taken. Two angles (θ_{BXY} and θ_{WXY}) are obtained from these cosines

$$\theta_{BXY} = \cos^{-1}|r_{BXY}|$$
$$\theta_{WXY} = \cos^{-1}|r_{WXY}|$$

The angles, expressed in degrees or radians, are subtracted from each other, as indicated in Equation 5.14:

$$\theta_{WXY} - \theta_{BXY} = A_{BWXY}$$

As indicated previously, because a larger angle indicates a smaller correlation, the A test takes on a negative value when the within-cell correlation is larger and a positive value when the between-cell correlation is larger in magnitude. In addition, an indicator from the statistical paradigm for expressing the difference between the within- and between-cell correlations is necessary.

In the traditional statistical paradigm, the differences between two independent correlations is obtained by converting correlations to Fisher's Z' scores and then performing a subtraction and adjusting for degrees of freedom. Because the within- and between-cell correlations are independent and can be shown to vary freely from each other (see section 7 of Appendix D), this Z test procedure is appropriate. Since we are interested in the differences between the magnitudes of these correlations, only the absolute value of the correlation is of interest. Once the absolute value is taken, each correlation is converted to a Z' score by taking the inverse hyperbolic tangent of the absolute value of the correlation (see Guilford, 1965):

$$Z'_B = \text{Tanh}^{-1}|r_B|$$
$$Z'_W = \text{Tanh}^{-1}|r_W|$$

Values for this transformation are presented in Table A.2 in Appendix A.

Once these correlations are transformed to Z' scores, a standard Z test for the differences of correlations is performed.[1] In this test, one degree of freedom is lost for the conversion to Z' scores in addition to the degrees of freedom that are lost for the correlation. For example, in the traditional case when a correlation has $N - 2$ degrees of freedom, the degrees of freedom for the Z test are $N - 3$. The formula for this Z_{BW} indicator for the **difference of the within- and between-cell correlations** is written as:

$$Z_{BW} = \frac{Z'_B - Z'_W}{\sqrt{1/(N - J - 2) + 1/(J - 3)}} \qquad (5.15)$$

In this case, as with the A test, a negative sign indicates that a within-cell correlation is greater in magnitude than a between-cell correlation and a positive sign indicates a between-cell correlation is greater than a within-cell correlation. The range of this indicator is from $-\infty$ to $+\infty$, as is required in order for a Z distribution to be approximated. The values of correlations (rather than Z' scores), as suggested by Arnold (1982), are not used in this analysis because their use does not result in Z scores that range from $-\infty$ to $+\infty$. Therefore, Fisher's (1925) transformation is retained to approximate a normal distribution.

Degree of Association and Lack of Association   In addition to the differences between the within- and between-cell correlations, indicators can be derived for each correlation in order to assess the degree of association or lack of association.

Specifically, the **between-cell R ratio** can be defined by substitution into Equation 5.2, as follows:

$$\cot \theta_{BXY} = R_{BXY} = \frac{r_{BXY}}{\sqrt{1 - r_{BXY}^2}} \qquad (5.16)$$

The t test for the correlation is dependent on the degrees of freedom for the between-cell deviations, which according to McNemar (1955) equal $J - 2$ (see

---

[1] Fisher's (1973) work demonstrates the geometric basis of this Z test. The $\hat{Z}'$ distribution is an approximation of the t distribution, which in turn is equal to a cotangent multiplied by degrees of freedom.

Appendix E). Therefore, the **between-cell *t* test** is written

$$t_{BXY} = R_{BXY}\sqrt{J - 2} \qquad (5.17)$$

The **within-cell *R* ratio** is written as

$$\cot \theta_{WXY} = R_{WXY} = \frac{r_{WXY}}{\sqrt{1 - r_{WXY}^2}} \qquad (5.18)$$

The degrees of freedom from McNemar (1955) for a within-cell correlation are known to be $N - J - 1$ (see Appendix E). Therefore, the **within-cell *t* test** is written as follows:

$$t_{WXY} = R_{WXY}\sqrt{N - J - 1} \qquad (5.19)$$

Summary of WABA II   The set of key geometric indicators for WABA II and their ranges is summarized in Table 5.6. The nature of these indicators should be clarified by the following illustration.

Illustrative Data Reduction   The synthetic data presented in Tables 5.5a, 5.5b, and 5.5c illustrate the calculation of these indicators. The only summations that are not available from performing WABA I on variables X and Y are the summations of the between- and within-cell cross products between X and Y, which are necessary for calculating the numerator of the between- and within-cell correlations. These summation results are shown in Table 5.5c; the calculations of the between- and within-cell correlations are also shown in the table. The values that result for all indicators are presented in the last column of Table 5.6.

TABLE 5.6.   Illustration of WABA II

	EQUATION	MATHEMATICAL INDICATOR	RANGE	ILLUSTRATIVE RESULTS (TABLES 5.5a, 5.5b, 5.5c)
Degree of Association				
Between-cell deviations on *X* and between-cell deviations on *Y*	5.12	r_{BXY}	−1 to 1	−0.548
Within-cell deviations on *X* and within-cell deviations on *Y*	5.13	r_{WXY}	−1 to 1	1.000
Differences				
Angular difference	5.14	A_{BW}	−90° to 90°	−0.99 radians
Adjustment for degrees of freedom	5.15	Z_{BW}	−∞ to ∞	*l*
Degree of Association Relative to Lack of Association				
Between-cell correlation				
One correlation	5.16	R_{BXY}	0 to ∞[a]	−0.655
Adjustment for degrees of freedom	5.17	t_{BXY}	0 to ∞	−0.655
Within-cell correlation				
One correlation	5.18	R_{WXY}	0 to ∞	∞
Adjustment for degrees of freedom	5.19	t_{WXY}	0 to ∞	∞

[a]See footnote to Table 5.1.

The values for the between- and within-cell correlations are

$$r_{BXY} = -0.548$$
$$r_{WXY} = 1.000$$

Given just these two correlations, the values for the indicators of their differences (A_{BW} and Z_{BW}) and the indicators for the degree of association and lack of association (R_{BXY}, t_{BXY}, R_{WXY}, t_{WXY}) can be calculated.

Specifically, the differences between the two correlations can be calculated as follows: The between and within angles are obtained

$$\theta_{BXY} = \cos^{-1}|r_{BXY}| = 56.8° = 0.99 \text{ radians}$$
$$\theta_{WXY} = \cos^{-1}|r_{WXY}| = 0° = 0 \text{ radians}$$

and the difference of these angles (A) is calculated:

$$A_{BW} = \theta_{WXY} - \theta_{BXY} = 0° - 56.8° = -56.8°$$
$$= 0 - 0.99 = -0.99 \text{ radians}$$

The negative sign indicates that the within-cell correlation is larger than the between-cell correlation.

In terms of statistical tests, the correlations are converted to Z' scores (see Table A.2 in Appendix A), as follows:

$$|r_{BXY}| = 0.548 \quad \therefore \quad Z'_{BXY} = 0.62$$
$$|r_{WXY}| = 1.00 \quad \therefore \quad Z'_{WXY} = \infty$$

The Z_{BW} value in this case is indeterminate (I). This result for the Z illustrates two key points about this indicator. First, there must be four or more cells in order for the term $1/(J - 3)$ to be meaningful and for the test to be used appropriately. Second, when a correlational value of 1 is obtained, the Z test is problematic. Both characteristics for the Z test are generally known (see Guilford, 1965). The two conditions are met when there are more than three cells and when obtained correlations do not equal 1.

For illustrative purposes, assume that in the example in Table 5.6, a correlational value of 0.99 had been obtained, four rather than three cells and nine rather than seven scores had been employed, and the between-cell correlation had equaled 0.548. The following calculations and results would then be obtained:

$$r_{BXY} = 0.548 \quad \therefore \quad Z'_B = 0.62$$
$$r_{WXY} = 0.990 \quad \therefore \quad Z'_W = 2.65$$
$$Z_{BW} = \frac{0.62 - 2.65}{\sqrt{1/1 + 1/3}} = -1.76$$

The two limitations of the Z test do not apply to the E, A, or R tests or to the F and t tests.

In terms of the indicators of the degree of association relative to lack of association, the values obtained in this case are shown in the lower right portion of Table 5.6.

Combining WABA I and II

Essentially, WABA I and WABA II determine the value of the total correlation. At one extreme, a total correlation may be completely represented by a between-cell correlation. At the other extreme, a total correlation may be completely represented by a within-cell correlation. The WABA equation demonstrates that the use of a total correlation is ambiguous because it can be based mainly on differences between or within cells. Therefore both WABA I and II must be performed in assessments of the correlation between two variables.

This point can be illustrated further by defining the between-cell components of the total correlation as

$$\eta_{BX}\eta_{BY}r_{BXY} \tag{5.20}$$

As is shown in Table 5.5c, in the illustrative case this between-cell component equals -0.0885. In addition, the within-cell component can be defined as

$$\eta_{WX}\eta_{WY}r_{WXY} \tag{5.21}$$

As is shown in Table 5.5c, in the illustrative case the within component equals 0.7673. Using the WABA equation (Equation 5.7), these two values sum to the total correlation. As should be apparent for the illustrative case, these two values add to 0.679, which was the value obtained for the total correlation based on the synthetic data presented in Table 5.2.

Summary of WABA

The entire set of indicators employed whenever WABA is used is summarized in Table 5.7. Specifically, in WABA I the relationships of within-eta correlations to between-eta correlations are estimated on a practical basis with an E ratio and on a statistical basis with an F ratio. In WABA II, the relationships of the within- and between-cell correlations are obtained by an A test in a practical sense and by a Z test in a statistical sense. In addition, in WABA II the magnitudes of the within- and between-cell correlations are examined independently of each other. Since the E, A, R indicators are not calculated with the use of degrees of freedom and are purely geometric, these indicators are used as tests of practical significance. In contrast, since degrees of freedom are included in calculations of the F, Z, t indicators, these indicators are used as tests of statistical significance. Finally, as is shown in the table, the within and between components are calculated, and they sum to the total correlation.

TABLE 5.7. Key empirical and inferential indicators in WABA

	EQUATION	INDICATOR	RANGE Metric	RANGE Geometric
WABA I Difference Tests				
η between ($df = J - 1$)	5.8	η_B	0 to 1	0° to 90° (cos)
η within ($df = N - J$)	5.9	η_W	0 to 1	0° to 90° (cos)
E ratio	5.10	$E = \eta_B / \eta_W$	0 to ∞	0° to 90° (cot)
F ratio	5.11	$F = (E^2)(N - J)/(J - 1)$	0 to ∞	—
WABA II Difference Tests				
r between ($df = J - 2$)	5.12	r_{BXY}	-1 to 1	180° to 0° (cos)
r within ($df = N - J - 1$)	5.13	r_{WXY}	-1 to 1	180° to 0° (cos)
Angular difference	5.14	$A_{BW} = \cos^{-1}|r_W| - \cos^{-1}|r_B|$	-1.57 to 1.57	$-90°$ to 90° ($\theta_W - \theta_B$)
Statistical difference	5.15	$Z_{BW} = \dfrac{Z'_B - Z'_W}{\sqrt{1/(N - J - 2) + 1/(J - 3)}}$	$-\infty$ to ∞	
WABA II Magnitude Tests				
Between R	5.16	$R_B = r_B/\sqrt{1 - r_B^2}$	0 to ∞[a]	0° to 90° (cot)
Between t	5.17	$t_B = R_B\sqrt{J - 2}$	0 to ∞	—
Within R	5.18	$R_W = r_W/\sqrt{1 - r_W^2}$	0 to ∞[a]	0° to 90° (cot)
Within t	5.19	$t_W = R_W\sqrt{N - J - 1}$	0 to ∞	—
WABA II Components				
Between	5.20	$\eta_{BX}\eta_{BY}r_{BXY}$	-1 to 1	—
Within	5.21	$\eta_{WX}\eta_{WY}r_{WXY}$	-1 to 1	—

[a]See footnote to Table 5.1.

As an extension of the general linear tensor, WABA is a geometrically based procedure for analyzing data. As Appendix F illustrates, it can be viewed as underlying the traditional one-way analysis of variance and correlational analyses. The link of WABA with multivariate methods such as multiple regression, multivariate analysis of variance, and covariance is presented in Chapter 13. The meaning of the indicators in WABA, however, depends on an alignment of theory with various values of these indicators. In Chapter 6 we will consider ideal or extreme values that correspond to theoretical conditions. In Chapter 7, we will characterize all values that can be taken on by these indicators in terms of the degree to which they approximate the ideal values presented in Chapter 6. Our purpose at this point is to provide an overview of the ways WABA can be used explicitly to consider variables and entities simultaneously in data analysis.

VARIENT APPLICATIONS OF WABA

In the varient paradigm, cells are constructed based on the assertion of a particular level of analysis, not on the values taken on by a variable of interest. For example, suppose dyads are the level of analysis of interest. Then each cell is constructed so that it contains reports or observations about or from only *two* individuals. The notion of aligning cells with entities is not new (Robinson, 1950; Schriesheim, 1980; Sheridan and Vredenburgh, 1979). However, the ability to reject an alignment (or level of analysis) based on practical significance tests is an extension of traditional approaches. This ability to test such assertions is due to the identification and development of indicators that align with the varient paradigm. An overview of the alignment is useful before we present it in Chapters 6 and 7.

Single-Level Analysis

If wholes are asserted, the focus is between entities rather than within entities; therefore, the within-cell component should make little contribution to the total correlation. One way to express this assertion of wholes is with the following WABA equation in which the within-cell component equals zero:

$$r_{TXY} = \eta_{BX}\eta_{BY}r_{BXY} + (0)(0)(0)$$

In such a case, the between-eta correlations equal 1, and the total correlation is actually a between-cell correlation:

$$r_{TXY} = r_{BXY}$$

If parts are asserted, the between-cell component should make little contribution to the total correlation, as in the following equation in which the between-cell component equals zero:

$$r_{TXY} = (0)(0)(0) + \eta_{WX}\eta_{WY}r_{WXY}$$

In this case, the within-eta correlations equal 1, and the total correlation is actually a within-cell correlation:

$$r_{TXY} = r_{WXY}$$

In the equivocal condition, both components contribute about equally:

$$r_{TXY} = \eta_{BX}\eta_{BY}r_{BXY} + \eta_{WX}\eta_{WY}r_{WXY}$$

In this case, the total correlation is an aggregate of both the within and between components. In an ideal case, this equation reduces to

$$r_{TXY} = 0.50 + 0.50 = 1$$

In the inexplicable case, both components should result in a lack of relationship between and within cells:

$$r_{TXY} = 0 + 0 = 0$$

From this illustration, the ambiguity of any empirically calculated total correlation should be clear—it can be interpreted in any one of the four ways. Therefore, to make an inference about the relationship between two variables, assumptions must be made about the eta and within- and between-cell correlations, or these indicators can be examined directly. In some traditional work, a whole condition is assumed because one score is assigned to each entity. In contrast to this assumptive approach, the illustrative synthetic data used in this chapter can be employed to illustrate how such an assumption might be tested.

For the purpose of illustration, assume that three entities are aligned with three cells (I, II, and III). In an assumptive approach, each of the three entities is characterized by an average. Therefore, the following values would be asserted for variables X and Y (see Tables 5.5a and 5.5b).

	Entity I	*Entity II*	*Entity III*
Variable X	5	4	6
Variable Y	8	6	3

In contrast, in the varient approach the assertion of a whole condition must be tested. For the synthetic data presented in the chapter, most of the variation on the scores seemed to occur within entities ($\eta_{WX} = 0.964$ and $\eta_{WY} = 0.796$). Likewise, the within-entity correlation ($r_{WXY} = 1.0$) was larger than the between-entity correlation ($r_{BXY} = -0.548$). Thus, although all variation did not occur within entities, there appeared to be more variation within than between entities. Therefore the between-entity scores do not seem to represent the scores for the three entities. Indeed, the within-cell component (0.7673) seemed to be much larger than the between-cell component (-0.0885). The total correlation (0.679) thus seems to be better represented by the within-cell deviations than by averages.

Despite the fact that an inference toward parts (valid within-entity deviations) seems reasonable for the data presented in this chapter, the decision rules for drawing such a conclusion must be made explicit. In Chapter 6, for single-level analysis, ideal conditions are defined, and in Chapter 7, interpretations for values that vary from such ideal values—as in the illustrative case in this chapter—are presented. Nevertheless, it should be apparent that WABA seems to permit the empirical testing of assumptions that are made in traditional approaches.

Multiple-Level Analysis

For an overview of multiple-level analysis, it is helpful to recognize that between- or within-cell deviations at a lower level of analysis theoretically could be used in analyses at the next higher level of analysis. However, it is important always to use between-cell and not within-cell scores at the next higher level of analysis. A set of illustrations provides a rationale for this choice. For each illustration, assume the following alignment of cells where lower-level cells (entities) are contained in higher-level cells:

HIGHER LEVEL OF ANALYSIS:	**CELL I**		**CELL II**	
LOWER LEVEL OF ANALYSIS:	*Cell 1*	*Cell 2*	*Cell 3*	*Cell 4*
Scores	$X_1 X_2$	$X_3 X_4$	$X_5 X_6$	$X_7 X_8$

In this case, cell I at the higher level of analysis contains cells 1 and 2 at the lower level of analysis, and cell II at the higher level of analysis contains cells 3 and 4. Using this construction of cells, the consequences of employing between and within scores at the higher level of analysis can now be illustrated.

The advantage of analyzing between-cell scores from a lower level of analysis at a higher level of analysis is that either parts or wholes can be obtained at the higher level. Synthetic data compatible with cross-level wholes and parts illustrate this point. First, consider the case of a cross-level wholes condition shown in the upper portion of Table 5.8. In this case, the set of lower-level between-cell scores is completely represented by between-cell scores at the higher level. Second, consider the cross-level parts case shown in the middle portion of Table 5.8. In this example, the set of lower-level between-cell scores is represented completely by the within-cell scores at the higher level. It should be apparent that between-cell scores at a lower level of analysis can result in either parts or wholes at a higher level.

In contrast, when cells are embedded in this way, within-cell scores at a lower level of analysis can result only in within-cell deviations at the next higher level. This is the case because the average of within-cell scores at the lower level is 0. If the higher-level cells are constructed so that they contain complete cells from the lower level of analysis, the between-cell scores at the higher level of analysis must also equal 0. Essentially, new information is not

TABLE 5.8. Illustration of alternative approaches to multiple-level analysis

HIGHER-LEVEL CELLS:	CELL I				CELL II			
LOWER-LEVEL CELLS:	Cell 1		Cell 2		Cell 3		Cell 4	
Cross-Level Wholes								
Higher-level scores (wholes)								
Between cell	−1	−1	−1	−1	1	1	1	1
Within cell	0	0	0	0	0	0	0	0
Lower-level scores (wholes)								
Between cell	−1	−1	−1	−1	1	1	1	1
Within cell	0	0	0	0	0	0	0	0
Cross-Level Parts								
Higher-level scores (parts)								
Between cell	0	0	0	0	0	0	0	0
Within cell	−1	−1	1	1	−1	−1	1	1
Lower-level scores (wholes)								
Between cell	−1	−1	1	1	−1	−1	1	1
Within cell	0	0	0	0	0	0	0	0
Within-Cell Scores at a Higher Level								
Higher-level scores								
Between cell	0	0	0	0	0	0	0	0
Within cell	−1	1	−1	1	−1	1	−1	1
Lower-level scores								
Between cell	A	B	C	D	E	F	G	H
Within cell	−1	1	−1	1	−1	1	−1	1

obtained by examining within-cell scores at the next higher level of analysis. This can be illustrated with the example shown in the lower portion of Table 5.8. For purposes of illustration, assume in this example that between-cell scores at a lower level of analysis take on any value (A, B, C). Nevertheless, when the within-cell scores from a lower level are examined at the higher level, the between-cell scores must equal 0, and the same within-cell scores occur at the higher level of analysis. In other words, new information is not obtained by examining the within-cell scores at a higher level of analysis.

We have just demonstrated another reason that traditional approaches tend to assume wholes for a single level of analysis of interest. At one (higher) level of analysis of interest, the total correlation is assumed to be equal to the between-cell correlation (or to represent wholes) from a lower level of analysis. From this perspective, traditional approaches, by assigning one score to each object, assume that any deviation within an entity on that score is error. Once this assumption is made, the total correlation always equals a between-cell correlation, given the WABA equation. Alternatively, it can be argued that traditional approaches also allow for an equivocal condition at a lower level of analysis and therefore for emergent effects. *Therefore, in traditional approaches (1) at the level of analysis of interest, wholes are assumed; and (2) at the lower level of analysis, a whole or an equivocal condition is assumed. In addition, traditional approaches tend to assume that entities at the level of analysis of interest are "independent." This latter assumption means that an equivocal condition is assumed at a higher level of analysis.*

Of course, we prefer to test assertions of level-specific wholes by considering both within- and between-cell scores at single and multiple levels of analysis. From our perspective, the total correlation is viewed as inappropriate and ambiguous because a variety of conditions other than those assumed by a researcher may be obtained in a set of data. In the varient paradigm, assumptions about levels of analysis or entities are viewed as theoretical assertions to be tested empirically. In the synthetic data presented in this chapter, the inference of a parts condition at one level of analysis results in attempts to test whether wholes or an equivocal condition are more likely at a lower level of analysis, and a demonstration that between-cell scores at the level of analysis of interest are error at the next higher level (that parts are always followed by an inexplicable condition at the next higher level of analysis).

Therefore, multiple-level analysis involves a sequence of tests. Specifically, once a condition is identified at a lower level of analysis, between-cell scores are examined at the next higher level of analysis. In these analyses, the total correlation at higher level of analysis always equals the between-cell correlation at a lower level of analysis. Moreover, at each level of analysis, a choice is made among the four alternatives based on data at each level. Data are thus located along the entity axis of the varient matrix using the inductive procedures described in Chapters 6 and 7.

Multiple-Variable Analysis

As indicated in Chapter 2, the different cases in multiple-variable analysis (related, generally related, generally unrelated, and unrelated) are distinguishable by the magnitude and differences between correlations. An overview of procedures for locating data along the variable axis is simplified by focusing on one set of correlations (either between or within cells) and on the three-variable case. Given three variables (X, Y, and Z), three correlations are calculated, specifically:

$$r_{BXY}, r_{BXZ}, r_{BYZ}$$

or

$$r_{WXY}, r_{WXZ}, r_{WYZ}$$

The magnitudes of one of these sets of correlations are examined by using values for R and t for within- and between-cell correlations. The three differences that must be examined in this case are

$$r_{XY} - r_{XZ}$$
$$r_{XY} - r_{YZ}$$
$$r_{XZ} - r_{YZ}$$

The meaning of differences of this type can be clarified by considering the three differences separately. Specifically, the difference $r_{XY} - r_{XZ}$ can be viewed schematically as follows:

$$
\begin{array}{c}
Z \\
\bullet \\[4pt]
r_{XZ} \ \bullet \\[10pt]
X \bullet \quad \bullet \quad \bullet\, Y \\
\quad\quad r_{XY}
\end{array}
$$

In this case, the key question is whether variable X is better explained by Z or by Y. In a similar fashion, the difference between r_{XY} and r_{YZ} indicates whether variable Y is better explained by X or by Z. Finally, the difference $r_{XZ} - r_{YZ}$ addresses the question of whether variable Z is better explained by X or by Y.

The differences between these correlations can be calculated using **angular differences (A) between correlations**, for which two correlations are converted to angles that are subtracted from each other. In general, given the symmetrical nature of correlations, the differences between the magnitudes of the correlations are of interest. Therefore, as is the case in all our calculations of the angle associated with the difference between two correlations, the absolute value of each correlation is employed and the subtraction is reversed because larger angles indicate smaller correlations. For example,

$$A_{XY-XZ} = \cos^{-1}|r_{XZ}| - \cos^{-1}|r_{XY}| \tag{5.22}$$

In this case the angular difference is based on the differences between two correlations between one variable (X) and two other variables (Y and Z), rather than on between- and within-cell correlations.

In terms of statistical tests, a standard Z test is not appropriate because the three correlations are not independent of each other. However, Hotelling (1940) developed a test for such a situation (see Guilford, 1965). When the question is whether one variable (X) is more strongly correlated with one or another variable (Y or Z), **Hotelling's t'** is calculated in the following way:

$$t' = (r_{XY} - r_{XZ})\sqrt{\frac{(N-3)(1+r_{YZ})}{2(1 - r_{YZ}^2 - r_{XY}^2 - r_{XZ}^2 + 2r_{YZ}r_{XY}r_{XZ})}} \qquad (5.23)$$

The result is a t test with 1 and $N - 3$ degrees of freedom. In this case, interest is in whether the difference between r_{XY} and r_{XZ} is statistically significant. Similar equations can be derived to test the differences $r_{XY} - r_{YZ}$ and $r_{XZ} - r_{YZ}$. Of course, given the relationship between t and Z in the statistical paradigm, Z tests can also be used to test these differences (Glass and Stanley, 1970). When sample sizes are large, the two tests (Z and t') converge; either test is appropriate, depending on the assumption one is willing to make. Finally, because correlations are symmetrical, in general we prefer to use the absolute value of correlations in the A and t' tests.

Multiple-Relationship Analysis

When an empirical identification has been made of at least a third variable that is independent of two other variables (for example, unrelated and generally unrelated cases), multiple-relationship analysis is performed. Correlations in conditions defined by values of a third variable are examined in terms of their magnitude by calculating values for R and t in each condition. The correlations or Fisher's Z' scores (such as Z_1' and Z_2') in each condition are independent. Therefore, their difference is examined by calculating values for A and Z, as indicated in the lower portion of Table 5.9.

Review of Varient Applications of WABA

The indicators employed in single- and multiple-level analyses were listed in Table 5.7. The indicators employed in multiple-variable and multiple-relationship analyses are enumerated in Table 5.9. For all these indicators, we define ideal conditions in Chapter 6; then we provide a way to assess whether data approximate these conditions in Chapter 7. First, a brief review of its traditional uses, described in Appendix F, may help to clarify the nature of WABA.

TRADITIONAL APPLICATIONS OF WABA

Since levels of analysis are not often explicitly considered, contemporary applications of the WABA equation focus almost exclusively on variables rather than on variables *and* entities.

TABLE 5.9. Key empirical and inferential indicators in multiple-variable and multiple-relationship analysis

INDICATOR		EQUATION	RANGE	
			Metric	*Geometric*
Multiple-Variable Analysis				
Magnitude tests				
Between R	$R_B = r_B / \sqrt{1 - r_B^2}$	5.16	0 to ∞^a	0° to 90° (cot)
Between t	$t_B = R_B \sqrt{J - 2}$	5.17	0 to ∞	—
Within R	$R_W = r_W / \sqrt{1 - r_W^2}$	5.18	0 to ∞^a	0° to 90° (cot)
Within t	$t_W = R_W \sqrt{N - J - 1}$	5.19	0 to ∞	—
Difference tests				
Angular difference	$A = \cos^{-1}|r_{XZ}| - \cos^{-1}|r_{XY}|$	5.22	−1.57 to 1.57	−90° to 90°
Statistical difference	t'	5.23	−∞ to ∞	—
Multiple-Relationship Analysis				
Magnitude tests				
Between R	$R_B = r_B / \sqrt{1 - r_B^2}$	5.16	0 to ∞^a	0° to 90° (cot)
Between t	$t_B = R_B \sqrt{J - 2}$	5.17	0 to ∞	—
Within R	$R_W = r_W / \sqrt{1 - r_W^2}$	5.18	0 to ∞^a	0° to 90° (cot)
Within t	$t_W = R_W \sqrt{N - J - 1}$	5.19	0 to ∞	—
Difference tests				
Angular difference	$A = \cos^{-1}|r_2| - \cos^{-1}|r_1|$	5.24	−1.57 to 1.57	−90° to 90°
Statistical difference	$Z = (Z_1' - Z_2') / \sqrt{1/(df_1 - 1) + 1/(df_2 - 1)}$	5.25	−∞ to ∞	—

^{a}See footnote to Table 5.1.

Analysis of Variance

In a traditional **analysis of variance (ANOVA)**, for example, cells are not usually formed based on a hypothesis about entities. Instead, cells are formed by the values taken on by at least one independent variable (X). As a result, this variable does not vary within cells; thus $\eta_{WX} = 0$ and $\eta_{BX} = 1$. Therefore, the WABA equation reduces to

$$r_{TXY} = \eta_{BY} r_{BXY}$$

Any variation of a dependent variable (Y) within cells has a correlation of 0 with variable X, and the between-cell scores or averages of the dependent variable serve as indicators of the degree of association between variables. Three cases demonstrate an exact mathematical link between the ANOVA and correlation.

First, in the case with two cells, the between-cell correlation must equal 1 (see Appendix F). Therefore, the following equation results:

$$r_{TXY} = \eta_{BY}$$

Two consequences of this two-cell case are of particular importance in traditional work. First, as indicated in Appendix F, the square root of the F ratio equals t, so that the F ratio is actually a test of the significance of one correlation in the ANOVA; second, given this equality, the use of dummy codes (scores of 0 and 1) for the independent variable in a correlational analysis provides identical results to the ANOVA.

Second, in the case where a dependent variable Y varies only between cells ($\eta_{BY} = 1$), the total correlation equals the between-cell correlation:

$$r_{TXY} = r_{BXY}$$

In Appendix F an illustration is presented of how to translate into a total correlation of 1 a case in which the between-eta correlation equals 1 and the between-cell correlation equals 0. One key implication of this translation is that correlational analysis can be used to estimate nonlinear relationships between variables.

Third, cases in which the general equation holds in the ANOVA ($r_{TXY} = \eta_{BY}r_{BXY}$) require the calculation of both a between-eta correlation and a between-cell correlation for an accurate interpretation of the results of an ANOVA. In this way, the ANOVA is extended rather than modified. The implications of the WABA equation for multivariate analysis are presented in Chapter 13. In Appendix F, the focus is on extending the one-way analysis of variance.

It should be apparent from this discussion that in the analysis of variance, the F ratio can be viewed as a test of the significance of the between-eta correlation. Since the within-eta correlation represents the correlation of a dependent variable with itself, it represents error in this special use of WABA. In contrast, in the varient use of WABA, within-cell deviations may be valid (as in a parts condition). In the varient approach, a larger eta correlation defines which type of deviation (within or between) should be viewed as error or not error. Therefore, since tests of practical significance (such as an E ratio) indicate which type of deviation is error, tests of statistical significance always follow tests of practical significance. In contrast, when cells are aligned with variables, the between-eta correlation is used to estimate the correlation between two variables, and the traditional F ratio is employed. However, even in this case the magnitude of the (eta) correlation should be evaluated.

Correlational Analysis

Appendix F also shows that the components of the WABA equation can be viewed as six different beta weights from three different (multiple) regression equations. The WABA equation is, after all, not a multiple regression equation involving variables, but an equation involving correlations. One key implication of this formulation is again that either the between- or the within-eta correlations can be tested for statistical significance. As a result, it is the eta correlation of greater value, as indicated by the E ratio, whose statistical significance is tested. Therefore, again tests of practical significance always precede tests of statistical significance in the varient paradigm. This requirement can be viewed as a response to the problem that correlations of very small magnitude (such as 0.08) can be significant statistically, but probably should not be interpreted as significant in a practical sense.

SUMMARY

Geometric principles underlie the general linear tensor and the calculation of correlations. In addition, WABA, which uses the calculation procedures specified by the general linear tensor, has a geometric basis from which the empirical indicators for reducing data and the procedures for performing single- and multiple-level analyses and multiple-variable and multiple-relationship analyses are derived. As a result, all indicators are based on mathematical theory. Linkages between WABA and traditional approaches have been summarized in this chapter and are discussed in greater detail in Appendix F and Chapter 13. The procedures described in the next two chapters are developed from the mathematically based indicators described in this chapter and from the varient conceptualization of variables and entities presented in Chapter 2.

REVIEW QUESTIONS

1. Why is the general linear tensor an important concept?
2. How are total correlations computed?
3. (a) What is the purpose of WABA? (b) How do WABA I and WABA II differ?
4. (a) How are within- and between-eta correlations and within- and between-cell correlations calculated? (b) What is their relationship to the E ratio and A?
5. Why is the A test viewed as a test of "practical" significance?
6. Why can traditional analytical approaches be viewed as assuming whole conditions at single levels of analysis?
7. Why should between-cell rather than within-cell deviation scores be used when moving to the next higher level of analysis?
8. What is the relationship between WABA and the analysis of variance?
9. How are the differences between correlations assessed in two independent conditions?
10. Does the use of signed deviation scores preclude a consideration of the magnitude of an event? For example, can assessment of the degree to which an entity is very high or low on a scale be assessed?

6

DEDUCTIVE ALIGNMENT

Key decision alternatives in single- and multiple-level analyses and multiple-variable and multiple-relationship analyses were identified in the varient conceptualizations presented in Chapter 2. The values taken on by empirical indicators (E, A, R, and F, Z, t) when different alternatives are more likely must now be developed. From a deductive perspective, the values of indicators that are expected to occur under ideal conditions must be derived. From an inductive perspective, the degree to which any value taken on by an indicator approximates these ideal conditions must be specified. A deductive derivation of ideal values for indicators in single- and multiple-level analyses and multiple-variable and multiple-relationship analyses is presented in this chapter.

SINGLE-LEVEL ANALYSIS

For a single level of analysis, four key alternative conditions have been presented and defined, as follows:

	BETWEEN FOCUS	WITHIN FOCUS
Wholes	Valid	Error
Parts	Error	Valid
Equivocal	Valid	Valid
Inexplicable	Error	Error

From an empirical perspective, **error** is defined **for WABA I** as the lack of deviations, and **validity for WABA I** is defined as the presence of deviations for a variable. For **WABA II, error** is defined as a zero correlation between variables, and **validity** is defined as a nonzero correlation. When these empirical definitions of error and validity are substituted into the definitions of the whole, parts, equivocal, and inexplicable conditions, **ideal empirical conditions** are derived. A presentation of this derivation for WABA I and WABA II and their combination will be helpful in explaining our approach to single-level analysis. In all cases, cells are aligned with an entity of interest (for example, if dyads are of interest, then one cell contains the scores for the two individuals in that dyad, and so on for each cell and dyad).

WABA I

In an **ideal whole condition for WABA I,** deviations within cells should be lacking and deviations between cells should be present. Therefore, in the ideal case the between-eta correlation (η_B) should equal its maximum value of 1, and the within-eta correlation (η_W) should equal its minimum value of 0. As a result, the E ratio (η_B/η_W) takes on a maximum value of infinity, and since the F ratio is a multiplicative function of the E ratio, it too equals infinity.[1]

In an **ideal parts condition for WABA I,** deviations between cells should be lacking and deviations within cells should be present. Therefore, the within-eta correlation should take on a maximum value of 1 and the between-eta correlation should take on a minimum value of 0. As a result, the E and F ratios should equal their minimum values of zero.

In an **ideal equivocal condition for WABA I,** deviations within and between cells should be equal. This equality occurs when $\eta_{BX}^2 = 0.50$ and $\eta_{WX}^2 = 0.50$ (since $\eta_{BX}^2 + \eta_{WX}^2 = 1$). Under ideal conditions, the between-eta correlation should equal 0.7071, and the within-eta correlation should also equal 0.7071. Therefore, the E ratio must equal 1 (which will be referred to as the midpoint of the range), and the F ratio as a function of the E ratio equals $(N - J)/(J - 1)$ because $E^2 = 1$.

Finally, in an **ideal inexplicable condition for WABA I,** there is a complete lack of deviations. As a result, the E and F ratios are indeterminate.

These four ideal conditions can be viewed in a somewhat different light. Specifically, a set of scores is totally represented by averages when the between-eta correlation equals 1. In this case, no information is lost by employing an average. Therefore, in the ideal whole condition, cell averages are a perfect representation of scores in the cells (since no deviations occur within cells). In contrast, when the within-eta correlation equals 1, averages are not representative of the differences in the scores, and all information is lost by their use. Therefore, in the ideal parts condition the cell averages perfectly misrepresent the scores, and within-cell deviations are used instead. The ideal equivocal condition is halfway between the ideal parts and whole conditions; therefore, both the between- and the within-cell deviations are needed to represent the total deviations. In the inexplicable condition, there are no deviations to represent.

The values taken on by the eta correlations and E and F ratios for the four ideal conditions are summarized in the upper portion of Figure 6.1. Notice that in this illustration two variables are considered in each case. In the middle portion of the figure, each case is located along the entity axis of the

---

[1] Strictly speaking, the E ratio is undefined at this point. As correlations approach 1 and 0, the E ratio approaches infinity. We will say $E = \infty$ to express the extreme of its range.

	CASE W		CASE P		CASE E		CASE I	
	Variable X	Variable Y	Variable X	Variable Y	Variable X	Variable Y	Variable X	Variable Y
Data								
η between ($df = J - 1$)	1	1	0	0	0.7071	0.7071	I[a]	—
η within ($df = N - J$)	0	0	1	1	0.7071	0.7071	—	—
E ratio	∞	∞	0	0	1	1	—	—
F ratio	∞	∞	0	0	$(N-J)/(J-1)$	$(N-J)/(J-1)$	—	—
Choices								
Wholes								
Between (valid)	#	#						
Within (error)									
Parts								
Between (error)			#	#				
Within (valid)								
Equivocal								
Between (valid)					#	#		
Within (valid)								
Inexplicable								
Between (error)							#	#
Within (error)								
Diagrams	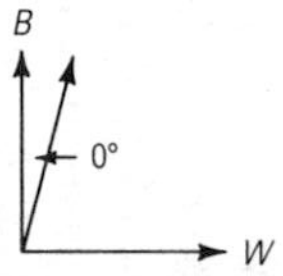 B, W (0°)		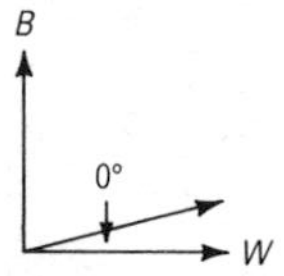 B, W (0°)		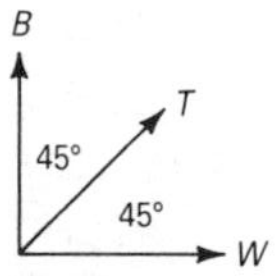 B, T, W (45°, 45°)			

[a]Indicates indeterminate.

FIGURE 6.1. Ideal conditions in WABA I

147

varient matrix by choosing among the four conditions based on both within- and between-cell indicators. For example, in case W for variable Y, the between-eta correlation is 1 (valid), and the within-cell correlation is 0 (error). This corresponds to a whole case, which is indicated in the figure by the location of the double lines and number signs. The meaning of these conditions is illustrated in geometric terms in the lower portion of the figure. In the case of wholes, the total deviations are represented completely by the between-cell vector ($\theta_{TB} = 0°$). In the case of parts, the total deviations are represented completely by the within-cell vector ($\theta_{TW} = 0°$). In the ideal equivocal condition, the total deviations are at an equal distance (45°) from the within- and between-cell vectors ($\cos 45° = 0.7071$; see Table A.1). In general, the E ratio (or cotangent) is used to distinguish among the four conditions, since it is a function of both between- and within-cell scores and indicators.

WABA II

In WABA II, the focus is on the correlation between two variables. To indicate error, the widely known proof that the correlation between two independent random variables equals zero is used. For the purpose of simplifying the ideal conditions, we prefer to view a correlational value of 1 as indicating validity. In subsequent chapters, this requirement will be relaxed.

In a whole condition, a focus between cells is valid and a focus within cells is error. Therefore, in an **ideal whole condition for WABA II**, the between-cell correlation should equal 1 and the within-cell correlation should equal 0. In this case ($r_{BXY} = 1$ and $r_{WXY} = 0$), the A value for the difference between the absolute values of these correlations takes on a maximum value of 1.57 radians, and the Z takes on a maximum value of plus infinity.

In the parts condition, between-cell deviations are error and within-cell deviations are valid. Therefore, in an **ideal parts condition for WABA II**, the between-cell correlation equals 0 and the within-cell correlation equals 1. As a result, the value for A takes on a minimum value of -1.57, and Z takes on a minimum value of minus infinity.

In the equivocal condition, differences both within and between cells are valid. Therefore, in an **ideal equivocal condition for WABA II**, both the between- and within-cell correlations take on a value of 1. As a result, the A and Z tests take on a midpoint value of 0.

In the inexplicable condition, deviations between and within entities are error. Therefore, in an **ideal inexplicable condition for WABA II**, both the within- and between-cell correlations should equal 0. In this case A and Z also take on a midpoint value of 0.

The values derived for these key indicators (within- and between-cell correlations and the A and Z tests) for the four ideal conditions are summarized in the upper portion of Figure 6.2. As should be apparent from the figure, A and Z take on their maximum values in the case of wholes and their minimum values in the case of parts. In the equivocal and inexplicable conditions, A and Z take on their midpoint values of 0. These cases and each pair of correlations are located along the entity axis by considering both the between-cell and the within-cell correlations. For example, in case W shown in

	CASE W	CASE P	CASE E	CASE I
	Variables X and Y	Variables X and Y	Variables X and Y	Variables X and Y
Data				
r between $(df = J - 2)$	1	0	1	0
r within $(df = N - J - 1)$	0	1	1	0
A	1.57	-1.57	0	0
Z	∞	$-\infty$	0	0
Choices				
Wholes				
Between (valid)	#			
Within (error)	|			
Parts				
Between (error)		#		
Within (valid)		|		
Equivocal				
Between (valid)			#	
Within (valid)			|	
Inexplicable				
Between (error)				#
Within (error)				|
Diagrams				

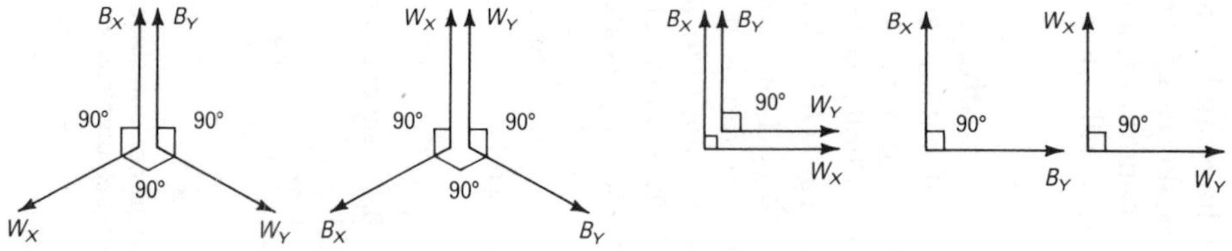

FIGURE 6.2. Ideal conditions in WABA II: Difference tests

the figure, a between-cell correlation of 1 is viewed as indicating valid between-cell deviations, and a within-cell correlation of 0 is viewed as indicating error within cells. Therefore, this case is located as wholes in the figure by the double lines and number sign. A geometric representation of the four conditions is shown in the lower portion of Figure 6.2. In the equivocal and inexplicable conditions, a two-dimensional space is defined by variables X and Y. In the parts and whole cases, a three-dimensional space is defined by X, Y, and error.

Unlike the eta correlations, however, within- and between-cell correlations take on positive and negative signs. As a result, a more complete specification of within- and between-cell correlations must be considered to define ideal conditions. The within- and between-cell correlations compatible with the ideal whole, parts, equivocal, and inexplicable conditions can be listed as shown in Table 6.1. Notice that for each of these cases, the absolute value is taken of each correlation before A and Z are calculated. This is appropriate because our interest is in whether one correlation is greater than the other correlation in magnitude, and not in sign. Also, as mentioned before, a positive value for A always indicates a greater between-cell correlation, and a negative value for A always indicates a greater within-cell correlation.

It may be helpful to view the four ideal conditions in a somewhat different way. In the whole and parts conditions, respectively, a between-cell or within-cell correlation is valid. In other words, one correlation in these two

TABLE 6.1.   Set of plausible alternative ideal cases for WABA II

	PLAUSIBLE ALTERNATIVES			
	A	*B*	*C*	*D*
Wholes				
Between-cell correlation	1.00	−1.00		
Within-cell correlation	0	0		
A	1.57	1.57		
Z	∞	∞		
Parts				
Between-cell correlation	0	0		
Within-cell correlation	1.00	−1.00		
A	−1.57	−1.57		
Z	−∞	−∞		
Equivocal				
Between-cell correlation	1.00	1.00	−1.00	−1.00
Within-cell correlation	1.00	−1.00	1.00	−1.00
A	0	0	0	0
Z	0	0	0	0
Inexplicable				
Between-cell correlation	0			
Within-cell correlation	0			
A	0			
Z	0			

conditions equals 0, and little information about the correlation between two variables is lost by interpreting only the nonzero correlation. In contrast, in the equivocal condition no choice is possible between these two correlations. According to Dansereau et al. (1982a), attempts are sometimes made to interpret the equivocal condition at one level of analysis. Such interpretations are called **double fallacies** because the interpretation is usually that there are parts and wholes at one level of analysis at the same time on one variable. Such a set of results is equivocal precisely because it is impossible to decide whether parts or wholes better represent the data at that level of analysis. In general, the angular difference (A) is used to distinguish among the four conditions, since it is a function of both within and between indicators.

In addition to a consideration of the differences between within-cell and between-cell correlations, the magnitude of these correlations must also be examined, because they are free to vary from each other (see section 7 of Appendix D). In an ideal whole condition, R and t equal infinity for a between-cell correlation and 0 for a within-cell correlation. In an ideal parts condition, R and t equal 0 for a between-cell correlation and infinity for a within-cell correlation. In the ideal inexplicable case, the R and t for both the between- and within-cell correlations equal 0. In the ideal equivocal case, given two correlations of 1, R and t should equal infinity for the within- and between-cell correlations. These values are shown in the upper portion of Figure 6.3, and they are represented geometrically in the lower portion of the figure.

Combining WABA I and II

The within and between components for the ideal cases for WABA I and II can be calculated in the following way. In the case of wholes, the total correlation equals 1 because the between-cell component equals 1 and the within-cell component equals 0. In the case of parts, the total correlation equals 1 because the within-cell component equals 1 and the between-cell component equals 0. In the equivocal condition, both the between- and the within-cell components equal 0.50, and the total correlation equals 1. In the inexplicable condition, the between and within components and the total correlation equal 0. In addition to the presentation in Figure 6.3, the following summary may be helpful:

WABA equation	(η_{BX})	(η_{BY})	(r_{BXY}) +	(η_{WX})	(η_{WY})	(r_{WXY}) = r_{XY}
Wholes	(1)	(1)	(1) +	(0)	(0)	(0) = 1
Parts	(0)	(0)	(0) +	(1)	(1)	(1) = 1
Equivocal	(0.7071)	(0.7071)	(1) +	(0.7071)	(0.7071)	(1) = 1
Inexplicable	(I)	(I)	(0) +	(I)	(I)	(0) = 0

It is convenient to remember that the ranges for the E ratio and A test are constructed such that the ideal whole condition defines one extreme of the range, and the ideal parts condition defines the other extreme. The equivocal condition is in the middle of the range. This alignment between conditions and

	CASE W	CASE P	CASE E	CASE I
	Variables X and Y	Variables X and Y	Variables X and Y	Variables X and Y
Between-cell values				
R_{BXY}	∞ ∞	0 0	∞ ∞	0 0
t_{BXY}				
Within-cell values				
R_{WXY}	0 0	∞ ∞	∞ ∞	0 0
t_{WXY}				
Components				
Between	1	0	0.50	0
Within	0	1	0.50	0
Diagrams				
Between				
Within				

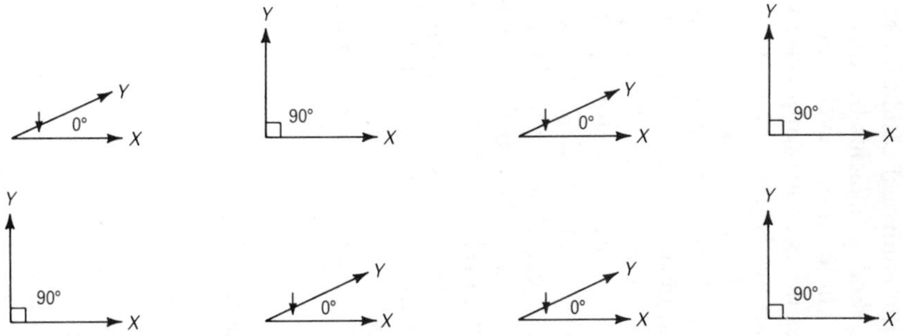

FIGURE 6.3. Ideal conditions in WABA II: Magnitude tests and components

the ranges of the E ratio and of A is illustrated as follows:

	WABA I (E RATIO)	WABA II (A)
Wholes	∞	1.57
Equivocal	1	0
Parts	0	−1.57

This alignment will be particularly useful in attempting to assess the degree to which a set of results is more compatible with the ideal wholes or parts conditions (see Chapter 7). Illustrating some of the distributions of scores that are compatible with each condition may clarify these four ideal conditions.

Numerical Illustration of Ideal Cases

A variety of distributions of scores will result in the ideal values shown for the eta correlations, the between- and within-cell correlations, and the E, A, R, and F, Z, t sequence of tests. For example, distributions of scores compatible with the ideal whole, parts, equivocal, and inexplicable conditions are shown in Table 6.2. A greater amount of detail is shown in the table for the ideal equivocal case to facilitate the calculation of the between- and within-eta correlations, which both equal 0.7071. Of particular interest in this table is that the same cells, entities, and components are used to illustrate all the ideal conditions. The various distributions of scores allow for a distinction among the ideal conditions. In other words, the values for E, A, R, and F, Z, t differ, depending on which of the distributions are examined. Therefore, even with ideal data, an empirically based choice between the four conditions must be made to interpret a set of obtained scores.

In general, in order to simplify the illustrations in this chapter, the notions of indeterminate and zero relationships are used interchangeably. One advantage of using examples with a lack of deviations either within or between cells is that in these ideal conditions, it is obvious that only one set of deviations (or correlations) need be considered. Numerous examples can be constructed for these ideal conditions in addition to the ones shown in Table 6.2.

MULTIPLE-LEVEL ANALYSIS

Ideal whole, parts, equivocal, and inexplicable conditions have been defined for any level of analysis. A consideration of these ideal cases for two levels of analysis using the principles presented in Chapter 2 illustrates the way ideal conditions are derived for multiple-level analysis. In the case of two levels of analysis, eight conditions are of interest (see Table 2.1). The E ratio and A are used as summarizing indicators at each level of analysis because whole and parts conditions are indicated by extreme values of these indicators.

The simplest case in multiple-level analysis occurs when wholes ($E = \infty$, $A = 1.57$) are obtained at a lower level of analysis. In this case, the between-cell

TABLE 6.2. Numerical illustration of ideal cases for single-level analysis

LEVEL: COMPONENTS:	CELL I		CELL II		CELL III		Summations Σ
	A	**B**	**C**	**D**	**E**	**F**	
Ideal Whole Condition							
Variable X	6	6	7	7	8	8	42
Variable Y	6	6	7	7	8	8	42
Ideal Parts Condition							
Variable X	5	9	6	8	4	10	42
Variable Y	5	9	6	8	4	10	42
Ideal Equivocal Condition							
Variable X							
X	3	5	6	10	6	12	42
$\bar{X}$	7	7	7	7	7	7	42
$\bar{X}_J$	4	4	8	8	9	9	42
$X - \bar{X}$	−4	−2	−1	3	−1	5	0
$\bar{X}_J - \bar{X}$	−3	−3	1	1	2	2	0
$X - \bar{X}_J$	−1	1	−2	2	−3	3	0
$(X - \bar{X})^2$	16	4	1	9	1	25	56
$(\bar{X}_J - \bar{X})^2$	9	9	1	1	4	4	28
$(X - \bar{X}_J)^2$	1	1	4	4	9	9	28
Variable Y							
Y	3	5	6	10	6	12	42
Ideal Inexplicable Condition							
Variable X	7	7	7	7	7	7	42
Variable Y	7	7	7	7	7	7	42

Note: The values for E, A, R and F, Z, t obtained for each condition are presented in Figures 6.1, 6.2, and 6.3.

deviations represent the entire set of scores and can be viewed as total scores at the next higher level of analysis. The results of a WABA at the next higher level can result in whole ($E = \infty$, $A = 1.57$), parts ($E = 0$, $A = -1.57$), or equivocal ($E = 1$, $A = 0$) conditions (or cross-level wholes, parts, or level-specific whole conditions, respectively). These three ideal multiple-level conditions can be defined as follows:

	Lower Level		Higher Level	
Ideal cross-level wholes	$E = \infty$	$A = 1.57$	$E = \infty$	$A = 1.57$
Ideal cross-level parts	$E = \infty$	$A = 1.57$	$E = 0$	$A = -1.57$
Ideal level-specific wholes	$E = \infty$	$A = 1.57$	$E = 1$	$A = 0$

When parts are obtained at a lower level of analysis ($E = 0$, $A = -1.57$), the between-cell scores are equal to 0 (error) at this level of analysis and therefore should be equal to 0 at the next higher level of analysis. Therefore, an inexplicable condition should occur ($E = I$, $A = 0$) at the next higher level of analysis, since parts are level-specific. This ideal multiple-level condition is defined as follows:

	Lower Level		Higher Level	
Ideal level-specific parts	$E = 0$	$A = -1.57$	$E = I$	$A = 0$

In contrast, an analysis at a lower level may result in an equivocal ($E = 1, A = 0$) condition. There are at least two ways in which this condition at a lower level of analysis may result in the emergence of a parts or whole condition at a higher level. First, given equivocal results at a lower level of analysis, the between-cell deviations can be examined at a higher level. As a result, either an ideal whole ($E = \infty, A = 1.57$) or parts ($E = 0, A = -1.57$) condition can occur at a higher level of analysis. Second, an equivocal condition may be obtained at a lower level of analysis and the components at this lower level of analysis may be examined in order to assess whether they are components of entities at the higher level. Therefore, the total deviations (components) at a lower level of analysis are employed at a higher level in order to assess whether these deviations are components at the higher level. In this case, either wholes or parts are viable in an analysis based on the components at a lower level of analysis. These two conditions can be defined as follows:

	Lower Level		Higher Level	
Ideal equivocal-emergent wholes	$E = 1$	$A = 0$	$E = \infty$	$A = 1.57$
Ideal equivocal-emergent parts	$E = 1$	$A = 0$	$E = 0$	$A = -1.57$

Finally, when an inexplicable condition ($E = I, A = 0$) is obtained at a lower level of analysis, another type of emergent condition can occur. In the ideal inexplicable case, at least in terms of WABA I, there is a lack of deviations within and between cells. As a result, additional scores would have to be added to the original set of scores to obtain deviations; then an ideal whole ($E = \infty, A = 1.57$) or parts ($E = 0, A = -1.57$) condition can be obtained. These two conditions can be defined as follows:

	Lower Level		Higher Level	
Ideal inexplicable-emergent wholes	$E = I$	$A = 0$	$E = \infty$	$A = 1.57$
Ideal inexplicable-emergent parts	$E = I$	$A = 0$	$E = 0$	$A = -1.57$

This set of eight ideal conditions for multiple-level analysis can be summarized along the entity axis of a varient matrix, as shown in Table 6.3, using values for E and A. Using these two indicators, eta correlations, within- and between-cell correlations, and F and Z tests are derivable.

TABLE 6.3. Illustration of ideal cross-level, emergent, and level-specific results for two levels of analysis

ENTITY AXIS	CROSS-LEVEL				LEVEL-SPECIFIC				EMERGENT[a]				EMERGENT[a]			
	Wholes		Parts		Wholes		Parts		Wholes		Parts		Wholes		Parts	
	E	A	E	A	E	A	E	A	E	A	E	A	E	A	E	A
Higher Level[b]																
Wholes	∞	1.57							∞	1.57			∞	1.57		
Parts			0	−1.57							0	−1.57			0	−1.57
Equivocal					1	0										
Inexplicable							I	0								
Lower Level																
Wholes	∞	1.57	∞	1.57	∞	1.57										
Parts							0	−1.57								
Equivocal									1	0	1	0				
Inexplicable													I	0	I	0

[a]Units are added to examine higher levels of analysis in these cases.
[b]All analyses at higher levels are based on between-cell scores from the lower level of analysis.

Numerical Illustration of Ideal Cases

A set of numerical illustrations for multiple-level analysis is presented in Table 6.4. The first four illustrations, shown in the upper portion of the table, are compatible with the ideal cross-level whole and parts and level-specific whole and parts conditions. Notice that in these four cases, six cells are defined at the lower level of analysis and three cells are defined at the higher level of analysis. Any one of these four ideal cases can occur given this configuration of cells. The values for the key indicators (E and A) for these cases were summarized in Table 6.3 and will not be further explained here.

The lower portion of Table 6.4 illustrates the ideal emergent conditions. When an equivocal condition is obtained at a lower level of analysis, both between-cell and within-cell scores should be considered. As a result, the total scores can be viewed as potentially representing the components at higher levels of analysis. An equivocal condition at a lower level of analysis is illustrated in the equivocal-emergent case shown in Table 6.4. If additional scores and entities are added, these original scores may be viewed as components at a higher level of analysis. In fact, an ideal whole condition at the higher level of analysis occurs in this case, as is shown in Table 6.4. Notice that the higher level of analysis results in more scores than the lower level. The need for additional entities and scores illustrates that the analysis at the lower level may have been incomplete. An analysis to test for emergent wholes will be illustrated in Chapter 10.

A similar type of numerical illustration for emergents, for the case in which an inexplicable condition is obtained at a lower level of analysis, is illustrated in the lower portion of Table 6.4. In this case, the between-cell scores are identical to each other and to the grand mean at a lower level of analysis. However, as shown in the table, if the four scores on each variable actually represent only one whole entity, then the addition of more entities and

TABLE 6.4. Numerical illustration of ideal cases for multiple-level analysis

HIGHER LEVEL OF ANALYSIS:	CELL I		CELL II		CELL III	
LOWER LEVEL OF ANALYSIS:	*Cell A*	*Cell B*	*Cell C*	*Cell D*	*Cell E*	*Cell F*

Cross-Level Wholes												
Variable *X*	6	6	6	6	7	7	7	7	8	8	8	8
Variable *Y*	6	6	6	6	7	7	7	7	8	8	8	8
Cross-Level Parts												
Variable *X*	5	5	9	9	6	6	8	8	4	4	10	10
Variable *Y*	5	5	9	9	6	6	8	8	4	4	10	10
Level-Specific Wholes												
Variable *X*	3	3	5	5	6	6	10	10	6	6	12	12
Variable *Y*	3	3	5	5	6	6	10	10	6	6	12	12
Level-Specific Parts												
Variable *X*	5	9	5	9	6	8	6	8	4	10	4	10
Variable *Y*	5	9	5	9	6	8	6	8	4	10	4	10

Equivocal-Emergent

Higher-level (wholes)	*Cell 1*	*Cell 2*	*Cell 3*	*Cell 4*	*Cell 5*	*Cell 6*
Variable *X*	3 3	5 5	6 6	10 10	6 6	12 12
Variable *Y*	3 3	5 5	6 6	10 10	6 6	12 12
Lower-level (equivocal)	*Cell A*		*Cell B*		*Cell C*	
Variable *X*	3	5	6	10	6	12
Variable *Y*	3	5	6	10	6	12

Inexplicable-Emergent

Higher-level (wholes)	*Cell 1*	*Cell 2*
Variable *X*	1 1 1 1	2 2 2 2
Variable *Y*	1 1 1 1	2 2 2 2
Lower level (inexplicable)	*Cell A*	*Cell B*
Variable *X*	1 1	1 1
Variable *Y*	1 1	1 1

scores will result in between-cell deviations and, in this case, in wholes at a higher level of analysis. In general, additional scores are usually necessary if interest is in examining emergents at a higher level of analysis. It is also possible that scores may be distributed in a capricious fashion at a lower level. In this latter case, WABA II can be used to identify an emergent parts or whole condition at a higher level of analysis.

MULTIPLE-VARIABLE ANALYSIS

Now that ideal conditions along the entity axis of the varient matrix have been defined, ideal conditions must also be derived for the variable axis. WABA II is a two-variable case, and the alternatives are the related and unrelated cases (see Chapter 2). To allow for an inference of either parts or wholes, one correlation should indicate that two variables are related and one should indicate that the same two variables are not related. The two-variable case is straightforward in that as the R or t test for one correlation reaches its maximum value, the other correlation results in a minimum value; consequently, the difference between the within-cell and between-cell correlations is at a maximum. A similar description of the equivocal and inexplicable conditions is possible using the two alternatives in the two-variable case.

As more variables are considered, the process of generating ideal conditions increases in complexity. To simplify the presentation and yet retain a somewhat general illustration, we will use a chosen focus (either between or within entities or cells). We assume for this purpose that all the variables are unrelated for the other focus. An additional simplification results by focusing on the three-variable case.

For a chosen focus and three variables in the **ideal related case**, and using for the moment the general assertion that an ideal valid correlation equals 1, the correlations among all the variables should equal 1. Therefore, the magnitude indicators (R and t) take on a maximum value of infinity and there are no differences between any of the correlations.

In the **ideal generally related case**, the correlation between two of the variables equals 0 and these two variables are correlated (0.7071) with a third variable. Presumably, in an ideal condition, two independent variables should completely determine a third variable. Although other ideal formulations are clearly possible in the three-variable case, we prefer to define this ideal condition as containing two correlations that both take on a value of 0.7071 and one correlation that takes on a value of 0. Therefore, the practical magnitude indicator R equals 1 and the value for t is determined by degrees of freedom for two of the correlations. The A tests of the differences between these two correlations of 0.7071 and the zero correlation take on a value of 45° (0.785 radians), and t' equals infinity.

In the **ideal generally unrelated case**, the correlation between two of the variables equals 1, and the correlation of these two variables with a third variable equals 0. Therefore, the magnitude indicators (R and t) take on a maximum value of infinity for one of the correlations and a minimum value for the two other correlations. As a result, two of the differences between the correlations take on a maximum value in terms of magnitude ($A = 1.57$, $t' = \infty$), and one difference equals 0 ($A = 0$, $t' = 0$).

In the **ideal unrelated case**, the three correlations among three variables equal 0. Therefore, the magnitude indicators (R and t) take on their minimum value of 0, and differences between any of the correlations equal 0.

The ideal values taken on by the various indicators in each of these four general cases (related, generally related, generally unrelated, and unrelated) are summarized in Table 6.5. As shown in the table, the conditions are distinguishable from each other by the number of zero and nonzero correlations. The magnitude and difference indicators allow for an empirical distinction to be made among these cases.

TABLE 6.5. Illustration of ideal conditions along a three-variable axis (chosen focus)

VARIABLE AXIS

	Related	Generally Related			Generally Unrelated			Unrelated
	$X \leftrightarrow Y \leftrightarrow Z$	$(X \perp Y) \leftrightarrow Z$	$(X \perp Z) \leftrightarrow Y$	$(Y \perp Z) \leftrightarrow X$	$(X \leftrightarrow Y) \perp Z$	$(X \leftrightarrow Z) \perp Y$	$(Y \leftrightarrow Z) \perp X$	$X \perp Y \perp Z$
Correlations								
r_{XY}	1	0	0.7071	0.7071	1	0	0	0
r_{XZ}	1	0.7071	0	0.7071	0	1	0	0
r_{YZ}	1	0.7071	0.7071	0	0	0	1	0
Magnitude Tests								
R values for (r)								
XY	∞	0	1	1	∞	0	0	0
XZ	∞	1	0	1	0	∞	0	0
YZ	∞	1	1	0	0	0	∞	0
t values for (r)								
XY	∞	0	$\sqrt{df}$	$\sqrt{df}$	∞	0	0	0
XZ	∞	$\sqrt{df}$	0	$\sqrt{df}$	0	∞	0	0
YZ	∞	$\sqrt{df}$	$\sqrt{df}$	0	0	0	∞	0
Difference Tests								
A values								
$-(|XY| - |XZ|)$	0	-0.785	0.785	0	1.57	-1.57	0	0
$-(|XY| - |YZ|)$	0	-0.785	0	0.785	1.57	0	-1.57	0
$-(|XZ| - |YZ|)$	0	0	-0.785	0.785	0	1.57	-1.57	0
t' values								
$|XY| - |XZ|$	0	$-\infty$	∞	(0)	∞	$-\infty$	0	0
$|XY| - |YZ|$	0	$-\infty$	(0)	∞	∞	0	$-\infty$	0
$|XZ| - |YZ|$	0	(0)	$-\infty$	∞	0	∞	$-\infty$	0

TABLE 6.6. Numerical illustration of ideal conditions for multiple-variable analysis (chosen focus)

Entity	RELATED CASE Variable X	Variable Y	Variable Z	GENERALLY RELATED CASE Variable X	Variable Y	Variable Z	GENERALLY UNRELATED CASE Variable X	Variable Y	Variable Z	UNRELATED CASE Variable X	Variable Y	Variable Z
A	1	1	1	2	3	3	1	1	1	1	1	1
B	2	2	2	2	3	3	1	1	1	1	1	2
C	3	3	3	3	2	3	2	2	1	1	2	1
D	4	4	4	3	2	3	2	2	1	1	2	2
E	5	5	5	1	2	1	1	1	2	2	1	1
F	6	6	6	1	2	1	1	1	2	2	1	2
G	7	7	7	2	1	1	2	2	2	2	2	1
H	8	8	8	2	1	1	2	2	2	2	2	2
Correlation												
r_{XY}	1			0			1			0		
r_{XZ}	1			0.7071			0			0		
r_{YZ}	1			0.7071			0			0		

Numerical Illustration of Ideal Cases

Distributions of scores compatible with the related, generally related, generally unrelated, and unrelated cases are presented in Table 6.6. As shown in the table, given a chosen focus, scores from one set of eight entities can be compatible with any of the four conditions shown in the table.

MULTIPLE-RELATIONSHIP ANALYSIS

When at least one variable is distinguishable from other variables (as in the generally unrelated and unrelated cases), ideal contingent and multiplexed conditions can be defined. In a multiplexed condition, the same results are predicted for all conditions defined by a third variable. In an **ideal multiplexed case**, a correlation of 1 is expected in each condition. Therefore, in each condition defined by values of at least a third variable, the magnitude tests (R and t) take on maximum values of infinity. Likewise, the differences (as indicated by A and Z values) between the correlations from different conditions equal 0. In an **ideal contingent case**, the correlation between two variables should differ maximally depending on the values taken on by a third variable. For example, in the case of a third variable that defines two conditions Z_1 and Z_2, the correlation in one condition (Z_1) should equal 1 and the magnitude tests (R and t) should take on maximum value of infinity. In the second condition (Z_2) the correlation should equal 0, and therefore the magnitude tests (R and t) should take on a minimum value of 0. Finally, the differences between the correlations in the two conditions Z_1 and Z_2 should take on their maximum values ($A = 1.57$ and $Z = \infty$).

An illustrative case in which two conditions are defined by values of a third variable is presented in the upper portion of Table 6.7. There are two contingent cases illustrated in the table; case A involves a relationship that holds in condition Z_1 but not in condition Z_2, and case B involves a relationship that holds in condition Z_2 but not in condition Z_1. In the two multiplexed cases shown in the table, the same correlational values are obtained in each condition defined by values of a third variable (Z). The values under these ideal conditions for the magnitude and difference tests are also shown in the upper portion of the table.

Additional analyses are necessary when each condition defined by a third variable is viewed as creating a new study. For example, when two conditions are defined, the results obtained can be considered to be from two different studies. From this perspective, the level of analysis underlying the results in each study should be assessed. Specifically, for the case in which two studies are defined, within- and between-cell correlations are obtained: two for condition Z_1 and two for condition Z_2, making a total of four correlations. The comparisons of the within- and between-cell correlations that can be made and tested are listed in the matrix shown in Figure 6.4.

In this case, two of the six possible comparisons (those contained in the triangles in Figure 6.4) involve an entity focus or a consideration of the differences between within- and between-entity correlations in each condition

TABLE 6.7.   Illustration of ideal multiplexed and contingent cases for two condition case

| | VARIABLE FOCUS | | | |
| | Contingent | | Multiplexed | |
	Case A	Case B	Case C	Case D
Correlations				
r in Condition Z_1 [$r(1)$]	1	0	0	1
r in Condition Z_2 [$r(2)$]	0	1	0	1
Magnitude Tests				
R in Condition Z_1	∞	0	0	∞
R in Condition Z_2	0	∞	0	∞
t in Condition Z_1	∞	0	0	∞
t in Condition Z_2	0	∞	0	∞
Difference Tests [$r(1) - r(2)$]				
A	1.57	−1.57	0	0
Z	∞	−∞	0	0

	ENTITY FOCUS						
	Contingent				Multiplexed		Error
Condition Z_1:	E or I	E or I	Parts	Wholes	Parts	Wholes	E or I
Condition Z_2:	Parts	Wholes	E or I	E or I	Parts	Wholes	E or I
Inside Conditions							
Condition Z_1							
r between [$r_B(1)$]	0	0	0	1	0	1	0
r within [$r_W(1)$]	0	0	1	0	1	0	0
A	0	0	−1.57	1.57	−1.57	1.57	0
Z	0	0	−∞	∞	−∞	∞	0
Condition Z_2							
r between [$r_B(2)$]	0	1	0	0	0	1	0
r within [$r_W(2)$]	1	0	0	0	1	0	0
A	−1.57	1.57	0	0	−1.57	1.57	0
Z	−∞	∞	0	0	−∞	∞	0
Among Conditions							
$r_B(1)$ minus $r_W(2)$							
A	−1.57	0	0	1.57	−1.57	1.57	0
Z	−∞	0	0	∞	−∞	∞	0
$r_B(2)$ minus $r_W(1)$							
A	0	1.57	−1.57	0	−1.57	1.57	0
Z	0	∞	−∞	0	−∞	∞	0

Note: E indicates equivocal and I indicates inexplicable.

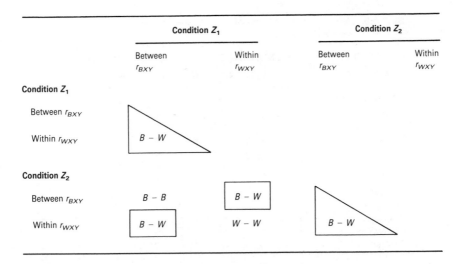

	Condition Z_1		Condition Z_2	
	Between r_{BXY}	Within r_{WXY}	Between r_{BXY}	Within r_{WXY}
Condition Z_1				
Between r_{BXY}				
Within r_{WXY}	$B - W$			
Condition Z_2				
Between r_{BXY}	$B - B$	$B - W$		
Within r_{WXY}	$B - W$	$W - W$	$B - W$	

FIGURE 6.4. Comparisons of correlations from two settings

defined by values of a third variable. In addition, a between-cell correlation in condition Z_1 can be compared to a within-cell correlation in condition Z_2. Likewise, a within-cell correlation in condition Z_1 can be compared to a between-cell correlation in condition Z_2. (The last two comparisons are contained in the rectangles shown in the matrix in Figure 6.4.) The ideal results that can occur from this type of entity-focused analysis are shown in the lower portion of Table 6.7. For example, in a multiplexed case, an ideal parts condition can be obtained in both conditions. As a result, all the indicators are at a minimum value. For the purpose of consistency in all analyses, the within-cell correlation is always subtracted from a between-cell correlation.

In addition to these four comparisons of within- and between-cell correlations, between-cell correlations in condition Z_1 can be compared to between-cell correlations in condition Z_2. Likewise, the within-cell correlations in condition Z_1 can be compared to the within-cell correlations in condition Z_2. These comparisons involve a focus on variables, and the ideal values presented in the upper portion of Table 6.7 apply to comparisons of this type. (The uses of these ideal conditions and associated tests are illustrated in Chapter 11.)

Numerical Illustration of Ideal Cases

Although a number of distributions of scores are compatible with the ideal multiplexed and contingent conditions, a focus on ideal whole conditions provides one example. In this ideal case, the within-cell scores are ignored because they result in indeterminate correlations. Distributions of scores compatible with the multiplexed and contingent conditions are presented in Table 6.8. In both cases, the conditions are formed by the between-cell values

TABLE 6.8. Numerical illustration of ideal cases for multiple-relationship analysis

CONDITIONS: ENTITIES:	CONDITION Z_1				CONDITION Z_2			
	A	**B**	**C**	**D**	**E**	**F**	**G**	**H**
Multiplexed Case								
Z between	1	1	1	1	−1	−1	−1	−1
Y between	−1	−1	1	1	−1	−1	1	1
X between	−1	−1	1	1	−1	−1	1	1
Z within	0	0	0	0	0	0	0	0
Y within	0	0	0	0	0	0	0	0
X within	0	0	0	0	0	0	0	0
Contingent Case								
Z between	1	1	1	1	−1	−1	−1	−1
Y between	−1	−1	1	1	−1	−1	1	1
X between	−1	1	−1	1	−1	−1	1	1
Z within	0	0	0	0	0	0	0	0
Y within	0	0	0	0	0	0	0	0
X within	0	0	0	0	0	0	0	0

of variable Z. Moreover, in both cases the correlations of variable Z with variables X and Y equal 0. In the multiplexed example, however, the between-cell correlation between X and Y equals 1 in both conditions. In contrast, in the contingent example, variables X and Y are correlated 0 in condition Z_1 and 1 in condition Z_2. This illustration demonstrates that tests for contingent relationships are necessary only when the correlation between the variables of interest (X and Y) is less than 1 across all conditions. Finally, as should be apparent from the table, since conditions are defined in the same way for both cases (Z_1 and Z_2), it is the correlation in each condition that indicates whether a relationship should be viewed as contingent or multiplexed.

SUMMARY

The ideal values defined for a single level of analysis permit a distinction to be made among the whole, parts, equivocal, and inexplicable conditions based on the values taken on by the E, A, R, and F, Z, t indicators. These key values also permit a distinction to be made among eight formulations of multiple levels of analysis. The ideal values presented for multiple-variable analysis permit a distinction between the related, generally related, generally unrelated, and unrelated cases based on the values taken on by the R, t and A, t' indicators. The ideal values defined for multiple-relationship analysis allow distinctions between contingent and multiplexed cases based on the values taken on by the R, t and A, Z indicators. The focus of the next chapter is on assessing the degree to which less than ideal values approximate these ideal conditions.

REVIEW QUESTIONS

1. In what two ways is error defined in WABA?

2. When all the variation in a variable occurs within entities, will the E or the A indicate an ideal parts condition and equal 0?

3. When the between-cell correlation between two variables equals 1 and the within-cell correlation equals 0, as in an ideal whole condition, will the A or the R equal 1.57 radians?

4. What is a double fallacy, and how does the varient approach address this problem?

5. What are three ways a total correlation of 1 could be interpreted at one level of analysis (for example, at the group level)?

6. What is an example of a distribution of scores compatible with the ideal whole condition?

7. How would a distribution of scores compatible with an ideal cross-level whole, dyad, and group formulation appear?

8. What are three ways a between-cell correlation of 1 (and a within-cell correlation of 0) can be interpreted at a higher level of analysis?

9. What problem would arise if a multiple regression equation were imposed on an *ideal* related variables case?

10. If a correlation of 1 were obtained across a set of conditions, would the relationship be multiplexed with or contingent on the conditions in the set of data?

7

INDUCTIVE ALIGNMENT

From an inductive and data analytic perspective, the entire range of values that can be taken on by key empirical indicators must be considered in order to assess the degree to which any obtained value of an indicator approximates the ideal conditions presented in Chapter 6. For example, assume that an indicator has a range from 0 to 1 and that a value of 0.87 is obtained. If the range of this indicator is divided into intervals, the value 0.87 becomes interpretable. From a practical perspective, a value of 0.87 seems closer to 1 than to 0. However, from a statistical perspective, a value of 0.87 may be attributable to statistical artifacts (or to a small number of degrees of freedom). Therefore, tests of both practical and statistical significance are required. An overview of our approach to these two types of tests of significance may be helpful before we describe the intervals used to locate data in a varient matrix.

TESTS OF SIGNIFICANCE

Statistical Significance

In terms of tests of statistical significance, Bakan (1966), among others, has suggested that when the statistical paradigm is used, inductions are contingent on a decision about whether a one- or two-tail test is appropriate and about the level of probability ($p \leq 0.05$ or $p \leq 0.01$), which is taken to indicate that a statistical explanation is unlikely. To understand how these decisions are made in the varient paradigm, a perspective on tests of statistical significance is necessary. Essentially, in the statistical paradigm, theoretical distributions of the $\hat{F}$, $\hat{t}$, and $\hat{Z}$ indicators are available. A hat ($\char`\^$) is used to indicate that values for $\hat{F}$, $\hat{t}$, and $\hat{Z}$ are derived from statistical theory. These theoretical distributions associate a probability with each of the values taken on by F, Z and t, given the specification of a certain number of degrees of freedom. A portion of the theoretical $\hat{F}$ distribution is presented in Table A.3

in Appendix A. Essentially, the $\hat{F}$ values listed in this table have a 0.05 or 0.01 probability for the degrees of freedom shown in the table. Such distributions result from a statistical conceptualization of the entire range of values that may be taken on by $\hat{F}$; they are totally independent of any values obtained in a study.

The values obtained in a particular study (F, Z, t) are compared to these theoretical values ($\hat{F}$, $\hat{Z}$, $\hat{t}$). As a result, a value obtained for an indicator is assigned a probability of occurrence due to what we have called statistical artifacts. To find the probability, a choice must be made between a one- and a two-tail test. The $\hat{F}$ and $\hat{t}$ indicators are often viewed as one-tail tests. In addition, since our focus is on half (on one tail) of the distribution of correlations (from 0 to 1 rather than from -1 to 1), **one-tail tests** are used in the paradigm. The 0.05 and 0.01 levels of significance are taken to indicate a low probability that a value obtained for an indicator is due to statistical artifacts in a particular study.

As should be apparent, decisions induced from the values taken on by indicators vary, depending on which level of significance is adopted and whether a one- or two-tail test is used. In general, the hypothesis that results are due to statistical artifacts is a question of degree, not kind. In other words, the choice of a probability of 0.05 or 0.01 is arbitrary. When an obtained value (F) for an indicator is compared to a theoretical value ($\hat{F}$), the hypothesis that an obtained result can be predicted based on statistical theory is rejected if the likelihood is less than or equal to 0.05 or 0.01. This rejection of a statistical hypothesis is made with full knowledge that some likelihood (5 in 100 or 1 in 100) remains that obtained values are due to statistical artifacts. This way of testing statistical significance is compatible with contemporary approaches. However, we prefer to retain a distinction between results that are statistically significant at the 0.01 and 0.05 levels of significance.

Practical Significance

Practical significance can also be viewed as a matter of degree. In contrast to tests of statistical significance, practical significance tests should not be sensitive to degrees of freedom. A review of key geometric as opposed to statistical properties, which were presented in Chapters 2 and 5 and which underlie tests of practical significance, should be helpful here.

In general, a natural midpoint is identifiable in the case of correlations. Specifically, the case in which a correlation between two variables X and Y equals 0.7071 is illustrated by the drawing of a 45° angle between two variables expressed as vectors. If a third vector e is added so that $\theta_{ex} = 90°$, variable Y is equidistant from vector X and from vector e. This can be illustrated as shown in Figure 7.1. From this geometric perspective, when a correlation is greater than 0.7071, two variables are more related than unrelated. If a correlation is less than 0.7071, two variables are more unrelated than related. Our view of correlations also has meaning in more traditional variance terms.

Specifically, when a correlation is squared, it is taken to represent the percentage of variance accounted for in one variable by a second variable. The

FIGURE 7.1. Geometric illustration of midpoint in the magnitude of correlations

square of 0.7071 (or cos 45°) is 0.50. When a correlation is greater than 0.7071, more than 50 percent of the variance in one variable is explained by another variable and less than 50 percent is unexplained. In contrast, when a correlation is less than 0.7071, more than 50 percent of the variance in one variable is unexplained by another variable. Ideally, one would like more explained than unexplained variance.

As pointed out previously, a correlational value of 0.7071 is a natural midpoint. The problems with using this midpoint in social science and organizational behavior studies should be apparent. Correlations below 0.7071 are routinely obtained and interpreted in these fields. For example, Roberts et al. (1978) suggest that correlational values of 0.30 are considered reasonable in organizational behavior. At least two possibilities account for this fact. First, the measurement and nature of the variables may be so imprecise that stronger correlations are not obtained. Second, human beings may be so complex that two variables will never be strongly correlated; therefore, multiple variables should always be employed to reflect the complexity. We do not intend to respond to these two different positions about the nature of the research process and human beings. Instead, when possible the natural midpoint is retained, and when necessary adjustments are made so that correlations of a lesser magnitude than 0.7071 can also be interpreted. In this way, both philosophical positions remain viable.

Tests of practical significance are similar to tests of statistical significance in that decisions must be made so that intervals of values that correspond to ideal conditions can be identified. The whole and parts conditions have been aligned with the endpoints of the E and A indicators. Therefore, a key question is the degree to which obtained data approximate these ideal conditions and endpoints. Although the four analyses (single and multiple level and multiple variable and relationship) use tests of practical and statistical significance, the derivation of these intervals for interpreting obtained values is accomplished mainly by focusing on WABA and single-level analysis.

SINGLE-LEVEL ANALYSIS

The tests of statistical significance used in WABA I and II for single-level analysis can be found in most statistics books. In terms of practical significance, the midpoint value of 0.7071 provides a reasonable basis on which to make decisions about the degree to which data align with one of the ideal conditions in WABA I. In contrast, in WABA II the midpoint value of 0.7071 is problematic, and an adjustment procedure is necessary. In addition, the use of WABA I and II on real data requires consideration of issues beyond those described for the ideal cases.

WABA I

In WABA I, when an E ratio equals a maximum value of infinity, an ideal whole condition is defined and the between-cell deviation scores completely represent the scores. When an E ratio equals a minimum value of 0, an ideal parts condition is defined and the within-cell deviation scores completely represent the scores. Furthermore, when an E ratio equals 1, an ideal equivocal condition is defined; the between- and within-entity correlations both equal 0.7071, and the scores are represented equally well by the within- and between-cell deviation scores.

Practical Significance Tests   For E values, at least three different intervals can be defined that allow for making a decision that an obtained E ratio indicates a parts, whole, or equivocal condition.

First, when a particular level of analysis is defined as of importance, an equivocal condition may be viewed as irrelevant; in this case, the equivocal condition can be limited to obtained E values of exactly 1. Then obtained E values greater than 1 are taken to indicate wholes and values less than 1 to indicate parts. This results in a **0° test in WABA I** because no (or a zero) range of values is given for the equivocal condition.

A second alternative is to view the equivocal condition as equally plausible with the parts and whole conditions. Since an E ratio is a cotangent of an angle between 0° to 90°, the range of the E ratio can be divided into three subranges, each of which is 30° in length (0° to 30°, 30° to 60°, and 60° to 90°). Cosines of 30° and 60° form two cutoff points. As a result, E ratios greater than 1.73 (cot 30°) approximate a whole condition; E ratios less than 0.577 (cot 60°) approximate a parts condition; E ratios between these two points approximate an equivocal condition. This results in a **30° test in WABA I** because a 30° range of values is given for the equivocal condition.

A third alternative is to take a middle position between the first formulation—in which an equivocal condition will rarely be induced from data—and the second formulation—in which an equivocal condition will be as often induced as the whole and parts conditions. In this third case, a 15° range that is symmetric around a midpoint of 45° is defined for the equivocal condition. Therefore, the two angles of 52.5° (45° + 7.5°) and 37.5° (45° − 7.5°) define cutoff points. Then E ratios greater than 1.303 are viewed as approximating a whole condition; E ratios less than 0.767 as approximating a parts condition; and any E ratios between these two values as approximating an equivocal condition. This results in a **15° test in WABA I** because a 15° range of values is given to the equivocal condition.

These three approaches for making decisions based on obtained E ratios are distinguishable in terms of the range of angles assigned to the equivocal condition. Specifically, in the 0° test, only the value at the midpoint ($E = 1$) is viewed as approximating the equivocal condition. In the 30° test, a 30° range symmetric around the midpoint is associated with the equivocal condition. In the 15° test, a 15° interval symmetric around the midpoint is associated with the equivocal condition. The intervals for E ratios that result from these three approaches are illustrated in the upper portion of Table 7.1. The lower portion

TABLE 7.1.   Illustration of intervals for practical and statistical significance tests in WABA I

	E RATIO (η_B/η_W)	0° TEST	15° TEST	30° TEST	F RATIO (E^2)$(N-J)/(J-1)$
Ranges					
Wholes	∞	0°	0°	0°	$F_{J-1,\,N-J} = \infty$
	1.73			30°	
	1.30		37.5°		
Equivocal	1.00	45°			
	0.77		52.5°		
	0.58			60°	
Parts	0.00	90°	90°	90°	$F_{N-J,\,J-1} = 0$
Choices					
Wholes					
η between ($J-1$)		> 0.71	≥ 0.79	≥ 0.87	
η within ($N-J$)		< 0.71	≤ 0.61	≤ 0.50	
E ratio		> 1.00	≥ 1.30	≥ 1.73	
F ratio					$F \geq \hat{F}_{0.05,\,0.01}$
Parts					
η between		< 0.71	≤ 0.61	≤ 0.50	
η within		> 0.71	≥ 0.79	≥ 0.87	
E ratio		< 1.00	≤ 0.77	≤ 0.58	
F ratio					$F \leq \dfrac{1}{\hat{F}_{0.05,\,0.01}}$
Equivocal					
η between		= 0.71	All others	All others	
η within		= 0.71	All others	All others	
E ratio		= 1.00	All others	All others	
F ratio					All others

Note: $\hat{F}$ ratio is obtained in the case of wholes for $J-1$ and $N-J$ degrees of freedom. $\hat{F}$ ratio is obtained in the case of parts for $N-J$ and $J-1$ degrees of freedom.

of the table lists the values that must be exceeded by an obtained eta correlation in order to pass each test.

The geometric basis of these tests is illustrated in Figure 7.2. In the 0° test, an equivocal condition is induced when obtained between- and within-eta correlations are equal to 0.7071. As a result, when a total vector falls in the area above the line representing the equivocal condition, a whole condition is induced; and when a total vector falls below this line, a parts condition is

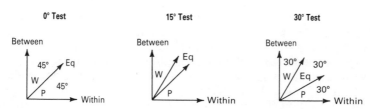

FIGURE 7.2.   Geometric illustration of the ranges in the 0°, 15°, and 30° tests

induced. In the 30° test, any total vector that falls in the range delineated by the two vectors forming 30° angles with the between- and within-cell vectors is viewed as indicating an equivocal condition. Total vectors that fall in the area above these lines are viewed as approximating an ideal whole condition, and vectors that fall below these lines are viewed as approximating an ideal parts condition. Correspondingly, in the 15° test, the vectors that fall in the 15° range around the midpoint of 45° are defined as approximating an equivocal condition; total vectors that fall in the area above these lines approximate an ideal whole condition; and total vectors that fall in the area below these lines approximate an ideal parts condition.

Of these sets of intervals, the 30° test is the most natural way to divide the 0° to 90° range of the E ratio and eta correlations, since equal intervals are defined for each condition (wholes, parts, and equivocal). Moreover, in order to infer wholes in this test, 75 percent of the variance must occur between cells (η_B^2), and thus only 25 percent of the variance occurs within cells (η_W^2). Likewise, in order to infer parts, 75 percent of the variance must occur within cells and only 25 percent can occur between cells.

As a second alternative, it might be argued that the intervals for the three conditions should be equal in terms of the percentage of variance contained in each interval. In other words, the argument might be made that the following intervals should be employed in evaluating the between-eta correlation *squared*:

Wholes	$1 \quad \geq \eta_B^2 \geq 0.666$	$\infty \quad \geq E \geq 1.41$
Equivocal	$0.666 > \eta_B^2 > 0.333$	$1.41 \quad > E > 0.707$
Parts	$0.333 \geq \eta_B^2 \geq 0$	$0.707 \geq E \geq 0$

Clearly, this argument has some merit, but its geometric properties are less clear than we find desirable. In contrast, the 15° test, which has a geometric basis, results in the following intervals:

Wholes	$1 \quad \geq \eta_B^2 \geq 0.63$	$\infty \quad \geq E \geq 1.30$
Equivocal	$0.63 > \eta_B^2 > 0.37$	$1.30 > E > 0.77$
Parts	$0.37 \geq \eta_B^2 \geq 0$	$0.77 \geq E \geq 0$

These intervals are very close to those obtained using the variance argument. In addition, these intervals for the 15° test provide ranges that neither completely ignore the equivocal condition nor give it equal status with the other conditions in terms of geometry.

Although the range of E ratios can be divided in a variety of ways, we prefer to use the intervals from the 15° and 30° tests. There should be little disagreement that the ranges formed by the 30° test are straightforward; the ranges formed by the 15° test serve as a compromise position. Notice, however, that when obtained values exceed the values specified by the 30° test, the requirements of the 15° test are also met.

The usefulness of the intervals specified in the 15° and 30° tests can be illustrated by assuming that a between-eta correlation of 0.81 and a within-eta correlation of 0.59 are obtained. Therefore, the E ratio equals 1.37. This E value is greater than the E ratio of 1.30 required in the 15° test to induce a whole condition. The E value of 1.37 is neither greater than or equal to ($\geq$) 1.73 or less than or equal to ($\leq$) 0.58, the values required to induce whole or parts conditions using a 30° test. Therefore, using the 30° test, the value of this indicator is viewed as approximating an equivocal condition.

The upper portion of Table 7.2 illustrates how an obtained E value of 1.37 is located along the entity axis of a varient matrix. An obtained E value (in this case of 1.37) is compared to the requirements for each condition shown in the table based on the 15° and 30° tests, and data are located by the insertion of number signs, as shown in this example along the entity axis.

Statistical Significance Tests   In addition to these tests of practical significance, F ratios can be used to test the significance of either a between- or a within-eta correlation (see Appendix F). A between-eta correlation is tested using the following equation:

$$F_B = \frac{\eta_B^2}{\eta_W^2} \frac{N-J}{J-1} = \frac{\eta_B^2/(J-1)}{\eta_W^2/(N-J)} \tag{7.1}$$

A within-eta correlation is tested using the following equation:

$$F_W = \frac{\eta_W^2}{\eta_B^2} \frac{J-1}{N-J} = \frac{\eta_W^2/(N-J)}{\eta_B^2/(J-1)} \tag{7.2}$$

Notice that Equations 7.1 and 7.2 are the inverse of each other:

$$F_B = \frac{1}{F_W} \quad \text{and} \quad F_W = \frac{1}{F_B} \tag{7.3}$$

Therefore, only one equation (7.1) need be considered when analyzing data. The process of assessing whether an obtained F ratio has a probability less than or equal to 0.05 or 0.01 is complicated somewhat by this inverse property of F ratios and requires further consideration.

For a whole condition, any obtained F ratio using Equation 7.1 is compatible with standard tests of between-eta correlations. Therefore, given $J-1$ and $N-J$ degrees of freedom for the numerator (η_B^2) and denominator (η_W^2), respectively, the values required for $\hat{F}$ at the 0.05 and 0.01 levels of statistical significance are obtained from Table A.3 in Appendix A. For a parts condition, the numerator in the F ratio should be the within-eta correlation according to Equation 7.2. Therefore, an $\hat{F}$ ratio is obtained for $N-J$ and $J-1$ degrees of freedom for the numerator and denominator, respectively, from Table A.3 in Appendix A. The inverse of the $\hat{F}$ values obtained from the table for the 0.05 and 0.01 levels of significance is taken to conform with the equation used in calculating the F ratio.

TABLE 7.2. Location of data on the entity axis using practical and statistical tests in WABA I

DATA AND CHOICES	LOCATION OF DATA
Practical Significance Tests:	
Data	
$E = 1.37$	
Choices	
Wholes	
15° $E \geq 1.30$	#
30° $E \geq 1.73$	
Parts	
15° $E \leq 0.77$	
30° $E \leq 0.58$	
Equivocal	
15° (all others)	
30° (all others)	#
Statistical Significance Tests:	
Data	
$F = 4.42$ ($df = 82, 193$)	
Choices	
Wholes	
$0.05\ F \geq \hat{F}_{J-1,\,N-J} \geq 1.35$	#
$0.01\ F \geq \hat{F}_{J-1,\,N-J} \geq 1.53$	#
Parts	
$0.05\ F \leq 1/\hat{F}_{N-J,\,J-1} \leq 0.72$	
$0.01\ F \leq 1/\hat{F}_{N-J,\,J-1} \leq 0.64$	
Equivocal	
0.05 (all others)	
0.01 (all others)	
Practical and Statistical Tests:	
Data	
$E = 1.37$	
$F = 4.42$	
Choices	
Wholes	
15° $E \geq 1.30$	#
30° $E \geq 1.73$	
$0.05\ F \geq 1.35$	#
$0.01\ F \geq 1.53$	#
Parts	
15° $E \leq 0.77$	
30° $E \leq 0.58$	
$0.05\ F \leq 0.72$	
$0.01\ F \leq 0.64$	
Equivocal	
15° (all others)	
30° (all others)	#
0.05 (all others)	
0.01 (all others)	

To summarize, $\hat{F}$ ratios compatible with a parts condition are obtained by the following equation:

$$\hat{F}_{\text{parts}} = \frac{1}{\hat{F}_{N-J, J-1}}$$

$\hat{F}$ ratios for wholes are obtained directly from Table A.3 in the Appendix A because

$$\hat{F}_{\text{wholes}} = \hat{F}_{J-1, N-J}$$

An example will illustrate this procedure.

If there are 276 individuals embedded in 83 work groups, the cells are aligned with 83 work groups. In this case, the between-group scores have $J - 1$ (82) degrees of freedom, and the within-cell scores have $N - J$ (193) degrees of freedom. Using the table of critical $\hat{F}$ values presented in Table A.3 for degrees of freedom of 82 and 193, an $\hat{F}$ ratio of approximately 1.35 at the 0.05 level of significance and 1.53 at the 0.01 level of significance is required. In contrast, if a within- rather than between-eta correlation is of interest, as in the case of parts, an $\hat{F}$ ratio for 193 and 82 degrees should be obtained. In this case $\hat{F}$ ratios of 1.38 and 1.57 are required at the 0.05 and 0.01 levels of significance, respectively. However, to test F_W, the inverses of these values are required. Therefore, the critical values of 0.72 ($p \le 0.05$) and 0.64 ($p \le 0.01$) are obtained. These critical values then determine ranges for wholes and parts. Any obtained values not within the ranges for parts or wholes are viewed as equivocal.

The usefulness of these ranges can be illustrated with the case in which an E ratio of 1.37 was obtained ($\eta_B = 0.81$, $\eta_W = 0.59$) based on 276 scores within 83 cells. The F ratio equals $4.42 = [(1.37)^2(193/82)]$. This obtained F value is greater than the theoretically based values required for the 0.05 and 0.01 levels of statistical significance (1.35 and 1.53), which are associated with wholes. Therefore, the greater between-eta correlation is viewed as statistically significant, indicating that a whole condition is viable from a statistical perspective.

This case is presented in tabular form, as shown in the middle portion of Table 7.2. The value of the obtained F ratio is compared to the intervals for the three conditions shown in the table. In this illustration, given 82 between and 193 within degrees of freedom, the values from Table A.3 of 1.35, 1.53, 0.72, and 0.64 required at the 0.01 and 0.05 levels specify the intervals used to make an induction about the obtained F ratio. The locations of the number signs indicate the induction drawn from the data.

Summary of WABA I Tests In order to test for statistical significance, however, one eta correlation should be viewed as error, or smaller in magnitude than the other eta correlation. This requirement is analogous to the traditional rule that the larger value should be divided by a lesser value in forming an F ratio. *Therefore, tests of practical significance always precede tests* *of statistical significance because the practical tests provide an indication of which eta correlation is larger (not error).* Once a practical test is concluded, a statistical test is performed.

The practical and statistical tests for the illustrative case can be summarized as shown in the lower portion of Table 7.2. As should be apparent from this tabular summary, once values are obtained for an E and F ratio, a variable is located along the entity axis in terms of both practical and statistical significance. In the illustrative example we have been using, E equaled 1.37 and F equaled 4.42. This result is interpreted as closer to a whole condition on a practical 15° test basis and as equivocal on a 30° test basis. From a statistical perspective, the probability that the greater between-eta correlation is due to statistical artifacts is low ($p \leq 0.05$ and $p \leq 0.01$). In this case, the induction process results in a statement that a tendency toward a whole condition is present, but this statement must take into account the inability to pass the 30° test.

In summary, the intervals shown in Table 7.1 allow the categorization of any value taken on by an E or F ratio. In addition, the inexplicable condition occurs in WABA I when no deviations are obtained either within or between cells and the values for the E and F are indeterminate. Moreover, because wholes and parts are aligned with the maximum and minimum values of the E and F ratios, this induction procedure can be applied regardless of the basis used to construct cells. Since our interest is in the case in which cells are aligned with entities, the intervals are used to locate data along the entity axis of the varient matrix (see Table 7.2). A consideration of two variables with WABA II is now appropriate.

WABA II

The mathematics of the eta correlations are such that the difference and magnitude of the correlations are interchangeable. Specifically, as the magnitude of one correlation increases the other decreases, and the difference between them changes accordingly. The magnitudes of the within- and between-cell correlations, however, are free to vary from each other (see section 7 of Appendix D). Therefore, both the magnitudes of and the differences between correlations must be examined. And as is always the case in the varient paradigm, tests of practical significance are considered before tests of statistical significance. We will consider difference tests before magnitude tests.

Difference Tests (Practical Significance) In WABA II an A value obtained by ignoring the signs of correlations is used to indicate the difference between within-cell and between-cell correlations. The range of A is from -1.57 to 1.57 radians or from $-90°$ to 90°. The midpoint is a value of 0 degrees or radians. Three sets of intervals of A are of particular interest for testing purposes.

When A $(\theta_W - \theta_B)$ takes on a positive value, a between-cell correlation is larger than a within-cell correlation. Therefore, positive A values can be viewed as indicating that data approximate an ideal whole condition. A negative value for A results when a within-cell correlation is greater than a between-cell correlation. Therefore, negative A values can be viewed as indicating that data are compatible with a parts condition. As a result of this construction of intervals, the inexplicable and equivocal conditions are limited to the case in which A equals 0. One advantage of this set of intervals is that wholes or parts are always induced except in the one case. This construction of intervals is called a **0° test for WABA II** because no range of values is given to the equivocal and inexplicable conditions.

Given that the range of A is 180°, a second set of (equal) intervals of 60° each can be constructed. This results in a 30° interval above and below the ideal equivocal and inexplicable conditions (when $A = 0$). As a result, a difference greater than or equal to 30° or 0.52 radians is taken to indicate a stronger between-cell correlation (or a whole condition). A difference less than or equal to $-30°$ or -0.52 radians is taken to indicate a stronger within-cell correlation (or parts). Finally, differences between these two values (-0.52 and $+0.52$ radians) are taken to indicate an equivocal or inexplicable condition. This set of intervals forms a **30° test for WABA II** because angles defined by the within- and between-cell correlations must differ by at least 30°.

A third approach—which is more biased toward parts or wholes than the 30° test and less biased than the 0° test—is called the 15° test. In this test, a 30° interval is formed around the midpoint of 0. This results in a 15° interval above and below the zero midpoint. Using this set of categories, an A value greater than 15° or 0.26 radians is taken to indicate wholes and an A value less than $-15°$ or -0.26 radians is taken to indicate parts. The range around 0 (-0.26 to 0.26 radians) is taken to represent the equivocal or inexplicable condition. This set of intervals forms a **15° test for WABA II** because angles defined by the within- and between-cell correlations must differ by at least 15°.

These three ways in which the range of the A test is divided into three intervals are illustrated by the figures shown in the upper portion of Table 7.3. The resulting cutoff points for the wholes, parts, and equivocal or inexplicable conditions are listed in the lower portion of the table.

Of the three tests, the 30° test seems most advantageous because the intervals for A are equal in size. A similar argument as the one made for WABA I in variance terms can be made for using the 15° test. In general, although the 0° test is straightforward, the intervals do not give the equivocal and inexplicable conditions fair play. Therefore, we chose the 15° and 30° tests in interpreting A values.

The use of these decision criteria can be illustrated by assuming that values for a between-cell correlation of 0.80 and for a within-cell correlation of 0.10 are obtained. A correlation of 0.80 results in an angle of 36.9° or 0.64 radians; a correlation of 0.10 results in an angle of 84.3° or 1.47 radians. The difference between these angles is 0.83 radians. This value is greater than the values of 0.26 and 0.52 radians required in the 15° and 30° tests. Therefore, the value of 0.83 radians is interpreted as approximating a whole condition. The location of this result along the entity axis of a varient matrix is shown in the upper portion of Table 7.4. In this case, the number signs are located in rows associated with the whole condition. In addition to the differences between the within-cell and between-cell correlations, the statistical significance of such differences must also be assessed.

TABLE 7.3.   Illustration of intervals for practical and statistical significance tests of differences in WABA II

	A TEST[a] $(\theta_W - \theta_B)$	0° TEST	15° TEST	30° TEST	Z
Distribution of Scores					
Wholes	1.57	90°	90°	90°	
	0.52			30°	
	0.26		15°		
Equivocal	0.00	0°			
	−0.26		−15°		
	−0.52			−30°	
Parts	−1.57	−90°	−90°	−90°	
Choices					
Wholes					
A		> 0.00	≥ 0.26	≥ 0.52	
0.05 Z					≥ 1.66
0.01 Z					≥ 2.33
Parts					
A		< 0.00	≤ −0.26	≤ −0.52	
0.05 Z					≤ −1.66
0.01 Z					≤ −2.33
Equivocal (or inexplicable)					
A		= 0.00	All others	All others	
0.05 Z					All others
0.01 Z					All others

[a] Expressed in radians.

Difference Tests (Statistical Significance)   A theoretical distribution of Z scores is available from the statistical paradigm and can be found in statistics books. For a one-tail test, $\hat{Z}$ values greater than 1.66 and 2.33 are viewed as statistically significant for $p \leq 0.05$ and $p \leq 0.01$, respectively. A Z score obtained by taking the difference between obtained within-cell and between-cell correlations is compared to the theoretical values of $\hat{Z}$ in order to determine the likelihood that obtained differences are due to statistical artifacts. As a result, obtained Z values greater than or equal to 1.66 and 2.33 indicate that a between-cell correlation is stronger than a within-cell correlation and are viewed as statistically significant and as compatible with an inference of wholes. Obtained Z values less than or equal to −1.66 and −2.33 are viewed as statistically significant and as indicating parts. Values between these points are viewed as equivocal or inexplicable.

These intervals can be summarized in tabular form with an example in which a between-cell correlation with 81 degrees of freedom equals 0.80, a within-cell correlation with 192 degrees of freedom equals 0.10, and Z equals 7.50. In this illustrative case, the Z value of 7.50 is statistically significant ($p \leq 0.05$ and $p \leq 0.01$), and it is compatible with an induction of wholes, as indicated by the locations of the number signs in the middle portion of Table 7.4.

TABLE 7.4. Location of data on the entity axis using practical and statistical tests in WABA II (difference tests)

DATA AND CHOICES	LOCATION OF DATA
Practical Significance Tests:	
Data	
$A = 0.83$	
Choices	
Wholes	
15° $A \geq 0.26$	#
30° $A \geq 0.52$	#
Parts	
15° $A \leq -0.26$	
30° $A \leq -0.52$	
Equivocal or inexplicable	
15° (all others)	
30° (all others)	
Statistical Significance Tests:	
Data	
$Z = 7.50$	
Choices	
Wholes	
0.05 $Z \geq 1.66$	#
0.01 $Z \geq 2.33$	#
Parts	
0.05 $Z \leq -1.66$	
0.01 $Z \leq -2.33$	
Equivocal or inexplicable	
0.05 (all others)	
0.01 (all others)	
Practical and Statistical Tests:	
Data	
$A = 0.83$	
$Z = 7.50$	
Choices	
Wholes	
15° $A \geq 0.26$	#
30° $A \geq 0.52$	#
0.05 $Z \geq 1.66$	#
0.01 $Z \geq 2.33$	#
Parts	
15° $A \leq -0.26$	
30° $A \leq -0.52$	
0.05 $Z \leq -1.66$	
0.01 $Z \leq -2.33$	
Equivocal or inexplicable	
15° (all others)	
30° (all others)	
0.05 (all others)	
0.01 (all others)	

Summary of Difference Tests   The results from testing the practical and statistical significance in our example ($A = 0.83$ and $Z = 7.50$) can be summarized as shown in the lower portion of Table 7.4. In this case the data are located in the whole condition. These choices are, of course, based on the intervals presented in the upper portion of Table 7.3. In addition to the differences of between- and within-cell correlations, their magnitudes must also be considered.

Magnitude Tests (Practical Significance)   A straightforward way of testing an assertion that two variables are related is to require that an obtained correlation be greater than 0.7071 and that the corresponding cotangent of the angle defined by a correlation (R value) be greater than 1. In this case, a correlation less than 0.7071 is viewed as closer to 0 than to 1. One consequence of this approach is that a correlation of 0.72 is interpreted as practically significant and a correlation of 0.70 is interpreted as closer to 0. To offset this problem, a range of ambiguous correlational values can be constructed, again using 15° and 30° ranges. The results of creating these intervals can be summarized as follows:

	30° RANGES		15° RANGES	
	Correlation	*R Values*	*Correlation*	*R Values*
Closer to $r = 1$	$r \geq 0.87$	$R \geq 1.73$	$r \geq 0.79$	$R \geq 1.30$
Closer to $r = 0$	$r \leq 0.50$	$R \leq 0.58$	$r \leq 0.61$	$R \leq 0.77$
Ambiguous	all others	all others	all others	all others

When these intervals for zero and nonzero correlations are substituted into the ideal whole, parts, equivocal, and inexplicable conditions, the result is shown in Table 7.5. The ability of the resulting intervals to permit distinctions between the ideal conditions should be apparent. Moreover, differences of 0°, 15°, and 30° between the within-cell and between-cell correlations are required in order to infer wholes and parts in each of the three tests. For example, in the 30° test, in order to infer wholes a between-cell correlation should be at least 0.87 and a within-cell correlation should be at most 0.50. Differences between these two correlations in these intervals are at least 30° or 0.52 radians. Unlike the case of WABA I, where eta correlations must sum to 1 and where ratios of the two correlations form cotangents, in WABA II the between- and within-cell correlations can both be 0 or $+1$, or they can take on other combinations of values. This makes the ranges shown in Table 7.5 somewhat problematic, since correlations of 0.30 are often considered of reasonable magnitude (Roberts et al., 1978). An ability to interpret correlations of magnitudes less than 0.7071 is accomplished by relying more on the difference (A) than magnitude (R) indicators.

As an illustration, assume that either a between-cell or a within-cell correlation equals exactly 0. If there is a difference of 0° between these correlations, both correlations equal 0. If there is a difference of 15° and one of the correlations equals 0, the other must equal 0.26. If there is a 30° difference,

TABLE 7.5. Illustration of rigorous criteria for practical tests of magnitude of correlations

	IDEAL CASES		30°		15°		0°	
	Between	**Within**	**Between**	**Within**	**Between**	**Within**	**Between**	**Within**
Correlational Values								
Wholes	1	0	$r \geq 0.87$	$r \leq 0.50$	$r \geq 0.79$	$r \leq 0.61$	$r > 0.7071$	$r < 0.7071$
Parts	0	1	$r \leq 0.50$	$r \geq 0.87$	$r \leq 0.61$	$r \geq 0.79$	$r < 0.7071$	$r > 0.7071$
Equivocal	1	1	$r \geq 0.87$	$r \geq 0.87$	$r \geq 0.79$	$r \geq 0.79$	$r > 0.7071$	$r > 0.7071$
Inexplicable	0	0	$r \leq 0.50$	$r \leq 0.50$	$r \leq 0.61$	$r \leq 0.61$	$r < 0.7071$	$r < 0.7071$
Ambiguous			All others		All others		All others	
Magnitude Values								
Wholes			$R \geq 1.73$	$R \leq 0.58$	$R \geq 1.30$	$R \leq 0.77$	$R > 1.00$	$R < 1.00$
Parts			$R \leq 0.58$	$R \geq 1.73$	$R \leq 0.77$	$R \geq 1.30$	$R < 1.00$	$R > 1.00$
Equivocal			$R \geq 1.73$	$R \geq 1.73$	$R \geq 1.30$	$R \geq 1.30$	$R > 1.00$	$R > 1.00$
Inexplicable			$R \leq 0.58$	$R \leq 0.58$	$R \leq 0.77$	$R \leq 0.77$	$R < 1.00$	$R < 1.00$

one of the correlations must equal 0.50. Therefore, for our purposes, in order to be viewed as greater than 0, a correlation must be greater than 0.26 or 0.50, depending on whether a 15° or 30° test is used.

The ranges that result for testing the practical significance of within- and between-cell correlations with an R indicator are shown in the upper portion of Table 7.6. The values of correlations and R indicators that must be obtained in order to infer that a correlation is greater than 0 are shown in the middle portion of the table. This approach is less rigorous than the one summarized in Table 7.5, because interpretations are possible when correlations of smaller magnitude are obtained. Therefore, testing the practical significance of the magnitude of the within- and between-cell correlations involves two steps. First, the degree to which an obtained set of correlations approximates the more rigorous criteria shown in Table 7.5 is ascertained. Second, when results do not meet these criteria, the magnitude of the larger correlation is examined to assess whether it can be viewed as being greater than zero.

TABLE 7.6. Chosen definition of a correlation of zero

$R = \dfrac{\sqrt{r^2}}{\sqrt{1-r^2}}$	BETWEEN				WITHIN			
	0°	15°	30°	t	0°	15°	30°	t
∞	0°	0°	0°		0°	0°	0°	
0.58			60°				60°	
0.27		75°				75°		
0.00	90°				90°			
Correlational Values								
Nonzero	$r > 0.00$	$r \geq 0.26$	$r \geq 0.50$		$r > 0.00$	$r \geq 0.26$	$r \geq 0.50$	
Near zero	$r = 0.00$	$r < 0.26$	$r < 0.50$		$r = 0.00$	$r < 0.26$	$r < 0.50$	
Magnitude Tests								
Nonzero	$R > 0.00$	$R \geq 0.27$	$R \geq 0.58$	$t \geq \hat{t}_{0.05,0.01}$	$R > 0.00$	$R \geq 0.27$	$R \geq 0.58$	$t \geq \hat{t}_{0.05,0.01}$
Near zero	$R = 0.00$	$R < 0.27$	$R < 0.58$	$t < \hat{t}_{0.05,0.01}$	$R = 0.00$	$R < 0.27$	$R < 0.58$	$t < \hat{t}_{0.05,0.01}$
Choices								
Wholes		$R \geq 0.27$	$R \geq 0.58$	$t \geq \hat{t}_{0.05,0.01}$				
Parts	—	—	—		$R \geq 0.27$	$R \geq 0.58$	$t \geq \hat{t}_{0.05,0.01}$	
Equivocal	—	—	—		—	—	—	
Inexplicable	—	—	—		—	—	—	

For example, again assume that the within- and between-cell correlations equal 0.10 and 0.80, respectively. In terms of the rigorous criteria (Table 7.5), the correlations meet the 15° and 30° tests, and a whole condition is induced as more likely. In terms of the less rigorous test (Table 7.6), the between-cell *R* value (chosen focus) of 1.33 is greater than 0.27 and 0.58, and thus is interpreted as greater than zero. The latter induction can be illustrated in tabular form, as shown in the upper portion of Table 7.7. The location of number signs in the table for these tests of practical significance simply indicates that the between-cell correlations are greater than zero.

Magnitude Tests (Statistical Significance)   A theoretical distribution of $\hat{t}$ values is available from the statistical paradigm. These values can be found from any $\hat{F}$ table (such as the one presented in Appendix A) in the following way. A $\hat{t}$ test equals the square root of an $\hat{F}$ ratio with 1 and k degrees of freedom:

$$\hat{t} = \sqrt{\hat{F}_{1,k}} \qquad (7.4)$$

The between-cell and within-cell correlations with 1 and $J - 2$ and 1 and $N - J - 1$ degrees of freedom, respectively, are compared against a set of theoretical $\hat{t}$ values to test their magnitudes. For example, the case in which a between-cell correlation with 81 degrees of freedom equals 0.80 and a within-cell correlation with 192 degrees of freedom equals 0.10 can be summarized as shown in the middle portion of Table 7.7. The t value when compared to $\hat{t}$ provides a test of whether a correlation is greater than zero based on statistical artifacts. In this way it is similar to the less rigorous practical test of significance that also tests the likelihood that a correlation equals zero. As a result, the t test is only useful in rejecting the hypothesis that a correlation equals zero, not for asserting that a correlation is equal to zero. In other words, a null hypothesis is not accepted when the statistical paradigm is used (see Chapter 1). Therefore, as shown in the middle portion of Table 7.7, number signs are inserted only for the statistically significant between-cell correlation.

Summary of Magnitude Tests   Tests of practical and statistical significance of the magnitude of correlations are summarized in the lower portion of Table 7.7.

Steps in Testing with WABA II   As we have demonstrated, a three-step procedure is employed in testing the within- and between-cell correlations in WABA II in terms of practical significance. First, the difference between the within-cell and between-cell correlations is given by A, and it is compared to the values required to infer parts, wholes, or an equivocal condition. Second, the magnitudes of the correlations are examined to ascertain whether the more rigorous criteria are met. If they are met, an induction is made. If they are not met, in the third step the significance of the greater correlation is tested using the values for the 15° and 30° tests as the minimum necessary to infer a nonzero correlation. When step 3 is necessary, the difference test permits the

TABLE 7.7.   Illustration of tests of significance in WABA II (magnitude tests)

DATA AND CHOICES		LOCATION OF DATA
Practical Significance Tests:		
Data		
$R_B = 1.33, R_W = 0.10$		
Choices		
Between cell (R_B)		
15° $R \geq 0.27$		#
30° $R \geq 0.58$		#
Within cell (R_W)		
15° $R \geq 0.27$		
30° $R \geq 0.58$		
Statistical Significance Tests:		
Data		
$t_B = 12, t_W = 1.39$		
Choices		
Between cell (t_B)		
0.05 $t \geq \hat{t}_{1, J-2}$	$t_B \geq 1.99$	#
0.01 $t \geq \hat{t}_{1, J-2}$	$t_B \geq 2.64$	#
Within cell (t_W)		
0.05 $t \geq \hat{t}_{1, N-J-1}$	$t_W \geq 1.97$	
0.01 $t \geq \hat{t}_{1, N-J-1}$	$t_W \geq 2.60$	
Practical and Statistical Tests:		
Data		
Between: $R_B = 1.33, t_B = 12$		
Within: $R_W = 0.10, t_W = 1.39$		
Choices		
Between cell (R_B and t_B)		
15° $R \geq 0.27$		#
30° $R \geq 0.58$		#
0.05 $t \geq 1.99$		#
0.01 $t \geq 2.64$		#
Within cell (R_W and t_W)		
15° $R \geq 0.27$		
30° $R \geq 0.58$		
0.05 $t \geq 1.97$		
0.01 $t \geq 2.60$		

parts and whole conditions to be distinguished from the equivocal and inexplicable conditions. However, a distinction between the equivocal and inexplicable conditions is not possible, because the magnitude of only one correlation (the greater correlation) is tested. When an induction is based on the third step, it is always questionable because the percentage of explained variance is small. Nevertheless, we prefer to use these three steps to allow inductions from data when obtained correlations are somewhat low in magnitude.

The tests for the statistical significance of the differences between the within- and between-cell correlations and of the magnitudes of these correlations are analogous to tests of practical significance. The simplest way to illustrate this point is to summarize all the intervals that have been developed for both WABA I and II.

Combining WABA I and II

The intervals compatible with the whole, parts, equivocal, and inexplicable conditions given any and all values taken on by any of the individual tests (E, A, R, and F, Z, t) are summarized in Table 7.8. In other words, given a set of eta correlations and between- and within-cell correlations, this table is used to choose among the four conditions based on the values taken on by the empirical indicators in WABA I and II and for the WABA components. The use of these intervals with synthetic and real data is illustrated in the next four chapters.

Using these intervals, however, can be problematic because they permit interpretations of less than ideal results. In dealing with less than ideal results, the inductions from WABA I and WABA II are compared. Since the use of these intervals in WABA I and II permits an induction of one of four conditions (wholes, parts, equivocal, and inexplicable) in both analyses, at least 16 inductions are possible. A discussion of these simultaneous inductions is simplified by assuming that two variables X and Y result in the same induction in WABA I. As a result, the 16 conditions listed in Table 7.9 need to be considered.

When inductions from WABA I and II result in the same conclusion, the overall induction is straightforward (see **category I inductions** listed in Table 7.9 for a definition of these four straightforward inductions).

When an analysis using WABA I results in the induction of an inexplicable condition (no deviation within or between cells), the analysis from WABA II should not result in an induction of a parts, whole, or equivocal condition; according to WABA I, scores do not vary either within or between cells. When

TABLE 7.8. Summary of intervals for making inductions in WABA

WABA I	WABA II (DIFFERENCE TESTS)	WABA II (MAGNITUDE TESTS)
Wholes	*Wholes*	*Between*
15° $E \geq 1.30$	15° $A \geq 0.26$	†15° $R \geq 0.27$
30° $E \geq 1.73$	30° $A \geq 0.52$	††30° $R \geq 0.58$
0.05 $F \geq \hat{F}_{J-1, N-J}$	0.05 $Z \geq 1.66$	*0.05 $t \geq \hat{t}_{1, J-2}$
0.01 $F \geq \hat{F}_{J-1, N-J}$	0.01 $Z \geq 2.33$	**0.01 $t \geq \hat{t}_{1, J-2}$
Parts	*Parts*	*Within*
15° $E \leq 0.77$	15° $A \leq -0.26$	†15° $R \geq 0.27$
30° $E \leq 0.58$	30° $A \leq -0.52$	††30° $R \geq 0.58$
0.05 $F \leq 1/\hat{F}_{N-J, J-1}$	0.05 $Z \leq -1.66$	*0.05 $t \geq \hat{t}_{1, N-J-1}$
0.01 $F \leq 1/\hat{F}_{N-J, J-1}$	0.01 $Z \leq -2.33$	**0.01 $t \geq \hat{t}_{1, N-J-1}$
Equivocal	*Equivocal or Inexplicable*	*Components*
All others	All others	$B > W$: Wholes
		$W > B$: Parts
		$W = B$: Equivocal

Note: $\hat{t}_{1, J-2} = \sqrt{\hat{F}_{1, J-2}}$ and $\hat{t}_{1, N-J-1} = \sqrt{\hat{F}_{1, N-J-1}}$

TABLE 7.9.   Illustration of inductions from WABA I and II at one level of analysis

	WABA I INDUCTION	WABA II INDUCTION	FINAL INDUCTION
Category I (stronger)			
	Wholes	Wholes	Wholes
	Parts	Parts	Parts
	Equivocal	Equivocal	Equivocal
	Inexplicable	Inexplicable	Inexplicable
Category II (weaker)			
	Equivocal	Wholes	Wholes (weaker)
	Wholes	Inexplicable	Wholes (weaker)
	Equivocal	Parts	Parts (weaker)
	Parts	Inexplicable	Parts (weaker)
Category III (range restriction)			
	Wholes	Parts	None
	Parts	Wholes	None
	Wholes	Equivocal	None
	Parts	Equivocal	None
Category IV (ambiguous and inconsistent)			
	Inexplicable	Parts	None
	Inexplicable	Wholes	None
	Inexplicable	Equivocal	None
	Equivocal	Inexplicable	None

an analysis using WABA I results in an induction of an equivocal condition and an analysis using WABA II indicates an inexplicable condition (within- and between-cell correlations of 0), no substantive interpretation is made because an entity has not been identified empirically (see **category IV inductions** listed in Table 7.9 for a definition of these four ambiguous outcomes).

In cases in which an analysis results in the induction of an equivocal condition using WABA I and wholes or parts using WABA II, a whole or parts condition is induced. This induction, however, is weaker than one based on results where wholes or parts are induced with both WABA I and II. In addition, when wholes or parts are induced using WABA I, and an inexplicable condition is induced using WABA II, the result can be viewed as compatible with a whole or parts condition. An induction of this type is also weaker than one based on results that permit an induction of wholes or parts using both WABA I and II (see **category II inductions** presented in Table 7.9 for a definition of these weaker outcomes).

A final set of inductions may occur when the range of variables is restricted (see **category III inductions** in Table 7.9). Specifically, if wholes are induced based on WABA I, the within-cell deviations are restricted relative to between-cell deviations by definition. This relative (rather than absolute) restriction of range makes an interpretation of the within-cell correlations in WABA II problematic, because a within-cell correlation greater than zero in magnitude could be due to range restriction. Therefore, the parts and equivocal conditions that involve nonzero within-cell correlations should not be induced from WABA II when wholes are induced in WABA I, because the obtained within-cell correlations could be due to restriction of within-cell deviations. The same requirement applies if parts are induced with WABA I. In this case, the whole and equivocal conditions that rely on nonzero between-cell correlations should not be induced with WABA II, because nonzero between-cell correlations could be due to range restrictions of between-cell deviation scores.

Therefore, only inductions compatible with the eight conditions shown in the upper portion of Table 7.9 should be interpreted. As an additional check, a consideration of the between ($\eta_{BX} \cdot \eta_{BY} \cdot r_{BXY}$) and within ($\eta_{WX} \cdot \eta_{WY} \cdot r_{WXY}$) components of the WABA equation provides an indication of whether a total relationship is based mainly on between- or within-cell deviations.

MULTIPLE-LEVEL ANALYSIS

Inductions for multiple-level analysis are based on the same criteria used in single-level analysis. Although the values of these criteria will change due to differing degrees of freedom at different levels of analysis, the practical significance tests remain constant across all levels. Since the same criteria are used at each level of analysis, a choice among the four conditions at each level is made, and data are located on the entity axis of a varient matrix at multiple levels of analysis.

When ideal data are employed at all levels of analysis and when two levels of analysis are considered, eight ideal multiple-level conditions are plausible. When data are less than ideal, and particularly when the inductions at one level of analysis are very weak, problems can occur. In general, Table 7.10 can be used to check inductions for analyses at multiple levels.

The first eight inductions shown in the upper portion of the table are not problematic. Moreover, Chapter 6 explained why an inexplicable condition at a lower level of analysis does not permit an induction of wholes or parts at a higher level unless entities are added. Therefore, only the last six uninterpretable conditions presented in Table 7.10 require further discussion.

When an induction is drawn that parts are more likely at a lower level of analysis, the between-cell deviations should be error. Therefore parts, wholes, or equivocal conditions should not be obtained at a higher level of analysis because the analysis at the higher level is based on between-cell scores from the lower level. In a similar vein, an induction of wholes at a lower level of analysis implies systematic deviations between cells that should not disappear at a higher level and that therefore result in an inexplicable condition. This may seem to occur when a relationship at a lower level of analysis is weak ($p \le 0.05$) and at a higher level of analysis the relationship is weak, but just misses passing a criterion ($p \le 0.05$). Such a result should not be induced as compatible with a level-specific condition, but rather should be interpreted as indicating a weak set of results. These four conditions are listed in the lowest portion of Table 7.10. Two conditions now remain to be described.

When an equivocal condition is induced at a lower level of analysis, the nonzero between-cell correlations at a lower level should not disappear at a

TABLE 7.10. Interpretation of outcomes from two-level analysis in a single study

INDUCTION		INTERPRETATION	
Lower Level	*Higher Level*	*WABA I*	*WABA II*
Wholes	Wholes	Cross-level wholes	Same as WABA I
Wholes	Parts	Cross-level parts	Same as WABA I
Wholes	Equivocal	Level-specific wholes	Same as WABA I
Parts	Inexplicable	Level-specific parts	Same as WABA I
Equivocal	Equivocal	Equivocal	Same as WABA I
Inexplicable	Inexplicable	Inexplicable	Same as WABA I
Equivocal	Wholes	Emergent wholes	Same as WABA I
Equivocal	Parts	Emergent parts	Same as WABA I
Inexplicable	Wholes	Not feasible[a]	Emergent wholes
Inexplicable	Parts	Not feasible[a]	Emergent parts
Equivocal	Inexplicable	Not feasible	Reject both levels
Inexplicable	Equivocal	Not feasible	Reject both levels
Parts	Parts	Inconsistent	Same as WABA I
Parts	Equivocal	Inconsistent	Same as WABA I
Parts	Wholes	Inconsistent	Same as WABA I
Wholes	Inexplicable	Inconsistent	Same as WABA I

[a]Additional entities are required to induce emergent wholes or parts.

higher level and should not result in an induction of an inexplicable condition. The same logic in reverse applies in terms of an inexplicable condition at a lower level of analysis and an equivocal condition at a higher level. These conditions are not very likely to occur; when they do occur, it is helpful to remember that correlations and deviations do not magically disappear from one level of analysis to another. Data, however, may be quite weak and may not result in substantive interpretations. Clearly, withholding judgment when results of this type are obtained does not preclude an inference of emergent wholes or parts when the varient paradigm is used.

MULTIPLE-VARIABLE ANALYSIS

Since intervals have been derived for correlations, locating data along a variable axis is a matter of using the same intervals in a somewhat different way. In multiple-variable analysis, conditions are distinguished in terms of the magnitude of obtained correlations and in terms of the differences between obtained correlations. Two methods for testing the practical significance of the magnitude of correlations have been presented. In general, in order to test for practical significance, the less rigorous 15° and 30° criteria for the R test are used. In terms of statistical significance, the magnitude of correlations is tested by comparing the obtained t value to the theoretical $\hat{t}$ value.

In terms of tests of differences between correlations, criteria for testing the practical significance of A values have been presented. In terms of

TABLE 7.11. Summary of intervals for multiple-variable and multiple-relationship analyses[a]

MULTIPLE-VARIABLE ANALYSIS	MULTIPLE-RELATIONSHIP ANALYSIS
Magnitude Tests	*Magnitude Tests*
15° $R \geq 0.27$	15° $R \geq 0.27$
30° $R \geq 0.58$	30° $R \geq 0.58$
0.05 $t \geq \hat{t}_{1,df}$	0.05 $t \geq \hat{t}_{1,df}$
0.01 $t \geq \hat{t}_{1,df}$	0.01 $t \geq \hat{t}_{1,df}$
Difference Tests	*Difference Tests*
15° $A \geq 0.26$ and ≤ -0.26	15° $A \geq 0.26$ and ≤ -0.26
30° $A \geq 0.52$ and ≤ -0.52	30° $A \geq 0.52$ and ≤ -0.52
0.05 $t' \geq \hat{t}_{1,df}$ and $\leq -\hat{t}_{1,df}$	0.05 $Z \geq 1.66$ and ≤ -1.66
0.01 $t' \geq \hat{t}_{1,df}$ and $\leq -\hat{t}_{1,df}$	0.01 $Z \geq 2.33$ and ≤ -2.33

[a]$\hat{t}_{1,df} = \sqrt{\hat{F}_{1,df}}$ at the 0.05 and 0.01 level of statistical significance and *df* indicates the appropriate degrees of freedom for correlations and Hotelling's *t'* test.

statistical significance, Hotelling's t' test results in values that have 1 and $N - 3$ degrees of freedom. The theoretical values of $\hat{t}$ to which obtained t' values are compared are available from Table A.3 in Appendix A, using the standard conversion of $\hat{F}$ to $\hat{t}$:

$$\hat{t}_{1,N-3} = \sqrt{\hat{F}_{1,N-3}}$$

The intervals used in multiple-variable analysis are summarized in the first column of Table 7.11. Essentially, obtained correlations (using R and t) are compared against the intervals shown in the table for these indicators. Obtained differences are compared against the difference test intervals (A and $\hat{t}$) shown in the table. In this way, various conditions along the variable axis are identified empirically based on practical and statistical tests of magnitudes and differences.

MULTIPLE-RELATIONSHIP ANALYSIS

Once data are located on the variable axis, multiple-relationship analysis may be necessary. The contingent and multiplexed conditions are distinguished from each other in terms of both the magnitude of and the differences between correlations obtained in different conditions defined by values of at least a third variable. Procedures for assessing the magnitude of any correlation have been presented. Again, the less rigorous 15° and 30° tests of practical significance can be employed in addition to the rigorous tests. In multiple-relationship analysis, the difference between two correlations from different conditions can be calculated using A and Z values. Intervals have been derived for these values; however, the intervals for these differences are used in a special way.

From a variable focus, differences are calculated after the absolute values of the correlations are taken. As a result, the signs of these difference scores (A and Z) indicate the condition defined by a third variable (Z_1 or Z_2) that shows a stronger correlation. A contingent condition is induced when the obtained differences between the correlations from different conditions are statistically and practically significant; a multiplexed condition is induced when obtained differences are not significant. In this analysis, practically and statistically significant differences are inferred based on the magnitude of the difference between correlations, regardless of sign.

From an entity focus, in testing the differences between the within-cell and between-cell correlations from different conditions, the standard A and Z test criteria described for WABA II are employed. The sign of difference indicators and their magnitude result in an induction of one of the four conditions (wholes, parts, equivocal, or inexplicable).

The intervals used in multiple-relationship analysis are summarized in the right side of Table 7.11 and are identical to the intervals presented previously.

SUMMARY

Intervals have been presented that permit any value taken on by an indicator (E, A, R, and F, Z, t) to be located in a varient matrix based on tests of practical and statistical significance. These intervals permit data to be located along the entity axis of the varient matrix or in one of four conditions at a single level of analysis and in a variety of ways at multiple levels of analysis. In addition, these intervals are used to assess the magnitude of and differences between obtained correlations. As a result, data are also located along the variable axis of the varient matrix. The entire inferential procedure (using induction and deduction) is summarized and illustrated in the next chapter.

REVIEW QUESTIONS

1. How are tests of statistical significance viewed from an inferential perspective?
2. What serves as the basis for tests of practical significance?
3. How are tests of practical significance related to E ratios of between- and within-eta correlations?
4. Why should tests for the significance of both the magnitudes of and differences between correlations be used in WABA II?
5. Why should tests of practical significance precede tests of statistical significance?

6. What is the induction when an equivocal condition is induced with WABA I and a whole condition is induced with WABA II?

7. When wholes are induced at one level of analysis, what is the next analytical step?

8. How are values of $\hat{r}$ at the 0.05 level of significance determined?

9. Why are $\hat{Z}$ values of 1.66 and 2.33 required to induce a significant difference between correlations on a statistical basis?

10. What concern is the foundation for the varient approach to practical and statistical significance?

8

INFERENCES

The inference process in the varient paradigm is based on the varient conceptualization presented in Chapter 2. Specifically, the intervals and decision-making processes described in the previous chapter and based on a consideration of ideal conditions (see Chapter 6) for key geometrically determined indicators (see Chapter 5) are used in drawing inferences from data collected in a particular context. The starting point in the inference process, however, is a theory formulated in the way illustrated in Chapters 3 and 4. From such a theory, definitions of variables and entities are deduced for a particular setting. Based on these deductions, cells are aligned with hypothesized entities and scores are obtained for variables. The data are then analyzed, and an induction is made about the characteristics of the data. Finally, an inference is drawn by comparing obtained to predicted results using a varient matrix.

In this approach, a theory is inferred to be supported when theoretical predictions and obtained data occupy the same space (are isomorphic) in a varient matrix. A theory is replaced when obtained data have substantive meaning, but are not compatible with the predictions of the theory. For example, the original theoretical formulation is rejected in favor of another substantive theoretical hypothesis when parts are hypothesized and wholes seem more likely empirically; when a cross-level relationship is hypothesized and a level-specific relationship seems more likely empirically; when a related case is hypothesized and a generally unrelated one seems more likely empirically; or when a contingency formulation is hypothesized and a multiplexed formulation seems more likely empirically. Of course, when results are not practically or statistically significant, no inference can be drawn because results of this type can be due to poor theory or poor data collection techniques. In other words, as in traditional approaches, poor results from a study cannot be used to replace a theory, since poor results have no meaning.

In the varient paradigm, three steps are used in testing theories or drawing inferences. First, a theory is used to obtain scores on variables and to identify entities in a particular setting. In this theory and deduction step, the predictions for all analyses to be performed on data collected from a particular setting are specified by the use of double lines in a varient matrix. Second, data analysis is performed and inductions are made. In this data analysis and induction step, the results from each data analysis are located with the use of number signs in a varient matrix. Third, inductions are compared to the theoretical predictions and inferences are drawn. In this inference step, predictions are compared with obtained results. The degree to which data (indicated by number signs) align with the predictions from theory (indicated by double lines) is readily apparent using a varient matrix. These three steps and the ways in which the varient matrix is used in each step are examined in depth using synthetic data in this chapter and real data in Chapters 9, 10, and 11.

THEORY AND DEDUCTION

For the purpose of illustration, assume we have a theory (such as theory A presented in Chapter 4) not only about work groups (single-level analysis), but also about collectivities and persons (multiple-level analysis). Moreover, assume we predict that two variables X and Y are related to each other but independent of a third variable Z (multiple-variable analysis). Finally, with multiple-relationship analysis in mind, assume that the relationship of interest between X and Y will hold regardless of the values taken on by a third variable Z.

Having formulated such a theory, a researcher should be able to define persons, groups, and collectivities in a precise way in a particular setting. For the purpose of illustration, we will use the number of entities we identified in a setting to be discussed in the following three chapters. In this setting, 276 individuals were contained in 83 supervisory work groups, which in turn were contained in 8 collectivities. A researcher should also be able to obtain scores for variables of interest from this formulation. For this illustration, assume that scores have been obtained by asking 276 individuals to respond to questions which are thought to measure three variables X, Y, and Z. Our theory has therefore been used to define entities and obtain scores in a particular setting.

In addition, our theory should predict exactly what should happen when data from a particular setting are analyzed. According to our theory, whole groups should underlie obtained relationships between the three variables when a single-level analysis is performed using WABA I and WABA II. This prediction for a single-level analysis is indicated in Table 8.1 by the placement of double lines at the whole condition. Likewise, wholes are predicted at the collectivity and person levels of analysis when multiple-level analysis is performed. The double lines in Table 8.2, in which results from a multiple-level analysis are presented, indicate these predictions. In terms of multiple-variable analysis, from this theory the three variables are predicted to be generally unrelated. The double lines in Table 8.3 indicate this prediction. In addition, the double lines in the lower portion of Table 8.4 indicate that variables X and Y are predicted to be multiplexed with values of variable Z. Theoretically, we have predicted a generally unrelated and multiplexed set of three variables will be obtained at the whole person, work group, and collectivity levels of analysis. These predictions are indicated by the double lines in Table 8.5.

Empirically, data may be located anywhere in the varient matrix. It is not until data have also been located in the matrix (with number signs) that our theory can be viewed as tested. In other words, a theory specifies how to define entities and measure variables, and it is these specifications that are tested with data. We know nothing about the accuracy of our theoretical predictions until after empirical analyses are performed.

DATA ANALYSIS AND INDUCTION

The analysis of data involves the use of single- and multiple-level analyses and multiple-variable and multiple-relationship analyses. In each analysis, cells are aligned with entities, values for correlations are obtained, and an induction is made. Inductions from data are indicated by the number signs as opposed to double lines in the varient matrix.

Single-Level Analysis

In making a single-level analysis, we prefer to begin with the lowest level of analysis specified by a theory for a particular setting. In our theoretical formulation, the starting point is 276 individuals. If these individuals were viewed as whole persons, then one cell would be formed for each individual. The contents of each cell would be scores thought to represent parts for each individual. For the purpose of simplifying this illustration, assume that a hypothesized relationship based on whole persons is obtained. As a result, the new starting point is now the 276 between-cell scores for persons comprising 83 work groups. The prediction of the theory is that when cells are aligned with 83 work groups and within- and between-work-group scores are calculated, WABA I and II will result in an induction of whole work groups.

WABA I Using WABA I, a set of within- and between-eta correlations and their associated E and F ratios are presented in the upper left portion of Table 8.1. In this fictional set of results, the E and F ratios both equal infinity. In the lower left portion of the left side of the table, the three alternative conditions (wholes, parts, and equivocal) and the intervals required to induce each condition are presented in the same fashion as in Chapter 7. As shown in the table by the number signs, the E and F values exceed the critical values required to induce that a whole rather than parts or equivocal condition is more likely. An induction of whole work groups is therefore made for each variable, X and Y.

We use averages when there is a need to summarize a set of similar results. **Average within-** and **average between-eta correlations** are calculated by transforming the correlations into angles, taking an average of these angles, and transforming this average into an average for within- and between-eta correlations. From these averages, **E and F ratios** are calculated. In the case illustrated in Table 8.1, the averages of the between- and within-cell correla-

TABLE 8.1. Format for drawing inferences at one level of analysis

WABA I

	Variables		
	X	Y	Avg.
Data			
η between (82)	1	1	1
η within (193)	0	0	0
E ratio	∞	∞	∞
F ratio	∞	∞	∞
Inferences			
Wholes			
15° E ≥ 1.30	#	#	#
30° E ≥ 1.73	#	#	#
0.05 F ≥ 1.35	#	#	#
0.01 F ≥ 1.53	#	#	#
Parts			
15° E ≤ 0.77			
30° E ≤ 0.58			
0.05 F ≤ 0.72			
0.01 F ≤ 0.64			
Equivocal			
15° (all others)			
30 ° (all others)			
0.05 (all others)			
0.01 (all others)			
Overall Inference			
Theory Wholes			
Data Wholes			

WABA II DIFFERENCE TESTS

	Variables X and Y Average		
	r	Prac.	Stat.
Data			
r between (81)	1	1	1
r within (192)	0	0	0
A	1.57	1.57	
Z	∞		∞
Inferences			
Wholes			
15° A ≥ 0.26	#	#	
30° A ≥ 0.52	#	#	
0.05 Z ≥ 1.66	#		#
0.01 Z ≥ 2.33	#		#
Parts			
15° A ≤ −0.26			
30° A ≤ −0.52			
0.05 Z ≤ −1.66			
0.01 Z ≤ −2.33			
Equivocal			
15° (all others)			
30° (all others)			
0.05 (all others)			
0.01 (all others)			
Overall Inference			
Theory Wholes			
Data Wholes			

WABA II MAGNITUDE TESTS AND SUMMARY

	Variables X and Y Average		
	r	Prac.	Stat.
Between data			
R	∞††	∞††	
t	∞**		∞**
Inferences			
†15° R ≥ 0.27			
††30° R ≥ 0.58			
*0.05 t ≥ 1.99			
**0.01 t ≥ 2.64			
Within data			
R	0	0	
t	0		0
Inferences			
†15° R ≥ 0.27			
††30° R ≥ 0.58			
*0.05 t ≥ 1.97			
**0.01 t ≥ 2.60			
Components			
Between	1	1	
Within	0	0	
Inference			
B > W	#		
W > B			
W = B			

tions for variables X and Y are 1 and 0, respectively. Therefore, the average E and F ratios equal infinity. These values are shown in the upper left portion of the table. An induction of whole work groups is again indicated by the location of the number signs in the lower left portion of Table 8.1.

WABA II   Using WABA II, a fictional set of values for the between- and within-cell correlations and their associated A and Z values is presented in the upper middle portion of Table 8.1. In this case, A and Z take on their maximum values (1.57 and ∞). As is shown in the lower middle portion of the table by the number signs, these values are within the intervals described in Chapter 7 required for inducing a whole rather than a parts or equivocal condition.

On occasion, a summary value for a set of these correlations is desirable. Two types of averages serve this purpose. The first, **a statistical average of a set of correlations**, is obtained by transforming each correlation to a Z' within or between score (see Appendix A), taking the average of the within and between Z' scores separately, and then converting averages back to an average correlation (see Guilford, 1965). The second, the **practical average**, is obtained by converting correlations into angles, taking an average of these angles, and converting the average angle to an average correlation. This procedure is used for within- and between-cell correlations separately. In the case in Table 8.1, only one within-cell and one between-cell correlation is presented; therefore, the value for the averages is the same as for the obtained correlations. The finding that the values based on the averages for A and Z result in an induction of whole work groups is indicated by the location of number signs in the lower middle portion of the table.

In WABA II, the magnitudes of the within- and between-cell correlations must be considered in addition to the differences between these correlations. As is shown in Table 8.1, the obtained between-cell correlation of 1 is greater than the value required by the rigorous (30°) test (0.866) in order to infer a relationship between variables X and Y. The results from applying less rigorous tests are presented in the right portion of the table. As is shown by the use of daggers and asterisks, using these practical and statistical criteria, the between-cell correlations are systematic. Finally, as shown in the lower right portion of the table, the between-cell component equals 1, and the within-cell component equals 0, as predicted. These components are summarized by using averages.

Combining WABA I and II   The results from this work-group-level analysis lead to an induction of wholes using both WABA I and WABA II. Empirically, X and Y are related based on differences between work groups; this result was predicted by the theory, as indicated by the double lines in Table 8.1. Data, however, need not align with such predictions. For example, despite a prediction of wholes, the data could have resulted in an induction of parts or an equivocal condition.

Setting up an analysis such as that illustrated in Table 8.1 is considerably simpler than may appear at first glance. The within- and between-eta and work-group correlations are obtained from data. The intervals required for the E, A, R, and $\hat{Z}$ tests are the same regardless of degrees of freedom. Only the intervals for the $\hat{F}$ ratio and $\hat{t}$ change, based on the degrees of freedom in a data set. The degrees of freedom for each correlation are shown in parens in the table. The results presented in Table 8.1 are for one level of analysis. In this case, between-work-group scores completely represent the total deviations in the two variables of interest ($\eta_{BX} = \eta_{BY} = 1$); therefore, multiple-level analysis is very appropriate.

Multiple-Level Analysis

At the collectivity level of analysis, such between-work-group scores with 82 degrees of freedom can be partitioned into between-collectivity scores with 7 degrees of freedom ($J - 1$), and within-collectivity scores with 75 degrees of freedom ($N - J$). At this higher level of analysis, the format presented in Table 8.1 is again employed. WABA I and II are repeated at this higher level of analysis by calculating within- and between-collectivity scores from between-work-groups scores. For the purpose of simplifying this illustration,

TABLE 8.2.   Illustrative format for summarizing inferences for multiple-level analysis

ENTITY AXIS	EMPIRICAL		INFERENTIAL		
	E ratio	A value	WABA I	WABA II	WABA I and II
Collectivities					
Wholes ($J - 1 = 7$)	∞	1.57	#	#	#
Parts ($N - J = 75$)					
Equivocal ($N - 1 = 82$)					
Inexplicable					
Groups					
Wholes ($J - 1 = 82$)	∞	1.57	#	#	#
Parts ($N - J = 193$)					
Equivocal ($N - 1 = 275$)					
Inexplicable					
Persons					
Wholes ($J - 1 = 275$)	∞	1.57	#	#	#
Parts					
Equivocal					
Inexplicable					
Inferences			Wholes across levels	Wholes across levels	Wholes across levels

assume that the collectivity level of analysis results in an induction of whole collectivities.

Fictitious results from a three-level analysis (persons, groups, and collectivities) are summarized in Table 8.2. Essentially, an entity axis from the varient matrix defines the rows of the table. The E ratios and A values are employed as summary indicators at each level of analysis for WABA I and WABA II, respectively (assuming that all the results reach statistical significance). The number signs in the table indicate that the data are more compatible with a whole condition at each level of analysis. Using both WABA I and II, therefore, the overall induction shown in the last column of the table is that the relationship between the two variables of interest is based on differences between whole collectivities, work groups, and persons. Since this induction is identical to the original hypothesis, the illustrative theory withstood the test, at least in terms of entities. A consideration of variables is now appropriate.

Multiple-Variable Analysis

According to the theoretical formulation, a third variable Z was hypothesized to be unrelated to the two variables of interest X and Y. Actually, variable Z should have been included in the analyses presented in Tables 8.1 and 8.2. To simplify the illustration, however, assume that variable Z was included in the analyses, that it was found to vary between entities using WABA I at each level of analysis, and that it was correlated 0 with variables X and Y at each level of analysis. In other words, assume that the following three between-cell correlations were obtained at each level of analysis:

$$r_{BXY} = 1.00$$

$$r_{BXZ} = 0.00$$

$$r_{BYZ} = 0.00$$

TABLE 8.3. Format for drawing inferences with multiple-variable analysis

	OBTAINED VALUES	INFERRED MEANING	Related X ↔ Y ↔ Z	Generally Related (X ⊥ Y) ↔ Z / (X ⊥ Z) ↔ Y	Generally Related (Y ⊥ Z) ↔ X	Generally Unrelated (X ↔ Y) ⊥ Z	Generally Unrelated (X ↔ Z) ⊥ Y / (Y ↔ Z) ⊥ X	Unrelated X ⊥ Y ⊥ Z
Magnitude Tests								
R values								
XY (1.00)	∞††	+	o	o o	o o	o o	o o	o o
XZ (.00)	0	o		o	o o	o o	o o	o o
YZ (.00)	0	o		o				o o
t values								
XY	∞**	+	o	o o	o o	o o	o o	o o
XZ	0	o		o	o o	o o	o o	o o
YZ	0	o		o				o o
Difference Tests								
A values								
−(|XY| − |XZ|)	1.57††	+	o	+ (0)	+ +	− +	− o	o o
−(|XY| − |YZ|)	1.57††	+	o	− (0)	+ −	− o	o −	o −
−(|XZ| − |YZ|)	0	o	o	(0) −	o o	(0) o	o o	o o
t′ values								
|XY| − |XZ|	∞**	+	o	+ (0)	+ +	− +	− o	o o
|XY| − |YZ|	∞**	+	o	− (0)	+ −	− o	o −	o −
|XZ| − |YZ|	0	o	o	(0) −	o o	(0) o	o o	o o
Inference							#	

Note: Whole work groups are assumed ($df = J - 2 = 81$).

†15° $R \geq 0.27$; $A \geq 0.26$.

*0.05 $t \geq 1.99$.

††30° $R \geq 0.58$; $A \geq 0.52$.

**0.01 $t \geq 2.64$.

These correlations show that the three variables are generally unrelated and that variable Z is independent of variables X and Y. When results are not this straightforward, the format for presenting the results from multiple-variable analysis given in Table 8.3 is particularly useful.

The values for the three correlations (r_{BXY}, r_{BXZ}, and r_{BYZ}) are shown in parens in the upper left portion of Table 8.3. Values for R, t, A, and t' are presented in the column labeled "Obtained Values." The footnotes to the table provide the critical values necessary to infer that correlations are significant in magnitude and that their differences are significant. Using these criteria, an inferred meaning is given to each indicator (R, t, A, and t'). For example, the obtained R value of infinity is taken to mean that the correlation of 1 indicates a positive relationship. Likewise, obtained R values of 0 are taken to mean a lack of relationship or a value of zero. The same procedure is used for all the tests.

The remaining columns of the table contain the values indicators should take on for each of the eight plausible locations listed along the variable axis of this three-variable varient matrix. As shown in the table, the obtained values—given their inferred meaning—correspond to the values specified for the generally unrelated case. This induction is indicated in the last row of the table by the number sign found under the column labeled "Generally Unrelated." The fact that this generally unrelated case was predicted on a theoretical basis is indicated by the location of the double lines in the same row and column. Clearly, the synthetic data and theoretical predictions are isomorphic.

Multiple-Relationship Analysis

Since the correlation between the two variables of interest that are independent of a third variable equals 1, the relationship is multiplexed, because the correlation between the two variables of interest (X and Y) must equal 1 in all conditions defined by any third variable Z. To illustrate the procedure for choosing between multiplexed and contingent conditions, assume that interest is in the work-group level of analysis and that four conditions are defined by values of a third variable Z. Assume that 20, 21, 21, and 21 work groups are contained in conditions Z_1, Z_2, Z_3, and Z_4, respectively, and that a between-cell correlation of 1 between variables X and Y is obtained in each condition. These correlational values are presented in parens in the upper left portion of Table 8.4.

The R, t, A, and Z values that result are presented in the column labeled "Obtained Values" in Table 8.4. Using the ranges shown in the table footnotes, decisions are made about both the magnitude of and the differences between the correlations. These decisions are shown in the column labeled "Inferred Meaning." Values compatible with multiplexed and contingent hypotheses are shown in the next two columns. A comparison of the inferred meaning of the obtained results with the multiplexed and contingent cases leads to the induction that the obtained results are compatible with a multiplexed case. This is indicated in the last row of the table by the number sign. In addition, the double lines indicate that a multiplexed case was also hypothesized on a theoretical basis.

TABLE 8.4.   Illustration of format for drawing inferences with multiple-relationship analysis (variable focus)

	EMPIRICAL		VARIABLE AXIS		
BETWEEN (CHOSEN FOCUS)	Obtained Values	Inferred Meaning	Multiplexed $(X \leftrightarrow Y) \perp Z$	Contingent $[(X \leftrightarrow Y) \perp Z]$	Degrees of Freedom
Magnitude Tests					
R values					
Condition Z_1 (1.00)	$\infty^{\dagger\dagger}$	+	+ or −	+ or −	18
Condition Z_2 (1.00)	$\infty^{\dagger\dagger}$	+	+ or −	0	19
Condition Z_3 (1.00)	$\infty^{\dagger\dagger}$	+	+ or −	0	19
Condition Z_4 (1.00)	$\infty^{\dagger\dagger}$	+	+ or −	0	19
t values					
Condition Z_1	∞^{**}	+	+ or −	+ or −	18
Condition Z_2	∞^{**}	+	+ or −	0	19
Condition Z_3	∞^{**}	+	+ or −	0	19
Condition Z_4	∞^{**}	+	+ or −	0	19
Difference Tests					
A values					
Condition Z_1 minus					
Condition Z_2	0	0	0	+	18
Condition Z_3	0	0	0	+	19
Condition Z_4	0	0	0	+	19
Condition Z_2 minus					
Condition Z_3	0	0	0	0	19
Condition Z_4	0	0	0	0	19
Condition Z_3 minus					
Condition Z_4	0	0	0	0	19
Z values					
Condition Z_1 minus					
Condition Z_2	0	0	0	+	18
Condition Z_3	0	0	0	+	19
Condition Z_4	0	0	0	+	19
Condition Z_2 minus					
Condition Z_3	0	0	0	0	19
Condition Z_4	0	0	0	0	19
Condition Z_3 minus					
Condition Z_4	0	0	0	0	19
Inference			#		

†15° $A \geq 0.26$; $R \geq 0.27$.
*0.05 $Z \geq 1.66$; $t \geq \hat{t}$ (for degrees of freedom shown).
††30° $R \geq 0.58$; $A \geq 0.52$.
**0.01 $Z \geq 2.33$; $t \geq \hat{t}$ (for degrees of freedom shown).

INFERENCES

All the results and inferences presented in Tables 8.1 to 8.4 are used to locate data in a varient matrix. The single- and multiple-level analyses locate data along the entity axis. In the analyses, whole persons, work groups, and collectivities were chosen as more compatible with the variables than the parts

TABLE 8.5. Illustration of procedure for locating theory and data in a varient matrix

ENTITY AXIS	Related	Generally Related	Generally Unrelated Contingent or Multiplexed $(X \leftrightarrow Y) \perp Z$	Unrelated Contingent or Multiplexed
Collectivities				
Wholes			# # #	
Parts				
Equivocal				
Inexplicable				
Groups				
Wholes			# # #	
Parts				
Equivocal				
Inexplicable				
Persons				
Wholes			# # #	
Parts				
Equivocal				
Inexplicable				

Tables 8.1 and 8.2 ◄─────────── Tables 8.3 and 8.4 ───────────►

or equivocal conditions. In the multiple-variable and multiple-relationship analyses, a generally unrelated and multiplexed case was induced as more likely than the related, generally related, and unrelated or contingent cases. The data are summarized by the number signs in Table 8.5 for each variable; the predictions of the theoretical specifications are illustrated by the double lines. In terms of inferences, data and theory align perfectly. To summarize, as is shown in the last row of Table 8.5, the results from the analyses presented in Tables 8.1 and 8.2 are used to locate data along the entity axis of the varient matrix, and the results presented in Tables 8.3 and 8.4 are used to locate data along the variable axis.

SUMMARY

Theory is the starting point in any empirical investigation because it defines measures of variables and entities. In addition, predictions are derived from theory for measures and entities in a specific setting and these are specified in a varient matrix using single- and multiple-level analyses and multiple-variable and multiple-relationship analyses. Data are then located in a varient matrix using empirical procedures in single- and multiple-level and multiple-variable and multiple-relationship analyses. A comparison of theoretically predicted results (indicated by double lines in a varient matrix) with obtained results (indicated by number signs in a varient matrix) indicates the degree to which data are compatible with a preferred theory or some other formulation. In the fictitious example presented in this chapter, theory and data were isomorphic. In the next three chapters, the degree to which the real theoretical predictions presented in Chapter 4 align with real data is examined.

REVIEW QUESTIONS

1. What is the basis on which inferences are drawn about theory and data?
2. In what way could the inferential process be thought of as based on inconsistencies?
3. How can theory testing be simplified into three steps?
4. In what ways do WABA I and WABA II still depend on the averaging of scores?
5. How do differing degrees of freedom affect the inference process?
6. When A and E are used as key indicators in summarizing results from multiple levels of analysis, what should be kept in mind?
7. If correlations in two conditions defined by a third variable equal zero, is such a case multiplexed or contingent?
8. Why should theory testing usually begin with assessment of appropriate levels of analysis and then move to a consideration of relationships between variables?
9. What is the inference when results are practically but not statistically significant?
10. What is the inference when results are statistically but not practically significant?

9

TESTING THEORIES:
A Group – Collectivity Illustration

The inferential procedures in the varient paradigm are now illustrated by testing the predictions of theory A and theory B separately and then in combination. Theory A (the focus of this chapter) predicts that titles and expectations will be related based on differences among whole persons, whole dyads, whole groups, and whole collectivities. To test this assertion, data collected in a setting about 10 miles outside a major metropolitan area in the northeastern United States were employed. In this setting the person, group, and collectivity levels of analysis were defined and measures believed to assess titles and expectations were identified. Data were then collected and analyzed, and inductions were made based on the results of the analyses. Finally, inferences were drawn by comparing the predictions of theory A to the results from analyzing data. A description of the results of applying these steps (theory and deduction, data analysis and induction, and inferences) to one setting is now presented.

THEORY AND DEDUCTION

Entities and variables were defined in the setting of interest based on our theory. Admittedly, our theoretical formulation was somewhat less articulated before we began the study, and our initial observations clarified ideas. Nevertheless, the process of defining variables and entities involves a consideration of single- and multiple-level analyses and multiple-variable and multiple-relationship analyses.

Single-Level Analysis

Our initial contact with the setting we investigated was with the manager of a division of a large conglomerate. To maintain the anonymity of the setting, we refer to it as the metals company or MCO. Of course, this organization could be viewed as one collectivity (MCO); however, an examination of organization records and discussions with all the managers in the organization suggested that the setting could also be viewed in a variety of ways in terms of entities. The division manager was interested in seeking aid in defining the training needs of the managers, and our study was thus confined to a consideration of the entire managerial corps. At the time of the study, 307 managers were on the payroll. Of this total, 90 percent agreed to answer all our questions. These 276 individuals can be viewed as persons, components of work groups, and/or members of collectivities.

Persons   At the person level of analysis, 552 scores result when two different reports are associated with each of the 276 individuals. Scores concerning these individuals may reflect the characteristics of the 276 (J) whole persons or 276 ($N - J$) reports within persons (person parts). This person-level conceptualization of the setting at MCO can be illustrated by listing the total number of scores and degrees of freedom appropriate at this level of analysis as follows:

		DEGREES OF FREEDOM	
PERSON	**TOTALS**	*WABA I*	*WABA II*
Level total	$N = 552$		
Parts	$N - J = 276$	276	275
Wholes	$J = 276$	275	274

Work Groups   The 276 individuals can also be conceptualized in terms of work groups as identified from organization records. Each work group is defined as the set of individuals who report to the same superior. To check on the accuracy of our initial understanding of the setting, during our interviews each of the superiors drew a picture of his or her work group and indicated who reported to him or her. As an additional procedural check on this identification of work groups, all individuals were asked whether our view of who was their superior was accurate. Ten individuals indicated that our understanding was in error. In some cases, this "error" was due to transfers in the organization. In other cases, the respondents preferred to believe they reported not to the superior we listed, but to their superior's boss. The data from these 10 individuals were not included in any analyses and are not included in the 276 reports, since we chose not to follow up on the accuracy of these reports. The results of these procedures for identifying work groups suggested that the 276 individuals could be viewed as comprising 83 work groups. The consequences of this work-group conceptualization of the setting at MCO can be illustrated by representing the total number of scores and degrees of freedom at this level of analysis as follows:

		DEGREES OF FREEDOM	
WORK GROUP	**TOTALS**	*WABA I*	*WABA II*
Level total	276		
Parts	193	193	192
Wholes	83	82	81

Collectivities   In addition, records and the physical layout of the setting suggested that eight collectivities could be identified at MCO. Mechanical equipment used to transform ore into metal in a continuous metal extraction process was located in one area, with the offices and desks of a number of individuals nearby. Most observers would probably infer that the individuals in these offices were involved in moving ore through a set of complicated mechanical operations and in extracting various metals at different points in the process. In this production collectivity, 107 individuals were organized into 30 work groups.

A building containing the research and development collectivity was a short walk from all other buildings in the division. Most observers would probably infer that the library and research facilities in the building were characteristic of a setting with an adaptive function (Katz and Kahn, 1978). Fifty-one individuals comprising 19 managerial work groups were housed in this adaptive collectivity.

Old and new parts and test benches were contained in a separate maintenance building. In addition to maintenance facilities, drafting and engineering tables were contained in a separate floor in the main building of the division. The function here was to design and redesign the equipment as it deteriorated from the intense heat of the extraction process. Eighty individuals were divided into 21 work groups in this maintenance collectivity.

A quality control department as well as various customer service work groups involved in controlling inputs and outputs were located in another building. Thirty-eight individuals were divided into 13 work groups in this support collectivity.

The integration of these functions at MCO (production, adaptive, maintenance, and support) was hierarchical. Any individual's level *in the hierarchy* was defined by the number of individuals between that individual and the division manager. Upper-level collectivities were defined as containing those individuals who reported to the division manager and those who were one individual removed from the division manager. All other managers were conceptualized as being contained in lower-level collectivities. This conceptualization of the setting results in the following 8 functional collectivities: upper- and lower-level production, upper- and lower-level support, upper- and lower-level maintenance, and upper- and lower-level adaptive. One of the consequences of this collectivity-level conceptualization at MCO can be illustrated by beginning with the 83 work groups contained in the 8 collectivities. These 83 work groups are then conceptualized as comprising 75 different parts in 8 collectivities or as the 8 whole collectivities themselves. The consequences of this conceptualization can also be illustrated by the following list of degrees of freedom at the collectivity level of analysis:

		DEGREES OF FREEDOM	
COLLECTIVITY	TOTALS	*WABA I*	*WABA II*
Level total	83		
Parts	75	75	74
Wholes	8	7	6

TABLE 9.1.   Number of units at various levels of analysis

	TOTAL	PRODUCTION Lower	PRODUCTION Upper	SUPPORT Lower	SUPPORT Upper	MAINTENANCE Lower	MAINTENANCE Upper	ADAPTIVE Lower	ADAPTIVE Upper
Person (dyad)									
Level total (N)	552	156	58	40	36	134	26	76	26
Parts ($N - J$)	276	78	29	20	18	67	13	38	13
Wholes (J)	276	78	29	20	18	67	13	38	13
Group									
Level total (N)	276	78	29	20	18	67	13	38	13
Parts ($N - J$)	193	55	22	13	12	48	11	21	11
Wholes (J)	83	23	7	7	6	19	2	17	2
Collectivity (group)									
Level total (N)	83	23	7	7	6	19	2	17	2
Parts ($N - J$)	75	22	6	6	5	18	1	16	1
Wholes (J)	8	1	1	1	1	1	1	1	1

Multiple-Level Analysis

The consequences for data analysis of this formulation of three levels of analysis at MCO are summarized in Table 9.1. The values shown in the left portion of the table are identical to those presented for the person, group, and collectivity levels of analysis. The values shown in the right portion represent the number of collectivity, work group, and person parts and wholes within each collectivity. From a different perspective, these values illustrate the distribution of work groups and persons (wholes and parts) within collectivities.

In this setting, the entire set of 276 individuals can be conceptualized as 276 whole persons, 193 independent parts of groups, or as 83 whole work groups. Moreover, the 83 work groups can be conceptualized as 75 independent parts of collectivities or as 8 whole collectivities. Empirically, any set of scores obtained from these 276 individuals can be viewed in any one or combination of these ways. Theory A predicts that whole persons, work groups, and collectivities will be more likely bases for the differences underlying any obtained relationships between titles and expectations. To test this hypothesis, variables must also be defined and measured.

Multiple-Variable Analysis

In addition to organization records, variables were measured using questionnaires administered during structured interviews completed on company time. Each individual's responses were identified so that analyses could assess whether responses should be associated with the individual as a person or as a member of a work group or collectivity. Several steps were taken to emphasize that although each individual's responses were identified, they would be held in strict confidence. First, a meeting was held with the division manager and his subordinates. In this meeting, in addition to outlining the purpose of the study, we emphasized that data would be reported to them in such a way that no individual's responses would be identifiable. Second, the division manager introduced the study to the 276 managers with a memo that stressed the confidential nature of their responses. Third, in each interview session we explained the purpose of the study and again stressed the confidential nature of the responses. The 276 individuals seemed quite supportive and willing to be interviewed (at times, for 3 to 4 hours), so much so that the interview schedule had to be extended. During these interviews, measures of titles and expectations were employed. All these measures of individuals' reports and their alpha coefficients are presented in Appendix G. The scales were formed by adding together the responses for each item shown in the appendix based on factor analysis techniques (each item can be viewed as weighted by a value of 1 or by unit weights, since factor weights were not employed. See Chapter 14 for a discussion and extension of this traditional approach to scale formation).

Titles Functional and professional titles were assessed in different ways. First, functional titles seemed to align naturally with collectivities in this setting. In addition to the different geographic locations of the functional collectivities, records indicated that the organization was structured around these functions, with one individual heading a particular function or subfunction. Although this natural clustering of individuals is somewhat supportive of our original notions of titles, a key disadvantage is that the strength of the relationship between functional titles and expectations is difficult to assess independent of collectivities. In this setting, functional titles are by definition collectivity-based (**collectivity functional titles**). To assess functional titles at other levels of analysis, a second set of measures was employed. Each individual at MCO was now also classified in two ways: as technical or nontechnical, and at one of three skill levels based on organization records. We called this measure **individual functional titles**, since level of analysis is not defined.

To assess professional orientation, a procedure similar to that employed by Haga, Graen, and Dansereau (1974) was used. Within an organization, an individual can be viewed as more or less attached to professional associations. In order for us to assess this attachment, each manager indicated the number of **professional associations (PA)** in which he or she held paid memberships. In addition, the **level of education (Ed)**, indicated by each manager, can be viewed as the degree to which an individual buys a particular title (such as high school graduate, B.S., M.A., Ph.D.).

Although a key question is whether these four measures of titles are related at the collectivity level of analysis, a more important issue is whether these titles are related to measures of expectations.

Expectations Three expectations were of particular interest to us. First, **freedom from superior (FS)** refers to the extent to which an individual perceives his or her superior as insisting that standard procedures be followed and the extent to which this superior checks the work. A higher score on the set of items in this scale means that a superior is reported as spending less time checking the subordinate's work and insisting that the subordinate follow standard operating procedures. Therefore, the scale attempts to measure the degree to which an individual perceives he or she is free from the superior. Second, **freedom from machine determination (FM)** refers to the degree to which an individual perceives that machines determine the pace and order in which the job is done. A higher score indicates more freedom from machines is reported by an individual and a lower score means that an individual perceives less freedom. These two measures are similar to those used by Bell (1965, 1966). A third measure, **freedom preferences (FP)**, is defined as the extent to which an individual believes a superior should be willing to allow an effective performer to make various changes in his or her job. A high score indicates that an individual believes effective subordinates should be allowed to make changes in their own jobs. A low score indicates that the individual believes effective subordinates should not be allowed to make such changes.

Titles and Expectations   Theoretically, all these measures are hypothesized to form one network of variables. In other words, theory A predicts that a related rather than generally related, generally unrelated, or unrelated set of results will be obtained and that these relationships will be based on differences among whole collectivities, work groups, and persons.

Multiple-Relationship Analysis

According to theory A, these variables are not expected to be correlated so that a distinctive set of two or a subset of variables will be identifiable; therefore, multiple-relationship analysis is not required.

Summary of Theory and Deduction Steps

From theory A, we believe the various measures of titles and expectations will be related (multiple-variable and multiple-relationship analyses) based on differences among the 8 whole collectivities, the 83 whole work groups, and the 276 whole persons (single- and multiple-level analyses). Of course, we do not really *know* whether these results will be obtained from this data set until the analyses have been completed. Empirically, a number of alternative theoretical conditions can occur. To illustrate this point, the presentation of the outcome of the data analysis begins with results considered ambiguous in the varient paradigm. Of particular importance is the fact that the induction process can be performed without any consideration of the preferred theoretical conditions. Therefore, in the presentation of the results of the analysis, little attention is given to our preferred theoretical predictions other than to indicate the exact predictions based on theory A with double lines in each table.

DATA ANALYSIS AND INDUCTION

Ambiguous Person-Level Analysis

The data relevant to theory A were collected from the 276 individuals. Each responded only once to each item, making any attempt to analyze data at the person level ambiguous. (The results from a person-level analysis of other data collected in this setting will be presented in the next chapter.) The total

TABLE 9.2. Ambiguous analysis of title and expectation measures

	CORRELATIONS	R TEST	t TEST	INFERENCE[a]
Education (Ed) and	*(df = 274)*			
Freedom from superior	0.43	0.48[†]	7.88**	S
Freedom from machines	0.40	0.44[†]	7.22**	S
Freedom preferences	0.32	0.34[†]	5.59**	S
Professional associations	0.59	0.73[††]	12.10**	S
Professional Associations (PA) and				
Freedom from superior	0.34	0.36[†]	5.98**	S
Freedom from machines	0.35	0.37[†]	6.18**	S
Freedom preferences	0.28	0.29[†]	4.83**	S
Freedom from Superior (FS) and				
Freedom from machines	0.47	0.53[†]	8.81**	S
Freedom preferences	0.36	0.39[†]	6.39**	S
Freedom from Machines (FM) and				
Freedom preferences (FP)	0.25	0.26	4.27**	NS
Averages				
Practical	0.38	0.41[†]		S
Statistical	0.38		6.80**	S

[a]S indicates practical and statistical significance. NS indicates a lack of significance.
[†] $15° \ R \geq 0.27$.
[††] $30° \ R \geq 0.58$.
* $0.05 \ \ t \geq 1.97$.
**$0.01 \ \ t \geq 2.60$.

correlations between the title and expectation measures based on the reports of 276 individuals can be calculated despite the inadequacy of the data collection and are presented in Table 9.2. It may be useful to recall that the use of total correlations is quite common in traditional work and that we are illustrating here why such analyses are ambiguous.

All the total correlations based on the reports of the 276 individuals achieve statistical significance. This induction is indicated by the asterisks shown for the *t* values presented in Table 9.2. In terms of practical significance, none of the correlations is greater than 0.7071. Nevertheless, all but one correlation achieve practical significance using a less rigorous test (15°). This induction is indicated by the daggers shown with the *R* values presented in the table. These results suggest a network of related variables, but any attempt to interpret these total correlations is problematic at best. Admittedly, freedom from machines sounds like it might be a collectivity-level variable, freedom from superior sounds like it might be a work-group-level variable, and freedom preferences sounds like it might be a person-level variable. The results presented in Table 9.2 do not permit such interpretations about the units of analysis that may underlie these total correlations. Therefore this one traditional type of analysis is viewed as ambiguous.

An assumption could, of course, be made that these reports do not vary within persons or that if they do, such variation is error. Based on this assumption, the correlations could be interpreted as being based on differences between whole persons. From an empirical perspective, however, either these correlations could be based on differences between whole persons or they could be the result of an equivocal condition at the person level of analysis. In either event, the results would remain ambiguous, because it is unclear whether these correlations hold at the work-group or collectivity levels.

Specifically, the correlations presented in Table 9.2 could be based solely on differences among 276 independent persons. In other words, persons who report a professional orientation may tend to report more freedom from constraints in this setting. Empirically, an equivocal condition should be obtained in work-group and collectivity-level analyses before interpreting these correlations in this way or as level-specific.

As another alternative, the correlations shown in Table 9.2 could be based on differences among work-group parts. For example, the relationship between titles and expectations could be contingent on some individuals being more professional and reporting more freedom from constraints than others in the same work group. This might occur because superiors offer more freedom to more professional subordinates than to others. Theoretically, this interpretation is plausible. Empirically, a work-group parts condition should be obtained at the work-group level of analysis before such an induction is drawn. Another possible explanation (whole work groups) for the total correlations shown in Table 9.2 is that professional work groups have more freedom from constraints and may tend to demand more latitude independent of their membership in a collectivity. This type of interpretation implies a whole condition at a work-group level of analysis and an equivocal condition at the collectivity level of analysis. Empirically, data should be shown to be compatible with this interpretation before results are discussed in this way.

Other interpretations or speculations about these total correlations can be created using the collectivity rather than work-group or person level of analysis. For example, the total correlations might be viewed as being based on work-group differences within functional collectivities; within each collectivity, some work groups may be more professional and free from constraints than others. This interpretation means that a whole condition at the work-group level of analysis and a part condition at the collectivity level should be empirically demonstrated. As a final alternative explanation, differences among whole collectivities might be hypothesized to underlie the correlations shown in Table 9.2. From this perspective, the more professional collectivities (for example, the adaptive) may have greater freedom from constraints than the less professional collectivities (such as production).

As should be apparent, these total correlations based on the reports from 276 individuals are ambiguous despite any traditional assumptive basis for interpreting them. These correlations can be viewed as between-person correlations and can be clarified to some extent by examining the correlations at the work-group and then at the collectivity levels of analysis.

Work-Group Analysis

At the work-group level of analysis, one cell is formed for each of the 83 work groups in the setting. The 276 between-cell scores (or individuals' reports) are then located in their respective cells. The prediction from theory A is that whole work groups will underlie the correlations between titles and expectations and that these variables will be related rather than generally related, generally unrelated, or unrelated. These predictions are now tested, beginning with single-level analysis.

Single-Level Analysis The within- and between-work-group eta correlations and the associated E and F ratios, indicating the degree to which the within- and between-cell scores represent the 276 scores, are presented in the upper portion of Table 9.3. Instead of using asterisks and daggers, in the lower portion of the table number signs locate data in the varient matrix in terms of statistical and practical significance. In this work-group analysis, only the difference between the within-eta and between-eta correlations for education is practically significant (15° test). The eta correlations for the other variables fail to demonstrate a significant difference (the E ratio is less than 1.30 and 1.73 and not less than 0.77 or 0.58). All the F ratios are statistically significant. However, recall that statistical tests are based on a demonstration or assumption that one of the eta correlations is error and the other is valid. In this case, such an assertion is not justifiable; therefore, the induction is that these variables are more compatible with an equivocal (rather than whole or parts) condition based on WABA I. A comparison of the number signs with the double lines in the table indicates that this result is not compatible with the prediction of theory A.

TABLE 9.3. WABA I: Within and between work group analysis

	VARIABLES					
	Education (Ed)	Prof. Assoc. (PA)	Freedom from Superior (FS)	Freedom from Machines (FM)	Freedom Preferences (FP)	Averages
Data						
η between (82)	0.79	0.73	0.68	0.78	0.64	0.72
η within (193)	0.61	0.68	0.74	0.63	0.77	0.69
E ratio	1.30	1.07	0.92	1.24	0.83	1.04
F ratio	3.95	2.71	1.99	3.61	1.63	2.56
Inferences						
Wholes						
15° $E \geq 1.30$	#					
30° $E \geq 1.73$						
0.05 $F \geq 1.35$	#	#	#	#	#	#
0.01 $F \geq 1.53$	#	#	#	#	#	#
Parts						
15° $E \leq .77$						
30° $E \leq .58$						
0.05 $F \leq .72$						
0.01 $F \leq .64$						
Equivocal						
15° (all others)		#	#	#	#	#
30° (all others)	#	#	#	#	#	#
0.05 (all others)						
0.01 (all others)						
Overall inference			Equivocal			

TABLE 9.4. WABA II: Within and between work group analysis (difference tests)

		VARIABLES										
	Education (Ed) and				Prof. Assoc. (PA) and			Freedom from Superior (FS) and		Freedom from Machines (FM) and	Averages	
	FS	FM	FP	PA	FS	FM	FP	FM	FP	FP	Practical	Statistical
Data												
r between (81)	0.55	0.53	0.54	0.72	0.52	0.51	0.48	0.66	0.66	0.43	0.56	0.57
r within (192)	0.29	0.18	0.09	0.42	0.17	0.15	0.10	0.25	0.13	0.08	0.19	0.19
A	0.29	0.38	0.48	0.37	0.38	0.38	0.40	0.45	0.59	0.36	0.40	
Z	2.40	3.07	3.86	3.46	3.04	3.09	3.18	4.04	4.98	2.85		3.31
Inferences												
Wholes												
15° $A \geq 0.26$	#	#	#	#	#	#	#	#	#	#	#	
30° $A \geq 0.52$									#			
0.05 $Z \geq 1.66$	#	#	#	#	#	#	#	#	#	#		#
0.01 $Z \geq 2.33$	#	#	#	#	#	#	#	#	#	#		#
Parts												
15° $A \leq -0.26$												
30° $A \leq -0.52$												
0.05 $Z \leq -1.66$												
0.01 $Z \leq -2.33$												
Equivocal and inexplicable												
15° (all others)												
30° (all others)	#	#	#	#	#	#	#	#		#	#	
0.05 (all others)												
0.01 (all others)												
Overall inference	Weak (15° test) whole work groups											

For WABA II, the within- and between-work-group correlations and their associated A and Z values are presented in the upper portion of Table 9.4. As is shown in the lower portion of the table, for all the correlations the difference between the within- and between-work-group correlations as represented by the A values is greater than that required for a 15° test but does not exceed the value required for a 30° test. In terms of practical significance, the difference between these correlations is interpreted as weak. As is shown in the table, the values of the Z tests of the difference between the within- and between-work-group correlations all reach an acceptable level of statistical significance ($p \leq 0.01$). Therefore, the relationship among the titles and expectations measures is induced to be more likely based on differences between whole work groups (rather than on differences between parts within work groups). This induction is weak because the 30° test of practical significance has not been passed.

Except for one correlation, the between-work-group correlations presented in Table 9.4 are not greater than 0.7071 and therefore do not exceed the rigorous criteria. Consequently, the question is whether the between-cell correlations are systematic. The values of the magnitude indicators (R and t) for these correlations are presented in Table 9.5. As the table shows, each of the between-work-group correlations reaches an acceptable level of statistical and practical significance. Moreover, the average of the between-work-group correlations indicate statistically ($p \leq 0.01$) and practically (30° test) significant correlations. The magnitude tests for the within-work-group correlations are

TABLE 9.5. WABA II: Within and between work group analysis (magnitude tests and components)

	BETWEEN (df = 81)			WITHIN (df = 192)			COMPONENTS		
	R Test	t Test	Inferences	R Test	t Test	Inferences	Between	Within	Inference
Education and									
Freedom from superior	0.66††	5.93**	S	0.30†	4.20**	S	0.295	0.131	B
Freedom from machines	0.63††	5.63**	S	0.18	2.54**	NS	0.327	0.069	B
Freedom preferences	0.64††	5.77**	S	0.09	1.25	NS	0.273	0.042	B
Professional associations	1.04††	9.34**	S	0.46†	6.41**	S	0.415	0.174	B
Professional Associations and									
Freedom from superior	0.61††	5.48**	S	0.17	2.39*	NS	0.258	0.086	B
Freedom from machines	0.59††	5.34**	S	0.15	2.10*	NS	0.290	0.064	B
Freedom preferences	0.55†	4.92**	S	0.10	1.39	NS	0.224	0.052	B
Freedom from Superior and									
Freedom from machines	0.88††	7.91**	S	0.26	3.58**	NS	0.350	0.117	B
Freedom preferences	0.88††	7.91**	S	0.13	1.82	NS	0.287	0.074	B
Freedom from Machines and									
Freedom preferences	0.48†	4.29**	S	0.08	1.11	NS	0.215	0.039	B
Averages (see Table 9.4)									
Practical	0.68††		S	0.19		NS	0.293	0.085	B
Statistical		6.24**	S		2.68**	S			

† 15° test: between $R \geq 0.27$ within $R \geq 0.27$.
†† 30° test: between $R \geq 0.58$ within $R \geq 0.58$.
* 0.05 test: between $t \geq 1.99$ within $t \geq 1.97$.
**0.01 test: between $t \geq 2.64$ within $t \geq 2.60$.

also shown in the table and do not reach an acceptable level of practical significance. In addition, the between-cell components are larger than the within-cell components for all correlations. Of course, the addition of these components equals the total correlations presented in Table 9.2.

At a single level of analysis, an equivocal condition was induced using WABA I and a whole condition was induced using WABA II. As indicated in Table 7.9, this outcome is feasible and is interpreted as a weak whole condition. The results suggest that although these variables deviate about the same within and between work groups, the correlations among the variables are based mainly on between-work-group deviations, so that a *weak whole condition* is induced.

Multiple-Level Analysis   The 83 whole groups are contained in 8 collectivities. Therefore, the induction of whole work groups could be specific to that level of analysis or could be a manifestation of relationships based on differences within or between collectivities. To address this issue, the 83 between-cell scores must be analyzed at the collectivity level. Before we test this collectivity-level hypothesis, the question of whether these variables can be viewed empirically as one network of variables (compatible with a related case) must be addressed.

Multiple-Variable and Multiple-Relationship Analyses   The results from WABA II showed that all the between-cell correlations were significantly different from the within-cell correlations and reached an acceptable level of practical and statistical significance. The between-work-group correlations are therefore the chosen focus for multiple-variable analysis. Based on rigorous criteria, all the correlations could be viewed as rather small, because only one exceeded a value of 0.7071, and the set of variables could be viewed as compatible with an unrelated case. However, because the between-cell correlations are greater than the within-cell correlations, for our purposes all the correlations are viewed as significant. The unrelated case is therefore rejected.

Since 10 correlations are used to assess the relationship between titles and expectations, 45 comparisons can be made among the between-group correlations. Of these, only five result in a practically significant difference greater than 0.26 radians (15° test). Specifically, the correlation between education and membership in professional associations (the measures of the degree of professionalism of groups in this case) is stronger than the relationships among the expectations measures. Moreover, the correlations among the expectation measures can be summarized as follows, and indicate the significantly different correlation between freedom from machines and freedom preferences:

VARIABLES	CORRELATIONS (r_B)
Freedom from superior and	
Freedom from machines	0.66
Freedom preferences	0.66
Freedom from machines and	
Freedom preferences	0.43

Although these correlations among the expectation measures could be viewed as compatible with a generally related case, the finding that 89 percent of the comparisons of the correlations resulted in differences which were not practically significant leads to an induction that the variables are compatible with the related case (rather than the unrelated, generally unrelated, and generally related cases). Therefore, one titles-expectations network at the work-group level of analysis is induced from multiple-variable analysis. Finally, since the variables are viewed as forming one network at the work-group level of analysis, multiple-relationship analysis is not employed.

Collectivity Analysis

The 276 between-work-group scores that vary only between work groups can be conceptualized as potentially belonging to 8 collectivities. The results from analyzing these scores at the collectivity level are now presented. In this analysis, 8 cells are formed and the 83 different work-group scores are located in their appropriate cells. The 276 scores are retained, however, in order to generate results that are weighted by the number of individuals in each work group. An alternative unweighted analysis could also be employed, in which case only 83 between-work-group scores need be analyzed. Since the inductions from both analyses were similar, only the results of the weighted analysis are presented.

Single-Level Analysis   The within- and between-collectivity eta correlations and their associated E and F ratios are presented for each scale in the upper portion of Table 9.6. For only one scale, the difference (E ratio) between the eta correlations reached an acceptable level of practical significance (15° test). Therefore, "despite statistical significance," an induction is made that the scales are equivocal (rather than representing parts or wholes) using WABA I.

Using WABA II, the obtained values for the within- and between-collectivity correlations and their associated A and Z values are presented in the upper portion of Table 9.7. For all these correlations, the between-collectivity correlations are greater than the within-collectivity correlations in a practical sense (15° test). In all but one case, the differences between these correlations also exceed the values required to pass the 30° test. Since the between-collectivity correlations are based on 6 degrees of freedom, their magnitude is likely to be inflated according to the statistical paradigm. Thus, tests of the statistical significance of the difference between the within- and between-collectivity correlations are of particular importance. In all but two comparisons, the Z test of the difference between the correlations reaches an acceptable level of statistical significance ($p \leq 0.05$). Since these differences do not permit a rejection of the statistical hypothesis at the 0.01 level, these results are interpreted as indicating relationships based on somewhat weak differences between whole collectivities (rather than, for example, between collectivity parts).

The magnitudes of the between-collectivity correlations approximate the rigorous criteria required for inferring wholes ($r = 0.7071$). However, these correlations are based on 6 degrees of freedom. A test of the statistical significance of these correlations is therefore particularly important. The results

TABLE 9.6. WABA I: Within and between collectivity analysis

			VARIABLES			
	Education	Professional Associations	Freedom from Superior	Freedom from Machines	Freedom Preferences	Averages
Data						
η between (7)	0.72	0.73	0.67	0.68	0.55	0.67
η within (75)	0.70	0.69	0.74	0.74	0.84	0.74
E ratio	1.03	1.06	0.91	0.92	0.65	0.91
F ratio	11.34	11.99	8.78	9.05	4.59	8.78
Inferences						
Wholes						
15° $E \geq 1.30$						
30° $E \geq 1.73$						
0.05 $F \geq 2.13$	#	#	#	#	#	#
0.01 $F \geq 2.89$	#	#	#	#	#	#
Parts						
15° $E \leq 0.77$					#	
30° $E \leq 0.58$						
0.05 $F \leq 0.30$						
0.01 $F \leq 0.17$						
Equivocal						
15° (all others)	#	#	#	#		#
30° (all others)	#	#	#	#	#	#
0.05 (all others)						
0.01 (all others)						
Overall inference			Equivocal			

TABLE 9.7. WABA II: Within and between collectivity analysis (difference tests)

	VARIABLES											
	Education (Ed) and				Prof. Assoc. (PA) and			Freedom from Superior (FS) and		Freedom from Machines (FM) and	Averages	
	FS	FM	FP	PA	FS	FM	FP	FM	FP	FP	Practical	Statistical
Data												
r between (6)	0.83	0.77	0.98	0.87	0.78	0.78	0.90	0.87	0.92	0.80	0.85	0.87
r within (74)	0.29	0.29	0.26	0.55	0.27	0.24	0.20	0.48	0.52	0.21	0.33	0.34
A	0.68	0.58	1.11	0.47	0.62	0.65	0.92	0.55	0.62	0.72	0.68	
Z	1.92	1.56	4.39	1.55	1.66	1.73	2.75	1.75	2.19	1.92		2.12
Inferences												
Wholes												
15° $A \geq 0.26$	#	#	#	#	#	#	#	#	#	#	#	
30° $A \geq 0.52$	#	#	#		#	#	#	#	#	#	#	
0.05 $Z \geq 1.66$	#		#		#	#	#	#	#	#		
0.01 $Z \geq 2.33$			#			#						#
Parts												
15° $A \leq -0.26$												
30° $A \leq -0.52$												
0.05 $Z \leq -1.66$												
0.01 $Z \leq -2.33$												
Equivocal and inexplicable												
15° (all others)												
30° (all others)			#									
0.05 (all others)		#		#								
0.01 (all others)	#	#	#	#	#		#	#	#			#
Overall inference					Weak ($p \leq 0.05$) whole collectivities							

TABLE 9.8.   WABA II: Within and between collectivity analysis (magnitude tests and components)

	BETWEEN ($df = 6$)			WITHIN ($df = 74$)			COMPONENTS		
	R Test	t Test	Inference	R Test	t Test	Inference	Between	Within	Inference
Education and									
Freedom from superior	1.49††	3.65*	S	0.30†	2.61*	S	0.400	0.150	B
Freedom from machines	1.21††	2.96*	S	0.30†	2.61*	S	0.377	0.150	B
Freedom preferences	4.92††	12.06**	S	0.27†	2.32*	S	0.388	0.153	B
Professional associations	1.76††	4.32**	S	0.66††	5.67**	S	0.457	0.266	B
Professional Associations and									
Freedom from superior	1.25††	3.05*	S	0.28†	2.41*	S	0.381	0.138	B
Freedom from machines	1.25††	3.05*	S	0.25	2.13*	NS	0.387	0.123	B
Freedom preferences	2.06††	5.06**	S	0.20	1.76	NS	0.361	0.116	B
Freedom from Superior and									
Freedom from machines	1.76††	4.32**	S	0.55†	4.71**	S	0.396	0.263	B
Freedom preferences	2.35††	5.75**	S	0.61††	5.24**	S	0.339	0.323	B
Freedom from Machines and									
Freedom preferences	1.33††	3.27*	S	0.21	1.85	NS	0.299	0.131	B
Averages (see Table 9.7)									
Practical	1.61††		S	0.35†		S	0.379	0.181	B
Statistical		4.32**	S		3.11**	S			

†   15° test: between $R \geq 0.27$ within $R \geq 0.27$.
†† 30° test: between $R \geq 0.58$ within $R \geq 0.58$.
* 0.05   test: between $t \geq 2.45$ within $t \geq 1.99$.
**0.01   test: between $t \geq 3.71$ within $t \geq 2.64$.

from the tests are presented in Table 9.8. As the table shows, all the between-collectivity correlations reach an acceptable level of practical and statistical significance. Moreover, the averages of these between-collectivity correlations also reach an acceptable level of practical and statistical significance. From the perspective of practical significance, these results approximate an ideal set of values. The between-cell correlations approximate 0.866 in value, and the within-cell correlations are less than 0.50. Statistically, the finding of results at the 0.05 level suggests lack of an effect due to statistical artifacts. An inability to reject the statistical hypothesis at the 0.01 level suggests that the degrees of freedom may have somewhat inflated the values of the between-collectivity correlations. Finally, an examination of the within and between components listed in Table 9.8 indicates that the between component is larger than the within component for all correlations. (These within- and between-collectivity components, of course, add to the between-work-group correlations presented in Table 9.4.)

The induction of whole collectivities from the analysis of the within- and between-collectivity correlations using WABA II must be tempered because of the results from examining each scale separately using WABA I. In WABA I, each scale showed deviations both within and between collectivities, and an equivocal condition was induced. In WABA II, whole collectivities were induced. Although this is an interpretable outcome (see Table 7.9), the results would have been stronger if a whole-collectivity condition had also been induced in WABA I. With due regard for this weakness, *whole collectivities* are induced from this analysis.

TABLE 9.9.   Summary of inferences for multiple-level analysis

	EMPIRICAL		INFERENTIAL		
ENTITY AXIS	**E Ratio**	**A Values**	**WABA I**	**WABA II**	**WABA I and II**
Collectivities					
(Tables 9.6 and 9.7)					
Wholes (7)		0.68	——	#	#
Parts (75)			——		
Equivocal (82)	0.91		#		
Inexplicable					
Groups (Subordinates)					
(Tables 9.3 and 9.4)					
Wholes (82)		0.40	——	#	#
Parts (193)			——		
Equivocal (275)	1.04		#		
Inexplicable					
Persons					
Wholes (275)			?	?	?
Parts					
Equivocal					
Inexplicable					
Inferences			Equivocal	Wholes across levels	Wholes across levels

Multiple-Level Analysis   The results from the collectivity level of analysis should be interpreted in light of the work-group-level analysis. The two analyses are summarized by considering the values of A and the E ratio based on the averages of correlations. The values for the work group and collectivity levels of analysis are shown in Table 9.9. WABA I was used in both analyses, and an equivocal condition was induced based on the E ratios. In contrast, using WABA II in both the work-group and the collectivity-level analyses, whole conditions were induced based on the values of A. With full recognition of the weakness of the induction from WABA I, a relationship between the titles and expectation measures at the *whole group* and *whole collectivity* unit of analysis is induced. This relationship is indicated in Table 9.9 by the number signs in the rows labeled "Wholes." Although Table 9.9 provides a partial summary of the cross-level (rather than, for example, a level-specific) induction from the data, several issues need further attention.

Multiple-Variable and Multiple-Relationship Analyses   Since the between-collectivity correlations were significantly larger than the within-collectivity correlations, the between-collectivity correlations are the focus for multiple-variable analysis. The magnitude tests indicate that, based on rigorous criteria, all the between-collectivity correlations are systematic. An examination of all the possible differences between the correlations revealed that only 10 of 45 possible differences (22 percent) were greater than 0.26 radians, and none of the differences was greater than 0.52 radians, as required to exceed the 30° test. In general, then, we view these correlations as indicating that the variables are all related in one network (rather than as unrelated, generally unrelated, or generally related).

Because a related case has been induced, multiple-relationship analysis is not necessary. We can therefore proceed to summarize and draw inferences from the results of the work-group- and collectivity-level analyses, after considering one additional issue.

Functional Titles and Expectations Revisited   Because the functional title variable is aligned with collectivities, the results presented in this chapter may appear to be based on correlations of reports about professional orientation and freedom from various constraints. These analyses can be viewed in a somewhat different way if the 8 cells defined by functional titles are considered in light of a more traditional analysis of variance (ANOVA). The averages of the between-work-group deviation scores in each collectivity are presented in the upper portion of Table 9.10 in a format similar to that used in the ANOVA.

The totals of the average deviation scores indicate that the upper-level adaptive collectivity tends to contain reports of more education and professional orientation than the other collectivities (such as lower-level production). The between-cell eta correlations provide an estimation of the relationship between these scores and the 8 functional titles expressed as a categorical variable. Since the functional titles do not vary within cells, the values of these correlations from Table 9.6 can be summarized as follows:

VARIABLES	CORRELATIONS (η_B)
Functional Titles and	
Freedom from superior	0.67
Freedom from machines	0.68
Freedom preferences	0.55
Education	0.72
Professional associations	0.73

These eta correlations can be viewed as representing the relationship between the self-report variables and the functional title classification. (The statistically significant F ratios for these analyses of variance are presented in Table 9.6.) Therefore, a relationship between functional titles and the reports of professionalism and freedom from various constraints is induced at the collectivity level. It is clear that this induction is weak because these between-collectivity eta correlations are less than 0.79 and 0.866 and therefore do not pass the 15° and 30° tests, respectively, in WABA I. However, if within-collectivity scores are viewed as error, as in the ANOVA, these correlations can be viewed as statistically and practically significant (greater than 0.26 and 0.50).

One way to examine the assertion that the variation of titles within collectivities may be correlated 0 with the expectation measures is to use a

TABLE 9.10. Between-cell scores for collectivities and additional F tests

	BETWEEN-CELL SCORES							
	Upper Level				Lower Level			
VARIABLES	Adaptive	Maintenance	Support	Production	Adaptive	Maintenance	Support	Production
Education	1.80	0.42	0.30	0.26	1.48	−0.17	−0.39	−1.21
Prof. associations	2.06	−0.09	0.44	0.05	0.69	−0.20	−0.28	−5.39
Freedom from superior	1.79	0.72	0.71	0.93	2.14	0.20	−2.14	−1.61
Freedom from machines	2.36	1.59	1.66	0.30	0.61	0.41	−1.20	−1.38
Freedom preferences	5.95	0.64	0.93	1.12	5.25	−0.40	−0.92	−3.73
Totals	13.96	3.28	4.04	2.66	10.17	−0.16	−4.93	−13.32

	F RATIOS					
	Total Scores		Within Work Group Scores		Between Work Group Scores	
VARIABLES	Job Function	Job Level	Job Function	Job Level	Collectivity Function	Collectivity Level
Degrees of freedom ($J − 1, N − J$)	(1,274)	(2,273)	(1,274)	(2,273)	(3,79)	(1,81)
Education	33.9*	22.5*	2.8	1.0	18.5*	5.8*
Prof. associations	25.2*	18.3*	3.7	0.8	15.9*	29.3*
Freedom from superior	13.9*	22.8*	1.6	0.8	9.7*	7.3*
Freedom from machines	18.3*	17.5*	0.2	0.0	8.4*	16.2*
Freedom preferences	17.4*	15.3*	0.2	0.7	8.4*	3.3

*$p \leq 0.05$.

second classification of titles derived from organization records. To clarify the results of this type of analysis, the collectivity-level classification of titles we have been using is viewed as distributing the 276 individuals in the following way:

COLLECTIVITY LEVEL	COLLECTIVITY FUNCTION			
	Production	Maintenance	Support	Adaptive
Upper	29	13	18	13
Lower	78	67	20	38

In the second classification, the same individuals are categorized as being in technical or nontechnical jobs and in high, medium, or low skill jobs. Using this individual or job classification, the 276 individuals are distributed in the following way:

JOB LEVEL	JOB FUNCTION	
	Technical	Nontechnical
Upper	20	40
Middle	43	101
Lower	52	20

The relationships between these classifications of titles can be summarized with contingency correlations as follows:

	JOB FUNCTION	JOB LEVEL	COLLECTIVITY FUNCTION	COLLECTIVITY LEVEL
Job Function	—			
Job level	0.35	—		
Collectivity function	0.46	0.25	—	
Collectivity level	0.14	0.60	0.21	—

An examination of the frequencies on which these contingency correlations are based indicates that the production collectivity contained mainly nontechnical jobs and the adaptive collectivity contained mainly technical jobs. Maintenance and support collectivities tend to be more heterogeneous because there is a mix of different types of jobs. Considering the contingency coefficient of 0.60 between the job skill level and the collectivity classification, higher- and lower-skill jobs tend to be at higher and lower levels of the hierarchy in collectivities.

The contingency correlations between the two classifications of titles are less than 1, indicating that the six job title categories are somewhat similar to, but not identical with, the collectivity-level classification of titles. Therefore, an obtained relationship of job classification with the self-report variables (based on the 276 reports of individuals) could be due either to a collectivity-level relationship that holds across levels, or to differences among persons. The results from a test of this hypothesis are presented in the lower portion of Table 9.10.

For the purpose of this illustration, two one-way analyses of variance are employed. Job function is an independent variable forming two cells, and job level is an independent variable forming three cells. In the first set of analyses, reports from the 276 individuals about their professional orientation and their expectations are viewed as the dependent variables. The F ratios that result are shown in the lower portion of Table 9.10 in the columns labeled "Total Scores." Since we desired a test compatible with traditional work, only the F ratios are presented, and all reach an acceptable level of statistical significance ($p \leq 0.05$). When the same independent variables are used but the dependent variables are expressed as within-work-group scores, all the F ratios fail to reach an acceptable level of statistical significance. These results are shown in the lower portion of Table 9.10 in the columns labeled "Within Work Group Scores."

Where did the significant F ratios go? When 276 scores were analyzed, significant F ratios were obtained; and when the within-work-group scores were analyzed, nonsignificant F ratios were obtained. One answer to this question can be found in the last two columns in the lower portion of Table 9.10 labeled "Between Work Group Scores." As is shown in the table, the between-work-group scores on these variables show a statistically significant relationship with collectivity function and level. Obviously, F ratios do not magically disappear in a data set. Indeed, the significant F ratios based on total deviations appear to be based on differences between work groups.

This finding may be quite important: When a functional classification of titles that varies both between and within collectivities is used, relationships are obtained with the self-report measures; however, the lack of a significant relationship is obtained by examining within-work-group deviation scores when the differences between work groups are removed from the self-reports. One particularly interesting implication of this finding is that when a cross-level relationship is operating, an ability to obtain a relationship empirically depends on the representation of the higher level of analysis in the data. For example, unless future studies contain data incorporating differences between collectivities, the results presented here will probably not be replicable; such is the nature of a cross-level effect.

INFERENCES AND SUMMARY

Using theory A, titles and expectations were predicted to be related based on differences among whole collectivities, work groups, dyads, and persons. These predictions are indicated by the double lines in the varient matrix presented in

TABLE 9.11. Location of theory A and data in a varient matrix

	VARIABLE AXIS			
ENTITY AXIS	*Related* $T \leftrightarrow E$	*Generally Related*	*Generally Unrelated*	*Unrelated* $T \perp E$
Collectivities				
Wholes	# #			
Parts				
Equivocal				
Inexplicable				
Groups				
Wholes	# #			
Parts				
Equivocal				
Inexplicable				
Dyads				
Wholes	‾‾‾‾			
Parts				
Equivocal				
Inexplicable				
Persons				
Wholes	‾‾‾‾			
Parts				
Equivocal				
Inexplicable				

Table 9.11. The data presented in this chapter provide little information about the relationship of titles and expectations at the person and dyad levels of analysis. This is indicated in the table by the lack of number signs at these levels of analysis. At the next two levels of analysis is an induction, although weak, that whole collectivities and work groups underlie the relationship between titles and expectations. This induction about entities was drawn by using the inferential processes of the paradigm. In terms of the variable axis, the magnitudes of the correlations among the variables are very similar in value, suggesting that the variables are more compatible with the related case and form one network. These inductions about variables and entities are indicated by the location of number signs under the column labeled "Related" and the rows labeled "Whole Collectivities" and "Whole Work Groups."

The data therefore provide some support for the notion that professional orientation in an organization is related to the type of functional title an individual holds and that these titles are related to the degree of freedom people report they have in a setting. These data, however, suggest that such relationships are based on differences between whole collectivities and whole work groups. One implication of these findings is that the relationship between titles and expectations may be contingent on the operation of collectivities. For example, in situations where such collectivities are not sampled, relationships between title and expectation measures are not necessarily expected to be obtained. The meaning of these results is enhanced somewhat by the tests of theory B presented in the next chapter.

REVIEW QUESTIONS

1. How do theoretical predictions about variables and entities enter into data analysis?
2. (a) Why were responses identified with individuals in this study? (b) Can analyses be performed when responses are not identified with individuals?
3. What is the problem with the consistently robust total correlations presented in Table 9.2?
4. Why were the variables listed in Table 9.3 interpreted as most compatible with an equivocal condition based on WABA I?
5. Which levels of analysis were empirically justified in the study?
6. How can a collectivity-level analysis be justified?
7. Why was multiple-relationship analysis not performed?
8. How was the relationship of analysis of variance with WABA I and WABA II illustrated in this study?
9. How does the possibility of cross-level effects constrain research design?
10. The data in this chapter could have been analyzed in ways that would have resulted in questionable interpretations. Describe two of these ways.

10

TESTING THEORIES:
A Person–Dyad–Group Illustration

Although the basic inferential procedures remain the same for testing theory B as for theory A, their use is extended by including a consideration of the dyad level of analysis at MCO. This extension is necessary because theory B specifies that investments and returns are related based *only* on differences between whole dyads. In specific terms, measures of investments and returns are predicted to be correlated based on differences between whole superior-subordinate dyads. First, therefore, the theory relating to measures and entities must be defined. Second, an empirical test of whether the measures are correlated at the whole-dyad unit of analysis must be performed. Third, the theoretical predictions of theory B must be compared to empirical results in order to draw an inference. These three steps together are the basis for the presentation of the results from testing theory B at MCO.

THEORY AND DEDUCTION

Although the group and collectivity levels of analysis have been defined at MCO, a definition of the dyad level of analysis (single-level analysis) and the way in which dyads are linked with other levels of analysis (multiple-level analysis) must be specified. In terms of variables (multiple-variable and multiple-relationship analyses), measures of investments and returns believed to differ from titles and expectations must be defined.

Single-Level Analysis

In the hierarchical work setting at MCO, each individual reports to one superior. Since there are 276 subordinates, the setting at MCO can be conceptualized as containing 276 dyads, each including one subordinate and one superior. At MCO, each of the 276 subordinates reports to 1 of only 83 superiors; thus the total number of subordinates and superiors is not equal.

However, from the perspective of superiors, each relationship between a superior and a subordinate makes up a dyad, so that the 83 superiors can be potentially viewed as forming 276 relationships with the 276 subordinates. In this way, each dyad can be viewed as containing a superior and a subordinate, even though some different dyads contain the same superiors. This formulation of dyads was used as a basis for collecting data at MCO.

The 276 individuals at MCO reported in their capacities as subordinates about their superiors. Since 83 of the 276 individuals were also superiors of other managers, these 83 managers responded about each of their subordinates as well. A simplified illustration of this interview strategy is presented in Figure 10.1. A structure containing seven individuals is shown in the upper portion of the figure. In this case six individuals (excluding Helen) respond as subordinates. In addition, as a superior, Helen describes her relationship with

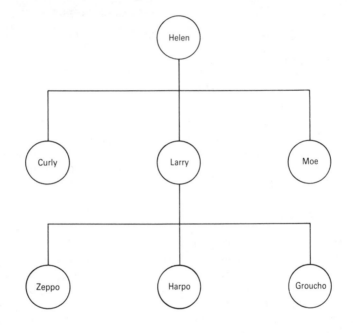

	Responds about self	In addition responds about subordinates
Helen	No	Larry, Moe, and Curly
Larry	Yes	Zeppo, Harpo, and Groucho
Moe	Yes	No one
Curly	Yes	No one
Harpo	Yes	No one
Zeppo	Yes	No one
Groucho	Yes	No one

FIGURE 10.1. Interview strategy in the hierarchy at MCO

Larry, Curly, and Moe, who report to her, and Larry also describes his relationship with Groucho, Zeppo, and Harpo. Moe, Curly, Zeppo, Groucho, and Harpo do not supervise other managers and thus do not respond as superiors, but only as subordinates. Therefore, six superior-subordinate dyads are identified in this case: Helen-Curly, Helen-Larry, Helen-Moe, Larry-Zeppo, Larry-Harpo, and Larry-Groucho.

At MCO, the 83 superiors generate 276 reports by responding about each of their subordinates on each variable of interest. These supervisory reports are then paired with the 276 reports from all subordinates to form 552 scores on each variable (one from a superior and one from a subordinate). The consequences of this dyadic conceptualization for viewing the setting at MCO and for degrees of freedom for WABA I and II are illustrated as follows:

| | | DEGREES OF FREEDOM | |
DYADS	TOTALS	*WABA I*	*WABA II*
Level total	552		
Parts	276	276	275
Wholes	276	275	274

Two hundred seventy-six cells are thus defined at the dyad level of analysis. Each cell contains two scores: one from a superior and another from a subordinate on each variable of interest. Analyses can be performed at the dyad level of analysis, but since a superior can be a member of multiple dyads, an additional set of analyses at the person level is appropriate.

Multiple-Level Analysis

The 276 reports of the 83 superiors can be examined at a person level of analysis. At this level 83 cells are formed, each containing one superior's responses about his or her subordinates. This type of analysis permits an induction to be made about whether the 276 superiors' reports should be viewed as reflecting differences among 83 whole superiors, differences within superiors (parts), or as independent of superiors (an equivocal condition). An equivocal condition was predicted by theory B for this analysis because each report is viewed as a reflection of dyad-level processes (superiors and subordinates), and not of each superior's view of the situation.

A second analysis, based on the 276 subordinate reports, is appropriate for our test of theory B. Although these subordinates' reports cannot be analyzed at the person level, a within- and between-work-group analysis can be performed. For this analysis, the 276 reports can be viewed as being contained in 83 work groups. This work-group analysis is identical to that presented in the previous chapter. An equivocal condition is also predicted at the work-group level of analysis by theory B.

A third key analysis is performed by constructing cells containing both superior and subordinate reports. This dyad-level analysis permits a choice as to whether the 552 scores from superiors and subordinates are more likely to represent 276 whole dyads, differences inside dyads (parts), or simply independent superior and subordinate reports (an equivocal condition). As a fourth analysis, if whole dyads are induced empirically as predicted by theory B, then between-dyad scores can be partitioned into within- and between-work-group scores, because superior and subordinate dyads are embedded in supervisory work groups. Theory B predicts that an equivocal condition is more likely at the work-group level of analysis based on dyads. The last analysis is referred to as a dyad–work-group level analysis to distinguish it from the other work-group analysis, which is based on individual reports.

In summary, then, four different types of analysis are necessary to test theory B: (1) Reports from superiors are examined at the person level of analysis; (2) reports from subordinates are examined at the work-group level; (3) reports from superiors and subordinates are examined simultaneously at the dyad level; and (4) between-cell scores or averages of reports from superiors and subordinates in the same dyad are examined at the work-group level. This more complex conceptualization of levels of analysis was presented in Chapter 3.

The consequences of these conceptualizations of multiple levels of analysis can be illustrated by using 12 fictitious scores, which we will assume have been obtained from 6 subordinates and the 2 superiors to whom they report. Such a set of scores from superiors and subordinates is shown in the heading of Table 10.1. Using this data set, at least three ambiguous analyses can be performed. First, the subordinates' reports can be analyzed as one set of data. Second, the superiors' reports can be analyzed as another set of data. Third,

TABLE 10.1.   Conceptualization underlying person, group, dyad, and dyad – work group analysis

	Helen (1)	Larry (1)	Helen (2)	Curly (2)	Helen (3)	Moe (3)	Larry (4)	Zeppo (4)	Larry (5)	Harpo (5)	Larry (6)	Groucho (6)
				SOURCES AND SCORES								
Conceptualization												
Person (superior)	Helen		Helen		Helen		Larry		Larry		Larry	
Work group (subordinate)		Larry		Curly		Moe		Zeppo		Harpo		Groucho
Dyad	Helen	Larry	Helen	Curly	Helen	Moe	Larry	Zeppo	Larry	Harpo	Larry	Groucho
Dyad-group	Dyad I		Dyad II		Dyad III		Dyad IV		Dyad V		Dyad VI	
Scores												
Person (superior)	1		2		3		4		5		6	
Work group (subordinate)		1		2		3		4		5		6
Dyad	1	1	2	2	3	3	4	4	5	5	6	6
Dyad-group	1		2		3		4		5		6	

Results and Location of Analyses

All scores: no prediction (see Table 10.2)
Person analysis: equivocal (see Tables 10.3, 10.4, and 10.6)
Work-group analysis: equivocal (see Tables 10.3, 10.5, and 10.6)
Dyad analysis: wholes (see Tables 10.7, 10.8, and 10.9)
Dyad – work-group analysis: equivocal (see Table 10.11)

since the reports of superiors and subordinates are about the same variables, the data set can be viewed as 12 reports based on one variable. In this "dyadic" configuration, the 12 scores are viewed as representing deviations on one variable.

As an alternative to these ambiguous analyses, the data presented in Table 10.1 can be viewed in two different ways. First, the superiors' reports can be analyzed at the person level and the subordinates' reports can be analyzed at the group level. Second, these scores can be viewed as 12 reports on one variable and analyzed at the dyad and work-group levels. Dotted lines in Table 10.1 indicate the way scores and individuals are clustered into cells. The lower portion of Table 10.1 lists the predictions from theory B for each of these analyses and cross references to the tables in which the results of these analyses are presented for the MCO data.

Multiple-Variable Analysis

To perform these analyses, the set of variables hypothesized to represent investments and returns (latitude and attention given by a superior to subordinates, superior satisfaction with subordinates, and subordinate congruence with superior) must be measured. At MCO, the **attention (AT)** given by superiors to subordinates was measured by a set of nine items that focused on the degree to which superiors provided assurance of confidence, support for a subordinate's actions, encouragement to solve problems, and the like. **Latitude (LA)** given to subordinates by superiors was measured by a set of items that focused on the degree to which a superior allowed a subordinate to make changes in his or her job under various conditions. In addition, the degree of a **superior's satisfaction with subordinates (SS)** and the degree of **congruence of a subordinate's actions with a superior's preferences (SC)** were also assessed. These measures were factor analytically derived, and the responses on items presented in Appendix G were summed to form a scale.

Using these measures, the 276 managers as subordinates reported how much attention and latitude they received from their superior, how satisfied they felt their superior was with their performance, and the degree to which they felt their actions were congruent with their superior's preferences. In addition, the same measures were employed in the second part of the interview for the 83 superiors. In this case, for *each* of his or her subordinates, a superior indicated the degree of attention and latitude a subordinate felt the superior offered. Superiors also reported the degree to which they were satisfied with each subordinate's performance and the degree to which they felt each subordinate's actions were congruent with the superior's own preferences.

Multiple-Relationship Analysis

Theory B specifies that this set of measures should be related at the dyad level of analysis, since the constructs measure investments and returns (see Chapter 4). Therefore, no indirect contingencies are specified and multiple-relationship analysis is not used. The question at this point is whether the data collected at MCO are compatible with the predictions from theory B. In each of the four nonambiguous analyses, predictions from theory B are indicated by the location of the double lines along the variable and entity axes of the varient matrix. At this point, however, the object is to present the results from analyzing the data.

DATA AND INDUCTION

Ambiguous Analysis

From a more traditional perspective, the reports of superiors and sub-ordinates can be examined in three ambiguous ways. First, the total correlations based on the subordinates' reports are ambiguous for the reasons described in Chapter 9. Second, the total correlations among the superiors' reports are ambiguous because these correlations could reflect differences among the 83 whole superiors, differences perceived by each superior between his or her subordinates (parts), or nothing having to do with superiors as persons. Third, since the same measures were evaluated for superiors and subordinates, each of the four measures can be viewed as having 552 responses (as four variables with 552 responses). The total correlations among these four variables are ambiguous because they could be based on differences among 276 whole dyads, differences within dyads, or 552 differences among reports that are independent of superior-subordinate dyadic relationships.

The total correlations based on these three ambiguous analyses are presented in Table 10.2. As is shown in the table, all the correlations are less than 0.7071. However, when less rigorous criteria for testing the practical significance of the R values are employed in combination with standard t tests, only two of the correlations are *not* significant in magnitude. Although these total correlations are not interpretable, the results serve as a starting point for the person, work-group, and dyad analyses. To condense the presentation, we will present the results from the analyses at the person and work-group levels simultaneously.

Person and Work-Group Analyses

In the person and work-group analyses, 83 cells are formed containing 276 scores. The analysis of the 276 reports from 83 superiors is a person-level analysis, whereas the analysis of the 276 reports from subordinates comprising 83 work groups is a work-group-level analysis.

Single-Level Analysis   The eta correlations from WABA I performed at the person and work-group levels of analysis are presented in Table 10.3. As is shown in the left portion of the table, for the subordinate reports the E ratios do not reach an acceptable level of practical significance. An equivocal condition is therefore induced for the subordinate reports at the work-group level of analysis. The results from the analysis of the superiors' reports are shown in the right side of the table. The E ratios are practically and statistically significant for two variables; the superiors' reports of the attention and

TABLE 10.2. Ambiguous analysis of superior and subordinate reports of investments and returns

VARIABLES	CORRELATIONS	R TEST	t TEST	INFERENCE[a]
Subordinate Reports (groups)	($df = 274$)			
Sup. sat. with sub. (SS) and				
Sub. cong. with sup. (SC)	0.41	0.45[†]	7.44**	S
Attention (AT)	0.48	0.55[†]	9.06**	S
Latitude (LA)	0.30	0.31[†]	5.21**	S
Sub. cong. with sup. (SC) and				
Attention (AT)	0.36	0.39[†]	6.39**	S
Latitude (LA)	0.10	0.10	1.66	NS
Attention and latitude				
(AT) and (LA)	0.52	0.61[††]	10.08**	S
Practical average	0.36	0.39[†]		S
Statistical average	0.37		6.59**	S
Superior Reports (persons)	($df = 274$)			
Sub. sat. with sub. and				
Sub. cong. with sup.	0.68	0.93[††]	15.35**	S
Attention	0.39	0.42[†]	7.01**	S
Latitude	0.31	0.33[†]	5.40**	S
Sub. cong. with sup. and				
Attention	0.38	0.41[†]	6.80**	S
Latitude	0.38	0.41[†]	6.80**	S
Attention and latitude	0.54	0.64[††]	10.62**	S
Practical average	0.45	0.50[†]		S
Statistical average	0.46		8.58**	S
Dyads	($df = 550$)			
Sup. sat. with sub. and				
Sub. cong. with sup.	0.56	0.68[††]	15.85**	S
Attention	0.42	0.46[†]	10.85**	S
Latitude	0.30	0.31[†]	7.38**	S
Sub. cong. with sup. and				
Attention	0.35	0.37[†]	8.76**	S
Latitude	0.19	0.19	4.54**	NS
Attention and latitude	0.49	0.56[†]	13.18**	S
Practical average	0.39	0.42[†]		S
Statistical average	0.39		9.93**	S

[a]S indicates practically and statistically significant.
[†]   15° $R \geq 0.27$.
[††] 30° $R \geq 0.58$.
* 0.05 $t \geq 1.97$.
**0.01 $t \geq 2.60$.

latitude they offered to subordinates varied mostly among superiors. In other words, a whole-person induction that some superiors report themselves as more attentive and as offering more latitude to subordinates than others seems plausible. The averages of the eta correlations for all the variables based on the superiors' reports, however, are compatible with an induction that an equivocal condition is more likely at the person level of analysis. Moreover, an equivocal condition is compatible with subordinate reports on the same measures at the

TABLE 10.3. WABA I: Within- and between-person (superior) and work-group (subordinate) analyses

	SUBORDINATE REPORTS (WORK GROUP LEVEL)					SUPERIOR REPORTS (PERSON LEVEL)				
	SS	SC	AT	LA	Average	SS	SC	AT	LA	Average
Data										
η between (82)	0.58	0.63	0.73	0.72	0.67	0.59	0.56	0.83	0.85	0.71
η within (193)	0.81	0.78	0.69	0.69	0.74	0.81	0.83	0.56	0.53	0.68
E ratio	0.72	0.81	1.06	1.04	0.91	0.73	0.67	1.48	1.60	1.04
F ratio	1.21	1.54	2.63	2.56	1.93	1.25	1.07	5.17	6.05	2.57
Inferences										
Wholes										
15° $E \geq 1.30$								#	#	
30° $E \geq 1.73$										
0.05 $F \geq 1.35$		#	#	#	#			#	#	#
0.01 $F \geq 1.53$		#	#	#	#			#	#	#
Parts										
15° $E \leq 0.77$	#					#	#			
30° $E \leq 0.58$										
0.05 $F \leq 0.72$										
0.01 $F \leq 0.64$										
Equivocal										
15° (all others)		#	#	#	#					#
30° (all others)	#	#	#	#	#	#	#	#	#	#
0.05 (all others)	#					#	#			
0.01 (all others)	#					#	#			
Overall Inference (person and group)	Equivocal					Equivocal				

229

work-group level of analysis. We therefore interpret both the superiors' and the subordinates' reports as equivocal (with the caveat that two of the superiors' reports are compatible with a whole-person condition). Given this caveat, in Table 10.3 most of the number signs locate the data in the equivocal condition, and this is viewed as compatible with predictions of theory B, indicated by the double lines in the table.

The results from WABA II of the superiors' reports are presented in Table 10.4. The differences between two of the within- and between-superior correlations reach an acceptable level of practical and statistical significance at the person level of analysis (the correlations of latitude with superior satisfaction and latitude with the congruence of a subordinate with the superior's preference). In these two cases, since the within-person correlations are larger than the between-person correlations, a parts condition seems more likely. Although all but one of the within-superior correlations tend to be larger than the between-superior correlations, the average of all correlations does not result in an induction that there is a significant difference between these correlations. As is shown in the lower portion of Table 10.4, an equivocal condition is induced at the person level of analysis (given the caveat that there is a tendency toward a parts condition for two correlations).

TABLE 10.4. WABA II: Within- and between-person (superior) analysis (difference tests)

	VARIABLES							
	SS and			SC and		AT and	Averages	
	SC	AT	LA	AT	LA	LA	Prac.	Stat.
Data								
r between (81)	0.60	0.31	0.19	0.33	0.27	0.57	0.38	0.39
r within (192)	0.72	0.53	0.50	0.48	0.57	0.46	0.54	0.55
A	−0.16	−0.24	−0.33	−0.16	−0.33	0.13	−0.18	
Z	−1.61	−2.02	−2.68	−1.35	−2.78	1.13		−1.55
Inferences								
Wholes								
$\quad$ 15° $A \geq 0.26$								
$\quad$ 30° $A \geq 0.52$								
$\quad$ 0.05 $Z \geq 1.66$								
$\quad$ 0.01 $Z \geq 2.33$								
Parts								
$\quad$ 15° $A \leq -0.26$			#		#			
$\quad$ 30° $A \leq -0.52$								
$\quad$ 0.05 $Z \leq -1.66$		#	#		#			
$\quad$ 0.01 $Z \leq -2.33$			#		#			
Equivocal and inexplicable								
$\quad$ 15° (all others)	#	#		#		#	#	
$\quad$ 30° (all others)	#	#	#	#	#	#	#	
$\quad$ 0.05 (all others)	#			#		#		#
$\quad$ 0.01 (all others)	#	#		#		#		#
Overall Inference				Equivocal				

TABLE 10.5. WABA II: Within- and between-group (subordinate) analysis (difference tests)

	SS and			SC and		AT and	Averages	
	SC	AT	LA	AT	LA	LA	Prac.	Stat.
Data								
r between (81)	0.50	0.53	0.37	0.41	0.18	0.67	0.44	0.46
r within (192)	0.36	0.45	0.26	0.31	0.03	0.35	0.29	0.30
A	0.16	0.09	0.12	0.11	0.15	0.38	0.15	
Z	1.30	0.79	0.92	0.86	1.14	3.34		1.41
Inferences								
Wholes								
15° $A \geq 0.26$						#		
30° $A \geq 0.52$								
0.05 $Z \geq 1.66$						#		
0.01 $Z \geq 2.33$						#		
Parts								
15° $A \leq -0.26$								
30° $A \leq -0.52$								
0.05 $Z \leq -1.66$								
0.01 $Z \leq -2.33$								
Equivocal and inexplicable								
15° (all others)	#	#	#	#	#		#	
30° (all others)	#	#	#	#	#	#	#	
0.05 (all others)	#	#	#	#	#			#
0.01 (all others)	#	#	#	#	#			#
Overall Inference				Equivocal				

The within- and between-work-group correlations from WABA II based on subordinate reports are presented in Table 10.5. As is shown in this table, only one difference between the within- and between-work-group correlations reaches an acceptable level of statistical and practical significance. The remaining differences are more compatible with an equivocal condition than with a whole or parts condition. As is shown in the lower portion of the table, an equivocal condition is induced at the work-group level of analysis.

The magnitude of the within- and between-cell correlations from both the person and the work-group analyses suggests that an induction of a relationship between investments and returns is plausible. The results from employing the magnitude tests (R and t) at the person and work-group levels of analysis are presented in Table 10.6. Only two of the between-superior and work-group correlations fail to reach an acceptable level of practical and statistical significance when the less rigorous criteria are used. Likewise, the within-cell correlations are statistically and practically significant except for one correlation (using the less rigorous criteria). This set of results is compatible with an induction that an equivocal condition is more likely the basis for these correlations than a parts or whole condition.

The within- and between-superior and work-group components are presented in the last columns of Table 10.6. The sum of these components equals

TABLE 10.6. WABA II: Within- and between-person and work-group analyses (magnitude tests and components)

	BETWEEN ($df = 81$)			WITHIN ($df = 192$)			COMPONENTS		
	R Test	t Test	Inferences	R test	t Test	Inferences	Between	Within	Inferences
Person Level									
SS and									
SC	0.75††	6.75**	S	1.04††	14.38**	S	0.198	0.484	W
AT	0.33†	2.93**	S	0.63††	8.66**	S	0.152	0.240	W
LA	0.19	1.74	NS	0.58††	8.00**	S	0.095	0.215	W
SC and									
AT	0.35†	3.15**	S	0.55††	7.58**	S	0.153	0.223	W
LA	0.28†	2.52*	S	0.69††	9.61**	S	0.129	0.251	W
LA and									
AT	0.69††	6.24**	S	0.52†	7.18**	S	0.402	0.137	B
Averages (See Table 10.4)									
Practical	0.41†		S	0.64††		S	0.188	0.258	W
Statistical		3.81**	S		9.13**	S			
Work-Group Level									
SS and									
SC	0.58††	5.20**	S	0.39†	5.35**	S	0.183	0.227	W
AT	0.63††	5.63**	S	0.50†	6.98**	S	0.224	0.252	W
LA	0.40†	3.58**	S	0.27†	3.73**	S	0.155	0.145	B
SC and									
AT	0.45†	4.05**	S	0.33†	4.52**	S	0.189	0.167	B
LA	0.18	1.65	NS	0.03	0.42	NS	0.082	0.016	B
LA and									
AT	0.90††	8.12**	S	0.37†	5.18**	S	0.352	0.167	B
Averages (See Table 10.5)									
Practical	0.49†		S	0.30†		S	0.198	0.162	B
Statistical		4.66**	S		4.36**	S			

†15° test.
††30° test.
* $p \leq 0.05$.
**$p \leq 0.01$.

the values for the total correlations presented in Table 10.2. The within-superior (person) components tend to be larger than the between-superior components, whereas the between-work-group components tend to be larger than the within-work-group components.

Multiple-Level Analysis The tests of practical and statistical significance in WABA I and WABA II do not support an induction that either the between- or within-work-group or superior correlations are larger. For this set of variables and their relationships, therefore, an equivocal condition is induced at both levels of analysis, as predicted by theory B.

Multiple-Variable and Multiple-Relationship Analyses Since an equivocal condition is induced, a focus (within or between) cannot be chosen, and multiple-variable analysis is not performed based on either the superior (person) or subordinate (work group) level of analysis. Therefore, multiple-relationship analysis is also not performed.

Dyad Analysis

In the dyad-level analysis, 276 cells are formed and each cell contains reports about a subordinate from that subordinate and his or her superior.

Single-Level Analysis   In terms of WABA I, only one of the differences between the eta correlations reaches an acceptable level of statistical and practical significance. The between-eta correlations, however, are larger than the within-eta correlations for all the variables, and the average of the eta correlations results in an E ratio of 1.30 and an F ratio of 1.68. These averages, although very weak, are compatible with a whole condition (based on a 15° test). The results from this analysis and the inductions derived from it are shown in Table 10.7.

Using WABA II, all the between-dyad correlations are greater than the within-dyad correlations. Although these differences between the within- and between-dyad correlations achieve an acceptable level of statistical significance, only three pass the 15° test. The averages of the between- and within-dyad correlations are 0.48 and 0.23, respectively. The difference between the average of these two correlations is 0.27 radians and is thus statistically and practically significant. Although certainly *very* weak, an inference toward whole dyads

TABLE 10.7.   WABA I: Within- and between-dyad analysis

	VARIABLES				
	SS	*SC*	*AT*	*LA*	*Average*
Data					
η between (275)	0.84	0.75	0.78	0.78	0.79
η within (276)	0.54	0.66	0.62	0.63	0.61
E ratio	1.56	1.14	1.26	1.24	1.30
F ratio	2.43	1.30	1.59	1.54	1.68
Inferences					
Wholes					
15° $E \geq 1.30$	#				#
30° $E \geq 1.73$					
0.05 $F \geq 1.26$	#	#	#	#	#
0.01 $F \geq 1.39$	#		#	#	#
Parts					
15° $E \leq 0.77$					
30° $E \leq 0.58$					
0.05 $F \leq 0.79$					
0.01 $F \leq 0.72$					
Equivocal					
15° (all others)		#	#	#	
30° (all others)	#	#	#	#	#
0.05 (all others)					
0.01 (all others)		#			
Overall Inference	Very weak whole dyads				

TABLE 10.8. WABA II: Within- and between-dyad analysis (difference tests)

| | VARIABLES | | | | | | | |
| | SS and | | | SC and | | AT and | Averages | |
	SC	AT	LA	AT	LA	LA	Prac.	Stat.
Data								
r between (274)	0.62	0.54	0.39	0.44	0.31	0.58	0.48	0.49
r within (275)	0.46	0.19	0.13	0.23	0.03	0.36	0.23	0.24
A	0.19	0.38	0.27	0.22	0.29	0.25	0.27	
Z	2.66	4.82	3.29	2.78	3.40	3.34		3.41
Inferences								
Wholes								
15° $A \geq 0.26$		#	#		#		#	
30° $A \geq 0.52$								
0.05 $Z \geq 1.66$	#	#	#	#	#	#		#
0.01 $Z \geq 2.33$	#	#	#	#	#	#		#
Parts								
15° $A \leq -0.26$								
30° $A \leq -0.52$								
0.05 $Z \leq -1.66$								
0.01 $Z \leq -2.33$								
Equivocal and inexplicable								
15° (all others)	#			#		#		
30° (all others)	#	#	#	#	#	#	#	
0.05 (all others)								
0.01 (all others)								
Overall Inference	Very weak (15° test) whole dyads							

seems plausible. The results of this analysis and the bases of this induction are presented in Table 10.8.

Considering this induction, the magnitudes of the between-cell correlations certainly do not exceed the rigorous criteria (greater than 0.7071 or 0.866). The results from using less rigorous criteria and the R and t values are presented in Table 10.9. In this analysis, the average of the between-dyad correlations reaches an acceptable level of practical (15°) and statistical ($p \leq 0.01$) significance, but the average of the within-dyad correlations fails to reach an acceptable level of practical significance.

The within- and between-dyad components are also presented in Table 10.9. For each of the correlations, the between-dyad component is greater than the within-dyad component. The sum of these components equals the total correlations presented in the lower portion of Table 10.2. This set of results is compatible with an induction that whole dyads are more likely because the results from WABA I and WABA II lead to the same induction. The induction of whole dyads, however, is based on the averages of correlations.

Multiple-Level Analysis   Since an equivocal condition was induced at the person and work-group levels of analysis, the reports of subordinates and

TABLE 10.9. WABA II: Within- and between-dyad analysis (magnitude tests and components)

	BETWEEN ($df = 274$)			WITHIN ($df = 275$)			COMPONENTS		
	R test	*t Test*	*Infer.*	*R Test*	*t Test*	*Infer.*	*Between*	*Within*	*Infer.*
SS and									
SC	$0.79^{\dagger\dagger}$	13.08**	S	$0.52^{\dagger}$	8.59**	S	0.391	0.164	B
AT	$0.64^{\dagger\dagger}$	10.62**	S	0.19	3.21**	NS	0.354	0.064	B
LA	$0.42^{\dagger}$	7.01**	S	0.13	2.17*	NS	0.256	0.044	B
SC and									
AT	$0.49^{\dagger}$	8.11**	S	0.24	3.92**	NS	0.257	0.094	B
LA	$0.33^{\dagger}$	5.40**	S	0.03	0.50	NS	0.181	0.012	B
LA and									
AT	$0.71^{\dagger\dagger}$	11.79**	S	$0.39^{\dagger}$	6.40**	S	0.353	0.141	B
Average									
Practical	$0.55^{\dagger}$		S	0.24		NS	0.299	0.087	B
Statistical		9.30**	S		4.10**	S			

$\dagger$15° test within and between $R \geq 0.27$.
$\dagger\dagger$30° test within and between $R \geq 0.58$.
*$p < 0.05$ between $t \geq$ and within $t \geq 1.97$.
**$p < 0.01$ between $t \geq$ and within $t \geq 2.60$.

superiors can be viewed as two different ways of representing investments and returns. In addition, wholes were induced at the dyad level of analysis; therefore, between-dyad scores provide a third way to represent investments and returns. The correlations between these representations provide some clarification of the induction that whole dyads are a more likely basis for the obtained correlations. Also, the correlations of the superior and subordinate reports with the between-dyad scores indicate the degree to which superiors' and subordinates' reports are represented by between-dyad scores. These correlations are shown in the upper portion of Table 10.10.

The results suggest that the between-dyad scores equally represent the superiors' and subordinates' reports. In an ideal case, the correlations of superiors' and subordinates' reports with the between-cell scores on one variable should equal 1. In the results shown in Table 10.10, these correlations (0.70, 0.74, 0.87, 0.78, and 0.87; 0.85, 0.81, and 0.73) do not equal 1, which is not surprising, considering the weakness of the induction that whole dyads underlie these correlations.

An additional analysis of interest deals with the correlations of the superiors' reports with the subordinates' reports. To interpret the total correlations, an assumption must be made that the total scores represent the components of each dyad. Each correlation then indicates the degree to which these components are related as one. In light of the weakness of the between-eta correlations in WABA I, the magnitude of the correlations between superiors' and subordinates' reports shown in the lower portion of Table 10.10 is low, as expected.

Nevertheless, some evidence for a relationship between investments and returns can be presented by considering the relationships between superiors'

TABLE 10.10.　Correlations between superior-subordinate and between-dyad scores

	SUPERIOR REPORTS				SUBORDINATE REPORTS			
	AT	*LA*	*SS*	*SC*	*AT*	*LA*	*SS*	*SC*
Between-Dyad Scores								
AT	0.70†*	0.42†*	0.42†*	0.38†*	0.87†*	0.48†*	0.43†*	0.33†*
LA	0.44†*	0.74†*	0.33†*	0.35†*	0.47†*	0.85†*	0.29†*	0.16*
SS	0.51†*	0.34†*	0.87†*	0.57†*	0.41†*	0.31†*	0.81†*	0.48†*
SC	0.36†*	0.14*	0.32†*	0.78†*	0.31†*	0.31†*	0.61†*	0.73†*
Superior Reports								
AT					0.24*			
LA					0.18*	0.26†*		
SS					0.28†*	0.20*	0.32†*	
SC					0.16*	0.15*	0.31†*	0.14*
Subordinate Reports								
AT	0.24*							
LA	0.22*	0.26†*						
SS	0.32†*	0.23*	0.32†*					
SC	0.20*	0.13*	0.28†*	0.14*				

†15° test.
*$p < 0.05$.

and subordinates' reports of attention and superiors' satisfaction with sub-ordinates. The total correlations can be summarized by inserting them in the investment-return model, as illustrated in Figure 10.2. All but one of the correlations shown in the figure are significant both practically and statistically using the less rigorous test. As should be apparent from the figure, the between-dyad correlations reflect a blend of the correlations of investments and returns based on superiors' *and* subordinates' reports separately and in combination. The use of the total correlations in the schematic diagram is simply a way to express the three bases of the between-dyad correlations. Of course, without the previous analyses, the level of analysis underlying the total correlations would be empirically untested. For example, the total correlations could represent differences between or within work groups, superiors, and/or dyads. The previous analyses clarify these correlations, demonstrating that the dyad level of analysis is a plausible basis for the total correlations between investments and returns. It is important to recognize, however, that this induction is very weak.

Multiple-Variable and Multiple-Relationship Analyses　The six between-dyad correlations presented in Table 10.8 provide the basis for the induction that whole dyads are more likely: therefore, the between-dyad scores and correlations serve as the focus for multiple-variable analysis. In terms of the less rigorous magnitude test (Table 10.9), all the between-dyad correlations are practically (15°) and statistically ($p \leq 0.01$) significant. Moreover, of the 15 possible comparisons between these 6 correlations, only 3 differences result in an angular difference greater than 15° or 0.26 radians; these 3 cases can be

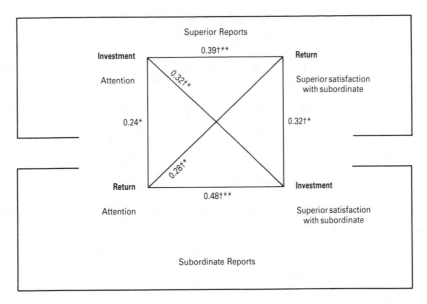

Superior Reports

Investment   0.39†**   Return

Attention   0.32†*   Superior satisfaction
with subordinate

0.24*   0.32†*

0.28†*

Return   Investment
0.48†**

Attention   Superior satisfaction
with subordinate

Subordinate Reports

FIGURE 10.2.   Summary of results in terms of the investment-return model

attributed to the weak correlations of latitude with other measures. If the measures other than latitude were considered, then an induction that the variables form one set of related variables would be straightforward. However, it seems inappropriate to omit this latitude measure because the between-dyad correlation of latitude and the attention measure equals 0.58. The induction from multiple-variable analysis is therefore that the variables seem to be related, recognizing the weakness of this induction in three cases. Given this induction, one network of related variables is induced at the dyad level of analysis, and multiple-relationship analysis is not performed.

Dyad-Group Analysis

As a final analysis, the between-dyad scores are examined at the group level of analysis. In this analysis, the 276 between-dyad scores are contained in the 83 superior work-group cells.

Single-Level Analysis   The results from analyzing the between-dyad scores at the work-group level based on WABA I are presented in the upper portion of Table 10.11. All of the *E* ratios fail to reach practical *and* statistical significance; therefore, an equivocal condition based on WABA I is induced at the work-group level of analysis.

In terms of WABA II, all the differences between the within- and between-work-group correlations fail to achieve practical or statistical significance. In terms of the magnitude of these correlations, using the less rigorous tests, both the between- and the within-work-group correlations reach practical and statistical significance.

TABLE 10.11. Within- and between-dyad work group analysis[a]

	SS	SC	AT	LA	AVERAGES Prac.	AVERAGES Stat.
WABA I						
η between (82)	0.56	0.58	0.74	0.78	0.67	NA
η within (193)	0.83	0.81	0.67	0.63	0.74	NA
E ratio	0.67[†]	0.72[†]	1.10	1.24	0.91	NA
F ratio	1.07	1.21	2.87**	3.61**	1.93	NA
Inference	Eq	Eq	Eq	Eq	Eq	

	SS AND SC	SS AND AT	SS AND LA	SC AND AT	SC AND LA	LA AND AT	AVG.
WABA II Differences							
r between (81)	0.59	0.56	0.36	0.46	0.28	0.64	0.48[b]
r within (192)	0.64	0.55	0.44	0.44	0.36	0.50	0.49
A	−0.06	0.01	−0.09	0.02	−0.08	0.17	−0.01
Z	−0.60	0.11	−0.72	0.19	−0.67	1.57	0.00
Inference	Eq/I	Eq/I	Eq/I	Eq/I	Eq/I	Eq/I	Eq/I
WABA II Magnitude							
Between R	0.73[††]	0.68[††]	0.39[†]	0.52[†]	0.29[†]	0.83[††]	0.55[†]
Between t (df = 81)	6.58**	6.08**	3.47**	4.66**	2.63**	7.50**	5.06**
Inference	S	S	S	S	S	S	S
Within R	0.83[††]	0.66[††]	0.49[†]	0.49[†]	0.39[†]	0.58[††]	0.56[†]
Within t (df = 192)	11.54**	9.13**	6.79**	6.79**	5.35**	8.00**	7.79**
Inference	S	S	S	S	S	S	S
Components							
Between	0.192	0.232	0.157	0.197	0.127	0.369	0.212
Within	0.430	0.306	0.230	0.239	0.184	0.211	0.267
Inference	W	W	W	W	W	B	W

[a] Eq indicates equivocal, I indicates inexplicable, B indicates between, and W indicates within.
[b] The statistical average equals 0.49.
[†] 15° test.
[††] 30° test.
* $p < 0.05$.
** $p < 0.01$.

Finally, the within- and between-work-group components are shown in the lower portion of Table 10.11. These components add to the between-dyad correlations presented in Table 10.8. Although the within-cell components (with one exception) tend to be slightly higher in value than the between-cell components, this set of results appears to be compatible with an induction of an equivocal condition at the work-group level using both WABA I and WABA II.

Multiple-Level Analysis The within and between analyses at the person, work-group, dyad, and dyad–work-group levels of analysis can be summarized with the averages for E and A from each analysis, using the procedure shown

TABLE 10.12. Summary of inferences for multiple-level analysis

ENTITY AXIS	EMPIRICAL		INFERENTIAL		
	E Ratio	A Test	WABA I	WABA II	WABA I and II
Groups — Dyads (Table 10.11)					
Wholes (82)					
Parts (193)					
Equivocal (275)	0.91	−0.01	#	#	#
Inexplicable					
Groups — sub. (Tables 10.3 and 10.5)					
Wholes (82)					
Parts (193)					
Equivocal (275)	0.91	0.15	#	#	#
Inexplicable					
Dyads (Tables 10.7 and 10.8)					
Wholes (275)	1.30[†]	0.27[†]	#	#	#
Parts (276)					
Equivocal (551)					
Inexplicable					
Persons (Tables 10.3 and 10.4)					
Wholes (82)					
Parts (193)					
Equivocal (275)	1.04	−0.18	#	#	#
Inexplicable					
Inference	Emergent and level-specific whole dyads				

[†]$15°$ test.

in Table 10.12. Based on superiors' reports, at the person level of analysis the induction is an equivocal condition. Based on subordinates' reports and the work-group analysis of between-dyad scores, at the group level of analysis the induction is also an equivocal condition. Finally, at the dyad level of analysis, the induction is whole dyads.

Multiple-Variable and Multiple-Relationship Analyses   Since an equivocal condition has been induced for the work-group level of analysis, a between- or within-work-group focus cannot be chosen; therefore, multiple-variable analysis is not applied in the dyad–work-group analysis. In addition, since no induction has been made that any variable was different from any other variable, multiple-relationship analysis is not performed at the dyad–work-group level of analysis.

INFERENCES AND SUMMARY

Theoretically, a set of measures has been hypothesized to be related only at the dyad level of analysis. These hypotheses are summarized in Table 10.13 with the location of the double lines in the varient matrix. Empirically, the correlations between these measures seem more likely (with notable exceptions) to be

TABLE 10.13.   Location of theory B and data in a varient matrix

	VARIABLE AXIS			
ENTITY AXIS	Related $I \leftrightarrow R$	Generally Related	Generally Unrelated	Unrelated $I \perp R$
Collectivities				
Wholes				
Parts				
Equivocal	(NA)			
Inexplicable				
Groups				
Wholes				
Parts				
Equivocal	# #			
Inexplicable				
Dyads				
Wholes	# #			
Parts				
Equivocal				
Inexplicable				
Persons (superiors only)				
Wholes				
Parts				
Equivocal	# #			
Inexplicable				

based on differences between whole dyads. At the work-group and person levels of analysis, an equivocal condition seems more likely. Given an equivocal condition at the work-group level of analysis, an analysis at the collectivity level is not necessary. In addition, in terms of variables, an induction was made that investments and returns are related rather than generally related, generally unrelated, or unrelated. (This inference is not based on a rigorous test.) These data are summarized by the number signs in Table 10.13.

The theoretical predictions and obtained results are essentially isomorphic. This inference of support for theory B is weak, however, since the inductions at the dyad level of analysis are based only on the averages of correlations. The reasons for the weakness of these results are unclear. One hypothesis is that a significant relationship between investments and returns may have occurred in only some collectivities. As a result, the correlations based on all collectivities may have been weak because of the inclusion of correlations of low and high magnitude. This is a contingency hypothesis. An alternative, multiplexed hypothesis is that the correlations between investments and returns are weak in all collectivities. The results from testing for the multiplexed versus the contingent alternative hypotheses are presented in the next chapter.

REVIEW QUESTIONS

1. Why is the dyad level of analysis critical for any test of theory B?
2. How does interest in one-on-one interpersonal relationships impose constraints on data collection procedures?
3. What types of analysis in this setting were used to test the efficacy of theory B?
4. What types of analysis in this study would lead to ambiguous findings?
5. How is it that total correlations can yield highly significant findings that seem to disappear when within- and between-cell deviations are considered?
6. Why was the dyadic inference considered to be weak in this study?
7. Why were the results not interpreted as supportive of the VDL or ALS models of leadership?
8. Why was a collectivity-level analysis not conducted?
9. Why was multiple-relationship analysis not performed on the data set?
10. Why is this type of analysis not limited to the use of Likert-type scales, which are illustrated in Appendix G?

11

TESTING THEORIES:
Completing the Analysis

THEORY AND DEDUCTION

Single-Level Analysis

A correlation between investments and returns based on differences among whole superior-subordinate dyads at MCO is predicted by theory B. In contrast, theory A predicts a correlation between titles and expectations based on differences among whole collectivities, groups, dyads, and persons. The two theories thus intersect at the dyad level of analysis. At this level, reports of investments and returns should not be related to titles and expectations. Unfortunately, in the data collected at MCO, titles and expectations were assessed only from the perspective of subordinates; therefore, between-dyad scores for titles and expectations measures cannot be calculated or correlated with between-dyad scores for investments and returns. Nevertheless, the data can be analyzed in two ways that approximate a dyad-level analysis.

First, superiors' and subordinates' reports of investments and returns can be correlated with subordinates' reports of titles and expectations. In this case, an assumption must be made that subordinate reports reflect differences among whole dyads. Second, and more important, the between-dyad scores on investments and returns based on superiors' and subordinates' reports can be correlated with the subordinates' reports of titles and expectations. In this case, subordinate reports on titles and expectations are assumed to reflect differences among whole dyads.

Multiple-Level Analysis

These two analyses permit an assessment of the degree to which titles and expectations are correlated with investments and returns. In addition, in theory A the collectivity level of analysis is of particular importance, because titles and expectations are characterizations of whole collectivities. In contrast, according to theory B, investments and returns are characterizations of whole dyads. Since collectivities contain dyads and not vice versa, the correlations of investments and returns at the dyad level of analysis can be examined in different collectivities.

Multiple-Variable Analysis

This type of multiple-level investigation, however, is possible only when the variables specified by theory A are independent of the variables specified by theory B. In other words, titles and expectations can be related and investments and returns can be related. However, investments and returns must be correlated near 0 with titles and expectations. Therefore, when the two theories are considered simultaneously, a generally unrelated case is hypothesized as more likely than unrelated, generally related, or related cases.

Multiple-Relationship Analysis

If a generally unrelated case is induced, the correlations between the investments and returns measures should be examined within collectivities of different titles and expectations. The hypothesis we chose (see Chapter 4) is that the correlations between investments and returns at the dyad level of analysis will be of the same magnitude in each collectivity—that is, theory A and theory B are multiplexed.

DATA ANALYSIS AND INDUCTION

Two hypotheses or key questions from theories A and B remain to be tested empirically. First, are the four variables (titles, expectations, investments, and returns) generally unrelated, unrelated, generally related, or related? Second, does the relationship between investments and returns hold in all collectivities (a multiplexed formulation) or in only some collectivities (a contingency formulation)?

Single- and Multiple-Level Analyses

The data at MCO have been interpreted as compatible with the whole-collectivity and whole-dyad predictions from theory A and theory B, respectively (see Chapters 9 and 10). Since we have made a cross-level inference for titles and expectations (see Chapter 9), an examination of the correlations of investment and return measures with titles and expectations at the dyad level of analysis is appropriate. In addition, an examination of the correlations of investments and returns in different collectivities is appropriate.

Multiple-Variable Analysis

The results of the multiple-variable analyses presented in the previous two chapters can be viewed as incomplete because the correlations between the variables specified by the two theories were not presented. The correlations of the subordinates' reports of titles and expectations measures with the superiors' and subordinates' reports of investments and returns are presented in the upper portion of Table 11.1. The averages of subsets of these correlations are also presented in this table to simplify testing procedures. The results from a second analysis, in which the between-dyad scores for the investment and return measures are correlated with the subordinate reports of titles and expectations, are presented in the lower portion of Table 11.1. The average of all the correlations equals 0.13. The averages for the various subsets of correlations are also presented.

From previous analyses, the average of the correlations between the investment and return measures based on between-dyad scores is known to be 0.48, and the average of the correlations between the titles and expectations measures based on the subordinates' reports is 0.38. The averages of subsets of the between-dyad correlations are presented in Table 11.1; these correlations can be summarized as follows:

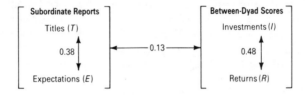

From this summary, the results seem to be compatible with an induction that the two networks of variables (*TE* and *IR*) differ from each other. The following two tests of this assertion are required because titles and expectations may be viewed as alternative explanations for investments and returns, and vice versa.

First, using the average correlational values presented in Table 11.1, when titles and expectations are viewed as one network of variables, the correlations between them and investments and returns are summarized in the following way:

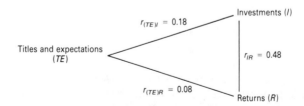

Taking this perspective, the following three questions arise:

1. Are investments (*I*) more highly correlated with titles and expectations (*TE*) than with returns (*R*)? Using the notation from the schematic diagram, is the difference $r_{(IR)} - r_{(TE)I}$ significant? In other words, are the correlational values of 0.48 and 0.18 significantly different?

TABLE 11.1. Correlations of titles and expectations with investments and returns based on individuals' reports

INVESTMENTS AND RETURNS	TITLES		EXPECTATIONS			AVERAGES
	Ed	*PA*	*FS*	*FM*	*FP*	
Person-Work Group Analysis						
Investments (sup. reports)						
AT	0.08	0.15	0.05	0.03	0.00	
LA	0.18	0.18	0.29	0.22	0.14	
Returns (sup. reports)						
SS	0.12	0.17	0.10	0.08	0.00	
SC	0.01	0.02	0.06	0.10	0.01	
Investments (sub. reports)						
SS	0.02	0.04	0.11	0.00	0.04	
SC	0.21	0.15	0.00	0.11	0.05	
Returns (sub. reports)						
AT	0.21	0.10	0.03	0.03	0.05	
LA	0.12	0.23	0.36	0.24	0.43	
Averages (Practical)						
Investments (and titles and expectations) $I(TE)$						0.10
Returns (and titles and expectations) $R(TE)$						0.12
Titles (and investments and returns) $T(IR)$						0.12
Expectations (and investments and returns) $E(IR)$						0.11
All correlations						0.11
Dyad Analysis (Between Dyad)						
Investments						
AT	0.11	0.00	0.05	0.03	0.04	
LA	0.18	0.26	0.41	0.29	0.38	
Returns						
SS	0.09	0.13	0.13	0.05	0.02	
SC	0.14	0.11	0.04	0.00	0.04	
Averages (Practical)						
Investments (and titles and expectations) $I(TE)$						0.18
Returns (and titles and expectations) $R(TE)$						0.08
Titles (and investments and returns) $T(IR)$						0.13
Expectations (and investments and returns) $E(IR)$						0.12
All correlations						0.13

Average Correlation of Investments and Returns (Whole Dyads) 0.48
(See Table 10.8)
Average Correlation of Titles and Expectations (Persons) 0.38 (See Table 9.2)

TABLE 11.2. Inference from multiple-variable analysis of investments and returns

	OBTAINED VALUES	INFERRED MEANING	VARIABLE AXIS — Related I ↔ R ↔ (TE)	Generally Related (I ⊥ R) ↔ (TE)	Generally Related (I ⊥ TE) ↔ R	Generally Related (R ⊥ TE) ↔ I	Generally Unrelated (I ↔ R) ⊥ TE	Generally Unrelated (I ↔ TE) ⊥ R	Generally Unrelated (R ↔ TE) ⊥ I	Unrelated I ⊥ R ⊥ TE
Magnitude Tests										
R values for (r)										
IR (.48)	0.55†	+	o	0	o	o	o	0	0	0
I(TE) (.18)	0.18	0	o	o	0	o	0	o	0	0
R(TE) (.08)	0.08	0	o	o	o	0	0	0	o	0
t test (df = 274)										
IR	9.06**	+	o	0	o	o	o	0	0	0
I(TE)	3.03**	NA	o	o	0	o	0	o	0	0
R(TE)	1.33	NA	o	o	o	0	0	0	o	0
Difference Tests										
A values										
−[|R| − |(TE)|]	0.32†	+	o	−	+	(0)	+	−	o	o
−[|R| − |R(TE)|]	0.42†	+	o	−	(0)	+	+	o	−	o
−[|(TE)| − |R(TE)|]	0.10	0	o	(0)	−	+	o	+	+	o
t′ values (df = 273)										
|IR| − |I(TE)|	4.22**	+	o	−	+	(0)	+	−	o	o
|IR| − |R(TE)|	5.88**	+	o	−	(0)	+	+	o	−	o
|(TE)| − |R(TE)|	1.65	NA	o	(0)	−	+	o	+	+	o
Inference								#			

† 15° R ≥ 0.27.   †† 30° R ≥ 0.58.
*0.05 t ≥ 1.97.   **0.01 t ≥ 2.60.
† 15° A ≥ 0.26.   †† 30° A ≥ 0.52.
*0.05 t′ ≥ 1.97.   **0.01 t′ ≥ 2.60.

2. Are returns more highly correlated with investments than with titles and expectations? (That is, is the difference $r_{IR} - r_{(TE)R}$ significant?)

3. Are titles and expectations more highly correlated with investments or returns? (That is, is the difference $r_{(TE)I} - r_{(TE)R}$ significant?)

Under our hypothesis of a generally unrelated set of variables, in terms of the differences between correlations, the answer should be "yes" to questions 1 and 2 and "no" to question 3 because the investment-return and the title-expectation measures are hypothesized to be unrelated. An answer to the three questions about the differences between these correlations is presented in Table 11.2.

The values of the three correlations of interest are shown in parens in the upper left portion of Table 11.2. In terms of the magnitude tests, only the correlation of 0.48 between investments and returns achieves an acceptable level of practical and statistical significance. The inferred meaning of this result is indicated in the table by the location of a plus sign after the correlation labeled *IR*. In terms of the differences between these correlations, the first two differences listed in the table reach an acceptable level of practical and statistical significance, and the remaining difference is not practically or statistically significant. The inferred meaning of this set of results is indicated in Table 11.2 by the use of two plus signs. The last eight columns contain the values required to induce one of the cases along the variable axis (see Table 2.6). The values in the column labeled "Inferred Meaning" correspond to the values shown under the heading "Generally Unrelated"; therefore, a generally unrelated case is induced as more likely. This induction is indicated in the last row of the table.

A second analysis is performed by again using averages of the between-dyad correlations and by viewing the correlations among the variables in the following way:

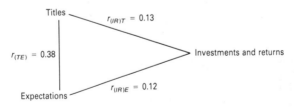

The results from this second multiple-variable analysis are presented in Table 11.3. Again, the results seem to be more compatible with the generally unrelated case. This induction is indicated in the last row of the table.

In light of these two tests, an induction is made that the four variables are generally unrelated rather than unrelated, generally related, or related; multiple-relationship analysis is therefore appropriate.

Multiple-Relationship Analysis

In multiple-relationship analysis, correlational analyses are performed in each of a number of settings. Based on previous results, the settings at MCO are defined by the title variable, which is aligned perfectly with the collectivi-

TABLE 11.3. Inference from multiple-variable analysis of titles and expectations

	OBTAINED VALUES	INFERRED MEANING	Related $T \leftrightarrow E \leftrightarrow (IR)$	Generally Related $(T \perp E) \leftrightarrow (IR)$	Generally Related $T \perp (IR) \leftrightarrow E$	Generally Related $E \perp (IR) \leftrightarrow T$	Generally Unrelated $(T \leftrightarrow E) \perp IR$	Generally Unrelated $T \leftrightarrow (IR) \perp E$	Generally Unrelated $E \leftrightarrow (IR) \perp T$	Unrelated $T \perp E \perp IR$
										VARIABLE AXIS
Magnitude Tests										
R values for (r)										
TE (0.38)	0.41†	+		0			0			0 0
$T(IR)$ (0.13)	0.13	0			0			0		0 0
$E(IR)$ (0.12)	0.12	0				0			0	0 0
t values ($df = 274$)										
TE	6.80**	+		0			0			0 0
$T(IR)$	2.17*	NA			0			0		0 0
$E(IR)$	2.00*	NA				0			0	0 0
Difference Tests										
A values										
$-[|TE - T(IR)|]$	0.26†	+	0	−	+	(0)	+	−	0	0 0
$-[|TE - E(IR)|]$	0.27†	+	0	−	(0)	+	+	0	−	0 0
$-[|T(IR) - E(IR)|]$	0.01	0	0	(0)	−	+	0	+	+	0 0
t' values ($df = 273$)										
$|TE| - |T(IR)|$	3.38**	+	0	−	+	(0)	+	−	0	0 0
$|TE| - |E(IR)|$	3.53**	+	0	−	(0)	+	+	0	−	0 0
$|T(IR)| - |E(IR)|$	0.15	NA	0	(0)	−	+	0	+	+	0 0
Inference								#		

Note: see footnotes in Table 11.2 for ranges for tests of significance.

† 15° *A* and *R* tests.

* 0.05 *t* test.

†† 30° *A* and *R* tests.

** 0.01 *t* test.

ties. Although the correlations between the investment and return measures have been examined at the dyad level in each of the eight functional collectivities, the correlations are similar in the upper- and lower-level collectivities. Therefore, the results from analyses of only the four functional collectivities (production, support, maintenance, and adaptive) are presented here. Although complete person, dyad, and group-level analyses have been performed on data collected from each collectivity, various summarizing devices (such as averages) are used to simplify the presentation of the results.

Ambiguous Analysis   From a traditional perspective, one way to illustrate multiple-relationship analysis is to focus on the total correlations of the investment and return measures based on the reports of superiors, subordinates, and superior-subordinates. Such an analysis is identical to the ambiguous analyses described in testing theory B across all collectivities. In these analyses, total correlations are calculated from data collected from each of the four collectivities. The results, presented in Table 11.4, indicate that in all the collectivities, most of the correlations between investment and return measures reach an acceptable though not rigorous level of practical and statistical significance. These total correlations are as uninterpretable for each collectivity as when calculated across all collectivities. Nevertheless, the results from an analysis for testing the differences between these ambiguous total correlations (obtained in different collectivities) provide an overview of the general testing procedure used in multiple-relationship analysis.

For our purposes, the analysis of interest is one based on data in which the reports from superiors and subordinates are viewed as 552 reports using one set of variables. As shown in the lower portion of Table 11.4, these 552 reports are distributed among collectivities according to the differing degrees of freedom for the correlations. To simplify this illustration, the practical averages of the total correlations of 0.50, 0.35, 0.35, and 0.32 are used for the support, production, maintenance, and adaptive collectivities, respectively. To test whether these total correlations differ or are similar from one collectivity to the next, it is necessary to generate predictions for the multiplexed and contingent hypotheses.

If the relationship between investments and returns is multiplexed, the correlations between investments and returns should be about equal in each collectivity. Obviously, the differences between any of these correlations should also be equal to or near 0. Theoretically, in terms of ideal values, a correlation of 1 between investments and returns is expected in each collectivity:

Support	$r = 1$
Production	$r = 1$
Maintenance	$r = 1$
Adaptive	$r = 1$

The six differences that can be examined between these four total correlations are expected to equal 0 and are summarized in a matrix format, as shown in the upper portion of Table 11.5.

TABLE 11.4. Total correlations among investments and returns in each collectivity

	SUPPORT	PRODUCTION	MAINTENANCE	ADAPTIVE
Superior Reports: Df	36	105	78	49
Superior sat. with sub. (SS) and				
Sub. cong. with sup. (SC)	$0.68^{††**}$	$0.68^{††**}$	$0.64^{††**}$	$0.77^{††**}$
Attention (AT)	$0.47^{†**}$	$0.44^{†**}$	$0.43^{†**}$	$0.30^{†*}$
Latitude (LA)	$0.40^{†*}$	$0.36^{†**}$	$0.29^{†*}$	$0.28^{†*}$
Sub. cong. with sup. (SC) and				
Attention (AT)	$0.40^{†*}$	$0.37^{†**}$	$0.31^{†**}$	$0.51^{††**}$
Latitude (LA)	$0.37^{†*}$	$0.39^{†**}$	$0.43^{†**}$	$0.38^{†**}$
Attention (AT) and (LA)	$0.46^{†**}$	$0.43^{†**}$	$0.42^{†**}$	$0.55^{††**}$
Averages (practical)	$0.46^{†}$	$0.45^{†}$	$0.42^{†}$	$0.49^{†}$
Averages (statistical)	0.47^{**}	0.45^{**}	0.43^{**}	0.49^{**}
Inference	Systematic in all collectivities			
Subordinate Reports: Df	36	105	78	49
Superior sat. with sub. (SS) and				
Sub. cong. with sup. (SC)	$0.61^{††**}$	$0.28^{†**}$	$0.43^{†**}$	$0.44^{†**}$
Attention (AT)	$0.68^{††**}$	$0.47^{†**}$	$0.35^{†**}$	$0.35^{†**}$
Latitude (LA)	$0.55^{††**}$	0.24^{*}	0.23^{*}	0.14
Sub. cong. with sup. (SC) and				
Attention (AT)	$0.51^{††**}$	$0.33^{†**}$	$0.40^{†**}$	0.22
Latitude (LA)	$0.40^{†*}$	0.04	0.15	−0.01
Attention (AT) and (LA)	$0.70^{††**}$	$0.39^{†**}$	$0.53^{†**}$	$0.35^{†**}$
Averages (practical)	$0.58^{††}$	$0.29^{†}$	$0.35^{†}$	0.25
Averages (statistical)	0.58^{**}	0.30^{**}	0.35^{**}	0.25
Inference	Systematic in all collectivities except adaptive			
Dyadic Arrangement: Df	74	212	158	100
Superior sat. with sub. (SS) and				
Sub. cong. with sup. (SC)	$0.56^{††**}$	$0.56^{††**}$	$0.50^{††**}$	$0.67^{††**}$
Attention (AT)	$0.57^{††**}$	$0.44^{†**}$	$0.31^{†**}$	$0.33^{†**}$
Latitude (LA)	$0.44^{†**}$	$0.27^{†**}$	0.24^{**}	0.19
Sub. cong. with sup. (SC) and				
Attention (AT)	$0.43^{†**}$	$0.37^{†**}$	$0.32^{†**}$	$0.35^{†**}$
Latitude (LA)	$0.27^{†*}$	0.12	$0.26^{†**}$	0.16
Attention (AT) and (LA)	$0.71^{††**}$	$0.33^{†**}$	$0.49^{†**}$	0.19
Averages (practical)	$0.50^{††}$	$0.35^{†}$	$0.35^{†}$	$0.32^{†}$
Averages (statistical)	0.51^{**}	0.36^{**}	0.36^{**}	0.33^{**}
Inference	Systematic in all collectivities			

† 15° Test.
†† 30° Test.
* $p \leq 0.05$.
** $p \leq 0.01$.

In contrast, if total correlations are contingent on the title of the collectivity in which the data have been obtained, some of the differences between the total correlations obtained in different collectivities should be greater than 0. To illustrate this point, given that the obtained total correlation of investments and returns in the support collectivity is the largest, assume that a relationship between investments and returns holds only in this collectivity

TABLE 11.5. Traditional method for developing differences between total correlations in matrix form

		SUPPORT	PRODUCTION	MAINTENANCE	ADAPTIVE
Multiplexed		$r = 1$	$r = 1$	$r = 1$	$r = 1$
Support	$r = 1$				
Production	$r = 1$	0			
Maintenance	$r = 1$	0	0		
Adaptive	$r = 1$	0	0	0	
Contingent		$r = 1$	$r = 0$	$r = 0$	$r = 0$
Support	$r = 1$				
Production	$r = 0$	+			
Maintenance	$r = 0$	+	0		
Adaptive	$r = 0$	+	0	0	

and not in the production, maintenance, or adaptive collectivities. Predicted differences between correlations are then generated in the following way for a contingency formulation.

Theoretically, using ideal values, a total correlation of 1 between investments and returns is hypothesized in the support collectivity and correlations of 0 or near 0 are hypothesized in the other collectivities. These predictions can be stated as follows:

Support	$r = 1$
Production	$r = 0$
Maintenance	$r = 0$
Adaptive	$r = 0$

A comparison of these ideal total correlational values results in the matrix of six predicted differences shown in the lower portion of Table 11.5.

The predictions for the multiplexed and contingent cases presented in Table 11.5 are contained in the columns labeled "Multiplexed" and "Contingent" in Table 11.6. In addition, the degrees of freedom for each correlation in the different collectivities are shown in the last column of the table. The obtained correlations are shown in parens in the upper left portion of the table. Based on the magnitude tests, the four total correlations are all interpreted as being greater than zero. In addition, all the differences between these total correlations, as shown in the lower portion of the table, are inferred to equal zero. Therefore, as shown in the last row of the table, the results of this ambiguous analysis of total correlations are induced to be compatible with the predictions for the multiplexed case.

Single-Level Analysis As in the traditional approach, the results presented in Table 11.6 are ambiguous because the level of analysis was not examined for the data collected in each collectivity. The results of employing WABA I on the data collected in each collectivity at the dyad level of analysis are summarized in Table 11.7. The averages of the within- and between-eta correlations for each collectivity are presented in the upper portion of the

TABLE 11.6. Comparison of total correlations from different collectivities (dyad level of analysis)

| | OBTAINED VALUES | | INFERRED | VARIABLE AXIS | | |
	Practical	Statistical	MEANING	Multiplexed $(X \leftrightarrow Y) \perp Z$	Contingent $[(X \leftrightarrow Y) \perp Z]$	$df = N - 2$
Magnitude Tests	**R**	**t**				
Support (0.50)	0.58††	4.97**	+	+	+	74
Production (0.35)	0.37†	5.44**	+	+	0	212
Maintenance (0.35)	0.37†	4.85**	+	+	0	158
Adaptive (0.32)	0.34†	3.38**	+	+	0	100
Difference Tests	**A**	**Z**				
Support (0.50 minus)						74
Production (0.35)	0.17	1.35	0	0	+	212
Maintenance (0.35)	0.17	1.22	0	0	+	158
Adaptive (0.32)	0.20	1.41	0	0	+	100
Production (0.35 minus)						212
Maintenance (0.35)	0.00	−0.11	0	0	0	158
Adaptive (0.32)	0.03	0.28	0	0	0	100
Maintenance (0.35 minus)						158
Adaptive (0.32)	0.03	0.35	0	0	0	100
Inference				$\overline{\#}$		

† 15° test.   * $p \leq 0.05$.
††30° test.   **$p \leq 0.01$.

TABLE 11.7. WABA I: Results of within- and between-dyad analysis in each collectivity

	SUPPORT	PRODUCTION	MAINTENANCE	ADAPTIVE
Data				
η between	0.82	0.75	0.78	0.76
η within	0.57	0.66	0.63	0.65
E ratio	1.44†	1.14	1.24	1.17
F ratio	2.13*	1.30	1.55*	1.39

| | E RATIO | | F RATIO | | INFERENCES | |
CHOICES	15°	30°	0.05	0.01	15°	30°
Inside Conditions						
Support (37, 38)						
Wholes	≥ 1.30	≥ 1.73	≥ 1.71	≥ 2.14	$\overline{\#}$	___
Parts	≤ 0.77	≤ 0.58	≤ 0.58	≤ 0.47		
Equivocal	All other results		All other results			#
Production (106, 107)						
Wholes	≥ 1.30	≥ 1.73	≥ 1.39	≥ 1.59	___	___
Parts	≤ 0.77	≤ 0.58	≤ 0.72	≤ 0.63		
Equivocal	All other results		All other results		#	#
Maintenance (79, 80)						
Wholes	≥ 1.30	≥ 1.73	≥ 1.45	≥ 1.70	___	___
Parts	≤ 0.77	≤ 0.58	≤ 0.69	≤ 0.59		
Equivocal	All other results		All other results		#	#
Adaptive (50, 51)						
Wholes	≥ 1.30	≥ 1.73	≥ 1.60	≥ 1.94	___	___
Parts	≤ 0.77	≤ 0.58	≤ 0.63	≤ 0.52		
Equivocal	All other results		All other results		#	#

table. As is shown in the lower portion of the table, only in the support collectivity is the difference between the averages of the between-eta correlations and the within-eta correlations practically and statistically significant. Therefore, only in the support collectivity are whole dyads induced to be more likely, based on WABA I.

Using WABA II and multiple-relationship analysis, it is possible to draw inductions based not only on differences between the within- and between-cell correlations in each collectivity, but also on the differences between correlations from different collectivities. These predictions must be generated for the multiplexed and contingent conditions.

In an ideal multiplexed case, whole dyads are inferred in each collectivity, based on the within- and between-cell correlations of investments and returns. This prediction is stated using ideal values, as follows:

	BETWEEN-CELL CORRELATIONS	WITHIN-CELL CORRELATIONS
Support	$r = 1$	$r = 0$
Production	$r = 1$	$r = 0$
Maintenance	$r = 1$	$r = 0$
Adaptive	$r = 1$	$r = 0$

The differences that would be expected under these ideal conditions are shown for the multiplexed case in the upper portion of Table 11.8.

Since whole dyads have been induced only in the support collectivity and since the between-dyad correlations are larger in this collectivity than in others, a contingency formulation seems plausible. Specifically, investments and returns can be predicted to be correlated only in the support collectivity. The predicted values for the within- and between-dyad correlations for data collected in each collectivity are stated as follows:

	BETWEEN-CELL CORRELATIONS	WITHIN-CELL CORRELATIONS
Support	$r = 1$	$r = 0$
Production	$r = 0$	$r = 0$
Maintenance	$r = 0$	$r = 0$
Adaptive	$r = 0$	$r = 0$

These predicted magnitudes can be translated into the predicted differences shown for the contingent case in the lower portion of Table 11.8.

The predicted differences for the contingent and multiplexed conditions contained in the triangles in Table 11.8 focus on variables, because in each of these comparisons a between-cell correlation is compared to another between-cell correlation, or a within-cell correlation is compared to another within-cell correlation. As a result, these comparisons do not permit assessment of whether a within- or between-cell correlation is a better representation of the correlation. Only inferences about variables or about the degree to which correlations differ in data collected from different collectivities can therefore be drawn. In contrast, the differences not included in the triangles compare within

TABLE 11.8.   Method for developing predicted differences between correlations in matrix form

		BETWEEN-CELL CORRELATIONS				WITHIN-CELL CORRELATIONS			
		Supp.	*Pro.*	*Maint.*	*Adp.*	*Supp.*	*Pro.*	*Maint.*	*Adp.*
Multiplexed		$(r=1)$	$(r=1)$	$(r=1)$	$(r=1)$	$(r=0)$	$(r=0)$	$(r=0)$	$(r=0)$
Between									
Support	$r=1$								
Production	$r=1$	0							
Maintenance	$r=1$	0	0						
Adaptive	$r=1$	0	0	0					
Within									
Support	$r=0$	+	+	+	+				
Production	$r=0$	+	+	+	+	0			
Maintenance	$r=0$	+	+	+	+	0	0		
Adaptive	$r=0$	+	+	+	+	0	0	0	
Contingent		$(r=1)$	$(r=0)$	$(r=0)$	$(r=0)$	$(r=0)$	$(r=0)$	$(r=0)$	$(r=0)$
Between									
Support	$r=1$								
Production	$r=0$	+							
Maintenance	$r=0$	+	0						
Adaptive	$r=0$	+	0	0					
Within									
Support	$r=0$	+	0	0	0				
Production	$r=0$	+	0	0	0	0			
Maintenance	$r=0$	+	0	0	0	0	0		
Adaptive	$r=0$	+	0	0	0	0	0	0	

and between correlations, a comparison that permits an inference to be made about entities.

The results from analyzing the data collected at MCO from a variable perspective are presented in Table 11.9. The average of the within- and between-dyad correlations of investments with returns obtained for each collectivity are shown in the parens in the upper left portion of the table. The values of between-dyad correlations (0.62, 0.45, 0.42, and 0.44) all reach an acceptable level of statistical and practical significance in each collectivity, using the less rigorous tests of the R and t values. The between-dyad correlations are therefore interpreted as indicating a relationship between investments and returns in each collectivity. This induction is indicated by insertion of the four plus signs shown under the column labeled "Inferred Meaning." The differences between these between-dyad correlations from different collectivities, shown in the lower left portion of Table 11.9, fail to reach an acceptable level of practical and statistical significance. Therefore, as shown in the column labeled "Inferred Meaning," the values for the differences among the between-dyad correlations from different collectivities are near zero. These results seem more compatible with the prediction associated with the multiplexed than the contingent case (see also Table 11.8). This induction is indicated in the lower left portion of the last row of Table 11.9 by the location of the number sign under the column labeled "Multiplexed" rather than under "Contingent."

TABLE 11.9. Comparison of correlations from different collectivities at dyad level of analysis (variable focus)

	BETWEEN-DYAD CORRELATIONS						WITHIN-DYAD CORRELATIONS					
	Obtained		Inferred Meaning	Multiplexed[a] $(X \leftrightarrow Y) \perp Z$	Contingent[a] $[(X \leftrightarrow Y) \perp Z]$	df $(J-2)$	Obtained		Inferred Meaning	Multiplexed[a]	Contingent[a]	df $(N-J-1)$
	Prac.	Stat.					Prac.	Stat.				
Magnitude Tests	**R**	**t**					**R**	**t**				
Support (0.62, 0.25)	0.79††	4.74**	+	+	+	36	0.26	1.57	0	0	+	37
Production (0.45, 0.23)	0.50†	5.16**	+	+	0	105	0.24	2.43*	0	0	0	106
Maintenance (0.42, 0.24)	0.46†	4.09**	+	+	0	78	0.25	2.20*	0	0	0	79
Adaptive (0.44, 0.22)	0.49†	3.43**	+	+	0	49	0.23	1.60	0	0	0	50
Difference Tests[b]	**A**	**Z**					**A**	**Z**				
Support minus												
Production (0.62, 0.45)	0.20	1.23	0	0	+	105	0.02	0.11	0	0	+	106
Maintenance (0.62, 0.42)	0.24	1.36	0	0	+	78	0.01	0.05	0	0	+	79
Adaptive (0.62, 0.44)	0.21	1.14	0	0	+	49	0.03	0.14	0	0	+	50
Production minus												
Maintenance (0.45, 0.42)	0.03	0.25	0	0	0	78	−0.01	−0.07	0	0	0	79
Adaptive (0.45, 0.44)	0.01	0.07	0	0	0	49	0.01	0.06	0	0	0	50
Maintenance minus												
Adaptive (0.42, 0.44)	−0.02	−0.13	0	0	0	49	0.02	0.12	0	0	0	50
Inference				⧧						⧧		

[a]The predictions shown in this table are identical to those presented in Table 11.8.
[b]Values shown in parens are between-cell correlations.
† Exceeds 15° test.   ††Exceeds 30° test.   *p < 0.05.   **p < 0.01.

255

The results of examining the within-dyad correlations (0.25, 0.23, 0.24, and 0.22) and the tests of the differences among these correlations are shown in the right portion of Table 11.9. As shown here, the value of these within-dyad correlations is induced to be near zero and indicates a lack of relationship between investments and returns in each collectivity. In addition, the tests of differences permit an induction that the values of these correlations are similar. As shown in the table, an induction is therefore drawn that the within-dyad correlations are multiplexed, and investments and returns are unrelated across the collectivities.

The results presented in Table 11.9 may seem to be idealized because all the between-dyad correlations are greater than zero and all the within-dyad correlations approximate zero. Therefore, it might seem that investments and returns are correlated based on whole dyads in all collectivities (a multiplexed inference). Such an inference is based on a variable focus and must be tested by turning to entities and comparing the within- and between-dyad correlations.

The results from testing the 16 differences between the within- and between-dyad correlations are presented in Table 11.10. As is shown in the upper portion of the table, only in the support collectivity is the difference of the averages of the within- as compared to the between-dyad correlations of sufficient magnitude to be considered statistically and practically significant. Moreover, only the differences of the between-dyad correlations in the support collectivity as compared to the within-dyad correlations in the production, maintenance, and adaptive collectivities reach an acceptable level of practical and statistical significance. Therefore, as is shown in the column labeled "Inferred Meaning," only 4 of the 16 potential differences between the within- and between-cell correlations are inferred to be greater than zero. As shown by the number signs, these results are more compatible with a contingent formulation than a multiplexed formulation.

Empirically, a formulation which asserts that investments and returns are related based on differences between whole dyads *only* in the support collectivity seems more likely. With the benefit of hindsight, the rationale for such an assertion seems obvious; investments and returns measured in this setting involve interpersonal and supportive characterizations of an exchange. With roles that involve support of the other collectivities, it is not surprising that the support collectivity is more likely to exhibit supportive interpersonal relationships. Although the implications of these results will be discussed in more detail in subsequent chapters, additional analyses were performed for each collectivity to complete the entire analysis.

Multiple-Level Analysis Since whole dyads have been inferred only in the support collectivity, the question of whether these results are level-specific and emergent must be addressed for this collectivity. As is shown in Table 11.11, for the support collectivity, the averages of all the correlations in WABA I and WABA II are equivocal at all levels of analysis except the dyad level. At least in the support collectivity, therefore, the hypothesis of a level-specific and emergent relationship between investments and returns based on whole dyads seems plausible.

TABLE 11.10.   Comparison of correlations from different collectivities at dyad level of analysis (entity focus)

	B		INFERRED	VARIABLE AXIS		
	OBTAINED DIFFERENCES[b]			*Multiplexed*[a]	*Contingent*[a]	
	A Values	*Z Values*	**MEANING**	$(X \leftrightarrow Y) \perp Z$	$[(X \leftrightarrow Y) \perp Z]$	*df*
Inside Conditions						
Support (0.62, 0.25)	0.42[†]	1.98*	+	+	+	(36, 37)
Production (0.45, 0.23)	0.23	1.81	0	+	0	(105, 106)
Maintenance (0.42, 0.24)	0.19	1.26	0	+	0	(78, 79)
Adaptive (0.44, 0.22)	0.23	1.22	0	+	0	(49, 50)
Among Conditions						
Support (between) minus						
Production (*W*) (0.62, 0.23)	0.44[†]	2.51**	+	+	+	(36, 106)
Maintenance (*W*) (0.62, 0.24)	0.43[†]	2.36**	+	+	+	(36, 79)
Adaptive (*W*) (0.62, 0.22)	0.45[†]	2.27**	+	+	+	(36, 50)
Production (between) minus						
Support (*W*) (0.45, 0.25)	0.21	1.19	0	+	0	(105, 37)
Maintenance (*W*) (0.45, 0.24)	0.22	1.60	0	+	0	(105, 79)
Adaptive (*W*) (0.45, 0.22)	0.24	1.51	0	+	0	(105, 50)
Maintenance (between) minus						
Support (*W*) (0.42, 0.25)	0.18	0.95	0	+	0	(78, 37)
Production (*W*) (0.42, 0.23)	0.20	1.42	0	+	0	(78, 106)
Adaptive (*W*) (0.42, 0.22)	0.21	1.23	0	+	0	(78, 50)
Adaptive (between) minus						
Support (*W*) (0.44, 0.25)	0.20	0.98	0	+	0	(49, 37)
Production (*W*) (0.44, 0.23)	0.22	1.37	0	+	0	(49, 106)
Maintenance (*W*) (0.44, 0.24)	0.21	1.24	0	+	0	(49, 79)
Inference				—	#	

[a] The predictions shown in this table are identical to those presented in Table 11.8.
[b] Within-cell correlations are always subtracted from between-cell correlations for Z values and between-cell angles are always subtracted from within-cell angles for A values. As a result, positive values indicate a larger between-cell correlation.
[†] 15° test.   [††] 30° test.   *$p \leq 0.05$.   **$p \leq 0.01$.

For the purpose of comparison with the results presented in the previous chapter, the correlations between attention and superior satisfaction with subordinates based on superior and subordinate reports can be summarized in the schematic diagram shown in Figure 11.1. All the correlations shown in the figure reach an acceptable level of statistical and practical significance and are considerably higher than the same correlations presented in the previous chapter, which were based on reports from all the collectivities. These results support an inference that the relationship between investments and returns at the dyad level of analysis is contingent on the title of the collectivity investigated in the study.

Multiple-Variable and Multiple-Relationship Analyses   The correlations presented in Figure 11.1 are similar in magnitude. Of the 15 possible comparisons between these correlations, only one difference was greater than 15° (0.41 versus 0.68). Therefore, in the support collectivity these variables are viewed as related rather than as unrelated, generally unrelated, or generally related.

Because titles, expectations, investments, and returns are viewed as a set of generally unrelated variables, the relationship between investments and

TABLE 11.11.   Summary of inferences for multiple-level analysis in the support collectivity

	EMPIRICAL		INFERENTIAL		
ENTITY AXIS	*E Ratio*	*A Values*	*WABA I*	*WABA II*	*WABA I and II*
Collectivities (NA)					
Wholes					
Parts					
Equivocal			——	——	——
Inexplicable			——	——	——
Groups (Dyad)					
Wholes (12)					
Parts (25)					
Equivocal (37)	0.94	0.13	#	#	#
Inexplicable					
Groups (Subordinates)					
Wholes (12)					
Parts (25)					
Equivocal (37)	0.84	0.14	#	#	#
Inexplicable					
Dyads					
Wholes (37)	1.44[†]	0.42[†]	#	#	#
Parts (38)					
Equivocal (75)					
Inexplicable					
Persons					
Wholes (12)					
Parts (25)					
Equivocal (37)	1.04	0.18	#	#	#
Inexplicable					
Inference			Emergent, level specific whole dyads.		

[†]$15°$ test.

returns is induced to be contingent on rather than multiplexed with different titles. This induction is, of course, somewhat weakened by a lack of significant differences between the between-dyad correlations from the different collectivities. Nevertheless, whole dyads can be induced only when WABA I and WABA II are performed. Therefore, this induction seems plausible only for the support collectivity.

INFERENCES AND SUMMARY

The title and expectation measures were predicted by theory A to be related based on differences among whole persons, dyads, groups, and collectivities. Investments and returns were predicted by theory B to be related based on

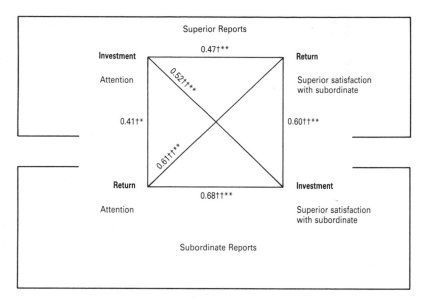

FIGURE 11.1. Summary of results in the support collectivity in terms of investments and returns

differences among whole dyads and to emerge and be specific to that level. In terms of both theories, titles and expectations were predicted to be unrelated to investments and returns, and therefore the set of variables was predicted to be generally unrelated. In addition, the relationship between investments and returns at the dyad level of analysis was predicted to hold across different collectivities (to be multiplexed). These predictions are summarized by the location of double lines in the varient matrix in Table 11.12.

Empirically, titles and expectations were induced to be related at the whole-group and whole-collectivity levels of analysis. The investment and return measures were induced to be related at the whole-dyad level of analysis. Titles and expectations were induced to be unrelated to investments and returns. As a result, the four variables were induced to be generally unrelated. A correlation between investments and returns based on differences among whole dyads was obtained only in the support collectivity; therefore, a contingency formulation was induced to be more likely than a multiplexed formulation. This set of inductions is indicated by the location of the number signs in Table 11.12.

A comparison of the theoretical predictions and the obtained results shows a slight discrepancy. In terms of entities, the theoretical predictions and empirical results are isomorphic. In terms of variables, however, our initial hypothesis was that investments and returns are multiplexed with titles and expectations. The multiplexed assertion is rejected in favor of a contingency formulation because of the results obtained from analyzing the data at MCO. Some of the key implications of these results and analyses are presented in the next chapter.

TABLE 11.12. Location of theory A, theory B, and data in a varient matrix

VARIABLE AXIS

ENTITY AXIS	Related [T ↔ E ↔ I ↔ R]	Generally Related (T ⊥ E) ↔ (I ↔ R)	Generally Unrelated Contingent [(T ↔ E) ⊥ (I ↔ R)]	Generally Unrelated Multiplexed (T ↔ E) ⊥ (I ↔ R)	Unrelated Contingent [T ⊥ E / I ⊥ R]	Unrelated Multiplexed T ⊥ E / I ⊥ R
Collectivities						
Wholes		#	#			
Parts				‖		
Equivocal			#	‖		
Inexplicable						
Groups						
Wholes		#	#			
Parts				‖		
Equivocal			#	‖		
Inexplicable						
Dyads						
Wholes		?	?			
Parts			#	#	‖	
Equivocal				‖		
Inexplicable						
Persons						
Wholes		?	?			
Parts			#	#	‖	
Equivocal				‖		
Inexplicable						

Inference: Emergent and level-specific whole dyads contingent on whole collectivities

REVIEW QUESTIONS

1. How does the dyad level of analysis provide a focal point for the testing of theory A relative to theory B?

2. What was the critical shortcoming in data collection in terms of the dyad level of analysis?

3. How is the assertion of generally unrelated variables reflected in data analytic processes?

4. How were theories A and B tested against each other on substantive grounds?

5. What problem occurs when only the differences between total correlations from different conditions are compared?

6. Why was the conclusion drawn that the within-dyad correlations were multiplexed?

7. Why does an emergent and level-specific formulation of investments and returns at the dyad level appear plausible only for the support collectivity?

8. How do multiplexed and contingent formulations differ?

9. Did the empirical results fail to support any hypotheses that were asserted for theory A and theory B?

10. What implications does the inference of generally unrelated variables have for issues of multicollinearity?

12

SUMMARY AND EXTENSIONS
OF THE
VARIENT PARADIGM

The results from the analyses of the data collected at MCO should have provided answers to a number of questions as well as raised additional concerns about the nature of theory, data analysis, and their alignment in the varient paradigm. This chapter, with a focus on the additional issues raised by the illustration, provides an overview of the way in which the varient paradigm can be extended to address a number of theoretical, empirical, and time-based issues. Additional approaches to drawing conclusions about theory and data are presented in this and the remaining chapters of the book.

In terms of the illustrative data and theory A, a weak inference from the results at MCO is that different collectivities are composed of individuals with different titles and expectations. One of the interesting aspects of this finding is that the freedom an individual experiences in his or her role may not be totally dependent on that individual's personal preferences, but rather on the titles and expectations shared by members of a collectivity. For example, an individual who develops new methods and ideas in an adaptive function may have more freedom (considering his or her professional training) than individuals who operate equipment in a production function. If the freedom an individual experiences in a role is contingent on agreement among a large number of individuals, then changes in roles are hypothesized to involve collectivity-level processes. For example, consider attempts to change titles and expectations by blacks and women who formed collectivities of their own, such as the NAACP and NOW, rather than rely solely on themselves as independent persons.

Contrary to our prediction from theory B that a relationship between investments and returns would hold in all collectivities, it was inferred only in the support collectivity. With the benefit of hindsight, this inference seems quite reasonable. In the production and maintenance collectivities, for example, work is organized around equipment; therefore, individuals may have less of a need to form relationships with others. Instead, they may be able to rely on more obvious and impersonal role requirements. In the adaptive collectivity, individuals may experience "pressure" to create new ideas and bring about changes based on their own professional training and skills, rather than on interpersonal relationships. In contrast, in the support collectivity, where the focus is on managing inputs and outputs in an advisory fashion, the character or quality of interpersonal relationships may be essential.

Any enthusiasm for this interpretation must be tempered by the problems raised by the results of the analyses. We will demonstrate that these problems are characteristic of the illustration instead of the varient paradigm after presenting a more general conceptualization of WABA.

WABA IN MORE GENERAL TERMS

As we have shown, when a between-cell focus is valid, homogeneity or similarity should occur within cells. When a within-cell focus is valid, heterogeneity or differences should occur within cells. With this in mind, special cases that involve similarities or differences within cells can be viewed as whole and parts conditions. This more general conceptualization can be summarized as follows:

BETWEEN CELL	WITHIN CELL	GENERAL FORMULATION	ENTITY FORMULATION
Valid	Error	Similarities	Wholes
Error	Valid	Differences	Parts
Valid	Valid	Equivocal	Reject entity
Error	Error	Inexplicable	Reject entity

From this general perspective, WABA can be viewed as a procedure to assess the degree to which scores are similar or different within cells.

Each variable is expressed in terms of total, within-cell, and between-cell scores in WABA. Of the 15 possible correlations among two variables expressed in these three ways, 7 correlations are included in the WABA equation and 4 are known to equal zero (see Chapter 5). The following four correlations therefore require further consideration in order to demonstrate that the analyses of data collected at MCO completely represent all the possible correlations:

r_{TBXY}: total score T on X correlated with between score on Y
r_{BTXY}: total score T on Y correlated with between score on X
r_{TWXY}: total score T on X correlated with within score on Y
r_{WTXY}: total score T on Y correlated with within score on X

These four correlations are mathematically identical to the multiplication of a between- or within-cell correlation by an eta correlation; therefore these correlations are called **composite correlations**. These correlations and their composites are written

$$r_{TBXY} = \eta_{BX} \cdot r_{BXY}$$
$$r_{BTXY} = \eta_{BY} \cdot r_{BXY}$$
$$r_{TWXY} = \eta_{WX} \cdot r_{WXY}$$
$$r_{WTXY} = \eta_{WY} \cdot r_{WXY}$$

An illustrative proof and a general procedure for proving these equations is presented in Appendix D.

Two features of these four composite correlations make them undesirable for testing theories. First, these correlations are redundant in that they are functions of the eta and between- and within-cell correlations. It has been shown that the 15 correlations among the total, between-, and within-cell deviation scores for two variables are completely determined by the eta and the within- and between-cell correlations. Second, the degrees of freedom for the four composite correlations are rather difficult to determine. In each case, total deviation scores having $N - 1$ degrees of freedom are correlated either with between-cell deviations with $J - 1$ degrees of freedom or with within-cell deviations with $N - J$ degrees of freedom. In contrast, the degrees of freedom for the eta and within- and between-cell correlation are widely known from the traditional statistical paradigm. Moreover, from these six basic indicators —r_{BXY}, r_{WXY}, η_{BX}, η_{WX}, η_{BY}, η_{WY}—values for the 9 remaining correlations are known.

Therefore, a focus on these six indicators is sufficient to summarize empirically the 15 correlations that can be examined when two variables are of interest and to choose among the four theoretical conditions. This general perspective on WABA is useful for dealing with a number of problems with the illustration, on which we will focus in the remainder of this chapter.

TIME IN THE VARIENT PARADIGM

The formulations of theories A and B can be viewed as somewhat inadequate because only relationships among variables and associated entities were specified. The specification of a relationship between variables and associated entities can be clarified by a consideration of the time-related processes hypothesized to underlie such relationships.

In a sense, the procedures used in the illustration focus on the structure of a setting at *one* point in time. In other words, the paradigm has been described as a way to take a snapshot: a picture of a setting at a point in time. In this structural approach, correlations are examined using the differences between entities at a particular time. When interest is in processes, difference scores over time should serve as the basis for correlations. A complete articulation of the way in which this view of time is incorporated in the varient paradigm could form material for at least one more book; however, some of the key implications of this view of time for single- and multiple-level analyses and multiple-variable and multiple-relationship analyses will be discussed here.

Single-Level Analysis

Theoretically, when two variables are hypothesized to be related, at least three different assertions are plausible. First, two variables may be specified as being related in a reciprocal fashion so that a change in one variable (X) results in a change in the other (Y), and vice versa. This case is written in terms of changes Δ for two variables X and Y as follows:

$$\Delta X \rightarrow \Delta Y$$
$$\Delta X \leftarrow \Delta Y$$

Second, in a nonreciprocal case, a change in one variable X is viewed as preceding a change in a second variable Y, but not vice versa, or

$$\Delta X \rightarrow \Delta Y$$
$$\Delta X \nleftarrow \Delta Y$$

Third, in another nonreciprocal case, the same variables are viewed as related; however, the direction of the relationships is specified so that changes in variable Y are followed by changes in variable X, but not vice versa, or

$$\Delta X \nrightarrow \Delta Y$$
$$\Delta X \leftarrow \Delta Y$$

The differences among these three formulations can be illustrated by considering the hypothesized relationship between titles and expectations. First, in a reciprocal formulation, changes in titles are hypothesized as being followed by changes in expectations, and vice versa. Second, in one nonreciprocal formulation, changes in titles are hypothesized as being followed by changes in expectations, although changes in expectations are hypothesized as not being followed by changes in titles. Third, in the other nonreciprocal formulation, changes in titles are hypothesized as not being followed by changes in expectations, but changes in expectations are hypothesized as being followed by changes in titles.

Although reasonably complex, an overview of an empirical procedure for distinguishing among these three conditions will now be presented. For the purpose of simplifying the presentation of the procedure, it is helpful to begin with an assertion that a particular unit of analysis at one level (parts or wholes) has been identified and that scores are characterizations of these units. Then each cell is aligned with one entity and contains the scores for that entity from multiple time periods. If the focus is whole entities, then each whole entity defines one cell, and the cell contains between-cell scores for that entity from multiple time periods. If the focus is parts, each part defines a cell, and within-entity scores for that part from multiple time periods are contained in each cell. With this alignment, WABA I and WABA II are performed, and at least one of the following three ideal conditions is identified.

1. **Stable condition**   The same value is assigned to each entity on a variable at each time period (within-cell deviations are error), and the entities differ from each other (between-cell deviations are valid).

2. **Change condition**   A different value is assigned to each entity on a variable at each time period (within-cell deviations are valid), and each entity changes to the same degree (between-cell deviations are error).

3. **Equivocal condition**   A different value is assigned to each entity at each time period (valid within-cell deviations), and each entity differs from other entities (valid between-cell deviations). In this case, the entities differ from each other and from themselves, so that each time period must be considered separately.

WABA I   Table 12.1 provides an illustration of the way in which cells are constructed in this type of analysis and demonstrates results compatible with the three ideal conditions using WABA I.

For the stable condition, the scores are similar within cells, but differ among the three entities. In this case, the between-eta correlation equals 1, the within-eta correlation equals 0, and the E ratio equals a maximum value of infinity.

For the change conditions illustrated in Table 12.1, the deviations between entities equal zero, and the deviations within entities are systematic. As is shown in the table, in this case the between-eta correlation equals 0, the within-eta correlation equals 1, and the E ratio equals 0. Two change conditions are illustrated in the table. In the first case (type A), each entity changes in the same way (has a score of 1 at time 1 and score of 3 at time 2). In the second case (type B), the entities change so that the average for all entities is the same, but lower scores increase and higher scores decrease from time 1 to time 2.

Finally, in the equivocal condition, the scores vary both between and within cells. As a result, the scores cannot be characterized as stable or changing over time. As shown for this illustrative equivocal case, the between- and within-cell etas are equal in value (0.7071), and the result is an E ratio of 1. Since the inexplicable condition results in indeterminate values for all indicators, it is not presented in the table.

As should be apparent, the synthetic data presented in Table 12.1 illustrate the ideal conditions that can be identified with the use of WABA I. In the stable condition, the E ratio takes on a maximum value of infinity, and in the change condition the E ratio takes on a minimum value of zero.

TABLE 12.1.   Ideal stable, change, and equivocal conditions over time for WABA I

CONDITION	RESULTS (WABA I)				SCORES (PARTS OR WHOLES)					
					Entity A		Entity B		Entity C	
	η_B	η_W	E ratio	F ratio	T 1	T 2	T 1	T 2	T 1	T 2
Stable	1.00	0.00	∞	∞	3	3	2	2	1	1
Change type A	0.00	1.00	0.00	0.00	1	3	1	3	1	3
Change type B	0.00	1.00	0.00	0.00	1	3	2	2	3	1
Equivocal	0.7071	0.7071	1.00	$N - J / J - 1$	2	4	3	5	5	5

Therefore the intervals described previously (see Chapter 7) for assessing the degree to which an E ratio approximates either endpoint are used to make inductions about change and stability.

WABA II   When two variables are considered using WABA I, an induction is made about the degree to which each variable is stable or has changed. As a result, one of the four key conditions listed in the upper portion of Table 12.2 is identified using WABA I. When variables change, within-cell scores are used to represent the scores; and when variables are stable, between-cell scores are used to represent the scores. In WABA II, because the correlation between within- and between-cell scores must equal zero, the correlation between two variables, one of which changes and one of which remains stable over the same time period, must equal zero. When both variables change or are stable, the correlations between the variables are not necessarily equal to zero but can vary between zero and one. Specifically, when two variables are stable, the within-cell correlation should equal zero or be indeterminate, but the between-cell correlation should be free to vary from zero to one. When both variables change, the between-cell correlation is indeterminate or zero, and the within-cell correlation is free to vary from zero to one. These characteristics of WABA II are illustrated by the ideal values shown in the middle portion of Table 12.2. The degree to which a data set approximates these ideal conditions can also be determined using the intervals presented previously for WABA II (see Chapter 7).

The illustrations presented in the lower portion of Table 12.2 provide a way to conceptualize the results of using WABA I and WABA II when cells are constructed in this way. Specifically, when two variables are stable over time, an induction that a change in one variable precedes a change in another variable is not plausible, since neither variable changes. In other words, between-cell correlations by definition provide no information about changes in or the temporal ordering of variables. In contrast, when an induction that two variables change is made using WABA I, the within-cell scores can be correlated. However, these correlations provide only an indication of the degree to which two variables change over the same time period; they do not specify the temporal ordering of such changes. By the process of elimination, therefore, the two cases in which one variable is stable and the other changes may allow for an assessment of the temporal ordering of variables.

Combining WABA I and II   The temporal ordering of variables can be examined when changes in one variable over two time periods are correlated with changes in another variable over two subsequent time periods. To perform this type of analysis, cells are again aligned with entities, but this time in a special way. In this case, each entity has four scores (one for each of four time periods) on each variable X and Y. For one entity, two scores X_1 and X_2 on one variable from the first and second time periods are viewed as a set of scores for that entity, as follows:

	ENTITY A	
One view of variable X	X_1	X_2

TABLE 12.2. Ideal stable and change conditions for WABA I and WABA II

	VARIABLE X — Stable	VARIABLE Y — Stable	VARIABLE X — Stable	VARIABLE Y — Change	VARIABLE Y — Stable	VARIABLE X — Change	VARIABLE Y — Change	VARIABLE X — Change
WABA I								
η between	1.00	1.00	1.00	0.00	1.00	0.00	0.00	0.00
η within	0.00	0.00	0.00	1.00	0.00	1.00	1.00	1.00
E ratio	∞	∞	∞	0.00	∞	0.00	0.00	0.00
F ratio	∞	∞	∞	0.00	∞	0.00	0.00	0.00
WABA II								
Alternative one[a]								
r between	1.00		0.00		0.00		0.00	
r within	0.00		0.00		0.00		1.00	
A	1.57		0.00		0.00		−1.57	
Z	∞		0.00		0.00		−∞	
Alternative two								
r between	0.00						0.00	
r within	0.00						0.00	
A	0.00						0.00	
Z	0.00						0.00	

Schematic[b] illustrations

Condition 1 — X: T_1 X_1 ——— X_2 T_2 (Stable); Y: Y_1 ——— Y_2 (Stable); r_{BXY}

Condition 2 — X: T_1 X_1 ——— X_2 T_2 (Stable); Y: Y_1 ——— Y_2 (Change); $r = 0$

Condition 3 — X: T_1 X_1 ——— X_2 T_2 (Change); Y: Y_1 ——— Y_2 (Stable); $r = 0$

Condition 4 — X: T_1 X_1 ——— X_2 T_2 (Change); Y: Y_1 ——— Y_2 (Change); r_{WXY}

[a] Alternative two is used to illustrate that the between-cell correlation when both variables are stable can vary from 0 to 1. Likewise, when both variables change, the within-cell correlation can vary from 0 to 1.

[b] T_1 and T_2 indicate time periods 1 and 2, respectively. X_1 and X_2 indicate values for X at time 1 and 2, respectively.

The scores for the same entity at times 3 and 4 on the same variable, X_3 and X_4, are viewed as another set of scores on the variable embedded in an entity. Taken together, these two perspectives result in the following tabular organization of the data:

	ENTITY A	
First view of variable X	X_1	X_2
Second view of variable X	X_3	X_4

In this case, the two views of one variable form two different "variables" that can then be correlated.

This conceptualization for the case of four time periods, three entities, and two variables (X and Y) is illustrated in Table 12.3. As a result of this conceptualization, three analyses are possible. First, variables X and Y can be examined using WABA I and WABA II based on scores from time 1 and time 2. Second, variables X and Y can be examined using WABA I and WABA II, based on scores from time 3 and time 4. Third, variable X, based on scores from time 1 and time 2, can be correlated with variable Y, based on scores from times 3 to 4; and variable X, based on scores for time 3 and time 4, can be correlated with variable Y, based on scores for times 1 and 2 in four ways shown in the lower portion of Table 12.4. Ideal results from these three analyses permitting an assessment of the temporal ordering of variables are also presented in the upper portion of Table 12.4.

This type of analysis can be summarized in a somewhat different, perhaps simpler way. If one variable X changes from time 1 to time 2 and a second variable Y changes from time 3 to time 4, then a change in variable X, as represented by within-cell scores from time 1 to time 2, can be correlated with a change in variable Y, as represented by within-cell scores from time 3 to time 4. This can be illustrated by the case in which changes in variable X precede changes in variable Y, as shown in the upper portion of Figure 12.1. In this case, the correlation of the between-cell scores for variable X from time 1 to time 2 with between-cell scores on variable Y from time 3 to time 4 should equal zero or be indeterminate, because the two variables are not stable over these time periods. A comparison of this between-cell correlation ($r_{B X_{12} Y_{34}}$) with the within-cell correlation ($r_{W X_{12} Y_{34}}$) should therefore result in a significant

TABLE 12.3. Arrangement of cells for examination of correlations across four time periods

	ENTITY A		ENTITY B		ENTITY C	
Times 1 and 2						
Variable X	X_1	X_2	X_1	X_2	X_1	X_2
Variable Y	Y_1	Y_2	Y_1	Y_2	Y_1	Y_2
Times 3 and 4						
Variable X	X_3	X_4	X_3	X_4	X_3	X_4
Variable Y	Y_3	Y_4	Y_3	Y_4	Y_3	Y_4

practical and statistical difference, with the within-cell correlation being of greater value if changes in variable X precede changes in variable Y.

A second set of within- and between-cell correlations is also examined in this type of analysis. Although it is not critical, ideally variable Y should be stable from time 1 to time 2 and variable X should be stable from time 3 to time 4. In this case, the correlation of the within-cell scores for variable Y from time 1 to time 2 and variable X from time 3 to time 4 should equal zero ($X \nleftrightarrow Y$). As a result, the between-cell correlation indicates the degree to which the two variables are correlated when they are stable. This relationship of interest in this part of the analysis is illustrated in the lower portion of Figure 12.1.

The values taken on by between-cell correlations of this type ($r_{BY_{12}X_{34}}$) are not critical for purposes of drawing an induction (as indicated by question marks in Table 12.4). In order to induce that a change in variable X precedes a change in variable Y, however, the other between-cell correlation, $r_{BX_{12}Y_{34}}$, should equal zero or be indeterminate. This critical requirement is indicated by

TABLE 12.4. Ideal outcomes from examination of correlations across four time periods

	CASE $X \to Y$		CASE $Y \to X$	
	Variable X	**Variable Y**	**Variable X**	**Variable Y**
Times 1 and 2				
WABA I				
η between	0.00	1.00	1.00	0.00
η within	1.00	0.00	0.00	1.00
WABA II				
r between		0.00		0.00
r within		0.00		0.00
Inferences	Change	Stable	Stable	Change
Times 3 and 4				
WABA I				
η between	1.00	0.00	0.00	1.00
η within	0.00	1.00	1.00	0.00
WABA II				
r between		0.00		0.00
r within		0.00		0.00
Inferences	Stable	Change	Change	Stable
Cross-Time Correlations[a]				
Within $T_1T_2(X)$ and Within $T_3T_4(Y)$		1.00		0.00
Between $T_1T_2(X)$ and Between $T_3T_4(Y)$		0.00		?
Within $T_3T_4(X)$ and Within $T_1T_2(Y)$		0.00		1.00
Between $T_3T_4(X)$ and Between $T_1T_2(Y)$		?		0.00

[a]$T_1T_2(X)$ indicates that values for variable X at times 1 and 2 are used; $T_3T_4(Y)$ indicates that values for variable Y at times 3 and 4 are used.

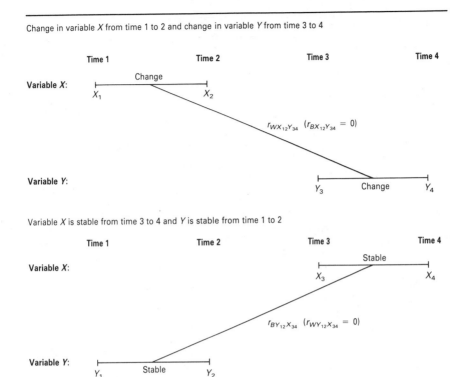

Change in variable X from time 1 to 2 and change in variable Y from time 3 to 4

Variable X is stable from time 3 to 4 and Y is stable from time 1 to 2

FIGURE 12.1. A change in variable Y preceded by a change in variable X

the location of double lines in Table 12.4. Ideal results necessary to induce that a change in variable X is followed by a change in variable Y are summarized in the left portion of Table 12.4. Using the same logic, the ideal values that should be obtained if a change in variable Y leads to a change in variable X are presented in the right side of the table. In this case, variable Y changes from time 1 to 2, and the change is correlated with a change in variable X from time 3 to time 4.

As should be apparent from an examination of Table 12.4, the cases $X \rightarrow Y$ and $Y \rightarrow X$ are distinguishable in two ways. First, in WABA I the variables change over different time periods; obviously, if the variables changed simultaneously, no temporal ordering could be established. Second, in WABA II the correlations across time, as is shown in the lower portion of Table 12.4, differ depending on which case is more likely. This is indicated by the location of double lines in the table.

These two cases ($X \rightarrow Y$ and $X \leftarrow Y$) are illustrated in the upper portion of Figure 12.2. When eight time periods are considered, it is possible to test whether a reciprocal relationship between the two variables is a more likely explanation. For example, a change in variable X from time 1 to time 2 may be related to a change in variable Y from time 3 to time 4 ($X \rightarrow Y$). Likewise, a

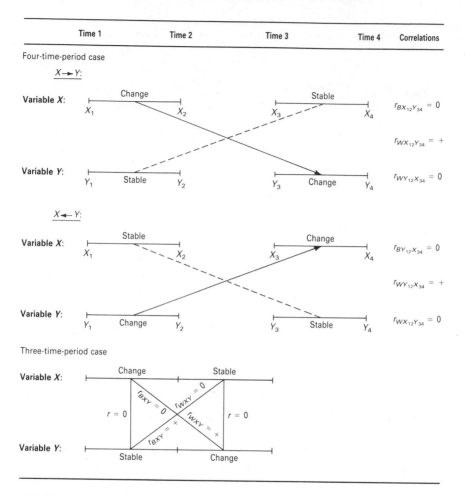

FIGURE 12.2. Correlations of changes over time

change in variable Y from time 5 to time 6 may be related to a change in variable X from time 7 to time 8 ($X \leftarrow Y$), so that a reciprocal relationship is induced.

A number of variations on this approach to testing for the temporal ordering of variables are possible. For example, as shown in the lower portion of Figure 12.2, changes can be examined over three time periods. This case is somewhat problematic because the scores at time 2 are used in the analyses for time 1 to time 2 and time 2 to time 3. The eight-time-period analysis, which is clearly preferable to the three-time-period analysis, provides an overview of this approach for testing assertions that (1) changes in variable X are followed by changes in variable Y; (2) changes in variable Y are followed by changes in variable X; and (3) changes in either variable result in changes in the other.

Multiple-Level Analysis

The procedures that have been described for use at one level of analysis are also applicable to multiple levels of analysis. Therefore, the temporal ordering of variables can be hypothesized to hold across levels of analysis or to be specific to one or several levels of analysis. These hypotheses are tested sequentially at each level of analysis.

Multiple-Variable Analysis

Multiple-variable analysis takes on fuller meaning when time is included in the analysis. The presentation of this extension is simplified by focusing on the three-variable case and by assuming that a stable or change condition has been identified as more likely (using WABA). The related, generally related, generally unrelated, and unrelated cases are then reconceptualized using this simplified perspective.

In the related case, a number of additional theoretical specifications are possible when time is incorporated into multiple-variable analysis. For example, changes in one variable X can be hypothesized as being followed by changes in a second variable Y, and these changes in turn can be hypothesized as being followed by changes in a third variable Z. This theoretical formulation can be illustrated in the following way:

$$X \rightarrow Y \rightarrow Z$$

Not only can such a set of relationships be hypothesized as being nonreciprocal ($X \leftrightarrow Y \leftrightarrow Z$), but the ordering of the sequence of changes in variables can also be hypothesized. For example, if changes in variable X are not followed by changes in variable Y, it can be hypothesized that no change occurs in variable Z ($X \nrightarrow Z$). Likewise, a change in variable Y without a prior change in variable X may be hypothesized not to result in a change in variable Z. The related case, therefore, can be extended by including a consideration of time. The upper portion of Figure 12.3 presents results that are compatible with a hypothesis that a change in variable X is followed by a change in variable Z, which is in turn followed by a change in variable Y. In this case, a change in variable X is not followed by a change in variable Y; instead, changes in variable Z occur before changes in variable Y. In such a formulation, variable Z can be viewed as an intervening third variable.

The generally related case is also extended by incorporating time into the analysis. For example, changes in two variables X and Y over an earlier time period may be correlated zero, but these earlier changes may be correlated with changes in a third variable Z that occur in a later time period. A generally related case of this type is illustrated in the middle portion of Figure 12.3.

In the unrelated case, changes in variables are not related to each other, and in the generally unrelated case changes in some variables are related to changes in other variables. The unrelated and generally unrelated cases require multiple-relationship analysis.

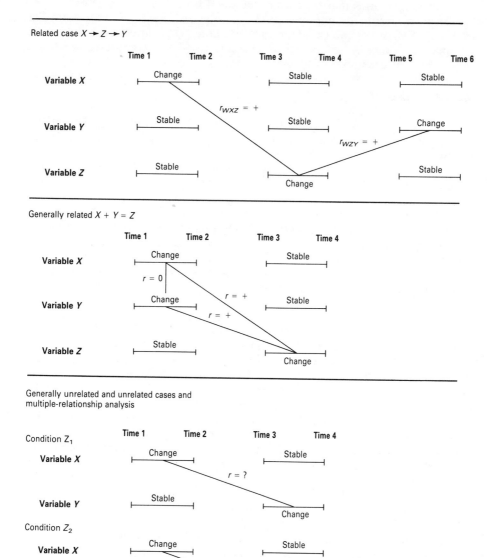

FIGURE 12.3.   Multiple-variable and multiple-relationship analyses over time

Multiple-Relationship Analysis

A consideration of time can be used to extend multiple-relationship analysis. Assume that two conditions, Z_1 and Z_2, are identified for a third variable Z which is stable across time periods. In one condition Z_1, a change in one variable X may be followed by a change in a second variable Y; in a second condition Z_2, a change in one variable X may not be followed by a change in a second variable Y. This type of result indicates that a temporal relationship of variables is contingent on values taken on by a third variable Z. In contrast, in a multiplexed case, a change in one variable X is followed by a change in a second variable Y regardless of the conditions defined by a third variable. An illustration of this type of analysis is shown in the lower portion of Figure 12.3.

THE EXTENDED VARIENT PARADIGM

The entire varient paradigm can now be extended to permit the simultaneous consideration of variables, entities, and time. In terms of entities, it should be apparent that single-level analysis is actually just one component of multiple-level analysis, resulting in the location of theory and data along the entity axis of the varient matrix. Likewise, multiple-variable and multiple-relationship analyses locate theory and data along the variable axis of the varient matrix. In general, to clarify and simplify the presentation of the paradigm, the notion of a chosen focus was introduced for multiple-variable and multiple-relationship analyses, but this is unnecessary. The location of data along the entity axis involves a consideration of relationships among variables. Therefore, multiple-variable and multiple-relationship analyses can be performed on two focuses (within- and between-cell correlations) simultaneously, and the results from each focus can be compared.

When multiple-variable and multiple-relationship analyses are performed in this way, the definitions of validity and error for between- and within-cell deviations are extended to include definitions for any number of variables (such as three, four, and five). Extensions of this multivariate type are referred to as WABA III, WABA IV, and so on. In these extensions, variables and entities are considered simultaneously rather than in the step-by-step fashion illustrated with the data collected at MCO.

In addition, the incorporation of time into the paradigm need not be restricted, since time-based analysis can be performed on both within- and between-entity scores. The results based on within-entity scores over time may be quite different from results based on between-entity scores over time. A time-based analysis is therefore performed simultaneously with multiple-variable and multiple-relationship analyses and single- and multiple-level analyses.

From this perspective, the theoretical formulations and empirical tests presented in Chapters 9, 10, and 11 represent only a first step and illustrate a very narrow use of the varient paradigm. Only one time period was considered, for example. Moreover, the definition of error and valid deviations was based solely on one- and two-variable relationships. Nevertheless, our analysis of the data from MCO provides a basic procedure for testing differences between within-cell and between-cell deviations. These basic procedures should be included as special cases in more advanced work (for example, in developing WABA III). In a real sense, the conceptualization of variables and entities used in the paradigm is one way to view space. The incorporation of time, then, provides one way to examine and test theories in what physicists call space-time. Obviously, other paradigms for testing theories in space-time are also plausible; however, before we consider this issue in Chapter 15, we will return to several additional theoretical and empirical issues raised by the analyses at MCO.

THEORETICAL ISSUES

Both theory A and theory B were actually formulated at three, not two, levels of abstraction. At the lowest level of abstraction, the specification of measures and entities for the setting at MCO was derived from the specific-level formulation of theory A and theory B (see Chapter 4). At this level of abstraction, other entities and measures that might be compatible with other role and exchange theory formulations or views of the setting were not considered. To some extent, this is a valid criticism of almost any study, because alternative hypotheses and therefore measures and entities are always viewed as plausible until tested in the varient paradigm. In any one study, only a subset of perhaps an infinite set of alternative hypotheses can be tested, so inferences are always limited. In the varient paradigm, however, a specific set of plausible alternatives is defined by the number of variables and types of entities specified, and those alternatives are tested. A more valid criticism of the analyses is that traditional measurement issues were apparently almost totally disregarded.

At the next higher level of abstraction, variables and levels of analysis were specified for each theory. Of course, other entities (such as subordinate-subordinate dyads) and variables could have been specified at this higher level of abstraction and then tested with the data collected at MCO. Moreover, the inference that a relationship between investments and returns is probably valid only in support collectivities does not preclude an alternative explanation—that the correlation of measures of investments and returns, other than attention, latitude, superior's satisfaction with a subordinate, and subordinate's congruence with a superior, could result in an inference of interpersonally based superior-subordinate dyads in all the collectivities. For example, if different investments and returns are exchanged in different collectivities, then different measures of the variables should be used in each collectivity. Although the particular measures used in a study can always be criticized, a key issue that was not addressed in the analyses was the degree to which a different method of theory testing (such as experimental) might have produced clearer results. In addition to this methodological issue, a consideration of the implications of the results for theory A and theory B at a still higher level of abstraction suggests a third set of theoretical issues.

Additional studies are necessary in order to assess to what extent the content of exchanges can be viewed as contingent on the nature of the roles within which they occur. Considering the results of the study at MCO, however, the weight of the evidence at this point is in favor of a specific-level formulation of investments and returns involving whole superior-subordinate dyads contingent on a cross-level formulation of titles and expectations. The results from the study at MCO raise a number of questions about role and exchange theory; however, the two theoretical formulations (A and B) presented in Chapter 4 are worthy of further testing at least until other formulations are better able to explain such results. As should be apparent, the generalization from the study at MCO is from data to theory. This approach to drawing inferences from data was not discussed in the MCO analysis.

In summary, the following set of three key issues has been raised by the analyses at MCO: first, little attention has been given to traditional measurement issues, and this may limit the implications of the results; second, the use of a survey method instead of a laboratory or experimental method may limit the implications of the study; third, although generalizations were made from data to theory, the issue of making such generalizations was not considered. These three issues (measurement, methods, and generalizability) seem to be valid limitations of the illustration. However, we believe these limitations are not applicable to the varient paradigm. Chapter 14 demonstrates the way in which the varient paradigm clarifies and extends traditional approaches to measurement, methodology, and generalizability or inferences.

EMPIRICAL ISSUES

An additional set of empirical rather than theoretical issues is raised by the analyses and can be summarized by considering multiple-variable and multiple-relationship analyses and single- and multiple-level analyses.

Multiple-Variable and Multiple-Relationship Analyses

Based on the analyses of the data at MCO, a generally unrelated case was inferred and an unrelated case was rejected. Given the near zero correlations of the investment and return measures with the titles and expectations measures, any attempt to remove the deviations of titles and expectations from the investment and return measures would have little impact on the correlations between the investment and return measures. Therefore, given the equations presented in the next chapter, any attempt to control, hold constant, or partial out the variables specified by one theory (such as theory A) would have little impact on the variables specified by the other (such as theory B). In other words, the results of applying traditional tools such as the partial correlation and the analysis of covariance to hold one set of variables constant would have little impact on the magnitude of the correlations among the other variables.

In contrast, when the variables specified by only one theory were considered, a network of *related* variables was inferred. In cases in which variables are related and form one network, the consequences of holding any one of the variables in the network constant on the relationships between the other variables can be examined using partial correlations or analyses of covariance. In addition to these two tools, other applications might seem to be appropriate for use on the data collected at MCO. For example, an analysis could have been imposed on the data based on an assumption of a generally related case. To illustrate, let T stand for titles, E for expectations, I for investments, and R for returns; any of the following additive models could have been imposed on the data:

$$T = I + R + E$$
$$I = R + E + T$$
$$R = I + E + T$$
$$E = T + R + I$$

A variety of readily available tools compatible with these equations, such as multiple regression or two- or three-way analyses of variance, could have been imposed on the data from MCO.

In terms of multiple-variable analysis, therefore, a question that must be addressed is why the standard methods and tools such as partial and multiple correlation and analyses of variance and covariance were not imposed on the data from MCO. In addition, in terms of multiple-relationship analysis, the notion of an interaction usually associated with analyses of variance and moderated regression analysis seems to have linkages with contingency and multiplexed formulations; but these linkages between the traditional tools and the varient paradigm seem to have been ignored. If these traditional techniques (partial correlation and multiple regression, analysis of covariance, and n-way analysis of variance) are based on correlation matrices, then the analyses at MCO are quite compatible with traditional procedures. A demonstration that these traditional tools are indeed based on correlation matrices is presented in Chapter 13.

Single- and Multiple-Level Analyses

Traditional tools can be readily extended to include an explicit consideration of single and multiple levels of analysis. The importance of including an explicit consideration of entities in any analysis should be clear from the results obtained at MCO. Basically, the empirical finding that whole dyads were more likely in the support collectivity than in the others was based on the tests for levels of analysis. Chapter 13 also focuses on incorporating an explicit consideration of levels of analysis into traditional techniques.

SUMMARY

The varient paradigm can readily be extended to include time. This extension involves the use of WABA, which permits stability or change over time to be inferred and allows for the possibility that each time period is unique (an equivocal condition). Moreover, the paradigm can be extended to include a simultaneous consideration of variables and entities (space) with time. Several implications of the varient paradigm for contemporary and traditional approaches to data analysis (such as analysis of variance and covariance and partial and multiple correlation) are presented in the next chapter. The implications of the paradigm for contemporary problems in measurement, methodology, and generalizing from data to theory are presented in Chapter 14. In all cases, traditional and contemporary approaches are extended and not necessarily contradicted by the use of the general varient paradigm summarized in this chapter.

REVIEW QUESTIONS

1. What problems arise when composite correlations are used to test theories?
2. How does the inclusion of the temporal ordering of variables affect tests for entities and networks of variables?
3. Does consideration of temporal factors alter the basic logic of the inference process?
4. Ideally, at how many time periods should data be collected to assess the temporal ordering of variables?
5. What is the relationship between many traditional views of individual differences and the stable condition at the person level of analysis?
6. Why is a chosen focus on either within- or between-cell deviations or correlations not necessary?
7. How are intervening variables conceptualized?
8. How are multiplexed and contingent formulations extended by a consideration of the temporal ordering of variables?
9. How can the varient approach be used to test whether results are replicable over time?
10. What are some of the theoretical limitations affecting the interpretation of the findings based on MCO data?

13

IMPLICATIONS

A complete articulation of the implications of the varient paradigm for the large number of data analytic techniques used in organizational behavior and the social sciences is beyond the scope of one chapter in a book. However, six data analytic techniques that are widely used in examining hypotheses about variables and entities are identified in this chapter. These six techniques are based on signed deviation scores and are compatible with the general linear tensor and WABA.

Two of these techniques, **bivariate correlations** and the **analysis of variance**, assess the degree of correlation between two variables. Two other techniques, **partial correlations** and the **analysis of covariance**, adjust correlations between two variables so that a correlational value is independent of the values taken on by a third variable. The last two techniques, **multiple regressions** and the **n-way analysis of variance**, permit the addition of variables and a consideration of interactions (contingencies). The correlational techniques will be considered before the analysis of variance techniques.

BIVARIATE CORRELATIONS

The Varient Approach

Bivariate (two-variable) correlations are used extensively in the varient paradigm to characterize networks of variables in multiple-variable and multiple-relationship analyses. In terms of single- and multiple-level analyses, between-cell, within-cell, and eta correlations are always used to test assertions about levels of analysis. Therefore, bivariate correlations have been extended in the paradigm to include an explicit consideration of entities. Although within- and between-entity scores and correlations can be calculated for one time period, the uses of bivariate correlations have been extended through the time-based analysis described in Chapter 12.

Other Approaches

The use of bivariate correlations to locate data along a variable axis may appear to be somewhat new. However, an examination of relationships among variables using bivariate correlations is not unusual in contemporary and traditional approaches. The use of WABA to test assertions about the *entities* that may underlie variables and their relationships differs, however, from most contemporary approaches. Two examples should illustrate this point.

First, Epstein (1980), among others, has proposed that correlations based on multiple assessments of variables over time be calculated for each entity. The correlations for each entity are then converted to Fisher's Z' scores and averaged. The average serves as a summary or overall intraperson (or intra-entity) correlation. The procedure can be illustrated with the following synthetic data, in which the correlation for each person based on three time periods equals 1 and the average of the correlations for all persons equals 1.

		SCORE		
PERSON	TIME	X	Y	CORRELATION
Abe	1	1	5	
Abe	2	2	6	
Abe	3	3	7	$r_A = 1$
Cathy	1	4	8	
Cathy	2	5	9	
Cathy	3	6	10	$r_C = 1$

Epstein's approach does not permit a consideration of the variation that occurs between persons. In addition, the basis of the inference process is the statistical significance of one correlation rather than the significance of the difference between obtained correlations. Therefore, this procedure requires an assumption that only intraperson correlations are valid. In the varient paradigm, inferences are drawn based on the degree to which one hypothesis (such as wholes) is more likely than another hypothesis (such as parts), rather than on assumptions about the validity of a level of analysis. Nevertheless, an examination of intraperson correlations might be interesting after an induction is made that these correlations are a better explanation of the deviations.

A second general approach to assessing levels of analysis, called contextual analysis (see Kraemer, 1978), also seems to be based on bivariate correlations. **Contextual analysis** uses composite correlations in which one variable expressed as a total score is correlated with another variable expressed as a between-cell score. In this approach, within- and between-eta and within- and between-cell correlations are multiplied to form composite correlations.

Although they are perhaps not readily apparent, a number of interesting assumptions underlie the contextual analysis approach to levels of analysis. Apparently, total deviation scores on one variable are assumed to represent between-cell scores or wholes at a lower level of analysis. A second variable of interest is apparently assumed to represent whole entities at the next higher level of analysis, and between-cell scores are used for this variable. The conceptualization that seems to underlie this approach can be illustrated as shown in the upper portion of Figure 13.1. The composite correlation r_{TBXY} shown in the diagram is apparently assumed to be some type of cross-level correlation. This correlation, however, is a composite (see Chapter 12) of a between-eta correlation and a between-cell correlation at the higher level of analysis. Schematically, the components of the composite correlation can be illustrated as shown in the middle portion of Figure 13.1. As shown in the lower portion of the figure, the composite correlation can be written as:

$$r_{TBXY} = \eta_{BX} r_{BXY}$$

In other words, the composite correlation r_{TBXY} is an adjusted between-cell correlation at the higher level of analysis. We call the interpretation of this correlation as indicating a cross-level effect the **composite fallacy**. Nevertheless, if composite correlations are of interest, they can be calculated from the indicators used in WABA I and II. Therefore, no information is lost when WABA is employed. In contrast, when only composite correlations are reported, a substantial amount of information is lost about the correlations and deviations at each level of analysis.

In addition to their uses in examining variables and entities, bivariate correlations are also used in traditional approaches to examine data that have been collected over time. For example, when two variables are assessed at each of two time periods, the following bivariate correlations are examined in a

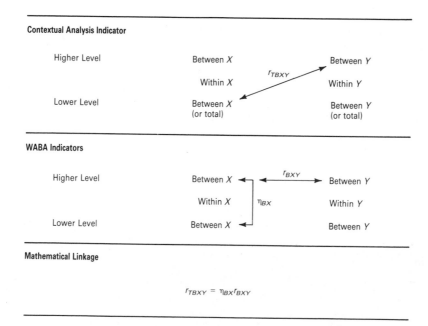

FIGURE 13.1. Linkage between contextual analysis and WABA

traditional **cross-lagged correlational analysis** (see Kenny, 1975):

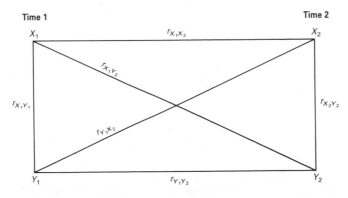

Since bivariate correlations are used in analyses of this type, two sets of correlations and cross-lagged tests can be calculated based on both within- and between-entity scores, and their results can be compared (see Nachman, Dansereau, and Naughton, 1980). Rogosa (1980), however, has shown that the cross-lagged approach to assessing the temporal ordering of variables has a number of deficiencies. One key deficiency is that these correlations are based on differences between entities and not on changes in variables. In contrast, tests of the degree of stability or change can be performed using WABA, and the relationship among changes in scores can then be examined, if appropriate. Nevertheless, when cross-lagged analysis is viewed as desirable, at a minimum it can be extended by using within- and between-entity cross-lagged correlations. Obviously, we believe that the procedures outlined in Chapter 12 are preferable, particularly in light of Rogosa's (1980) remarks.

PARTIAL CORRELATIONS

When interest is in three rather than two variables, partial rather than bivariate correlations are often used in traditional analyses. Given three variables, X, Y, and Z, the following three bivariate correlations can be examined:

$$X$$
$$r_{XY} \qquad r_{XZ}$$
$$Y \quad \cdots \quad Z$$
$$r_{YZ}$$

Using the traditional formula for partial correlations, three different partial correlations can be calculated. First, the correlation of variable X with variable Y partialing out variable Z is calculated using the following formula:

$$r_{XY \cdot Z} = \frac{r_{XY} - r_{XZ}r_{YZ}}{\sqrt{\left(1 - r_{XZ}^2\right)\left(1 - r_{YZ}^2\right)}}$$

Second, the correlation of variable X with variable Z, with variable Y partialed out, is written:

$$r_{XZ \cdot Y} = \frac{r_{XZ} - r_{XY}r_{YZ}}{\sqrt{\left(1 - r_{XY}^2\right)\left(1 - r_{YZ}^2\right)}}$$

Third, the correlation between variables Y and Z, partialing out variable X, is written:

$$r_{YZ \cdot X} = \frac{r_{YZ} - r_{XY}r_{XZ}}{\sqrt{\left(1 - r_{XY}^2\right)\left(1 - r_{XZ}^2\right)}}$$

As should be apparent from these three equations, when the values for the three bivariate correlations are known, the value taken on by any of these partial correlations is determined. In contrast, given a value for a partial correlation, the values taken on by the three bivariate correlations are not necessarily known. Therefore, the matrix of bivariate correlations among variables determines the values of all partial correlations. For this reason, we prefer to focus on matrices of correlations among variables rather than only on partial correlations.

The Varient Approach

Partial correlations can also be calculated using WABA, by aligning cells with the values of a third variable that is to be partialed out from two variables of interest. In this case, the between-cell deviation scores for the two variables of interest represent the deviations of the variables of interest that covary with a third variable. In contrast, the within-cell deviations represent the deviations of the variables of interest that do not covary with a third variable; in this case, within-cell correlations are partial correlations. In fact, McNemar (1955) has derived the traditional formula for partial correlations from the formula for within-cell correlations by assuming that any common variation of two variables of interest with a third variable is linear. A test of this assumption is not available. In contrast, in the WABA approach to partial correlations an assumption need not be made that the relationships among variables are linear. Moreover, using WABA, the degrees of freedom are reduced for each cell defined by one value of a variable—in other words, according to the number of conditions (cells) held constant. In contrast, the number of degrees of freedom for the standard partial correlation is calculated based on a series of assumptions in which one degree of freedom is lost for each variable held constant.

One advantage of the WABA approach to partial correlations is that a test can be performed to assess whether the imposition of cells, and therefore the partialing procedure, has an impact on a set of scores. In this approach, all the indicators from WABA are used, and inductions are based on the following conceptualization:

	BETWEEN Z	WITHIN Z	INDUCTION
Condition 1	Systematic	Near zero	Effect of partialing
Condition 2	Near zero	Systematic	No effect of partialing
Condition 3	Systematic	Systematic	Equivocal
Condition 4	Near zero	Near zero	Inexplicable

When this procedure is used, one of the four conditions is chosen based on a comparison of obtained values with the intervals used for the E, A, R, and F, Z, t indicators (see Chapter 7). In this way, the degree to which a third variable affects a relationship between two variables of interest is tested. This partialing procedure can be employed using any variable as a third variable. In addition, the procedure can be applied sequentially where several variables are partialed out of one relationship of interest. At each step, when a new variable is partialed out the degrees of freedom for the within-cell correlations are adjusted by the number of cells within which the variables of interest are held constant.

Multiple-Variable and Multiple-Relationship Analyses   Partial correlations are particularly useful in multiple-variable analysis when variables are directly contingent (in the related and generally related cases). Given a network of related variables, when any one of the variables is partialed out, the correlations among the variables should reduce in value *significantly*. In contrast, when variables are indirectly contingent, a partialing procedure should have little impact on the relationship between them.

Single- and Multiple-Level Analyses   The partialing procedure described thus far has been limited to cases in which the units of analysis for all variables are identified before the application of the procedure. It should be apparent, however, that partial correlations can be calculated based on both within- and between-entity scores. In other words, the identification of entities (parts or wholes) does not prohibit the use of partialing procedures on both within- and between-entity scores.

In addition, the WABA approach to partial correlations provides a somewhat different perspective on the WABA approach to levels of analysis. Specifically, WABA results in the following two adjustments of scores. First, within-entity deviation scores make total scores compatible with a parts condition, since within-entity deviation scores are independent of any deviations between entities and are constant across cells. In the second adjustment, between-entity deviation scores make total scores compatible with a whole condition, since between-entity deviation scores are independent of any deviations within entities and take on the same values within cells. As a result, a comparison of these two representations of scores indicates which condition seems more likely.

Time   It should be apparent that partial correlations can also be calculated for data collected over time. However, because space and time are conceptualized as interwoven in the varient paradigm (see Chapter 12), the effect of different time periods need not be partialed out. Of course, analysis of this type can be performed on within- and between-entity scores if it seems desirable.

Other Approaches

Multiple-Variable and Multiple-Relationship Analyses   In contemporary studies, partial correlations typically tend to be calculated based on assumptions of linearity. Within-cell scores, however, are sometimes used as the basis for partial correlations in studies of organizational behavior (see Parasuraman and Alutto, 1981). In these cases, however, WABA I and II can be used to test whether a third variable affects the correlation between two variables of interest. Actually, in most contemporary research reports, total correlations are presented first and are followed by partial correlations. As a result, tests of whether holding a third variable constant affects the relationship between two variables of interest are not performed, and levels of analysis are ignored by using total correlations.

Single- and Multiple-Level Analyses   A partialing perspective is also useful in understanding a seminal paper written by Robinson (1950) on the ecological fallacy and levels of analysis. According to Robinson, correlations based on total deviation scores are not necessarily identical with correlations based on between-cell scores. An interpretation of total correlations as identical to the between-cell correlations is called the **ecological fallacy**. To illustrate his point, Robinson (1950) analyzed 1940 U.S. Census data and presented a total correlation between literacy and race of 0.203; he showed that this correlation was not equal to a between-cell correlation of 0.946. WABA provides additional information about Robinson's results.

In WABA terminology, nine regions of the United States were used to construct nine cells. The percentage of individuals who were illiterate and black served as an indicator of literacy and race. The results from analyzing the census data using WABA I and WABA II are summarized in Table 13.1. In terms of WABA I, both literacy and race tend to be better represented by within- rather than between-region deviations using tests of practical significance. However, the stronger within-eta correlations are not statistically significant. This should not be surprising, because the between-region deviations have 8 degrees of freedom and the within-region deviation scores have 97,272,000 degrees of freedom. Therefore, the finding that more deviation occurs within regions can be viewed as due to statistical artifacts and as quite likely, since the number of degrees of freedom for the within-cell deviations is very large. In terms of WABA II, as shown in the table, the greater magnitude of the between-region correlation between race and literacy is significantly different from the within-region correlation.

TABLE 13.1.   Results of reanalysis of 1940 census data used by Robinson

WABA Iᵃ	LITERACY	RACE	WABA IIᵇ	LITERACY AND RACE
Data				
η between	0.092	0.524	*r* between	0.946
η within	0.996	0.852	*r* within	0.185
E ratio	0.092	0.615	*A*	1.055
F ratio	103,742	4,599,189	*Z*	3.932
Inferences				
Practical	Parts	Parts		Wholes
Statistical	Wholes	Wholes		Wholes
Total		Inconsistent		Spurious
Components				
Between				0.046
Within				0.157
Total *r*				0.203

ᵃ$df = 8$ and 97,272,000
ᵇ$df = 7$ and 97,271,999

In terms of WABA I and II, the results from WABA II lead to an induction of whole regions, whereas WABA I leads to an induction of parts (in terms of practical significance). This set of findings is compatible with the inference that range restriction in the between-cell scores could account for the difference between the within-cell correlation of 0.185 and the between-cell correlation of 0.946. Indeed, the components of the total correlation suggest that the between-cell component (0.046) is not as strong as the within-cell component (0.157). Therefore, using WABA, inductions are made that the ranges of the variables are restricted because of lack of variation between cells and that the between-cell correlation should not be interpreted.

Essentially, the conclusion from the analysis of this data using WABA is identical to that proposed by Robinson (1950). In this case, a cross-level relationship is not induced, and therefore the between-cell and total correlations are not similar. Moreover, the particular classification of regions used in Robinson's analysis fails to clarify the relationship between race and literacy (other classifications, of course, could result in a different inference). Because Robinson's example was based on dichotomized variables for race and literacy, some problems occur because the average of dichotomized $(0 - 1)$ variables is related to the within-cell deviations of variables expressed in this way. Nevertheless, despite this problem WABA provides an explanation of why the between-cell and total correlations are not equal in this case.

Time   The notion of partialing out a variable has also been applied to attempts to measure change. For example, residual gain scores are sometimes calculated by transforming a variable measured at two time periods to standard scores at each time period; then the standard scores at one time period are multiplied by the correlation of a variable with itself over time; then the variable at one time period is subtracted from the values at other time periods. Cronbach and Furby (1970) have raised a number of questions about this type of partialing procedure. Although within-cell scores can be viewed as change scores in the varient paradigm, these scores are used in such a way only if a test indicates that variables seem to change rather than remain stable over time.

MULTIPLE CORRELATION AND REGRESSION

As should be apparent, traditional uses of partial correlations are totally determined by the matrix of correlations among a set of variables. In a similar vein, multiple correlation and regression are also known to be determined by a matrix of bivariate correlations. For example, Guilford (1965, p. 409) illustrates this point by using the following regression equation with four independent variables (X_2, X_3, X_4, X_5) and one dependent variable (X_1):

$$X_1 = X_2 + X_3 + X_4 + X_5$$

A set of simultaneous equations is employed in the Doolittle method to obtain values for beta weights (β). According to Guilford (1965, p. 409), these equations are written:

$$\beta_{12} + r_{23}\beta_{13} + r_{24}\beta_{14} + r_{25}\beta_{15} = r_{12}$$
$$r_{23}\beta_{12} + \beta_{13} + r_{34}\beta_{14} + r_{35}\beta_{15} = r_{13}$$
$$r_{24}\beta_{12} + r_{34}\beta_{13} + \beta_{14} + r_{45}\beta_{15} = r_{14}$$
$$r_{25}\beta_{12} + r_{35}\beta_{13} + r_{45}\beta_{14} + \beta_{15} = r_{15}$$

The beta coefficients are symbolized in abbreviated form by Guilford (1965) in order to conserve space. For example, β_{12} can be written as $\beta_{12.345}$ or as the beta weight for variable X_2 in the regression equation, partialing out variables 3, 4, and 5. The value for the bivariate correlations r must be known in order to solve this set of equations. Therefore, the entire solution of this set of simultaneous equations is based completely on bivariate correlations. In addition, once these simultaneous equations are solved, a multiple correlation (R) is obtained from the beta weights and correlations in the following manner (Guilford, 1965):

$$R^2 = \beta_{12}r_{12} + \beta_{13}r_{13} + \beta_{14}r_{14} + \beta_{15}r_{15}$$

Because values for these beta weights are determined by bivariate correlations, multiple correlations and beta weights are determined by bivariate correlations, and not vice versa.

Multiple regression, like partial correlations, can be viewed as one way to summarize a matrix of correlations among variables. Consider the following case, in which a multiple regression perfectly summarizes a matrix of correlations with no loss of information.

	VARIABLE 1	VARIABLE 2	VARIABLE 3	VARIABLE 4	VARIABLE 5
VARIABLE 1	—				
VARIABLE 2	r_{12}	—			
VARIABLE 3	r_{13}	0	—		
VARIABLE 4	r_{14}	0	0	—	
VARIABLE 5	r_{15}	0	0	0	—

In this case, the correlations among all the independent variables (variables 2 to 5) equal zero. Therefore, only the correlations between the independent variables and dependent variables are greater than zero. In this case, the beta weights are written:

$$\beta_{12} = r_{12}$$

$$\beta_{13} = r_{13}$$

$$\beta_{14} = r_{14}$$

$$\beta_{15} = r_{15}$$

and the equation for the squared multiple correlation is written:

$$R^2 = r_{12}^2 + r_{13}^2 + r_{14}^2 + r_{15}^2$$

In this case, the entire matrix of correlations is completely represented by a regression equation; the squared multiple correlation is simply a summation of the squared bivariate correlations, and the beta weights equal the bivariate correlations.

When there is lack of multicollinearity in a set of independent variables, no information about the matrix of correlations is lost by using a multiple regression equation, and the beta weights are simply bivariate correlations. The requirement of a lack of multicollinearity in a multiple-regression analysis is well known (see Heise, 1975). In addition to this general approach to multiple regression, two versions of regression called hierarchical and stepwise regression are sometimes used in contemporary approaches. If there is a lack of multicollinearity, values for the multiple correlation and beta weights will be identical regardless of which version is used to derive the values. If the independent variables are correlated, however, the order in which variables are entered into a multiple regression equation will influence the magnitude of the beta weights. Specifically, although the definitions are sometimes reversed in traditional work, in **hierarchical regression**, variables are entered in an order that depends on a user's preference; in **stepwise regression**, the variable with the largest correlation is entered first. In these two versions of regression, partial correlations are used to estimate beta weights and therefore assumptions of linearity are again made. Nevertheless, since partial correlations are based on bivariate correlations, multiple regression also rests on matrices of bivariate correlations.

The Varient Approach

In the varient paradigm, the use of multiple regression is viewed as being contingent on the degree to which a matrix of correlations can be adequately summarized by a multiple-regression equation. Moreover, the interpretation of any multiple-regression equation changes depending on the type of network of variables identified before it is imposed on data. This approach can be illustrated by considering the three-variable case with multiple-variable and multiple-relationship analyses.

Multiple-Variable and Multiple-Relationship Analyses   Clearly, multiple-regression equations can be used to summarize the generally related case (such as two variables are correlated zero, but both contribute to a third variable). From a theoretical perspective, any number of multiple-regression equations can be hypothesized. For example, any of the following three equations can be specified for the case of three variables:

$$X + Y = Z$$
$$X + Z = Y$$
$$Y + Z = X$$

It should be possible to show empirically that one of these equations is more likely. The purpose of multiple-variable analysis, as described previously, is to test which of these equations is more likely. Therefore, in the varient paradigm the choice of a particular multiple regression is based not only on theory, but also on data.

Multiple regression can also be viewed as a data-reduction device rather than as a way to construct a theoretical assertion. As such, it can be employed on data when the generally unrelated, related, or unrelated case seems more likely. For example, when multiple regression is imposed on a network of unrelated variables, there is no empirical basis on which to decide which variables should serve as independent or dependent variables. Nevertheless, arbitrary decisions can be made, and a multiple-regression equation can be imposed on the data. In the generally unrelated case, a third variable is unrelated to two variables of interest; when multiple regression is imposed on data, the results should indicate that the third variable makes little contribution to the dependent variable.

The application of multiple regression in the generally unrelated case can be quite problematic. As an illustration, suppose that the bivariate correlations among three variables take on the following values: $r_{XY} = +$, $r_{YZ} = 0$, $r_{XZ} = 0$. Two multiple-regression equations ($X + Z = Y$ and $Y + Z = X$) are straightforward because the correlation among the independent variables is zero. In these two cases, the application of a multiple-regression equation will result in an inference that a third variable (Z) makes little contribution to the dependent variable. However, the following multiple-regression equation will result in multicollinearity problems because variables X and Y are correlated:

$$X + Y = Z$$

In this case, a multiple correlation is likely to be inflated in value due to multicollinearity.

Finally, in the related case, the choice of which variables should serve as independent or dependent variables cannot be made based on data. Since all the variables are interrelated in this case, two variables cannot be identified as contributing independently to a third variable. Of course, a stepwise or hierarchical multiple regression can be employed. In these procedures, the unique contribution of each independent variable to the dependent variable is assessed by partialing out the contribution of all other variables to the dependent variable. In the related case, the order in which variables are entered into a regression equation affects the value for the beta weights.

From an empirical perspective, a consideration of the matrix of correlations that determines the values for a multiple regression is clearly necessary when using the technique. Moreover, when interest is in multiple-relationship analysis, different multiple-regression equations can be examined in the different conditions defined by values of a third variable.

Single- and Multiple-Level Analyses   Since the values for any multiple-regression equation are determined by the values of the bivariate correlations, within- and between-entity multiple regressions can be specified and examined. In other words, in the varient paradigm, because multiple regression is viewed as a type of correlational analysis, entities must be specified and tests performed to assess the accuracy of such specifications.

Time   As indicated previously, when time is included in the paradigm, within- and between-cell scores are calculated such that they represent change and stability. Therefore, multiple-regression equations can be constructed using both sets of scores. For example, the within-cell scores on two variables (over two time periods) can serve as the independent variables in a regression equation, and the within-cell scores on a third variable can serve as the dependent variable (assuming between-cell scores are also examined in a second multiple-regression equation).

Other Approaches

Frequently, multiple regression is used for demonstration rather than testing purposes. In such a case, one multiple-regression equation and one unit of analysis are assumed to hold in a data set. The issue addressed by this type of data analysis seems to be whether an assumed truth does better than what would be predicted by chance or the statistical paradigm. An examination of this demonstration approach from the perspective of the varient paradigm provides some additional insights into the nature of theory testing in the varient paradigm.

Multiple-Variable and Multiple-Relationship Analyses   For purposes of demonstration alone, once a multiple-regression equation is assumed to be true, problems of multicollinearity—and most other problems with entities and variables—are assumed away (at least in the mind of the demonstrator).

Regardless of the assumptions usually made by a demonstrator, data can be located along the variable axis by considering the matrix of bivariate correlations. Moreover, a matrix of obtained correlations can be tested using multiple-variable analysis, even if a demonstrator believes that his or her multiple-regression equation is true. An examination of the matrix of correlations, however, may result in evidence for or against a demonstrator's hypothesis. At a minimum, a consideration of the matrix of correlations among a set of variables provides information about the nature of the network of variables that underlies any multiple-regression equation.

In terms of multiple-relationship analysis, moderated multiple regression is sometimes viewed as a way to incorporate a consideration of interactions (contingency formulations) into data analysis. We will defer a consideration of interactions until the n-way analysis of variance is discussed. At this point, it is important to note that multiplying two variables together and entering them into a multiple-regression equation does not always result in a test for interactions or provide another approach to multiple-relationship analysis.

Single- and Multiple-Level Analyses   In terms of entities, as should be apparent, in the varient paradigm multiple regression can be applied using within-cell *and* between-cell (entity) scores. The bivariate case of two variables can be expressed at one level of analysis as follows:

$$\text{Between:} \quad \beta(\bar{X}_J - \bar{X}) = (\bar{Y}_J - \bar{Y})$$
$$\text{Within:} \quad \beta(X - \bar{X}_J) = (Y - \bar{Y}_J)$$

and a three-variable multiple-regression equation can be written as follows:

$$\text{Between:} \quad \beta(\bar{X}_J - \bar{X}) + \beta(\bar{Z}_J - \bar{Z}) = (\bar{Y}_J - \bar{Y})$$
$$\text{Within:} \quad \beta(X - \bar{X}_J) + \beta(Z - \bar{Z}_J) = (Y - \bar{Y}_J)$$

These deviation scores are used in a variety of other ways in contemporary approaches to levels of analysis. For example, the following multiple-regression equation, presented in our notation, is the basis for Firebaugh's (1978) $\bar{X}$ rule.

$$Y = \beta_1 X + \beta_2 \bar{X}_J$$
$$(Y - \bar{Y}) = \beta_1(X - \bar{X}) + \beta_2(\bar{X}_J - \bar{X})$$

In this equation, the total deviations on one variable (X) at a lower level of analysis plus the between-cell deviations on the same variable ($\bar{X}_J$) at a higher level of analysis are viewed as summing to another variable Y at a lower level of analysis. Firebaugh's rule (1978) can now be stated as follows: When between-cell scores at a higher level of analysis ($\bar{X}_J$) make no contribution to a regression equation beyond that explained by the total deviations (X, assumed to represent between-cell deviations at a lower level of analysis), then a lack of cross-level effects can be inferred.

On the surface, this rule may seem reasonable. Consider the extreme case in which the correlation of the total deviations (X) with between-cell deviations ($\overline{X}_J$) equals zero. In this case, the between-cell eta correlation equals zero. Therefore, the correlation between X and Y based on total deviations at the lower level of analysis must represent a within-cell correlation. This means that a parts condition is more likely; since by definition parts are level-specific (not cross-level), the inferred lack of cross-level effects makes sense.

In another extreme case, the correlation between the total deviations (X) and the between-cell deviations ($\overline{X}_J$) equals one. Here the between-cell deviations make the same contribution to variable Y as do the total deviations. As a result, a problem arises with Firebaugh's rule. Specifically, the rule requires that if the between-cell scores contribute anything beyond the total deviation scores, then a cross-level effect should be inferred. In this admittedly extreme case, the between-cell deviation scores are identical to the total deviation scores; thus the between-cell scores contribute nothing beyond what is known from the total deviations. In this case, a variable is identical at two levels of analysis. Using the varient paradigm, a cross-level effect would be inferred; whereas if Firebaugh's rule were used, a cross-level effect presumably would not be inferred.

Another interesting situation occurs when a parts condition as conceptualized in the varient paradigm occurs at a higher level of analysis. In an ideal case, the between-cell scores at a higher level of analysis are correlated zero with any total deviation scores at a lower level of analysis. According to the $\overline{X}$ rule, no cross-level effect would be inferred. Apparently, in Firebaugh's approach parts are not permitted across levels of analysis.

Perhaps the major problem with the Firebaugh rule is that the formulation is based on composite correlations. In other words, the correlation of one variable based on *total* deviations is correlated with another variable based on *between-cell* deviations. It has been shown that such correlations are aggregates of between-eta and between-cell correlations at a higher level of analysis (see Chapter 12). Further problems arise in connection with this use of multiple regression. Specifically, the variables in the regression equation have different degrees of freedom. For example, the between-cell scores ($\overline{X}_J$) are based on $J - 1$ degrees of freedom, and the total scores have $N - 1$ degrees of freedom. An appropriate way to test the significance of beta weights in such regression equations, even in a statistical sense, is not clear. In addition, considering the characteristics of the statistical paradigm, the exclusive use of statistical tests of significance means that the larger the sample size, the more likely one is to find a significant beta-weight effect for the between-cell correlation and the more likely a cross-level effect is to be inferred.

In the varient paradigm, inferences of cross-level, level-specific, and emergent relationships are all based on at least one practically and statistically significant finding. In Firebaugh's approach, an inference of a lack of a cross-level effect (such as a level-specific effect) is based on a finding of a lack of statistical significance. The logic underlying this approach is unclear. Nevertheless, several contemporary approaches to levels of analysis are modeled after Firebaugh's (1978) thinking.

For example, the conclusions of Lincoln and Zeitz (1980) seem to underscore the problems inherent in this contextual approach to levels of analysis. They indicate that an attempt to apply their analysis to two levels of analysis would be too complicated to discuss and that no tests of statistical significance could be employed. Their conclusion that the use of tests of statistical significance is inappropriate seems to be correct, because the number of degrees of freedom used to test for statistical significance is unclear in this approach. As a result, when this approach is used, the basis of any inferences drawn from data is unclear. In addition, Lincoln and Zeitz (1980) present eta correlations, ignore them, and then include them in their path model by including the correlations between total scores and between cell scores. Finally, their path model seems to contain an incomprehensible assertion that *both* the between-eta and the within-eta correlations on one variable can equal one when it is known that the sum of two squared eta correlations must equal one (see Appendix D).

Katerburg and Hom (1981) and Vecchio (1982) have advocated another variation on this approach to levels of analysis. In their approach, only some within- and between-cell and eta correlations are considered. For example, the following submatrix of correlations is presented:

	TOTAL SCORES	BETWEEN-CELL SCORES	OTHER TOTAL SCORES (DEPENDENT VARIABLES)
TOTAL SCORES	r_T		
BETWEEN SCORES	η_B	r_B	
OTHER TOTAL SCORES (DEPENDENT VARIABLES)	r_T	r_{TB}	r_T

In this mixed approach, within-cell correlations are ignored and between-cell and composite correlations are presented. Given these correlations, it is apparent that no empirical or systematic comparisons or tests of statistical significance can be performed. Apparently, as a result, the following regression equation—which is the epitome of the composite fallacy—is examined:

$$\beta\bar{X} + \beta\bar{Z} = Y \tag{13.1}$$

In this case, the degrees of freedom for the independent variables $(J-1)$ are different than for the dependent variable $(N-1)$ and, of course, no tests of significance could be employed. The composite fallacy is then extended by allowing for multicollinearity, since the total deviation scores for the two independent variables are added into the regression equation, as follows:

$$\beta\bar{X} + \beta X + \beta\bar{Z} + \beta Z = Y \tag{13.2}$$

In Equation 13.2, multicollinearity is quite likely because the total and between-cell scores (the between-eta correlations) can be highly correlated on the same variable. The basis of inferences in this approach is a comparison of the squared multiple correlations from Equations 13.1 and 13.2. Inferences are based on a visual inspection of the degree to which the two multiple correlations seem similar or different in magnitude. The criteria for decision making are therefore unclear.

At this point, it should be clear that within- and between-entity scores can be created and used in a number of ways. All these other formulations can be derived from WABA if needed. If interest is in using the composite correlations, for example, then at a minimum the composites (between- and within-cell and eta correlations) should be presented, in addition to the results from multiplying the composites.

Time   Finally, a more complex use of multiple regression called path analysis is often employed to attempt to assess the ordering of variables with and without the consideration of time periods in a data set. Such analyses can be performed on within- and between-entity scores, if interest is in levels of analysis. In addition, however, a consideration of the bivariate correlations on which any multiple-regression equation is based seems appropriate. In general, path analysis tends to be used for demonstration purposes. For example, a particular path (network) of variables is assumed to hold, and then data are used to demonstrate the consequences of assuming that this path or network is true. Only tests of statistical significance seem to be employed in path analysis. Again, before performing path analysis, it would be appropriate to consider examining a matrix of obtained within- and between-entity correlations.

ONE-WAY ANALYSIS OF VARIANCE (ANOVA)

The mathematical similarity of the one-way analysis of variance and correlational analysis is presented in Appendix F. Specifically, when between $(\overline{Y}_J - \overline{Y})$- and within $(Y - \overline{Y}_J)$-cell scores are viewed as independent variables and the total deviations $(Y - \overline{Y})$ are viewed as the dependent variable, the one-way analysis of variance is written in multiple-regression terms as follows:

$$\beta(\overline{Y}_J - \overline{Y}) + \beta(Y - \overline{Y}_J) = (Y - \overline{Y})$$

The values for the beta coefficients in this equation equal the within- and between-eta correlations. Therefore, since multiple regression is based on bivariate correlations, the one-way analysis of variance is also based on these correlations.

The Varient Approach

In the varient paradigm, the between-cell eta correlations are used in the one-way analysis of variance as a way to estimate the relationship between two variables. The ANOVA is particularly useful in multiple-variable and multiple-relationship analyses when an independent variable is categorical rather than continuous. In the illustrative tests on the data collected at MCO, an ANOVA was performed on within- and between-work-group scores. Since the ANOVA can be used with both between- and within-entity scores, it also is useful in single- and multiple-level analyses.

In the varient paradigm, time is incorporated in a special way into traditional experimental designs that typically employ an ANOVA. The basic design of an experiment is similar to that required to use an ANOVA. However, the inferences drawn from an experiment using the varient paradigm are based on a different set of procedures. In designs of this type, an experimental condition is defined such that an independent variable X changes from one time period to the next. At the first time period, a set of objects usually receives no amount of an independent variable X. Before the second time period, the objects in this experimental condition receive some amount of an independent variable. Therefore, an independent variable is made to change from the first to the second time period. In a second condition (control), a different set of objects receives no amount of a particular variable at any time period. This situation for an independent variable (X) can be illustrated schematically as follows:

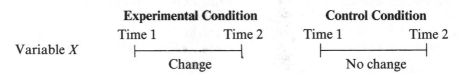

The focus of studies of this type is on the degree to which a dependent variable Y is influenced by changes in an independent variable X. Therefore, if there is an effect of X on Y, the dependent variable should change in the experimental condition, and the dependent variable should remain stable in the control condition.

Using WABA, a dependent variable can be examined in the experimental and control conditions separately to assess the degree of stability or change. This analysis is accomplished by constructing cells for the objects in the experimental group such that each cell contains scores for one object at two time periods. The within- and between-eta correlations from employing WABA I then indicate the degree of change or stability on the dependent variable in the experimental condition. The same procedure is used to assess stability and change in the control condition. A finding of change (mainly within-cell deviations) in the experimental condition indicates the possibility that the change in the dependent variable (Y) in the experimental condition *may* be correlated with a change in the independent variable. WABA II is used to test this possibility further.

WABA II is of particular importance in this type of analysis because only one type of change in the experimental group is compatible with an inference of an effect of X on Y. Specifically, a within-eta correlation significantly greater than a between-eta correlation in an experimental condition can be due to two very different types of changes. In one type of change, all entities increase or decrease to the same degree over time. In the experimental condition, this type of change is desirable because the independent variable changes over the two time periods for all objects. The following example illustrates this type of change.

	ENTITY I		ENTITY II	
VARIABLE Y	*Time 1*	*Time 2*	*Time 1*	*Time 2*
Score	1	3	1	3
Within	−1	1	−1	1
Between	0	0	0	0

In this case, the scores for each object change from 1 to 3 from the first to the second time periods. When WABA II is applied using variables X and Y, the within-cell correlation in the experimental group represents the correlation of the change in X (experimental manipulation) with variable Y. In the illustrative case, the within-cell correlation equals one. An inference that there was an effect due to the manipulation of variable X, however, is appropriate only when the dependent variable is stable over time in the control condition. When stability is obtained in the control condition, the scores can be viewed as independent of any changes in the experimental condition.

In a second type of change, values increase for some entities and decrease for other entities, and within-cell correlations should equal zero. The following synthetic data illustrate this type of change:

	ENTITY I		ENTITY II	
VARIABLE Y	*Time 1*	*Time 2*	*Time 1*	*Time 2*
Scores	1	3	3	1
Within	−1	1	1	−1
Between	0	0	0	0

In this case, for entity I scores increase from time 1 to time 2, whereas for entity II, the scores decrease. Although a set of scores of this type will show mainly within-cell deviations using WABA I, such a distribution of scores is not compatible with an inference that changes in a dependent variable are correlated with changes in an independent variable, since the independent variable changes in the same way for all entities. As a result, the within-cell correlation using WABA II equals zero in this case.

In this type of analysis, WABA I and II are employed based on scores in the experimental and control conditions. The results from the analysis in each condition indicate the degree to which the independent and dependent variables are correlated. In general, in order to infer an effect of X on Y, the within-cell correlations in the experimental group should be larger than the within-cell correlations in the control group as induced from tests of the practical and statistical significance of these differences.[1]

Other Approaches

Although a wide variety of applications to the analysis of data collected in an experimental setting can be developed from this perspective on the ANOVA, other, more contemporary uses of the ANOVA require further discussion.

---

[1] When an independent variable is categorical or indeterminate (as is often the case in control groups) *and* when a change is induced, further analysis with WABA I rather than II can be performed. In this analysis, within-cell scores for the dependent variable are located in cells formed by time periods, and the likelihood of each of the two types of changes illustrated in the tables in the text is assessed with WABA I.

Multiple-Variable and Multiple-Relationship Analyses In traditional applications of the one-way analysis of variance, the between-eta correlation is used as an estimate of the relationship between an independent and a dependent variable (see Appendix F). In addition, between-eta correlations are often adjusted by degrees of freedom in some way. Such adjustments usually result in an estimate of the relationship between the two variables that is less than the between-eta correlation. For example, intraclass correlations (Fisher, 1925) are calculated from an F ratio as follows:

$$\text{Intraclass correlation} = \frac{F - 1}{F + (k - 1)}$$

$$k = \frac{\Sigma n}{J - 1} - \frac{\Sigma n^2}{(\Sigma n)(J - 1)}$$

where in this case n equals the number of objects in each cell. It should be apparent that since the F ratio is a one-tail test and can be written in terms of the eta correlations, the intraclass correlation is a function of the between-eta correlations and degrees of freedom. A variety of other adjustments have been suggested (see Maxwell, Camp, and Arvey, 1981).

A key problem with adjustments of a between-eta correlation is that negative values can occur. When this happens, some kind of argument must be made to reset the correlation to zero. Since such adjusted correlations (for example, the intraclass correlations, omega squared, epsilon squared) are simply a function of the within- and between-eta correlations and since the between-eta correlation is never less than zero, these adjusted correlations are simply other ways to express the eta correlation based on some set of assumptions. Adjustments of this type can be made after an eta correlation is found to be significant in the varient paradigm.

The analysis of variance is used in a variety of additional ways in contemporary approaches. In multivariate analysis of variance, cells are constructed based on the values of one independent variable X and then a number of dependent variables are analyzed with an ANOVA. Although the correlations among the dependent variables based on within-cell scores are sometimes considered in this type of analysis (see Finn, 1974), tests of these correlations (such as WABA II) are usually not performed. Another approach, discriminant analysis, can be viewed as being simply a variation on the multivariate one-way analysis of variance.

Single- and Multiple-Level Analyses In most traditional approaches, the analysis of variance is used to estimate the relationship between two variables. On occasion, however, cells are aligned with entities and an F ratio is used as an indicator of the correlation of a group variable and a dependent variable (see Schriesheim, 1980; Stogdill, 1974). Although cells are formed based on entities in the varient paradigm, the ANOVA model, which requires an assumption that within-cell deviations are error (only wholes are valid), does not seem to be appropriate for testing assertions about levels of analysis.

Time In traditional approaches to experimental work, a repeated-measures analysis of variance is sometimes employed. In this procedure, the observations at one time period are contained in one cell and the observations at another time period are contained in another cell (and so on for as many time periods as are included in a study). Although WABA can be employed on data that are conceptualized in this way in the varient paradigm, the focus is on the degree to which each of a set of entities changes on a variable, rather than on overall changes for an entire set of data from one time period to the next. In the varient paradigm, time is considered to be an integral component of entities and continuously flowing. In contrast, in a repeated-measures analysis of variance, time is apparently viewed as some type of variable.

ANALYSIS OF COVARIANCE (ANCOVA)

One variation on the analysis of variance is the analysis of covariance (ANCOVA). When this tool is employed, results from an ANOVA are adjusted by correlations of a dependent variable with a third variable (called a covariate). This type of analysis differs from partial correlations in that an attempt is made to assess what the results of an ANOVA would be if a third variable did not vary between cells. Essentially, a standard analysis of variance is performed and then adjustments are made to various indicators. The typical analysis (see McNemar, 1955) requires that a covariate Z and a dependent variable Y be continuous so that a correlation between these two variables (r_{TZY}) can be used to make adjustments in the one-way analysis of variance. The adjusted sums of squares used in this procedure are written as follows:

$$\widehat{SS}_T = SS_T - \left(r_{TYZ}^2\right)\left(SS_T\right)$$

$$\widehat{SS}_W = SS_W - \left(r_{WYZ}^2\right)\left(SS_W\right)$$

$$\widehat{SS}_B = SS_T - SS_W - \left(r_{TYZ}^2\right)\left(SS_T\right) + \left(r_{WYZ}^2\right)\left(SS_W\right)$$

$$= SS_B - \left(r_{TYZ}^2\right)\left(SS_T\right) + \left(r_{WYZ}^2\right)\left(SS_W\right)$$

These adjusted sum of squares terms are used in the analysis of covariance as the bases on which to calculate F ratios. In terms of the adjustments, the squared correlation between a dependent variable Y and the covariate Z is written r_{TYZ}^2, and the squared correlation between two continuous variables based on within-cell scores is written r_{WYZ}^2. From these equations, it should be apparent that the ANCOVA is based on correlations and is simply another way to use WABA.

The purpose of the ANCOVA can be achieved, we believe, in a somewhat more effective way through the use of the WABA. Specifically, cells can be formed based on the values of the covariate Z, and within- and between-covariate deviations can be calculated for a dependent variable Y. Then the relationship of these deviations with an independent variable can be assessed. In this case, an analysis of the within-covariate deviations of the dependent variable indicates the degree of relationship of the independent variable with the dependent variable, holding the covariate constant. (A complete elaboration of this approach is beyond the scope of this chapter.)

Because the ANCOVA is a variation of WABA, the analysis of covariance is not used as a basic tool in the varient paradigm. The ANCOVA requires a number of assumptions to justify the adjustments of the sum of squares terms by correlational values; fortunately, it is not used very often in contemporary approaches. It can be performed on between- and within-entity deviation scores separately, and in this way it may be useful in testing assertions about levels of analysis.

THE *n*-WAY ANALYSIS OF VARIANCE

The *n*-way analysis of variance, which is used more frequently in contemporary approaches than the ANCOVA, can be viewed as an extension of the one-way analysis of variance. As in any analysis of variance, cells are constructed such that the independent variables (such as J and K) vary between and not within cells. As a result, only the between-cell deviations of a dependent variable Y can covary with values of independent variables. In the two- (or *n*-) way analysis of variance, cells are constructed based on the values of two (or *n*) independent variables. We will briefly describe a simple two-way analysis of variance to illustrate both the calculations and the notations we use for this analysis.

For this purpose, assume that two independent variables J and K, each with two values (J_1, J_2, K_1, and K_2), are of interest and that cells are defined as follows:

	J_1	J_2
K_1	Y_{I11}	Y_{I21}
K_2	Y_{I12}	Y_{I22}

Scores for the dependent variable Y are contained in each cell. A subscript indicates each score (I) and the number of the J cell and K cell in which the score is embedded (Y_{IJK}). This construction of cells can be conceptualized in the following three ways.

First, the set of scores can be viewed from the perspective of a one-way analysis of variance with four cells. As a result, total $(Y - \bar{Y})$, within-cell $(Y - \bar{Y}_{JK})$, and between-cell $(\bar{Y}_{JK} - \bar{Y})$ scores are calculated as in any one-way analysis of variance with four cells. This is called an overall analysis.

Second, the set of scores can be viewed as a one-way analysis of variance with two cells defined by values of variable K. This can be illustrated as follows:

K_1	Y_{11}	Y_{21}	$\bar{Y}_{K1}$
K_2	Y_{12}	Y_{22}	$\bar{Y}_{K2}$

In this case, between $(\overline{Y}_K - \overline{Y})$- and within $(Y - \overline{Y}_K)$-cell scores are calculated.

Third, the set of scores can be viewed as a one-way analysis of variance with two cells defined by values of variable J. This is illustrated in schematic form as follows:

J_1	J_2
Y_{11}	Y_{21}
Y_{12}	Y_{22}
$\overline{Y}_{J1}$	$\overline{Y}_{J2}$

In this case, within $(Y - \overline{Y}_J)$- and between $(\overline{Y}_J - \overline{Y})$-cell scores are calculated. The calculation of a total of seven scores from all the analyses is illustrated in Table 13.2. As the table shows, these three conceptualizations result in deviation scores that can be used to represent overall (JK), K, and J effects on variable Y.

To examine fully a set of data configured in this way, the correlations among the seven deviation scores should be examined. It is beyond the scope of this section to articulate how these 21 correlations among the seven deviations are used to draw inferences. It should be sufficient to indicate that each of the 21 correlations is useful in interpreting results when a two-way analysis of variance is used. Moreover, as the number of independent variables

TABLE 13.2. Illustrative two-way analysis of variance

	CELL I		CELL II		CELL III		CELL IV		SQUARED SUMMATIONS
Scores									
J	1	1	1	1	2	2	2	2	
K	1	1	2	2	1	1	2	2	
Y	1	2	3	4	5	6	7	8	
$\overline{Y}$	4.5	4.5	4.5	4.5	4.5	4.5	4.5	4.5	
$\overline{Y}_J$	2.5	2.5	2.5	2.5	6.5	6.5	6.5	6.5	
$\overline{Y}_K$	3.5	3.5	5.5	5.5	3.5	3.5	5.5	5.5	
$\overline{Y}_{JK}$	1.5	1.5	3.5	3.5	5.5	5.5	7.5	7.5	
Overall JK									
$Y - \overline{Y}$	−3.5	−2.5	−1.5	−0.5	0.5	1.5	2.5	3.5	42
$Y - \overline{Y}_{JK}$	−0.5	0.5	−0.5	0.5	−0.5	0.5	−0.5	0.5	2
$\overline{Y}_{JK} - \overline{Y}$	−3	−3	−1	−1	1	1	3	3	40
J effects									
$Y - \overline{Y}_J$	−1.5	−0.5	0.5	1.5	−1.5	−0.5	0.5	1.5	10
$\overline{Y}_J - \overline{Y}$	−2	−2	−2	−2	2	2	2	2	32
K effects									
$Y - \overline{Y}_K$	−2.5	−1.5	−2.5	−1.5	1.5	2.5	1.5	2.5	34
$\overline{Y}_K - \overline{Y}$	−1	−1	1	1	−1	−1	1	1	8
Interaction									
$\overline{Y} + \overline{Y}_{JK} - \overline{Y}_J - \overline{Y}_K$	0	0	0	0	0	0	0	0	0

increases, the number of deviation scores increases and the correlation matrix increases in size. Nevertheless, the importance of some of these 21 correlations can be illustrated by limiting the discussion to the subset of correlations employed in a traditional *n*-way analysis of variance.

Traditional approaches use an extension of the multiple-regression formulation of the one-way analysis of variance to test for effects in the two- and *n*-way analyses of variance. In traditional approaches interest is in the degree to which the total deviation scores $(Y - \bar{Y})$ can be represented by between-cell scores where cells are formed based on values of variables J and K ($\bar{Y}_J - \bar{Y}$ and $\bar{Y}_K - \bar{Y}$). The following multiple-regression-type equation serves as a starting point in understanding the traditional multiple-regression formulation of an *n*-way analysis of variance.

$$\text{total} = \text{overall within} + \text{between } K + \text{between } J$$
$$Y - \bar{Y} = \beta(Y - \bar{Y}_{JK}) + \beta_K(\bar{Y}_K - \bar{Y}) + \beta_J(\bar{Y}_J - \bar{Y}) \qquad \textbf{(13.3)}$$

When the correlation of the between-cell deviation scores of variable Y based on cells formed by values of variables J and K equals zero, the beta weights (β_K and β_J) equal the between-eta correlations. However, Equation 13.3 is not the equation for the *n*-way analysis of variance and is not yet identical to the one-way analysis of variance formulation. This point can be illustrated using simple algebra and canceling terms.

Specifically, Equation 13.3 does not hold because it has a remainder of

$$-\bar{Y}_{JK} - \bar{Y} + \bar{Y}_K + \bar{Y}_J$$

By subtracting this remainder from the right side of Equation 13.3, the following equation for a two-way analysis of variance results:

$$(Y - \bar{Y}) = \beta_W(Y - \bar{Y}_{JK}) + \beta_J(\bar{Y}_J - \bar{Y})$$
$$+ \beta_K(\bar{Y}_K - \bar{Y}) + \beta_I(\bar{Y} + \bar{Y}_{JK} - \bar{Y}_K - \bar{Y}_J) \qquad \textbf{(13.4)}$$

The last term in Equation 13.4 is traditionally called an interaction term and is required because the total between-cell deviation scores do not necessarily equal the sum of the two between-cell deviations based on values of J and K. Therefore, interaction terms can be viewed as the deviations in a dependent variable Y that cannot be explained by variables J or K.

The traditional two-way analysis of variance is expressed in multiple-regression terms by Equation 13.4. Since any multiple regression is determined by the bivariate correlations among the variables in the equation, a consideration of the matrix of correlations among deviation scores is appropriate in interpreting the results of a two-way analysis of variance. In addition, since multicollinearity is a problem for multiple regressions, it is also a problem for *n*-way analyses of variance. In the one-way analysis of variance, multicollinearity is not an issue because the correlation between the independent variables (within- and between-cell scores on one variable) always equals zero. In contrast, in the *n*-way analysis of variance, the correlation among the independent variables need not equal zero. Therefore, a consideration of a complete matrix of correlations among the deviation scores provides one way to assess the degree of multicollinearity in a particular analysis. In the traditional statistical paradigm, this problem is addressed by requiring (although sometimes it is only assumed) that the two independent variables J and K be orthogonal or independent. However, an examination of the obtained correlations among the between-cell deviations is preferable because it provides an empirical assessment of the degree of multicollinearity in the regression equation and in the n-way analysis of variance.

In traditional approaches to the n-way analysis of variance, the results from testing for statistical significance seem to depend on the number of independent variables included in the analysis. Specifically, in the traditional paradigm, the tests of statistical significance vary depending on whether a one- or two-way analysis of variance is employed. The synthetic data presented in Table 13.2 can be used to illustrate this key point.

Three different sets of eta correlations can be calculated on the data in Table 13.2. First, based on the overall (one-way analysis of variance) model in which four cells are constructed, the between- and within-cell eta-squared correlations and corresponding degrees of freedom can be summarized as follows:

$$\eta^2_{BY} = 0.95 \qquad df = JK - 1 = 3$$
$$\eta^2_{WY} = 0.05 \qquad df = N - JK = 4$$

Second, when the cells are viewed as being constructed based on values of variable J, the squared eta correlations and corresponding degrees of freedom can be written:

$$\eta^2_{BJY} = 0.76 \qquad df = J - 1 = 1$$
$$\eta^2_{WJY} = 0.24 \qquad df = N - J = 6$$

Third, when the cells are viewed as being constructed based on values of variable K, the squared eta correlations and corresponding degrees of freedom can be written:

$$\eta^2_{BKY} = 0.19 \qquad df = K - 1 = 1$$
$$\eta^2_{WKY} = 0.81 \qquad df = N - K = 6$$

When two one-way analyses of variance are used, the F ratios to test the statistical significance of the relationship between variables K and J with Y are calculated as follows:

$$F_J = \frac{\eta^2_{BJY}}{\eta^2_{WJY}} \frac{N - J}{J - 1} = \frac{0.76}{0.24}(6) = 19.0$$

$$F_K = \frac{\eta^2_{BKY}}{\eta^2_{WKY}} \frac{N - K}{K - 1} = \frac{0.19}{0.81}(6) = 1.41$$

Tests of the same relationship using the traditional formulas for a two-way analysis of variance are calculated as follows:

$$F_J = \frac{\eta_{BJY}^2}{\eta_{TWY}^2} \frac{N - JK}{J - 1} = \frac{0.76}{0.05}(4) = 60.8$$

$$F_K = \frac{\eta_{BKY}^2}{\eta_{TWY}^2} \frac{N - JK}{K - 1} = \frac{0.19}{0.05}(4) = 15.2$$

As should be apparent, the values for the F ratios obtained using the formulas for the n-way analysis of variance are significantly higher than those obtained based on the multiple one-way analyses of variance, even though the same cells and between-eta correlations are used in both sets of calculations. This discrepancy is to be expected in each analysis because even though the same between-eta correlations are used, different within-eta correlations are used. Specifically, the overall within-cell deviations $(Y - \overline{Y}_{JK})$ are employed in the n-way analysis of variance. In contrast, overall within-cell deviations plus all other within-cell deviations are used in each one-way analysis of variance.

Therefore, the magnitude of the between-eta correlations should always be considered in drawing inferences from an ANOVA, because tests of statistical significance vary depending on the number of variables included in the design. The formulation that uses two one-way analyses of variance is preferable in the varient paradigm, because this approach retains the geometric basis of the E ratio, which in turn is the basis for the F ratio.

The Varient Approach

A consideration of those correlations from the n-way analysis of variance that are of interest in traditional approaches illustrates some additional linkages between the varient paradigm and contemporary work.

Multiple-Variable and Multiple-Relationship Analyses To reduce the complexity of the presentation, this discussion will be limited to three variables. In the related case, a correlation of one independent variable with a dependent variable as indicated by between-eta correlations could be influenced by the other independent variables. Therefore, the partialing procedures described previously may be useful in the related case. In the generally related case, the two variables that are unrelated should be viewed as independent variables in an n-way analysis of variance. In the generally unrelated case, only one of the between-eta correlations should be significant. In the unrelated case, all the between-eta correlations should approximate zero.

In addition to allowing for a focus on the direct relationships between variables by the use of the between-eta correlations, the n-way analysis of variance also permits interactions to be examined. Statisticians differ a little in their interpretation of interactions. From a mathematical perspective, interaction terms are scores that are not due to direct relationships between the independent and the dependent variables. The interpretation of interaction scores depends in part on the nature of the relationships among all the variables of interest. In both the related and generally related cases, an interaction is quite difficult to interpret because in both cases the independent variables are directly related to the dependent variable, whereas interaction implies that the independent variables are indirectly related with the dependent variable. Some statisticians recommend that when an interaction is obtained, an interpretation of direct relationships (such as J and K main effects) is inappropriate (see Finn, 1974). When interactions are obtained in the related or generally related cases, it is difficult to isolate the unique contribution of an interaction term from other effects.

In contrast, in the unrelated and generally unrelated cases, the unique contribution of an interaction seems to be identifiable. For example, in the three-variable, generally unrelated case, a third variable Z is unrelated to two related variables X and Y. Therefore, the relationship of the two variables of interest can be examined within values of the third variable. This view of interactions is illustrated for the unrelated case with the synthetic data presented in Table 13.3. In the illustration shown in the table, total deviations are represented perfectly by the interaction scores. This interaction can be translated into correlational terms, as shown in the middle portion of Table 13.3.

TABLE 13.3. Illustration of two approaches to an interaction

	CELL I		CELL II		CELL III		CELL IV	
Scores								
J	1	1	1	1	2	2	2	2
K	1	1	2	2	1	1	2	2
Y	8	8	2	2	2	2	8	8
Overall $\bar{Y}_{JK} - \bar{Y}$	3	3	−3	−3	−3	−3	3	3
J between $\bar{Y}_J - \bar{Y}$	0	0	0	0	0	0	0	0
K between $\bar{Y}_K - \bar{Y}$	0	0	0	0	0	0	0	0
Interaction $\bar{Y} + \bar{Y}_{JK} - \bar{Y}_J - \bar{Y}_K$	3	3	−3	−3	−3	−3	3	3
K in J	*Condition J_1*				*Condition J_2*			
$Y - \bar{Y}$	3	3	−3	−3	−3	−3	3	3
$\bar{Y}_K - \bar{Y}$	3	3	−3	−3	−3	−3	3	3
Correlations	$\eta_B = -1$[a]				$\eta_B = 1$[a]			
J in K	*Condition K_1*				*Condition K_2*			
	Cell I		Cell III		Cell II		Cell IV	
K	1	1	1	1	2	2	2	2
J	1	1	2	2	1	1	2	2
Y	8	8	2	2	2	2	8	8
$Y - \bar{Y}$	3	3	−3	−3	−3	−3	3	3
$\bar{Y}_J - \bar{Y}$	3	3	−3	−3	−3	−3	3	3
Correlations	$\eta_B = -1$[a]				$\eta_B = 1$[a]			

[a] The sign of these correlations can be inferred from the between-cell deviation scores—in this two-cell case, by calculating bivariate correlations.

Specifically, the correlation of one independent variable K with a dependent variable Y can be examined within the two conditions defined by another independent variable J. In condition J_1 the correlation between variable K and variable Y equals -1, and in condition J_2 the correlation between variable K and variable Y equals 1. The results of a similar analysis of the relationships of variable J with variable Y in conditions defined by different values of K are shown in the lowest portion of the table.

From this illustration, it should be apparent that the two variables Y and K are correlated in the conditions defined by different values of a third variable J and that two variables Y and J are correlated in conditions defined by different values of a third variable K. The results presented in Table 13.3 illustrate one type of statistical interaction. In this unrelated case, the variables are indirectly related, not directly related, because an interpretation of the relationship between any two variables requires consideration of a third variable.

In the generally unrelated case, conditions are defined by the variable that is unrelated to the two variables of interest. For example, in the illustrative analysis of data collected at MCO, conditions were defined by values of a third variable at a higher level of analysis. Therefore, certain interactions are similar to the contingency formulations specified in multiple-relationship analysis, and others are not. If a relationship is hypothesized to be contingent on values of a third variable, an interaction is expected; if a relationship is hypothesized to be multiplexed with a third variable, an interaction is not expected. In the varient paradigm, interactions are always translated into correlations so that the meaning of an interaction can be tested in both practical and statistical terms.

Single- and Multiple-Level Analyses and Time   Analyses of variance, since they are multiple regressions, are not designed to test assertions about levels of analysis. This should be apparent because the n-way analysis of variance can be performed based on within- and between-entity deviation scores. In terms of time, the repeated-measures analysis of variance discussed previously can also be viewed as a special form of an n-way analysis of variance. However, time is again viewed as a variable rather than as interwoven with variables and entities.

Other Approaches

Multiple-Variable and Multiple-Relationship Analyses   In many contemporary uses of the analysis of variance, inferences may be based solely on the value obtained for an F ratio. This is somewhat disconcerting in light of the fact that the magnitude of the F ratio depends on the number of independent variables included in the design of an ANOVA. One might suggest cynically that if one-way analyses of variance do not produce statistically significant results, then independent variables are added to obtain statistically significant relationships between two variables. (The same criticism holds for multiple regression as well.) In order to offset such criticism, a consideration of the values of the between-eta correlations (bivariate correlations in multiple regression) seems necessary, since these values do not change as the number of independent variables is increased. Likewise, if an interaction is inferred, a consideration of the meaning of an interaction in correlation terms seems appropriate.

Various other linkages between the ANOVA and multiple regressions have been proposed by various individuals (see Cohen and Cohen, 1975). In the one-way analysis of variance, when the values of an independent variable define two cells, the total correlation between the independent and dependent variables equals a between-eta correlation (see Appendix F). In a similar fashion, dummy codes (two categories for each independent variable) can be employed for multiple independent variables. However, as in the case of the one-way analysis of variance, dummy codes in multiple regressions do not always provide results identical to those obtained from an analysis of variance (see Appendix F). The exact multiple-regression formulation of any analysis of variance follows the form of Equation 13.4.

Single- and Multiple-Level Analyses   In terms of entities, Bass (1982), among others, has suggested the use of n-way analysis of variance where independent variables at different levels of analysis define cells. An assumption that a particular level of analysis underlies a particular variable is clearly required in this approach. Therefore, the procedure suggested by Bass (1982) does not provide a test of an assertion that a particular level of analysis is appropriate.

Time   Although perhaps not apparent, the F ratios used in the repeated-measures analysis of variance differ from the F ratios obtained when a one-way analysis of variance is used at each time period. In a sense, statistically significant results seem more likely when the number of independent variables (including time) is increased in an analysis. Of course, by using WABA the more fundamental correlation matrix from which all these tests and indicators are derived can be examined.

SUMMARY

The general linear tensor and WABA have been shown to underlie six tools that are often used in contemporary work: bivariate, partial, and multiple correlations; and one-way analysis of variance, covariance, and n-way analysis of variance. The values taken on by the indicators used in these analyses are determined by the matrix of correlations that specify the structure of the relationships between variables. In terms of multiple-variable and multiple-relationship analyses, the usefulness of the six tools varies depending on the structure of the relationship between variables or the location of data along the variable axis of the varient matrix. Since the general linear tensor underlies these tools, each can be extended to include an explicit consideration of single and multiple levels of analysis using WABA. The way these tools and the more fundamental within- and between-entity deviations and correlations underlie contemporary and traditional approaches to measurement, methods and generalizability is presented in the next chapter.

REVIEW QUESTIONS

1. How are bivariate, partial, and multiple correlations and the one- and n-way analyses of variance and covariance similar?
2. What is the relationship of WABA I and WABA II to composite correlations?
3. How is the WABA approach to the analysis of the temporal ordering of variables related to the cross-lagged correlation approach?
4. How does one avoid the ecological fallacy?
5. In what way does WABA extend the usefulness of partial correlations?
6. How does WABA extend multiple regression?
7. What problems arise in Firebaugh's $\overline{X}$ rule?
8. Why can path analysis techniques be used in conjunction with WABA?
9. Why is the ANOVA model inappropriate for testing assertions about levels of analysis?
10. What is a problem that occurs in judging the statistical significance of results with the n-way analysis of variance?

14

COMPARISON TO OTHER APPROACHES

Our view is that theory and data are linked by paradigms that permit multiple-hypothesis testing; our approach differs from some traditional approaches in which measurements, methodologies, or inferences are individually conceptualized as providing a link between theory and data. The focus of this chapter is on illustrating that the basic mathematics (such as WABA) underlying the varient paradigm can be used to extend and integrate various traditional approaches to measurement, methodology, and inferences.

MEASUREMENT

In order to focus on measurement issues, it is useful to make a simple distinction between the analysis of items and of scales. Items are responses (behaviors) whose values are added together to form a scale (see Dubno et al., 1978). In one view of scaling, the values for a number of items are added together to reduce redundancy. In other words, items that are highly correlated are added together because the correlation of any one item in a set with a different set of items would be about the same as that for any other item. In another approach to scaling, each item is viewed as containing a true and an error component; when items are added together, the errors cancel each other out so that nonsystematic error is removed. Questions have been raised about assumptions that error components tend to cancel each other out; Zeller and Carmines (1980), for example, argue that error can be systematic, so that such additions can result in systematic bias in scales.

    Regardless of how scales are conceptualized, correlations are typically employed to assess empirically the nature of scales. Since WABA calculations are central to correlational studies, a consideration of single- and multiple-level analyses and multiple-variable and multiple-relationship analyses may be used to extend the traditional approaches to measurement.

Single- and Multiple-Level Analyses

Most approaches to measurement tend to ignore levels of analysis. WABA provides one way to incorporate an explicit consideration of entities in approaches to measurement.

WABA I The degree to which each item in a scale seems to be more compatible with the whole, parts, or equivocal conditions can be assessed using WABA I. If a set of items is inferred to be compatible with one condition, the scale that results from adding these items has a clear meaning. In this way, only items that tend to be associated with similar units of analysis can be used to form scales; other, less pure, items can be deleted from a scale. Thus WABA I is employed to build scales that are characterizations of one or several levels of analysis.

This type of analysis of items is compatible with traditional approaches to content validity. **Content validity** is defined as the degree to which an item taps the content of some domain (for example, see Zeller and Carmines, 1980). From this perspective, an item can be viewed as a member of a domain, where the domain is defined by levels of analysis. An item, for example, might be hypothesized to be contained in a domain defined as level-specific whole persons (traditional individual differences). Using WABA I, the unit of analysis associated with each item can be assessed, and the likelihood that it fits in this domain can be examined empirically. Items that do not fall into a hypothesized domain are viewed as lacking content validity.

An illustration from the MCO data set of the results from applying WABA I on the items that composed the freedom from machines and freedom from superior scales based on within- and between-work-group scores is presented in Table 14.1. As is shown in the table, the items tend to vary both within and between work groups, and are therefore equivocal. The scales based on these items are also equivocal at the group level (see Chapter 9). When WABA I is used, these scales seem to present problems. But when we created these scales using traditional methods without WABA (see Cronbach et al., 1972), they seemed adequate.

TABLE 14.1. WABA I: Within and between work-groups analysis

	ETA			
SCALES AND ITEMS	*Between*	*Within*	*E* RATIO	*F* RATIO
Freedom from Machines	($df = 82$)	($df = 193$)		
Machines determine order of work	0.76	0.65	1.17	3.22
Machines determine pace of work	0.76	0.65	1.17	3.22
Freedom from Superior				
Superior observes subordinate's work	0.60	0.80	0.75[†]	1.32
Superior determines subordinate's work	0.67	0.74	0.91	1.93
Regulation and rule usage	0.64	0.77	0.83	1.63
Superior insists on standard procedures	0.62	0.79	0.78	1.45

[†]15° test exceeded.

WABA II   Most contemporary approaches to measurement focus on the relationship between items that compose a scale. Since these approaches tend to concentrate on more than two variables, a consideration of multiple-variable analysis using WABA II is appropriate.

Multiple-Variable Analysis

Related Case   A popular approach to measurement involves a demonstration of the internal consistency (redundancy) of the items in a scale, as indicated by the correlations among the items. It should be apparent that internal consistency is most compatible with the related case in multiple-variable analysis. In traditional approaches to internal consistency, items in a scale are often divided such that two scales are formed, and the correlation among two scales is used to indicate the degree of internal consistency of the total scale. Numerous variations on this approach can be found in statistics books. For example, the even-numbered items in a scale can be considered as forming one scale and the odd-numbered items as forming another scale. The correlation between these two scales then indicates the internal consistency of the overall scale. In other variations of this approach to internal consistency, an average of the intercorrelation matrix among a set of items (inter-item correlations) is used to estimate the reliability of a scale (see Cronbach's alpha coefficient). Obtained correlations are then adjusted so that the greater the number of items included in a scale, the greater the value taken on by the adjusted correlations. As a result, the adjusted correlation that represents internal consistency tends to take on larger values than do the obtained correlations.

These approaches to assessing the internal consistency of a scale can be extended by using both within-entity and between-entity correlations. For example, Cronbach's alpha coefficient can be calculated based on both within- and between-cell correlations. In the varient paradigm, whether the related case is more likely is a theoretical and empirical question. In contrast, in traditional approaches it seems that the different cases in multiple-variable analysis are viewed as different approaches to reliability or validity, and empirical tests of which case seems more likely tend not to be performed.

Generally Related Case   Guilford (1965) has suggested that most approaches to reliability favor the use of similar (homogeneous) or highly intercorrelated items (the related case). However, according to Guilford (1965), heterogeneous items that are correlated near zero can also be used to form scales when items are independent but additive in the sense that all items contribute to a dependent variable, as in the generally related case. In a similar vein, approaches to **predictor-criterion validity** can be viewed as making an assertion that the generally related case is more likely because predictors are viewed as independent variables and the criterion is viewed as a dependent variable. In the varient paradigm, predictor-criterion equations (such as multiple-regression equations) can be employed using both within- and between-entity deviation scores. In addition, a choice to use this formulation of variables can also be made based on data by examining scores and/or items.

Generally Unrelated Case   Still another viable approach to measurement is called **construct validity**, which is defined by Zeller and Carmines (1980, p. 81) as follows: "Construct validity focuses on the assessment of whether a particular measure relates to other measures consistent with theoretically derived hypotheses concerning the concepts (or constructs) that are being measured." In general, construct validity includes the concept of convergent and discriminant validity, in which one set of measures is hypothesized to converge and be different from another set of measures, as in the generally unrelated case in multiple-variable analysis. The results from the study at MCO can be viewed from this perspective on validity. In that study, the within-cell correlations were all near zero and failed to show discriminant and convergent validity. In contrast, the between-cell correlations indicated that titles and expectations measures which converged were different from the investments and returns measures.

Factor analysis can be viewed as a variation on the construct validity approach to measurement. In this approach, when factors are formed, the items that load on one factor should intercorrelate (converge) with each other and differ from (discriminate between) other items that load on other factors. Essentially, a model is imposed on the matrix of correlations among items and factors are extracted. Different models are available (such as principal components or common factor analysis with varimax or oblique rotation). Since factor analysis can be viewed as a way to summarize a correlation matrix, it can be performed using a matrix of within- and between-entity correlations (see also Markham and Scott, 1983). In this type of analysis, all items are transformed into within- and between-entity scores and the correlations among these scores are factor analyzed. Error is viewed as producing near-zero correlations among items. Table 14.2 shows the factor analysis results expected for the four conditions in single-level analysis for the case of two items.

The determination of whether a particular factor should be called a whole, parts, equivocal, or inexplicable factor depends on the loadings of items on factors. For the two-variable case presented in Table 14.2, in the whole condition the first factor is a between-entity factor and both items load on this factor. In addition, two within-cell factors are shown for the case of wholes, since within-entity scores are viewed as error. In the case of parts, the within-cell correlations are expected to be valid and form the first factor, whereas the between-cell scores should tend to be error and not form one factor. For the equivocal condition, the same items load on each of two factors. Finally, in an inexplicable condition, all items are independent and each item forms one factor.

Factor analysis is not an inferential procedure, so no decision-making criteria are readily available for choosing among the four conditions. Table 14.3 presents the three-factor solution, which was obtained from applying a principal component factor analysis with varimax rotation to the items that composed the freedom from machines and freedom from superior scales used at MCO. All the between-work-group versions of the items loaded on the first factor and failed to load on the second or third factors. The within-cell version of the items on the freedom from superior scale loaded on a second factor, and the items on the freedom from machines scale loaded on a third factor.

TABLE 14.2. Illustration of ideal conditions in within- and between-factor analysis

	WITHIN- AND BETWEEN-FACTOR ANALYSIS			
	Factor I	*Factor II*	*Factor III*	*Factor IV*
Whole Condition				
Between item 1	+	0	0	
Between item 2	+	0	0	
Within item 1	0	+	0	
Within item 2	0	0	+	
Parts Condition				
Between item 1	0	+	0	
Between item 2	0	0	+	
Within item 1	+	0	0	
Within item 2	+	0	0	
Equivocal Condition				
Between item 1	+	0		
Between item 2	+	0		
Within item 1	0	+		
Within item 2	0	+		
Inexplicable Condition				
Between item 1	+	0	0	0
Between item 2	0	+	0	0
Within item 1	0	0	+	0
Within item 2	0	0	0	+

TABLE 14.3. Illustration of factor analysis of items at the work-group level of analysis

	FACTOR I	FACTOR II	FACTOR III
Between-Group Items			
Freedom from machines			
Machines determine order of work	0.84	0.00	0.00
Machines determine pace of work	0.88	0.00	0.00
Freedom from superior			
Superior observes subordinate's work	0.55	0.00	0.00
Superior determines subordinate's work	0.58	0.00	0.00
Regulation and rule usage	0.62	0.00	0.00
Superior insists on standard procedures	0.72	0.00	0.00
Within-Group Items			
Freedom from machines			
Machines determine order of work	0.00	0.13	0.84
Machines determine pace of work	0.00	0.21	0.73
Freedom from superior			
Superior observes subordinate's work	0.00	0.51	0.12
Superior determines subordinate's work	0.00	0.64	0.07
Regulation and rule usage	0.00	0.51	0.08
Superior insists on standard procedures	0.00	0.52	0.03
Factor	Between	Within	Within
Inference		Whole Groups	

Therefore, one between-cell factor and two within-cell factors are obtained from this factor analysis, and the results seem to be more compatible with the whole-work-group condition.

The results of this analysis illustrate that different factor structures can result for the same items, depending on whether within- or between-cell scores are examined. In addition, the conclusion that these two sets of items seem to form a whole-work-group factor is compatible with the inferences drawn based on these two scales in previous analyses (see Chapter 9). Therefore, in this case, factor analysis and WABA II result in the same conclusion.

In summary, various contemporary approaches to measurement seem to focus on one of the four cases identifiable in multiple-variable analysis, and thus can be extended by using WABA. We prefer to choose among at least these four cases and their corresponding notions of validity and reliability based on both theory and data.

Multiple-Relationship Analysis

Until recently, measurement theorists seem to have favored formulations in which measures are expected to have the same characteristics under a variety of conditions. Indeed, results are often viewed as cross-validated when the same results are obtained in all conditions. One of the difficulties with the use of these approaches is that the conditions (or samples) employed quite frequently are defined by some assertion rather than by the values taken on by a specific variable. Nevertheless, making a multiplexed assertion that measures operate in the same way across different settings (conditions) is one way to deal with measurement issues. Assertions of contingencies, of course, are also permissible in the varient paradigm. In other words, under some conditions measures may operate in one way, and under other conditions the measures may operate in a different way. As far as we can determine, the notion of conditions of measurement (Cronbach et al., 1972) allows for multiplexed and contingency formulations in measurement approaches.

Essentially, conditions of measurement can be viewed as variables and as such may be related, generally related, generally unrelated, or unrelated to other variables. Using the varient paradigm, it is possible to assess the way in which these variables are related to variables of interest, as well as whether items or scales and their relationships are multiplexed with or contingent on these variables. However, in such assessments, levels of analysis are always considered explicitly. Thus most traditional approaches to measurement can be employed in new and extended ways.

Time

A somewhat complicated set of issues involving time and other matters arises in traditional approaches to measurement at the person level of analysis. Applying WABA to examine the internal consistency of a scale is helpful as a starting point in attempting to clarify some points relevant to these issues. For the purpose of illustration, assume that either a parts or a whole condition has been inferred and that cells are then constructed so that each cell represents one entity and contains items which supposedly comprise a scale. In this illustration, between-cell scores represent the differences between entities on a scale and within-cell scores represent the deviations of each item from the scale average. A larger between- than within-eta correlation should be obtained when a scale is homogeneous or internally consistent. The way cells are constructed in this analysis can be illustrated as follows:

Cell I		Cell II		Cell III	
Entity A		Entity B		Entity C	
Item 1	Item 2	Item 1	Item 2	Item 1	Item 2

When WABA I and II are performed based on cells constructed in this way, an estimate of the degree of similarity among items is provided. To perform this analysis, it must be possible to calculate within- and between-entity deviations independent of the items contained in the cells. At the person level of analysis parts are difficult to define independent of the variables. The physiological components that define parts of persons are usually not of interest in organizational behavior and the social sciences. As a result, at the person level of analysis multiple items or some notions of time are traditionally used to test whether whole persons are a more likely unit of analysis.

For example, the illustrative person-level analysis based on the data collected at MCO involved multiple responses made over time on the same items. Specifically, each superior responded about a set of subordinates, and the reports from one superior formed one cell that contained his or her reports. Since the superior's reports were generated over time, a time-based analysis was performed. In other words, the analysis tested whether these reports were stable for superiors (represented whole superiors), changed (represented differences within superiors), or neither.

This type of person-level analysis is compatible with traditional approaches to individual differences (whole persons). In these approaches, a measure is often viewed as reliable when it is stable over time. In this case, stability and reliability are viewed as equivalent because it is assumed that whole persons (or individual differences) are valid and that any variation that is not stable is error by definition. The key difficulty that arises for the person level of analysis is that the components at this level are defined as measures. At higher levels of analysis, an assumption of this type is not necessary, since the components can be identified at a lower level of analysis. For example, at the collectivity level of analysis, the components are groups.

Confusion about these issues arises when the concepts of internal consistency, stability, and levels of analysis are blurred. At the person level of analysis, since it is not possible to define components, assertions about levels of analysis are not directly tested. Nevertheless, the degree of stability of scores is assessed and at the same time the internal consistency of scales based on between- and within-entity scores is examined. At other levels of analysis, entities can be defined independently of variables and assertions about levels of analysis are tested directly. In addition, the degree of stability or internal consistency of items based on both between- and within-entity scores can be examined. In all cases, lack of stability can be viewed as lack of reliability when stability is viewed as a preferred condition. In this way, one individual's reliability (stability) may be another individual's error term (change).

METHODOLOGICAL APPROACHES

In addition to considering measurement issues, the varient paradigm provides a way to address various methodological questions. For example, it is sometimes argued that studies of human beings in experimental settings present more problems than field studies, and vice versa. Indeed, the characterization of a setting or study as experimental or nonexperimental can be rather difficult because a number of entities and associated variables could differ from one setting to another. From the perspective of the varient paradigm, entities in the different settings can be assessed through single- and multiple-level analyses. In addition, key variables that distinguish between these settings should be identifiable. Using multiple-relationship analysis, attempts can be made to assess the degree to which different conditions defined by variables indirectly affect relationships obtained in different types of studies. The degree to which the variables that distinguish between these settings or studies are directly related to some and not to other variables of interest can be assessed using multiple-variable analysis.

In order to address methodological questions, theories that specify variables and entities are necessary. Once specified, these theories of methodology can be tested using the varient paradigm. From this perspective, contemporary and traditional approaches to specifying the differences and similarities between experimental and nonexperimental studies (see Campbell and Stanley, 1966) can be viewed as first steps in generating hypotheses about the nature of data collected in different settings.

Comparison of Methods

Experimental and nonexperimental settings seem to offer complementary limitations and advantages in testing substantive rather than methodological theories. In **experimental studies**, independent variables are forced to change over time, whereas in **nonexperimental (field) studies**, changes in variables are viewed as occurring naturally. Therefore, in nonexperimental studies a fortuitous change must occur for the temporal ordering of variables to be examined. In experimental work, the forced changes in an independent variable need not be followed by changes in dependent variables. Therefore, the approach to assessing changes over time used in the varient paradigm can be employed even in experimental studies. Specifically, one can begin with naturally occurring phenomena and then attempt to induce such phenomena using an experimental method. Alternatively, one can begin with an experimental approach to see whether certain relationships can be made to occur. The theories that underlie these experimentally induced phenomena can then be tested to see whether such phenomena occur naturally without experimental intervention.

One advantage of the experimental method is that relationships which may not occur naturally may successfully be induced in an experimental setting. In this way, experimental studies can be viewed as permitting innovative types of research. Of course, data collected in such experimental settings, as well as the theoretical formulations that are of interest, can be subjected to single- and multiple-level analyses and multiple-variable and multiple-relationship analyses.

Methods and Multiple-Hypothesis Testing

Attempts to understand and use experimental and nonexperimental designs with human beings involve the specification and testing of theories. We believe this approach to experimental and nonexperimental work is in the very early stages of development and is compatible with a multiple-hypothesis testing approach to research.

One approach to methodological issues has been suggested by Campbell and Stanley (1966). They propose that there are a number of threats to internal validity in research conducted in experimental settings. In general, they state that inferences can be based on the comparison of a control group or condition (where a particular treatment is absent) with experimental or treatment groups or conditions. The use of control groups can be viewed as one way to offset a number of alternative explanations. For example, when a variable of interest is measured before and after a treatment, a change in this variable could be due to the passage of time or historical effects rather than to a treatment. Therefore, if there is an effect of history, changes should occur in both the control and the experimental conditions. The assumption that underlies this test for the effects of history (and other threats to internal validity) is that the control and experimental conditions are subject to a similar set of effects except for the degree of change in one variable in the experimental condition.

A second set of methodological issues involves a variety of arguments about the efficacy of observers. For example, Argyris (1980) argues that systematic insights should be developed from an observer's own experience and that these insights should be shared with the participants in a study. The varient paradigm is somewhat compatible with this observational approach, since in order to do empirical testing a theory must be developed; the work of Argyris, among others, suggests ways to develop theories. At some point, however, the varient paradigm requires that such theories be tested against other theories. Indeed, a focus on only one theory or explanation may very well be compatible with Argyris' (1980) notion of closed rather than open thinking. Unless observer insights are tested, any insight is as plausible as any other insight (or theory). In the varient paradigm, a set of data is the arbitrator of insights and theories.

A similar issue arises when overemphasis is placed on data collected by observers rather than through reports of respondents about themselves and others. Even observers may respond based on their own style (whole-person unit of analysis), or based on a comparison among the objects observed (person-parts unit of analysis), or simply as a function of objects outside the observer (an equivocal condition at the person level of analysis). Clearly,

WABA can be employed to test these alternative views of observer reports. Moreover, reports of an observer about individuals embedded in, for example, dyads, groups, and collectivities, may reflect any one or a number of these levels of analysis.

In summary, the varient paradigm is compatible with interview, questionnaire, and observational methods in experimental and nonexperimental studies. In all cases, single- and multiple-level analyses and multiple-variable and multiple-relationship analyses can be performed to extend traditional approaches.

INFERENCES

In all these analyses, generalizations are made from data about the predictive ability of one theory relative to another. Specifically, different theories are conceptualized as specifying different variables, entities, and conditions (if any) under which a theory is expected to be predictive (multiple-relationship analysis). Data are then used to generalize to theory.

For example, if a theory is hypothesized to apply to all levels of analysis, variables, and conditions, a demonstration that the theory does not hold in one condition should be sufficient to raise questions about it. However, most theories (particularly in the social sciences) are not specified as applying to the entire physical universe, and the level and units of analysis are often unclear. A theory is typically tested by demonstrating its ability to predict in relation to the statistical theory of randomness. Only in this way can it be seen that generalizations are made about one theory in relation to another theory. These generalizations, however, are never totally justifiable because alternative explanations for results can almost always be generated. It is important to remember that the strength of a study depends on the number of competing hypotheses which are included in the design of study and not solely on the sample size. Indeed, in the varient paradigm, although traditional approaches to "statistical power" can be employed, a study can also be viewed as more powerful as more data and subjects are included. In a sense, it is possible to argue the more data (the larger the sample size), the better, because the likelihood that results are due to statistical artifacts decreases. Simply stated, the greater the number of alternative hypotheses shown to be less likely in a study, the greater the strength of inferences from a study about a theory.

In the varient paradigm, since results are allowed to be interpreted as not significant in both a practical and a statistical sense, it is possible for no inference to be drawn from a study. As an illustration of the rationale for this approach to nonsignificant results, consider a situation in which one study provides significant results and a second study provides nonsignificant results. The nonsignificant results could be due to poor data or poor theory or both. In addition, the theory under consideration could be contingent on factors that occurred in the second study but not in the first study. In order to examine this contingency hypothesis, it is necessary to conduct a third study incorporating the contingencies (variables) expected to serve as a boundary on the relationships between the variables of interest. In the varient paradigm, a theory is rejected only if it can be replaced by another substantive theory. When results are nonsignificant on a statistical basis, an alternative substantive theory has not been shown to be more likely and an induction is inappropriate. In this way, the research process is deliberately biased in favor of theory, because any theory is viewed as better than no theory.

Although we use a particular perspective to generalize from data to theory, the varient paradigm is compatible with other approaches to generalizing from data. For example, in **infinite sampling theory** (Fisher, 1973), a population of similar studies is defined. Generalizations are then made based on tests of statistical significance about the likelihood that the results of a study fit a population of similar studies. This theoretical population of studies is distributed so that the most likely event is a statistically nonsignificant result; the probabilities obtained are interpreted as indicating the likelihood that results can be viewed as compatible with a set of studies which produce nonsignificant results. In this traditional approach, once statistically significant results are obtained, a generalization is sometimes made that the same results will be obtained in future studies and therefore that replications are not necessary. In contrast, in the varient paradigm the purpose of replication is continually to test the results from previous studies by subjecting them to alternative explanations. As a result, theories are continuously placed in jeopardy. The purpose of a series of studies and replications is to sort out old theories and develop new theories that can withstand rigorous testing. Nevertheless, the infinite sampling theory approach to generalizing from data is viable in the varient paradigm.

A second traditional approach to generalizing from data is called the **representativeness approach**. Since tests of statistical significance can also be used to assess representativeness and since these tests are not modified in the varient paradigm, this approach is also viable in the varient paradigm. However, the varient paradigm provides an additional perspective on the representativeness approach to generalizations. In the representativeness approach a population is defined, a sample is taken from the population, and generalizations are made from the sample to the population. The definition of a population usually requires the specification of entities (single- and multiple-level analyses), the variables that characterize entities (multiple-variable analysis), and the bounds of a population (multiple-relationship analysis). In an ideal sense, the representativeness approach should be based on theoretical specifications of populations that, in turn, are based on previous studies in which variables and entities have been identified as more likely on an empirical basis. Regardless of whether theoretical specifications have been tested, theory guides the definition of populations, and the degree to which a theory is inaccurate or incomplete influences the results from studies using the representativeness approach.

For example, in the Literary Digest Public Opinion Poll during the 1936 presidential campaign, a sample of voters was generated based on the list of names in the telephone directory and automobile registrations; the results of the poll were not representative of the votes that were later obtained. The rationale for this error is that individuals with telephones and automobiles voted for the candidate who lost. The theory that initially guided the polling procedure (voters have telephones and automobiles) was inadequate (see Guilford, 1965, p. 140, for additional theoretical explanations). We believe this theoretical perspective on the representativeness approach to making generalizations is helpful because it implies that solid applied research and polls can be based on theoretical *and* empirical work which specifies the entities to which variables may apply. Nevertheless, since tests of statistical significance have not been modified in the varient paradigm, it can be used by individuals with interest in investigating the representativeness of the responses of a sample for a population. Also, individuals with our interest in generalizing from theory to data to theory can use the varient paradigm.

SUMMARY

Theoretical approaches to measurement are extended and integrated by the use of the varient paradigm; the study of methodological issues is extended by using both a theoretical and an empirical perspective. Moreover, experimental methods seem to be particularly useful in attempting to assess the temporal ordering of variables, because in much of this work at least one variable is forced to change. Finally, various approaches to generalizing from data have been shown to be compatible with the varient approach. A final set of the implications of the use of the varient paradigm is presented in the next chapter.

REVIEW QUESTIONS

1. What issues arise when levels of analysis are considered in attempts to measure variables?
2. How can content validity be defined to include levels of analysis?
3. How can the definition of construct validity be extended to include levels of analysis?
4. How can stability be viewed as a limited approach to demonstrating the validity of scales?
5. How can WABA be used to clarify the meaning of observational or interview data?
6. What is a special role for replication in theory building?
7. How is the issue of the representativeness of results addressed in the varient approach?
8. How is the matter of generalizability of results addressed in the varient approach?
9. How does one evaluate the criticism that when WABA is used, results are due to method variance or are sample-specific?
10. How does one evaluate the results obtained based on the MCO data in terms of (1) the replication and (2) the representativeness approach to drawing inferences?

15

THE VARIENT PARADIGM
AND THEORY TESTING
IN THE FUTURE

In the varient paradigm, a conceptualization of variables, entities, and time is interwoven into theory formulation and data analysis in a way that allows for the inferences flowing from any study to be based on multiple-hypothesis testing. Since many of the implications of the paradigm for contemporary and traditional approaches to research have been discussed, the focus of this chapter is on identifying some of the implications of the paradigm for formulating theory, analyzing data, drawing inferences, and dealing with practical problems in the future.

VARIENT CONCEPTUALIZATIONS

Single- and Multiple-Level Analyses

In this book persons, dyads, groups, and collectivities have been viewed as physical objects composed of human beings. Clearly, these four levels of analysis do not exhaust all the possible ways to define entities at one or several time periods. However, in our view, an ability to focus on physical entities rather than on nonphysical entities is an advantage of the paradigm. For example, we believe notions such as task or role are concepts located inside human beings; as such, they are not viewed as entities. Others apparently disagree (for example, Van de Ven and Astley, 1981) and seem to argue, for example, that tasks exist in space and time independent of human beings. Regardless of a researcher's preferences, the varient paradigm requires testable assertions that a particular entity is relevant.

It should be apparent from the paradigm that an evaluation of entities is enhanced by considering higher and lower levels of analysis. Essentially, the entity axis, regardless of the definitional basis, permits a choice to be made among four alternatives at each level of analysis. The diagram shown in the upper portion of Figure 15.1 for two levels of analysis illustrates this multiple-level conceptualization. A variety of decision trees can be generated from the four basic decisions at each level of analysis (see, for example, the lower portion of Figure 2.1). For example, a certain condition may be viewed as necessary before the next higher level of analysis is considered. Of course, variables are always examined in addition to entities in the varient paradigm.

Multiple-Variable and Multiple-Relationship Analyses

Hunt et al. (1982) suggest that WABA may be problematic in dealing with what they call "difficult to interpret variables" (such as job satisfaction or unit output). Actually, one purpose of the varient paradigm is to reduce some of the ambiguity in variables by requiring a specification of underlying units of analysis. Indeed, many measures currently in use may contain items that

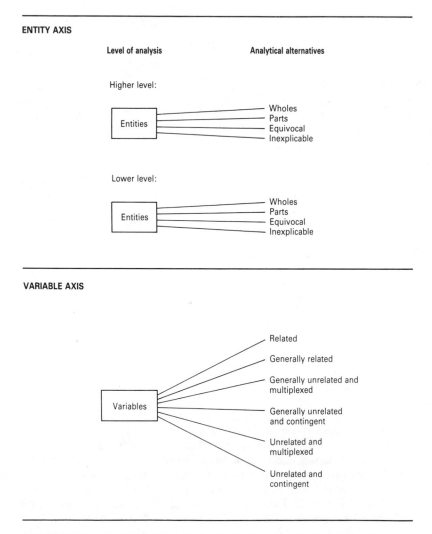

ENTITY AXIS

Level of analysis   Analytical alternatives

Higher level:

Entities
- Wholes
- Parts
- Equivocal
- Inexplicable

Lower level:

Entities
- Wholes
- Parts
- Equivocal
- Inexplicable

VARIABLE AXIS

Variables
- Related
- Generally related
- Generally unrelated and multiplexed
- Generally unrelated and contingent
- Unrelated and multiplexed
- Unrelated and contingent

FIGURE 15.1. Summary of basic decisions for entity and variable axes

operate at different levels of analysis and that therefore may be difficult to interpret. For example, feelings of job satisfaction may reflect satisfaction with collectivities or satisfaction with interpersonal relationships, as well as personal factors. In this case, a specification may be appropriate of different measures of satisfaction for different levels of analysis or of measures of satisfaction that hold across levels. In the varient paradigm, the decomposition of a concept into variables that involve different levels of analysis is viewed as being part of the process of increasing the precision of a concept and not merely as an exercise in measurement development.

As an example, consider the salary an individual receives in a job. One variable can be constructed that reflects the dollars associated with an individual's function in a collectivity; a second variable can be constructed that reflects differentials based on groups or dyads; and a third variable may reflect an individual's abilities. Although each of the variables is measured in dollars, the dollars have different meanings, depending on which variable or unit of analysis is considered. In general, we believe greater precision in meaning and measurement may be obtained for new as well as traditional variables by employing the varient paradigm.

Presumably, one could argue that a problem occurs when the paradigm is used because the magnitudes of obtained correlations are unlikely to equal ideal values. One response to this criticism is that the use of the paradigm may actually increase the precision of measures and therefore the magnitudes of the relationships that will be obtained over a series of studies. Furthermore, the varient paradigm guards against a cavalier use of multiple regression to obtain multiple correlations of a higher magnitude. When multicollinearity occurs in data a regression analysis is problematic, and such conditions can be anticipated on theoretical grounds and assessed empirically. However, regression equations can be justified in some cases (such as the generally related case) as a way of summarizing a set of correlations and indicating that several variables contribute to a dependent variable. The varient paradigm encourages explicit decisions about networks of variables based on theoretical and empirical considerations.

Moreover, when different variables are identified (as in the generally unrelated and unrelated cases when three variables are considered) in the varient paradigm, additional analyses are performed and a choice is made between the contingent and the multiplexed formulations. The choices made in multiple-variable and multiple-relationship analyses can be summarized for the three-variable case in the decision format shown in the lower portion of Figure 15.1. A number of variations on this decision format can be developed, depending on the number of variables of interest.

Time

Since a time-based analysis can be performed on both within- and between-entity scores, it is performed simultaneously with single- and multiple-level analyses and multiple-variable and multiple-relationship analyses. As a result, the varient paradigm is viewed as a conceptualization compatible with space-time metrics. In this manner, researchers should be better able to assess the efficacy of (causal) models for the temporal ordering of variables.

Perhaps of equal importance, the paradigm allows a perspective on changes in variable values that goes beyond issues of reliability by including matters of entity delineation.

THEORY

Although the varient paradigm provides an integrated system for theory testing, our approach may or may not be useful in creating theories. For example, Mintzberg (1982) has argued that constructs, instruments, measurements, variables, and perhaps even definitions should be ignored in attempting to generate theories. It is possible that the creation of theories may very well not be accomplished by starting with variables and entities in a formal way. Clearly, if the varient paradigm inhibits an individual's ability to create theories, the paradigm should not be considered at the formative stages of theory development. In addition, creative processes can result in theories so innovative in focus or scope that contemporary methods for testing cannot be employed. Such a new theory may require the development of new testing procedures. Since the varient paradigm is highly compatible with the widely used statistical paradigm, it should, however, be applicable to a broad range of theoretical formulations, including those inductively or deductively generated, simple or grand in scope and inclusiveness, and entity-specific or uncertain as to level effects.

DATA ANALYSIS

Although in a general sense theories provide the basis for data analysis in the varient paradigm, it must be remembered that no one theory is permitted to dominate or determine data analysis. Through the researcher's continuous examination of multiple theories, data are free to vary and support one theory over another. Therefore, data analysis in the varient paradigm, which uses tests of practical and statistical significance, is inherently tied to multiple-hypothesis testing and multiple theories.

The data analytic techniques in the varient paradigm, however, could probably be forced to favor data over theory. For example, from the perspective of dust bowl empiricism, one could develop empirical procedures that would take a data set and attempt to define units of analysis based on the heterogeneity or homogeneity in obtained scores. Such procedures would involve the manipulation of numbers rather than tests for a hypothesized unit or level of analysis. Although one can misuse any technique, the flaws of such an atheoretical approach would be rather clear to anyone familiar with the varient paradigm.

INFERENCES

Since the varient paradigm can be viewed as a logical extension of contemporary and traditional approaches to theory building, it will rise or fall in part depending on the strength of these traditional approaches. In fact, when many traditional data analytical manipulations are performed (see Chapter 13), the procedures in the varient paradigm can be viewed as applicable, even if only for highlighting assumptions made in a more traditional analysis. When the varient paradigm is used in a series of studies, however, in every study the degree to which one theory of variables and entities seems more appropriate than another is specified. Therefore, studies that test more than one theoretical specification and theories that consistently pass such tests should be given more weight than studies in which theories are used to justify assumptions left untested.

This strategy for evaluating theory based on relationships between different studies can be seen in the work of Markham (1978), Nachman (1982), and Naughton (1982). Markham (1978), using some of the WABA procedures on data collected in an organization in the aerospace industry, found a network of relationships that was quite similar to the relationship between titles and expectations found in the data collected at MCO. In a similar vein, Nachman (1982), using some of the WABA procedures for a nonsupport collectivity, failed to find a dyadic-level relationship between investments and returns. Naughton (1982), using WABA, examined a person-level theory and found stability over time for a set of reports on what he defined as option cutting and commitment. Although these works were conducted while the varient paradigm was being developed, the objective in each case was to formulate a theory in a way in which alternative hypotheses could be tested rather than simply assumed away.

One consequence of conducting a series of studies that employ the varient paradigm is that the results from each study can be located in a varient matrix. The frequency with which the results of studies fall in different or similar cells of the varient matrix provides a way to draw conclusions about theories. Over a series of studies, a great majority of results may fall into a particular cell of a varient matrix, thus providing support for one theory over others. Anomalies that tend not to be consistent with the great majority of results from a series of studies may serve to stimulate additional theorizing and empirical work. In this way, the contribution each study makes to knowledge can be identified. From this perspective, reviews of empirical studies should be simplified, since some cells will remain empty—indicating a lack of support for one theory—and other cells may regularly appear to be more likely, indicating support for another theory. Of course, in the varient paradigm, support for a theory is tentative because alternative explanations not included in a particular study are viewed as plausible and testable. Nevertheless, the results from employing the paradigm over a series of studies and the resulting identification of continuously supported theories can serve as a basis for applied work.

APPLIED ISSUES

One of the traditional dilemmas for those interested in the social sciences or studies of organizational behavior is the question of how to prescribe solutions for practical or applied problems (such as absenteeism, turnover, low productivity) when theories are insufficiently articulated and tested. We believe that use of the varient paradigm can greatly assist in providing theoretical knowledge as a basis for interventions and for ensuring that the results of applying theory to problem resolution can be reflected in further refinement of theory.

In its most fundamental form, a continuous demonstration of support for one theory over others suggests that such a theory may serve (until perhaps replaced by another theory) as a basis for diagnosing problems and taking action. In addition, the procedures in the varient paradigm can be used to monitor phenomena that may occur in organizations and other social settings and as a basis for providing feedback to organizational participants about the nature of their situation.

For example, given a cross-level collectivity effect and a desire to bring about changes, a more sociological approach to, for instance, public policy formulation that focuses on large-scale social movements would seem to be appropriate. In such a case, an attempt to bring about changes at only the person level of analysis may be doomed to fail. Similarly, if discrimination against women or minorities is viewed as a collectivity-level phenomenon, then a focus on collectivity processes may be necessary to bring about change. As a result, emphasis may be placed on encouraging formation of collectivities for this purpose (such as NOW and NAACP) and on allowing individuals to gain titles through tuition assistance schemes rather than relying solely on each individual to bring about changes.

In contrast, if groups or dyads underlie a set of relationships, such as those concerning control over work-group output, and a change is desirable, social psychological approaches that involve the facilitation of group or dyadic processes may be appropriate. If the relationships or phenomena of interest are specific to the dyad or group level of analysis, an attempt to bring about changes at the collectivity level may be doomed to failure; such attempts may be seen simply as interference in the lives of individuals.

Moreover, when a relationship holds at only the person level of analysis, a psychological approach would be most appropriate for bringing about change. In this type of approach, the focus is on helping each individual, independent of other actors or groups. If such effects are level-specific, using group or dyadic processes to bring about change will fail, and such efforts could be viewed as inappropriate infringements on each person's individuality.

Of course, a variety of different variables may be associated with different levels of analysis, and any individual may be contained in a variety of entities. Therefore, an individual may experience little difficulty, for example, with collectivities, but a great deal of difficulty with interpersonal relationships. From a practical perspective, an individual's ability to cope may be dependent on his or her skills in dealing with the interplay of variables associated with all these levels of analysis encountered in everyday life. Future theories and research that employ the varient paradigm may begin to provide information about the nature of processes at and across various levels of analysis.

Although an ability to associate variables with entities may be useful from an applied perspective, the type of relationship that occurs among variables can also be important. For example, when a relationship between variables is multiplexed, it applies across a variety of conditions. When a relationship is contingent, the applicability of the theory is limited to certain conditions and these limits must be identified if one is to avoid problems. In addition, a theory may specify a sequence of variables in which one variable or set of variables must shift before a change in another variable occurs (related case). Alternatively, a dependent variable may be an additive function of a set of variables, as in a multiple regression; in this case, a change in a set of variables may be necessary to change a dependent variable. From a series of studies that employ the varient paradigm, a choice among these alternative views of the relationships among variables is possible.

The varient paradigm may generate knowledge about the nature of these relationships, but the end for which such knowledge is employed is beyond the scope of the paradigm. For example, an individual may attempt to use mass communication and a variety of other devices to bring about collectivity-level changes, and he or she may use exchanges to build a select group of individuals who will execute his or her preferences. These processes presumably can be used to produce outcomes that may be viewed as valuable by some and worthless by others. Nevertheless, knowledge about processes can be used in a functional way. For example, various requirements may have to be met for an organization to function at the collectivity, group, dyad, and person levels of analysis; and individuals may then be evaluated in terms of these needs. To some extent, many individuals in organizations are probably evaluated in this way: Some portion of an individual's performance is probably based on the requirements of the position; another portion may be based on interpersonal relationships; and yet another portion may be based on unique skills and abilities independent of other persons. From an organizational design perspective, attempts can be made to structure a situation in a way that enhances a blend of the different performance capabilities of individuals.

From our perspective, the basis for the practical application of knowledge should be theories that have been shown to be more likely than alternative theories. The notion that multiple-hypothesis testing should be the basis for developing applied approaches may seem to be too demanding. We obviously disagree; although the varient paradigm is only one approach to multiple-hypothesis testing, we tend to agree with the following remarks by Chamberlin (1965, p. 754):[1]

> It has not been our custom to think of the method of working hypotheses as applicable to instruction or to the practical affairs of life. We have usually regarded it as but a method of science. But I believe its application to practical affairs has a value coordinate with the importance of the affairs themselves. I refer especially to those inquiries and inspections that precede the coming out of an enterprise rather than to its actual execution. The methods which are superior in scientific investigation should likewise be superior in those investigations that are the necessary antecedents to an intelligent conduct of affairs.

Finally, use of the varient paradigm allows one more effectively to evaluate the effects of theoretical applications. Too often changes in behavior

[1] From "The Method of Multiple Working Hypotheses," by T. C. Chamberlin, *Science*, Vol. 148, pp. 754–59, May 1965. Copyright © 1965 by the American Association for the Advancement of Science. Used with the permission of the American Association for the Advancement of Science.

or attitude are assumed to be related to changes in collectivity, group or person levels, with little attempt made actually to explicate entity and variable relationships. The varient paradigm allows one systematically to assess the effects of theoretical applications in such a manner that theory development is enhanced. Indeed, a real advantage to the varient paradigm is that it highlights and takes advantage of the mutual dependence of application and theory development in all areas of the social sciences, including behavior in organizational contexts.

CONCLUSION

In the social sciences and organizational behavior, a theory can be tested relative to other theories using the varient paradigm. However, the varient paradigm is not an endpoint because the need for new and better paradigms is likely to be ever present (see Popper, 1957, 1959). As our paradigm is used and developed, we hope that new ways to test theories will evolve, incorporating the old (what may now seem to be the new) varient paradigm.

REVIEW QUESTIONS

1. What is one way to clarify ambiguous variables or theories?
2. What is one way to integrate different studies, in different settings, involving multiple-hypothesis testing?
3. Why might many practitioners be particularly interested in multiplexed relationships?
4. Since there are always alternative explanations for a preferred hypothesis, how does one decide which alternatives should be evaluated in a study?
5. How is the issue of the meaningfulness of a research question assessed in the varient approach?
6. How does one evaluate the following argument: If a leadership theory asserts that leaders cannot be trained to change their behavior, then that assertion should be tested, rather than focusing on a pattern of correlations at a point in time.
7. What is the usefulness of examining data when no measures are used other than questionnaires?
8. What is the varient approach to statistical power (too small or large a sample size) and null results?
9. (a) To what extent are levels of analysis important in fields other than organizational behavior? (b) How can human beings not be embedded in multiple levels of analysis?
10. How can the varient paradigm be integrated with previous work? That is, is it an extension or a rejection of previous work?

APPENDICES

A. Tables

B. Key Geometric Properties

C. Key Algebraic Properties

D. Mathematical Proofs

E. Degrees of Freedom

F. Traditional Applications of WABA

G. Measures Used at MCO

H. Computerized WABA

I. Answers to Review Questions

APPENDIX A   TABLES

1. Trigonometric Functions
2. Hyperbolic Tangents for Transforming a Correlation to a Z' Score
3. .05 and .01 Values for the $\hat{F}$ Ratio ($df = \nu_1, \nu_2$)

TABLE A.1.   Trigonometric functions

ANGLE					ANGLE				
Degrees	Radians	COSINE (r)	SINE	TANGENT	Degrees	Radians	COSINE (r)	SINE	TANGENT
0	.00	1.000	.000	.000	90	1.57	.000	1.000	∞
1	.02	1.000	.017	.017	89	1.55	.017	1.000	57.290
2	.03	.999	.035	.035	88	1.54	.035	.999	28.636
3	.05	.999	.052	.052	87	1.52	.052	.999	19.081
4	.07	.998	.070	.070	86	1.50	.070	.998	14.301
5	.09	.996	.087	.087	85	1.48	.087	.996	11.430
6	.10	.995	.105	.105	84	1.47	.105	.995	9.514
7	.12	.993	.122	.123	83	1.45	.122	.993	8.144
8	.14	.990	.139	.141	82	1.43	.139	.990	7.115
9	.16	.988	.156	.158	81	1.41	.156	.988	6.314
10	.17	.985	.174	.176	80	1.40	.174	.985	5.671
11	.19	.982	.191	.194	79	1.38	.191	.982	5.145
12	.21	.978	.208	.213	78	1.36	.208	.978	4.705
13	.23	.974	.225	.231	77	1.34	.225	.974	4.331
14	.24	.970	.242	.249	76	1.33	.242	.970	4.011
15	.26	.966	.259	.268	75	1.31	.259	.966	3.732
16	.28	.961	.276	.287	74	1.29	.276	.961	3.487
17	.30	.956	.292	.306	73	1.27	.292	.956	3.271
18	.31	.951	.309	.325	72	1.26	.309	.951	3.078
19	.33	.946	.326	.344	71	1.24	.326	.946	2.904
20	.35	.940	.342	.364	70	1.22	.342	.940	2.747
21	.37	.934	.358	.384	69	1.20	.358	.934	2.605
22	.38	.927	.375	.404	68	1.19	.375	.927	2.475
23	.40	.921	.391	.424	67	1.17	.391	.921	2.356
24	.42	.914	.407	.445	66	1.15	.407	.914	2.246
25	.44	.906	.423	.466	65	1.13	.423	.906	2.145
26	.45	.899	.438	.488	64	1.12	.438	.899	2.050
27	.47	.891	.454	.510	63	1.10	.454	.891	1.963
28	.49	.883	.469	.532	62	1.08	.469	.883	1.881
29	.51	.875	.485	.554	61	1.06	.485	.875	1.804
30	.52	.866	.500	.577	60	1.05	.500	.866	1.732
31	.54	.857	.515	.601	59	1.03	.515	.857	1.664
32	.56	.848	.530	.625	58	1.01	.530	.848	1.600
33	.58	.839	.545	.649	57	.99	.545	.839	1.540
34	.59	.829	.559	.675	56	.98	.559	.829	1.483
35	.61	.819	.574	.700	55	.96	.574	.819	1.428
36	.63	.809	.588	.727	54	.94	.588	.809	1.376
37	.65	.799	.602	.754	53	.93	.602	.799	1.327
38	.66	.788	.616	.781	52	.91	.616	.788	1.280
39	.68	.777	.629	.810	51	.89	.629	.777	1.235
40	.70	.766	.643	.839	50	.87	.643	.766	1.192
41	.72	.755	.656	.869	49	.86	.656	.755	1.150
42	.73	.743	.669	.900	48	.84	.669	.743	1.111
43	.75	.731	.682	.933	47	.82	.682	.731	1.072
44	.77	.719	.695	.966	46	.80	.695	.719	1.036
45	.79	.707	.707	1.000	45	.79	.707	.707	1.000

Note: The cotangent is the tangent of the other angle in the row. For example, the cotangent of an angle of 43° is the tangent for an angle of 47° or 1.072. The cotangent for an angle of 47° is the tangent of an angle of 43° or 0.933—all values were obtained from a Texas Instruments (TI-55) scientific calculator.

TABLE A.2. Hyperbolic tangents for transforming a correlation to a Z' score

r	Z'	r	Z'	r	Z'	r	Z'
.00	.00	.26	.27	.52	.58	.78	1.05
.01	.01	.27	.28	.53	.59	.79	1.07
.02	.02	.28	.29	.54	.60	.80	1.10
.03	.03	.29	.30	.55	.62	.81	1.13
.04	.04	.30	.31	.56	.63	.82	1.16
.05	.05	.31	.32	.57	.65	.83	1.19
.06	.06	.32	.33	.58	.66	.84	1.22
.07	.07	.33	.34	.59	.68	.85	1.26
.08	.08	.34	.35	.60	.69	.86	1.29
.09	.09	.35	.37	.61	.71	.87	1.33
.10	.10	.36	.38	.62	.73	.88	1.38
.11	.11	.37	.39	.63	.74	.89	1.42
.12	.12	.38	.40	.64	.76	.90	1.47
.13	.13	.39	.41	.65	.78	.91	1.53
.14	.14	.40	.42	.66	.79	.92	1.59
.15	.15	.41	.44	.67	.81	.93	1.66
.16	.16	.42	.45	.68	.83	.94	1.74
.17	.17	.43	.46	.69	.85	.95	1.83
.18	.18	.44	.47	.70	.87	.96	1.95
.19	.19	.45	.48	.71	.89	.97	2.09
.20	.20	.46	.50	.72	.91	.98	2.30
.21	.21	.47	.51	.73	.93	.99	2.65
.22	.22	.48	.52	.74	.95	.995	2.99
.23	.23	.49	.54	.75	.97	.999	3.80
.24	.24	.50	.55	.76	1.00	.9999	4.95
.25	.26	.51	.56	.77	1.02	1.00	—

Note: All values obtained from a Texas Instruments (TI-55) scientific calculator.

TABLE A.3. .05 and .01 values of the $\hat{F}$ ratio ($df = \nu_1, \nu_2$)

ν_2 \ ν_1	1	2	3	4	5	6	7	8	9	10	11	12
1	161	200	216	225	230	234	237	239	241	242	243	244
	4,052	**4,999**	**5,403**	**5,625**	**5,764**	**5,859**	**5,928**	**5,981**	**6,022**	**6,056**	**6,082**	**6,106**
2	18.51	19.00	19.16	19.25	19.30	19.33	19.36	19.37	19.38	19.39	19.40	19.41
	98.49	**99.00**	**99.17**	**99.25**	**99.30**	**99.33**	**99.34**	**99.36**	**99.38**	**99.40**	**99.41**	**99.42**
3	10.13	9.55	9.28	9.12	9.01	8.94	8.88	8.84	8.81	8.78	8.76	8.74
	34.12	**30.82**	**29.46**	**28.71**	**28.24**	**27.91**	**27.67**	**27.49**	**27.34**	**27.23**	**27.13**	**27.05**
4	7.71	6.94	6.59	6.39	6.26	6.16	6.09	6.04	6.00	5.96	5.93	5.91
	21.20	**18.00**	**16.69**	**15.98**	**15.52**	**15.21**	**14.98**	**14.80**	**14.66**	**14.54**	**14.45**	**14.37**
5	6.61	5.79	5.41	5.19	5.05	4.95	4.88	4.82	4.78	4.74	4.70	4.68
	16.26	**13.27**	**12.06**	**11.39**	**10.97**	**10.67**	**10.45**	**10.27**	**10.15**	**10.05**	**9.96**	**9.89**
6	5.99	5.14	4.76	4.53	4.39	4.28	4.21	4.15	4.10	4.06	4.03	4.00
	13.74	**10.92**	**9.78**	**9.15**	**8.75**	**8.47**	**8.26**	**8.10**	**7.98**	**7.87**	**7.79**	**7.72**
7	5.59	4.74	4.35	4.12	3.97	3.87	3.79	3.73	3.68	3.63	3.60	3.57
	12.25	**9.55**	**8.45**	**7.85**	**7.46**	**7.19**	**7.00**	**6.84**	**6.71**	**6.62**	**6.54**	**6.47**
8	5.32	4.46	4.07	3.84	3.69	3.58	3.50	3.44	3.39	3.34	3.31	3.28
	11.26	**8.65**	**7.59**	**7.01**	**6.63**	**6.37**	**6.19**	**6.03**	**5.91**	**5.82**	**5.74**	**5.67**
9	5.12	4.26	3.86	3.63	3.48	3.37	3.29	3.23	3.18	3.13	3.10	3.07
	10.56	**8.02**	**6.99**	**6.42**	**6.06**	**5.80**	**5.62**	**5.47**	**5.35**	**5.26**	**5.18**	**5.11**
10	4.96	4.10	3.71	3.48	3.33	3.22	3.14	3.07	3.02	2.97	2.94	2.91
	10.04	**7.56**	**6.55**	**5.99**	**5.64**	**5.39**	**5.21**	**5.06**	**4.95**	**4.85**	**4.78**	**4.71**
11	4.84	3.98	3.59	3.36	3.20	3.09	3.01	2.95	2.90	2.86	2.82	2.79
	9.65	**7.20**	**6.22**	**5.67**	**5.32**	**5.07**	**4.88**	**4.74**	**4.63**	**4.54**	**4.46**	**4.40**
12	4.75	3.88	3.49	3.26	3.11	3.00	2.92	2.85	2.80	2.76	2.72	2.69
	9.33	**6.93**	**5.95**	**5.41**	**5.06**	**4.82**	**4.65**	**4.50**	**4.39**	**4.30**	**4.22**	**4.16**
13	4.67	3.80	3.41	3.18	3.02	2.92	2.84	2.77	2.72	2.67	2.63	2.60
	9.07	**6.70**	**5.74**	**5.20**	**4.86**	**4.62**	**4.44**	**4.30**	**4.19**	**4.10**	**4.02**	**3.96**
14	4.60	3.74	3.34	3.11	2.96	2.85	2.77	2.70	2.65	2.60	2.56	2.53
	8.86	**6.51**	**5.56**	**5.03**	**4.69**	**4.46**	**4.28**	**4.14**	**4.03**	**3.94**	**3.86**	**3.80**
15	4.54	3.68	3.29	3.06	2.90	2.79	2.70	2.64	2.59	2.55	2.51	2.48
	8.68	**6.36**	**5.42**	**4.89**	**4.56**	**4.32**	**4.14**	**4.00**	**3.89**	**3.80**	**3.73**	**3.67**
16	4.49	3.63	3.24	3.01	2.85	2.74	2.66	2.59	2.54	2.49	2.45	2.42
	8.53	**6.23**	**5.29**	**4.77**	**4.44**	**4.20**	**4.03**	**3.89**	**3.78**	**3.69**	**3.61**	**3.55**
17	4.45	3.59	3.20	2.96	2.81	2.70	2.62	2.55	2.50	2.45	2.41	2.38
	8.40	**6.11**	**5.18**	**4.67**	**4.34**	**4.10**	**3.93**	**3.79**	**3.68**	**3.59**	**3.52**	**3.45**
18	4.41	3.55	3.16	2.93	2.77	2.66	2.58	2.51	2.46	2.41	2.37	2.34
	8.28	**6.01**	**5.09**	**4.58**	**4.25**	**4.01**	**3.85**	**3.71**	**3.60**	**3.51**	**3.44**	**3.37**
19	4.38	3.52	3.13	2.90	2.74	2.63	2.55	2.48	2.43	2.38	2.34	2.31
	8.18	**5.93**	**5.01**	**4.50**	**4.17**	**3.94**	**3.77**	**3.63**	**3.52**	**3.43**	**3.36**	**3.30**
20	4.35	3.49	3.10	2.87	2.71	2.60	2.52	2.45	2.40	2.35	2.31	2.28
	8.10	**5.85**	**4.94**	**4.43**	**4.10**	**3.87**	**3.71**	**3.56**	**3.45**	**3.37**	**3.30**	**3.23**
21	4.32	3.47	3.07	2.84	2.68	2.57	2.49	2.42	2.37	2.32	2.28	2.25
	8.02	**5.78**	**4.87**	**4.37**	**4.04**	**3.81**	**3.65**	**3.51**	**3.40**	**3.31**	**3.24**	**3.17**
22	4.30	3.44	3.05	2.82	2.66	2.55	2.47	2.40	2.35	2.30	2.26	2.23
	7.94	**5.72**	**4.82**	**4.31**	**3.99**	**3.76**	**3.59**	**3.45**	**3.35**	**3.26**	**3.18**	**3.12**
23	4.28	3.42	3.03	2.80	2.64	2.53	2.45	2.38	2.32	2.28	2.24	2.20
	7.88	**5.66**	**4.76**	**4.26**	**3.94**	**3.71**	**3.54**	**3.41**	**3.30**	**3.21**	**3.14**	**3.07**
24	4.26	3.40	3.01	2.78	2.62	2.51	2.43	2.36	2.30	2.26	2.22	2.18
	7.82	**5.61**	**4.72**	**4.22**	**3.90**	**3.67**	**3.50**	**3.36**	**3.25**	**3.17**	**3.09**	**3.03**
25	4.24	3.38	2.99	2.76	2.60	2.49	2.41	2.34	2.28	2.24	2.20	2.16
	7.77	**5.57**	**4.68**	**4.18**	**3.86**	**3.63**	**3.46**	**3.32**	**3.21**	**3.13**	**3.05**	**2.99**
26	4.22	3.37	2.98	2.74	2.59	2.47	2.39	2.32	2.27	2.22	2.18	2.15
	7.72	**5.53**	**4.64**	**4.14**	**3.82**	**3.59**	**3.42**	**3.29**	**3.17**	**3.09**	**3.02**	**2.96**

TABLE A.3. .05 and .01 values of the $\hat{F}$ ratio ($df = \nu_1, \nu_2$)

14	16	20	24	30	40	50	75	100	200	500	∞	ν_1 / ν_2
245	246	248	249	250	251	252	253	253	254	254	254	1
6,142	6,169	6,208	6,234	6,258	6,286	6,302	6,323	6,334	6,352	6,361	6,366	
19.42	19.43	19.44	19.45	19.46	19.47	19.47	19.48	19.49	19.49	19.50	19.50	2
99.43	99.44	99.45	99.46	99.47	99.48	99.48	99.49	99.49	99.49	99.50	99.50	
8.71	8.69	8.66	8.64	8.62	8.60	8.58	8.57	8.56	8.54	8.54	8.53	3
26.92	26.83	26.69	26.60	26.50	26.41	26.35	26.27	26.23	26.18	26.14	26.12	
5.87	5.84	5.80	5.77	5.74	5.71	5.70	5.68	5.66	5.65	5.64	5.63	4
14.24	14.15	14.02	13.93	13.83	13.74	13.69	13.61	13.57	13.52	13.48	13.46	
4.64	4.60	4.56	4.53	4.50	4.46	4.44	4.42	4.40	4.38	4.37	4.36	5
9.77	9.68	9.55	9.47	9.38	9.29	9.24	9.17	9.13	9.07	9.04	9.02	
3.96	3.92	3.87	3.84	3.81	3.77	3.75	3.72	3.71	3.69	3.68	3.67	6
7.60	7.52	7.39	7.31	7.23	7.14	7.09	7.02	6.99	6.94	6.90	6.88	
3.52	3.49	3.44	3.41	3.38	3.34	3.32	3.29	3.28	3.25	3.24	3.23	7
6.35	6.27	6.15	6.07	5.98	5.90	5.85	5.78	5.75	5.70	5.67	5.65	
3.23	3.20	3.15	3.12	3.08	3.05	3.03	3.00	2.98	2.96	2.94	2.93	8
5.56	5.48	5.36	5.28	5.20	5.11	5.06	5.00	4.96	4.91	4.88	4.86	
3.02	2.98	2.93	2.90	2.86	2.82	2.80	2.77	2.76	2.73	2.72	2.71	9
5.00	4.92	4.80	4.73	4.64	4.56	4.51	4.45	4.41	4.36	4.33	4.31	
2.86	2.82	2.77	2.74	2.70	2.67	2.64	2.61	2.59	2.56	2.55	2.54	10
4.60	4.52	4.41	4.33	4.25	4.17	4.12	4.05	4.01	3.96	3.93	3.91	
2.74	2.70	2.65	2.61	2.57	2.53	2.50	2.47	2.45	2.42	2.41	2.40	11
4.29	4.21	4.10	4.02	3.94	3.86	3.80	3.74	3.70	3.66	3.62	3.60	
2.64	2.60	2.54	2.50	2.46	2.42	2.40	2.36	2.35	2.32	2.31	2.30	12
4.05	3.98	3.86	3.78	3.70	3.61	3.56	3.49	3.46	3.41	3.38	3.36	
2.55	2.51	2.46	2.42	2.38	2.34	2.32	2.28	2.26	2.24	2.22	2.21	13
3.85	3.78	3.67	3.59	3.51	3.42	3.37	3.30	3.27	3.21	3.18	3.16	
2.48	2.44	2.39	2.35	2.31	2.27	2.24	2.21	2.19	2.16	2.14	2.13	14
3.70	3.62	3.51	3.43	3.34	3.26	3.21	3.14	3.11	3.06	3.02	3.00	
2.43	2.39	2.33	2.29	2.25	2.21	2.18	2.15	2.12	2.10	2.08	2.07	15
3.56	3.48	3.36	3.29	3.20	3.12	3.07	3.00	2.97	2.92	2.89	2.87	
2.37	2.33	2.28	2.24	2.20	2.16	2.13	2.09	2.07	2.04	2.02	2.01	16
3.45	3.37	3.25	3.18	3.10	3.01	2.96	2.89	2.86	2.80	2.77	2.75	
2.33	2.29	2.23	2.19	2.15	2.11	2.08	2.04	2.02	1.99	1.97	1.96	17
3.35	3.27	3.16	3.08	3.00	2.92	2.86	2.79	2.76	2.70	2.67	2.65	
2.29	2.25	2.19	2.15	2.11	2.07	2.04	2.00	1.98	1.95	1.93	1.92	18
3.27	3.19	3.07	3.00	2.91	2.83	2.78	2.71	2.68	2.62	2.59	2.57	
2.26	2.21	2.15	2.11	2.07	2.02	2.00	1.96	1.94	1.91	1.90	1.88	19
3.19	3.12	3.00	2.92	2.84	2.76	2.70	2.63	2.60	2.54	2.51	2.49	
2.23	2.18	2.12	2.08	2.04	1.99	1.96	1.92	1.90	1.87	1.85	1.84	20
3.13	3.05	2.94	2.86	2.77	2.69	2.63	2.56	2.53	2.47	2.44	2.42	
2.20	2.15	2.09	2.05	2.00	1.96	1.93	1.89	1.87	1.84	1.82	1.81	21
3.07	2.99	2.88	2.80	2.72	2.63	2.58	2.51	2.47	2.42	2.38	2.36	
2.18	2.13	2.07	2.03	1.98	1.93	1.91	1.87	1.84	1.81	1.80	1.78	22
3.02	2.94	2.83	2.75	2.67	2.58	2.53	2.46	2.42	2.37	2.33	2.31	
2.14	2.10	2.04	2.00	1.96	1.91	1.88	1.84	1.82	1.79	1.77	1.76	23
2.97	2.89	2.78	2.70	2.62	2.53	2.48	2.41	2.37	2.32	2.28	2.26	
2.13	2.09	2.02	1.98	1.94	1.89	1.86	1.82	1.80	1.76	1.74	1.73	24
2.93	2.85	2.74	2.66	2.58	2.49	2.44	2.36	2.33	2.27	2.23	2.21	
2.11	2.06	2.00	1.96	1.92	1.87	1.84	1.80	1.77	1.74	1.72	1.71	25
2.89	2.81	2.70	2.62	2.54	2.45	2.40	2.32	2.29	2.23	2.19	2.17	
2.10	2.05	1.99	1.95	1.90	1.85	1.82	1.78	1.76	1.72	1.70	1.69	26
2.86	2.77	2.66	2.58	2.50	2.41	2.36	2.28	2.25	2.19	2.15	2.13	

TABLE A.3. .05 and .01 values of the $\hat{F}$ ratio ($df = \nu_1, \nu_2$)

ν_2 \ ν_1	1	2	3	4	5	6	7	8	9	10	11	12
27	4.21	3.35	2.96	2.73	2.57	2.46	2.37	2.30	2.25	2.20	2.16	2.13
	7.68	**5.49**	**4.60**	**4.11**	**3.79**	**3.56**	**3.39**	**3.26**	**3.14**	**3.06**	**2.98**	**2.93**
28	4.20	3.34	2.95	2.71	2.56	2.44	2.36	2.29	2.24	2.19	2.15	2.12
	7.64	**5.45**	**4.57**	**4.07**	**3.76**	**3.53**	**3.36**	**3.23**	**3.11**	**3.03**	**2.95**	**2.90**
29	4.18	3.33	2.93	2.70	2.54	2.43	2.35	2.28	2.22	2.18	2.14	2.10
	7.60	**5.42**	**4.54**	**4.04**	**3.73**	**3.50**	**3.33**	**3.20**	**3.08**	**3.00**	**2.92**	**2.87**
30	4.17	3.32	2.92	2.69	2.53	2.42	2.34	2.27	2.21	2.16	2.12	2.09
	7.56	**5.39**	**4.51**	**4.02**	**3.70**	**3.47**	**3.30**	**3.17**	**3.06**	**2.98**	**2.90**	**2.84**
32	4.15	3.30	2.90	2.67	2.51	2.40	2.32	2.25	2.19	2.14	2.10	2.07
	7.50	**5.34**	**4.46**	**3.97**	**3.66**	**3.42**	**3.25**	**3.12**	**3.01**	**2.94**	**2.86**	**2.80**
34	4.13	3.28	2.88	2.65	2.49	2.38	2.30	2.23	2.17	2.12	2.08	2.05
	7.44	**5.29**	**4.42**	**3.93**	**3.61**	**3.38**	**3.21**	**3.08**	**2.97**	**2.89**	**2.82**	**2.76**
36	4.11	3.26	2.86	2.63	2.48	2.36	2.28	2.21	2.15	2.10	2.06	2.03
	7.39	**5.25**	**4.38**	**3.89**	**3.58**	**3.35**	**3.18**	**3.04**	**2.94**	**2.86**	**2.78**	**2.72**
38	4.10	3.25	2.85	2.62	2.46	2.35	2.26	2.19	2.14	2.09	2.05	2.02
	7.35	**5.21**	**4.34**	**3.86**	**3.54**	**3.32**	**3.15**	**3.02**	**2.91**	**2.82**	**2.75**	**2.69**
40	4.08	3.23	2.84	2.61	2.45	2.34	2.25	2.18	2.12	2.07	2.04	2.00
	7.31	**5.18**	**4.31**	**3.83**	**3.51**	**3.29**	**3.12**	**2.99**	**2.88**	**2.80**	**2.73**	**2.66**
42	4.07	3.22	2.83	2.59	2.44	2.32	2.24	2.17	2.11	2.06	2.02	1.99
	7.27	**5.15**	**4.29**	**3.80**	**3.49**	**3.26**	**3.10**	**2.96**	**2.86**	**2.77**	**2.70**	**2.64**
44	4.06	3.21	2.82	2.58	2.43	2.31	2.23	2.16	2.10	2.05	2.01	1.98
	7.24	**5.12**	**4.26**	**3.78**	**3.46**	**3.24**	**3.07**	**2.94**	**2.84**	**2.75**	**2.68**	**2.62**
46	4.05	3.20	2.81	2.57	2.42	2.30	2.22	2.14	2.09	2.04	2.00	1.97
	7.21	**5.10**	**4.24**	**3.76**	**3.44**	**3.22**	**3.05**	**2.92**	**2.82**	**2.73**	**2.66**	**2.60**
48	4.04	3.19	2.80	2.56	2.41	2.30	2.21	2.14	2.08	2.03	1.99	1.96
	7.19	**5.08**	**4.22**	**3.74**	**3.42**	**3.20**	**3.04**	**2.90**	**2.80**	**2.71**	**2.64**	**2.58**
50	4.03	3.18	2.79	2.56	2.40	2.29	2.20	2.13	2.07	2.02	1.98	1.95
	7.17	**5.06**	**4.20**	**3.72**	**3.41**	**3.18**	**3.02**	**2.88**	**2.78**	**2.70**	**2.62**	**2.56**
55	4.02	3.17	2.78	2.54	2.38	2.27	2.18	2.11	2.05	2.00	1.97	1.93
	7.12	**5.01**	**4.16**	**3.68**	**3.37**	**3.15**	**2.98**	**2.85**	**2.75**	**2.66**	**2.59**	**2.53**
60	4.00	3.15	2.76	2.52	2.37	2.25	2.17	2.10	2.04	1.99	1.95	1.92
	7.08	**4.98**	**4.13**	**3.65**	**3.34**	**3.12**	**2.95**	**2.82**	**2.72**	**2.63**	**2.56**	**2.50**
65	3.99	3.14	2.75	2.51	2.36	2.24	2.15	2.08	2.02	1.98	1.94	1.90
	7.04	**4.95**	**4.10**	**3.62**	**3.31**	**3.09**	**2.93**	**2.79**	**2.70**	**2.61**	**2.54**	**2.47**
70	3.98	3.13	2.74	2.50	2.35	2.23	2.14	2.07	2.01	1.97	1.93	1.89
	7.01	**4.92**	**4.08**	**3.60**	**3.29**	**3.07**	**2.91**	**2.77**	**2.67**	**2.59**	**2.51**	**2.45**
80	3.96	3.11	2.72	2.48	2.33	2.21	2.12	2.05	1.99	1.95	1.91	1.88
	6.96	**4.88**	**4.04**	**3.56**	**3.25**	**3.04**	**2.87**	**2.74**	**2.64**	**2.55**	**2.48**	**2.41**
100	3.94	3.09	2.70	2.46	2.30	2.19	2.10	2.03	1.97	1.92	1.88	1.85
	6.90	**4.82**	**3.98**	**3.51**	**3.20**	**2.99**	**2.82**	**2.69**	**2.59**	**2.51**	**2.43**	**2.36**
125	3.92	3.07	2.68	2.44	2.29	2.17	2.08	2.01	1.95	1.90	1.86	1.83
	6.84	**4.78**	**3.94**	**3.47**	**3.17**	**2.95**	**2.79**	**2.65**	**2.56**	**2.47**	**2.40**	**2.33**
150	3.91	3.06	2.67	2.43	2.27	2.16	2.07	2.00	1.94	1.89	1.85	1.82
	6.81	**4.75**	**3.91**	**3.44**	**3.14**	**2.92**	**2.76**	**2.62**	**2.53**	**2.44**	**2.37**	**2.30**
200	3.89	3.04	2.65	2.41	2.26	2.14	2.05	1.98	1.92	1.87	1.83	1.80
	6.76	**4.71**	**3.88**	**3.41**	**3.11**	**2.90**	**2.73**	**2.60**	**2.50**	**2.41**	**2.34**	**2.28**
400	3.86	3.02	2.62	2.39	2.23	2.12	2.03	1.96	1.90	1.85	1.81	1.78
	6.70	**4.66**	**3.83**	**3.36**	**3.06**	**2.85**	**2.69**	**2.55**	**2.46**	**2.37**	**2.29**	**2.23**
1,000	3.85	3.00	2.61	2.38	2.22	2.10	2.02	1.95	1.89	1.84	1.80	1.76
	6.66	**4.62**	**3.80**	**3.34**	**3.04**	**2.82**	**2.66**	**2.53**	**2.43**	**2.34**	**2.26**	**2.20**
∞	3.84	2.99	2.60	2.37	2.21	2.09	2.01	1.94	1.88	1.83	1.79	1.75
	6.64	**4.60**	**3.78**	**3.32**	**3.02**	**2.80**	**2.64**	**2.51**	**2.41**	**2.32**	**2.24**	**2.18**

TABLE A.3. .05 and .01 values of the $\hat{F}$ ratio ($df = \nu_1, \nu_2$)

14	16	20	24	30	40	50	75	100	200	500	∞	ν_2
2.08	2.03	1.97	1.93	1.88	1.84	1.80	1.76	1.74	1.71	1.68	1.67	27
2.83	**2.74**	**2.63**	**2.55**	**2.47**	**2.38**	**2.33**	**2.25**	**2.21**	**2.16**	**2.12**	**2.10**	
2.06	2.02	1.96	1.91	1.87	1.81	1.78	1.75	1.72	1.69	1.67	1.65	28
2.80	**2.71**	**2.60**	**2.52**	**2.44**	**2.35**	**2.30**	**2.22**	**2.18**	**2.13**	**2.09**	**2.06**	
2.05	2.00	1.94	1.90	1.85	1.80	1.77	1.73	1.71	1.68	1.65	1.64	29
2.77	**2.68**	**2.57**	**2.49**	**2.41**	**2.32**	**2.27**	**2.19**	**2.15**	**2.10**	**2.06**	**2.03**	
2.04	1.99	1.93	1.89	1.84	1.79	1.76	1.72	1.69	1.66	1.64	1.62	30
2.74	**2.66**	**2.55**	**2.47**	**2.38**	**2.29**	**2.24**	**2.16**	**2.13**	**2.07**	**2.03**	**2.01**	
2.02	1.97	1.91	1.86	1.82	1.76	1.74	1.69	1.67	1.64	1.61	1.59	32
2.70	**2.62**	**2.51**	**2.42**	**2.34**	**2.25**	**2.20**	**2.12**	**2.08**	**2.02**	**1.98**	**1.96**	
2.00	1.95	1.89	1.84	1.80	1.74	1.71	1.67	1.64	1.61	1.59	1.57	34
2.66	**2.58**	**2.47**	**2.38**	**2.30**	**2.21**	**2.15**	**2.08**	**2.04**	**1.98**	**1.94**	**1.91**	
1.98	1.93	1.87	1.82	1.78	1.72	1.69	1.65	1.62	1.59	1.56	1.55	36
2.62	**2.54**	**2.43**	**2.35**	**2.26**	**2.17**	**2.12**	**2.04**	**2.00**	**1.94**	**1.90**	**1.87**	
1.96	1.92	1.85	1.80	1.76	1.71	1.67	1.63	1.60	1.57	1.54	1.53	38
2.59	**2.51**	**2.40**	**2.32**	**2.22**	**2.14**	**2.08**	**2.00**	**1.97**	**1.90**	**1.86**	**1.84**	
1.95	1.90	1.84	1.79	1.74	1.69	1.66	1.61	1.59	1.55	1.53	1.51	40
2.56	**2.49**	**2.37**	**2.29**	**2.20**	**2.11**	**2.05**	**1.97**	**1.94**	**1.88**	**1.84**	**1.81**	
1.94	1.89	1.82	1.78	1.73	1.68	1.64	1.60	1.57	1.54	1.51	1.49	42
2.54	**2.46**	**2.35**	**2.26**	**2.17**	**2.08**	**2.02**	**1.94**	**1.91**	**1.85**	**1.80**	**1.78**	
1.92	1.88	1.81	1.76	1.72	1.66	1.63	1.58	1.56	1.52	1.50	1.48	44
2.52	**2.44**	**2.32**	**2.24**	**2.15**	**2.06**	**2.00**	**1.92**	**1.88**	**1.82**	**1.78**	**1.75**	
1.91	1.87	1.80	1.75	1.71	1.65	1.62	1.57	1.54	1.51	1.48	1.46	46
2.50	**2.42**	**2.30**	**2.22**	**2.13**	**2.04**	**1.98**	**1.90**	**1.86**	**1.80**	**1.76**	**1.72**	
1.90	1.86	1.79	1.74	1.70	1.64	1.61	1.56	1.53	1.50	1.47	1.45	48
2.48	**2.40**	**2.28**	**2.20**	**2.11**	**2.02**	**1.96**	**1.88**	**1.84**	**1.78**	**1.73**	**1.70**	
1.90	1.85	1.78	1.74	1.69	1.63	1.60	1.55	1.52	1.48	1.46	1.44	50
2.46	**2.39**	**2.26**	**2.18**	**2.10**	**2.00**	**1.94**	**1.86**	**1.82**	**1.76**	**1.71**	**1.68**	
1.88	1.83	1.76	1.72	1.67	1.61	1.58	1.52	1.50	1.46	1.43	1.41	55
2.43	**2.35**	**2.23**	**2.15**	**2.06**	**1.96**	**1.90**	**1.82**	**1.78**	**1.71**	**1.66**	**1.64**	
1.86	1.81	1.75	1.70	1.65	1.59	1.56	1.50	1.48	1.44	1.41	1.39	60
2.40	**2.32**	**2.20**	**2.12**	**2.03**	**1.93**	**1.87**	**1.79**	**1.74**	**1.68**	**1.63**	**1.60**	
1.85	1.80	1.73	1.68	1.63	1.57	1.54	1.49	1.46	1.42	1.39	1.37	65
2.37	**2.30**	**2.18**	**2.09**	**2.00**	**1.90**	**1.84**	**1.76**	**1.71**	**1.64**	**1.60**	**1.56**	
1.84	1.79	1.72	1.67	1.62	1.56	1.53	1.47	1.45	1.40	1.37	1.35	70
2.35	**2.28**	**2.15**	**2.07**	**1.98**	**1.88**	**1.82**	**1.74**	**1.69**	**1.62**	**1.56**	**1.53**	
1.82	1.77	1.70	1.65	1.60	1.54	1.51	1.45	1.42	1.38	1.35	1.32	80
2.32	**2.24**	**2.11**	**2.03**	**1.94**	**1.84**	**1.78**	**1.70**	**1.65**	**1.57**	**1.52**	**1.49**	
1.79	1.75	1.68	1.63	1.57	1.51	1.48	1.42	1.39	1.34	1.30	1.28	100
2.26	**2.19**	**2.06**	**1.98**	**1.89**	**1.79**	**1.73**	**1.64**	**1.59**	**1.51**	**1.46**	**1.43**	
1.77	1.72	1.65	1.60	1.55	1.49	1.45	1.39	1.36	1.31	1.27	1.25	125
2.23	**2.15**	**2.03**	**1.94**	**1.85**	**1.75**	**1.68**	**1.59**	**1.54**	**1.46**	**1.40**	**1.37**	
1.76	1.71	1.64	1.59	1.54	1.47	1.44	1.37	1.34	1.29	1.25	1.22	150
2.20	**2.12**	**2.00**	**1.91**	**1.83**	**1.72**	**1.66**	**1.56**	**1.51**	**1.43**	**1.37**	**1.33**	
1.74	1.69	1.62	1.57	1.52	1.45	1.42	1.35	1.32	1.26	1.22	1.19	200
2.17	**2.09**	**1.97**	**1.88**	**1.79**	**1.69**	**1.62**	**1.53**	**1.48**	**1.39**	**1.33**	**1.28**	
1.72	1.67	1.60	1.54	1.49	1.42	1.38	1.32	1.28	1.22	1.16	1.13	400
2.12	**2.04**	**1.92**	**1.84**	**1.74**	**1.64**	**1.57**	**1.47**	**1.42**	**1.32**	**1.24**	**1.19**	
1.70	1.65	1.58	1.53	1.47	1.41	1.36	1.30	1.26	1.19	1.13	1.08	1,000
2.09	**2.01**	**1.89**	**1.81**	**1.71**	**1.61**	**1.54**	**1.44**	**1.38**	**1.28**	**1.19**	**1.11**	
1.69	1.64	1.57	1.52	1.46	1.40	1.35	1.28	1.24	1.17	1.11	1.00	∞
2.07	**1.99**	**1.87**	**1.79**	**1.69**	**1.59**	**1.52**	**1.41**	**1.36**	**1.25**	**1.15**	**1.00**	

Note: .05 level in lightface type; .01 level in boldface type; ν_1 = degrees of freedom for numerator; ν_2 = degrees of freedom for denominator.

Reprinted by permission from *Statistical Methods* by George W. Snedecor and William G. Cochran, Seventh edition, © 1980 by the Iowa State University Press, Ames, IA 50010.

APPENDIX B   KEY GEOMETRIC PROPERTIES

1. Symmetry of Correlations
2. Relationship of Sines and Cosines of Angles
3. Derivation of Two Expressions for a Cotangent

1. SYMMETRY OF CORRELATIONS

The angle between two vectors or lines in space can vary not only from 0° to 90°, but also from 90° to 180° (see Smail, 1953). These two intervals are symmetrical in terms of magnitude. For example, suppose two vectors form a 150° angle, as is illustrated in the upper portion of Figure B.1. If the direction of one of the vectors (in this case vector X) is rotated 180°, the angle between the rotated vector X and Y is 30°. Schematically, this point can be illustrated as shown in the lower portion of Figure B.1. This example can be extended by considering the lower portion of Figure 5.2. When an angle of 150° is observed, the cosine equals -0.866, the sine equals $+0.500$, and cotangent (cosine/sine) equals -1.732. The magnitude of these values is identical to the magnitude for a 30° angle.

Original 150° angle between two vectors.

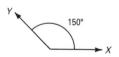

Resulting 30° angle between two vectors after rotation of vector X.

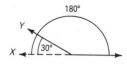

FIGURE B.1.   Illustration of the equivalence of 30° and 150° angles

This geometric characteristic of angles can be expressed by the following rule: If an angle occurs between 90° and 180°, then it can be transformed to an angle between 0° and 90° by subtracting the angle of interest from 180°:

$$180° - \theta° = \text{adjusted angle } 0° \text{ to } 90°$$

2. RELATIONSHIP OF SINES AND COSINES OF ANGLES

From geometry (Smail, 1953) the cosine squared plus the sine squared of an angle equals 1. Or, for example,

$$\cos^2\theta_{VY} + \sin^2\theta_{VY} = 1$$

Therefore, the cosine of an angle can be rewritten as:

$$\cos\theta_{VY} = \sqrt{1 - \sin^2\theta_{VY}}$$

In the case shown in Chapter 5:

$$\sin\theta_{VY} = \cos\theta_{XY}$$

Therefore

$$\cos\theta_{VY} = \sqrt{1 - \cos^2\theta_{XY}}$$

Moreover, the eta correlation follows this rule, because:

$$\eta^2_{BY} + \eta^2_{WY} = 1$$

Therefore, sine θ_{TB} equals cosine θ_{TW}, and sine θ_{TW} equals cosine θ_{TB}.

3. DERIVATION OF TWO EXPRESSIONS FOR A COTANGENT

The cosine of an angle θ equals the sine of 90° minus that angle $(90° - \theta)$. For example, in the illustrative case in Chapter 5:

$$\cos\theta_{XY} = \sin(90° - \theta_{XY}) \tag{B.1}$$

$$\cos\theta_{VY} = \sin(90° - \theta_{VY}) \tag{B.2}$$

In the illustrative case presented in Chapter 5, the two angles of interest can be defined by knowledge of the magnitude of either one of the angles:

$$\theta_{VY} = 90° - \theta_{XY} \tag{B.3}$$

$$\theta_{XY} = 90° - \theta_{VY} \tag{B.4}$$

Substituting Equations B.3 and B.4 into Equations B.1 and B.2:

$$\cos \theta_{XY} = \sin \theta_{VY} \qquad (\textbf{B.5})$$

$$\cos \theta_{VY} = \sin \theta_{XY} \qquad (\textbf{B.6})$$

It can now be shown that the ratio of the degree to which one variable is associated and not associated with another variable is the cotangent of the angle between the two variables of interest. Specifically,

$$\cot \theta_{XY} = \frac{\cos \theta_{XY}}{\sin \theta_{XY}}$$

and from Equation B.6 and given $\cos \theta_{XY} = r_{XY}$

$$\cot \theta_{XY} = \frac{\cos \theta_{XY}}{\cos \theta_{VY}} = \frac{r_{XY}}{r_{VY}} \qquad (\textbf{B.7})$$

In this case, the cotangent equals the ratio of two correlations and is called a general E ratio. From section 2 of this Appendix, the following is known:

$$\cos \theta_{VY} = \sqrt{1 - \cos^2 \theta_{XY}}$$

Therefore, Equation B.7 is rewritten as

$$\cot \theta_{XY} = \frac{\cos \theta_{XY}}{\sqrt{1 - \cos^2 \theta_{XY}}} = \frac{r_{XY}}{\sqrt{1 - r_{XY}^2}} \qquad (\textbf{B.8})$$

and is called a general R ratio.

APPENDIX C   KEY ALGEBRAIC PROPERTIES

1. Averages
2. Deviation Scores

Various proofs that follow from the basic definition of averages and deviation scores are presented in this appendix. These properties also underlie the proofs presented in Appendix D. To demonstrate these properties, let Y stand for a set of scores, $\overline{Y}_J$ for the average of the set of Y scores in each cell (J), and $\overline{Y}$ for the grand average of all Y scores across all cells. The grand average of N scores on Y can be expressed

$$\overline{Y} = \frac{\Sigma Y}{N} \qquad (C.1)$$

or

$$N\overline{Y} = \Sigma Y \qquad (C.2)$$

1. AVERAGES

If the grand average $\overline{Y}$ is distributed among all objects such that each of N objects has the same grand average score, Equation C.2 can be rewritten

$$\Sigma \overline{Y} = \Sigma Y \qquad (C.3)$$

In other words, the sum of N grand average scores on a variable Y equals the sum of N scores on that variable.

The same principle holds for each cell in a data set. Specifically, for any cell that contains scores (Y) and a cell average $(\overline{Y}_J)$ for each object in that cell, the following holds:

$$\Sigma \overline{Y}_J = \Sigma Y \qquad (C.4)$$

Since Equation C.4 holds for each cell in a set of data, it also holds for all cells combined; therefore, a double summation sign is not necessary.

Therefore, from Equations C.3 and C.4, the following holds:

$$\Sigma Y = \Sigma \overline{Y}_J = \Sigma \overline{Y} \qquad (C.5)$$

All components of Equation C.5 can be multiplied by a grand average (a constant, since the same value occurs for all objects), as follows:

$$\bar{Y}\Sigma Y = \bar{Y}\Sigma\bar{Y}_J = \bar{Y}\Sigma\bar{Y}$$

or

$$\Sigma Y\bar{Y} = \Sigma\bar{Y}_J\bar{Y} = \Sigma\bar{Y}^2 \qquad (\text{C.6})$$

Equation C.6 is of particular importance for various proofs presented in Appendix D. In a similar fashion, for a single cell, both sides of Equation C.4 can be multiplied by the cell average $(\bar{Y}_J)$ because it is a constant for that cell, or

$$\bar{Y}_J\Sigma\bar{Y}_J = \bar{Y}_J\Sigma Y$$

$$\Sigma\bar{Y}_J^2 = \Sigma Y\bar{Y}_J \qquad (\text{C.7})$$

An illustration of the three principles contained in Equations C.5, C.6, and C.7 is presented in the upper portion of Table C.1. The principles apply regardless of any assumption about variance or the number of objects in each cell because they are based on mathematics alone. As should be apparent from the table, scores are always distributed such that they are associated with a particular object. It should be apparent that all calculations are then based on weighted scores.

TABLE C.1.　Illustration of the properties of averages and deviations

	CELL I		CELL II		SUMMATIONS (Σ)	RELEVANT EQUATION	EQUATION NUMBER
	A	**B**	**C**	**D**			
Averages							
Y	1.00	2.00	3.00	4.00	10	$\Sigma Y = \Sigma\bar{Y}_J = \Sigma\bar{Y}$	C.5
$\bar{Y}_J$	1.50	1.50	3.50	3.50	10		
$\bar{Y}$	2.50	2.50	2.50	2.50	10		
$\bar{Y}_J^2$	2.25	2.25	12.25	12.25	29	$\Sigma\bar{Y}_J^2 = \Sigma Y\bar{Y}_J$	C.7
$Y\bar{Y}_J$	1.50	3.00	10.50	14.00	29		
$Y\bar{Y}$	2.50	5.00	7.50	10.00	25	$\Sigma Y\bar{Y} = \Sigma\bar{Y}_J\bar{Y} = \Sigma\bar{Y}^2$	C.6
$\bar{Y}_J\bar{Y}$	3.75	3.75	8.75	8.75	25		
$\bar{Y}^2$	6.25	6.25	6.25	6.25	25		
Deviations							
$Y - \bar{Y} = T^a$	−1.50	−0.50	0.50	1.50	0		
$Y - \bar{Y}_J = W^a$	−0.50	0.50	−0.50	0.50	0		
$\bar{Y}_J - \bar{Y} = B^a$	−1.00	−1.00	1.00	1.00	0		
$(\bar{Y}_J - \bar{Y})^2$	1.00	1.00	1.00	1.00	4	$\Sigma(\bar{Y}_J - \bar{Y})^2 =$	
$(Y - \bar{Y})(\bar{Y}_J - \bar{Y})$	1.50	0.50	0.50	1.50	4	$\Sigma(Y - \bar{Y})(\bar{Y}_J - \bar{Y})$	C.10
$(Y - \bar{Y}_J)^2$	0.25	0.25	0.25	0.25	1	$\Sigma(Y - \bar{Y}_J)^2 =$	
$(Y - \bar{Y})(Y - \bar{Y}_J)$	0.75	−0.25	−0.25	0.75	1	$\Sigma(Y - \bar{Y})(Y - \bar{Y}_J)$	C.11
$(Y - \bar{Y})^2$	2.25	0.25	0.25	2.25	5		
$(Y - \bar{Y}_J)(\bar{Y}_J - \bar{Y})$	0.50	−0.50	−0.50	0.50	0	$\Sigma(Y - \bar{Y}_J)(\bar{Y}_J - \bar{Y}) = 0$	C.12

[a]T indicates total deviations; W indicates within-cell deviations; and B indicates between-cell deviations.

2. DEVIATION SCORES

From any statistics book, the total deviations are known to equal the within-plus between-cell deviation scores:

$$\text{Total} = \text{within} + \text{between}$$
$$Y - \bar{Y} = \left(Y - \bar{Y}_J\right) + \left(\bar{Y}_J - \bar{Y}\right) \qquad \text{(C.8)}$$

Moreover, when these scores are squared and summed, the sums of squares are formed and the within plus between sum of squares equals the total sum of squares:

$$\Sigma\left(Y - \bar{Y}\right)^2 = \Sigma\left(Y - \bar{Y}_J\right)^2 + \Sigma\left(\bar{Y}_J - \bar{Y}\right)^2 \qquad \text{(C.9)}$$

Three correlations can be calculated among these three deviation scores, one of which equals zero and two of which are the between- and within-eta correlations. To prove the latter statement, equations that show the equivalence of various multiplications are necessary. To simplify the presentation of proofs in Appendix D, a series of algebraic identities are presented in Table C.2. For example, for the first case shown in the table, the between sum of squares is extended as follows:

$$\Sigma\left(\bar{Y}_J - \bar{Y}\right)^2 = \Sigma\bar{Y}_J^2 - \Sigma\bar{Y}_J\bar{Y} - \Sigma\bar{Y}_J\bar{Y} + \Sigma\bar{Y}^2$$

This equation is reduced in step A by using Equation C.6, which leaves the following portion of the equation:

$$\Sigma\bar{Y}_J^2 - \Sigma\bar{Y}_J\bar{Y}$$

However, using Equation C.6, in step B this expression may be rewritten

$$\Sigma\bar{Y}_J^2 - \Sigma\bar{Y}^2$$

TABLE C.2. Simplification of component summations

	PROPERTY EMPLOYED		STARTING POINT	EXTENSION	SIMPLIFIED VALUE		EQUATION
Step	Identities	Equation			Step A	Step B	
A	$\Sigma\bar{Y}^2 - \Sigma\bar{Y}_J\bar{Y} = 0$	C.6	$\Sigma(\bar{Y}_J - \bar{Y})^2$	$\Sigma\bar{Y}_J^2 - \Sigma\bar{Y}_J\bar{Y} - \Sigma\bar{Y}_J\bar{Y} + \Sigma\bar{Y}^2$	$\Sigma\bar{Y}_J^2 - \Sigma\bar{Y}_J\bar{Y}$	$\Sigma\bar{Y}_J^2 - \Sigma\bar{Y}^2$	C.10
B	$\Sigma\bar{Y}_J\bar{Y} = \Sigma\bar{Y}^2$	C.6					
A	$\Sigma\bar{Y}^2 - \Sigma\bar{Y}_J\bar{Y} = 0$	C.6	$\Sigma(Y - \bar{Y})(\bar{Y}_J - \bar{Y})$	$\Sigma Y\bar{Y}_J - \Sigma\bar{Y}_J\bar{Y} - \Sigma Y\bar{Y} + \Sigma\bar{Y}^2$	$\Sigma Y\bar{Y}_J - \Sigma Y\bar{Y}$	$\Sigma\bar{Y}_J^2 - \Sigma\bar{Y}^2$	
B	$\Sigma Y\bar{Y}_J = \Sigma\bar{Y}_J^2$	C.7					
	$\Sigma Y\bar{Y} = \Sigma\bar{Y}^2$	C.6					
A	$\Sigma\bar{Y}_J^2 - \Sigma Y\bar{Y}_J = 0$	C.7	$\Sigma(Y - \bar{Y}_J)^2$	$\Sigma Y^2 - \Sigma Y\bar{Y}_J - \Sigma Y\bar{Y}_J + \Sigma\bar{Y}_J^2$	$\Sigma Y^2 - \Sigma Y\bar{Y}_J$	$\Sigma Y^2 - \Sigma\bar{Y}_J^2$	C.11
B	$\Sigma Y\bar{Y}_J = \Sigma\bar{Y}_J^2$	C.7					
A	$\Sigma\bar{Y}_J\bar{Y} - \Sigma Y\bar{Y} = 0$	C.6	$\Sigma(Y - \bar{Y})(Y - \bar{Y}_J)$	$\Sigma Y^2 - \Sigma Y\bar{Y}_J - \Sigma Y\bar{Y} + \Sigma\bar{Y}_J\bar{Y}$	$\Sigma Y^2 - \Sigma Y\bar{Y}_J$	$\Sigma Y^2 - \Sigma\bar{Y}_J^2$	
B	$\Sigma Y\bar{Y}_J = \Sigma\bar{Y}_J^2$	C.7					
A	$\Sigma\bar{Y}^2 - \Sigma Y\bar{Y} = 0$	C.6	$\Sigma(Y - \bar{Y})^2$	$\Sigma Y^2 - \Sigma Y\bar{Y} - \Sigma Y\bar{Y} + \Sigma\bar{Y}^2$	$\Sigma Y^2 - \Sigma Y\bar{Y}$	$\Sigma Y^2 - \Sigma\bar{Y}^2$	
B	$\Sigma Y\bar{Y} = \Sigma\bar{Y}^2$	C.6					
A	$\Sigma Y\bar{Y}_J - \Sigma\bar{Y}_J^2 = 0$	C.7	$\Sigma(Y - \bar{Y}_J)(\bar{Y}_J - \bar{Y})$	$\Sigma Y\bar{Y}_J - \Sigma\bar{Y}_J^2 - \Sigma Y\bar{Y} + \Sigma\bar{Y}_J\bar{Y}$	$\Sigma\bar{Y}_J\bar{Y} - \Sigma Y\bar{Y}$	0	C.12
B	$\Sigma\bar{Y}_J\bar{Y} - \Sigma Y\bar{Y} = 0$	C.6					

An examination of the table results in the following key identities:

$$\Sigma(\overline{Y}_J - \overline{Y})^2 = \Sigma(Y - \overline{Y})(\overline{Y}_J - \overline{Y}) \qquad \text{(C.10)}$$

$$\Sigma(Y - \overline{Y}_J)^2 = \Sigma(Y - \overline{Y})(Y - \overline{Y}_J) \qquad \text{(C.11)}$$

$$\Sigma(Y - \overline{Y}_J)(\overline{Y}_J - \overline{Y}) = 0 \qquad \text{(C.12)}$$

An illustration of these identities is presented in the lower portion of Table C.1. Again, in all cases the scores are distributed among all objects and then summed. In Appendix D, Equations C.10, C.11, and C.12, which are based on Equations C.5, C.6, and C.7, are employed in various proofs.

APPENDIX D   MATHEMATICAL PROOFS

1. Independence of Within- and Between-Cell Scores
2. Between-Eta Correlations
3. Within-Eta Correlations
4. Relationship of the Between- and the Within-Eta Correlations
5. The WABA Equation
6. Correlations of Total X with Between-Y or Within-Y Scores
7. Independence of Between- and Within-Cell Correlations

The mathematical proofs presented and the notations used in this appendix are based on the algebraic proofs presented in Appendix C. A consideration of the mathematics of the correlations of total, between-cell, and within-cell deviation scores results in several proofs that highlight the nature of within- and between-cell deviation scores.

1. INDEPENDENCE OF WITHIN- AND BETWEEN-CELL SCORES

Using the total correlational formula, the correlation between within-cell and between-cell scores for one variable Y is written

$$r_{WB} = \frac{\Sigma(Y - \overline{Y}_J)(\overline{Y}_J - \overline{Y})}{\sqrt{\Sigma(Y - \overline{Y}_J)^2 \Sigma(\overline{Y}_J - \overline{Y})^2}} = 0$$

From Equation C.12, the numerator for this correlation must equal zero. Therefore, the correlation of within- and between-cell scores always equals zero.

2. BETWEEN-ETA CORRELATIONS

Using the total correlational formula, the correlation of the total and between-cell deviations for one variable Y is written

$$r_{TB} = \frac{\Sigma(Y - \overline{Y})(\overline{Y}_J - \overline{Y})}{\sqrt{\Sigma(Y - \overline{Y})^2 \Sigma(\overline{Y}_J - \overline{Y})^2}}$$

However, from Equation C.10, the numerator is rewritten with the following result:

$$r_{TB} = \frac{\Sigma(\overline{Y}_J - \overline{Y})^2}{\sqrt{\Sigma(Y - \overline{Y})^2 \Sigma(\overline{Y}_J - \overline{Y})^2}}$$

Since only squared deviations are employed in this equation, this correlation must be positive in value. If this correlation is squared, the following equation results:

$$r_{TB}^2 = \frac{\Sigma(\bar{Y}_J - \bar{Y})^2 \Sigma(\bar{Y}_J - \bar{Y})^2}{\Sigma(Y - \bar{Y})^2 \Sigma(\bar{Y}_J - \bar{Y})^2}$$

which can be rewritten

$$r_{TB}^2 = \frac{\Sigma(\bar{Y}_J - \bar{Y})^2}{\Sigma(Y - \bar{Y})^2} = \eta_{BY}^2 \qquad \textbf{(D.1)}$$

In other words, the square of the correlation between the total deviation and the between-cell deviation scores equals the between sum of squares divided by the total sum of squares, which is the traditional formula for eta squared. The between-eta correlation is the correlation of the total deviation scores with the between-cell scores.

3. WITHIN-ETA CORRELATIONS

The same logic applies to within-eta correlations. Specifically,

$$r_{TW} = \frac{\Sigma(Y - \bar{Y})(Y - \bar{Y}_J)}{\sqrt{\Sigma(Y - \bar{Y})^2 \Sigma(Y - \bar{Y}_J)^2}}$$

However, from Equation C.11 the numerator may be rewritten as

$$r_{TW} = \frac{\Sigma(Y - \bar{Y}_J)^2}{\sqrt{\Sigma(Y - \bar{Y})^2 \Sigma(Y - \bar{Y}_J)^2}}$$

Since only squared deviations are employed in the equation, the correlation must take on positive values. The square of this correlation is written

$$r_{TW}^2 = \frac{\Sigma(Y - \bar{Y}_J)^2 \Sigma(Y - \bar{Y}_J)^2}{\Sigma(Y - \bar{Y})^2 \Sigma(Y - \bar{Y}_J)^2}$$

which is rewritten

$$r_{TW}^2 = \frac{\Sigma(Y - \bar{Y}_J)^2}{\Sigma(Y - \bar{Y})^2} = \eta_{WY}^2 \qquad \textbf{(D.2)}$$

In other words, the square of the correlation between the total and the within-cell deviation scores equals the within sum of squares divided by the total sum of squares and is equal to the formula for within-eta squared. The within-eta correlation is the correlation of the total with the within-cell scores.

4. RELATIONSHIP OF THE BETWEEN- AND THE WITHIN-ETA CORRELATIONS

The addition of the squared within- and between-eta correlations ($\eta_{BY}^2 + \eta_{WY}^2$) is written using Equations D.1 and D.2, as follows:

$$\frac{\Sigma(\overline{Y}_J - \overline{Y})^2}{\Sigma(Y - \overline{Y})^2} + \frac{\Sigma(Y - \overline{Y}_J)^2}{\Sigma(Y - \overline{Y})^2}$$

which may be rewritten

$$\frac{\Sigma(\overline{Y}_J - \overline{Y})^2 + \Sigma(Y - \overline{Y}_J)^2}{\Sigma(Y - \overline{Y})^2}$$

From Equation C.9, the numerator in this equation equals the total sum of the squares, which also is the denominator. Therefore,

$$\eta_{BY}^2 + \eta_{WY}^2 = 1 \qquad \textbf{(D.3)}$$

Since the correlation between the within- and between-cell scores always equals zero, the characteristics of all three correlations and their relationships have been demonstrated.

5. THE WABA EQUATION

Robinson (1950) provides the following equation for any total correlation between two variables X and Y.

$$r_{TXY} = \eta_{BX}\eta_{BY}r_{BXY} + \sqrt{1 - \eta_{BX}^2}\sqrt{1 - \eta_{BY}^2}\,r_{WXY}$$

From Equation D.3, the following is known to hold:

$$\eta_{WX} = \sqrt{1 - \eta_{BX}^2}$$

$$\eta_{WY} = \sqrt{1 - \eta_{BY}^2}$$

The following WABA equation results by substitution:

$$r_{TXY} = \eta_{BX}\eta_{BY}r_{BXY} + \eta_{WX}\eta_{WY}r_{WXY} \qquad \textbf{(D.4)}$$

The within and between components of the correlations may be rewritten and reduced as follows:

$$\eta_{BX}\eta_{BY}r_{BXY} = \frac{\sqrt{\Sigma(\bar{X}_J - \bar{X})^2}}{\sqrt{\Sigma(X - \bar{X})^2}} \frac{\sqrt{\Sigma(\bar{Y}_J - \bar{Y})^2}}{\sqrt{\Sigma(Y - \bar{Y})^2}} \frac{\Sigma(\bar{X}_J - \bar{X})(\bar{Y}_J - \bar{Y})}{\sqrt{\Sigma(\bar{X}_J - \bar{X})^2\Sigma(\bar{Y}_J - \bar{Y})^2}}$$

$$= \frac{\Sigma(\bar{X}_J - \bar{X})(\bar{Y}_J - \bar{Y})}{\sqrt{\Sigma(X - \bar{X})^2\Sigma(Y - \bar{Y})^2}} \tag{D.5}$$

$$\eta_{WX}\eta_{WY}r_{WXY} = \frac{\sqrt{\Sigma(X - \bar{X}_J)^2}}{\sqrt{\Sigma(X - \bar{X})^2}} \frac{\sqrt{\Sigma(Y - \bar{Y}_J)^2}}{\sqrt{\Sigma(Y - \bar{Y})^2}} \frac{\Sigma(X - \bar{X}_J)(Y - \bar{Y}_J)}{\sqrt{\Sigma(X - \bar{X}_J)^2\Sigma(Y - \bar{Y}_J)^2}}$$

$$= \frac{\Sigma(X - \bar{X}_J)(Y - \bar{Y}_J)}{\sqrt{\Sigma(X - \bar{X})^2\Sigma(Y - \bar{Y})^2}} \tag{D.6}$$

The addition of the two components expressed in Equations D.5 and D.6, since there is the same denominator in each component, is rewritten

$$\frac{\Sigma(\bar{X}_J - \bar{X})(\bar{Y}_J - \bar{Y}) + \Sigma(X - \bar{X}_J)(Y - \bar{Y}_J)}{\sqrt{\Sigma(X - \bar{X})^2\Sigma(Y - \bar{Y})^2}} \tag{D.7}$$

The numerator can be expanded as follows:

$$\left(\Sigma\bar{X}_J\bar{Y}_J - \Sigma\overline{XY}_J - \Sigma\overline{YX}_J + \Sigma\overline{XY}\right) + \left(\Sigma XY - \Sigma\bar{X}_J Y - \Sigma\bar{Y}_J X + \Sigma\bar{X}_J\bar{Y}_J\right)$$

By extension of Equation C.4

$$\Sigma\bar{X}_J\bar{Y}_J = \bar{X}_J\Sigma\bar{Y}_J = \bar{X}_J\Sigma Y = \Sigma\bar{X}_J Y$$
$$\Sigma\bar{X}_J\bar{Y}_J = \bar{Y}_J\Sigma\bar{X}_J = \bar{Y}_J\Sigma X = \Sigma X\bar{Y}_J$$

Therefore

$$\Sigma\bar{X}_J Y = \Sigma X\bar{Y}_J$$

By appropriate cancellation of terms, the numerator of Equation D.7 becomes

$$-\Sigma\overline{XY}_J - \Sigma\overline{YX}_J + \Sigma\overline{XY} + \Sigma XY$$

By extension of Equation C.3

$$\Sigma\overline{YX}_J = \bar{Y}\Sigma\bar{X}_J = \bar{Y}\Sigma X = \Sigma\bar{Y}X$$
$$\Sigma\overline{XY}_J = \bar{X}\Sigma\bar{Y}_J = \bar{X}\Sigma Y = \Sigma\bar{X}Y$$

Therefore the numerator may be rewritten

$$\Sigma XY - \Sigma\bar{X}Y - \Sigma\bar{Y}X + \Sigma\overline{XY}$$

By collecting terms, the numerator equals

$$\Sigma(X - \bar{X})(Y - \bar{Y})$$

By substitution into Equation D.7, the standard formula for the total correlation results:

$$r_{TXY} = \frac{\Sigma(X - \bar{X})(Y - \bar{Y})}{\sqrt{\Sigma(X - \bar{X})^2 \Sigma(Y - \bar{Y})^2}}$$

This proof of the WABA equation is totally compatible with Robinson's (1950) result.

6. CORRELATIONS OF TOTAL *X* WITH BETWEEN-*Y* OR WITHIN-*Y* SCORES

As indicated in Chapter 12, all correlations of total deviations with between-cell or within-cell deviation scores are determined by the correlations in the WABA equation. A proof that a correlation between one variable (such as X) expressed as a total score $(X - \bar{X})$ and a second variable (such as Y) expressed as a between-cell score $(\bar{Y}_J - \bar{Y})$ is exactly equal to the multiplication of a between-eta correlation (η_{BX}) by the between-cell correlation (r_{BXY}) should be sufficient to illustrate a general procedure that results in proofs that all correlations are a function of the correlations in the WABA equation.

Specifically, an assertion can be stated as follows:

$$r_{TBXY} = \eta_{BX} r_{BXY} \qquad \qquad \textbf{(D.8)}$$

or that

$$\frac{\Sigma(X - \bar{X})(\bar{Y}_J - \bar{Y})}{\sqrt{\Sigma(X - \bar{X})^2 \Sigma(\bar{Y}_J - \bar{Y})^2}} = \frac{\sqrt{\Sigma(\bar{X}_J - \bar{X})^2}}{\sqrt{\Sigma(X - \bar{X})^2}} \frac{\Sigma(\bar{X}_J - \bar{X})(\bar{Y}_J - \bar{Y})}{\sqrt{\Sigma(\bar{X}_J - \bar{X})^2 \Sigma(\bar{Y}_J - \bar{Y})^2}}$$

$$= \frac{\Sigma(\bar{X}_J - \bar{X})(\bar{Y}_J - \bar{Y})}{\sqrt{\Sigma(X - \bar{X})^2 \Sigma(\bar{Y}_J - \bar{Y})^2}}$$

The denominators for the formulas are identical; therefore, only the equality of the numerators remains to be demonstrated:

$$\Sigma(X - \bar{X})(\bar{Y}_J - \bar{Y}) = \Sigma(\bar{X}_J - \bar{X})(\bar{Y}_J - \bar{Y})$$

These terms can be expanded as follows:

$$\Sigma(X\bar{Y}_J - \bar{Y}_J\bar{X} - X\bar{Y} + \overline{XY}) = \Sigma(\bar{X}_J\bar{Y}_J - \bar{Y}_J\bar{X} - \bar{X}_J\bar{Y} + \overline{YX})$$

By combining and canceling terms the following equality remains to be shown:

$$\Sigma X\bar{Y}_J - \Sigma X\bar{Y} = \Sigma \bar{X}_J \bar{Y}_J - \Sigma \bar{X}_J \bar{Y}$$

From Equations C.3 and C.5, the following holds:

$$\Sigma X\bar{Y}_J = \Sigma \bar{X}_J \bar{Y}_J$$
$$\Sigma X\bar{Y} = \Sigma \bar{X}_J \bar{Y}$$

Therefore, the original assertion holds, namely:

$$r_{TBXY} = \eta_{BX} r_{BXY}$$

The same procedure can be employed to prove all of the three remaining assertions presented in Chapter 12.

TABLE D.1. Demonstration of the independence of between- and within-cell correlations

	CELL I		CELL II		
	A	B	C	D	SUMMATION
Variable X					
Scores X	1	2	3	4	10
Total average $\bar{X}$	2.5	2.5	2.5	2.5	10
Cell average $\bar{X}_J$	1.5	1.5	3.5	3.5	10
Total deviations $X - \bar{X}$	-1.5	-0.5	0.5	1.5	0
Between deviations $\bar{X}_J - \bar{X}$	-1.0	-1.0	1.0	1.0	0
Within deviations $X - \bar{X}_J$	-0.5	0.5	-0.5	0.5	0
Squared (B) deviations $(\bar{X}_J - \bar{X})^2$	1.0	1.0	1.0	1.0	4
Squared (W) deviations $(X - \bar{X}_J)^2$	0.25	0.25	0.25	0.25	1
Squared total $(X - \bar{X})^2$	2.25	0.25	0.25	2.25	5
Variable Y					
Scores Y	5	6	3	4	18
Total average $\bar{Y}$	4.5	4.5	4.5	4.5	18
Cell average $\bar{Y}_J$	5.5	5.5	3.5	3.5	18
Total deviations $Y - \bar{Y}$	0.5	1.5	-1.5	-0.5	0
Between deviations $\bar{Y}_J - \bar{Y}$	1.0	1.0	-1.0	-1.0	0
Within deviations $Y - \bar{Y}_J$	-0.5	0.5	-0.5	0.5	0
Squared (B) deviations $(\bar{Y}_J - \bar{Y})^2$	1.0	1.0	1.0	1.0	4
Squared (W) deviations $(Y - \bar{Y}_J)^2$	0.25	0.25	0.25	0.25	1
Squared total $(Y - \bar{Y})^2$	0.25	2.25	2.25	0.25	5
Variables X and Y					
Within $(X - \bar{X}_J)(Y - \bar{Y}_J)$	0.25	0.25	0.25	0.25	1
Between $(\bar{X}_J - \bar{X})(\bar{Y}_J - \bar{Y})$	-1.0	-1.0	-1.0	-1.0	-4
Correlations					

Within r_{WXY} $\quad \left[\Sigma(X - \bar{X}_J)(Y - \bar{Y}_J) \right] \Big/ \sqrt{\Sigma(X - \bar{X}_J)^2 \Sigma(Y - \bar{Y}_J)^2} = \dfrac{1}{\sqrt{(1)(1)}} = +1$

Between r_{BXY} $\quad \left[\Sigma(\bar{X}_J - \bar{X})(\bar{Y}_J - \bar{Y}) \right] \Big/ \sqrt{\Sigma(\bar{X}_J - \bar{X})^2 \Sigma(\bar{Y}_J - \bar{Y})^2} = \dfrac{-4}{\sqrt{(4)(4)}} = -1$

7. INDEPENDENCE OF BETWEEN- AND WITHIN-CELL CORRELATIONS

The independence of the within- and between-cell correlations can be proven by simply illustrating in one case that a between-cell correlation can equal -1 and at the same time a within-cell correlation can equal $+1$. As a result of such a demonstration, one correlation is shown to be able to take on any value independent of the value taken on by the other correlation. This independence is demonstrated with an oversimplified example, presented in Table D.1.

APPENDIX E   DEGREES OF FREEDOM

1. Deviation Scores
2. Total Correlations
3. Between- and Within-Cell Deviations
4. Eta Correlations
5. Between- and Within-Cell Correlations

When degrees of freedom equal zero, the value of a particular indicator or score is known to be a function of the characteristics of the indicator and not of the data being examined. The degrees of freedom described in this book correspond to the formulas given in the majority of statistics books. From our perspective, degrees of freedom are mathematically determined, independent of inference processes, because they are properties of particular indicators.

1. DEVIATION SCORES

The sum of signed deviation scores always equals zero. Mathematically,

$$\Sigma(X - \bar{X}) = \Sigma\left(X - \frac{\Sigma X}{N}\right)$$

which can be rewritten by distributing the summation sign as

$$\Sigma X - \Sigma\left(\frac{\Sigma X}{N}\right)$$

However, an average (the $\Sigma X/N$ component) is a constant over all scores. The summation of a constant number equals that number multiplied by the number (N) of times it appears, so that

$$\Sigma X - N\left(\frac{\Sigma X}{N}\right) = \Sigma X - \Sigma X = 0$$

Essentially, when all but one of the signed deviation scores $(N - 1)$ are known, the value of the remaining score is determined. Therefore, signed deviation scores have $N - 1$ degrees of freedom where N equals the number of scores.

For example, consider the following set of signed deviation scores:

$$-2 \quad -1 \quad 0 \quad 1 \quad 2$$

If any four of these five scores $(N - 1 = 4)$ are known, the fifth score is obtained by using the following equation, where $\Sigma(d)$ is the sum of all but one deviation:

$$\Sigma(d) + K = 0$$

In contrast, if only three scores are known, the remaining two scores cannot be obtained.

2. TOTAL CORRELATIONS

The degrees of freedom for a total correlation can be derived in a similar way. Specifically, given only two ($N = 2$) pairs of scores on two variables (X and Y), the total correlation must equal one. Given just two pairs of scores (X_1 and Y_1; X_2 and Y_2), the correlation is written as:

$$
\begin{aligned}
r_{TXY} &= \frac{\Sigma(X - \bar{X})(Y - \bar{Y})}{\sqrt{\Sigma(X - \bar{X})^2 \Sigma(Y - \bar{Y})^2}} \\
&= \frac{(X_1 - \bar{X})(Y_1 - \bar{Y}) + (X_2 - \bar{X})(Y_2 - \bar{Y})}{\sqrt{\left[(X_1 - \bar{X})^2 + (X_2 - \bar{X})^2\right]\left[(Y_1 - \bar{Y})^2 + (Y_2 - \bar{Y})^2\right]}}
\end{aligned}
\quad \text{(E.1)}
$$

In this case, the averages can be written as $\bar{X} = (X_1 + X_2)/2$ and $\bar{Y} = (Y_1 + Y_2)/2$. Then, by substitution, Equation E.1 reduces to

$$
r_{TXY} = \frac{(X_1 - X_2)(Y_1 - Y_2) + (X_2 - X_1)(Y_2 - Y_1)}{\sqrt{\left[(X_1 - X_2)^2 + (X_2 - X_1)^2\right]\left[(Y_1 - Y_2)^2 + (Y_2 - Y_1)^2\right]}} \frac{\sqrt{4}}{2}
$$

Assume the following definitions:

$$
\begin{aligned}
k_x &= (X_1 - X_2) \\
-k_x &= (X_2 - X_1) \\
k_y &= (Y_1 - Y_2) \\
-k_y &= (Y_2 - Y_1)
\end{aligned}
$$

By substitution, Equation E.1 is written as:

$$
\begin{aligned}
r_{TXY} &= \frac{(k_x)(k_y) + (-k_x)(-k_y)}{\sqrt{\left[k_x^2 + (-k_x)^2\right]\left[k_y^2 + (-k_y)^2\right]}} \\
&= \frac{2k_x k_y}{\sqrt{4k_x^2 k_y^2}} = \pm 1
\end{aligned}
$$

Clearly, when two scores on variable X and two scores on variable Y are correlated, the *magnitude* of the correlation must always equal one. In other words, given two pairs of scores ($N = 2$), there are no degrees of freedom, and a correlation with a magnitude of one is always obtained. Thus a correlation has $N - 2$ degrees of freedom.

3.   BETWEEN- AND WITHIN-CELL DEVIATIONS

Within each cell, the sum of the within-cell deviation scores must equal zero. Therefore the degrees of freedom within each cell equal $n - 1$, where n equals the total number of scores in that cell. The summation of degrees of freedom for each cell across all cells equals $\sum_{j}(n - 1)$, which in turn can be rewritten as

$$\sum_{j} n - \sum_{j} 1 = N - J$$

where N equals the total number of scores across all cells and J equals the number of cells. The between-cell deviation scores do not differ within cells, but only between cells. Therefore, given J cells, the between-cell deviations have $J - 1$ degrees of freedom. The total deviation scores, which have $N - 1$ degrees of freedom, equal the between-cell plus within-cell deviations, or

$$\text{Total} = \text{between} + \text{within}$$
$$N - 1 = (J - 1) + (N - J)$$

4.   ETA CORRELATIONS

The between-eta correlation (η_B) is equal to the correlation of the total deviations with the between-cell deviations. If there is only one cell, the total deviations are represented by the within-cell deviations, the between-eta correlation equals zero, and the within-eta correlation equals one. Therefore, the between-eta correlation equals zero when $J = 1$. If there are as many scores as cells ($N = J$), all within-cell deviations equal zero (all are equal to the average), the within-eta correlation is fixed at zero, and the between-eta correlation equals one. Therefore, both correlations must be considered simultaneously, and the degrees of freedom are $J - 1$ and $N - J$.

5.   BETWEEN- AND WITHIN-CELL CORRELATIONS

Since the between-cell deviation scores have $J - 1$ degrees of freedom, the between-cell correlation is analogous to the general case where the total deviations have $N - 1$ degrees of freedom and the correlation has $N - 2$ degrees of freedom. Therefore, the between-cell correlation has $J - 2$ degrees of freedom. The within-cell correlations are generally, though not always, thought to have $N - J - 1$ degrees of freedom. The accuracy of this formula can be illustrated in the following way. When the number of cells equals the number of scores, there is one score for each cell and all the within-cell deviation scores on X and Y equal zero. When only one cell contains two scores and all others contain one score, there will be one degree of freedom for the within-cell deviation scores ($N - J = 1$), and deviations occur only within one cell. In this case, however, the within-cell correlation is based on two pairs of scores on X and Y in one cell and must equal one. As a result, within-cell correlations have $N - J - 1$ degrees of freedom.

APPENDIX F   TRADITIONAL APPLICATIONS OF WABA

1. Analysis of Variance
2. Correlation and Multiple Regression

To illustrate several contemporary data analytic procedures, a mathematical articulation of the way in which WABA links the analysis of variance and correlational analysis is presented in this appendix. A discussion of the implications of WABA for multivariate analysis is presented in Chapter 13.

1.   ANALYSIS OF VARIANCE

The purpose of a one-way analysis of variance is to calculate the relationship between an independent variable (X) and a dependent variable (Y). As a result, cells usually are not formed based on a hypothesis about entities. Instead, cells are formed by values taken on by at least one independent variable. For example, one variable may take on five different values (such as $1, 2, 3, 4, 5$) and define five different cells. In a similar fashion, in a laboratory study an independent variable may equal zero for one (control) condition and take on some other value or values in an experimental condition. As a result of this construction of cells, an independent variable X varies only between cells and not within cells. In other words, the between-cell eta correlation on an independent variable equals one ($\eta_{BX} = 1$). The within-cell eta correlation equals zero ($\eta_{WX} = 0$). In addition, a within-cell correlation of a dependent variable with an independent variable must equal zero ($r_{WXY} = 0$). By substitution, the WABA equation is written

$$r_{TXY} = 1\eta_{BY}r_{BXY} + (0)(\eta_{WY})(0)$$

In this application of WABA, interest is in the relationship between two variables X and Y. Therefore, deviations of Y within cells are considered error, because these within-cell deviations must be correlated zero with the independent variable and must represent variation in Y independent of X. Since within-eta correlations are a function of between-eta correlations, $\left(\sqrt{1 - \eta_{WY}^2} = \eta_{BY}\right)$, information is not lost by ignoring within-cell deviations on a dependent variable (η_{WY}) and focusing on only the between-eta correlation (η_{BY}). The WABA equation is then written as follows for a one-way analysis of variance:

$$r_{TXY} = \eta_{BY}r_{BXY} \qquad (F.1)$$

As should be apparent from this equation, between-cell deviation scores determine the total correlation (r_{TXY}). Since between-cell deviation scores are based on averages, the analysis of variance is typically described in terms of tests of the difference between means. We prefer to retain a more general perspective and view the analysis of variance in terms of between-cell deviation scores. The following three examples demonstrate various linkages between the ANOVA and correlations.

First, if an independent variable (X) forms only two cells, then the between-cell correlation (r_{BXY}) must equal one, since the degrees of freedom equal zero $(J - 2 = 0)$. Therefore, Equation F.1 is rewritten

$$r_{TXY} = \eta_{BY}$$

In this case, the value for the correlation between the two variables is identical to the value for the between-eta correlation. An illustration of the exact mathematical linkage between the analysis of variance and correlations in this special case may be helpful at this point. Specifically, consider the set of scores shown in the upper portion of Table F.1. In this example, a value for the *total* correlation is determined as follows:

$$r_{TXY} = \frac{\Sigma(X - \bar{X})(Y - \bar{Y})}{\sqrt{\Sigma(X - \bar{X})^2 \Sigma(Y - \bar{Y})^2}}$$

$$r_{TXY} = \frac{2.00}{\sqrt{(1)(5)}} = 0.8944$$

Using the same set of scores, cells can be aligned with values for variable X, and the WABA calculations are performed as shown in the lower portion of Table F.1. The between-cell eta correlation is calculated as follows:

$$\eta_{BY} = \sqrt{\eta_{BY}^2} = \frac{\sqrt{\Sigma(\bar{Y}_J - \bar{Y})^2}}{\sqrt{\Sigma(Y - \bar{Y})^2}} = \frac{\sqrt{4}}{\sqrt{5}} = \sqrt{0.8} = 0.8944$$

This case can be summarized using WABA I and II, as shown in the upper portion of Table F.2. WABA, of course, provides both the total correlation and the eta correlations.

Therefore, in the case in which two cells are constructed and dummy coding is used, the total and between-eta correlations are identical. In this special case with two cells $(J = 2)$, the F ratio is written

$$F = \frac{\eta_{BY}^2}{1 - \eta_{BY}^2} \frac{N - 2}{2 - 1} = \frac{\eta_{BY}^2}{1 - \eta_{BY}^2}(N - 2)$$

Taking the square root of the F ratio,

$$\sqrt{F} = \frac{\eta_{BY}}{\sqrt{1 - \eta_{BY}^2}} \sqrt{N - 2}$$

Substituting the total correlation for the eta correlation, since $r_{TXY} = \eta_{BY}$,

$$\sqrt{F} = \frac{r_{TXY}}{\sqrt{1 - r_{TXY}^2}} \sqrt{N - 2} = t$$

TABLE F.1. Illustration of calculations for a total correlation and a between-eta correlation for one data se

| | CELL 1 | | CELL 2 | | |
	A	B	C	D	SUMMATION
Calculations for a Total Correlation					
Independent variable					
X	0	0	1	1	2
$X - \bar{X}$	−0.5	−0.5	0.5	0.5	0
$(X - \bar{X})^2$	0.25	0.25	0.25	0.25	1
Dependent variable					
Y	1	2	3	4	10
$Y - \bar{Y}$	−1.5	−0.5	0.5	1.5	0
$(Y - \bar{Y})^2$	2.25	0.25	0.25	2.25	5
Cross products					
$(X - \bar{X})(Y - \bar{Y})$	0.75	0.25	0.25	0.75	2
Calculations for an Eta Correlation					
Scores (Y)	1	2	3	4	10
Total average $(\bar{Y})$	2.5	2.5	2.5	2.5	10
Cell average $(\bar{Y}_J)$	1.5	1.5	3.5	3.5	10
Total deviation					
$(Y - \bar{Y})$	−1.5	−0.5	0.5	1.5	0
Between deviation					
$(\bar{Y}_J - \bar{Y})$	−1.0	−1.0	1.0	1.0	0
Within deviation					
$(Y - \bar{Y}_J)$	−0.5	0.5	−0.5	0.5	0
Squared between deviation					
$(\bar{Y}_J - \bar{Y})^2$	1.0	1.0	1.0	1.0	4
Squared total deviation					
$(Y - \bar{Y})^2$	2.25	0.25	0.25	2.25	5

TABLE F.2. Summaries of data in WABA terms

| | WABA I | | | WABA II | |
Indicators	Variable X	Variable Y	Indicators	Obtained Values	Components
Summary of Results from Table F.1					
Between					
$\eta_B (df = 1)$	1.00	0.8944	r_{BXY}	1.00	(1)(0.8944)(1)
Within					
$\eta_W (df = 2)$	0.00	0.4472	r_{WXY}	0.00	(0)(0.4472)(0)
E ratio	∞	2.00	A	∞	
F ratio	∞	8.00	Z	∞	
Total of components r_{TXY}					0.8944
Summary of Results from Table F.3					
Between					
$\eta_B (df = 2)$	1	1	r_{BXY}	0	(1)(1)(0)
Within					
$\eta_W (df = 3)$	0	0	r_{WXY}	0	(0)(0)(0)
E ratio	∞	∞	A	0	
F ratio	∞	∞	Z	0	
Total of components r_{TXY}					0

We have just shown that the square root of the F ratio equals a t test in this case. This suggests that an F ratio is a test of the significance of one correlation.

Because of this special case, some methodologists seem to imply that dummy coding (the creation of only two cells) is one way to express the ANOVA in correlational form. Although that is correct, the analysis of variance is not restricted to the special case in which an independent variable takes on only two values.

Consider a second case in which three cells are defined by the values of an independent variable and in which the between-eta correlation equals one. In this special case the total correlation (r_{TXY}) between X and Y equals the between-cell correlation, or

$$r_{TXY} = r_{BXY}$$

An illustration of this case is presented in Table F.3.

The data shown in Table F.3 can be summarized in terms of WABA I and II, as shown in the lower portion of Table F.2. In this example, the between-eta correlation equals one and the total correlation equals zero. In

TABLE F.3.   Calculations for special ANOVA case

	CELL 1		CELL 2		CELL 3		
	A	B	C	D	E	F	SUMMATION
Variable X							
X	1	1	2	2	3	3	12
$\bar{X}$	2	2	2	2	2	2	12
$\bar{X}_J$	1	1	2	2	3	3	12
$X - \bar{X}$	-1	-1	0	0	1	1	0
$\bar{X}_J - \bar{X}$	-1	-1	0	0	1	1	0
$X - \bar{X}_J$	0	0	0	0	0	0	0
$(X - \bar{X})^2$	1	1	0	0	1	1	4
$(X - \bar{X}_J)^2$	0	0	0	0	0	0	0
$(\bar{X}_J - \bar{X})^2$	1	1	0	0	1	1	4
Variable Y							
Y	2	2	1	1	2	2	10
$\bar{Y}$	1.67	1.67	1.67	1.67	1.67	1.67	10
$\bar{Y}_J$	2.0	2.0	1.0	1.0	2.0	2.0	10
$Y - \bar{Y}$	0.33	0.33	-0.66	-0.66	0.33	0.33	0
$\bar{Y}_J - \bar{Y}$	0.33	0.33	-0.66	-0.66	0.33	0.33	0
$Y - \bar{Y}_J$	0	0	0	0	0	0	0
$(Y - \bar{Y})^2$	0.1089	0.1089	0.4356	0.4356	0.1089	0.1089	1.307
$(\bar{Y}_J - \bar{Y})^2$	0.1089	0.1089	0.4356	0.4356	0.1089	0.1089	1.307
$(Y - \bar{Y}_J)^2$	0	0	0	0	0	0	0
Cross products							
$(X - \bar{X})(Y - \bar{Y})$	-0.33	-0.33	0	0	0.33	0.33	0
$(X - \bar{X}_J)(Y - \bar{Y}_J)$	0	0	0	0	0	0	0
$(\bar{X}_J - \bar{X})(\bar{Y}_J - \bar{Y})$	-0.33	-0.33	0	0	0.33	0.33	0

addition, the F ratios for the eta correlations are undefined or approach infinity. In terms of WABA II, the between-cell correlation and total correlation equal zero. If a t test were performed on the total correlation or the between-cell correlation, the results would indicate a lack of relationship ($r_{TXY} = r_{BXY} = 0$). In contrast, the F ratio for the analysis of variance indicates a relationship of one ($\eta_{BY} = 1$). This appears to suggest that correlational and the analysis of variance procedures provide different results. Actually, the effect indicated by the significant eta correlation can be translated into a correlation in the following way. Specifically, the means for variable Y result in the following graph:

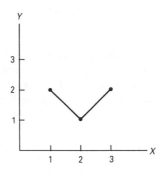

Such a graph is appropriate because in this case, the means totally represent the scores on the dependent variable ($\eta_{BY} = 1$). The following expression can be used to correct the X scores and create a linear relationship:

$$X^2 - 4X + 4$$

In cell 1, X is converted to a value of 1 ($1^2 - 4 + 4 = 1$). In cell 2, X is converted to a value of 0 ($4 - 8 + 4 = 0$). In cell 3, X is converted to a value of 1 ($9 - 12 + 4 = 1$). Therefore, the same case can be rewritten as:

	CELL 1		CELL 2		CELL 3	
	A	**B**	**C**	**D**	**E**	**F**
New variable X	1	1	0	0	1	1
$X - \bar{X}$	0.33	0.33	−0.66	−0.66	0.33	0.33
Variable Y	2	2	1	1	2	2
$Y - \bar{Y}$	0.33	0.33	−0.66	−0.66	0.33	0.33

Notice that based on this conversion, the total deviation scores on X and Y are equal. The same result occurs for the between-cell scores. The result of a calculation of the correlation of the new X values with the old Y values is a total correlation of one.

Essentially, a functional relationship was employed to convert the zero (curvilinear) total correlation between X and Y into one that is linear. By using this transformation, the eta correlation of one is captured in the new total correlation. We have just illustrated that the use of correlations is not limited to the assessment of linear relationships. By transforming variables, correlations can be used to assess a variety of functional relationships. In this book, however, only linear relationships are considered in order to simplify the presentation.

Nevertheless, this second special case of WABA illustrates another way in which the correlation and analysis of variance are linked. In this case, note that an F ratio of the eta correlation is not equal to a t test for the total correlation. However, by using a transformation, these two tests can be made to give equal results.

A final case of special interest occurs when both the between-cell correlation and the between-eta correlation contribute to the total correlation:

$$r_{TXY} = \eta_{BY} r_{BXY}$$

This situation occurs when there are more than two cells and the between-cell eta correlation for variable Y is not equal to one. Then it may not be possible to calculate a between-cell correlation, or the calculation may be meaningless because an independent variable X is a categorical variable (such as cell 1 = apples, cell 2 = oranges, cell 3 = plums). In such cases, the between-eta correlation (η_{BY}) is typically used as the basis for tests. When possible, however, a between-cell correlation should be calculated and a complete WABA presented in order to test fully the correlation between X and Y. Although various adjustments have been suggested for eta correlations, in fact the actual correlation in a data set can be obtained by using a complete set of indicators from WABA. In the case of categorical variables, the eta correlations are tested by the F ratio, as follows:

$$F = \frac{\eta_{BY}^2}{1 - \eta_{BY}^2} \frac{N - J}{J - 1}$$

In the three applications of WABA presented thus far, the F ratio has been shown to be a test of a particular correlation. An example of the implications of this characteristic of the F ratio illustrates an important point. Consider an analysis of variance with 1,002 cases in two cells and an obtained between-eta correlation of 0.10. In this case, the between-cell degrees of freedom ($J - 1$) equal one, and the within-cell degrees of freedom ($N - J$) equal 1,000. The resulting E ratio equals 0.10.

$$E = \frac{0.10}{\sqrt{1 - 0.10^2}} = 0.10$$

The F ratio is

$$F = (0.01) \frac{(1,000)}{1} = 10$$

In this illustrative case, 99 percent of the variance in the total deviations is contained in the within-cell scores ($\eta^2_W = 0.99$). This is indicated by the E ratio of 0.10. In contrast, the F ratio is substantially larger than 1.

The key point illustrated by this example is that in the traditional one-way analysis of variance, an F ratio is a test of the magnitude of the between-eta correlation and is not a test of the degree to which between- or within-cell deviations represent the total deviations. This is not a criticism of the analysis of variance or the F ratio. However, our interest in the varient paradigm is in testing whether the between-cell or the within-cell deviations better represent a set of total deviation scores. In our approach, unlike the analysis of variance, cells are not formed by scores on a variable, but rather by collecting individuals into cells. Therefore, we have no reason to ignore within-cell deviations or to treat them as error. As a result, the traditional one-way analysis of variance model is inappropriate. In varient analysis, a decision is made before employing an F ratio as to whether it is the between-cell eta correlation whose statistical significance is to be tested. Therefore, the examination of an F ratio is always preceded by examination of an E ratio. Although the WABA equation is totally consistent with the analysis of variance and permits the expression of the ANOVA in correlational terms, WABA is not limited to the analysis of variance.

2. CORRELATION AND MULTIPLE REGRESSION

Another way to illustrate WABA is to use a multiple-regression formulation. The eta correlations are mathematically identical to the standardized beta weights that would be obtained in a multiple regression in which the two independent variables are the between- and within-cell deviation scores, and the dependent variable is the total deviation score

$$\eta_{BY}(\overline{Y}_J - \overline{Y}) + \eta_{WY}(Y - \overline{Y}_J) = (Y - \overline{Y}) \qquad \textbf{(F.2)}$$

where the eta correlations are standardized regression coefficients. This is the case because the between- and within-cell scores are independent ($r_{BWY} = 0$). When this occurs, the standardized beta weights equal the correlation of each independent variable with the dependent variable (Guilford, 1965). Moreover, the total multiple correlation equals one in this case because the sum of the squared beta weights equals one. This multiple-regression formulation can be employed for a second variable X as follows:

$$\eta_{BX}(\overline{X}_J - \overline{X}) + \eta_{WX}(X - \overline{X}_J) = (X - \overline{X}) \qquad \textbf{(F.3)}$$

In the case of a one-way analysis of variance (given that X is an independent variable), Equation F.3 reduces to

$$(1)(\overline{X}_J - \overline{X}) = (X - \overline{X})$$

This equation is simply another way to state that all the variation in an independent variable $(X - \bar{X})$ occurs only between cells $(\bar{X}_J - \bar{X})$. In contrast, Equation F.2 remains the same and is an exact mathematical representation of a one-way analysis of variance in multiple-regression terms using the dependent variable.

In varient analysis, both Equations F.2 and F.3 must be considered because cells are not constructed based on a variable. This multiple-regression formulation illustrates another point about the use of the F ratio. The F ratio for the between (F_B) and within (F_W) beta weights is written as follows:

$$F_B = \frac{\eta_B^2}{\eta_W^2}\frac{N-J}{J-1} \quad \text{and} \quad F_W = \frac{\eta_W^2}{\eta_B^2}\frac{J-1}{N-J}$$

Notice, however, that the inverse of one F ratio equals the other F ratio:

$$F_B = \frac{1}{F_W}$$

Therefore, only one of these terms is necessary. The formula we use for the F ratio has the following characteristic: As the F ratio approaches zero, the within-cell correlation is approaching one $(F \rightarrow 0, \eta_W \rightarrow 1)$. Likewise, as the F ratio approaches infinity, the between-eta correlation approaches one $(F \rightarrow \infty, \eta_B \rightarrow 1)$. Therefore, one formula is used as a test of either the within- or the between-eta correlation.

In addition to Equations F.2 and F.3, the WABA equation includes within- and between-cell correlations that can also be expressed in terms of beta weights. In other words, the WABA equation can be viewed as including six beta weights, all of which are examined separately by comparing within-cell to between-cell indicators. Our choice to use bivariate (within and between) correlations, rather than two multiple regressions (within and between), is the result of traditional caveats that bivariate correlations should be considered before using multiple regression. In other words, after an examination of the network of relationships among a set of variables, one multiple-regression equation based on within-cell and another based on between-cell deviation scores can be examined. An attempt, however, to formulate the WABA equation in multiple-regression terms is problematic. The WABA equation contains correlations, not variables. The application of WABA to multiple regression is presented in Chapter 13.

APPENDIX G: MEASURES USED AT MCO

THEORY A MEASURES

Subordinate Reports

Titles
   Professional Associations (PA)
   Education (Ed)
Expectations
   Freedom from Machines (FM)
   Freedom from Superior (FS)
   Freedom Preferences (FP)

THEORY B MEASURES

Subordinate Reports

Superior Investments–Subordinate Returns
   Attention (AT)
   Latitude (LA)
Subordinate Investments–Superior Returns
   Superior Satisfaction with Subordinate (SS)
   Subordinate Congruence with Superior (SC)

Superior Reports

Superior Investments–Subordinate Returns
   Attention (AT)
   Latitude (LA)
Subordinate Investments–Superior Returns
   Superior Satisfaction with Subordinate (SS)
   Subordinate Congruence with Superior (SC)

THEORY A MEASURES

Subordinate Reports

Titles
   Professional Associations (PA)
      To how many professional or trade associations do you belong?
   Education (Ed)

Please circle highest level of education attained

1. Some high school
2. High school diploma
3. Technical training
4. Some college
5. College degree (B.S., B.A., etc.)
6. Some graduate work
7. Graduate degree (M.A., M.B.A., Ph.D., etc.)

Expectations

Freedom from Machines ($\alpha = 0.79$) (FM)

To what extent do machines determine the order in which you do things while on the job?

A great deal	Some	Little	Not at all
(1)	(2)	(3)	(4)

To what extent do machines determine the pace at which you work while on the job?

A great deal	Some	Little	Not at all

Freedom from Superior ($\alpha = 0.67$) (FS)

How often does your immediate supervisor check what you are doing or closely observe your work?

Never	Seldom	Occasionally	Quite often	Always
(5)	(4)	(3)	(2)	(1)

What percent of your activities does your immediate supervisor determine or directly influence on a typical work day?

0–20% (Almost none)	21–40% (Little)	41–60% (Some)	61–80% (Fair amount)	81–100% (Almost all)
(5)	(4)	(3)	(2)	(1)

To what extent do explicit rules, regulations, or policies determine or directly influence what you do on an average workday?

Never	Seldom	Occasionally	Quite often	Always

How often does your immediate supervisor insist that you follow standard procedures and practices?

Never	Seldom	Occasionally	Quite often	Always

Freedom Preferences ($\alpha = 0.86$) (FP)

If a subordinate has been *Very Effective* in the past, a superior should be willing to allow him to:

Make *minor* changes in his job.

Strongly agree (1)	Agree (2)	Slightly agree (3)	Slightly disagree (4)	Disagree (5)	Strongly disagree (6)

Make *major* changes in his job.

Strongly agree	Agree	Slightly agree	Slightly disagree	Disagree	Strongly disagree

Make *minor* changes in his job as long as those changes have "little cost for other areas outside the immediate work unit."

Strongly agree	Agree	Slightly agree	Slightly disagree	Disagree	Strongly disagree

Continue implementing *minor* changes in his job as long as he had "previously spoken to his superior about those changes."

Strongly agree	Agree	Slightly agree	Slightly disagree	Disagree	Strongly disagree

Continue implementing *minor* changes in his job as long as he had "not previously spoken to his superior about those changes."

Strongly agree	Agree	Slightly agree	Slightly disagree	Disagree	Strongly disagree

Continue implementing *major* changes in his job as long as he had "previously spoken to his superior about those changes."

Strongly agree	Agree	Slightly agree	Slightly disagree	Disagree	Strongly disagree

Continue implementing *major* changes in his job as long as he had "not previously spoken to his superior about those changes."

Strongly agree	Agree	Slightly agree	Slightly disagree	Disagree	Strongly disagree

Make *minor* changes in his job as long as those changes have "little impact on how the superior does his own job."

Strongly agree	Agree	Slightly agree	Slightly disagree	Disagree	Strongly disagree

Make *minor* changes in his job even if those changes have "a major impact on how his superior does his own job."

Strongly agree	Agree	Slightly agree	Slightly disagree	Disagree	Strongly disagree

Make *major* changes in his job as long as those changes have "little impact on how the superior does his own job."

Strongly agree	Agree	Slightly agree	Slightly disagree	Disagree	Strongly disagree

Make *major* changes in his job even if those changes have "a major impact on how the superior does his own job."

Strongly agree	Agree	Slightly agree	Slightly disagree	Disagree	Strongly disagree

THEORY B MEASURES

Subordinate Reports

Superior Investments–Subordinate Returns

Attention ($\alpha = 0.92$) (AT)

Input into decisions that affect my work given by superior.

Amount: (Circle one)	Almost none (1)	A little (2)	A fair amount (3)	Quite a bit (4)	A great deal (5)

Information from my superior about his assessment of my job performance.

Amount: (Circle one)	Almost none	A little	A fair amount	Quite a bit	A great deal

Assurance by my superior that he has confidence in my integrity, motivation, and ability.

Amount: (Circle one)	Almost none	A little	A fair amount	Quite a bit	A great deal

Attention by my superior to my feelings and needs.

Amount: (Circle one)	Almost none	A little	A fair amount	Quite a bit	A great deal

Information from my superior about the current and future state of our unit and/or division and my position in the unit.

Amount: (*Circle one*)	Almost none	A little	A fair amount	Quite a bit	A great deal

Support by my superior for my actions and ideas.

Amount: (*Circle one*)	Almost none	A little	A fair amount	Quite a bit	A great deal

Information from my superior about the scope of my job duties and authority.

Amount: (*Circle one*)	Almost none	A little	A fair amount	Quite a bit	A great deal

Freedom in doing my job from superior.

Amount: (*Circle one*)	Almost none	A little	A fair amount	Quite a bit	A great deal

Serious consideration by my superior of my suggestions and ideas.

Amount: (*Circle one*)	Almost none	A little	A fair amount	Quite a bit	A great deal

Encouragement by my superior to solve problems and generate new ideas.

Amount: (*Circle one*)	Almost none	A little	A fair amount	Quite a bit	A great deal

Explanations by my superior of the reasons behind programs and practices.

Amount: (*Circle one*)	Almost none	A little	A fair amount	Quite a bit	A great deal

Latitude ($\alpha = 0.91$) (LA)

In general, would your immediate superior let you implement "minor" changes you wanted to make in your job?

Certainly (4)	Probably (3)	Probably not (2)	No chance (1)

In general, would your immediate superior let you implement "major" changes you wanted to make in your job?

Certainly	Probably	Probably not	No chance

Would your immediate superior tend to let you implement "minor" changes in your job as long as those changes involved little cost to other areas outside your department?

> Certainly   Probably   Probably not   No chance

Would your immediate superior tend to let you implement "minor" changes in your job if you had previously spoken to him about those changes?

> Certainly   Probably   Probably not   No chance

Would your immediate superior tend to let you implement "minor" changes in your job even if you had not previously spoken to him about those changes?

> Certainly   Probably   Probably not   No chance

Would your immediate superior tend to let you implement "major" changes in your job if you had previously spoken to him about those changes?

> Certainly   Probably   Probably not   No chance

Would your immediate superior tend to let you implement "major" changes in your job if you had not previously spoken to him about those changes?

> Certainly   Probably   Probably not   No chance

Would your immediate superior tend to let you implement "minor" changes in your job as long as they had little impact on how he did his own job?

> Certainly   Probably   Probably not   No chance

Would your immediate superior tend to let you implement "minor" changes in your job even if those changes had a major impact on how he did his own job?

> Certainly   Probably   Probably not   No chance

Would your immediate superior tend to let you implement "major" changes in your job as long as they had little impact on how he did his own job?

> Certainly   Probably   Probably not   No chance

Would your immediate superior tend to let you implement "major" changes in your job even if they had a major impact on how he did his own job?

Certainly	Probably	Probably not	No chance

Subordinate Investments–Superior Returns

Superior Satisfaction with Subordinate (SS)

How satisfied do you think your superior is with your job performance? (*Circle one*)

Very dissatisfied	Dissatisfied	Neutral	Satisfied	Very satisfied
(1)	(2)	(3)	(4)	(5)

Subordinate Congruence with Superior (SC)

How often is the way you do your job in line with your superior's preferences? (*Circle one*)

Almost always	Usually	Fairly often	Occasionally	Seldom	Almost never
(6)	(5)	(4)	(3)	(2)	(1)

Superior Reports

Superior Investments–Subordinate Returns

Attention ($\alpha = 0.90$) (AT)

For each of the following questions please indicate how much (*insert name*) thinks you provide.

Input into decisions that affect his work.

Almost none	A little	A fair amount	Quite a bit	A great deal
(1)	(2)	(3)	(4)	(5)

Information from you regarding your assessment of his job performance.

Almost none	A little	A fair amount	Quite a bit	A great deal

Assurance that you have confidence in his integrity, motivation, and ability.

Almost none	A little	A fair amount	Quite a bit	A great deal

Attention by you to his feelings and needs.

Almost none	A little	A fair amount	Quite a bit	A great deal

Information from you about the current and future state of the unit and/or division and his position in the unit.

Almost none	A little	A fair amount	Quite a bit	A great deal

Support by you of his actions and ideas.

Almost none	A little	A fair amount	Quite a bit	A great deal

Information from you about the scope of his job duties and his authority.

Almost none	A little	A fair amount	Quite a bit	A great deal

Freedom in doing his job.

Almost none	A little	A fair amount	Quite a bit	A great deal

Serious consideration by you of his suggestions and ideas.

Almost none	A little	A fair amount	Quite a bit	A great deal

Encouragement by you for solving problems and generating ideas.

Almost none	A little	A fair amount	Quite a bit	A great deal

Explanations by you of the reasons behind programs and practices.

Almost none	A little	A fair amount	Quite a bit	A great deal

Latitude ($\alpha = 0.92$) (LA)

These questions concern how you might treat (*insert name*) under various conditions. Please circle the answer that best represents how you probably would react to him under each of the conditions listed below.

In general, would you tend to support this individual in implementing "minor" changes he wanted to make in his job?

Certainly (4)	Probably (3)	Probably not (2)	No chance (1)

In general, would you tend to support this individual in implementing "major" changes he wanted to make in his job?

        Certainly   Probably   Probably not   No chance

Would you tend to support this individual in implementing "minor" changes in his job as long as these changes involved little cost for other areas outside your department?

        Certainly   Probably   Probably not   No chance

Would you tend to support this individual in implementing "minor" changes in his job if he had previously spoken to you about them?

        Certainly   Probably   Probably not   No chance

Would you tend to support this individual in implementing "minor" changes in his job if he had not previously spoken to you about them?

        Certainly   Probably   Probably not   No chance

Would you tend to support this individual in implementing "major" changes in his job if he had previously spoken to you about them?

        Certainly   Probably   Probably not   No chance

Would you tend to support this individual in implementing "minor" changes in his job as long as these changes had little impact on how you do your own job?

        Certainly   Probably   Probably not   No chance

Would you tend to support this individual in implementing "minor" changes in his job even if these changes had a major impact on how you do your own job?

        Certainly   Probably   Probably not   No chance

Would you tend to support this individual in implementing "major" changes in his job as long as these changes had little impact on how you do your own job?

        Certainly   Probably   Probably not   No chance

Would you tend to support this individual in implementing "major" changes in his job even if he had not previously spoken to you about them?

        Certainly   Probably   Probably not   No chance

Would you tend to support this individual in implementing "major" changes in his job even if these changes had a major impact on how you do your own job?

Certainly   Probably   Probably not   No chance

Subordinate Investments–Superior Returns

Superior Satisfaction with Subordinate (SS)

Please answer these questions in terms of (*insert name*).

How satisfied are you with his job performance? (*Circle one*)

Very dissatisfied (1)	Dissatisfied (2)	Neutral (3)	Satisfied (4)	Very satisfied (5)

Subordinate Congruence with Superior (SC)

How often does this individual do his job the way *you* think he should? (*Circle one*)

Almost always (6)	Usually (5)	Fairly often (4)	Occasionally (3)	Seldom (2)	Almost never (1)

Note: All scales were formed by adding the values shown for each item which was checked. All alpha (α) coefficients are based on the reports of the 276 individuals. All of the managers at MCO were males; therefore, the terms "he" and "him" were employed.

APPENDIX H   COMPUTERIZED WABA

1. SPSS
2. FORTRAN

In addition to the traditional mathematical indicators associated with data analysis, others are available when a computer program is used to perform within and between analysis. Specifically, in program WABA (within and between analysis), it is necessary to code data such that each object (case) is identified by a unique individual descriptor (ID), as well as a group, cluster, or cell indicator (CID).

These identification variables are then followed by values of other variables of interest. This standard approach to coding data is illustrated in the upper portion of Table H.1. In this example, four objects (ID) are embedded in two cells (CID), each having two variables of interest (X and Y). Each row in the table appears as a separate computer card or row.

From this standard input, three scores are then computed for each variable. These are the total deviations ($X - \bar{X}$, $Y - \bar{Y}$), the between-cell deviations ($\bar{X}_J - \bar{X}$, $\bar{Y}_J - \bar{Y}$) and the within-cell deviations ($X - \bar{X}_J$, $Y - \bar{Y}_J$). The resulting values from calculating these scores from the synthetic data are also shown in the table. These total, between-, and within-cell deviations then serve as inputs to a correlation program. The correlation matrix resulting from the illustrative data is shown in the lower portion of Table H.1. The total correlation is contained in the upper left rectangle in the table, and the remaining rectangles indicate the location of the eta, between-, and within-cell correlations in the matrix. Values for these correlations can be obtained by using SPSS.

1. SPSS

The aggregation subroutine in SPSS can be used to calculate cell means (averages) from a set of data. Once these averages are calculated, they can be aligned with the original scores (X and Y). For the synthetic data presented in Table H.1, the following output results:

UNIQUE ID	CELL ID	X	Y	$\bar{X}_J$	$\bar{Y}_J$
01	01	1	1	1.5	1.5
02	01	2	2	1.5	1.5
03	02	3	3	3.5	3.5
04	02	4	4	3.5	3.5

Once this set of scores is created, then using the write cases procedure, the within-cell deviation scores can be calculated by subtracting the cell averages from the scores. For the synthetic data, the following rows and columns should

Table H.1. Steps in calculating total, within- and between-cell scores and correlations with a computer

Data Preparation (Figure H.1 and H.2)

A. Input

	ID	CID	X Y
Cols:	1 2	3 4	5 6
	0 1	0 1	1 1
	0 2	0 1	2 2
	0 3	0 2	3 3
	0 4	0 2	4 4

B. Output

	ID	CID	$X - \bar{X}$	$Y - \bar{Y}$	$X - \bar{X}_J$
Cols:	1 2	3 4	5 6 7 8	9 10 11 12	13 14 15 16
	0 1	0 1	− 1 . 5	− 1 . 5	− 0 . 5
	0 2	0 1	− 0 . 5	− 0 . 5	0 . 5
	0 3	0 2	0 . 5	0 . 5	− 0 . 5
	0 4	0 2	1 . 5	1 . 5	0 . 5

$Y - \bar{Y}_J$	$\bar{X}_J - \bar{X}$	$\bar{Y}_J - \bar{Y}$
17 18 19 20	21 22 23 24	25 26 27 28
− 0 . 5	− 1 . 0	− 1 . 0
0 . 5	− 1 . 0	− 1 . 0
− 0 . 5	1 . 0	1 . 0
0 . 5	1 . 0	1 . 0

Correlational Analysis (Figure H.3)

A. Input (see B above)
B. Output

	Total		Within		Between	
	$X - \bar{X}$	$Y - \bar{Y}$	$X - \bar{X}_J$	$Y - \bar{Y}_J$	$\bar{X}_J - \bar{X}$	$\bar{Y}_J - \bar{Y}$
$X - \bar{X}$	1.0					
$Y - \bar{Y}$	r_{TXY}	1.0				
$X - \bar{X}_J$	η_{WX}	r	1.0			
$Y - \bar{Y}_J$	r	η_{WY}	r_{WXY}	1.0		
$\bar{X}_J - \bar{X}$	η_{BX}	r	0.	0.	1.0	
$\bar{Y}_J - \bar{Y}$	r	η_{BY}	0.	0.	r_{BXY}	1.0

result:

UNIQUE ID	CELL ID	X	Y	$\bar{X}_J$	$\bar{Y}_J$	$X - \bar{X}_J$	$Y - \bar{Y}_J$
01	01	1	1	1.5	1.5	−0.5	−0.5
02	01	2	2	1.5	1.5	0.5	0.5
03	02	3	3	3.5	3.5	−0.5	−0.5
04	02	4	4	3.5	3.5	0.5	0.5

This matrix of total, between-, and within-cell scores is input into a correlation program in SPSS; the matrix of correlations shown in Table H.1 results. In this procedure, averages distributed among scores or between cell scores can be input into the program, because SPSS subtracts a grand mean from the scores when a correlation is calculated.

One note of caution is necessary. In SPSS, the degrees of freedom are based on the total number of rows (N) input into a correlation program. These degrees of freedom are appropriate for correlations based on total deviations. The eta correlations have $N - J$ and $J - 1$ degrees of freedom, and their significance should be tested using the E and F ratios. The within- and between-cell correlations have $N - J - 1$ and $J - 2$ degrees of freedom, respectively, and not $N - 2$ degrees of freedom as displayed in the computer printout for SPSS.

Essentially, using SPSS, tests of statistical significance must be recalculated based on correlations and degrees of freedom. Likewise, values for the tests of practical significance can also be obtained with a calculator. As an alternative, a FORTRAN program can be used to remove the need for hand calculations of these tests.

2. FORTRAN

The basic logic for performing such tests is presented in Table H.2. At Buffalo, a computer program written in FORTRAN (called WABA) permits a user on one card to specify all the calculations to be performed, and on additional cards to title the job and to employ label cards. In addition, when the data are not sorted based on the cell ID number, a sort utility program is employed to cluster the cases associated with each cell. Finally, a blank case is inserted at the end of the data set. These steps are illustrated in Figure H.1.

The next steps in the computer program begin with the reading of one case (row). A check is made to ascertain whether the case read is the last or the first in the entire data set. If it is the first case, the variables are written as an E vector. Then a second case (row) is read. Since this is not the first case in the data set, a comparison is made between the stored cell ID number for the first case and the cell ID of this case. If the second case has the same cell ID number as the stored cell ID number, the variables in the second case are added to the variables in the first case on a one-to-one basis. This procedure continues until a different cell ID number is reached. When this occurs, the new cell ID number and the data for the first card in this cell are retained, and

TABLE H.2. Steps in calculating tests of significance with a computer

Tests of Significance (Figure H.4)

A. Input from correlation analysis

	Total		Within		Between	
	$X - \bar{X}$	$Y - \bar{Y}$	$X - \bar{X}_J$	$Y - \bar{Y}_J$	$\bar{X}_J - \bar{X}$	$\bar{Y}_J - \bar{Y}$
$X - \bar{X}$	C(1)					
$Y - \bar{Y}$	C(2)	C(3)				
$X - \bar{X}_J$	C(4)	C(5)	C(6)			
$Y - \bar{Y}_J$	C(7)	C(8)	C(9)	C(10)		
$\bar{X}_J - \bar{X}$	C(11)	C(12)	C(13)	C(14)	C(15)	
$\bar{Y}_J - \bar{Y}$	C(16)	C(17)	C(18)	C(19)	C(20)	C(21)

B. Output

	Variable X	Variable Y
Eta correlations		
Between	C(11)	C(17)
Within	C(4)	C(8)
E ratio	C(11)/C(4) = E(2)	C(17)/C(8) = E(1)
F ratio	$E(2)^2(N - J)/(J - 1) = F(2)$	$E(1)^2(N - J)/(J - 1) = F(1)$
Within and between correlations		
Between	C(20)	
Within	C(9)	
A test	$\text{Cos}^{-1}|C9| - \text{Cos}^{-1}|C20|$	
Z test	$Z(20) - Z(9)/\sqrt{1/(N - J - 2) + 1/(J - 3)}$	
t_B test	$R(20) \cdot \sqrt{J - 2}$	
t_W test	$R(9) \cdot \sqrt{N - J - 1}$	
Between component	$C(20) \cdot C(17) \cdot C(11) = B(1)$	
Within component	$C(9) \cdot C(8) \cdot C(4) = B(2)$	
Total correlation	$C(2) = B(1) + B(2)$	

Note: R values are not calculated in WABA because the width of a computer printout is filled by the output from the calculations shown in this table.

the computer backspaces to the first case in the previous cell and reads that case. At this point, the number of objects in the first cell is known, and the cell means are calculated by dividing the E vector by the number of cases in the cell. The total, within-, and between-cell deviation scores are then calculated and written for this case. This procedure continues until each object in the first cell has a set of three deviation scores. (In addition, the squared deviations are also output on a separate tape.) Once all cases in a given cell have a set of scores, the entire procedure is repeated for the next cell. The logic of this approach to calculating total, within-cell and between-cell scores is shown in the flow diagram in Figure H.2. Given the calculation of the squared total,

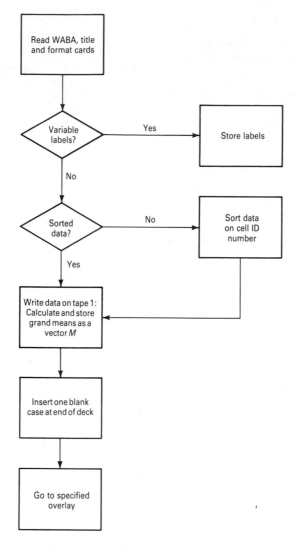

FIGURE H.1. Data preparation (WABA)

within-cell, and between-cell scores, correlations are calculated; a flow chart for these calculations is shown in Figure H.3.

A final set of calculations is necessary to obtain values for the tests of statistical and practical significance (see Table H.2). In these steps, a correlation matrix is written as one vector; the position of each correlation is then determined internally in the program by creating position indicators. (It is easier for programming purposes if the last variable is considered first and the correlation of the last variable with all other variables is then calculated.) Once positioning indicators are identified, one variable is identified, the eta correla-

FIGURE H.2. Calculation of within- and between-cell scores (WABA)

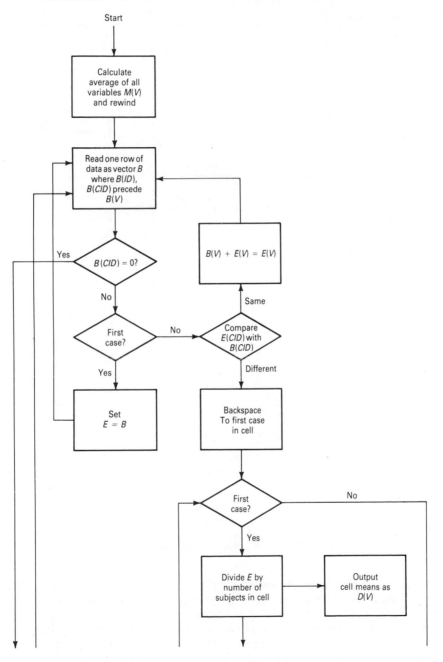

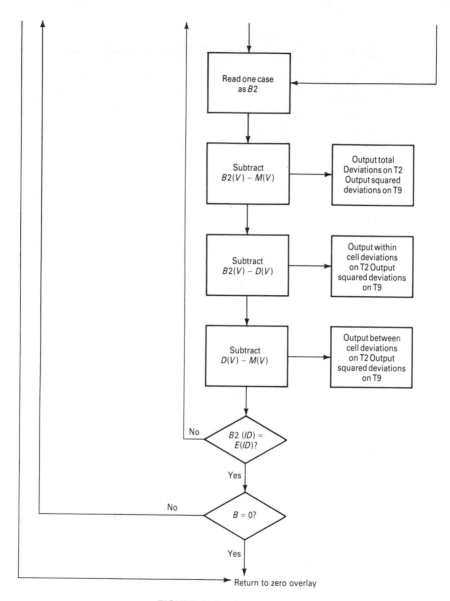

FIGURE H.2. (*continued*)

tions for this variable are obtained, and the E and F ratios are calculated. Then the correlations of this variable with all other variables are identified, the within- and between-cell correlations are printed, and the A, Z, and t tests, within and between components, and total correlations are calculated and printed. This procedure continues until all variables are considered. The output, for example, when five variables are input would appear as follows for

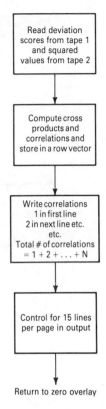

FIGURE H.3. Calculation of correlations (WABA)

the last variable (variable 5):

VARIABLE 5 AND	WABA I VALUES	WABA II VALUES
Variable 4		
Variable 3		
Variable 2		
Variable 1		

At this point, the program then repositions variables and the following output occurs:

VARIABLE 4 AND	WABA I VALUES	WABA II VALUES
Variable 3		
Variable 2		
Variable 1		

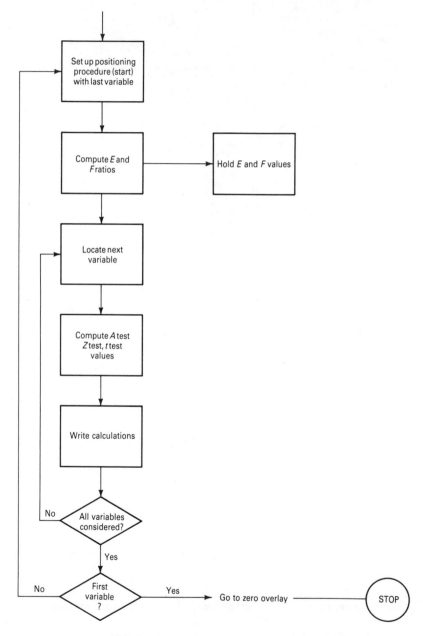

FIGURE H.4. Significance tests (WABA)

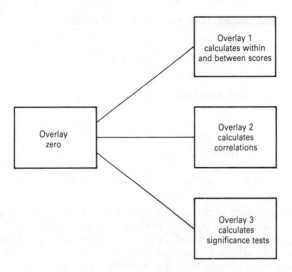

FIGURE H.5.   Overlay zero controls other overlays

This output continues until all the variables are considered. Each row of printed output contains all the correlations and indicators. A flow chart that illustrates this part of the program is presented in Figure H.4. In the WABA program at Buffalo, a series of overlays is employed to link these programs, as illustrated in Figure H.5. The program at Buffalo has been successfully employed over 500 times and provides results identical to those obtained with SPSS and BMD programs.

APPENDIX I   ANSWERS TO REVIEW QUESTIONS

CHAPTER 1

1. Traditionally, theories have been tested by comparing one substantive theory with a statistical theory. A conceptualization of variables and entities that allows for tests of one substantive theory relative to another has been lacking, but is necessary for any systematic theory building in the social sciences.

2. Testing of multiple substantive hypotheses has not been common, although it has often been recommended by theorists as essential for theory building. In its place has been a method of testing one substantive hypothesis against a statistically based hypothesis of random effects.

3. One could argue that all theory testing with the statistical paradigm is sample-dependent. As sample sizes increase, minor differences in effects and relationships of small magnitude between variables become susceptible to a decision that importance should be attached to related inferences. One consequence is that effort is focused on achieving large sample sizes rather than on the substantive hypotheses tested against the statistical standard. One can assume a particular set of entities without testing the assumption, and use the sample-size-dependent statistical paradigm to test variables alone. The resulting ambiguity can have lasting undesirable consequences.

4. Such an approach accomplishes two objectives. First, it controls for setting and contextual differences between different studies (such as time frames, subject characteristics), recognizing that in the social sciences exact replication is difficult, if not impossible. Second, the focus on multiple substantive hypotheses allows one to rule out or eliminate competing explanations for effects under identical conditions. Rather than simply comparing one theoretical explanation with a theory of randomness, the approach in this book places alternative theoretical assertions in competition with each other.

5. The phrase "unit of analysis" refers to the way in which one focuses on an entity within one level of analysis. Specifically, the unit of analysis at one level can be viewed as an undifferentiated whole, in which case the focus is on differences between entities; or the unit at the same level can be viewed as an internally differentiated entity or as parts, in which case the focus is on differences occurring within an entity.

6. (a) Clearly, variables can have cross-level effects. One strength of the varient approach is an ability to test for the strength of variable effects across multiple levels, regardless of the theoretical preferences or assumptions of a researcher.

   (b) By definition, single-level analysis precludes assertions of an emergent effect. Emergent effects can be ascertained only by systematic multiple-level analysis. Indeed, some of the confusion in social science research may result from the unexpected discovery of emergent effects with an absence of multiple-level (lower-level) considerations necessary to delineate the scope of such effects.

7. The assertion of the degree of relatedness is important if only because it imposes some limitations on the appropriateness of particular data analytic techniques (such as multiple regression). More to the point, based on theory, one should be able to assert variable relationships that are and are not expected to occur, thereby extending the comparisons of substantive hypotheses.

8. A moderated effect—the dependence of a relationship between two variables on a third variable—is equivalent to the concept of indirect contingency. In the multiplexed alternative, the relationships between variables are not dependent upon a third variable. In a direct contingency, the variables (not their relationships) are dependent.

9. Although many widely known ideas are used in the varient paradigm, precise definitions are required to permit the empirical testing of a hypothesis and also to allow for a rejection of that hypothesis. In other words, definitions are constructed such that what is and what is *not* meant by a term will be clear before the paradigm is used in testing theories. Definitions of terms also focus conscious attention on distinctions among variables, entities, and relationships.

10. The varient paradigm is not designed to be a new statistical theory or to be the only way to test theories. Instead, the varient paradigm is a response to specific problems with contemporary statistical approaches outlined in Chapter 1. Since it is compatible with widely used statistical methods (bivariate and multiple correlations, as well as univariate and multivariate analyses of variance), it can be applied whenever these methods are used in contemporary and previous work.

CHAPTER 2

1. The number of variables and types of entities determines a set of equally plausible alternative formulations for one set of variables and types of entities. The number is critical, because a test of one hypothesis involves a comparison of it with the other hypotheses in the set.

2. (a) A varient matrix is constructed by intersecting variable and entity axes. On a theoretical basis, predictions are made about levels and units of analysis at which particular types of variable relationships will be found. The results of data analyses are then superimposed, and the degree of correspondence is used to draw inferences about theory and data.

   (b) By comparing theoretical predictions with results of data analyses, one quickly sees areas of convergence or divergence. It is then possible to focus attention on exploring reasons for disjunctures, including entity definitions, variable measures, and characteristics of multiple-variable relationships.

3. The varient approach can be used to reorganize and develop ideas about abstract entities, but in order to actually use the paradigm in theory testing, some representations of entities must be identified. In a similar fashion, empirical measures for abstract variables must be generated to use the paradigm for theory-testing purposes.

4. This is referred to as a focus on whole units, or between-entity analysis. When the focus is on wholes, within-entity variations are viewed as error. In contrast, a focus on parts involves assuming that within-entity (such as person) or unit differences are critical in explaining some effects and involves an assertion that between-entity variation is error.

5. By definition, this is not appropriate. Such a finding constitutes an equivocal condition. In this case, multiple-level analysis would be an appropriate next step.

6. (a) Essentially, an inexplicable condition involves data that are uninterpretable. Nevertheless, inexplicable findings after a single-level analysis may be followed by higher- or lower-level analyses in order to attempt to clarify reasons

for such results (such as measurement problems or a parts condition at a lower level of analysis).

   (b) Averages may not adequately reflect a set of scores. Although averages are used in analytical procedures, in each case a demonstration that deviations around the averages are error is necessary before they are used.

7. When an effect or variable relationship is not obtained, one could stop and infer that the measures are not valid. Alternatively, one could explore whether the same results are obtained at other levels of analysis. A critical point is that if variable measures are sound, and level-unit definitions clear, any insignificant level effect eliminates the possibility of cross-level effects but leaves open the possibility of emergent or level-specific effects.

8. Without lower-level analyses, one cannot identify emergent effects. In addition, the degree of level-specificity remains unknown in the absence of lower-level analyses. Recall that if a particular level of analysis is of interest, then the analytical starting point is usually an assumption of a whole condition at a *lower* level of analysis. Finally, the interpretation of results at a lower level of analysis varies depending on assertions at a higher level of analysis.

9. The first example is a generally related variables case and the second is a related variables case. These two cases are distinguished in terms of (a) the magnitude of the relationships among the three variables and (b) the difference between the magnitudes of the relationships.

10. This example is a contingent formulation. A multiplexed formulation asserts that a relationship would hold in both conditions.

CHAPTER 3

1. A theory must specify at least two variables, their relationship, and one level of analysis.

2. **(a)** Theory formulation in the varient paradigm requires the specification of variables, networks of relationships, and entities.

   (b) Theory testing with the varient paradigm requires measurement of variables, indicators of relationships, and assessments of entities or levels represented by measures and indicators.

3. Either insider or outsider perspectives may be used for theory development. For theory *testing* purposes, an outsider perspective is adopted in the varient paradigm.

4. In addition to illustrating how to use the general conceptualization of levels of analysis, the simple and complex models can be used as a basis for examining data (see Chapters 9 and 10, respectively).

5. The complex illustration in this chapter demonstrates that one level of analysis can be pursued with this approach (for example, superiors as persons). One of the strengths of the approach, however, is that when levels of analysis are naturally embedded in each other, as in most organizations, multiple-level hypotheses can be generated.

6. The basic levels are persons, dyads, groups, and collectivities. Each level is then viewed as a whole or in terms of parts. These levels align with the traditional focuses of social science disciplines such as psychology, social psychology, and sociology. Furthermore, since much research activity in the social and behavioral

sciences focuses on aspects of human behavior in organizational contexts, these levels represent critical entities found in all such settings.

7. To begin with, all variables must be anchored in specific entities at a general level of analysis. Then relationships between pairs of variables must be postulated as related or unrelated. Finally, multiplexed or contingent conditions are postulated. These theory-based assertions are then tested with data against alternatives, and inferences are drawn.

8. The concept of lower levels being embedded in higher-level or larger units of analysis automatically begins to define relevant environments for entities. For example, dyads provide the most immediate, controllable environments for persons, groups provide the most immediate and influential environments for dyads, and so on. This notion of relative immediacy of environments is reflected in the orderly testing of multiple-level effects for variable relationships.

9. In terms of entities, the notion of attitude research probably suggests the hypothesis that attitudes are level-specific to the person level of analysis. In terms of variables, the notion of multicollinearity and multidimensionality probably suggests the hypothesis that variables are all related (a related variables case).

10. Levels of analysis and variables can be broadly defined to apply to any types of situation being studied (for example, variables that characterize societies or individual differences).

CHAPTER 4

1. Such a defect in theory construction forces consideration of levels of analysis in order to test theories. Indeed, in the testing of theory A, the apparent uncertainty about limits on level effects led to development of a cross-level formulation. If levels are not specified, there is always the danger that different researchers will test for variable relationships at different levels of analysis, assuming a specificity of effect that has been left untested.

2. Tests of these theories require interpreting, among other things, the appropriate levels at which one should anticipate critical variable relationships.

3. *Whole* collectivities were selected for theory A and *whole* dyads were selected for theory B.

4. Because it was reasoned that titles and expectations would be related based on characteristics of whole units at each level rather than on units at only one level of analysis. This position was the most consistent with existing theoretical developments.

5. This position was based on a reading of existing literature that postulated processes anchored primarily at dyadic levels.

6. In testing theories, one focuses on characteristics internal to each model but then also compares across theories. In this case, it was believed that variable relationships and level effects were unique to each model. Therefore, barring shortcomings in measurement technique, variables asserted in theories A and B should *not* be related to each other across theories, although relationships asserted within each theory should be represented in the data.

7. The assertion that variables are not related means that a lack of multicollinearity between those variables is expected on an empirical basis.

8. It is a contingent formulation of the variables.

9. If titles and expectations had been postulated to be emergent and level-specific for dyadic wholes and identical to investments and returns, Table 4.3 would be modified to be similar in terms of levels of analysis and the related condition would have been chosen ($T = E = I = R$). If such results were obtained they would then be inconsistent with the theoretical model presented in this chapter, and extensive revision would be required prior to further research. A theory compatible with the new results would need to be developed and then tested.

10. The variables described in the less abstract formulations can be measured in a variety of ways (such as questionnaires, interviews, unobtrusive measures). Moreover, various measures of titles and expectations, investments and returns can be generated.

CHAPTER 5

1. The general linear tensor based on geometry specifies the way to calculate the angle between two vectors. Since total, within- and between-cell vectors are examined in analyses, it specifies how within- and between-cell and eta correlations and total correlations are calculated.

2. One can calculate the total correlation by understanding the geometric basis for calculations of all correlations and the method involved in converting signed deviation scores into vectors. In addition, Equation 5.4 is used for such calculations and Table 5.2 illustrates its application.

3. (a) WABA is designed to generate information about within-cell, between-cell, and total signed deviation scores. It is a technique developed to focus attention on the relative importance of within and between sources of variance in signed deviation scores. WABA is particularly appropriate for analytical purposes in the varient paradigm because levels and units of analysis form naturally occurring cells.

   (b) In WABA I, the focus is on eta correlations or the relationships of the total scores with the between- or within-cell scores for any one variable. In the case of WABA II, the concern is on correlations involving two variables based on within- and between-cell deviations. When WABA I is used, the issue is a determination of the relative size of the correlations of total scores with within- and between-cell scores (with an E ratio). For WABA II, the concern is whether within- or between-cell correlations for specific variables are greater in value, as indicated by A. Thus, the two variations of WABA are designed to address different questions critical to the varient paradigm.

4. (a) Equation 5.8 is the formula for calculating a between-eta correlation. Equation 5.9 is the formula for calculating within-eta correlations. The calculations of these correlations for one variable (X) are shown in Table 5.5a. Equation 5.12 is the formula for calculating a between-cell correlation, and Equation 5.13 is the formula for calculating a within-cell correlation. The calculations are illustrated in Tables 5.5a, 5.5b, and 5.5c.

   (b) E equals a between-eta correlation divided by a within-eta correlation for one variable. The A ratio equals the angle defined by a within-cell correlation minus the angle defined by a between-cell correlation.

5. The A test is free from the artifacts of sample size and focuses on the absolute differences between correlations. It therefore best presents an answer to the

question of whether the magnitudes of between- and within-cell correlations differ in a practical rather than purely sample-size-induced way, as in the case of Z.

6. Primarily because the total correlation at a single level of study is assumed to be equal to the between-cell correlation for the next lower level of analysis. By assigning one score per entity at a particular level, traditional correlation studies *assume* that within-entity deviations at the next lower level represent error. In addition, by assuming that the scores are independent at a level of interest, an equivocal condition is assumed at the next higher level of analysis. In the varient approach, assumptions are not accepted but tested.

7. At the next higher level of analysis the between-cell, or whole entity (person), scores can be partitioned into within- *and* between-cell components at the next higher level (dyad). Thus, between-cell scores at a lower level of analysis can be used to discover either parts or whole conditions at higher levels. New information is not obtained at higher levels if only lower-level within-cell scores are used.

8. WABA is a more general formulation than the ANOVA. The ANOVA is a statistically based approach to assessing the statistical significance of a relationship between variables. In the ANOVA, cells are formed based on the values of a variable. WABA can be used in this way, but it can also be used to assess levels of analysis. Nevertheless, in multiple-variable analysis, the relationship between two variables can be assessed using the ANOVA (see Appendix F and Chapter 9).

9. A and Z are indicators of the difference between correlations and are used in multiple-relationship analysis.

10. Signed deviation scores can always be translated back to a score expressed in an original metric by adding the average to each score. This type of issue arises when individuals are to be selected for jobs, so that a cutoff point is necessary. In such cases, a distribution of scores can be derived and cutoff points can be determined. One can also examine the distribution of scores in a study to assess the degree to which extreme scores are represented in the data. The use of signed deviation scores also permits a consideration of scores in a relative sense.

CHAPTER 6

1. In WABA I, error is defined as a lack of deviation (either within or between cells), and validity is defined as systematic deviation. For WABA II, error is defined as zero correlations among variables (either within- or between-cell correlations), and validity is defined as nonzero correlations.

2. In WABA I, systematic deviations only within cells indicate a parts condition; systematic deviations only between cells indicate a whole condition. The E ratio is used in WABA I and equals zero in an ideal parts condition.

3. In WABA II, within-cell correlations and between-cell correlations are used. A is used to detect the difference between two angles measured in radians specified by these correlations, and in this case it will equal 1.57.

4. The double fallacy results from attempts to infer *both* parts and whole conditions for one variable in one entity during the same time period. This is generated by invalid interpretation of equivocal results and can be minimized through reliance on the A test.

5. A total correlation of 1 may reflect differences between (a) whole groups and (b) parts within groups. Or (c) it may not be based on group-level differences but, for example, reflect differences between dyads.

6. A distribution of scores is shown in Table 6.2.

7. See Table 6.4 for an illustration of such a distribution of scores.

8. Results of this type can be interpreted as part of a cross-level wholes or parts formulation or as level-specific.

9. A value for the multiple regression cannot be obtained because of multicollinearity.

10. In general, the relationship should be multiplexed because when pairs of scores are divided into conditions by a contingency variable, the one-to-one correspondence between the variables should remain.

CHAPTER 7

1. The inference to be drawn concerns the relationship between some indicator of an effect and the probability that the effect is more likely due to a series of statistical artifacts including sample size, accepted significance levels, and whether one- or two-tailed tests are appropriate.

2. Tests of practical significance are independent of degrees of freedom (sample size) and focus on the issue of estimating the degree to which data approximate ideal conditions. These tests can be understood by recalling the geometric basis for correlational analysis and thus tests of practical significance.

3. An eta value is a measure of correlation between total deviation scores and within or between scores. The test for practical significance involves a consideration of the location of an obtained E ratio in the range of possible values for the E ratio.

4. In the comparison of eta correlations in WABA I, the magnitudes of the correlations of within and between scores with total scores are dependent on each other. As one eta value increases, the other decreases. However, in the case of correlations among variables based on within-cell or between-cell (but not with total) deviations, the correlations are independent; therefore, tests for both the magnitude of correlations and the differences between correlations are required.

5. A test of practical significance identifies whether a within- or between-cell or eta correlation is larger (which is not error), thereby forming the basis of defining error for the F and Z values used in tests of statistical significance.

6. The induction is one of weak wholes, since WABA I does not support an induction of wholes. This induction is viable if one is willing to assert that although there may be deviations as indicated in WABA I, the within-cell deviations are error and thus should correlate near zero.

7. The next step is an analysis at the next higher or lower level of analysis.

8. Using the table of $\hat{F}$ ratios shown in Appendix A, the square root of these values equals values for $\hat{t}$. For example, if a t value for 1, and 200 degrees of freedom ($p \leq 0.05$) is desired, an F ratio of 3.89 is obtained from the table, which results in a t value of 1.972.

9. A one-tail test is used because only the magnitude of correlations is of interest. The values 1.66 and 2.33 are required for $\hat{Z}$ at the 0.05 and 0.01 level of significance. For a two-tail test, $\hat{Z}$ values of 1.96 ($p \leq 0.05$) and 2.58 ($p \leq 0.01$) would be used.

10. The focus on tests of practical and statistical significance is critical because all conclusions or inferences can be viewed as relative in the varient paradigm. That is, based on the interplay between practical and statistical significance tests in WABA I and II, a researcher draws inferences about the probability that effects are anchored in one or more entities. The use of multiple-significance tests to answer different substantive questions provides multiple points of comparison that serve as a basis for an induction from data.

CHAPTER 8

1. The entire paradigm, including the conceptualization of variables and entities and the associated method by which theories are formulated and data analyzed, serves as the basis of the inferential system. In addition, the statistical paradigm serves as a basis for drawing inferences.

2. The primary process involved in the varient paradigm is one of constantly comparing theoretical assertions with data. The varient matrix is simply a heuristic device for summarizing the degree of consistency between theory-based predictions and obtained results. To the extent that competing alternative explanations are eliminated as unlikely, more consistency between theoretical predictions and obtained results provides an indication of greater validity and less consistency indicates less validity.

3. First, a theory is used to guide the collection of scores for variables based on one or more entities. Second, data analysis consistent with theoretical assertions is performed. Finally, empirically based inductions are compared to theoretically based predictions and inferences are drawn.

4. Averaging is a critical activity in WABA, occurring in the creation of deviation scores and summarizing of statistical tests. However, in both WABA I and II, the entity or cell base for averaging activities and the degree to which scores deviate from the average (within-cell scores) is never lost.

5. Degrees of freedom are critical in all tests of statistical significance. Moreover, degrees of freedom are reflected in changes in intervals for $\tilde{F}$ and $\hat{\imath}$.

6. These two indicators indicate whether between- or within-cell deviations should be considered as valid at each level of analysis. However, the use of these indicators alone assumes that statistical significance has already been demonstrated.

7. It is a multiplexed case because the correlations do not differ in each condition.

8. It is the determination of levels of analysis that permits the analysis of relationships between variables. Unanchored consideration of variable relationships can yield uninterpretable results. Once an appropriate level of analysis has been identified, one can begin to interpret relationships between variables.

9. In such a case, the results are viewed as more likely to be explained by chance or statistical artifacts than by a substantive theory.

10. This outcome can be achieved by using large sample sizes. The inference is that the results are not interpretable as supportive of one theory relative to another, but they also do not seem to be due to statistical artifacts.

CHAPTER 9

1. Predicted variable and entity specification serve as a basis for data collection and analysis. They guide the development of variable scores and focus attention on units as well as levels of analysis.

2. **(a)** Since the possibility of relationships across all levels was specified in theory A, it was essential that we be able to identify responses with individuals and identify links between superiors and subordinates at all levels. This strategy resulted in data on persons nested in dyads nested in groups nested in collectivities.

   (b) If one is interested only in groups, then individuals need not be identified; only the group to which each individual belongs need be specified. Nevertheless, the approach requires the placement of individuals' responses into cells and the identification of cells. There is, of course, no reason that ambiguous results based on individuals' anonymous responses cannot be compared to results where between-cell scores are used.

3. There is (a) uncertainty as to the level of analysis reflected and (b) uncertainty as to the units of analyses involved.

4. Despite statistically significant F ratios, the E ratios were not practically significant; thus, an equivocal condition was inferred. Since we examined the assertion that either within- or between-cell deviations were error, no differentiation between these two types of deviations could be made. Therefore, no assertion was made that one type of deviation was error.

5. Based on data analysis, relationships among variables specified in theory A held for whole collectivities and whole work groups. No empirical assessment was performed at the person or dyad level.

6. Given an inference of whole-group effects, albeit a weak one, it was possible that this was an artifact of differences within or between collectivities. To determine the appropriate multiple-level inference and given the whole-group inference, a collectivity-level analysis was justified.

7. The results of multiple-variable analysis indicated that a related case seemed more likely. Therefore, multiple-relationship analysis was not performed.

8. The eight cells created by functional title categories were used in an ANOVA design to test for the relationship between titles and expectations. An assumption that the within-cell scores were error was necessary in this analysis and the implications of the need for this assumption were demonstrated in *tests* for a cross-level formulation.

9. If cross-level effects are possible, one should collect data based on the highest as well as lowest possible level. A finding of a whole effect at one level requires analysis at the next higher level if emergent or level-specific effects are to be identified. This means that many current methods of data collection (such as random sampling of individuals or groups) in the social sciences may unnecessarily inhibit the inferential potential of research projects.

10. An analysis could have been performed based on only (a) group averages or (b) collectivity averages. In both cases, a consideration of averages (between-cell scores) without the use of within-cell deviations would provide no justification for the averaging procedure. Moreover, a level-specific whole-group formulation or emergent collectivity-level formulation might have been asserted instead of the cross-level whole-collectivity effect if only averages had been employed.

CHAPTER 10

1. It is essential because theory B asserts that investments and returns are related only at the whole dyad level.

2. Obviously, one must collect data that can be analyzed at the dyad level of analysis. This means that, at a minimum, data must be collected about or from both members of each dyad.

3. Analyses were performed on (a) superior reports at the person level; (b) subordinate reports at the work-group level; (c) superior and subordinate reports at the dyad level, and (d) superior and subordinate reports at the work-group level.

4. Ambiguous results would be obtained if total correlations were used based on (a) only subordinate's reports, (b) only superior's reports, or (c) only on variables regardless of respondent.

5. This is really simply a matter of tracing the source of the total correlations back to within- or between-cell variance. When this is accomplished, one can begin to discover whether total correlations are based on multiple-level or other effects.

6. Both WABA I and II results were consistent with a whole-dyad formulation, but the average magnitudes of differences for eta correlations and between-cell correlations, respectively, were marginal, thus leading to a weakened inference.

7. At the group level of analysis, an equivocal condition was inferred (see Table 3.1 for the group-level predictions of the ALS and VDL models).

8. The discovery of an equivocal condition at the work-group level did not justify a collectivity-level analysis.

9. Once it was inferred that the variables were related at the whole-dyad level, a multiple relationship analysis was not performed at that level. The findings of equivocal conditions at the work-group and person levels eliminated the opportunity to pursue multiple relationships.

10. Variables can be assessed in any number of ways. The key requirement in the varient paradigm is that scores be distributed among entities in some way. For example, the results from an analysis of U.S. census data are presented in Chapter 13.

CHAPTER 11

1. Both theories predict relationships between variables at the dyad level, although cross-level effects are predicted by theory A. Thus, at the dyad level the degree of independence between the variables specified by the theories can be examined.

2. Between-dyad scores could not be assessed for titles and expectations because only subordinates responded to such questions. Thus, it was not possible to construct a clear dyadic alignment of cells, which illustrates that data collection procedures can impose constraints on theory testing.

3. The assertion is reflected in the prediction that titles and expectations will be unrelated to investments and returns at all levels.

4. The basis for anticipating generally unrelated variables at the dyad level was based on theory and not simply data manipulation. The one level asserted by both theories is the dyad level. The focus of analysis was on whether independence in

networks of variables was maintained even though both theories included assertions about the dyad level of analysis.

5. A test of such differences ignores the possibility that entities may be viable under only certain conditions.

6. When within-dyad correlations between investments and returns were examined, it was found that they remained fairly constant and near zero in value within all collectivities.

7. As indicated in Table 11.7, only for the support collectivity were the differences between the average between- and within-eta correlations practically and statistically significant. In all other collectivities, data analysis revealed equivocal conditions. Furthermore, the results presented in Table 11.10 indicate that a contingent formulation is more likely. Finally, the results in Table 11.11 indicate that an equivocal condition is more likely for all but the dyad level of analysis in the support collectivity.

8. In a multiplexed formulation, a relationship of interest holds under all conditions of a third variable. In a contingent formulation, relationships hold for only certain values of a third variable. If a third variable occurs at a higher level (such as a collectivity) than other variables (such as a work group), the third variable can be thought of as characterizing the environment which may (contingent) or may not (multiplexed) affect the relationship between variables of interest.

9. In Chapter 4, theory A and theory B were viewed as multiplexed. The results suggest a contingency formulation may be more appropriate, at least for these variables and measures.

10. The finding that some of the variables were unrelated to each other suggests that self-reports do not necessarily result in one network of variables, or multicollinearity.

CHAPTER 12

1. First, composite correlations are redundant since they are all functions of the eta and between- and within-cell correlations. Second, the degrees of freedom are difficult to determine for the composite correlations.

2. Temporal ordering simply adds a specification of predictions to be matched against inductions drawn from data. The identification of reciprocal or sequential relationships must still be anchored in specific units and levels of analysis.

3. Not really. The focus is still on identifying entities, variables, and relationships based on theory. The addition of a temporal dimension simply allows one to use the varient paradigm to address issues of causality effectively. In essence, the inclusion of time results in the creation of new cells for between and within analytic purposes.

4. Eight time periods are ideal because reciprocal effects can be obtained in this case. Of course, the analytical procedures can be used with as few time periods as are available.

5. At the person level of analysis, parts are difficult to define (see Chapter 14). Thus, some individuals believe that individual differences reflect characteristics which are stable over time. Thus, for example, if one individual were measured a number of times, the resulting scores are *assumed* to be the same over time, subject only to

measurement error. In the varient paradigm, the stable condition at the person level of analysis is viewed as only one alternative formulation.

6. The removal of this requirement is simply a recognition that between- and within-cell deviations and correlations can be examined simultaneously. Nevertheless, for theory development purposes, it is essential to specify a unit of analysis and level within which an effect or set of relationships is expected to be anchored.

7. An example of a case where variable Z intervenes between variable X and Y is presented in this chapter ($X \rightarrow Z \rightarrow Y$).

8. The temporal ordering of variables can be considered under different conditions defined by a third variable. In a multiplexed formulation, the same ordering occurs in each condition. In a contingent condition, a different temporal ordering occurs in different conditions.

9. When a stable condition is induced, the results are the same (replicated) across time. When a change occurs, the results may shift across time. Moreover, different types of changes can be identified with the use of the paradigm.

10. First, insufficient attention was devoted to alternative measures of variables. Second, data collection through survey techniques may be enhanced by other approaches (such as laboratory experiments). Third, the issue of generalizing from data was not fully explored. See Chapters 13, 14, and 15 for additional details on these issues.

CHAPTER 13

1. All these methods use at least total signed deviation scores and can be reduced to total correlations between two variables at a time. Therefore, each of the indicators in these methods can be extended to include a consideration of within- and between-cell deviations in addition to total deviations.

2. WABA I and II differentiate between the independent sources of variance that are commingled in composite correlations. Composite correlations can be reconstructed, if so desired, from WABA analyses.

3. WABA addresses a number of shortcomings in cross-lagged analysis by providing (a) tests of the degree of stability or change over time and (b) tests of the levels of analysis that may underlie a set of results.

4. When using WABA, one cannot commit the ecological fallacy of assuming that total correlations are identical to between-cell correlations because values for both correlations are considered.

5. By aligning cells with a third variable, it is possible to test whether a third variable significantly affects a relationship between other variables.

6. Separate multiple regressions can be performed on within- and between-cell deviation scores rather than based only on total deviations. In addition, an examination of the correlations between pairs of variables can be used to assess whether multiple regression is appropriate (whether there is a lack of multicollinearity).

7. Through the use of composite correlation, it is impossible clearly to identify cross-level effects because sources of variance are aggregated in composite correlations. Furthermore, no tests for practical significance are used in Firebaugh's approach.

8. Path analysis uses the multiple-regression method. Therefore it can be extended by using WABA.

9. The ANOVA model requires an assumption that within-cell deviations are error, making it inappropriate for testing assumptions about levels or units of analysis.

10. Judgments of statistical significance in the n-way ANOVA are influenced by the number of variables incorporated in the design of a study.

CHAPTER 14

1. Two issues are important. First, scales should be designed so that they are compatible with the theoretical assertions guiding their creation. If they are designed to measure variables asserted to be level-specific or cross level, then items, questions, and so on should be written accordingly. Second, regardless of design, for data analysis purposes only items relating to the same level and unit of analysis should be combined into scales.

2. Content validity refers to the determination of whether an item fits into the domain or level and unit of analysis as specified for a scale. In other words, domains are extended to include the specification of levels of analysis.

3. Construct validity involves a decision that the analysis of a set of measures leads to inferences (about whole, parts, equivocal, or inexplicable conditions) that were specified on substantive theoretical bases. To the extent that measures yield results consistent with theory, they can be said to be characterized as having achieved a certain degree of construct validity.

4. In traditional test development, instability in responses over time is often viewed as error. In WABA, the question posed is whether stability or instability should be viewed as valid. One chooses between these alternatives based on data analysis. Therefore, scale stability is only one view of a valid scale.

5. WABA allows a determination of whether observational or interview data are biased by perceptions or assumptions of the observer. Thus the effect of the observer on data is estimated. In all cases, the focus is on testing for the appropriate level and unit of analysis.

6. One purpose of replication is constantly to place theories in competition with alternative explanations. In the process, not only are measures refined (for example, levels and units of analysis are clarified), but inferences are drawn about multiple theoretical positions. This is compatible with but different from infinite sampling approaches, in which the objective is to define the minimum number of identical or similar studies needed to generalize to all such studies.

7. The varient paradigm assists in defining the essential characteristics of a population. This is accomplished by references to levels and units of analysis, as well as variables and characteristics of relationships.

8. The approach is compatible with the interests of those wishing to generalize from data to theory, from theory to data, or from sample to sample. In each case, the varient paradigm simply imposes some additional constraints or data points for comparison or generalization purposes. In this way, the varient paradigm assists in making more powerful and precise generalizations possible.

9. WABA is just as method-bound and sample-specific as the widely used techniques described in Chapter 13. The issue of whether similar results are obtained, for

example, when both self-reports and observational methods are used is not relevant to WABA because it can be used with both types of measurements. The degree to which results are specific to one sample can be assessed by replicating studies across samples.

10. All the bounds for theory A and theory B were not developed. (This criticism also applies to role and exchange theories.) Nevertheless, in future studies, for example, variables that may serve as contingencies on the degree to which titles and expectations are related can be hypothesized. Of course, empirical results may demonstrate that theory A is multiplexed with a variety of conditions. In a similar fashion, exchange theories may very well be contingent on the types of roles (titles) individuals occupy. Therefore, from a replication perspective, it is an empirical question for future research whether these two theories will hold across various contingencies. From an infinite sampling perspective, the obtained statistically significant results would be interpreted as indicating that the results at MCO will hold in similar types of studies. In terms of the representativeness approach to generalizations and issues of external validity, the results from testing theory A are viewed as generalizing to whole collectivities across levels and theory B is viewed as specific to dyads within certain collectivities. Again, there is a need to define with variables the limits on theories so that populations can be specified in more precise terms in the future.

CHAPTER 15

1. An explicit consideration of the level and unit of analysis at which a variable should manifest itself helps to clarify variables. By linking variables to levels and units in both theory building and data analysis, the varient approach assists in noting inconsistencies and ambiguities in both theory and inferences based on data.

2. Essentially, different studies can be used to fill out an extended varient matrix. Then, after plotting differences between theoretical predictions and findings, one can identify which of a series of competing theories appear to have greatest support and which have least support. On this basis, "critical experiments" can be designed to resolve ambiguities or incomplete cells in the matrix.

3. Multiplexed relationships are consistent under different conditions. This leads to fairly simple decision rules that are often attractive to individuals looking for quick and easy solutions (such as: satisfied workers are more productive workers). However, the danger is that relationships thought to be multiplexed often are not and actions taken based on this assumption of consistency can lead to unexpected results (such as: satisfied workers may be more productive only if they perceive a connection between sources of satisfaction and output).

4. The number of variables and types of entities indicate the number of explanations inherent in a formulation, and these alternatives should be examined (see Chapter 2).

5. The varient approach is indifferent to the value placed on a particular question. The meaningful question is how many alternative explanations have been rejected in a study and on what basis.

6. Both approaches are viable. In the first case, tests (described in Chapter 12) of whether variables are stable or change over time can be performed. In the second case, any examination of a pattern of correlations requires the use of within- and

between-cell deviations and thus a test is performed of one pattern relative to other patterns of correlations.

7. Although the use of multiple sources (see Chapter 9) of data and multiple raters (see Chapter 10) is certainly appropriate, even when self-reports are examined, alternative explanations can be tested. Obviously, such reports may be compatible with the equivocal condition; however, such an issue is an empirical question.

8. As the number of objects and degrees of freedom increase, statistical artifacts (sample size) influence the results less. Thus, more data is better than less data. Small samples in particular require *tests* of statistical significance. Moreover, null results are uninterpretable because they indicate an inability to reject a statistically based hypothesis.

9. **(a)** The varient paradigm is compatible with the statistical paradigm. Therefore, in fields where the statistical paradigm is used, levels of analysis are also of importance (for example, economics, political science, and some areas in biology).

   (b) Although human beings may be embedded in various levels of analysis, the varient approach requires that variables be identified that characterize such levels.

10. The varient paradigm provides an extension of previous work and a way to test assumptions that had to be made in previous work. Whether these assumptions, when they are tested in the future, will or will not be supported is an empirical question. Previous work can be rejected only by new empirical findings or reanalyses that fail to support the hypotheses asserted. Clearly, some previous theories may need to be rejected, but other theories may survive empirical tests of their assertions.

REFERENCES

ADAMS, J. S. "Toward an understanding of inequity." *Journal of Abnormal and Social Psychology,* 1963, 67, 422–36.

_____ "Injustice in social exchange." In L. Berkowitz (Ed.), *Advances in experimental social psychology.* New York: Academic Press, 1965, 2, 267–99.

_____ "A framework for the study of modes of resolving inconsistency." In R. P. Abelson et al. (Eds.), *Theories of cognitive inconsistency: A sourcebook.* Chicago: Rand McNally, 1968, 655–60.

ALDRICH, H. E. *Organizations and environment.* Englewood Cliffs, N.J.: Prentice-Hall, 1979.

ALEXANDER, C. N. and SIMPSON, R. L. "Balance theory and distributive justice." *Sociological Inquiry,* 1964, 34, 182–92.

ALUTTO, J. A. "Role propositions and the analysis of organizations." Unpublished doctoral dissertation, Cornell University, 1968.

ARGYRIS, C. "Some limitations of the case method: Experiences in a management development program." *Academy of Management Review,* 1980, 5, 291–98.

ARNOLD, H. J. "Moderator variables: A clarification of conceptual, analytic, and psychometric issues." *Organizational Behavior and Human Performance,* 1982, 29, 143–74.

BAKAN, D. "The test of significance in psychological research." *Psychological Bulletin,* 1966, 66, 423–37.

BANTON, M. P. *Roles: An introduction to the study of social relations.* London: Tavistock, 1965.

BARRETT, G. V. "Research models of the future for industrial and organizational psychology." *Personnel Psychology,* 1972, 25, 1–17.

BASS, B. M. "The substance and the shadow." *American Psychologist,* 1974, 29, 870–86.

_____ "Intensity of relations, dyadic-group considerations, cognitive categorization and transformational leadership." In J. Hunt, U. Sekaran, and C. Schreisheim (Eds.), *Leadership: Beyond establishment views.* Carbondale: Southern Illinois University Press, 1982.

BECHTOLDT, H. P. "Construct validity: A critique." *American Psychologist*, 1959, 14, 619–29.

BEHLING, O. "Some problems in the philosophy of science of organizations." *Academy of Management Review*, 1978, 3, 193–201.

_____ "The case for the natural science model for research in organizational behavior and organizational theory." *Academy of Management Review*, 1980, 5, 483–90.

BELL, G. D. "The influence of technological components of work upon management control." *Journal of the Academy of Management*, 1965, 8, 127–32.

_____ "Predictability of work demands and professionalism as determinants of workers' discretion." *Journal of the Academy of Management*, 1966, 9, 20–28.

BIDDLE, B. J. *Role theory: Expectations, identities and behavior.* New York: Academic Press, 1979.

_____ and THOMAS, E. J. (Eds.) *Role theory: Concepts and research.* New York: Wiley, 1966.

BLALOCK, H. M. *Causal inferences in nonexperimental research.* Chapel Hill: University of North Carolina Press, 1964.

_____ *Theory construction: From verbal to mathematical formulations.* Englewood Cliffs, N.J.: Prentice-Hall, 1969.

_____ "The presidential address: Measurement and conceptualization problems: The major obstacle to integrating theory and research." *American Sociological Review*, 1979, 44, 881–94.

BLAU, P. M. *Exchange and power in social life.* New York: Wiley, 1964.

_____ *On the nature of organizations.* New York: Wiley, 1974.

BOBBITT, H. R., BREINHOLT, R. H., DOKTOR, R. H., and McNAUL, J. P. *Organizational behavior: Understanding and prediction.* Englewood Cliffs, N.J.: Prentice-Hall, 1978.

BOLLES, R. C. "The difference between statistical hypotheses and scientific hypotheses." *Psychological Reports*, 1962, 11, 639–45.

BOULDING, K. E. "Science: Our common heritage." *Science*, 1980a, 207, 831–36.

_____ "Universal physiology." *Behavioral Science*, 1980b, 25, 35–39.

BRAITHWAITE, R. *Scientific explanation.* Cambridge, Eng.: Cambridge University Press, 1973.

BREDEMEIR, H. C. "Survey reviews." *Contemporary Sociology*, 1977, 6, 646–50.

BRONFENBRENNER, M. "The structure of revolutions in economic thought." *History of Political Economy*, 1971, 3, 136–51.

BROWN, R. and TURNER, J. "Interpersonal and intergroup behavior." In J. C. Turner and H. Giles (Eds.), *Intergroup behavior.* Oxford, Eng.: Basil Blackwell, in press.

BYRNE, D. and NELSON, D. "Attraction as a linear function of proportion of positive reinforcements." *Journal of Personality and Social Psychology*, 1965, 1, 659–63.

CAMPBELL, D. T. and FISKE, D. W. "Convergent and discriminant validation by the multitrait-multimethod matrix." *Psychological Bulletin*, 1959, 56, 81–105.

_____ and STANLEY, J. C. *Experimental and quasi-experimental designs for research.* Chicago: Rand McNally, 1963, 1966.

CAMPBELL, J. P. "Psychometric theory." In M. D. Dunnette (Ed.), *Handbook of industrial and organizational psychology*. Chicago: Rand McNally, 1976.

_____, DUNNETTE, M. D., LAWLER, E. E., and WEICK, K. E. *Managerial behavior, performance, and effectiveness*. New York: McGraw-Hill, 1970.

CARTWRIGHT, D. "Determinants of scientific progress: The case of research on the risky shift." *American Psychologist*, 1973, 28, 222–31.

CHADWICK-JONES, J. K. *Social exchange theory: Its structure and influence in social psychology*. London: Academic Press, 1976.

CHAMBERLIN, T. C. "The method of multiple working hypotheses." *Science*, 1965, 148, 754–59 (originally 1890).

COHEN, J. *Statistical power analysis for the behavioral sciences*. New York: Academic Press, 1977.

_____ and COHEN, P. *Applied multiple regression and correlation analysis in the behavioral sciences*. Hillsdale, N.J.: Erlbaum, 1975.

COHEN, M. R. and NAGEL, E. *An introduction to logic and scientific method*. New York: Harcourt Brace, 1934.

CONANT, J. B. *On understanding science: An historical approach*. New Haven, Conn.: Yale University Press, 1947.

COOK, T. D. and CAMPBELL, D. T. "The design and conduct of quasi-experiments and true experiments in field settings." In M. D. Dunnette (Ed.), *Handbook of industrial and organizational psychology*. Chicago: Rand McNally, 1976.

CRONBACH, L. J. "Test validation." In R. L. Thorndike (Ed.), *Educational measurement*. Washington, D.C.: American Council on Education, 1971.

_____ and FURBY, L. "How we should measure change—or should we?" *Psychological Bulletin*, 1970, 74, 68–80.

_____, GLESER, G. C., NANDA, H., and RAJARATNAM, N. *The dependability of behavioral measures: Theory of generalizability for scores and profiles*. New York: Wiley, 1972.

_____ and MEEHL, P. E. "Construct validity in psychological tests." *Psychological Bulletin*, 1955, 52, 281–302.

CUMMINGS, L. L. "State of the art: Organizational behavior in the 1980's." *Decision Sciences*, 1981, 12, 365–77.

DANSEREAU, F., ALUTTO, J. A., MARKHAM, S. E., and DUMAS, M. "Multiplexed leadership and supervision: An application of within and between analysis." In J. Hunt, U. Sekaran, and C. Schriesheim (Eds.), *Leadership: Beyond establishment views*. Carbondale: Southern Illinois University Press, 1982a.

DANSEREAU, F., ALUTTO, J. A., MARKHAM, S. E., and DUMAS, M. "A multiplexed response to Professors Bass and Morely." In J. G. Hunt, U. Sekaran, and C. Schriesheim (Eds.), *Leadership: Beyond establishment views*. Carbondale: Southern Illinois University Press, 1982b.

_____, CASHMAN, J., and GRAEN, G. "Instrumentality theory and equity theory as complementary approaches in predicting the relationship of leadership and turnover among managers." *Organizational Behavior and Human Performance*, 1973, 10, 184–200.

_____ and DUMAS, M. "Pratfalls and pitfalls in drawing inferences about leadership behavior in organizations." In J. G. Hunt and L. Larson (Eds.), *Leadership: The cutting edge*. Carbondale: Southern Illinois University Press, 1977, 68–83.

———, GRAEN, G., and HAGA, W. J. "A vertical dyad linkage approach to leadership within formal organizations: A longitudinal investigation of the role-making process." *Organizational Behavior and Human Performance*, 1975, 13, 46–78.

DIESING, P. *Patterns of discovery in the social sciences.* Chicago: Aldine, 1971.

DUBIN, R. *Theory building.* New York: Free Press, 1969.

——— "Theory building in applied areas." In M. D. Dunnette (Ed.), *Handbook of industrial and organizational psychology.* Chicago: Rand McNally, 1976.

DUBNO, P., HILLBURN, D., ROBINSON, G., SANDLER, D., TRANI, J., and WEINGARTEN, E. "An attitude toward behavior modification scale." *Behavior Therapy*, 1978, 9, 99–108.

DUNCAN, O. D., CUZZORT, R. P., and DUNCAN, B. D. *Statistical geography.* Glencoe: Free Press, 1961.

DUNNETTE, M. D. "Fads, fashions and folderol in psychology." *American Psychologist*, 1966, 21, 343–52.

DURKHEIM, E. *The division of labor in society.* New York: Free Press, 1933.

ECKBERG, D. L. and HILL, L. "The paradigm concept and sociology: A critical review." *American Sociological Review*, 1979, 44, 925–37.

EKEH, P. P. *Social exchange theory: The two traditions.* London: Heinemann, 1974.

EMMERSON, R. M. "Operant psychology and exchange theory." In R. L. Burgess and D. Bushell (Eds.), *Behavioral sociology.* New York: Columbia University Press, 1969.

EPSTEIN, S. "The stability of behavior II: Implications for psychological research." *American Psychologist*, 1980, 35, 790–806.

FESTINGER, L. *A theory of cognitive dissonance.* Stanford, Calif.: Stanford University Press, 1957.

FIEDLER, F. E. *A theory of leadership effectiveness.* New York: McGraw-Hill, 1967.

FINN, J. D. *A general model for multivariate analysis.* New York: Holt, Rinehart and Winston, 1974.

FIREBAUGH, G. "A rule for inferring individual-level relationships from aggregate data." *American Sociological Review*, 1978, 43, 557–72.

FISHER, R. A. "Frequency distribution of the values of the correlation coefficient in samples from an indefinitely large population." *Biometrika*, 1915, 10, 507–21.

——— *Statistical methods for research workers.* New York: Hafner, 1925.

——— *Statistical methods and scientific inferences.* New York: Hafner, 1973.

GERGEN, K. J., GREENBERG, M., and WILLIS, R. *Social exchange: Advances in theory and research.* New York: Plenum, 1980.

GHISELLI, E. E. "Some perspectives for industrial psychology." *American Psychologist*, 1974, 29, 80–87.

GLASS, G. and STANLEY, J. *Statistical methods in education and psychology.* Englewood Cliffs, N.J.: Prentice-Hall, 1970.

GNEDENKO, B. V. *The theory of probability.* New York: Chelsea Co., 1966.

GOULD, P. "The tyranny of taxonomy." *The Sciences*, 1982, 22, 5, 7–9.

GRAEN, G. "Role-making processes within complex organizations." In M. D. Dunnette (Ed.), *Handbook of industrial and organizational psychology.* Chicago: Rand McNally, 1976.

GROSS, N., MASON, W., and MCEACHERN, A. W. *Explorations in role analysis: Studies of the school superintendency role.* New York: Wiley, 1958.

GUILFORD, J. P. *Fundamental statistics in psychology and education.* New York: McGraw-Hill, 1965.

HAGA, W. J., GRAEN, G., and DANSEREAU, F. "Professionalism and role making in a service organization: A longitudinal investigation." *American Sociological Review,* 1974, 39, 122–33.

HAGE, J. and AIKEN, M. "Routine technology, social structure and organizational goals." *Administrative Science Quarterly,* 1969, 14, 366–76.

HALL, R. H. *Organizations: Structure and process.* Englewood Cliffs, N.J.: Prentice-Hall, 1977.

HANNAN, M. T. *Aggregation and disaggregation in sociology.* Lexington, Mass.: Heath-Lexington, 1971.

HARMAN, H. H. *Modern factor analysis.* Chicago: University of Chicago Press, 1970.

HARRIS, C. W. (Ed.) *Problems in measuring change.* Madison: University of Wisconsin Press, 1963.

HAYS, W. L. *Statistics for the social sciences.* New York: Holt, Rinehart and Winston, 1973.

HEIDER, F. *The psychology of interpersonal relations.* New York: Wiley, 1958.

HEISE, D. R. *Causal analysis.* New York: Wiley, 1975.

HELLRIEGEL, D. and SLOCUM, J. *Organizational behavior.* New York: West, 1979.

HOLLANDER, E. P. "Conformity, status and idiosyncrasy credit." *Psychological Review,* 1958, 65, 117–27.

_____ "Process of leadership emergence." *Journal of Contemporary Business,* 1974, 3, 19–33.

_____ *Leadership dynamics: A practical guide to effective relations.* New York: Free Press, 1978.

HOMANS, G. C. "Social behavior as exchange." *American Journal of Sociology,* 1958, 63, 597–606.

_____ *Social behavior: Its elementary forms.* New York: Harcourt, Brace and World, 1961.

_____ *Social behavior: Its elementary forms* (Revised edition). New York: Harcourt Brace Jovanovich, 1974.

HOTELLING, H. "The selection of variates for use in prediction with some comments on the general problem of nuisance parameters." *Annals of Mathematical Statistics,* 1940, 11, 271–83.

HOUSE, R. J. "A path-goal theory of leader effectiveness." *Administrative Science Quarterly,* 1971, 16, 321–39.

HUNT, J. G., SEKARAN, U., and SCHRIESHEIM, C. A. (Eds.) *Leadership: Beyond establishment views.* Carbondale: Southern Illinois University Press, 1982.

JACOBS, T. O. *Leadership and exchange in formal organizations.* Alexandria, Va.: Human Resources Research Organization, 1970.

JAMES, L. R. "Aggregation bias in estimates of perceptual agreement." *Journal of Applied Psychology,* 1982, 67, 219–29.

KAHN, R. L., WOLFE, D. M., QUINN, R. P., SNOEK, J. D., and ROSENTHAL, R. A. *Organizational stress: Studies in role conflict and ambiguity.* New York: Wiley, 1964.

KALLEBERG, A. L. and KLUEGEL, J. R. "Analysis of the multitrait-multimethod matrix: Some limitations and an alternative." *Journal of Applied Psychology*, 1975, 60, 1–9.

KAPLAN, A. *The conduct of inquiry: Methodology for behavioral science.* San Francisco: Chandler, 1964.

KATERBERG, R. and HOM, P. W. "The effects of within-group and between-group variation in leadership." *Journal of Applied Psychology*, 1981, 66, 218–23.

KATZ, D. and KAHN, R. L. *The social psychology of organizations.* New York: Wiley, 1978.

KENNY, D. A. "Cross-lagged panel correlation: A test for spuriousness." *Psychological Bulletin*, 1975, 82, 887–903.

KERLINGER, F. N. *Foundations of behavioral research.* New York: Holt, Rinehart and Winston, 1973.

KIMBERLY, J. R. "Issues in the design of longitudinal organizational research." *Sociological Methods and Research*, 1976, 4, 321–47.

———— "Data aggregation in organizational research: The temporal dimension." *Organization Studies*, 1980, 1, 367–77.

KORMAN, A. K. *Organizational behavior.* Englewood Cliffs, N.J.: Prentice-Hall, 1977.

KORNHAUSER, W. *Scientists in industry: Conflict and accommodation.* Berkeley: University of California Press, 1962.

KRAEMER, H. C. "Individual and ecological correlation in a general context." *Behavioral Science*, 1978, 23, 67–72.

KUHN, A. "Differences vs. similarities in living systems." *Behavioral Science*, 1980, 25, 40–45.

KUHN, T. S. *The structure of scientific revolutions.* Chicago: University of Chicago Press, 1970.

LAZARSFELD, P. F. and MENZEL, H. "On the relation between individual and collective properties." In A. Etzioni (Ed.), *Complex organizations: A sociological reader.* Glencoe, Ill.: Free Press, 1961, 422–40.

LERNER, D. (Ed.) *Evidence and inference.* Glencoe, Ill.: Free Press, 1959.

———— (Ed.) *Parts and wholes.* New York: Free Press, 1963.

LÉVI-STRAUSS, C. *The elementary structures of kinship.* Boston: Beacon Press, 1969.

LIKERT, R. *New patterns of management.* New York: McGraw-Hill, 1961.

———— *The human organization: Its management and values.* New York: McGraw-Hill, 1967.

LIN, N. *Foundations of social research.* New York: McGraw-Hill, 1976.

LINCOLN, J. R. and ZEITZ, G. "Organizational properties from aggregate data: Separating individual and structural effects." *American Sociological Review*, 1980, 45, 391–408.

LINDZEY, D. *The scientific publication system in social science.* San Francisco: Jossey-Bass, 1978.

LINTON, R. *The study of man.* Englewood Cliffs, N.J.: Prentice-Hall, 1936.

LOEVINGER, J. "Persons and population as psychometric concepts." *Psychological Review*, 1965, 72, 143–55.

MACKENZIE, K. D. and HOUSE, R. J. "Paradigm development in the social sciences: A proposed research strategy." *Academy of Management Review*, 1978, 3, 7–23.

MARCH, J. G. and SIMON, H. A. *Organizations*. New York: Wiley, 1958.

MARKHAM, S. E. "Leadership and motivation: An empirical examination of exchange and its outcomes." Unpublished doctoral dissertation, State University of New York at Buffalo, 1978.

_____, DANSEREAU, F., ALUTTO, J., and DUMAS, M. "Leadership convergence: An application of within and between analysis to validity." *Applied Psychological Measurement*, 1983, 7, 63–72.

_____ and SCOTT, K. D. "A component factor analysis of the initiating structure scale of the LBDQ Form XII." *Psychological Reports*, 1983, 52, 71–77.

MASTERMAN, M. "The nature of a paradigm." In I. Lakotos and A. Musgrave (Eds.), *Criticism and the growth of knowledge*. Cambridge, Eng.: Cambridge University Press, 1970, 59–89.

MAXWELL, S. E., CAMP, C. J., and ARVEY, R. D. "Measures of strength of association: A comparative examination." *Journal of Applied Psychology*, 1981, 66, 525–34.

McGUIRE, W. J. "The yin and yang of progress in social psychology: Seven koan." *Journal of Personality and Social Psychology*, 1973, 26, 446–56.

McNEMAR, Q. *Psychological statistics*. New York: Wiley, 1955.

MEEHL, P. E. "Theory-testing in psychology and physics: A methodological paradox." *Philosophy of Science*, 1967, 34, 103–15.

MERTON, R. K. *Social theory and social structure: Toward the codification of theory and research*. Glencoe, Ill.: The Free Press, 1949.

MILLER, J. G. *Living systems*. New York: McGraw-Hill, 1978.

_____ "Responses to the reviewers of *Living systems*." *Behavioral Science*, 1980, 25, 65–87.

MINTZBERG, H. "If you're not serving Bill and Barbara, then you're not serving leadership." In J. G. Hunt, U. Sekaran, and C. A. Schriesheim (Eds.), *Leadership: Beyond establishment views*. Carbondale: Southern Illinois University Press, 1982.

MISNER, C. W., THORNE, K. S., and WHEELER, J. A. *Gravitation*. San Francisco: Freeman, 1973.

MYRDAL, G. "How scientific are the social sciences?" *Bulletin of the Atomic Scientists*, 1973, 28, 31–37.

NACHMAN, S. "An empirical examination of the development of superior-subordinate interaction patterns in organizations: A test of a theory of investments and returns." Unpublished doctoral dissertation, State University of New York at Buffalo, 1982.

_____, DANSEREAU, F., and NAUGHTON, T. J. "Multiple hypothesis testing in leadership research: An empirical application of cross-lagged correlation analysis and within and between analysis." In W. Naumes and H. P. Sims (Eds.), *Proceedings of the Eastern Academy of Management*, May 1980, 117–22.

NAGEL, E. *The structure of science: Problems in the logic of scientific explanation*. New York: Harcourt, Brace and World, 1961.

_____ "Wholes, sums, and organic unities." In D. Lerner (Ed.), *Parts and wholes*. New York: Free Press, 1963.

NAUGHTON, T. J. "An empirical examination of a theory of option-cutting and commitment." Unpublished doctoral dissertation, State University of New York at Buffalo, 1982.

NEILSEN, E. H. "Contingency theory applied to small business organizations." *Human Relations*, 1974, 27, 357–79.

NEIMAN, L. J. and HUGHES, J. W. "The problems of the concept of role: A re-survey of the literature." *Social Forces*, 1951, 30, 141–49.

NEWCOMB, T. M. *Social psychology*. New York: Dryden, 1950.

_____ "An approach to the study of communicative acts." *Psychological Review*, 1953, 30, 393–404.

NUNNALLY, J. C. *Psychometric theory*. New York: McGraw-Hill, 1967.

OLMSTEAD, J. M. *Calculus with analytic geometry*. New York: Appleton-Century-Crofts, 1966.

PARASURAMAN, S. and ALUTTO, J. A. "An examination of the organizational antecedents of stressors at work." *Academy of Management Journal*, 1981, 24, 48–67.

PARSONS, T. "The relation between the small group and the larger social system." In R. Grinker (Ed.), *Toward a unified theory of behavior*. New York: Basic Books, 1956, 1967.

_____ *Structure and process in modern societies*. New York: Free Press, 1960.

_____ "Concrete systems and 'abstracted' systems." *Behavioral Science*, 1980, 25, 46–55.

PASCAL, B. *Pascal's pensées*. New York: Pantheon, 1950 (orginally, 1670).

PEPITONE, A. "Lessons from the history of social psychology." *American Psychologist*, 1981, 36, 972–85.

PLATT, J. R. "Strong inference." *Science*, 1964, 146, 347–53.

_____ *The step to man*. New York: Wiley, 1966.

POPPER, K. R. *The poverty of historicism*. Boston: Beacon Press, 1957.

_____ *The logic of scientific discovery*. New York: Basic Books, 1959.

RAPOPORT, A. "Philosophical perspectives on *Living systems*." *Behavioral Science*, 1980, 25, 56–64.

RIZZO, J. R., HOUSE, R. J., and LIRTZMAN, S. I. "Role conflict and ambiguity in complex organizations." *Administrative Science Quarterly*, 1970, 15, 150–63.

ROBERTS, K. H., HULIN, C. L., AND ROUSSEAU, D. M. *Developing an interdisciplinary science of organizations*. San Francisco: Jossey-Bass, 1978.

ROBINSON, W. S. "Ecological correlations and the behavior of individuals." *American Sociological Review*, 1950, 15, 351–57.

ROGOSA, D. "A critique of cross-lagged correlation." *Psychological Bulletin*, 1980, 88, 245–58.

ROSENZWEIG, J. E. "Editorial comment." *Academy of Management Review*, 1980, 5, 2, v.

ROZEBOOM, W. W. "The fallacy of the null-hypothesis significance test." *Psychological Bulletin*, 1960, 57, 416–28.

RUESCH, J. "Dialogue with Parsons and Rapoport." In R. Grinker (Ed.), *Toward a unified theory of human behavior*. New York: Basic Books, 1967, 328.

SARBIN, T. R. and ALLEN, V. L. "Role theory." In G. Lindzey and E. Aronson (Eds.), *The handbook of social psychology*. Reading, Mass.: Addison-Wesley, 1968.

SCHEIN, E. H. *Organizational psychology*. Englewood Cliffs, N.J.: Prentice-Hall, 1980.

SCHRIESHEIM, J. F. "The social context of leader-subordinate relations: An investigation of the effects of group cohesiveness." *Journal of Applied Psychology*, 1980, 65, 183–94.

SCHWAB, D. P. "Construct validity in organizational behavior." In B. M. Staw and L. L. Cummings (Eds.), *Research in organizational behavior*. Greenwich, Conn.: JAI Press, 1980, 2, 3–43.

SECORD, P. F. and BACKMAN, C. W. *Social psychology*. New York: McGraw-Hill, 1974.

SHERIDAN, J. E. and VREDENBURGH, D. J. "Structural model of leadership influence in a hospital organization." *Academy of Management Journal*, 1979, 22, 6–21.

SIENKO, M. J. and PLANE, R. A. *Chemistry: Principles and properties*. New York: McGraw-Hill, 1974.

SIGNORELLI, A. "Statistics: Tool or master of the psychologist?" *American Psychologist*, 1974, 29, 774–77.

SIMMEL, G. *Soziologie*. Leipzig: Duncker and Humbolt, 1908.

SKINNER, B. F. *Science and human behavior*. New York: Free Press, 1953.

SMAIL, L. *Analytic geometry and calculus*. New York: Appleton-Century-Crofts, 1953.

STANLEY, J. C. "Reliability." In R. L. Thorndike (Ed.), *Educational measurement*. Washington, D.C.: American Council on Education, 1971.

STARBUCK, W. H. *Organization theory from before Ptah-Hotep to beyond Pradip Khandwalla*. Berlin: International Institute of Management, 1972.

STAW, B. M. "Attitudinal and behavioral consequences of changing a major organizational reward: A natural field experiment." *Journal of Personality and Social Psychology*, 1974, 29, 742–51.

———— "Rationality and justification in organizational life." In B. M. Staw and L. L. Cummings (Eds.), *Research in organizational behavior*. Greenwich, Conn.: JAI Press, 1980, 2, 45–80.

———— and OLDHAM, G. R. "Reconsidering our dependent variables: A critique and empirical study." *Academy of Management Journal*, 1978, 21, 539–59.

———— and ROSS, J. "Commitment to a policy decision: A multitheoretical perspective." *Administrative Science Quarterly*, 1978, 23, 40–64.

————, SANDELANDS, L. E., and DUTTON, J. E. "Threat-rigidity effects in organizational behavior: A multilevel analysis." *Administrative Science Quarterly*, 1981, 26, 501–24.

STOGDILL, R. M. *Handbook of leadership: A survey of theory and research*. New York: Free Press, 1974.

STONE, E. F. *Research methods in organizational behavior*. Glenview, Ill.: Scott Foresman, 1978.

STUDENT. "Probable error of a correlation coefficient." *Biometrika*, 1908, 6, 302–10.

THIBAUT, J. W. and KELLEY, H. H. *The social psychology of groups*. New York: Wiley, 1959.

THORNDIKE, E. L. *Animal intelligence*. New York: Macmillan, 1911.

VAN DEN BERGHE, P. L. "Bridging the paradigms." *Society*, 1978, 15, 42–49.

VAN DE VEN, A. H. and ASTLEY, W. G. "A commentary on organizational behavior in the 1980's." *Decision Sciences*, 1981, 12, 388–98.

VECCHIO, R. P. "A further test of leadership effects due to between-group variation and within-group variation." *Journal of Applied Psychology*, 1982, 67, 200–08.

WATSON, J. S. "Publication delays in the natural and social-behavioral science journals: An indication of the presence or absence of a scientific paradigm?" *American Psychologist*, 1982, 37, 448–49.

WEBER, M. *The theory of social and economic organization.* New York: Oxford University Press, 1947.

WEICK, K. E. *The social psychology of organizing.* Reading, Mass.: Addison-Wesley, 1978.

YUKL, G. A. *Leadership in organizations.* Englewood Cliffs, N.J.: Prentice-Hall, 1981.

ZADEH, L. A. "Probability measures of fuzzy events." *Mathematical Analysis and Application*, 1968, 23, 421–27.

ZELLER, R. A. and CARMINES, E. G. *Measurement in the social sciences.* New York: Cambridge University Press, 1980.

ZIMAN, J. M. *Reliable knowledge: An exploration of the grounds for belief in science.* Cambridge, Eng.: Cambridge University Press, 1978.

INDEX

Name Index

A

Adams, J. S., 96, 397
Aiken, M., 10, 28, 401
Aldrich, H. E., 83, 397
Alexander, C. N., 96, 397
Allen, V. L., 88, 405
Alutto, J. A., 27, 88, 89, 91, 286, 397, 399, 403, 404
Argyris, C., 317, 397
Arnold, H. J., 16, 21, 131, 397
Arvey, R. D., 298, 403
Astley, W. G. 10–12, 321, 406

B

Backman, C. W., 89, 90, 91, 96, 97, 405
Bakan, D., 27, 39, 40, 166, 397
Banton, M. P., 88, 89, 397
Barrett, G. V., 1, 3, 16, 397
Bass, B. M., 3, 9, 16, 27, 307, 397
Bechtoldt, H. P., 27, 28, 398
Behling, O., 1, 3, 66, 398
Bell, G. D., 206, 398
Biddle, B. J., 88, 89, 90, 91, 398
Blalock, H. M., 3, 10, 66, 67, 398
Blau, P. M., 12, 87, 89, 96, 97, 99, 398
Bobbitt, H. R., 12, 398
Bolles, R. C., 4, 27, 398
Boulding, K. E., 10, 16, 27, 398
Braithwaite, R., 3, 66, 398
Bredemier, H. C., 98, 398
Breinholt, R. H., 398
Bronfenbrenner, M., 3, 398
Brown, R., 44, 398
Byrne, D., 12, 100, 398

C

Camp, C. J., 298, 403
Campbell, D. T., 16, 28, 316, 317, 398, 399
Campbell, J. P., 11, 28, 399
Carmines, E. G., 309, 310, 312, 406
Cartwright, D., 3, 399
Cashman, J., 73, 399
Chadwick-Jones, J. K., 95, 96, 399
Chamberlin, T. C., 3, 327, 399
Cohen, J., 27, 307, 399
Cohen, M. R., 3, 399
Cohen, P., 307, 399
Conant, J. B., 67, 399
Cook, T. D., 16, 399
Cronbach, L. J., 16, 27, 28, 288, 310, 311, 314, 399
Cummings, L. L., 10, 16, 399
Cuzzort, R. P., 120, 400

D

Dansereau, F., 27, 73, 151, 205, 283, 399, 400, 401, 403
Diesing, P., 3, 400
Doktor, R. H., 398
Dubin, R., 3, 66, 400
Dubno, P., 309, 400
Dumas, M., 27, 399, 403
Duncan, B. D., 120, 400
Duncan, O. D., 120, 400
Dunnette, M. D., 3, 27, 28, 399, 400
Durkheim, E., 12, 400
Dutton, J. E., 10, 405

E

Eckberg, D. L., 3, 400
Ekeh, P. P., 96, 97, 99, 400
Emmerson, R. M., 97, 400
Epstein, S., 10, 28, 281, 400

F

Festinger, L., 96, 400
Fiedler, F. E., 21, 400
Finn, J. D., 298, 305, 400
Firebaugh, G., 10, 28, 292, 293, 400
Fisher, R. A., 3–5, 9, 27, 111, 113, 131, 142,
    281, 298, 319, 400
Fiske, D. W., 16, 28, 398
Furby, L., 288, 399

G

Gergen, K. J., 95, 400
Ghiselli, E. E., 7, 16, 27, 400
Glass, G., 141, 400
Gleser, G. C., 399
Gnedenko, B. V., 44, 400
Gould, P., 45, 400
Graen, G., 3, 73, 205, 399, 400, 401
Greenberg, M., 95, 400
Gross, N., 88, 89, 401
Guilford, J. P., 7, 131, 133, 141, 194, 288, 311,
    320, 360, 401

H

Haga, W. J., 73, 205, 400, 401
Hage, J., 10, 28, 401
Hall, R. H., 93, 401
Hannan, M. T., 10, 13, 28, 401
Harman, H. H., 111–13, 115–17, 401
Harris, C. W., 28, 401
Hays, W. L., 4, 5, 7, 124, 401
Heider, F., 96, 401
Heise, D. R., 20, 289, 401
Hellriegel, D., 12, 21, 401
Hill, L., 3, 400
Hillburn, D., 400
Hollander, E. P., 12, 91, 100, 401
Hom, P. W., 10, 28, 294, 402
Homans, G. C., 10, 14, 66, 96, 97, 99, 401
Hotelling, H., 141, 187, 401
House, R. J., 3, 21, 88, 401, 403, 404
Hughes, J. W., 88, 404
Hulin, C. L., 1, 404
Hunt, J. G., 44, 322, 401

J

Jacobs, T. O., 73, 401
James, L. R., 10, 401

K

Kahn, R. L., 10, 11, 14, 88, 89, 91, 92, 93, 203,
    402
Kalleberg, A. L., 28, 402
Kaplan, A., 3, 12, 16, 402
Katerberg, R., 10, 28, 294, 402
Katz, D., 10, 11, 14, 88, 89, 91, 92, 93, 203,
    402
Kelley, H. H., 96, 405
Kenny, D. A., 283, 402
Kerlinger, F. N., 20, 27, 28, 402
Kimberly, J. R., 28, 45, 402
Kluegel, J. R., 28, 402
Korman, A. K., 12, 402
Kornhauser, W., 93, 402
Kraemer, H. C., 281, 402
Kuhn, A., 10, 402
Kuhn, T. S., 3, 402

L

Lawler, E. E., 399
Lazarsfeld, P. F., 10, 402
Lerner, D., 3, 12, 402
Lévi-Strauss, C., 97, 402
Likert, R., 11, 78, 402
Lin, N., 20, 402
Lincoln, J. R., 10, 28, 293, 294, 402
Lindzey, D., 3, 402
Linton, R., 89, 402
Lirtzman, S. I., 88, 404
Loevinger, J., 27, 28, 403

M

McEachern, A. W., 88, 89, 401
McGuire, W. J., 1, 3, 16, 403
MacKenzie, K. D., 3, 403
McNaul, J. P., 398
McNemar, Q., 27, 131, 132, 284, 299, 403
March, J. G., 98, 403
Markham, S. E., 27, 312, 325, 399, 403
Mason, W., 88, 89, 401
Masterman, M., 1, 403
Maxwell, S. E., 298, 403
Meehl, P. E., 3, 4, 8, 16, 27, 399, 403
Menzel, H., 10, 402
Merton, R. K., 66, 92, 403
Miller, J. G., 3, 7, 10–12, 14, 37, 67, 68, 70,
    83, 90, 403
Mintzberg, H., 70, 324, 403
Misner, C. W., 8, 110–12, 115, 403
Myrdal, G., 3, 9, 403

N

Nachman, S., 283, 325, 403
Nagel, E., 3, 4, 12, 399, 403, 404

Nanda, H., 399
Naughton, T. J., 283, 325, 403, 404
Neilsen, E. H., 21, 404
Neiman, L. J., 88, 404
Nelson, D., 12, 100, 398
Newcomb, T. M., 88, 96, 404
Nunnally, J. C., 16, 28, 404

O
Oldham, G. R., 10, 405
Olmstead, J. M., 111, 115, 404

P
Parasuraman, S., 286, 404
Parsons, T., 10, 13, 14, 90, 92, 404
Pascal, B., 67, 404
Pepitone, A., 96, 404
Plane, R. A., 12, 405
Platt, J. R., 4, 404
Popper, K. R., 4, 328, 404

Q
Quinn, R. P., 402

R
Rajaratnam, N., 399
Rapoport, A., 10, 404
Rizzo, J. R., 88, 404
Roberts, K. H., 1, 3, 10, 16, 168, 179, 404
Robinson, G., 400
Robinson, W. S., 10, 27, 42, 120, 123, 135, 286, 287, 345, 404
Rogosa, D., 283, 404
Rosenthal, R. A., 402
Rosenzweig, J. E., 21, 404
Ross, J., 4, 405
Rousseau, D. M., 1, 404
Rozeboom, W. W., 4, 27, 404
Ruesch, J., 90, 405

S
Sandelands, L. E., 10, 405
Sandler, D., 400
Sarbin, T. R., 88, 405
Schein, E. H., 12, 405
Schriesheim, C. A., 44, 401
Schriesheim, J. F., 135, 298, 405
Schwab, D. P., 16, 28, 405
Scott, K. D., 312, 403
Secord, P. F., 89, 90, 91, 96, 97, 405

Sekaran, U., 44, 401
Sheridan, J. E., 135, 405
Sienko, M. J., 12, 405
Signorelli, A., 27, 405
Simmel, G., 12, 405
Simon, H. A., 98, 403
Simpson, R. L., 96, 397
Skinner, B. F., 97, 405
Slocum, J., 12, 21, 401
Smail, L., 112, 115, 336, 337, 405
Snoek, J. D., 402
Stanley, J. C., 28, 141, 316, 317, 398, 400, 405
Starbuck, W. H., 9, 405
Staw, B. M., 4, 10, 405
Stogdill, R. M., 298, 405
Stone, E. F., 10, 405
Student, 118, 405

T
Thibaut, J. W., 96, 405
Thomas, E. J., 88, 89, 398
Thorndike, E. L., 96, 406
Thorne, K. S., 110, 403
Trani, J., 400
Turner, J., 44, 398

V
Van de Berghe, P. L., 3, 406
Van de Ven, A. H., 10–12, 321, 406
Vecchio, R. P., 10, 294, 406
Vredenburgh, D. J., 135, 405

W
Watson, J. S., 3, 406
Weber, M., 92, 406
Weick, K. E., 11, 83, 399, 406
Weingarten, E., 400
Wheeler, J. A., 110, 403
Willis, R., 95, 400
Wolfe, D. M., 402

Y
Yukl, G. A., 73, 406

Z
Zadeh, L. A., 29, 406
Zeitz, G., 10, 28, 293, 294, 402
Zeller, R. A., 309, 310, 312, 406
Ziman, J. M., 3, 406

Subject Index*

A

Adaptive titles:
  analyzed, 213–20, 249–58
  defined, 93
  measures of, 201–4
Aggregation, 43–46 (*see also* Multiple-level
  analysis)
Alternative hypotheses:
  creation of:
    multiple-level analysis, 51–52
    multiple-relationship analysis, 58–63
    multiple-variable analysis, 54–56
    single-level analysis, 38–41
  mutually exclusive, 33–37, 321–22
Analysis of covariance—ANCOVA, 299–300
Analysis of variance—ANOVA (*see also*
  WABA I)
  n-way:
    correlational basis of, 300–304
    defined, 300–304, 354
    traditional view of, 306–7
    varient view of, 304–6
  one-way:
    correlational basis of, 354–61
    defined, 295
    traditional view of, 297–99
    varient view of, 295–97
A test:
  and between-cell correlations, 129–30
  decision intervals for, 175–77, *178*, *183*,
    186–87
  defined, 130, 140
  differences between correlations, 130, 140
  examples of use, 193–99, 210, 212–16,

230–31, 233–34, 237–39, 246–49,
  251–59
ideal values for, 148–51, 158–63
and time, 267–71
and traditional approaches, 286–88
and within-cell correlations, 129–30
Attention:
  analyzed, 227–39
  defined, 102
  measures of, 226, 243–58, 365–66, 368–69
Average *E* ratio, defined, 192–93
Average *F* ratio, defined, 192–93
Average leadership style—ALS:
  defined, 73
  tested, 222–40
  and wholes, 73–78
Averages:
  defined, 41, 339–40
  limitations of, 44–46

B

Between-cell:
  component:
    defined, 123
    illustrated, 193, 211–12, 215, 232, 235,
     238
  correlation (*see* Correlation, between-cell)
  eta correlation (*see* Correlation, between-eta)
  R ratio, 131
  signed deviation scores:
    defined, 41, 350–51
    and higher levels of analysis, 137–39
  t test, 132

*Page numbers in italics denote tables or figures.

C

Causal analysis (*see* Time)
Cells, construction of, 135–36, 192, 202–3, 224–26, 354
Change condition, 266, 270–75
Chosen focus, 58, 275, 279
Collectivities:
  conceptualized, 67–68, 71, 80–82, 84–85
  defined, 11
  empirical tests for, 194–95, 213–20, 246–59
  number at the metals company, 203–4
  parts of, 12, 39
  whole, 12, 38–39, 70, 91
Collectivity functional titles:
  analyzed, 213–20, 249–58
  defined, 205
  measures of, 205
Composite fallacy:
  defined, 282
  and regression equations, 292–95
Computerized WABA:
  Fortran, 374–81
  SPSS, 372–74
Congruence of subordinate with superior:
  analyzed, 227–39
  defined, 103
  measures of, 226, 368, 371
Contextual analysis (*see also* Composite fallacy; Correlation, composite)
  defined, 281–82
Contingent variables:
  conceptualized, 58–63
  defined, 21
  empirical indicators for, 141–42
  empirical tests for, 251–56, 259–60
  ideal conditions for, 161–64
  inductions about, 187–88
  inferences about, 197–98
  theoretical illustrations of, 82–86, 106–8
  traditional views of, 16, 21, 326–27
Control groups, 296, 317
Correlation:
  and analysis of covariance, 299–300
  and analysis of variance, 142–43, 295, 301–4, 354–61
  average between-cell, 193–94
  average between-eta, 192
  average within-cell, 193–94
  average within-eta, 192
  between-cell:
    and A test, 129–30
    defined, 122, 129
    R test of, 131
    t test of, 131–32
    and Z test, 130–31
  between-eta:
    defined, 121, 124, 343–44
    and E ratio, 124

    and F ratio, 125
  bivariate:
    defined, 280
    geometric basis of, 114–17
    traditional view of, 280–83
    varient view of, 280
  composite:
    ambiguity of, 264, 281–82
    and contextual analysis, 281–82, 347–48
    defined, 263–64
    traditional view of, 292–95
    varient view of, 264
  cross lag, 283
  general, 113
  and general linear tensor, 111–16
  geometric basis of, 111–13
  interitem, 311
  and internal consistency, 311
  intraclass, 298
  midpoint of, 113, 167–68
  multiple:
    and bivariate correlations, 288
    correlational basis of, 288–89
    defined, 288
    traditional view of, 19–21, 291–95
    varient view of, 290–91
  partial:
    correlational basis of, 283–84
    defined, 283
    tests for, 284–88
    traditional view of, 286–88
    varient view of, 284–86
  and percent of variance, 115, 167–68, 171
  population, 6
  and sample size, 6–7
  total:
    ambiguity of, 119–20, 206–8, 227, 249–51
    defined, 116–19
  within-cell:
    and A test, 129–30
    defined, 122, 129
    R test of, 132
    t test of, 131–32
    and Z test, 130–31
  within-eta:
    defined, 121, 124, 344–45
    and E ratio, 124
    and F ratio, 125
  and Z' scores, 131, *331*
Cross-level approach, 13–14
Cross-level parts (*see also* Parts)
  conceptualized, 46, *50*
  defined, 46–47
  empirical indicators for, 137–39
  ideal conditions for, 154, *156*
  inductions about, 185–86
  theoretical illustrations of, 80–82
  traditional views of, 293

412   Subject Index

Cross-level wholes (*see also* Wholes)
  conceptualized, 46, *50*
  defined, 46–47
  empirical indicators for, 137–39
  ideal conditions for, 154, *156*
  inductions about, 185–86
  inferences about, 194–95, 216
  theoretical illustrations of, 80–82, 91–92, 94
  traditional views of, 139, 281–82, 292–93

D
Decision intervals (*see also* Practical
    significance tests; Statistical significance
    tests)
  A test, 175–77, *183*
  E ratio, 169–72, *183*
  F ratio, 172–74, *183*
  Hotellings *t'* test, 187
  R test, 179–81, *183*
  t test, 181, *183*
  Z test, 177–78, *183*
Degrees of freedom:
  for between-cell correlation, 131, 352–53
  for between-cell deviations, 352
  for between-eta correlation, 125, 352
  for *F* ratio, 172–74
  for Hotelling's *t'* test, 141
  for *t* test, 118, 131–32
  for within-cell correlation, 132, 352–53
  for within-cell deviations, 352
  for within-eta correlation, 125, 352
Dependent:
  variables, 19
  vectors, 112
Difference between two correlations, 131, 140
Direct contingency, 21
Discontinuity thesis, 14
Double fallacy, 151
Dyads:
  conceptualized, 67–68, 73–78, 84–85
  defined, 11
  empirical tests for, 233–36, 256–58
  number at the metals company, *224*
  parts of, 12, 39
  whole, 12, 38–39, 89, 91, 101

E
Ecological fallacy, 286–87
Education:
  analyzed, 206–21, 243–49
  defined, 205
  measures of, 205, 362–63
Emergent approach, 14
Emergent parts (*see also* Parts)

conceptualized, 48, *50*
  defined, 48–49
  empirical indicators for, 137–39
  ideal conditions for, 155–56
  inductions about, 185–86
  theoretical illustrations of, 80–82
  traditional views of, 44–46
Emergent wholes (*see also* Wholes)
  conceptualized, 48–49, *50*
  defined, 48–49
  empirical indicators for, 137–39
  ideal conditions for, 155–56
  inductions about, 185–86
  inferences about, 238–40, 256–58
  theoretical illustrations of, 78–82, 101, 103
  traditional views of, 44–46, 139
Entity axis:
  conceptualized, 37–52
  defined, 14–15
  illustrated, 90–92, 95, 99–101, 103–4, 107, 194–95, 198–99, 216, 220, 239, 240, 258, 260
Environments, defined, 83
Equity theory (*see also* Exchange theory)
  and hedonism, 97
Equivocal condition:
  conceptualized, 40
  defined, 40
  empirical indicators for, 41–42
  in general terms, 263
  ideal conditions for, 136, 146–54
  inductions about, 169–73, 175–81
  inferences about, 227–32, 237–40, 257–58
  and partial correlations, 284–85
  theoretical illustrations of, 73–75, 101, 103–4, 106–8
  and time, 266–67
  traditional views of, 151
E ratio:
  and between-eta correlations, 123–25
  decision intervals for, 169–75, *183*
  defined, 124
  differences between independent correlations, 114
  examples of use, 192–95, 209, 213–14, 227–30, 233, 237–38, 251–53, 266–68, 286–87
  general, 114
  ideal values for, 146–48
  and time, 266–67
  and traditional approaches, 286–87
  and within-eta correlations, 123–25
Error:
  component of scaling, 309
  meaning:
    one variable case, 41–42, 145
    two variable case, 42, 145, 148

Eta correlation:
  average, 192
  calculating, 128
  relation to F ratio, 125, 172, 174
Exchange theory:
  and equity, 96–97
  review of, 95–98
  and role theory, 104–8
  theory B formulation of, 95–104
Expectations:
  analyzed, 206–20, 243–58
  defined, 91, 93–94
  measures of, 205–6, 363–65
Experimental studies, 295–97, 316–17

F

Factor analysis, 312–14
F distribution:
  defined, 5
  table of, 332–35
  and t distribution, 5
  use of, 166–67
  and Z distribution, 5
15° test (*see* Practical significance tests)
Firebaugh's $\overline{X}$ rule, 292–93
Fisher's Z' scores, 130–31, 331
F ratio:
  and between-eta correlations, 125, 172–74
  decision intervals for, 166–67, *170*, 172–74, 332–35
  defined, 125, 172–73
  examples of use, 192–93, 209, 213–14, 217–20, 227–30, 233, 237–38, 251–53, 266–68, 286–87
  ideal values for, 146–48
  and time, 266
  and traditional approaches, 142–43, 217, 286–87, 298, 354–60
  and within-eta correlations, 125, 172–73
Freedom from constraints, defined, 93–94
Freedom from machine determination:
  analyzed, 206–20, 243–58
  defined, 93–94
  measures of, 206, 363
Freedom from superiors:
  analyzed, 206–20, 243–58
  defined, 93–94
  measures of, 205, 363
Freedom preferences:
  analyzed, 206–20, 243–58
  defined, 93–94
  measures of, 206, 364–65
Functional titles:
  analyzed, 206–20, 243–58
  defined, 92–93
  measures of, 205, 217–20

G

General E ratio, 114
Generalizations:
  data to populations, 319
  data to theory, 318–20
  study to study, 319
General-level theories:
  defined, 66
  illustrated, 90–92, 98–102
General linear tensor, 111–16
Generally related variables:
  conceptualized, 56–58
  defined, 19
  empirical indicators for, 139–41
  ideal conditions for, 157–61
  inductions about, 186–87
  inferences about, 195–97, 273–74
  theoretical illustrations of, 25, 273–74
  traditional views of, 20, 290–91, 311, 314
Generally unrelated variables:
  conceptualized, 56–58
  defined, 18
  empirical indicators for, 139–41
  ideal conditions for, 158–60
  inductions about, 186–87
  inferences about, 198–99, 258–60
  theoretical illustrations of, 106–8, 273
  traditional views of, 290–91, 312–14
Grand theories, defined, 65
Groups:
  conceptualized, 67–68, 71, 75–78, 84–85
  defined, 11
  empirical tests for, 192–95, 208–13, 227–33, 237–39, 256–57
  number at the metals company, 202
  parts of, 12, 39–40
  whole, 12, 38–39, 70, 89, 91–92, 94–95, 101

H

Hedonism and exchange, 97–98
Hierarchical regression, 289
Higher level of analysis, defined, 15
Homology thesis, defined, 13
Hotelling's t' test, 57, 141, 247, 248
Hypotheses:
  creation of, 33–37, 87–108
  defined, 3
  testing:
    with correlations (*see* Correlation)
    with WABA (*see* WABA)

I

Ideal empirical conditions:
  contingent, 161–63

cross-level parts, 154, 156–57
cross-level wholes, 154, 156–57
emergent parts, 155, 156–57
emergent wholes, 155, 156–57
equivocal, 145–54
generally related variables, 158–61
generally unrelated variables, 158–61
inexplicable, 145–54
level-specific parts, 154–55
level-specific wholes, 154
multiplexed, 161–64
parts, 145–54
related variables, 158–61
unrelated variables, 158–61
WABA I, 145–48, 153–54
WABA II, 148–54
wholes, 145–54
Idiosyncrasy credit theory, 100
Independent variables, defined, 19
Independent vectors, defined, 112–13
Inequity (*see* Exchange theory)
Inexplicable condition:
   conceptualized, 40
   defined, 40
   empirical indicators for, 41–42
   ideal conditions for, 136, 146–48
   inductions about, 169–81
   inferences about, *245*
   traditional view as a null hypothesis, 3–4
Infinite sampling theory, 319
Insider perspective:
   defined, 68–70
   and theory A, 90
   and theory B, 100
Internal consistency, 311
Intervening variables, 273
Investments:
   analyzed, 227–39, 243–58
   defined, 98
   measures of, 226, 365–71
Isomorphism, between theory and data, 190
Items:
   defined, 309
   illustrated, 362–71

J
Job (individual) titles:
   analyzed, 218–20
   defined, 205
   measures of, 218–19

L
Lack of association between vectors, 114, 124
Latitude:
   analyzed, 227–39, 243–57
   defined, 102
   measures of, 226, 366–68, 369–71

Leadership, 73–78
Levels of analysis (*see also* Collectivities;
   Dyads; Groups; Multiple-level analysis;
   Persons; Single-level analysis)
   defined, 9–10
   and exchange theory, 98–104
   higher, 15
   lower, 15
   and role theory, 89–92, 94–95
Levels of significance (*see* Practical significance
   tests; Statistical significance tests)
Level-specific parts (*see also* Parts)
   conceptualized, 48, *50*
   defined, 47–48
   empirical indicators for, 137–39
   ideal conditions for, 154–56
   inductions about, 185–86
   inferences about, 25
   theoretical illustrations of, 78–82
   traditional views of, 73, 75, 77
Level-specific wholes (*see also* Wholes)
   conceptualized, 46, *50*
   defined, 46–47
   empirical indicators for, 137–39
   ideal conditions for, 154–56
   inductions about, 185–86
   inferences about, 234–36, 256–57
   theoretical illustrations of, 78–82, 101, 103
   traditional views of, 139
Lower level titles, 93, 203, 218–19

M
Magnitude tests (*see* R test; t test)
Maintenance titles:
   analyzed, 213–20, 249–58
   defined, 93
   measures of, 205
Middle range theories, defined, 65
Moderator variable (*see* Contingent variables)
Multicollinearity, 20, 261, 289, 291–92
Multiple correlation (*see* Correlation, multiple)
Multiple-hypothesis testing:
   defined, 3–4
   and methods, 317–18
   in the statistical paradigm, 3–4
   in the varient paradigm, 33, 328
Multiple-level analysis:
   conceptualized, 33–36, 46–52, 321–22
   defined, 13–16
   empirical illustration of:
      real data, 204, 212, 216, 224–26, 232,
         234–36, 238–39, 242–43, 256–57
      synthetic data, 194–95
   empirical indicators for, 137–39
   ideal conditions for, 153–57
   inductions in, 185–86

inferences from, 194–95, 220–21, 232, 239–40, 258–60
and measurement, 310–11
practical implications of, 326
theoretical illustrations of, 71–78, 91–92, 94, 101, 103, 104
theory formulation, 80–82
time, 273
and traditional approaches, 278, 285–87, 291, 292–95, 298, 306, 307
Multiple regression (*see* Correlation, multiple)
Multiple-relationship analysis:
    conceptualized, 36, 58–63, 322–23
    defined, 21–24
    empirical illustration of:
        real data, 212–13, 216–17, 232, 236–37, 239, 247–58
        synthetic data, 197–98
    empirical indicators for, 141–42
    ideal conditions for, 161–63
    inductions in, 187–88
    inferences from, 197–98, 220–21, 239–40, 258–60
    and measurement, 314
    practical implications of, 326–27
    theoretical illustrations of, 92, 94–95, 101–3, 106
    theory formulation, 82–86
    time, 275
    and traditional approaches, 285, 286, 290–92, 298, 306–7
Multiple-variable analysis:
    conceptualized, 36, 53–58, 322–23
    defined, 17–21
    empirical illustrations of:
        real data, 212–13, 216–17, 232, 236–37, 239–40, 243–47, 257–58
        synthetic data, 195–97
    empirical indicators for, 139–41
    ideal conditions for, 157–61
    inductions in, 186–87
    inferences from, 195–97, 220–21, 239–40, 258–60
    and measurement, 311–14
    practical implications of, 326–27
    theoretical illustrations of, 92, 94–95, 101–6
    theory formulation, 82
    time, 273–74
    and traditional approaches, 285, 286, 290–92, 298, 304–7
Multiplexed variables:
    conceptualized, 58–63
    defined, 22
    empirical indicators for, 141–42
    empirical tests for, 251–58
    ideal conditions for, 161–64
    inductions about, 187–88
    inferences about, 197–98, 251–60

theoretical illustrations of, 82–86, 106
traditional views of, 16, 21, 275, 326–27
Mutually exclusive conditions, 39, 54

N
Non-experimental studies, 316
Non-reciprocal relationships, 265
Non-reductionist approach, 44–46
Normal distribution, 5
Null hypothesis, 4

O
Observational approach, 317
One-tail tests, 167
Other focus, 58, 275
Outsider perspective, defined, 68–70

P
Paradigm, 1–2
Partial correlation (*see* Correlation, partial)
Parts (*see also* Cross-level parts; Emergent parts; Level-specific parts)
    conceptualized, 39–40, 84–85
    defined, 12, 39
    empirical indicators for, 41–42
    ideal conditions for, 136, 146–49, 151–54
    inductions about, 169–85
    inferences about, 230, 287
    theoretical illustration of, 73–75, 90–91, 100
    traditional views of, 292–93, 315
Path analysis, 295
Persons:
    conceptualized, 67–68, 71, 73–77, 84, 85
    defined, 11
    empirical tests for, 227–32
    number at the metals company, 202
    parts of, 11, 39
    whole, 11, 38–39, 70, 73–74, 91, 101
Physical entities, defined, 37
Position, defined, 90
Practical significance tests:
    decision intervals:
        multiple-level analysis, 185–86
        multiple-relationship analysis, 187–88
        multiple-variable analysis, 186–87
        single-level analysis, 169–72, 175–77, 179–81
    0° test; 15° test; 30° test:
        WABA I, 169
        WABA II, 176, 179–81
Predictor-criterion validity, 311
Principle of parts, 48
Principle of wholes, 47

Production titles:
  analyzed, 213–20, 249–58
  defined, 92
  measures of, 205
Professional associations, 205
Professionalism, 93
Professional titles:
  analyzed, 206–17, 243–58
  defined, 93
  measures of, 205, 362–63

Q
Qualitative and quantitative methods, 70, 324

R
Reciprocal relationships, 265
Reductionist approach:
  and cross-level formulation, 91
  defined, 43–44
Regression (*see* Correlation, multiple)
Related variables:
  conceptualized, 53–54, 56–57
  defined, 18
  empirical indicators for, 139–41
  ideal conditions for, 157–61
  inductions about, 186–87
  inferences about, 212–13, 216–17, 220–21,
    236–37, 239–40, 257–58
  theoretical illustrations of, 25, 92, 94–95,
    101–4
  traditional views of, 291–92, 304–7, 311
Replication approach, 319
Representativeness approach, 319–20
Residual gain scores, 287–88
Returns:
  analyzed, 227–39, 243–58
  defined, 98
  measures of, 226, 365–71
Role taking, 89–90
Role theory:
  and exchange theory, 104–8
  review of, 88–90
  theory A formulation of, 88–95
R test:
  and between-cell correlations, 131
  decision intervals for, 179–81
  defined, 115, 131, 132
  examples of use, 194, 197, 207, 210–12,
    213–15, 227, 231–32, 234, 251, 254
  general, 115
  ideal cases for, 151–52, 158–59
  and total correlation, 117
  and traditional approaches, 206–8, 227,
    249–51
  and within-cell correlations, 132

S
Sampling:
  infinite, 319
  from a population, 319–20
Scalar product, 111, 116–17
Signed deviation scores, 41, 341–42, 350–52
Simple theories, defined, 65
Single-level analysis:
  conceptualized, 33–36, 38–42
  defined, 11–13
  empirical illustrations of:
    real data, 209–12, 213–15, 227–34,
      237–38, 243, 251–56, 286–87
    synthetic data, 192–94
  empirical indicators for, 136–37
  ideal conditions for, 145–54
  inductions in, 168–85
  inferences from, 192–94, 220–21, 239–40,
    258–60
  practical implications of, 325–27
  theoretical illustration of, 71–78, 90–91,
    94, 99–101, 103, 104
  theory formulation, 78–80
  time, 265–72
  and traditional approaches, 278, 281–83,
    286–87, 292–95, 298, 307
Specific-level theories:
  defined, 66
  illustrated, 92–95, 102–4
Stable condition, 266–72
Statistical artifacts, 6, 167
Statistical paradigm, 4–9
Statistical significance tests:
  decision intervals for:
    multiple-level analysis, 185–86
    multiple-relationship analysis, 187–88
    multiple-variable analysis, 186–87
    single-level analysis, 172–74, 177–78,
      181
  0.01 test; 0.05 test:
    WABA I, 166–67, 172–74, 332–35
    WABA II, 166–67, 177–81, 332–35
Stepwise regression, 289
Subordinate dyads, 276 (*see also* Dyads)
Subordinates and superiors, 71–78
Substantive hypothesis, defined, 3–4
Sum of squares:
  adjusted, 299
  and WABA, 343–47
Superior satisfaction with subordinate:
  analyzed, 227–39, 243–58
  defined, 102–3
  measures of, 226, 368, 371
Superior-subordinate dyads, 73–78 (*see also*
  Dyads)
Supervisory workgroups, 71 (*see also* Groups)
Support titles:
  analyzed, 213–20, 249–58

defined, 93
measures of, 205

T

Theory:
  and data alignment, 33–64, 145–89
  defined, 3
  grand, 65
  illustration of, 87–109
  middle range, 65
  physicalness of, 37
  simple, 65
  size, 65–66
  varient requirements for, 65–86
30° test (*see* Practical significance tests)
Time (*see* Multiple-level analysis; Multiple-relationship analysis; Multiple-variable analysis; Single-level analysis)
Titles:
  analyzed, 206–20, 243–58
  defined, 90
  measures of, 205
Total correlation (*see* Correlation, total)
Total *R* ratio, 117
Total signed deviation scores, 41, 116–18, 350–51
Trigonometric functions, 113, 330, 337–38
True component of scaling, 309
t test:
  and between-cell correlations, 132
  decision intervals for, 181
  defined, 117–19, 132
  examples of use, 194, 197, 207, 210–12, 213–15, 227, 231–32, 234, 251, 254
  ideal cases for, *152*
  and total correlation, 117–18
  and traditional approaches, 206–8, 227, 249–51
  and within-cell correlations, 132

U

Units of analysis (*see also* Parts; Wholes)
  defined, 11–12
Unit vectors, 116
  conceptualized, 54, 56–57
  defined, 18
  empirical indicators for, 139–41
  ideal conditions for, 157–59
  inductions about, 186–87
  inferences about, 195–97, 243–46
  theoretical illustration of, 92, 94–95, 101, 105
  time, 273
  traditional views of, 277–78, 290
Upper level titles, 93, 203–4, 217–20

V

Validity:
  construct, 312
  content, 310
  convergent, 312
  defined, 41–42, 145
  discriminant, 312
  for one variable, 41, 145
  predictor criterion, 311
  for two variables, 42, 145
Variable axis:
  conceptualized, 53–63
  defined, 23–24
  illustrated, 92, 94–95, 101–2, 103–4, 104–7, 195–98, 216–17, 220, 240, 251–58, 260
Variance, percent accounted for, 115, 167–68, 171
Varient matrix:
  conceptualized, 33–37, 321–24
  defined, 24–26
  illustrated, 25, 54, 77, 95, 104, 107, 199, 220, 240, 260
Vectors:
  and degree of association, 123–24, 129
  dependent, 112
  independent, 112–13
  unit length, 116
Vertical dyad linkage—VDL:
  defined, 73
  and parts, 73–78
  tested, 222–41

W

WABA:
  defined, 27, 119, 120–23
  in general terms, 263–64
WABA equation, 122, 345–47
WABA I:
  and analysis of variance, 295–308, 354–60
  formulas:
    correlation (between), 121, 124, 343–44
    correlation (within), 121, 124, 344–45
    E ratio, 124
    F ratio, 125
  ideal conditions for:
    defined, 136, 146–48, 153–56
    illustrated, 147, 153–54, 156–57
  illustration of calculations, 126–28
  illustration with data, 192–93, 209, 213–14, 227–30, 233, 237–38, 251–53, 286–87
  induction procedures in:
    defined, 169–75, 183–84
    illustrated, 173–75
  and measurement, 311–16
  and time, 266–72
  and traditional approaches, 139, 142–43, 282, 284–87, 295–307, 354–61

WABA II—difference tests:
  formulas:
    A test, 129–30
    correlations, 122, 129
    Z test, 130–31
  ideal conditions for:
    defined, 136, 148–53
    illustrated, *149*, 153–54
  illustration of calculations, *126–27*, 132–34
  illustration with data, 193–94, 210–12,
    213–15, 230–31, 233–34, 237–38, 253,
    286–87
  induction procedures in:
    defined, 175–77
    illustrated, 178
  and measurement, 310–16
  and time, 267–72, 283, 286, 291, 295–97,
    306
  and traditional approaches, 139, 143,
    281–83, 286–87, 291–95, 297–300,
    306–7, 360–61
WABA II—magnitude tests:
  formulas:
    correlations, 122, 129
    R tests, 131–32
    t tests, 132
  ideal conditions for, 150–53
  illustration of calculations, 132–34
  illustration with data, 193–94, 206–8,
    210–11, 213–15, 227, 231–32, 234, 238,
    247, 251, 254–55
  induction procedures in:
    defined, 179–83
  and measurement, 310–16
  and time, 267–69, 286, 291, 295–97, 306
  and traditional approaches, 143, 206–8,
    227, 249–51, 281–83, 286–88, 291–95,
    297–99, 306–7
Weak parts condition, 183–85
Weak whole condition, 183–85, 212
Wholes (*see also* Cross-level wholes; Emergent
  wholes; Level-specific parts)

  conceptualized, 38–39, 84–85
  defined, 12–13, 38
  empirical indicators for, 41–42
  ideal conditions for, 136, 146–53
  inductions about, 169–85
  inferences about, 192–94, 209–12, 213–16,
    220–21, 233–36, 239–40, 251–53, 256,
    258–60
  theoretical illustration of, 73–75, 90–91,
    94, 99–100, 103
  traditional views of, 11–12, 43–46, 139,
    206–8, 227, 249–51, 286–87, 291–95,
    297–99, 306–7
Within-cell:
  component:
    defined, 123
    illustrated, 193, 211–12, 215, 231–32,
    234–35, 238
  correlation (*see* Correlation, within-cell)
  eta correlation (*see* Correlation, within-eta)
  R ratio, 132
  signed deviation scores, 41, 132, 137–39,
    350–51
  t test, 132

Z

$\dot{Z}$ distribution and $\hat{F}$ distribution, 5
Z test:
  and between-cell correlations, 130–31
  decision intervals for, 177, 187
  defined, 130–31, 141
  differences between independent correlations,
    131, 141–42
  examples of use, 193, 197–98, 210–12,
    213–14, 230–31, 233–34, 237–38,
    251–57, 267–72, 286–87
  ideal cases for, 148–51, 161–63
  and time, 267–72
  and traditional approaches, 249–51
  and within-cell correlations, 130–31